Honda VT1100 Shadow V-Twins

Service and Repair Manual

by Mike Stubblefield

Models covered

VT1100C Shadow, 1985 through 1990 and 1992 through 1996
VT1100C2 and D2 Shadow American Classic Edition (ACE), 1995 through 1999
VT1100C Shadow Spirit, 1997 through 2007
VT1100T Shadow ACE Tourer, 1998 through 2001
VT1100C3 Shadow Aero, 1998 through 2002
VT1100C2 Shadow Sabre, 2000 through 2007

ABCD

2313-11S3-2

ISBN-10: **1-62092-146-4**
ISBN-13: **978-1-62092-146-3**

Library of Congress Control Number: 2010925930
Printed in Malaysia

Haynes Publishing
Sparkford, Nr Yeovil, Somerset BA22 7JJ, England

Haynes North America, Inc
859 Lawrence Drive, Newbury Park, California 91320, USA
www.haynes.com

10-272

A book in the **Haynes Service and Repair Manual Series**

Contents

Contents

REPAIRS AND OVERHAUL

Engine, transmission and associated systems

Chassis components

REFERENCE

The Birth of a Dream

by Julian Ryder

There is no better example of the Japanese post-war industrial miracle than Honda. Like other companies which have become household names, it started with one man's vision. In this case the man was the 40-year old Soichiro Honda, who had sold his piston-ring manufacturing business to Toyota in 1945 and was happily spending the proceeds on prolonged parties for his friends. However, the difficulties of getting around in the chaos of post-war Japan irked Honda, so when he came across a job lot of generator engines, he realized that here was a way of getting people mobile again at low cost.

A 12 by 18-foot shack in Hamamatsu became his first bike factory, fitting the generator motors into pushbikes. Before long he'd used up all 500 generator motors and started manufacturing his own engine, known as the "chimney," either because of the elongated cylinder head or the smoky exhaust, or perhaps both. The chimney made all of half a horsepower from its 50 cc engine but it was a major success and became the Honda A-type.

Less than two years after he'd set up in Hamamatsu, Soichiro Honda founded the Honda Motor Company in September 1948. By then, the A-type had been developed into the 90 cc B-type engine, which Mr. Honda decided deserved its own chassis, not a bicycle frame. Honda was about to become Japan's first post-war manufacturer of complete motorcycles. In August 1949 the first prototype was ready. With an output of three horsepower, the 98 cc D-type was still a simple two-stroke, but it had a two-speed transmission and, most importantly, a pressed steel frame with telescopic forks and hard tail rear end. The frame was almost triangular in profile with the top rail going in a straight line from the massively braced steering head to the rear axle. Legend has it that after the D-type's first tests, the entire workforce went for a drink to celebrate and try and think of a name for the bike. One man broke one of those silences you get when people are thinking, exclaiming "This is like a dream!" "That's it!" shouted Honda, and so the Honda Dream was christened.

Honda C70 and C90 OHV-engined models

Mr. Honda was a brilliant, intuitive engineer and designer, but he did not bother himself with the marketing side of his business. With hindsight, it is possible to see that employing Takeo Fujisawa - who would both sort out the home market and plan the eventual expansion into overseas markets - was a masterstroke. He arrived in October 1949 and in 1950 was made Sales Director. Another vital new name was Kiyoshi Kawashima, who along with Honda himself, designed the company's first four-stroke after Kawashima had told them that the four-stroke opposition to Honda's two-strokes sounded nicer and therefore sold better. The result of that statement was the overhead-valve 148 cc E-type, which first ran in July 1951 just two months after the first drawings were made. Kawashima was made a director of the Honda Company at 34 years old.

The E-type was a massive success, over 32,000 were made in 1953 alone, a feat of mass-production that was astounding by the standards of the day given the relative complexity of the machine. But Honda's lifelong pursuit of technical innovation sometimes distracted him from commercial reality. Fujisawa pointed out that they were in danger of ignoring their core business, the motorized bicycles that still formed Japan's main means of transport. In May 1952, the F-type Cub appeared, another two-stroke despite the top men's reservations. You could buy a complete machine or just the motor to attach to your own bicycle. The result was certainly distinctive, a white fuel tank with a circular profile went just below and behind the saddle on the left of the bike, and the motor with its horizontal cylinder and bright red cover just below the rear axle on the same side of the bike. This was the machine that turned Honda into the biggest bike maker in Japan, with 70% of the market for bolt-on bicycle motors. The F-type was also the first Honda to be exported. Next came the machine that would turn Honda into the biggest motorcycle manufacturer in the world.

> 'This is like a dream!' 'That's it' shouted Honda

The C100 Super Cub was a typically audacious piece of Honda engineering and marketing. For the first time, but not the last, Honda invented a completely new type of motorcycle, although the term "scooterette'" was coined to describe the new bike which had many of the characteristics of a scooter but the large wheels, and therefore stability, of a motorcycle. The first one was sold in August 1958; fifteen years later, over nine-million of them were on the roads of the world. If ever a machine can be said to have brought mobility

The CB250N Super Dream became a favorite with UK learner riders of the late seventies and early eighties

The GL1000 introduced in 1975, was the first in Honda's line of Gold Wings

to the masses, it is the Super Cub. If you add in the electric starter that was added for the C102 model of 1961, the design of the Super Cub has remained substantially unchanged ever since, testament to how right Honda got it first time. The Super Cub made Honda the world's biggest manufacturer after just two years of production.

Honda's export drive started in earnest in 1957 when Britain and Holland got their first bikes; America got just two bikes the next year. By 1962, Honda had half the American market with 65,000 sales. But Soichiro Honda had already travelled abroad to Europe and the USA, making a special point of going to the Isle of Man TT, then the most important race in the GP calendar. He realized that no matter how advanced his products were, only racing success would convince overseas markets for whom "Made in Japan" still meant cheap and nasty. It took five years from Soichiro Honda's first visit to the Island before his bikes were ready for the TT. In 1959 the factory entered five riders in the 125 class. They did not have a massive impact on the event, being benevolently regarded as a curiosity, but sixth, seventh and eighth were good enough for the team prize. The bikes were off the pace but they were well engineered and very reliable.

The TT was the only time the West saw the Hondas in '59, but they came back for more the following year with the first of a generation of bikes which shaped the future of motorcycling – the double-overhead-cam four-cylinder 250. It was fast and reliable – it revved to 14,000 rpm – but didn't handle anywhere near as well as the opposition. However, Honda had now signed up non-Japanese riders to lead their challenge. The first win didn't come until 1962 (Aussie Tom Phillis in the Spanish 125 GP) and was followed up with a world-shaking performance at the TT. Twenty-one year old Mike Hailwood won both 125 and 250 cc TTs and Hondas filled the top five positions in both races. Soichiro Honda's master plan was starting to come to fruition; Hailwood and Honda won the 1961 250 cc World Championship. Next year Honda won three titles. The other Japanese factories fought back and inspired Honda to produce some of the most fascinating racers ever seen: the awesome six-cylinder 250, the five-cylinder 125, and the 500 four, with which the immortal Hailwood battled Agostini and the MV Agusta.

Carl Fogarty in action at the Suzuka 8 Hour on the RC45

When Honda pulled out of racing in '67, they had won sixteen rider's titles, eighteen manufacturer's titles, and 137 GPs, including 18 TTs, and introduced the concept of the modern works team to motorcycle racing. Sales success followed racing victory as Soichiro Honda had predicted, but only because the products advanced as rapidly as the racing machinery. The Hondas that came to Britain in the early '60s were incredibly sophisticated. They had overhead cams where the British bikes had pushrods, they had electric starters when the Brits relied on the kickstart, they had 12V electrics when even the biggest British bike used a 6V system. There seemed no end to the technical wizardry. It wasn't that the technology itself was so amazing, but just like that first E-type, it was the fact that Honda could mass-produce it more reliably than the lower-tech competition that was so astonishing.

When, in 1968, the first four-cylinder CB750 road bike arrived, the world of motorcycling changed forever, they even had to invent a new word for it, "Superbike." Honda raced again with the CB750 at Daytona and won the World Endurance title with a prototype DOHC version that became the CB900 roadster. There was the six-cylinder CBX, the CX500T – the world's first turbocharged production bike. They invented the full-dress tourer with the Gold Wing, and came back to GPs with the

An early CB750 Four

revolutionary oval-pistoned NR500 four-stroke, a much-misunderstood bike that was more a rolling experimental laboratory than a racer. Just to show their versatility, Honda also came up with the weird CX500 shaft-drive V-twin, a rugged workhorse that powered a new industry: the courier companies that oiled the wheels of commerce in London and other big cities.

It was true, though, that Mr. Honda was not keen on two-strokes – early motocross engines had to be explained away to him as lawnmower motors! However, in 1982 Honda raced the NS500, an agile three-cylinder lightweight against the big four-cylinder opposition in 500 GPs. The bike won in its first year, and in '83 took the world title for Freddie Spencer. In four-stroke racing the V4 layout took over from the straight four, dominating TT, F1 and Endurance championships with the RVF750, the nearest thing ever built to a Formula 1 car on two wheels. And when Superbike arrived, Honda were ready with the RC30. On the roads the VFR V4 became an instant classic, while the CBR600 invented another new class of bike on its way to becoming a best-seller. The V4 road bikes had problems to start with, but the VFR750 sold world-wide over its lifetime while the VFR400 became a massive commercial success and cult bike in Japan. The original RC30 won the first two World Superbike Championships is 1988 and '89, but Honda had to wait until 1997 to win it again with the RC45, the last of the V4 roadsters. In Grands Prix, the NSR500 V4 two-stroke superseded the NS triple and became the benchmark racing machine of the '90s. Mick Doohan secured his place in history by winning five World Championships in consecutive years on it.

In yet another example of Honda inventing a new class of motorcycle, they came up with the astounding CBR900RR FireBlade, a bike with the punch of a 1000 cc motor in a package the size and weight of a 750. It became a cult bike as well as a best seller, and with judicious redesigns, it continues to give much more recent designs a run for their money.

When it became apparent that the high-tech V4 motor of the RC45 was too expensive to produce, Honda looked to a V-twin engine to power its flagship for the first time. Typically, the VTR1000 FireStorm was a much more rideable machine than its opposition, and once accepted by the market formed the basis of the next generation of Superbike racer, the VTR-SP-1.

One of Mr. Honda's mottos was that technology would solve the customers' problems, and no company has embraced cutting-edge technology more firmly than Honda. In fact, Honda often developed new technology, especially in the fields of materials science and metallurgy. The embodiment of that was the NR750, a bike that was misunderstood nearly as much as the original NR500 racer. This limited-edition technological tour-de-force embodied many of Soichiro Honda's ideals. It used the latest techniques and materials in every component, from the oval-piston, 32-valve V4 motor to the titanium coating on the windscreen, it was – as Mr Honda would have wanted – the best it could possibly be. A fitting memorial to the man who has shaped the motorcycle industry and motorcycles as we know them today.

The CX500 – Honda's first V-Twin and a favorite choice of dispatch riders

The VT1100

Honda's first entry in the heavyweight cruiser market appeared in 1985 with the introduction of the VT1100C Shadow. Several variations on the basic theme have been added over the years: the VT1100C2 Shadow American Classic Edition in 1995; The VT1100D2 Shadow American Classic Edition in 1999 (identical to the C2 except for two-tone paint); the VT1100C Shadow Spirit in 1997; The VT1100T Shadow American Classic Edition Tourer in 1997; The VT1100C3 Shadow Aero in 1998; and the VT1100C2 Shadow Sabre in 2002. The Spirit and Sabre continued in production through 2007, the last year the VT1100 was made.

All variations of the VT1100 are basically the same mechanically, with a liquid-cooled, V-twin engine that has a 52-degree angle between the cylinders. The engine has a single overhead cam and three valves (two intake, one exhaust) per cylinder.

Dual carburetors are used on all models.

Front suspension on all models is by damper rod forks. The rear suspension is equipped with a conventional swingarm and dual coil spring-shock absorber units.

The front brake on all models is a single hydraulic disc with a dual-piston caliper. The VT1100C uses a mechanical rear drum brake; all other models use a hydraulic disc brake with single-piston caliper at the rear. All VT1100 models use shaft final drive.

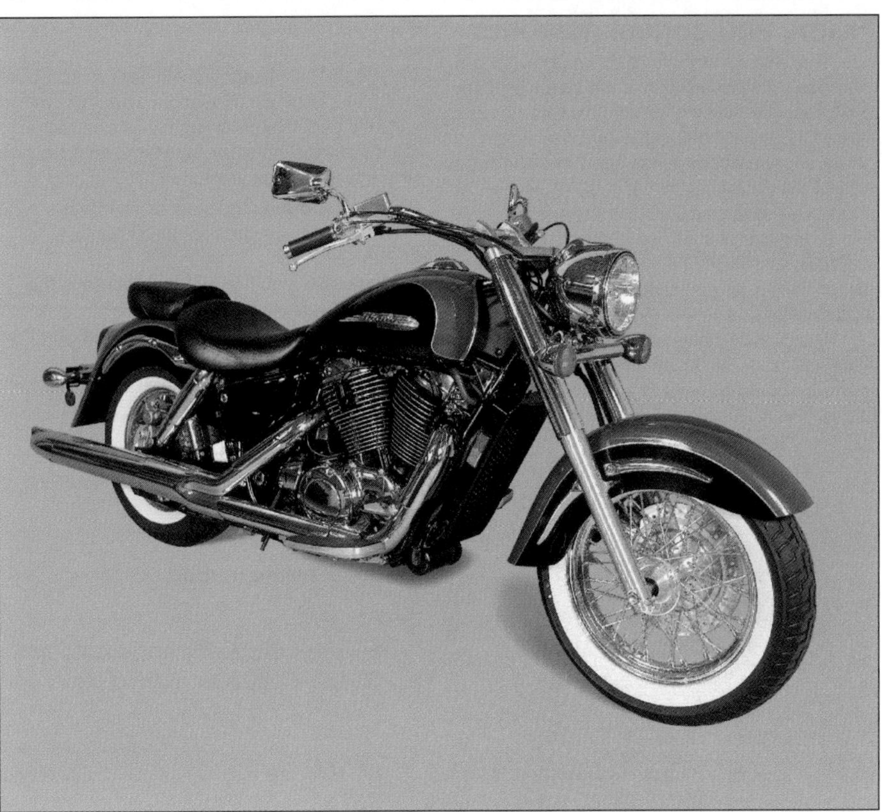

Honda Shadow VT1100

Acknowledgements

Our thanks to Honda of Milpitas, Milpitas, CA for providing the motorcycles used in the teardown photographs; to Pete Sirett, service manager, for arranging the facilities and fitting the project into his shop's busy schedule; and to Bruce Farley, service technician, for doing the mechanical work and providing valuable technical information. Thanks also to Fremont Honda Kawasaki, Fremont, California, for providing the 2002 VT1100C used in cover and maintenance photographs.

About this Manual

The aim of this manual is to help you get the best value from your motorcycle. It can do so in several ways. It can help you decide what work must be done, even if you choose to have it done by a dealer; it provides information and procedures for routine maintenance and servicing; and it offers diagnostic and repair procedures to follow when trouble occurs.

We hope you use the manual to tackle the work yourself. For many simpler jobs, doing it yourself may be quicker than arranging an appointment to get the motorcycle into a dealer and making the trips to leave it and pick it up. More importantly, a lot of money can be saved by avoiding the expense the shop must pass on to you to cover its labour and overhead costs. An added benefit is the sense of satisfaction and accomplishment that you feel after doing the job yourself.

References to the left or right side of the motorcycle assume you are sitting on the seat, facing forward.

We take great pride in the accuracy of information given in this manual, but motorcycle manufacturers make alterations and design changes during the production run of a particular motorcycle of which they do not inform us. No liability can be accepted by the authors or publishers for loss, damage or injury caused by any errors in, or omissions from, the information given.

Frame and engine numbers

The vehicle identification number (VIN) is stamped into the left side of the steering head, and/or is located on a label affixed to the right side of the frame, below the exhaust pipe. The frame serial number is stamped into the right side of the steering head and the engine serial number is stamped into the lower right side of the rear cylinder. These numbers should be recorded and kept in a safe place so they can be furnished to law enforcement officials in the event of theft.

The VIN, frame serial number, engine serial number and carburetor identification number should be kept in a handy place (such as your wallet) so they are always available when purchasing or ordering parts for your machine.

Other important identification numbers include the carburetor identification number and the color code. The carburetor identification number is stamped into the intake side of the carburetor.

The color code is located as follows:

1985 models - on the rear fender under the seat

1986 models - on the fuel tank (remove the left side cover for access)

1987 through 1996 VT1100C models - on the air cleaner housing

All other models - on the tool holder (remove the right side cover for access)

Always refer to the color code when buying painted parts such as the fuel tank, fenders or side covers.

The models covered by this manual are as follows:

VT1100C Shadow, 1985 through 1990 and 1992 through 1996

VT1100C2 and D2 Shadow American Classic Edition (ACE), 1995 through 1999

VT1100C Shadow Spirit, 1997 through 2007

VT1100T Shadow ACE Tourer, 1998 through 2001

VT1100C3 Shadow Aero, 1998 through 2002

VT1100C2 Shadow Sabre, 2000 through 2007

Year	Initial frame number	Initial engine number
1985		
VT1100C Shadow	SC180-FA002276 (non-California)	SC18E-2000078
VT1100C Shadow	SC181-FA002001 (California)	SC18E-2000058
1986		
VT1100C Shadow	SC180-GA100101 (non-California)	SC18E-2100001
VT1100C Shadow	SC181-GA102191 (California)	SC18E-2100382
1987		
VT1100C Shadow	SC180-HA200101 (non-California)	SC18E-2200048
VT1100C Shadow	SC181-HA200104 (California)	SC18E-2200051
1988		
VT1100C Shadow	SC180-JA300101 (non-California)	SC18E-2300001
VT1100C Shadow	SC181-JA300101 (California)	SC18E-2300025
1989		
VT1100C Shadow	SC180-KA400001 (non-California)	SC18E-2400001
VT1100C Shadow	SC181-KA400001 (California)	SC18E-2400851
1990		
VT1100C Shadow	SC180-LA500001 (non-California)	SC18E-2500001
VT1100C Shadow	SC181-LA500001 (California)	SC18E-2500361
1991		
No production		
1992		
VT1100C Shadow	SC181-NA600001 (California)	SC18E-2600001
1993		
VT1100C Shadow	SC181-PA700001 (California)	SC18E-2700001
1994		
VT1100C Shadow	SC180-RA800001 (non-California)	SC18E-2800001
VT1100C Shadow	SC181-RA800001 (California)	SC18E-2800001

Year	Initial frame number	Initial engine number
1995		
VT1100C Shadow	SC180-SA900001 (non-California)	SC18E-2900001
VT1100C Shadow	SC181-SA900001 (California)	SC18E-2900001
VT1100C2 Shadow ACE	SC320-SA000001 (non-California)	SC32E-2000001
VT1100C2 Shadow ACE	SC321-SA000001 (non-California)	SC32E-2000001
1996		
VT1100C Shadow	SC180-TA000001 (non-California)	SC18E-3000001
VT1100C Shadow	SC181-TA000001 (California)	SC18E-3000001
VT1100C2 Shadow ACE	SC320-TA100001 (non-California)	SC32E-2100001
VT1100C2 Shadow ACE	SC321-TA100001 (non-California)	SC32E-2100001
1997		
VT1100C Shadow Spirit	SC180-VA000001 (non-California)	SC18E-3000001
VT1100C Shadow Spirit	SC181-VA000001 (California)	SC18E-3000001
VT1100C2 Shadow ACE	SC320-VA200001 (non-California)	SC32E-2200001
VT1100C2 Shadow ACE	SC321-VA200001 (non-California)	SC32E-2200001
VT1100C2-2 Shadow ACE	SC323-VA240001 (non-California)	SC32E-2240001
VT1100C2-2 Shadow ACE	SC324-VA240001 (non-California)	SC32E-2240001
1998		
VT1100C Shadow Spirit	1HFSC180-WA200001 (non-California)	SC18E-3200001
VT1100C Shadow Spirit	1HFSC181-WA200001 (California)	SC18E-3200001
VT1100C2 Shadow ACE	SC320-WA300001 (non-California)	SC32E-2300001
VT1100C2 Shadow ACE	SC321-WA300001 (California)	SC32E-2300001
VT1100C2-2 Shadow ACE	SC323-WA300001 (non-California)	SC32E-2300001
VT1100C2-2 Shadow ACE	SC324-WA300001 (non-California)	SC32E-2300001
VT1100C3 Shadow Aero	1HFSC390-WA000001 (non-California)	SC39E-2000001
VT1100C3 Shadow Aero	1HFSC391-WA000001 (California)	SC39E-2000001
VT1100T Shadow ACE Touring	1HFSC370-WA000001 (non-California)	SC37E-2000001
VT1100T Shadow ACE Touring	1HFSC371-WA000001 (California)	SC37E-2000001
1999		
VT1100C Shadow Spirit	1HFSC180-XA300001 (non-California)	SC18E-3300001
VT1100C Shadow Spirit	1HFSC181-XA300001 (California)	SC18E-3300001
VT1100C2 Shadow ACE	SC320-XA400001 (non-California)	SC32E-2400001
VT1100C2 Shadow ACE	SC321-XA400001 (California)	SC32E-2400001
VT1100D2 Shadow ACE	SC323-XA400001 (non-California)	SC32E-2400001
VT1100D2 Shadow ACE	SC324-XA400001 (California)	SC32E-2400001
VT1100C3 Shadow Aero	1HFSC390-XA100001 (non-California)	SC39E-2100001
VT1100C3 Shadow Aero	1HFSC391-XA100001 (California)	SC39E-2100001
VT1100T Shadow ACE Touring	1HFSC370-XA100001 (non-California)	SC37E-2100001
VT1100T Shadow ACE Touring	1HFSC371-XA100001 (non-California)	SC37E-2100001
2000		
VT1100C Shadow Spirit	1HFSC180-YA400001 (non-California)	SC18E-3400001
VT1100C Shadow Spirit	1HFSC181-YA400001 (California)	SC18E-3400001
VT1100C2 Shadow Sabre	1HFSC430-YA000001 (non-California)	SC43E-2000001
VT1100C2 Shadow Sabre	1HFSC431-YA000001 (California)	SC43E-2000001
VT1100C3 Shadow Aero	1HFSC390-YA200001 (non-California)	SC39E-2200001
VT1100C3 Shadow Aero	1HFSC391-YA200001 (California)	SC39E-2200001
VT1100T Shadow ACE Touring	1HFSC370-YA200001 (non-California)	SC37E-2200001
VT1100T Shadow ACE Touring	1HFSC371-YA200001 (California)	SC37E-2200001

Year	Initial frame number	Initial engine number
2001		
VT1100C Shadow Spirit	1HFSC180-1A500001 (non-California)	SC18E-3500001
VT1100C Shadow Spirit	1HFSC181-1A500001 (California)	SC18E-3500001
VT1100C2 Shadow Sabre	1HFSC430-1A100001 (non-California)	SC43E-2100001
VT1100C2 Shadow Sabre	1HFSC431-1A100001 (California)	SC43E-2100001
VT1100C3 Shadow Aero	1HFSC390-1A300001 (non-California)	SC39E-2300001
VT1100C3 Shadow Aero	1HFSC391-1A300001 (California)	SC39E-2300001
VT1100T Shadow ACE Touring	1HFSC370-1A300001 (non-California)	SC37E-2300001
VT1100T Shadow ACE Touring	1HFSC371-1A300001 (California)	SC37E-2300001
2002		
VT1100C Shadow Spirit	1HFSC180-2A600001 (non-California)	SC18E-3600001
VT1100C Shadow Spirit	1HFSC181-2A600001 (California)	SC18E-3600001
VT1100C2 Shadow Sabre	1HFSC430-2A200001 (non-California)	SC43E-2200001
VT1100C2 Shadow Sabre	1HFSC431-2A200001 (California)	SC43E-2200001
VT1100C3 Shadow Aero	1HFSC390-2A400001 (non-California)	SC39E-2400001
VT1100C3 Shadow Aero	1HFSC391-2A400001 (California)	SC39E-2400001
2003		
VT1100C Shadow Spirit	1HFSC180-3A700001 (non-California)	SC18E-3700001
VT1100C Shadow Spirit	1HFSC181-3A700001 (California)	SC18E-3700001
VT1100C2 Shadow Sabre	1HFSC430-3A300001 (non-California)	SC43E-2300001
VT1100C2 Shadow Sabre	1HFSC431-3A300001 (California)	SC43E-2300001
2004		
VT1100C Shadow Spirit	1HFSC180-4A800001 (non-California)	SC18E-3800001
VT1100C Shadow Spirit	1HFSC181-4A800001 (California)	SC18E-3800001
VT1100C2 Shadow Sabre	1HFSC430-4A400001 (non-California)	SC43E-2400001
VT1100C2 Shadow Sabre	1HFSC431-4A400001 (California)	SC43E-2400001
2005		
VT1100C Shadow Spirit	1HFSC180-5A900001 (non-California)	SC18E-3900001
VT1100C Shadow Spirit	1HFSC181-5A900001 (California)	SC18E-3900001
VT1100C2 Shadow Sabre	1HFSC430-5A500001 (non-California)	SC43E-2500001
VT1100C2 Shadow Sabre	1HFSC431-5A500001 (California)	SC43E-2500001
2006		
VT1100C Shadow Spirit	1HFSC180-6A600001 (non-California)	SC18E-4000001
VT1100C Shadow Spirit	1HFSC181-6A600001 (California)	SC18E-4000001
VT1100C2 Shadow Sabre	1HFSC430-6A600001 (non-California)	SC43E-2600001
VT1100C2 Shadow Sabre	1HFSC431-6A600001 (California)	SC43E-2600001
2007		
VT1100C Shadow Spirit	1HFSC180-7A100001 (non-California)	Not available
VT1100C Shadow Spirit	1HFSC181-7A100001 (California)	Not available
VT1100C2 Shadow Sabre	1HFSC430-7A700001 (non-California)	Not available
VT1100C2 Shadow Sabre	1HFSC431-7A700001 (California)	Not available

The engine number location

The frame number location

Buying spare parts

Once you have found all the identification numbers, record them for reference when buying parts. Since the manufacturers change specifications, parts and vendors (companies that manufacture various components on the machine), providing the ID numbers is the only way to be reasonably sure that you are buying the correct parts.

Whenever possible, take the worn part to the dealer so direct comparison with the new component can be made. Along the trail from the manufacturer to the parts shelf, there are numerous places that the part can end up with the wrong number or be listed incorrectly.

The two places to purchase new parts for your motorcycle – the accessory store and the franchised dealer – differ in the type of parts they carry. While dealers can obtain virtually every part for your motorcycle, the accessory dealer is usually limited to normal high wear items such as shock absorbers, tune-up parts, various engine gaskets, cables, chains, brake parts, etc. Rarely will an accessory outlet have major suspension components, cylinders, transmission gears, or cases.

Used parts can be obtained for roughly half the price of new ones, but you can't always be sure of what you're getting. Once again, take your worn part to the breaker's yard for direct comparison.

Whether buying new, used or rebuilt parts, the best course is to deal directly with someone who specializes in parts for your particular make.

Professional mechanics are trained in safe working procedures. However enthusiastic you may be about getting on with the job at hand, take the time to ensure that your safety is not put at risk. A moment's lack of attention can result in an accident, as can failure to observe simple precautions.

There will always be new ways of having accidents, and the following is not a comprehensive list of all dangers; it is intended rather to make you aware of the risks and to encourage a safe approach to all work you carry out on your bike.

Asbestos

● Certain friction, insulating, sealing and other products - such as brake pads, clutch linings, gaskets, etc. - contain asbestos. Extreme care must be taken to avoid inhalation of dust from such products since it is hazardous to health. If in doubt, assume that they do contain asbestos.

Fire

● Remember at all times that gasoline is highly flammable. Never smoke or have any kind of naked flame around, when working on the vehicle. But the risk does not end there - a spark caused by an electrical short-circuit, by two metal surfaces contacting each other, by careless use of tools, or even by static electricity built up in your body under certain conditions, can ignite gasoline vapor, which in a confined space is highly explosive. Never use gasoline as a cleaning solvent. Use an approved safety solvent.

● Always disconnect the battery ground terminal before working on any part of the fuel or electrical system, and never risk spilling fuel on to a hot engine or exhaust.

● It is recommended that a fire extinguisher of a type suitable for fuel and electrical fires is kept handy in the garage or workplace at all times. Never try to extinguish a fuel or electrical fire with water.

Fumes

● Certain fumes are highly toxic and can quickly cause unconsciousness and even death if inhaled to any extent. Gasoline vapor comes into this category, as do the vapors from certain solvents such as trichloro-ethylene. Any draining or pouring of such volatile fluids should be done in a well ventilated area.

● When using cleaning fluids and solvents, read the instructions carefully. Never use materials from unmarked containers - they may give off poisonous vapors.

● Never run the engine of a motor vehicle in an enclosed space such as a garage. Exhaust fumes contain carbon monoxide which is extremely poisonous; if you need to run the engine, always do so in the open air or at least have the rear of the vehicle outside the workplace.

The battery

● Never cause a spark, or allow a naked light near the vehicle's battery. It will normally be giving off a certain amount of hydrogen gas, which is highly explosive.

● Always disconnect the battery ground terminal before working on the fuel or electrical systems (except where noted).

● If possible, loosen the filler plugs or cover when charging the battery from an external source. Do not charge at an excessive rate or the battery may burst.

● Take care when topping up, cleaning or carrying the battery. The acid electrolyte, even when diluted, is very corrosive and should not be allowed to contact the eyes or skin. Always wear rubber gloves and goggles or a face shield. If you ever need to prepare electrolyte yourself, always add the acid slowly to the water; never add the water to the acid.

Electricity

● When using an electric power tool, inspection light etc., always ensure that the appliance is correctly connected to its plug and that, where necessary, it is properly grounded. Do not use such appliances in damp conditions and, again, beware of creating a spark or applying excessive heat in the vicinity of fuel or fuel vapor. Also ensure that the appliances meet national safety standards.

● A severe electric shock can result from touching certain parts of the electrical system, such as the spark plug wires (HT leads), when the engine is running or being cranked, particularly if components are damp or the insulation is defective. Where an electronic ignition system is used, the secondary (HT) voltage is much higher and could prove fatal.

Remember...

✗ **Don't** start the engine without first ascertaining that the transmission is in neutral.

✗ **Don't** suddenly remove the pressure cap from a hot cooling system - cover it with a cloth and release the pressure gradually first, or you may get scalded by escaping coolant.

✗ **Don't** attempt to drain oil until you are sure it has cooled sufficiently to avoid scalding you.

✗ **Don't** grasp any part of the engine or exhaust system without first ascertaining that it is cool enough not to burn you.

✗ **Don't** allow brake fluid or antifreeze to contact the machine's paintwork or plastic components.

✗ **Don't** siphon toxic liquids such as fuel, hydraulic fluid or antifreeze by mouth, or allow them to remain on your skin.

✗ **Don't** inhale dust - it may be injurious to health (see Asbestos heading).

✗ **Don't** allow any spilled oil or grease to remain on the floor - wipe it up right away, before someone slips on it.

✗ **Don't** use ill-fitting wrenches or other tools which may slip and cause injury.

✗ **Don't** lift a heavy component which may be beyond your capability - get assistance.

✗ **Don't** rush to finish a job or take unverified short cuts.

✗ **Don't** allow children or animals in or around an unattended vehicle.

✗ **Don't** inflate a tire above the recommended pressure. Apart from overstressing the carcass, in extreme cases the tire may blow off forcibly.

✔ **Do** ensure that the machine is supported securely at all times. This is especially important when the machine is blocked up to aid wheel or fork removal.

✔ **Do** take care when attempting to loosen a stubborn nut or bolt. It is generally better to pull on a wrench, rather than push, so that if you slip, you fall away from the machine rather than onto it.

✔ **Do** wear eye protection when using power tools such as drill, sander, bench grinder etc.

✔ **Do** use a barrier cream on your hands prior to undertaking dirty jobs - it will protect your skin from infection as well as making the dirt easier to remove afterwards; but make sure your hands aren't left slippery. Note that long-term contact with used engine oil can be a health hazard.

✔ **Do** keep loose clothing (cuffs, ties etc. and long hair) well out of the way of moving mechanical parts.

✔ **Do** remove rings, wristwatch etc., before working on the vehicle - especially the electrical system.

✔ **Do** keep your work area tidy - it is only too easy to fall over articles left lying around.

✔ **Do** exercise caution when compressing springs for removal or installation. Ensure that the tension is applied and released in a controlled manner, using suitable tools which preclude the possibility of the spring escaping violently.

✔ **Do** ensure that any lifting tackle used has a safe working load rating adequate for the job.

✔ **Do** get someone to check periodically that all is well, when working alone on the vehicle.

✔ **Do** carry out work in a logical sequence and check that everything is correctly assembled and tightened afterwards.

✔ **Do** remember that your vehicle's safety affects that of yourself and others. If in doubt on any point, get professional advice.

● If in spite of following these precautions, you are unfortunate enough to injure yourself, seek medical attention as soon as possible.

Note: *The Pre-ride checks outlined in the owner's manual covers those items which should be inspected before riding the motorcycle.*

Engine oil level

Before you start:

Caution: Do not run the engine in an enclosed space such as a garage or workshop.

✔ Start the engine and let it idle for several minutes to allow it to reach normal operating temperature.

✔ Stop the engine and support the motorcycle in an upright position, using an auxiliary stand if required. Make sure it is on level ground.

✔ Leave the motorcycle undisturbed for a few minutes to allow the oil level to stabilize.

Bike care:

● If you have to add oil frequently, you should check whether you have any oil leaks. If there is no sign of oil leakage from the joints and gaskets the engine could be burning oil (see *Troubleshooting*).

The correct oil:

● Modern, high-revving engines place great demands on their oil. It is very important that the correct oil for your bike is used.

● Always top up with a good quality oil of the specified type and viscosity and do not overfill the engine.

Oil type	**API grade SF or SG meeting JASO standard MA**
Oil viscosity	**SAE 10W40 or 10W30**

1 Remove the oil filler cap (arrow) from the right-hand side of the engine. The dipstick is below and behind the cap and is used to check the engine oil level. Using a clean rag or paper towel, wipe all the oil off the dipstick. Insert the clean dipstick in the filler cap hole, but do not screw it in.

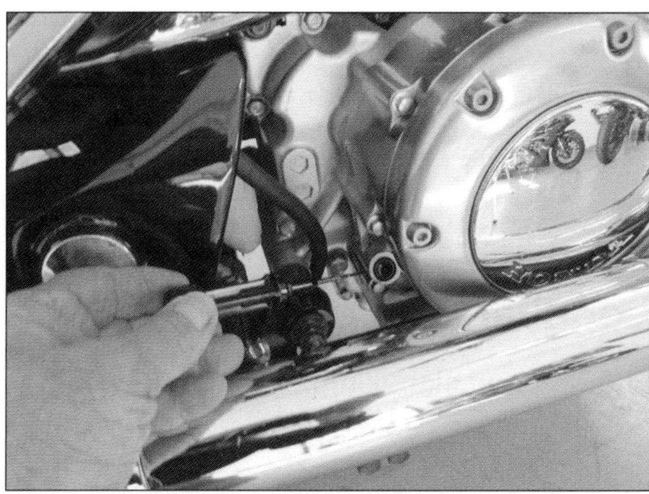

2 Remove the dipstick and observe the level of the oil, which should be somewhere in between the upper and lower lines. If the level is below the lower line, add the recommended grade and type of oil to bring the level up to the upper line on the dipstick. Do not overfill. Install the filler cap.

Coolant level

> ***Warning: DO NOT remove the radiator pressure cap to add coolant. Topping up is done via the coolant reservoir tank filler. DO NOT leave open containers of coolant about, as it is poisonous.***

Before you start:

✔ Make sure you have a supply of coolant available – a mixture of 50% distilled water and 50% corrosion inhibited ethylene glycol antifreeze is needed.
✔ Check the coolant level when the engine is at operating temperature and idling.
✔ Support the motorcycle in an upright position, using an auxiliary stand if required. Make sure it is on level ground.

Bike care:

● Use only the specified coolant mixture. It is important that antifreeze is used in the system all year round, and not just in the winter. Do not top the system up using only water, as the system will become too diluted.
● Do not overfill the reservoir. If the coolant is significantly above the FULL level line at any time, the surplus should be siphoned or drained off to prevent the possibility of it being expelled out of the overflow hose.
● If the coolant level falls steadily, check the system for leaks (see Chapter 1). If no leaks are found and the level continues to fall, it is recommended that the machine be taken to a Honda dealer for a pressure test.

1 The coolant reservoir filler cap (arrow) is located on the right side of the bike, near the passenger footpeg; the coolant level should be at the Upper mark on the reservoir. On disc brake models, it's beneath the same cover as the rear master cylinder reservoir.

Suspension, steering and final drive

Suspension and Steering:

● Check that the front and rear suspension operates smoothly without binding.
● Check that the suspension is adjusted as required.
● Check that the steering moves smoothly from lock-to-lock.

Final drive:

● Check the final drive unit for signs of oil leakage. If there's any oil on the outside of the final drive unit or on the ground beneath it, check the oil level as described in Chapter 1.

Legal and safety

Lighting and signalling:

● Take a minute to check that the headlight, tail light, brake light, instrument lights and turn signals all work correctly.
● Check that the horn sounds when the switch is operated.
● A working speedometer graduated in mph is a statutory requirement in the UK.

Safety:

● Check that the throttle grip rotates smoothly and snaps shut when released, in all steering positions. Also check for the correct amount of freeplay (see Chapter 1).
● Check that the engine shuts off when the kill switch is operated.
● Check that sidestand (and centerstand if equipped) return spring holds the stand up securely when it is retracted.

Fuel:

● This may seem obvious, but check that you have enough fuel to complete your journey. If you notice signs of fuel leakage – rectify the cause immediately.
● Ensure you use the correct grade unleaded fuel.

Brake fluid levels

> ⚠ ***Warning: Brake hydraulic fluid can harm your eyes and damage painted surfaces, so use extreme caution when handling and pouring it and cover surrounding surfaces with rag. Do not use fluid that has been standing open for some time, as it absorbs moisture from the air which can cause a dangerous loss of braking effectiveness.***

Before you start:

✔ Support the motorcycle in an upright position, using an auxiliary stand if required. Turn the handlebars until the top of the front master cylinder is as level as possible. The rear master cylinder is located behind a cover on the right side of the bike; unbolt the cover for access to the reservoir.

✔ Make sure you have the correct hydraulic fluid. DOT 4 is recommended.

✔ Wrap a rag around the reservoir being worked on to ensure that any spillage does not come into contact with painted surfaces.

Bike care:

- The fluid in the front and rear brake master cylinder reservoirs will drop slightly as the brake pads wear down.
- If any fluid reservoir requires repeated topping-up this is an indication of an hydraulic leak somewhere in the system, which should be investigated immediately.
- Check for signs of fluid leakage from the hydraulic hoses and brake system components – if found, rectify immediately (see Chapter 7).
- Check the operation of both brakes before taking the machine on the road; if there is evidence of air in the system (spongy feel to lever or pedal), it must be bled as described in Chapter 7.

1 The front brake fluid level is visible through the sight glass in the reservoir body - it must be above the LOWER reservoir line. If the fluid is below the line, remove the cap screws and lift off the reservoir cap, diaphragm plate and diaphragm. Top up with new, clean DOT 4 brake fluid, until the level is just below the upper level line cast on the inside of the reservoir. Take care to avoid spills (see WARNING above) and do not overfill. Be sure the diaphragm is correctly seated before installing the plate and cap, then tighten the screws securely.

2 If the motorcycle has a rear disc brake, remove the cover and unscrew the reservoir cap to add brake fluid - it should be at the upper mark on the reservoir.

3 If the motorcycle has a rear drum brake, press the brake pedal and look at the indicator. If the moving pointer (right arrow) aligns with the mark cast on the brake panel (left arrow), the brake shoes are worn and need to be replaced.

Tires

The correct pressures:

● The tires must be checked when **cold**, not immediately after riding. Note that low tire pressures may cause the tire to slip on the rim or come off. High tire pressures will cause abnormal tread wear and unsafe handling.

● Use an accurate pressure gauge. Many gas station gauges are wildly inaccurate. If you buy your own, spend as much as you can justify on a quality gauge.

● Correct air pressure will increase tire life and provide maximum stability, handling capability and ride comfort.

Tire care:

● Check the tires carefully for cuts, tears, embedded nails or other sharp objects and excessive wear. Operation of the motorcycle with excessively worn tires is extremely hazardous, as traction and handling are directly affected.

● Check the condition of the tire valve and ensure the dust cap is in place.

● Pick out any stones or nails which may have become embedded in the tire tread. If left, they will eventually penetrate through the casing and cause a puncture.

● If tire damage is apparent, or unexplained loss of pressure is experienced, seek the advice of a tire fitting specialist without delay.

Tire tread depth:

● Honda recommends a minimum of 1.5 mm for the front tire and 2 mm for the rear tire.

● Many tires now incorporate wear indicators in the tread. Identify the triangular pointer or TWI mark on the tire sidewall to locate the indicator bar and renew the tire if the tread has worn down to the bar.

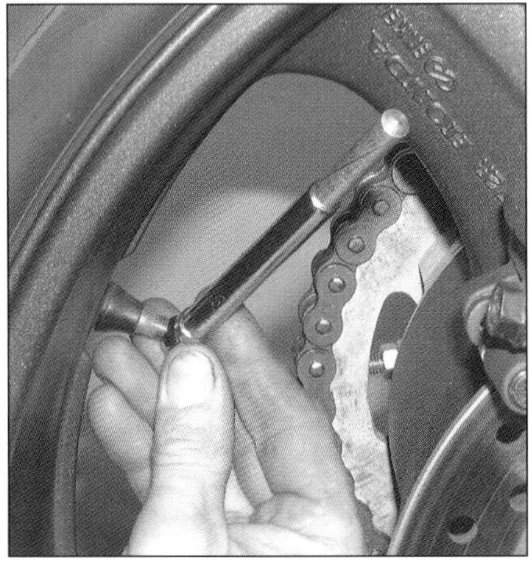

1 Check the tire pressures when the tires are cold and keep them properly inflated.

Front	
VT1100 C3	2.0 bars (29 psi)
1997 and later VT1100 C2 and D2	
Up to 90 kg (198 lbs)	2.0 bars (29 psi)
Up to maximum load	2.25 bars (33 psi)
All others	2.25 bars (33 psi)
Rear	
VT1100C, VT1100T	
Up to 90 kg (198 lbs)	2.25 bars (33 psi)
Up to maximum load	2.5 bars (36 psi)
VT1100C2	
Up to 90 kg (198 lbs)	2.25 bars (33 psi)
Up to maximum load	2.8 bars (41 psi)
VT1100C3	
Up to 90 kg (198 lbs)	2.0 bars (29 psi)
Up to maximum load	2.8 bars (41 psi)

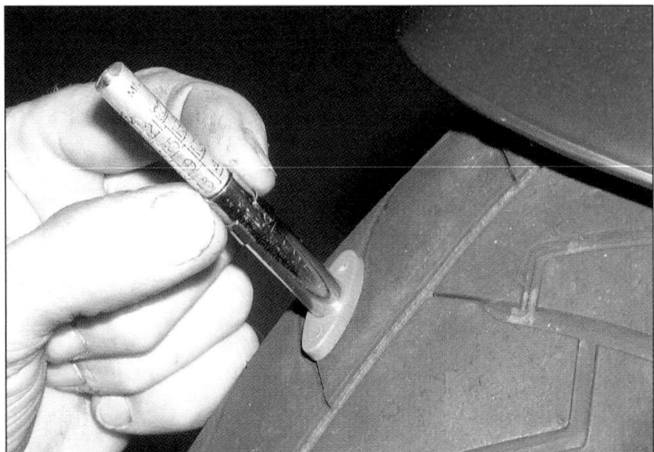

2 Measure tread depth at the center of the tire using a tread depth gauge.

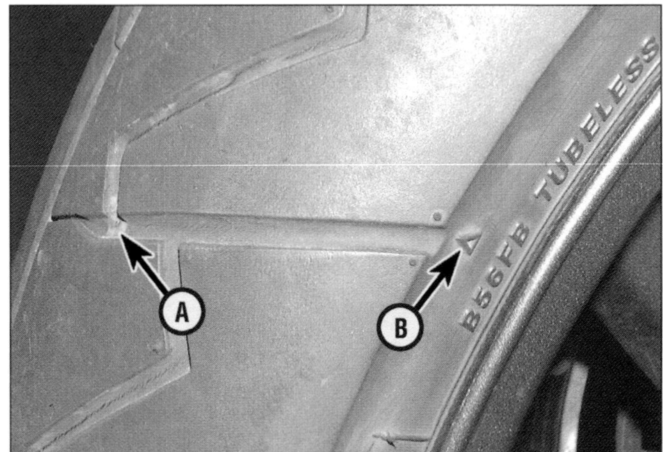

3 Tire tread wear indicator bar (A) and its location marking (B) – usually either an arrow, a triangle or the letters TWI – on the sidewall. Look for the tire information label on the chainguard or swingarm.

Chapter 1
Tune-up and routine maintenance

Contents

Degrees of difficulty

Easy, suitable for novice with little experience 	**Fairly easy,** suitable for beginner with some experience 	**Fairly difficult,** suitable for competent DIY mechanic 	**Difficult,** suitable for experienced DIY mechanic 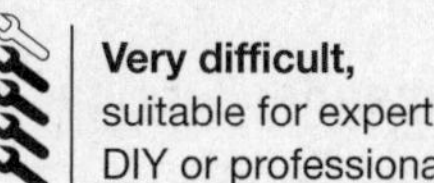	**Very difficult,** suitable for expert DIY or professional 

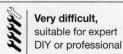

Specifications

Engine

Spark plugs	
Type	
Standard	NGK DPR7EA-9 or ND X22EPR-U9
Cold climate	NGK DPR6EA-9 or ND X20EPR-U9
Extended high-speed riding	NGK DPR8EA-9 or ND X24EPR-U9
Gap	0.8 to 0.9 mm (0.031 to 0.035 inch)
Engine idle speed	900 to 1100 rpm
Cylinder compression pressure	10.79 to 14.71 Bars (156 to 213 psi)
Maximum vacuum difference between cylinders (carburetor synchronization)	40 mm Hg (1.6 inches Hg)
Cylinder numbering	
Rear cylinder	1
Front cylinder	2

Miscellaneous

Battery electrolyte specific gravity	1.280 at 20 degrees C (68 degrees F)
Brake pedal position (models with rear drum brake)	
Pedal height (above top of footpeg)	
1985 and 1986	20 mm (3/4-inch)
1987 through 1996	35 mm (1-1/3 inches)
1995 and later VT1100C2, VT1100T	N/A (all models use rear disc brakes)
1997 and later VT1100C	Adjust to suit (no specified height)
Pedal freeplay	20 to 30 mm (3/4 to 1-1/4 inches)
Choke cable adjustment	SE valves 10 to 11 mm (0.39 to 0.43 inch) from end of threaded barrel
Clutch lever freeplay (cable-actuated clutch)	10 to 20 mm (3/8 to 3/4 inch)
Minimum tire tread depth	
Front	1.5 mm (0.06 inch)
Rear	2.0 mm (0.08 inch)
Throttle grip freeplay	2 to 6 mm (1/8 to 1/4 inch)
Tire pressures (cold)	
Front	
VT1100 C3	2.0 bars (29 psi)
1997 and later VT1100 C2 and D2	
Up to 90 kg (198 lbs)	2.0 bars (29 psi)
Up to maximum load	2.25 bars (33 psi)
All others	2.25 bars (33 psi)
Rear	
VT1100C, VT1100T	
Up to 90 kg (198 lbs)	2.25 bars (33 psi)
Up to maximum load	2.5 bars (36 psi)
VT1100C2	
Up to 90 kg (198 lbs)	2.25 bars (33 psi)
Up to maximum load	2.8 bars (41 psi)
VT1100C3	
Up to 90 kg (198 lbs)	2.0 bars (29 psi)
Up to maximum load	2.8 bars (41 psi)

Torque specifications

Engine oil drain plug	30 Nm (22 ft-lbs)
Final drive	
Filler cap	12 Nm (108 in-lbs)
Drain plug	12 Nm (108 in-lbs)
Spark plugs	14 Nm (120 in-lbs)
Steering head bearing adjustment nut	
1985 and 1986	23 to 27 Nm (17 to 20 ft-lbs)
1987 on	21 Nm (15 ft-lbs)
Water pump drain plug	13 Nm (108 in-lbs)

Recommended lubricants and fluids

Fuel type	Unleaded
Fuel capacity	
1985 and 1986	
Total	15 liters (4.0 gallons)
Reserve	3 liters (0.8 gallon)
1987 through 1996 VT1100C	
Total	13 liters (3.44 gallons)
Reserve	2.5 liters (0.64 gallon)
1995 and later VT1100C2	
Total	15.8 liters (4.17 US gallons)
Reserve	2.2 liters (0.58 gallon)
1997 and later VT1100C, VT1100T	
Total	15.8 liters (4.17 US gallons)
Reserve	2.2 liters (0.58 gallon)
Engine/transmission oil	
Type	API grade SG or higher, meeting JASO standard MA (the MA standard is required to prevent clutch slippage)
Viscosity	
Most conditions	SAE 10W-40
Cold weather	SAE 10W-30
Hot weather	SAE 20W-40
Very hot weather	SAE 20W-50

Capacity	
1985 and 1986	3.3 liters (4.0 quarts)
1987 through 1996 VT1100C	3.1 liters (3.26 quarts)
1995 and later VT1100C2, C3	
Oil change only	3.3 liters (3.5 quarts)
With filter change	3.5 liters (3.7 quarts)
1997 and later VT1100C, VT1100T; 2000 and earlier VT1100C3	
Oil change only	2.9 liters (3.1 quarts)
With filter change	3.1 liters (3.3 quarts)
Coolant	
Type	50/50 mixture of ethylene glycol-based antifreeze and distilled water
Capacity	
1985 through 1996 VT1100C	
Engine and radiator	1.86 liters (1.95 quarts)
Reservoir	0.34 liter (0.36 quart)
1995 and later VT1100C2, 1997 and later VT1100C, VT1100T	
Engine and radiator	2.0 liters (2.1 quarts)
Reservoir	0.39 liter (0.41 quart)
Final drive oil	
Type	Hypoid gear oil (API number not specified)
Viscosity	SAE 90
Capacity	150 cc (5.1 US fl oz)
Brake fluid	DOT 4
Wheel bearings	Medium weight, lithium-based multi-purpose grease
Swingarm pivot bearings	Medium weight, lithium-based multi-purpose grease
Cables and lever pivots	Chain and cable lubricant or 10W30 motor oil
Sidestand pivot	Chain and cable lubricant or 10W30 motor oil
Brake pedal/shift lever pivots	Chain and cable lubricant or 10W30 motor oil
Throttle grip	Multi-purpose grease or dry film lubricant

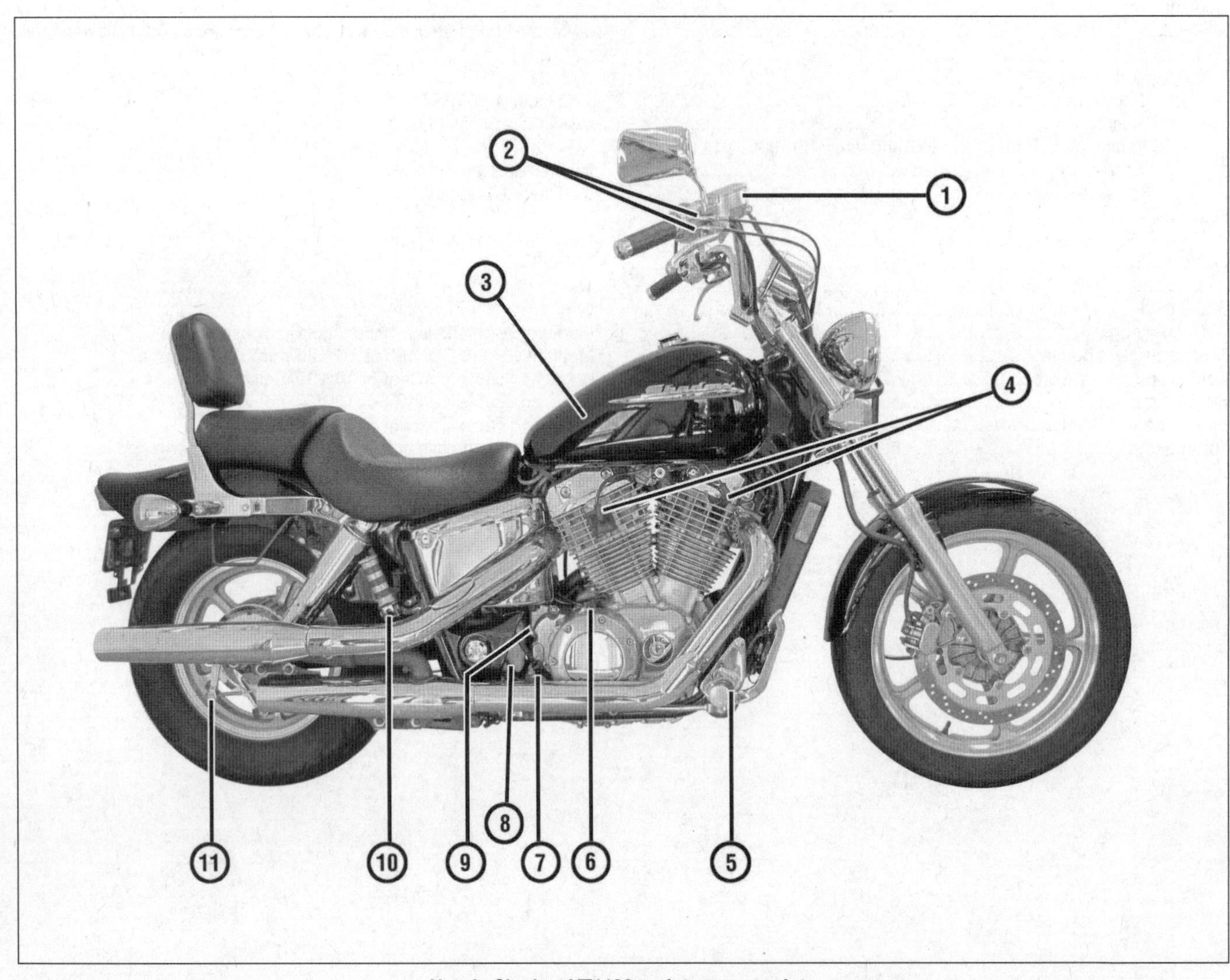

Honda Shadow VT1100 maintenance points

1 *Front brake fluid reservoir*
2 *Throttle cable adjusters*
3 *Air filter (beneath fuel tank)*
4 *Spark plugs (right side)*
5 *Front footpeg pivot*
6 *Engine oil filler cap*
7 *Engine oil dipstick*
8 *Coolant reservoir*
9 *Rear brake fluid reservoir (disc brake models)*
10 *Rear footpeg pivot*
11 *Rear brake adjuster (drum brake models)*

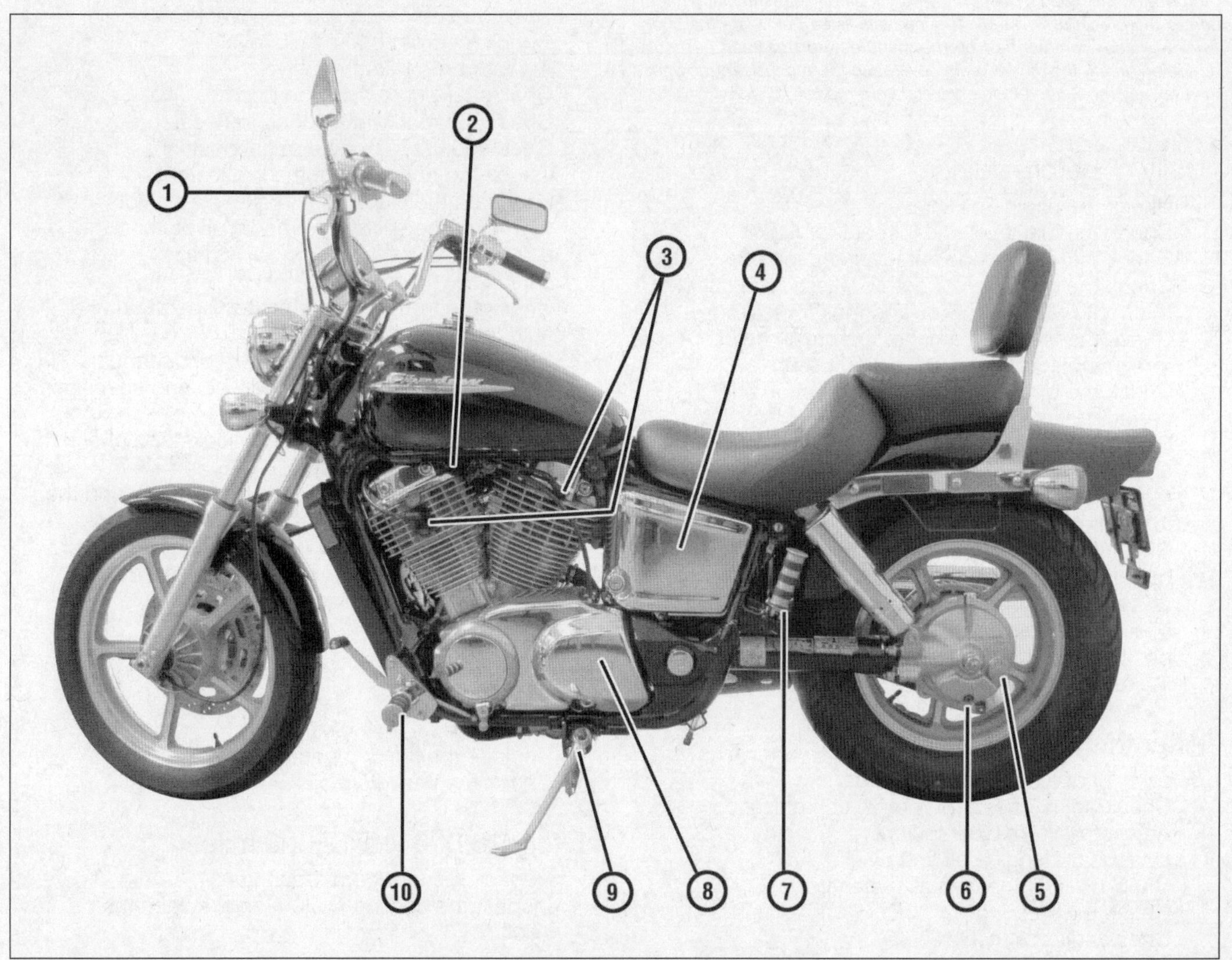

Honda Shadow VT1100 maintenance points

1 *Clutch cable adjuster (at handlebar)*
2 *Throttle stop screw*
3 *Spark plugs (left side)*
4 *Battery (inside left side cover)*
5 *Final drive fill/level plug*
6 *Final drive drain plug*
7 *Footpeg*
8 *Clutch cable adjuster (at engine, inside cover)*
9 *Sidestand*
10 *Footpeg*

1 Maintenance schedule

Note: *The pre-ride inspection outlined in the owner's manual covers checks and maintenance that should be carried out on a daily basis. It's condensed and included here to remind you of its importance. Always perform the pre-ride inspection at every maintenance interval (in addition to the procedures listed). The intervals listed below are the shortest intervals recommended by the manufacturer for each particular operation during the model years covered in this manual. Your owner's manual may have different intervals for your model.*

Daily or before riding

- ☐ Check the engine oil level
- ☐ Check the fuel level and inspect for leaks
- ☐ Check the engine coolant level and look for leaks
- ☐ Check the operation of both brakes - also check the front brake fluid level and look for leakage
- ☐ Check the tires for damage, the presence of foreign objects and correct air pressure
- ☐ Check the throttle for smooth operation and correct freeplay
- ☐ Check the operation of the clutch - make sure the freeplay is correct
- ☐ Make sure the steering operates smoothly, without looseness and without binding
- ☐ Check for proper operation of the headlight, taillight, brake light, turn signals, indicator lights and horn
- ☐ Make sure the sidestand fully returns to its "up" position and stays there under spring pressure
- ☐ Make sure the engine STOP switch works properly

After the initial 600 miles/1000 km

Perform all of the daily checks plus:

- ☐ Check/adjust the carburetor synchronization
- ☐ Adjust the valve clearances
- ☐ Change the engine oil and oil filter
- ☐ Check the tightness of all fasteners
- ☐ Check the steering
- ☐ Check/adjust clutch freeplay
- ☐ Check the front brake fluid level
- ☐ Check the cooling system hoses
- ☐ Inspect brake pads and shoes
- ☐ Check/adjust the brake pedal position
- ☐ Check the operation of the brake light
- ☐ Check the operation of the sidestand switch
- ☐ Lubricate the clutch cable, throttle cable(s) and speedometer cable

Every 4000 miles/6000 km or 6 months

- ☐ Change the engine oil and oil filter
- ☐ Clean the air filter element and replace it if necessary
- ☐ Adjust the valve clearances
- ☐ Clean and gap the spark plugs
- ☐ Lubricate the clutch cable, throttle cable(s) and speedometer cable
- ☐ Check/adjust throttle cable freeplay
- ☐ Check/adjust the idle speed
- ☐ Check/adjust the carburetor synchronization
- ☐ Check the front brake fluid level
- ☐ Adjust front brake freeplay
- ☐ Check the brake disc and pads
- ☐ Check the rear brake shoes for wear
- ☐ Check/adjust the brake pedal position
- ☐ Check the operation of the brake light
- ☐ Lubricate the clutch and brake lever pivots
- ☐ Lubricate the shift/brake pedal pivots and the sidestand pivot
- ☐ Check the steering
- ☐ Check the front forks for proper operation and fluid leaks
- ☐ Check the tires, wheels and wheel bearings
- ☐ Check the battery electrolyte level and specific gravity; inspect the breather tube
- ☐ Check the exhaust system for leaks and check the tightness of the fasteners
- ☐ Check the cleanliness of the fuel system and the condition of the fuel lines and vacuum hoses
- ☐ Inspect the crankcase ventilation system
- ☐ Check the operation of the sidestand switch
- ☐ Check and adjust clutch cable freeplay

Every 12,000 km/8,000 miles or 12 months

All of the items above plus:

- ☐ Replace the spark plugs
- ☐ Check the final drive oil level

Every 18,000 km/12,000 miles

- ☐ Repack the swingarm bearings
- ☐ Inspect the cooling system and replace the coolant

Every 24,000 km/15,000 miles or two years

- ☐ Clean and lubricate the steering head bearings

Every 50,000 km/30,000 miles

- ☐ Replace the drive chain

Every two years

- ☐ Replace the brake master cylinder and caliper seals and change the brake fluid

Every four years

- ☐ Replace the brake hose

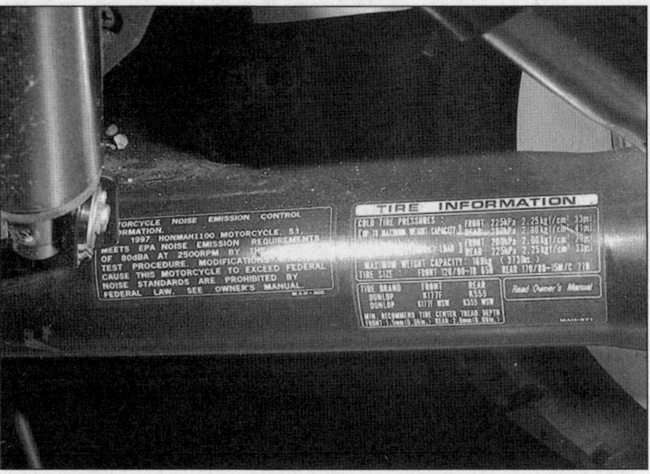

2.3 Decals at various locations on the motorcycle include such information as tire pressures and safety warnings

3.3a Remove the dipstick and verify that the oil level is at the upper mark

2 Introduction to tune-up and routine maintenance

This Chapter covers in detail the checks and procedures necessary for the tune-up and routine maintenance of your motorcycle. Section 1 includes the routine maintenance schedule, which is designed to keep the machine in proper running condition and prevent possible problems. The remaining Sections contain detailed procedures for carrying out the items listed on the maintenance schedule, as well as additional maintenance information designed to increase reliability.

Since routine maintenance plays such an important role in the safe and efficient operation of your motorcycle, it is presented here as a comprehensive checklist. For riders who do all their own maintenance, these lists outline the procedures and checks that should be done on a routine basis.

Maintenance information is printed on labels attached to the motorcycle **(see illustration)**. If the information on the labels differs from that included here, use the information on the label.

Deciding where to start, or "plug into," the routine maintenance schedule depends on several factors. If the warranty has recently expired, and if the motorcycle has been maintained according to the warranty standards, you may want to pick up routine maintenance as it coincides with the next mileage or calendar interval. If you have owned the machine for some time but have never performed any maintenance on it, then you may want to start at the nearest interval and include some additional procedures to ensure that nothing important is overlooked. If you have just had a major engine overhaul, then you may want to start the maintenance routine from the beginning. If you have a used machine and have no knowledge of its history or maintenance record, you may desire to combine all the checks into one large service initially and then settle into the maintenance schedule prescribed.

The Sections which outline the inspection and maintenance procedures are written as step-by-step comprehensive guides to the performance of the work. They explain in detail each of the routine inspections and maintenance procedures on the check list. References to additional information in applicable Chapters is also included and should not be overlooked.

Before beginning any maintenance or repair, the machine should be cleaned thoroughly, especially around the oil filter, spark plugs, cylinder head covers, side covers, carburetors, etc. Cleaning will help ensure that dirt does not contaminate the engine and will allow you to detect wear and damage that could otherwise easily go unnoticed.

3.3b If the oil level is low, remove the filler plug (arrow) and add enough oil to bring the level up the upper mark on the dipstick

3 Fluid levels - check

Engine oil

1 Run the engine and allow it to reach normal operating temperature.

Caution: Do not run the engine in an enclosed space such as a garage or shop.

2 Stop the engine and allow the machine to sit undisturbed for about five minutes.

3 Hold the motorcycle level. With the engine off, remove the filler cap from the right side of the crankcase and check the oil level on the dipstick. It should be between the Maximum and Minimum level marks on the dipstick **(see illustrations)**.

4 If the level is below the Minimum mark, add enough oil of the recommended grade and type to bring the level up to the Maximum mark. Do not overfill.

Brake fluid

5 In order to ensure proper operation of the hydraulic disc brake, the fluid level in the master cylinder reservoir must be properly maintained.

6 With the motorcycle held level, turn the handlebars until the top of the master cylinder is as level as possible.

7 Look closely at the inspection window in the master cylinder reservoir. Make sure that the fluid level is above the Lower mark

3.7a Brake fluid in the front master cylinder reservoir should be above the line next to the window; to remove the cover, remove these two screws (arrows)

3.7b The rear brake fluid reservoir (A) and coolant reservoir (B) are visible through slots; remove the cover bolt (C) to add brake fluid

on the reservoir **(see illustrations)**.

8 If the level is low, the fluid must be replenished. Before removing the master cylinder cover, cover the fuel tank to protect it from brake fluid spills (which will damage the paint) and remove all dust and dirt from the area around the cover.

9 To add brake fluid to the front brake master cylinder, remove the reservoir cover screws **(see illustration 3.7a)** and lift off the cover and rubber diaphragm **(see illustration)**.

Caution: Do not operate the front brake with the cover removed.

10 To add brake fluid to the rear brake master cylinder, remove the retaining bolt for the master cylinder cover **(see illustration 3.7b)**, then remove the cover and the rubber grommet for the cover upper positioning pin **(see illustration)**. Unscrew the reservoir cap.

11 Add new, clean brake fluid of the recommended type until the level is above the inspection window. Do not mix different brands of brake fluid in the reservoir, as they may not be compatible.

12 Reinstall the rubber diaphragm and the cover. Tighten the screws evenly, but do not overtighten them.

13 Wipe any spilled fluid off the reservoir body.

14 If the brake fluid level was low, inspect the brake system for leaks.

Clutch fluid

Note: *This procedure applies to 1985 through 1996 VT1100C models. Later VT1100C models, as well as all VT1100C2 and VT1100T models, use a cable-actuated clutch.*

15 With the motorcycle held level, turn the handlebars until the top of the clutch master cylinder is as level as possible.

16 Look closely at the inspection window in the master cylinder reservoir. Make sure that the clutch fluid level is above the Lower mark on the reservoir.

17 If the level is low, the fluid must be replenished. Before removing the master cylinder cover, cover the fuel tank to protect it from clutch fluid spills (which will damage the paint) and remove all dust and dirt from the area around the cover.

18 To add clutch fluid to the clutch master cylinder, remove the reservoir cover screws and lift off the cover, set plate and rubber diaphragm.

Caution: Do not operate the clutch lever with the cover removed.

19 Add new, clean clutch fluid of the recommended type until the level is above the inspection window. Do not mix different brands of clutch fluid in the reservoir, as they may not be compatible.

20 Reinstall the rubber diaphragm and the cover. Tighten the screws evenly, but do not overtighten them.

21 Wipe any spilled fluid off the reservoir body.

22 If the clutch fluid level was low, inspect the clutch system for leaks.

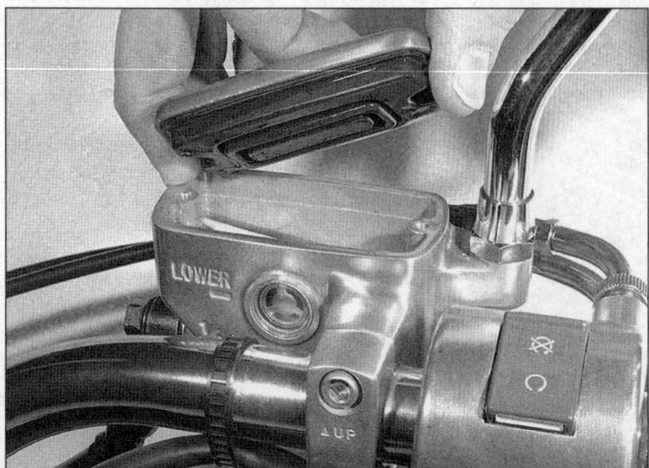

3.9 To add fluid to the front brake master cylinder, carefully remove the cover and diaphragm

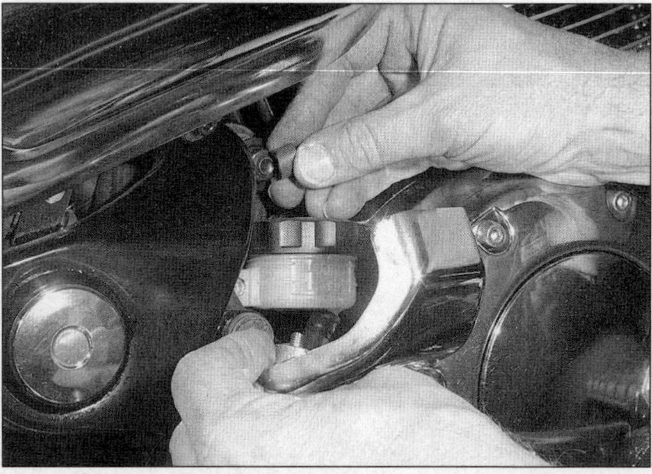
3.10 To add fluid to the rear brake master cylinder, remove the cover and unscrew the reservoir cap

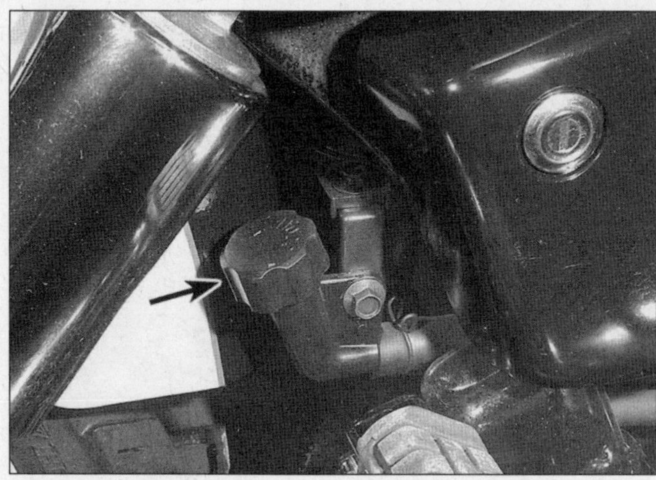

3.26 The coolant reservoir filler cap (arrow) is located on the right side of the bike, near the passenger footpeg

4.4 The electrolyte level should be between the marks on the battery case

Coolant

23 Warm up the engine and check the coolant level with the engine running at its normal temperature.

24 The UPPER and LOWER level marks for the coolant are on the front of the coolant reservoir, which is located right behind the oil filler cap/dipstick **(see illustration 3.7b)**.

25 The reservoir is translucent white plastic, so the coolant level is easily visible in relation to the marks. The coolant level should be at the Upper mark on the reservoir.

26 To add coolant, shut off the engine and remove the coolant reservoir filler cap **(see illustration)**. Using a 50/50 mixture of ethylene glycol and distilled water, bring the coolant level up to the Upper mark on the reservoir. Install the filler cap.

27 If the coolant level in the reservoir was low, or empty, inspect the cooling system (see Section 20). It might be leaking.

4 Battery electrolyte level/ specific gravity - check

Warning: Be extremely careful when handling or working around the battery. The electrolyte is very caustic and an explosive gas (hydrogen) is given off when the battery is charging.

1 This procedure applies to conventional batteries with filler caps which can be removed to add water to the battery cells.

2 Remove the battery (see Chapter 9).

3 Clean off the battery and place it on a workbench.

4 The electrolyte level, which is visible through the translucent battery case, should be between the Upper and Lower level marks **(see illustration)**.

5 If the electrolyte is low, remove the cell caps and fill each cell to the upper level mark with distilled water. Do not use tap water (except in an emergency), and do not overfill. The cell holes are quite small, so it may help to use a plastic squeeze bottle with a small spout to add the water. If the level is within the marks on the case, additional water is not necessary.

6 Next, check the specific gravity of the electrolyte in each cell with a small hydrometer made especially for motorcycle batteries. These are available from most dealer parts departments or motorcycle accessory stores.

7 Remove the caps, draw some electrolyte from the first cell into the hydrometer **(see illustration)** and note the specific gravity. Compare the reading to the Specifications listed in this Chapter. Add 0.004 points to the reading for every 10-degrees F above 20-degrees C (68-degrees F); subtract 0.004 points from the reading for every 10-degrees below 20-degrees C (68-degrees F). Return the electrolyte to the appropriate cell and repeat the check for the remaining cells. When the check is complete, rinse the hydrometer thoroughly with clean water.

8 If the specific gravity of the electrolyte in each cell is as specified, the battery is in good condition and is apparently being charged by the machine's charging system.

9 If the specific gravity is low, the battery is not fully charged. This may be due to corroded battery terminals, a dirty battery case, a malfunctioning charging system, or loose or corroded wiring connections. On the other hand, it may be that the battery is worn out, especially if the machine is old, or that infrequent use of the motorcycle prevents normal charging from taking place.

10 Be sure to correct any problems and charge the battery if necessary. Refer to Chapter 9 for additional battery maintenance and charging procedures.

11 Install the battery cell caps, tightening them securely.

12 Install the battery (see Chapter 9). When reconnecting the cables to the battery, attach the positive cable first, then the negative cable. Make sure to install the insulating boot over the positive terminal. Install all components removed for access. Be very careful not to pinch or otherwise restrict the battery vent tube, as the battery may build up enough internal pressure during normal charging system operation to explode.

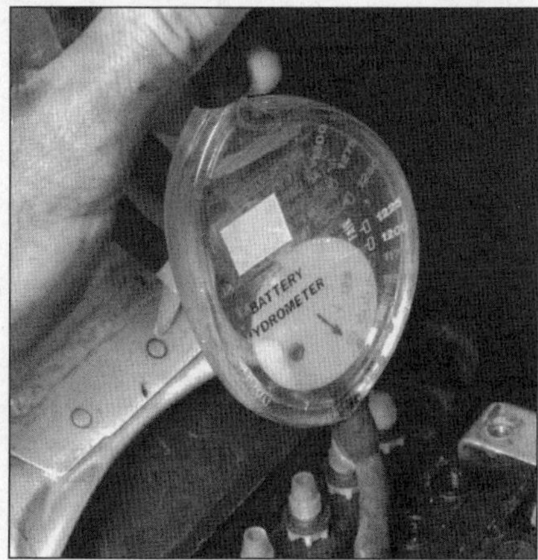

4.7 Check the specific gravity with a hydrometer

5 Brake pads and shoes - wear check

1 The front brake pads and the rear brake shoes or pads should be checked at the recommended intervals and replaced when worn beyond the limit listed in this Chapter's Specifications. Always replace pads and shoes as complete sets.

2 To check the thickness of the brake pads, squeeze the front brake lever or depress the rear brake pedal, and look at the pads. On pre-1994 models, the pads are visible through

5.2 If the pads are worn down to the wear indicator grooves (arrow), replace them

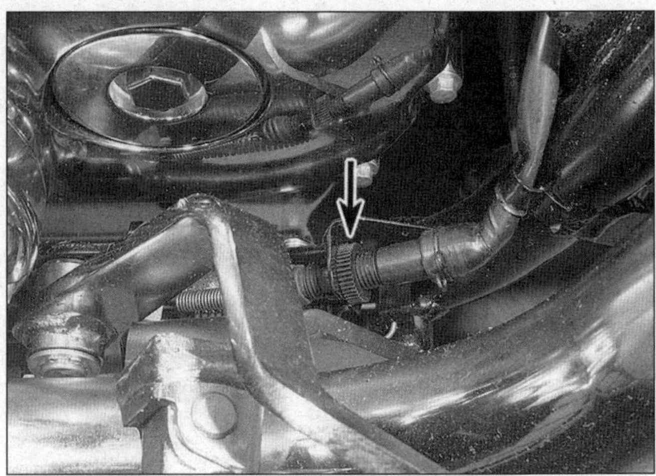

6.6 To adjust the rear brake light switch, hold the switch so it won't rotate and turn the adjustment nut (arrow)

the slot indicated by the arrow cast into the upper rear side of the caliper. On 1994 and later models, the brake pads are plainly visible **(see illustration)**. On all models, there are two ways to determine pad wear. On original-equipment Honda pads, simply note whether the pads are worn down to the wear indicator slots which run parallel to the pad backing plates. If the slots are exposed, replace the pads (see Chapter 7). If there are no wear indicator slots in the pads, note the small grooves in the surface of each pad. If these grooves are still visible, the pads have some service life remaining. If the grooves are gone, replace the pads (see Chapter 7).

3 To check the rear brake shoes, press the brake pedal firmly while you look at the wear indicator mark on the brake panel. If the indicator pointer on the brake arm is close to or at the wear indicator mark, replace the shoes (see Chapter 7).

6 Brake system - general check

1 A routine general check of the brakes will ensure that any problems are discovered and remedied before the rider's safety is jeopardized.

2 Check the brake lever and pedal for loose connections, excessive play, bends, and other damage. Replace any damaged parts (see Chapter 7).

3 Make sure all brake fasteners are tight. Check the brake pads or shoes for wear (see Section 5) and make sure the fluid level in the brake reservoir is correct (see Section 3). Look for leaks at the hose connections and check for cracks in the hose(s). If the lever or pedal is spongy, bleed the brakes (see Chapter 7).

4 Make sure the brake light operates when the brake lever is depressed.

5 Make sure the brake light operates when the brake pedal is depressed.

6 The rear brake light switch on 1985 and 1986 models is located on the right side, behind the passenger footpeg bracket. The rear brake light switch on all other models is located on the right side, at the rear brake pedal. To adjust the switch, hold the switch body so it won't rotate and turn the adjustment nut (don't try to turn the switch body). Turn the nut until the brake light comes on when it's supposed to **(see illustration)**. If the brake light doesn't work, check the switch and circuit (see Chapter 9).

7 The front brake light switch is not adjustable. If it fails to operate properly, replace it (see Chapter 9).

7 Brake pedal height and freeplay (drum brake models) - check and adjustment

Note: *This procedure does not apply to models with rear disc brakes.*

1 The rear brake pedal height, measured from the top of the footpeg to the top of the pedal, should be at the height listed in this Chapter's Specifications. If it isn't, adjust the pedal height. Loosen the locknut, turn the adjuster bolt to set the pedal height and tighten the locknut.

2 Check pedal freeplay (the distance the pedal travels downward before the brake shoes contact the drum) and compare it to the value listed in this Chapter's Specifications. If the pedal freeplay isn't within this dimension, adjust it by turning the nut at the rear end of the brake rod.

3 If necessary, adjust the brake light switch (see Section 6).

8 Tires/wheels - general check

1 Routine tire and wheel checks should be made with the realization that your safety depends to a great extent on their condition.

2 Check the tires carefully for cuts, tears, embedded nails or other sharp objects and excessive wear. Operation of the motorcycle with excessively worn tires is extremely hazardous, as traction and handling are directly affected. Measure the tread depth at the center of the tire **(see illustration)** and replace worn tires with new ones when the tread depth is less than specified.

3 Repair or replace punctured tires as soon as damage is noted. Do not try to patch a torn tire, as wheel balance and tire reliability may be impaired.

4 Check the tire pressures when the tires

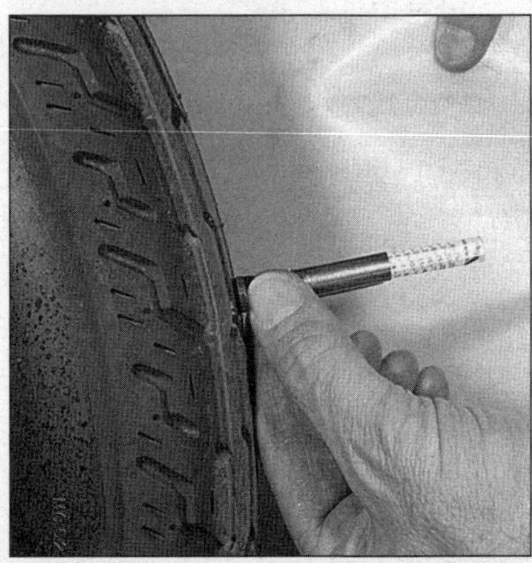

8.2 Measure tread depth at the center of the tire (tread depth gauges are available at most dealerships and motorcycle accessory shops)

8.4 Check tire pressures with an accurate gauge

8.5 Make sure the tire valve locknut (arrow) is snug and the valve cap is tight

are cold and keep them properly inflated **(see illustration)**. Proper air pressure will increase tire life and provide maximum stability and ride comfort. Keep in mind that low tire pressures may cause the tire to slip on the rim or come off, while high tire pressures will cause abnormal tread wear and unsafe handling.

5 Make sure the valve stem locknuts **(see illustration)** are tight. Also, make sure the valve stem cap is tight. If it is missing, install a new one made of metal or hard plastic.

9 Throttle cable and choke operation - check and adjustment

Throttle cable

1 Make sure the throttle grip rotates easily from fully closed to fully open with the front wheel turned at various angles. The grip should return automatically from fully open to fully closed when released. If the throttle sticks, check the throttle cables for cracks or kinks in the housings and make sure the inner cables are clean and well-lubricated.

2 Start the engine and warm it up. With the engine idling, turn the handlebars all the way to the left, then all the way to the right. The idle speed should not increase. If it does, check throttle grip freeplay.

3 Throttle grip freeplay is the distance the throttle grip can be rotated before resistance is felt, *i.e.* the point at which the throttle cable begins to open the carburetor throttle plates. Measure the throttle grip freeplay **(see illustration)** and compare your measurement to the value listed in this Chapter's Specifications.

4 There are actually *two* throttle cables - an "accelerator" cable and a "decelerator" cable. The accelerator cable opens the throttle plates; the decelerator cable closes them. If the throttle grip freeplay must be adjusted, it can be adjusted at either end of the accelerator cable, but only at the lower end of the decelerator cable. The upper adjuster at the throttle grip is used to make fine adjustments to the accelerator cable; throttle grip freeplay is usually adjusted here. The lower adjusters at the carburetors are only used to make major adjustments to the cables. Both cables can be adjusted at the carburetors, but the accelerator cable is the one that is adjusted to achieve correct throttle grip freeplay; the decelerator cable is adjusted only to compensate for the amount of freeplay that's added or subtracted from the accelerator cable. There should be no freeplay in the decelerator cable.

5 To adjust freeplay at the throttle grip, loosen the locknut **(see illustration)** and turn the adjuster until the freeplay is within the specified distance. Tighten the locknut.

9.3 Throttle grip freeplay is the distance the throttle grip can be turned before resistance is felt, as the throttle plates begin to open

9.5 Accelerator cable locknut (left arrow) and adjuster (right arrow) at the twist-grip end of the throttle cable

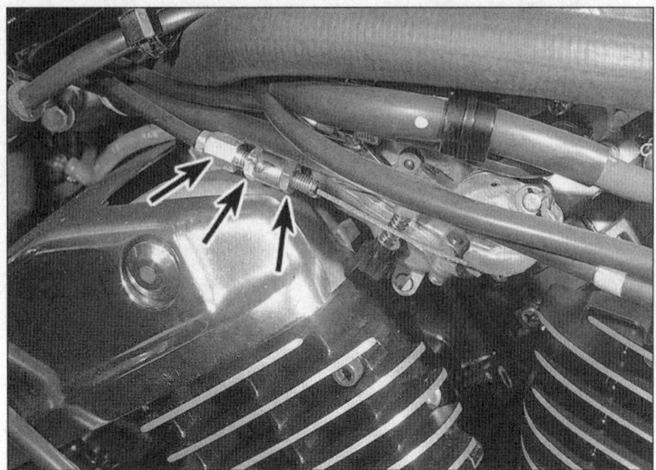
9.6 Carburetor-end cable adjuster (left arrow) and locknuts (right arrows)

9.11 Verify that the choke lever at the handlebar switch operates smoothly; if it doesn't, lubricate the choke cable

6 To adjust freeplay at the carburetors, loosen the cable adjuster locknuts **(see illustration)**, turn the adjuster nut on the decelerator cable to set freeplay to zero, tighten the decelerator cable adjuster locknut, then turn the accelerator cable adjuster nut to bring freeplay at the throttle grip within the range listed in this Chapter's Specifications. Once freeplay is correct, tighten the accelerator cable adjuster locknut.

7 Make sure the throttle grip is now in the fully-closed position.

8 Make sure the throttle linkage lever still contacts the idle adjusting screw when the throttle grip is in the fully-closed position.

9 Again, turn the handlebars all the way through their travel with the engine idling. Idle speed should not change. If it does, either the cables are incorrectly routed or freeplay is still insufficient.

Warning: Correct this condition before riding the bike.

Choke

10 The choke system consists of a pair of starting enrichment (SE) valves - one per carburetor - which control the fuel enrichment circuits in the carburetors. When the choke lever on the left handlebar switch is pulled back, the cable-actuated SE valves open the fuel enrichment circuits in the carburetors.

11 Make sure that the choke lever **(see illustration)** operates smoothly. If the lever is hard to operate, disconnect the upper end of the cable from the left handlebar switch (see Chapter 9) and lubricate the cable with cable lube or lightweight oil. Adjust the choke cable when you're done (see below). If lubricating the cable doesn't help, remove and inspect the SE valves (see below).

12 If the engine is hard to start when it's cold, but easy to start when it's warmed up, the SE valves are not opening completely. If the idle speed "wanders" up and down, even after the engine is warmed up, the SE valves are not closing completely. In either case, remove the SE valves and adjust the choke cable.

13 Remove the fuel tank (see Chapter 4).

14 Remove the SE valves from the carburetors **(see illustrations)**.

15 Before checking and adjusting the choke cable, make sure that the SE valves and springs are in good condition **(see illustration)**. If both valves are in good shape, reassemble them and proceed. If the springs and/or valves are damaged, replace them before continuing. Reassemble both SE valves.

16 Move the choke lever to its fully closed position and measure the distance between each SE valve and the threaded end of the cable. Compare your measurements to the distance listed in this Chapter's Specifications. If the distance that either SE valve protrudes from the threaded end of the cable is not within the specified range, adjust the choke cable.

17 To adjust the choke cable, turn the han-

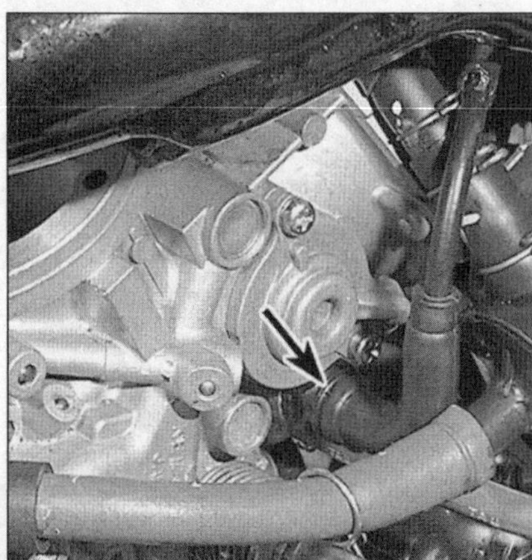
9.14a Unscrew the SE valve locknuts . . .

9.14b . . . and remove the SE valves (right carburetor shown)

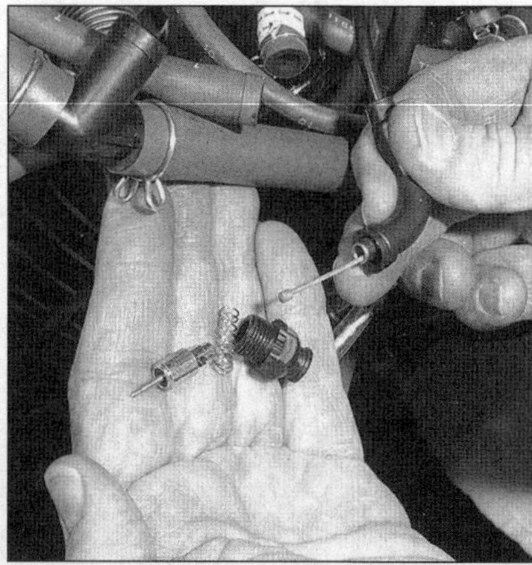
9.15 Before adjusting the choke cable, inspect the spring, valve and threaded barrel of each SE valve; replace any broken or worn pieces

10.3 To make clutch cable adjustments at the handlebar, loosen the lockwheel (right arrow) and turn the adjuster (left arrow); tighten the lockwheel after adjustment

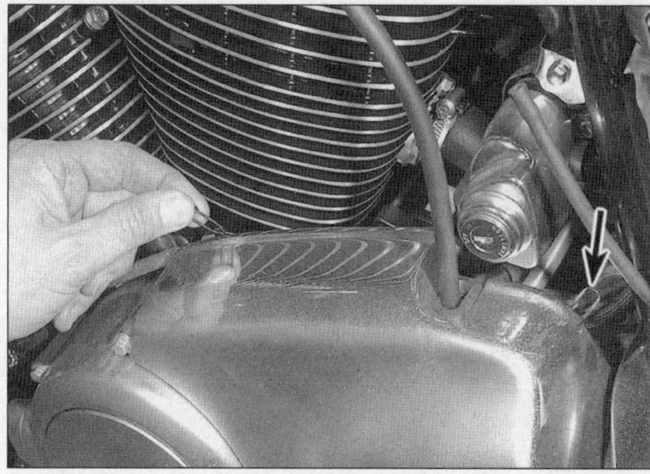

10.5a Remove the front retainer and the rear retainer (arrow) . . .

dlebar to the right side, loosen the locknut and turn the cable elbow until the SE valve distance is within specification. Tighten the locknut securely and recheck the SE valve distance and choke lever operation.

18 Install the SE valves and tighten the locknuts securely.

19 Install the fuel tank (see Chapter 4).

10 Clutch - check and adjustment

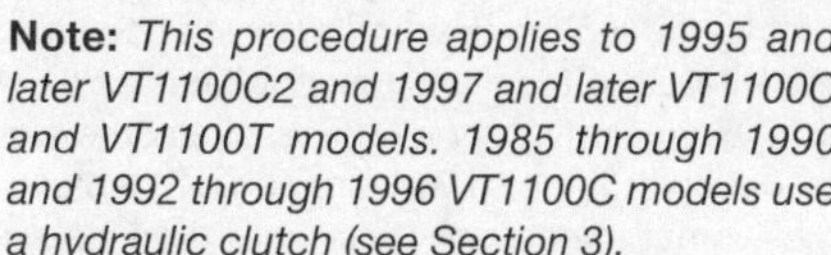

Note: *This procedure applies to 1995 and later VT1100C2 and 1997 and later VT1100C and VT1100T models. 1985 through 1990 and 1992 through 1996 VT1100C models use a hydraulic clutch (see Section 3).*

1 Correct clutch freeplay is necessary to ensure proper clutch operation and reasonable clutch service life. Freeplay normally changes because of cable stretch and clutch wear, so it should be checked and adjusted periodically.

2 Clutch cable freeplay is checked at the lever on the handlebar. Slowly pull in on the lever until resistance is felt, measure this distance and compare it with the value listed in this Chapter's Specifications. Too little freeplay might result in the clutch not engaging completely. If there is too much freeplay, the clutch might not release fully.

3 Normal freeplay adjustments are made at the clutch lever by loosening the lockwheel and turning the adjuster until the desired freeplay is obtained **(see illustration)**. Always retighten the lockwheel once the adjustment is complete.

4 If freeplay can't be adjusted at the handlebar, major adjustments can be made at the other end of the cable.

5 Remove the two retainer clips and washers from the upper edge of the left crankcase rear cover **(see illustrations)**.

6 Remove the nut from the lower edge of the rear cover **(see illustration)**.

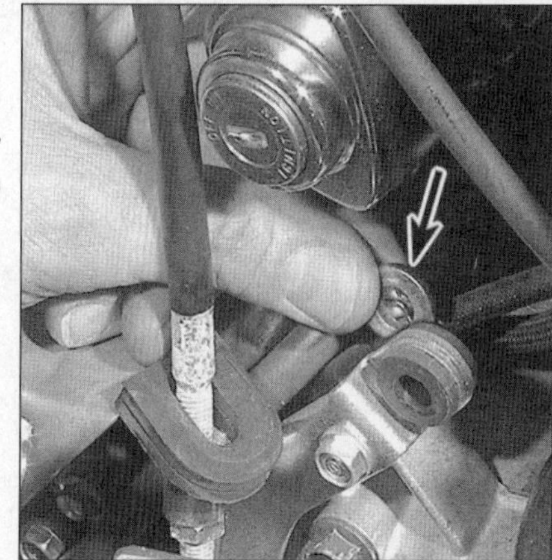

10.5b . . . and remove the washers (rear retainer washer shown)

7 Pull off the left crankcase rear cover.

8 To adjust cable freeplay, loosen the locknut and turn the adjusting nut **(see illus-**

10.6 Remove this nut (arrow) from the lower edge of the left crankcase rear cover and pull off the cover

10.8 To adjust clutch cable freeplay, loosen the locknut (arrow) and turn the adjuster nut

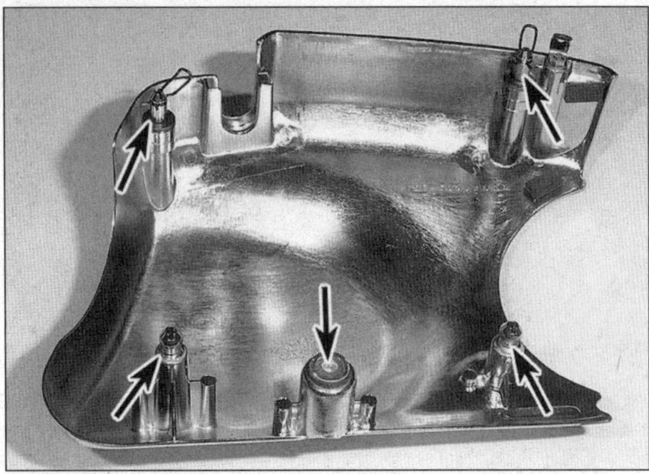

10.9 The left crankcase rear cover is attached to the engine by four positioning pins and a nut (arrows)

11.3 Here are the final drive housing check/fill plug (upper arrow) and drain plug (lower arrow)

tration). When cable freeplay is within the specified range, tighten the locknut.

9 Install the left crankcase rear cover **(see illustration)**.

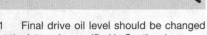

11 Final drive oil - check and change

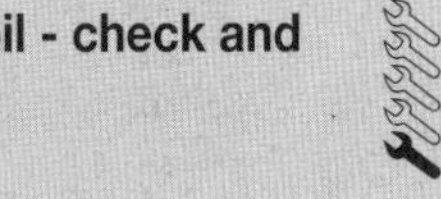

1 Final drive oil level should be changed at the intervals specified in Section 1.

Check

2 Support the bike securely in a level position.

Warning: When the bike is operated, the final drive unit gets hot enough to cause burns. If the machine has been ridden recently, make sure the final drive unit is cool to the touch before checking the level.

3 Remove the filler plug from the final drive housing **(see illustration)**.

4 Look inside the hole and check the oil level. It should be even with the top of the hole. If it's low, add oil of the type listed in this Chapter's Specifications with a funnel or hose, then reinstall the filler plug and tighten it to the torque listed in this Chapter's Specifications.

Oil change

5 Ride the bike to warm the oil so it will drain completely.

Warning: Be careful not to touch hot components (including the oil); they may be hot enough to cause burns.

6 Remove the filler plug **(see illustration 11.3)**.

7 Remove the drain plug **(see illustration 11.3)** and let the oil drain for 10 to 15 minutes.

8 Clean the drain plug, reinstall it and tighten it to the torque listed in this Chapter's Specifications.

9 Fill the final drive unit to the correct level with oil of the type listed in this Chapter's Specifications.

10 Install the filler plug and tighten it to the torque listed in this Chapter's Specifications.

12 Engine oil/filter - change

1 Regular oil and filter changes are the single most important maintenance procedure you can perform on a motorcycle. The oil not only lubricates the internal parts of the engine, transmission and clutch, but it also acts as a coolant, a cleaner, a sealant, and a protectant. Because of these demands, the oil takes a terrific amount of abuse and should be replaced often with new oil of the recommended grade and type. Saving a little money on the difference in cost between a good oil and a cheap oil won't pay off if the engine is damaged.

2 Before changing the oil and filter, warm up the engine so the oil will drain easily. Be careful when draining the oil; the exhaust pipes, the engine and the oil itself can cause severe burns.

3 Support the motorcycle securely over a clean drain pan. Remove the oil filler cap to vent the crankcase and act as a reminder that there is no oil in the engine.

4 Next, remove the drain plug from the lower left side of the engine **(see illustration)** and allow the oil to drain into the pan. Discard the sealing washer on the drain plug; it should be replaced every time the plug is removed. While the engine is draining, replace the oil filter.

5 The automotive style spin-on oil filter is located at the left lower rear part of the engine; with the bike leaned over to the left on its sidestand, it's easier to access the filter from the right side **(see illustration)**. Remove the filter from the engine with a filter wrench **(see illustration)**. If you don't have this type of filter wrench, use a pair of large water pump pliers to loosen the filter.

6 Coat the threads of the new oil filter and the new filter O-ring with clean engine oil.

7 Install the new filter and tighten it by hand.

8 Check the condition of the drain plug threads and the sealing washer.

9 Slip a new sealing washer over the drain plug, then install and tighten it to the torque listed in this Chapter's Specifications. Avoid overtightening the drain plug, which can strip the threads in the aluminum engine case.

10 Before refilling the engine, check the old oil carefully. If the oil was drained into a clean pan, small pieces of metal or other material can be easily detected. If the oil is very metallic colored, then the engine is experiencing wear from break-in (new engine) or from insufficient lubrication. If there are flakes

12.4 The engine oil drain plug (arrow) is on the lower left side of the engine, behind the lower coolant hose and below the upper coolant hose

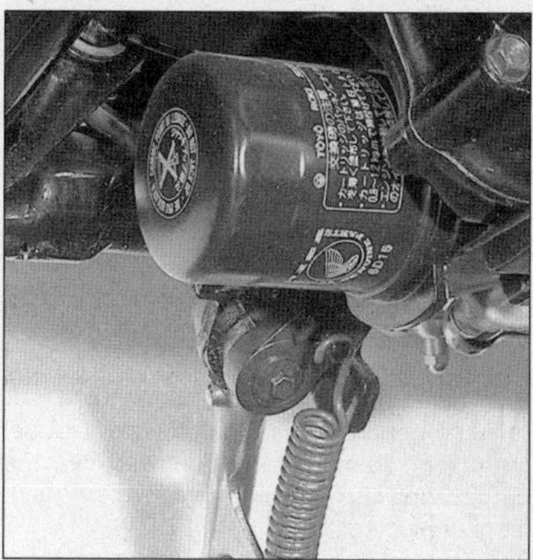

12.5a The oil filter (arrow) is at the left lower rear of the engine; the easiest way to reach it is from the right side, with the bike leaned over to the left on its sidestand

12.5b Use a filter wrench to remove the oil filter (if you don't have this type of filter wrench, use a pair of large water pump pliers)

13.5 On VT1100C2 models, unbolt the electrical connector bracket from the air cleaner housing cover and push it aside; it's not necessary to unplug any connectors

or chips of metal in the oil, then something is drastically wrong internally and the engine will have to be disassembled for inspection and repair.

11 If there are pieces of fiber-like material in the oil, the clutch is experiencing excessive wear and should be checked.

12 If the inspection of the oil turns up nothing unusual, refill the crankcase to the proper level with the recommended oil and install the filler cap. Start the engine and let it run for two or three minutes. Shut it off, wait a few minutes, then check the oil level. If necessary, add more oil to bring the level up to the Maximum mark. Check around the drain plug and filter housing for leaks.

13 The old oil drained from the engine cannot be reused in its present state and should be disposed of. Check with your local refuse disposal company, disposal facility or environmental agency to see whether they will accept the used oil for recycling. Don't pour used oil into drains or onto the ground. After the oil has cooled, it can be drained into a suitable container (capped plastic jugs, topped bottles, milk cartons, etc.) for transport to one of these disposal sites.

13 Air filter element - servicing

1985 and 1986 models

1 Remove the fuel tank cover (see Chapter 4).

2 Remove the three air cleaner housing cover screws and remove the air cleaner housing cover.

3 Remove the air filter element.

1987 and later models

4 Remove the seat(s) (see Chapter 8).

5 On VT1100C2 models, remove the electrical connector bracket bolt **(see illustration)** and push the bracket and connectors aside; it's not necessary to unplug any connectors.

6 Remove the four air cleaner housing cover screws and remove the air cleaner housing cover **(see illustration)**.

7 Remove the air filter element **(see illustration)**.

All models

8 Tap the filter element on a hard surface to shake out dirt. If compressed air is available, use it to clean the element by blowing from the inside out. If the element is extremely dirty or torn, or if dirt can't be blown or tapped out, replace the element.

9 Installation if the reverse of removal. Make sure the filter element is seated properly in the filter housing before installing the cover.

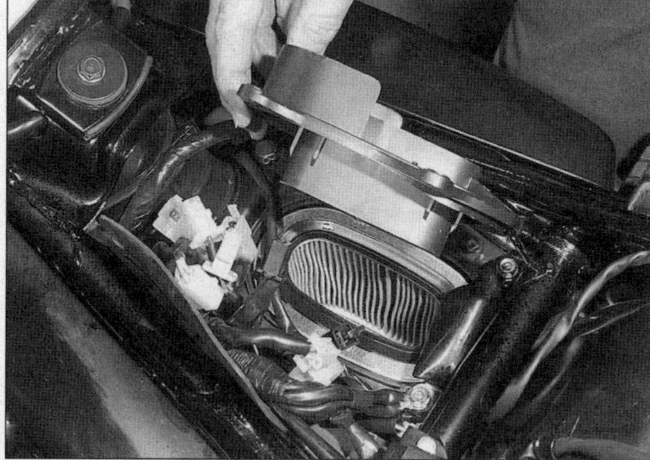

13.6 On 1987 and later models, remove the four cover screws and detach the air cleaner housing cover

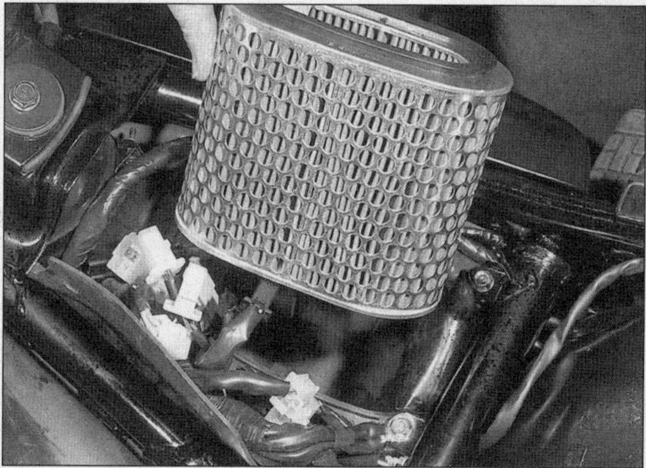

13.7 On 1987 and later models, remove the filter element

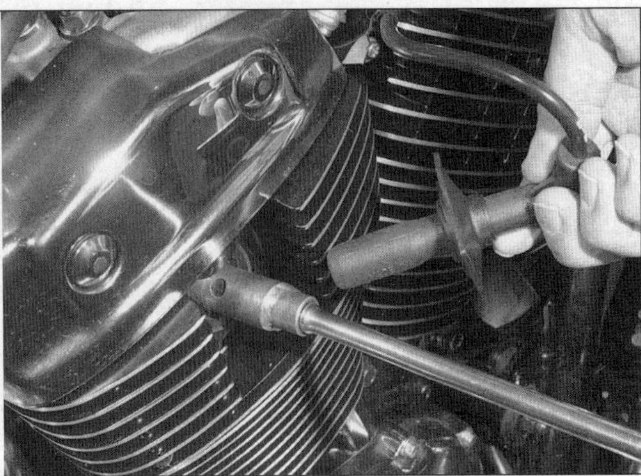
15.2 Remove the spark plug cap

14 Cylinder compression - check

1 Among other things, poor engine performance may be caused by leaking valves, incorrect valve clearances, a leaking head gasket, or worn pistons, rings and/or cylinder walls. A cylinder compression check will help pinpoint these conditions and can also indicate the presence of excessive carbon deposits in the cylinder heads.

2 The only tools required are a compression gauge and a spark plug wrench. Depending on the outcome of the initial test, a squirt-type oil can may also be needed.

3 Start the engine and allow it to reach normal operating temperature.

4 Support the bike securely so it can't be knocked over during this procedure.

5 Remove *one* spark plug from each cylinder (see Section 15). Work carefully - don't strip the spark plug hole threads and don't burn your hands.

6 Disable the ignition by unplugging the primary wires from the coils (see Chapter 5). Be sure to mark the locations of the wires before detaching them.

7 Install the compression gauge in one of the spark plug holes.

8 Hold or block the throttle wide open.

9 Crank the engine over a minimum of four or five revolutions (or until the gauge reading stops increasing) and observe the initial movement of the compression gauge needle as well as the final total gauge reading. Repeat the procedure for the other cylinder and compare the results to the value listed in this Chapter's Specifications.

10 If the compression in both cylinders built up quickly and evenly to the specified amount, you can assume the engine upper end is in reasonably good mechanical condition. Worn or sticking piston rings and worn cylinders will produce very little initial movement of the gauge needle, but compression will tend to build up gradually as the engine spins over. Valve and valve seat leakage, or head gasket leakage, is indicated by low initial compression which does not tend to build up.

11 To further confirm your findings, add a small amount of engine oil to each cylinder by inserting the nozzle of a squirt-type oil can through the spark plug holes. The oil will tend to seal the piston rings if they are leaking. Repeat the test for the other cylinder.

12 If the compression increases significantly after the addition of the oil, the piston rings and/or cylinders are definitely worn. If the compression does not increase, the pressure is leaking past the valves or the head gasket. Leakage past the valves may be due to insufficient valve clearances, burned, warped or cracked valves or valve seats or valves that are hanging up in the guides.

13 If compression readings are considerably higher than specified, the combustion chambers are probably coated with excessive carbon deposits. It is possible (but not very likely) for carbon deposits to raise the compression enough to compensate for the effects of leakage past rings or valves. Remove the cylinder head and carefully decarbonize the combustion chambers (see Chapter 2).

15.7a Spark plug manufacturers recommend using a wire type gauge when checking the gap - if the wire doesn't slide between the electrodes with a slight drag, adjustment is required

15 Spark plugs - replacement

1 Make sure your spark plug socket is the correct size before attempting to remove the plugs.

2 Disconnect the spark plug caps from the spark plugs **(see illustration)**. Inspect the caps for damage and wear.

3 Using compressed air, blow any accumulated debris from around the spark plugs. No dirt or debris must be allowed into the combustion chamber. Remove the plugs with a spark plug socket.

4 Inspect the electrodes for wear. Both the center and side electrodes should have square edges and the side electrode should be of uniform thickness. Look for excessive deposits and evidence of a cracked or chipped insulator around the center electrode. Compare your spark plugs to the color spark plug reading chart. Check the threads, the washer and the ceramic insulator body for cracks and other damage.

5 If the electrodes are not excessively worn, and if the deposits can be easily removed with a wire brush, the plugs can be regapped and reused (if no cracks or chips are visible in the insulator). If in doubt concerning the condition of the plugs, replace them with new ones, as the expense is minimal.

6 Cleaning spark plugs by sandblasting is permitted, provided you clean the plugs with a high flash-point solvent afterwards.

7 Before installing new plugs, make sure they are the correct type and heat range. Check the gap between the electrodes, as they are not preset. For best results, use a wire-type gauge rather than a flat gauge to check the gap **(see illustration)**. If the gap must be adjusted, bend the side electrode only and be very careful not to chip or crack the insulator nose **(see illustration)**. Make

15.7b To change the gap, bend the side electrode only, as indicated by the arrows, and be very careful not to crack or chip the ceramic insulator surrounding the center electrode

16.3a Lubing a cable with a pressure lube adapter is easier and less messy (available at most bike shops)

sure the washer is in place before installing each plug.

8 Since the cylinder head is made of aluminum, which is soft and easily damaged, thread the plugs into the heads by hand. Since the plugs are recessed, slip a short length of hose over the end of the plug to use as a tool to thread it into place. The hose will grip the plug well enough to turn it, but will start to slip if the plug begins to cross-thread in the hole - this will prevent damaged threads and the accompanying repair costs.

9 Once the plugs are finger tight, the job can be finished with a socket. If a torque wrench is available, tighten the spark plugs to the torque listed in this Chapter's Specifications. If you do not have a torque wrench, tighten the plugs finger tight (until the washers bottom on the cylinder head) then use a wrench to tighten them an additional 1/4 to 1/2 turn. Regardless of the method used, do not over-tighten them.

10 Reconnect the spark plug caps and reinstall the air ducts.

16 Lubrication - general

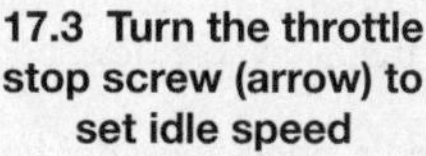

1 Since the controls, cables and various other components of a motorcycle are exposed to the elements, they should be lubricated regularly to ensure safe and trouble-free operation.

2 The clutch lever and brake lever pivots, the brake pedal, shift lever and sidestand pivots, the rear brake linkage, the shift linkage and the footpeg hinges should be lubricated frequently. In order for the lubricant to be applied where it will do the most good, the component should be disassembled. However, if chain and cable lubricant is being used, it can be applied to the pivot joint gaps and will usually work its way into the areas where friction occurs. If motor oil or

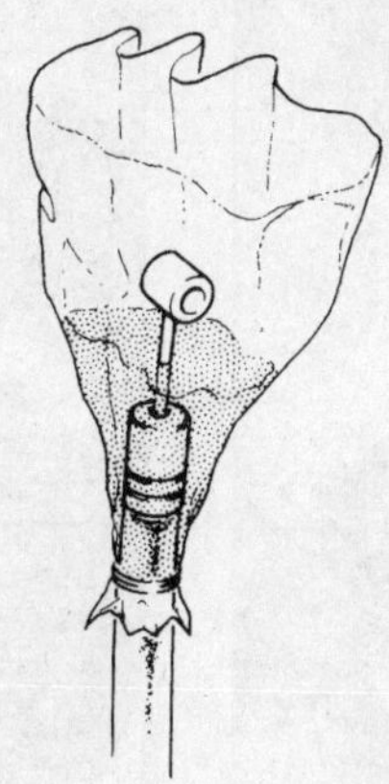

16.3b If you don't have a pressure lube adapter, make a funnel at one end of the cable with a small piece of plastic, tape it to the cable and carefully pour a small of oil into the funnel

light grease is being used, apply it sparingly as it may attract dirt (which could cause the controls to bind or wear at an accelerated rate). **Note:** *One of the best lubricants for the control lever pivots is a dry-film lubricant (available from many sources by different names).*

3 To lubricate the throttle cables, disconnect them at the lower end, then lubricate them with a pressure lube adapter **(see illustration)**. If you don't have one, disconnect both ends of the cable and use a funnel **(see illustration)**. It's a good idea to remove and lubricate the throttle twist grip whenever the throttle cables are lubricated (see the handlebar switch removal section of Chapter 9).

4 The choke cables should be lubricated the same way as the throttle cables (see Chapter 4 for the choke cable removal procedure).

5 The speedometer cable should be removed from its housing and lubricated with motor oil or cable lubricant (see Chapter 9 for speedometer cable removal).

6 The swingarm pivot ball and needle bearings should be lubricated with lithium-based multi-purpose grease (see Chapter 6 for the swingarm removal procedure).

17 Idle speed - check and adjustment

1 The idle speed should be checked and adjusted before and after the carburetors are synchronized and whenever it is obviously high or low. Before adjusting the idle speed, make sure the valve clearances and spark plug gaps are correct. Also, turn the handlebars back-and-forth and see if the idle speed changes as this is done. If it does, the throttle cables may not be correctly adjusted, or may be routed incorrectly. This is a dangerous condition that can cause loss of control of the bike. Be sure to correct this problem before proceeding.

2 The engine should be at normal operating temperature, which is usually reached after 10 to 15 minutes of stop and go riding. Put the transmission in Neutral and place the bike on its sidestand.

3 Turn the throttle stop screw **(see illustration)**, until the idle speed listed in this Chapter's Specifications is obtained.

4 Snap the throttle open and shut a few times, then recheck the idle speed. If necessary, repeat the adjustment procedure.

5 If a smooth, steady idle can't be achieved, the air/fuel mixture may be incorrect. Refer to Chapter 4 for additional carburetor information.

18 Carburetor synchronization - check and adjustment

Warning: Gasoline is extremely flammable, so take extra precautions when you work on any part of the fuel system.

17.3 Turn the throttle stop screw (arrow) to set idle speed

18.7 Remove the vacuum screw (arrow) from each intake port (rear cylinder port shown)

18.12 The carburetor synchronization screw (arrow) is located between the carburetors

Don't smoke or allow open flames or bare light bulbs near the work area, and don't work in a garage where a gas-type appliance (such as a water heater or clothes dryer) is present. If you spill any fuel on your skin, rinse it off immediately with soap and water. When you perform any kind of work on the fuel system, wear safety glasses and have a class B type fire extinguisher on hand.

1 Carburetor synchronization is simply the process of adjusting the carburetors so they pass the same amount of fuel/air mixture to each cylinder. This is done by measuring the vacuum produced in each cylinder. Carburetors that are out of synchronization will result in decreased fuel mileage, increased engine temperature, less than ideal throttle response and higher vibration levels.

2 To properly synchronize the carburetors, you will need some sort of vacuum gauge setup, preferably with a gauge for each cylinder, or a mercury manometer, which is a calibrated tube arrangement that utilizes columns of mercury to indicate engine vacuum. You'll also need an auxiliary fuel tank, since the bike's fuel tank must be removed for access to the vacuum fittings and synchronizing screws.

3 A manometer can be purchased from a motorcycle dealer or accessory shop and should have the necessary rubber hoses supplied with it for hooking into the vacuum hose fittings on the carburetors.

4 A vacuum gauge setup can also be purchased from a dealer or fabricated from commonly available hardware and automotive vacuum gauges.

5 The manometer is the more reliable and accurate instrument, and for that reason is preferred over the vacuum gauge setup; however, since the mercury used in the manometer is a liquid, and extremely toxic, extra precautions must be taken during use and storage of the instrument.

6 Because of the nature of the synchronization procedure and the need for special instruments, most owners leave the task to a dealer service department or a reputable motorcycle repair shop.

7 Remove the screws from the intake vacuum ports **(see illustration)** and install vacuum gauge adapters. Connect the vacuum gauges or manometer to the adapters.

8 Start the engine and let it run until it reaches normal operating temperature.

9 Make sure there are no leaks in the vacuum gauge or manometer setup, as false readings will result.

10 Start the engine and make sure the idle speed is correct. If it isn't, adjust it (see Section 17).

11 The carburetor for the rear cylinder is the "base" carburetor. In other words, vacuum at the front carburetor should be compared to vacuum at the rear carburetor. The vacuum readings for both of the cylinders should be within the allowable deviation listed in this Chapter's Specifications. If the variance in vacuum between the two carburetors exceeds the allowable deviation, synchronize the carburetors.

12 To perform the adjustment, synchronize the carburetors by turning the synchronizing screw **(see illustration)** until the vacuum is identical or within the allowable deviation for both cylinders.

13 Snap the throttle open and shut two or three times, then recheck synchronization and readjust if necessary.

14 When the adjustment is complete, recheck the vacuum readings and idle speed, then stop the engine. Remove the vacuum gauge or manometer and install the intake port screws.

19 Cooling system - check

Warning: The engine must be cool before beginning this procedure.

Note: *Check the coolant level before checking the cooling system (see Section 3).*

1 The cooling system should be checked carefully at the recommended intervals. Look for evidence of leaks, check the condition of the coolant, check the radiator for clogged fins and damage. Make sure the radiator cooling fan operates when the coolant gets hot. If it doesn't, either the fan motor, the fan switch or the circuit is defective (see Chapter 3).

2 Inspect the condition of the coolant hoses. Look for cracks, abrasions and any other damage that might cause a leak. Squeeze the hoses. They should feel firm yet pliable, and should return to their original shape when released. If they feel hard or stiff, replace them.

3 Look for signs of leaks at every cooling system joint (where the hoses are clamped to the radiator, thermostat and water pump). If a hose is leaking at one of these components, tighten the hose clamp. Of course, if a hose is in poor condition, tightening a hose clamp can tear the hose, making the leak worse. Such hoses must be replaced.

4 Inspect the radiator for signs of leaks and other damage. Leaks in the radiator leave tell-tale scale deposits or coolant stains on the outside of the core below the leak. If leaks are noted, remove the radiator and have it repaired or replace it (see Chapter 3). Do not use a liquid leak-stopping additive to try to repair leaks.

19.7 To remove the radiator cap, turn the cap counterclockwise to the first stop, let any residual pressure escape, then turn the cap counterclockwise until it's free

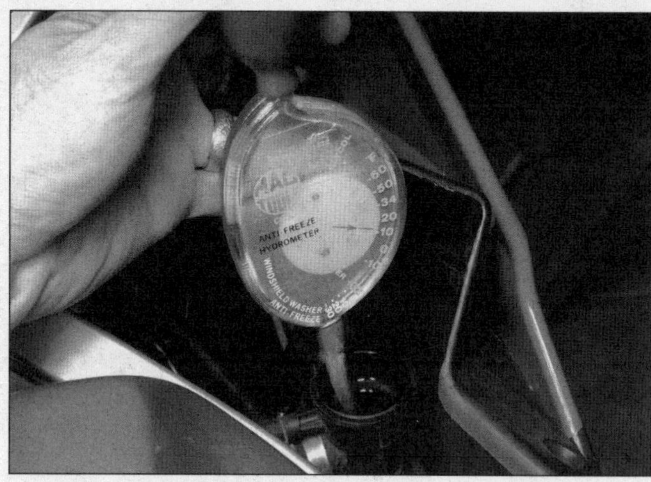

19.8 An antifreeze hydrometer is helpful for determining the condition of the coolant

5 Inspect the radiator fins for any debris - mud, dirt, insects, etc. - which impedes the flow of air through the radiator. If the fins are dirty, force water or low pressure compressed air through the fins from the backside. If the fins are bent or distorted, carefully straighten them with a small flat-blade screwdriver.

6 Remove the fuel tank (see Chapter 4) and the steering side covers (see Chapter 8).

7 Remove the radiator cap **(see illustration)** by turning it counterclockwise until it reaches a stop. If you hear a hissing sound, there's still pressure in the system. Wait until it stops. Then press down on the cap and continue turning it counterclockwise and remove it. Inspect the condition of the coolant in the radiator. If it's rust-colored, or if scale has accumulated inside the radiator, drain, flush and refill the system with a new 50/50 mixture of distilled water and ethylene glycol. Inspect the cap gasket for cracks and any other damage. If any damage is evident, have the cap pressure-tested by a dealer service department or replace it. Install the cap by turning it clockwise until it reaches the first stop, then push it down and continue turning it clockwise until it stops.

8 Check the antifreeze content of the coolant with an antifreeze hydrometer **(see illustration)**. Coolant might appear to be in good condition but might be too weak to offer adequate protection. If the hydrometer indicates a weak mixture, drain, flush and refill the cooling system (see Section 20).

9 Start the engine and let it reach normal operating temperature, then check for leaks again. As the coolant temperature reaches its upper operating temperature, the fan should come on automatically and the coolant temperature should begin to come back down. If it the fan doesn't come on, inspect the fan, the fan switch and the circuit (see Chapter 3).

10 If the coolant level is constantly low, and no evidence of leaks can be found, have the cooling system pressure checked by a Honda dealer service department or by a motorcycle repair shop.

20 Cooling system - draining, flushing and refilling

Warning: Allow the engine to cool completely before performing this maintenance operation. Also, don't allow antifreeze to come into contact with your skin or painted surfaces of the vehicle. Rinse off spills immediately with plenty of water. Antifreeze is highly toxic if ingested. Never leave antifreeze lying around in an open container or in puddles on the floor; children and pets are attracted by its sweet smell and may drink it. Check with local authorities about disposing used antifreeze. Many communities have collection centers that can dispose of antifreeze safely. Antifreeze is also combustible, so don't store it or use it near open flames.

Draining

1 Remove the fuel tank (see Chapter 4) and the steering covers (see Chapter 8).

2 Remove the radiator cap (see Section 20).

3 To drain the cooling system, remove the drain bolt from the water pump **(see illustration)**. Discard the drain bolt sealing washers. **Note:** *Initially, the coolant will rush out with some force, so be sure to position your drain pan accordingly.*

4 Remove the reservoir (see Chapter 3). Drain the reservoir into the drain pan and wash out the reservoir with clean water. Install the reservoir.

20.3 The cooling system drain bolt (arrow) is on the water pump

Flushing

5 Flush the system with clean tap water by inserting a garden hose into the radiator filler neck. Allow the water to run through the system until clear water comes out the drain hole. If the radiator is extremely corroded, remove it by referring to Chapter 3 and have it cleaned at a radiator shop.

6 Clean the drain bolt holes and install the drain bolts with new sealing washers. Tighten the drain bolts to the torque listed in this Chapter's Specifications.

7 Fill the cooling system with a mixture of clean water and flushing compound. Make sure that the flushing compound is compatible with aluminum components and follow the manufacturer's instructions carefully.

8 Install the radiator cap (see Section 21), start the engine and allow it to reach normal operating temperature. Let it run for about ten minutes.

9 Stop the engine. Let the machine cool for awhile, then cover the radiator cap with a heavy rag and turn it counterclockwise to the

21.2 Refer to the vacuum hose routing diagram label on the inside of the side cover for a schematic of the EVAP system on your machine

21.3a Locate the carburetor air vent control valve (left arrow) and the purge control valve (hidden behind frame gusset, right arrow), then inspect the hoses connecting these components with the rest of the system

first stop, wait for it to release any pressure in the system, then push down on the cap and remove it.

10 Drain the system again.

11 Fill the system with clean water, then repeat Steps 8, 9 and 10.

Refilling

12 Fill the system with a 50/50 mixture of distilled water and ethylene glycol until the system is full (all the way up to the top of the radiator filler neck).

13 Remove the cap from the cooling system reservoir (see Section 3) and fill the reservoir.

14 To bleed the cooling system of air, place the fuel tank in position (it's not necessary to bolt it down), hook up the fuel lines to the carburetors, put the transmission in Neutral, start the engine and let it idle for two to three minutes. Snap the throttle three or four times. Stop the engine and add coolant up to the top of the filler neck again. Install the radiator cap. Check the coolant level in the reservoir and, if necessary, fill it to the upper mark. Install the reservoir filler neck cap.

15 Install the steering side covers (see Chapter 8) and the fuel tank (see Chapter 4).

21 Evaporative emission control system (California models only) - inspection

1 Remove the fuel tank (see Chapter 4).

2 On 1985 and 1986 models, remove the right side cover; on all other models, remove the left side cover (see Chapter 8). Study the vacuum hose routing diagram on the inside of the side cover **(see illustration)**.

3 Inspect the hoses that connect the fuel tank, the EVAP canister, the EVAP purge control valve, the carburetor air vent control valve and the carburetors **(see illustrations)**. Look for loose or detached hoses and weak or missing clamps. Note the condition of the hoses themselves. There should be no cracks, tears or general deterioration. Make sure that none of the hoses are kinked or twisted, which will obstruct the passage of crankcase and fuel system emissions through the system. If any hose is damaged, replace it (see Chapter 4).

4 Lean the bike over to the left on its sidestand and inspect the EVAP canister, which is located underneath the radiator **(see illustration)**.

5 Install the left side cover and the fuel tank.

22 Exhaust system - check

1 Periodically check all of the exhaust system joints for leaks and loose fasteners. If tightening the clamp bolts fails to stop any

21.3b The EVAP canister hoses are routed along the right side of the frame (arrow)

21.4 The EVAP canister is beneath the radiator

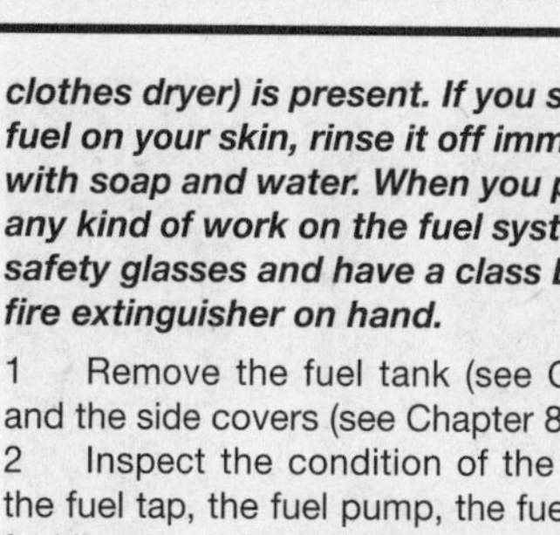

23.7 You'll need a special socket to torque the steering head bearing adjustment nut (it's available at Honda parts departments)

leaks, replace the gaskets with new ones (see Chapter 4).

2 The exhaust pipe flange nuts at the cylinder heads are especially prone to loosening, which could cause damage to the head. Check them frequently and keep them tight.

23 Steering head bearings - check, adjustment and lubrication

1 Steering head bearings can become dented, rough or loose as the machine ages. In extreme cases, worn or loose steering head bearings can cause steering wobble that is potentially dangerous.

Check

2 To check the steering head bearings, support the motorcycle securely and block the machine so the front wheel is in the air.

3 Point the wheel straight ahead and slowly move the handlebars from side-to-side. If there are any dents or rough spots in the bearing races, the front end will feel "rough" as the bearings roll over these spots when the handlebars are turned from side-to-side. If the front end feels rough, replace the steering head bearings and races (see Chapter 6).

4 Facing the bike from the front, grasp the fork legs firmly and try to move them forward and backward. If the steering head bearings are loose, you'll feel a "clunk" (freeplay) as the fork legs are moved back and forth. If there's freeplay in the steering head bearings, adjust the steering head as follows.

Adjustment

5 Remove the headlight (see Chapter 9).

6 Remove the handlebars, the upper triple clamp, the steering stem locknut and the lock washer (see Chapter 6).

7 Tighten the bearing adjustment nut **(see illustration)** to the torque listed in this Chapter's Specifications. To use a torque wrench on the nut, you'll need the Honda tool (07916-3710100, 07916-3710101, or equivalent). The tool can be ordered from a Honda dealer.

8 Turn the steering stem from lock to lock five or six times and check for binding.

9 If there is any binding in the steering stem, disassemble the steering stem assembly and inspect the bearings (see Chapter 6).

10 If the steering operates properly, verify that the adjustment nut is still tightened to the correct torque, then reassemble the front end.

11 Install the lock washer, locknut, upper triple clamp and handlebars (see Chapter 6).

12 Install the headlight (see Chapter 9).

Lubrication

13 Periodic cleaning and repacking of the steering head bearings is recommended by the manufacturer. Refer to Chapter 6 for steering head bearing lubrication and replacement procedures.

24 Fasteners - check

1 Since vibration of the machine tends to loosen fasteners, all nuts, bolts, screws, etc. should be periodically checked for proper tightness.

2 Pay particular attention to the following:

Brake caliper bolts and banjo bolts
Spark plugs
Engine oil drain plug
Oil drain plug
Cooling system drain plugs
Gearshift pedal (and linkage, if equipped)
Footpegs and sidestand
Engine mounting bolts
Shock absorber or rear suspension unit mounting bolts
Front axle (or axle nut) and axle pinch bolt
Rear axle nut

3 If a torque wrench is available, use it along with the torque specifications at the beginning of this and the other Chapters.

25 Fuel system - check and filter replacement

Warning: Gasoline is extremely flammable, so take extra precautions when you work on any part of the fuel system. Don't smoke or allow open flames or bare light bulbs near the work area, and don't work in a garage where a gas-type appliance (such as a water heater or clothes dryer) is present. If you spill any fuel on your skin, rinse it off immediately with soap and water. When you perform any kind of work on the fuel system, wear safety glasses and have a class B type fire extinguisher on hand.

1 Remove the fuel tank (see Chapter 4) and the side covers (see Chapter 8).

2 Inspect the condition of the fuel tank, the fuel tap, the fuel pump, the fuel filter, the fuel lines and the carburetors. Look for leaks and signs of damage or wear (see Chapter 4).

3 If the fuel tap is leaking, note whether the fuel tap-to-fuel tank locknut is tight. If leakage persists, the tap should be removed from the fuel tank, disassembled, cleaned and inspected (see Chapter 4).

4 If the fuel lines are cracked or otherwise deteriorated, replace them.

5 If the carburetor gaskets are leaking, the carburetors should be disassembled and rebuilt (see Chapter 4).

6 Install the fuel tank and side covers.

Fuel filter replacement

Warning: Make sure that the fuel valve is turned off before disconnecting any fuel lines. Do not smoke or perform any of the following procedures in the vicinity of an open flame.

1985 and 1986 models

7 Disconnect the fuel inlet line from the fuel pump (see Chapter 4).

8 Remove the regulator/rectifier from its mounting bracket (see Chapter 9).

9 Remove the fuel filter mounting bracket nut and detach the fuel filter and mounting bracket from the bottom of the auxiliary fuel tank.

10 Disconnect the fuel lines from the fuel filter and remove the fuel filter from the mounting bracket.

11 Installation is the reverse of removal. Be sure to install the new filter with the directional arrow pointing toward the fuel outlet line.

1987 through 1996 models

12 Locate the fuel filter, on the right side of the bike, right above the swingarm pivot bolt.

13 Disconnect the fuel lines from the fuel filter.

14 Remove the fuel filter.

15 Installation is the reverse of removal. Be sure to install the new filter with the directional arrow pointing toward the fuel outlet line.

1997 and later models

16 Remove the air cleaner housing (see Chapter 4).

17 Remove the two mounting nuts and detach the fuel pump/fuel filter assembly from the air cleaner housing.

18 Disconnect the inlet and outlet lines

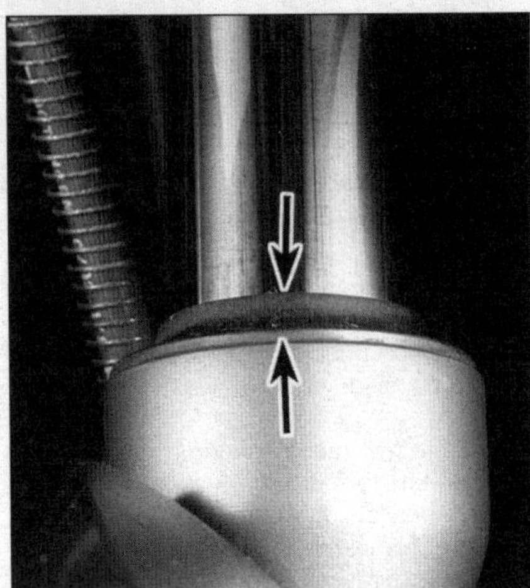

26.3 Inspect each fork seal for oil leaks in the indicated areas (arrows); if oil is leaking past either side of the seal, replace the seal

from the fuel filter.

19 Separate the fuel filter from the fuel pump/fuel filter bracket.

20 Installation is the reverse of removal. Be sure to install the new filter with the directional arrow pointing toward the fuel outlet line.

26 Suspension - check

1 The suspension components must be maintained in top operating condition to ensure rider safety. Loose, worn or damaged suspension parts decrease the vehicle's stability and control.

2 While standing alongside the motorcycle, lock the front brake and push on the handlebars to compress the forks several times. See if the fork tubes move up-and-down smoothly without binding. If the fork tubes stick in the sliders, disassemble and inspect the fork legs (see Chapter 6).

3 Carefully inspect the area around the fork seals for any signs of fork oil leakage **(see illustration)**. If leakage is evident, the seals must be replaced (see Chapter 6).

4 Check the tightness of all suspension nuts and bolts to be sure none have worked loose.

5 Inspect the shock absorber(s) for fluid leakage and tightness of the mounting nuts. If leakage is found, the shock(s) must be replaced.

6 Support the bike securely so it can't be knocked over during this procedure. Grab the swingarm on each side, just ahead of the axle. Rock the swingarm from side to side - there should be no discernible movement at the rear. If there's a little movement or a slight clicking can be heard, make sure the pivot bolt or shafts are tight. If they're tight but movement is still noticeable, remove the swingarm and replace the bearings (see Chapter 6).

7 Inspect the tightness of the rear suspension nuts and bolts (see Chapter 6).

27 Suspension adjustments

1 Rear spring preload can be adjusted on all models.

Warning: The rear shock absorber settings must be even to prevent unstable handling.

2 Adjust rear spring preload by turning the adjuster on the bottom of each shock absorber with the special pin spanner provided in the bike tool kit. The pin spanner fits into the holes in the lower part of the shock body.

3 The numerically lower settings are for lighter loads and smooth roads. The numerically higher settings are for heavier loads and rough roads. Position 2 is the standard position.

Chapter 2
Engine, clutch and transmission

Contents

Degrees of difficulty

Easy, suitable for novice with little experience 

Fairly easy, suitable for beginner with some experience 

Fairly difficult, suitable for competent DIY mechanic 

Difficult, suitable for experienced DIY mechanic 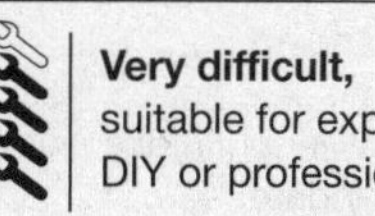

Very difficult, suitable for expert DIY or professional 

Specifications

General

Bore x stroke	87.5 x 91.4 mm (3.44 x 3.60 inches)
Displacement	1099 cc (67 cubic inches)

General (continued)

Compression ratio	
1985 and 1986	9 to 1
1987 through 1996 VT1100C	8.5 to 1
VT1100C2, VT1100T, 1997 and later VT1100C	8 to 1

Rocker arms

Hydraulic tappet compression stroke	0.2 mm (0.008 inch)
Tappet assist spring free length	
Standard	18.57 mm (0.731 inch)
Limit	17.80 mm (0.701 inch)
Rocker arm inside diameter	
Standard	13.750 to 13.768 mm (0.5413 to 0.5420 inch)
Limit	13.778 mm (0.5424 inch)
Rocker arm shaft diameter	
1985 through 1996 VT1100C	
Intake	
Standard	13.716 to 13.734 mm (0.5400 to 0.5407 inch)
Limit	13.796 mm (0.5396 inch)
Exhaust	
Standard	13.716 to 13.737 mm (0.5400 to 0.5408 inch)
Limit	13.706 mm (0.5396 inch)
VT1100C2, VT1100T, 1997 and later VT1100C	
Standard	13.716 to 13.734 mm (0.5400 to 0.5407 inch)
Limit	13.706 mm (0.5396 inch)
Rocker arm-to-rocker shaft clearance (VT1100C2, VT1100T, 1997 and later VT1100C)	
Standard	0.016 to 0.052 mm (0.0006 to 0.0020 inch)
Limit	0.072 mm (0.0028 inch)

Camshafts

Camshaft holder inside diameter (1985 through 1996 VT1100C)	
Standard	20.000 to 20.021 mm (0.7874 to 0.7882 inch)
Limit	20.031 mm (0.7886 inch)
Bearing oil clearance	
1985 through 1996	
A and B	
Standard	0.020 to 0.062 mm (0.0008 to 0.0024 inch)
Limit	0.072 (0.0028 inch)
C	
Standard	0.045 to 0.087 mm (0.0018 to 0.0034 inch)
Limit	0.097 mm (0.0038 inch)
1997 on	
A and B	
Standard	0.050 to 0.111 mm (0.0020 to 0.0044 inch)
Limit	0.130 mm (0.005 inch)
C	
Standard	0.065 to 0.126 mm (0.0026 to 0.0050 inch)
Limit	0.145 mm (0.006 inch)
Camshaft runout limit	0.05 mm (0.002 inch)
Camshaft lobe height	
1985 and 1986 (intake and exhaust)	
Standard	36.690 mm (1.4445 inches)
Limit	36.670 mm (1.4437 inches)
1987 through 1996 VT1100C	
Front cylinder (intake and exhaust)	
Standard	36.041 mm (1.4189 inches)
Limit	36.022 mm (1.4182 inches)
Rear cylinder (intake and exhaust)	
Standard	36.237 mm (1.4267 inches)
Limit	36.219 mm (1.4259 inches)
VT1100C2, VT1100T, 1997 and later VT1100C	
Intake	
Standard	38.021 to 38.181 mm (1.4969 to 1.5032 inches)
Limit	37.99 mm (1.496 inches)
Exhaust	
Standard	38.027 to 38.187 mm (1.4971 to 1.5034 inches)
Limit	38.00 mm (1.496 inches)
Cam chain tensioner wedge height limit	No more than 9 mm (0.35 inch)

Cylinder head, valves and valve springs (1985 through 1996 VT1100C)

Cylinder head warpage limit	0.05 mm (0.002 inch)
Valve stem diameter	
Intake	
Standard	6.670 to 6.595 mm (0.2587 to 0.2596 inch)
Limit	6.56 mm (0.258 inch)
Exhaust	
Standard	6.550 to 6.575 mm (0.2579 to 0.2589 inch)
Limit	6.54 mm (0.257 inch)
Valve guide inside diameter	
Intake	
Standard	6.600 to 6.615 mm (0.2598 to 0.2604 inch)
Limit	6.635 mm (0.2612 inch)
Exhaust	
Standard	6.600 to 6.615 mm (0.2598 to 0.2604 inch)
Limit	6.655 mm (0.2620 inch)
Stem-to-guide clearance	
Intake	
Standard	0.005 to 0.045 mm (0.0002 to 0.0018 inch)
Limit	0.075 mm (0.0030 inch)
Exhaust	
Standard	0.025 to 0.065 mm (0.0010 to 0.0026 inch)
Limit	0.115 (0.0045 inch)
Valve seat width (intake and exhaust)	
Standard	0.90 to 1.10 mm (0.035 to 0.043 inch)
Limit	1.50 mm (0.059 inch)
Valve spring free length	
Outer spring	
Intake	
Standard	45.70 mm (1.799 inches)
Limit	43.90 mm (1.728 inches)
Exhaust	
Standard	43.50 mm (1.713 inches)
Limit	41.80 mm (1.646 inches)
Inner spring	
Intake	
Standard	37.90 mm (1.492 inches)
Limit	36.40 mm (1.433 inches)
Exhaust	
Standard	37.90 mm (1.492 inches)
Limit	36.40 mm (1.433 inches)

Cylinder head, valves and valve springs (VT1100C2, VT1100T, 1997-on VT1100C)

Cylinder head warpage limit	0.05 mm (0.002 inch)
Valve stem diameter	
Intake	
Standard	6.575 to 6.590 mm (0.2589 to 0.2594 inch)
Limit	6.57 mm (0.259 inch)
Exhaust	
Standard	6.555 to 6.570 mm (0.2581 to 0.2587 inch)
Limit	6.54 mm (0.257 inch)
Valve guide inside diameter	
Intake	
Standard	6.600 to 6.615 mm (0.2598 to 0.2604 inch)
Limit	6.635 mm (0.2612 inch)
Exhaust	
Standard	6.600 to 6.615 mm (0.2598 to 0.2604 inch)
Limit	6.655 mm (0.2620 inch)
Stem-to-guide clearance	
Intake	
Standard	0.010 to 0.040 mm (0.0004 to 0.0016 inch)
Limit	0.08 mm (0.003 inch)
Exhaust	
Standard	0.030 to 0.060 mm (0.0012 to 0.0024 inch)
Limit	0.12 (0.005 inch)
Valve seat width (intake and exhaust)	
Standard	0.90 to 1.10 mm (0.035 to 0.043 inch)
Limit	1.50 mm (0.059 inch)

Cylinder head, valves and valve springs (VT1100C2, VT1100T, 1997-on VT1100C) (continued)

Valve spring free length	
Outer spring	
Intake	
Standard	45.70 mm (1.799 inches)
Limit	43.90 mm (1.728 inches)
Exhaust	
Standard	43.50 mm (1.713 inches)
Limit	41.80 mm (1.646 inches)
Inner spring (intake and exhaust)	
Standard	41.37 mm (1.629 inches)
Limit	39.9 mm (1.57 inches)

Cylinders

Bore diameter	
Standard	87.500 to 87.515 mm (3.4449 to 3.4466 inches)
Limit	87.545 mm (3.4466 inches)
Warpage (across top of cylinder)	0.05 mm (0.002 inch)
Taper and out-of-round limit	0.05 mm (0.002 inch)

Pistons

Piston diameter	
Standard	87.470 to 87.490 mm (3.4437 to 3.4445 inches) measured at 10 mm (0.4 inch) from the bottom of the skirt
Limit	87.41 mm (3.441 inches)
Piston-to-cylinder clearance	
Standard	0.010 to 0.045 mm (0.0004 to 0.0018 inch)
Limit	0.32 mm (0.013 inch)
Ring side clearance	
1985 through 1996 VT1100C	
Top and second rings	
Standard	0.015 to 0.045 mm (0.006 to 0.0018 inch)
Limit	0.25 mm (0.010 inch)
Oil ring	
Standard	0.030 to 0.035 mm (0.0012 to 0.0014 inch)
Limit	0.10 mm (0.004 inch)
VT1100C2, VT1100T, 1997 and later VT1100C	
Top ring	
Standard	0.020 to 0.050 mm (0.0008 to 0.0020 inch)
Limit	0.25 mm (0.010 inch)
Second ring	
Standard	0.015 to 0.045 mm (0.0006 to 0.0018 inch)
Limit	0.20 mm (0.008 inch)
Ring end gap	
Top and second rings	
Standard	0.20 to 0.35 mm (0.008 to 0.014 inch)
Limit	0.50 mm (0.020 inch)
Oil ring	
Standard	0.30 to 0.90 mm (0.012 to 0.035 inch)
Limit	1.1 mm (0.04 inch)
Piston pin bore	
Standard	22.002 to 22.008 mm (0.8662 to 0.8665 inch)
Limit	22.018 mm (0.8668 inch)
Piston pin diameter	
Standard	21.994 to 22.000 mm (0.8695 to 0.8661 inch)
Limit	21.984 mm (0.8655 inch)
Piston-to-piston pin clearance	
Standard	0.002 to 0.014 mm (0.0001 to 0.0005 inch)
Limit	0.034 mm (0.0013 inch)
Piston pin-to-connecting rod small end clearance	
Standard	0.020 to 0.047 mm (0.0008 to 0.0019 inch)
Limit	0.00 mm (0.003 inch)

Crankshaft, connecting rods and bearings

Connecting rod small end I.D.	
Standard	22.020 to 22.041 mm (0.8669 to 0.8678 inch)
Limit	21.051 mm (0.8681 inch)

Main bearing oil clearance	
Standard	0.030 to 0.046 mm (0.0012 to 0.0018 inch)
Limit	0.060 mm (0.0024 inch)
Connecting rod side clearance	
Standard	0.10 to 0.25 mm (0.004 to 0.010 inch)
Limit	0.28 mm (0.011 inch)
Connecting rod bearing oil clearance	
Standard	0.038 to 0.062 mm (0.0015 to 0.0024 inch)
Limit	0.070 mm (0.0028 inch)
Crankshaft runout limit	0.05 mm (0.002 inch)

Oil pump

Rotor tip clearance	
Standard	0.15 mm (0.006 inch)
Limit	0.20 mm (0.008 inch)
Pump body clearance	
Standard	0.15 to 0.22 mm (0.006 to 0.009 inch)
Limit	0.35 mm (0.014 inch)
Rotor-to-pump body end clearance	
Standard	0.02 to 0.07 mm (0.001 to 0.003 inch)
Limit	0.10 mm (0.004 inch)

Clutch (1985 through 1996 VT1100C)

Friction disc thickness	
Standard	3.72 to 3.88 mm (0.146 to 0.153 inch)
Minimum	3.1 mm (0.12 inch)
Steel plate warpage limit	0.30 mm (0.012 inch)

Master cylinder

Cylinder inside diameter	
Standard	14.000 to 14.043 mm (0.5512 to 0.5529 inch)
Limit	14.06 mm (0.554 inch)
Piston outside diameter	
Standard	13.957 to 13.984 mm (0.5495 to 0.5506 inch)
Limit	13.94 mm (0.549 inch)
Slave cylinder	
Cylinder inside diameter	
Standard	38.100 to 38.162 mm (1.5000 to 1.5024 inches)
Limit	38.18 mm (1.503 inches)
Piston outside diameter	
Standard	38.036 to 38.075 mm (1.4750 to 1.4990 inches)
Limit	38.02 mm (1.497 inches)
Clutch diaphragm spring free height	
Standard	4.9 mm (0.19 inch)
Minimum	4.5 mm (0.18 inch)
Clutch housing guide inside diameter	
Standard	24.995 to 25.012 mm (0.9841 to 0.9847 inches)
Limit	25.08 mm (0.987 inch)

Clutch (VT1100C2, VT1100T, 1997 and later VT1100C)

Spring free length	
Standard	44.0 mm (1.73 inches)
Minimum	42.5 mm (1.67 inches)
Mainshaft diameter (at clutch housing guide)	
Standard	27.980 to 27.993 mm (1.1016 to 1.1021 inches)
Minimum	27.93 mm (1.100 inches)
Clutch housing guide inside diameter	
Standard	27.955 to 28.012 mm (1.1006 to 1.1028 inches)
Limit	28.08 mm (1.106 inches)

Transmission

Gear inside diameter	
M3, M5, C4 (1985 and 1986)	
M3, M4 (1987 through 1996 VT1100C)	
M3, M5, C4 (VT1100C2, VT1100T, 1997 and later VT1100C)	
Standard	31.000 to 31.025 mm (1.2205 to 1.2215 inches
Limit	31.035 mm (1.2218 inches)
C1, C2	
Standard	33.000 to 33.025 mm (1.2992 to 1.3002 inches)
Limit	33.035 mm (1.3006 inches)

Transmission (continued)

Gear bushing	
Outside diameter	
M3, M5, C4 (1985 and 1986)	
M3, M4 (1987 through 1996 VT1100C)	
M5 (1998 VT1100C2, VT1100T, 1997 and later VT1100C)	
Standard	30.950 to 30.975 mm (1.2185 to 1.2195 inches)
Limit	30.94 mm (1.218 inches)
C1, C2 (1985 through 1996 VT1100C)	
C1 (VT1100C2, VT1100T, 1997 and later VT1100C)	
Standard	32.950 to 32.975 mm (1.2971 to 1.2982 inches)
Limit	32.94 mm (1.297 inches)
M3, C4 (VT1100C2, VT1100T, 1997 and later VT1100C)	
Standard	30.970 to 30.995 mm (1.2193 to 1.2203 inches)
Limit	30.94 mm (1.218 inches)
C2 (VT1100C2, VT1100T, 1997 and later VT1100C)	
Standard	32.955 to 32.980 mm (1.2974 to 1.2984 inches)
Limit	32.94 mm (1.297 inches)
Inside diameter	
M3 (1985 through 1996 VT1100C)	
Standard	27.995 to 28.016 mm (1.1022 to 1.1030 inches)
Limit	28.026 mm (1.1034 inches)
M3, C4 (VT1100C2, VT1100T, 1997 and later VT1100C)	
Standard	28.000 to 28.021 mm (1.1024 to 1.1032 inches)
Limit	28.04 mm (1.104 inches)
C2 (VT1100C2, VT1100T, 1997 and later VT1100C)	
Standard	29.985 to 30.006 mm (1.1805 to 1.1813 inches)
Limit	30.03 mm (1.182 inches)
Bushing-to-shaft clearance	
M3 (1985 through 1996 VT1100C)	
Standard	0.005 to 0.039 mm (0.0002 to 0.0015 inches)
Limit	0.059 mm (0.0023 inch)
M3 (VT1100C2, VT1100T, 1997 and later VT1100C)	
Standard	0.020 to 0.062 mm (0.0008 to 0.0024 inch)
Limit	0.082 mm (0.0032 inch)
C2 (VT1100C2, VT1100T, 1997 and later VT1100C)	
Standard	0.005 to 0.056 mm (0.0002 to 0.0022 inch)
Limit	0.076 mm (0.0030 inch)
C4 (VT1100C2, VT1100T, 1997 and later VT1100C)	
Standard	0.020 to 0.054 mm (0.0008 to 0.0021 inch)
Limit	0.074 mm (0.0029 inch)
Gear-to-bushing clearance	
M3, M5, C1, C2, C4 (1985 and 1986)	
M3, C1, C2 (1987 through 1996 VT1100C)	
M5, C1 (VT1100C2, VT1100T, 1997 and later VT1100C)	
Standard	0.025 to 0.075 mm (0.0010 to 0.0030 inch)
Limit	0.095 mm (0.0037 inch)
M3, C4 (VT1100C2, VT1100T, 1997 and later VT1100C)	
Standard	0.005 to 0.055 mm (0.0002 to 0.0022 inch)
Limit	0.075 mm (0.0030 inch)
C2 (VT1100C2, VT1100T, 1997 and later VT1100C)	
Standard	0.020 to 0.070 mm (0.0008 to 0.0028 inch)
Limit	0.090 mm (0.0035 inch)
Countershaft diameter (VT1100C2, VT1100T, 1997 and later VT1100C)	
At C2	
Standard	29.950 to 29.975 mm (1.1791 to 1.1801 inches)
Limit	29.94 mm (1.179 inches)
At C4	
Standard	27.967 to 27.980 mm (1.1011 to 1.1016 inches)
Limit	27.95 mm (1.100 inches)
Mainshaft diameter (at M3)	
1985 through 1996 VT1100C	
Standard	27.977 to 27.990 mm (1.1015 to 1.1020 inches)
Limit	27.967 mm (1.1011 inches)
VT1100C2, VT1100T, 1997 and later VT1100C	
Standard	27.959 to 27.980 mm (1.1007 to 1.1016 inches)
Limit	27.94 mm (1.100 inches)

Shift fork/shift fork shaft/shift drum

Shift fork tip thickness
- 1985 through 2000 VT1100C, all VT1100T, 1995 through 1999 VT1100C2, 2000 and earlier VT1100C3
  - Left .... 5.93 to 6.00 mm (0.233 to 0.236 inch)
  - Center and right .... 6.43 to 6.50 mm (0.253 to 0.256 inch)
- All others (left, center and right) .... 5.93 to 6.00 mm (0.233 to 0.236 inch)

Shift fork shaft diameter
- Left end
  - Standard .... 13.466 to 13.484 mm (0.5302 to 0.5309 inch)
  - Limit .... 13.456 mm (0.5289 inch)
- Right end
  - Standard .... 13.966 to 13.984 mm (0.5498 to 0.5506 inch)
  - Limit .... 13.956 mm (0.5494 inch)

Shift fork shaft journal inside diameter
- 1985
  - Left
    - Standard .... 13.500 to 13.527 mm (0.5315 to 0.5326 inch)
    - Limit .... 13.537 mm (0.5330 inch)
  - Right
    - Standard .... 14.000 to 14.027 mm (0.5512 to 0.5522 inch)
    - Limit .... 14.037 mm (0.5526 inch)
- 1986 through 1996 VT1100C
  - Left
    - Standard .... 13.466 to 13.484 mm (0.5302 to 0.5309 inch)
    - Limit .... 13.494 mm (0.5313 inch)
  - Right
    - Standard .... 13.966 to 13.984 mm (0.5498 to 0.5506 inch)
    - Limit .... 13.994 mm (0.5509 inch)
- VT1100C2, VT1100T, 1997 and later VT1100C
  - Left
    - Standard .... 13.500 to 13.527 mm (0.5315 to 0.5326 inch)
    - Limit .... 13.537 mm (0.5330 inch)
  - Right
    - Standard .... 14.000 to 14.027 mm (0.5512 to 0.5522 inch)
    - Limit .... 14.037 mm (0.5526 inch)

Shift drum diameter (at left end)
- Standard .... 13.966 to 13.984 mm (0.5498 to 0.5506 inch)
- Limit .... 13.956 mm (0.5494 inch)

Shift drum journal (left crankcase)
- Standard .... 14.000 to 14.018 mm (0.5512 to 0.5519 inch)
- Limit .... 14.028 mm (0.5523 inch)

Output gear

Output gear inside diameter
- Standard .... 25.000 to 25.021 mm (0.9843 to 0.9851 inch)
- Limit .... 25.031 mm (0.9855 inch)

Output gear bushing
- Outside diameter
  - Standard .... 24.959 to 24.980 mm (0.9826 to 0.9835 inch)
  - Limit .... 22.020 to 22.041 mm (0.8669 to 0.8678 inch)
- Inside diameter
  - Standard .... 22.020 to 22.041 mm (0.8669 to 0.8678 inch)
  - Limit .... 22.051 mm (0.8681 inch)

Output gear shaft outside diameter
- Standard .... 21.979 to 22.000 mm (0.0008 0.0024 inch)
- Limit .... 21.969 mm (0.8649 inch)

Gear-to-bushing clearance
- Standard .... 0.020 to 0.062 mm (0.0008 to 0.0024 inch)
- Limit .... 0.082 mm (0.0032 inch)

Gear bushing-to-shaft clearance
- Standard .... 0.020 to 0.062 mm (0.0008 to 0.0024 inch)
- Limit .... 0.082 mm (0.0032 inch)

Damper spring free length
- 1985 and 1986
  - Standard .... 58.5 mm (2.30 inches)
  - Limit .... 57.3 mm (2.26 inches)

Output gear (continued)

Damper spring free length (continued)	
1987 through 1994	
Standard	68.5 mm (2.70 inches)
Limit	67.3 mm (2.65 inches)
1995 on	
Standard	69.3 mm (2.73 inches)
Limit	68.1 mm (2.68 inches)
Backlash	
Standard	0.08 to 0.23 mm (0.003 to 0.009 inch)
Limit	0.40 mm (0.016 inch)
Difference between three measurements	0.10 mm (0.004 inch)

Torque specifications

Cylinder head cover bolts (all models)	
8 mm bolts/nuts	27 Nm (20 ft-lbs)
10 mm nut	40 Nm (29 ft-lbs)
Assist shaft caps	22 Nm (16 ft-lbs)
Rocker arm shaft hole plugs	40 Nm (29 ft-lbs)
Cylinder head bolts	12 Nm (108 in-lbs)
Cam chain tensioner bolts	12 Nm (108 in-lbs)
Camshaft sprocket bolts	18 Nm (156 it-lbs)
Spark plug sleeves	13 Nm (108 in-lbs)
Clutch master cylinder clamp bolts	12 Nm (108 in-lbs)
Fluid hose-to-master cylinder banjo bolt	30 Nm (22 ft-lbs)
Clutch slave cylinder mounting bolts	10 Nm (86 in-lbs)
Fluid hose-to-slave cylinder banjo bolt	30 Nm (22 ft-lbs)
Primary drive gear bolt	100 Nm (72 ft-lbs)
Clutch pressure plate bolts	12 Nm (108 in-lbs)
Clutch center locknut*	
2000 and earlier (except VT1100C2 Shadow Sabre)	100 Nm (72 ft-lbs)
2001 and later (except VT1100C2 Shadow Sabre)	127 Nm (94 ft-lbs)
VT1100C2 Shadow Sabre (2000 and later)	127 Nm (94 ft-lbs)
Oil pump driven sprocket bolt	15 Nm (132 in-lbs)
Clutch cover bolts	12 Nm (108 in-lbs)
Stopper arm bolt	10 Nm (84 in-lbs)
Oil pump mounting bolts	12 Nm (108 in-lbs)
Oil pump cover bolts	13 Nm (108 in-lbs)
Crankcase bolts	
1985 through 1996 VT1100C	
6 mm bolts	10 Nm (89 in-lbs)
8 mm bolts	27 Nm (20 ft-lbs)
VT1100C2, VT1100T, and 1997-on VT1100C	
6 mm bolts	12 Nm (106 in-lbs)
8 mm bolts	26 Nm (19 ft-lbs)
10 mm bolt	39 Nm (29 ft-lbs)
Output driven gear shaft bolt	50 Nm (36 ft-lbs)
Connecting rod bearing cap nuts	60 Nm (43 ft-lbs)
Transmission bearing set plate bolts	12 Nm (108 in-lbs)
Transmission bearing set plate screw	9 Nm (78 in-lbs)
Output gear assembly retaining bolts	32 Nm (23 ft-lbs)

** Apply clean engine oil to the threads and seating surface of the nut. Stake the nut after tightening.*

1 General information

The engine/transmission unit is a water-cooled V-twin. The valves are operated by overhead camshafts which are chain driven off the crankshaft. All models have three-valve heads (two intake and one exhaust valve per cylinder). The engine/transmission assembly is constructed from aluminum alloy. The crankcase is divided vertically.

The crankcase incorporates a wet sump, pressure-fed lubrication system which uses a gear-driven oil pump and an oil filter mounted on the rear of the crankcase.

Power from the crankshaft is routed to the transmission via a coil-spring, wet multi-plate type clutch, which is gear-driven off the crankshaft. The transmission on 1985 and 1986 models, VT1100C2, VT1100T and 1997-on VT1100C models is a five-speed, constant-mesh unit. 1987 through 1990 and 1992 through 1996 VT1100C models use a four-speed, constant-mesh unit.

2 Operations possible with the engine in the frame

The following components and assemblies can be serviced with the engine in the frame:

Alternator/flywheel
Camshafts/cam sprockets/cam chains
Carburetors
Clutch
Gearshift linkage
Ignition pulse generator(s)
Primary drive gear
Starter clutch
Starter motor

3 Operations requiring engine removal

The engine/transmission assembly must be removed from the frame to gain access to the following components:

Cylinder heads/cylinders/pistons
Water pump

The crankcase halves must be separated to gain access to the following components:

Crankshaft, connecting rods and bearings
Oil pump
Transmission
Shift drum and shift forks
Output gear assembly

4 Major engine repair - general note

1 It is not always easy to determine when or if an engine should be completely overhauled, as a number of factors must be considered.

2 High mileage is not necessarily an indication that an overhaul is needed, while low mileage, on the other hand, does not preclude the need for an overhaul. Frequency of servicing is probably the single most important consideration. An engine that has regular and frequent oil and filter changes, as well as other required maintenance, will most likely give many miles of reliable service. Conversely, a neglected engine, or one which has not been broken in properly, may require an overhaul very early in its life.

3 Exhaust smoke and excessive oil consumption are both indications that piston rings and/or valve guides are in need of attention. Make sure oil leaks are not responsible before deciding that the rings and guides are bad. Refer to Chapter 1 and perform a cylinder compression check to determine for certain the nature and extent of the work required.

4 If the engine is making obvious knocking or rumbling noises, the connecting rod and/or main bearings are probably at fault.

5 Loss of power, rough running, excessive valve train noise and high fuel consumption rates may also point to the need for an overhaul, especially if they are all present at the same time. If a complete tune-up does not remedy the situation, major mechanical work is the only solution.

6 An engine overhaul generally involves restoring the internal parts to the specifications of a new engine. During an overhaul the piston rings are replaced and the cylinder walls are bored and/or honed. If a rebore is done, then new pistons are also required. The main and connecting rod bearings are generally replaced with new ones and, if necessary, the crankshaft is also replaced. Generally the valves are serviced as well, since they are usually in less than perfect condition at this point. While the engine is being overhauled, other components such as the carburetors and the starter motor can be rebuilt also. The end result should be a like-new engine that will give as many trouble free miles as the original.

7 Before beginning the engine overhaul, read through all of the related procedures to familiarize yourself with the scope and requirements of the job. Overhauling an engine is not all that difficult, but it is time consuming. Plan on the motorcycle being tied up for a minimum of two weeks. Check on the availability of parts and make sure that any necessary special tools, equipment and supplies are obtained in advance.

8 Most work can be done with typical shop hand tools, although a number of precision measuring tools are required for inspecting parts to determine if they must be replaced. Often a dealer service department or motorcycle repair shop will handle the inspection of parts and offer advice concerning reconditioning and replacement. As a general rule, time is the primary cost of an overhaul so it doesn't pay to install worn or substandard parts.

9 As a final note, to ensure maximum life and minimum trouble from a rebuilt engine, everything must be assembled with care in a spotlessly clean environment.

5 Engine - removal and installation

Warning: Engine removal and installation should be done with the aid of an assistant to avoid damage or injury that could occur if the engine is dropped. A hydraulic floor jack should be used to support and lower the engine if possible (they can be rented at low cost).

Removal

1 Support the bike securely so it can't be knocked over during this procedure. Place a support under the swingarm pivot and be sure the motorcycle is safely braced.

2 Drain the engine oil and remove the oil filter (see Chapter 1). Remove the dipstick.

3 Drain the coolant (see Chapter 1).

4 Remove the seat and side covers (see Chapter 8).

5 Remove the fuel tank (see Chapter 4).

6 Disconnect the negative battery cable; on VT1100C2, VT1100T and 1997-on VT1100C models, remove the battery and the battery holder (see Chapter 9).

7 Remove the air cleaner housing cover and the filter element (see Chapter 1).

8 Remove the air cleaner housing and intake ducts, disconnect the throttle cables from the carburetors and remove the carburetors (see Chapter 4). On 1985 and 1986 models, detach the fuel pump from the frame without disconnecting the fuel lines.

9 Disconnect all four spark plug caps and set the spark plug leads aside. On 1985 and 1986 models, unplug the primary leads from the ignition coils and detach the coils from the frame (see Chapter 5).

5.10a Before removing the engine from a VT1100C2, VT1100T or a 1997-on VT1100C model, remove all four cylinder head cover shrouds: first, pry out the small plugs from each Allen bolt . . .

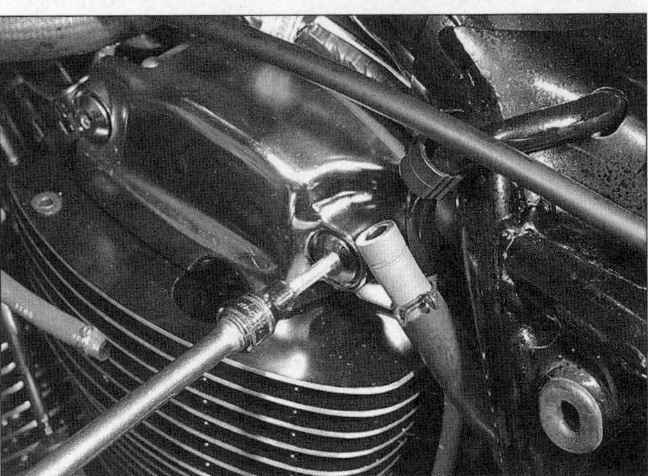

5.10b . . . Remove the Allen bolts . . .

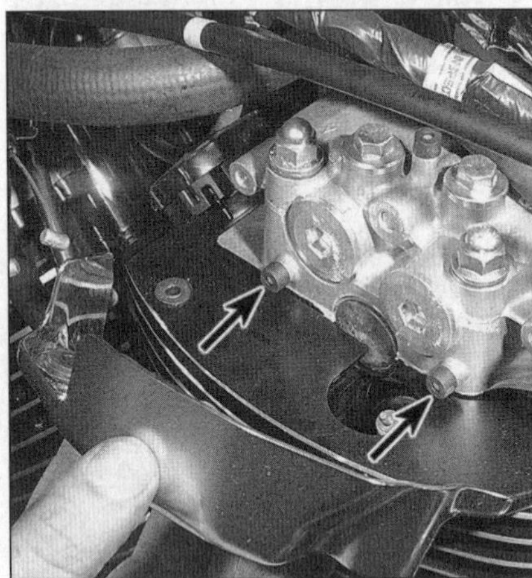

5.10c . . . and remove each shroud; pull off the rubber grommets (arrows) and bag them

10 On VT1100C2, VT1100T and 1997-on VT1100C models, remove all four cylinder head cover shrouds **(see illustrations)**.

11 Remove the exhaust pipes (see Chapter 4).

12 Remove the left and right footpegs and footpeg brackets (see Chapter 8). Remove the rear brake pedal (see Chapter 7). On VT1100C models, remove the gearshift arm from the shift spindle (see Section 22). On VT1100C2 and VT1100T models, remove the gearshift pedal from the gearshift spindle (see Section 22) and remove the rear brake master cylinder reservoir (see Chapter 7).

13 Remove the left crankcase rear cover (see Section 10 in Chapter 1). The stud for the rear cover retaining nut is screwed into the coolant pipe boss (part of the water pump). Remove this stud **(see illustration)** so the threads won't be damaged during engine removal.

14 On 1985 through 1996 VT1100C models, remove the clutch slave cylinder (see Section 17). On VT1100C2, VT1100T and 1997-on VT1100C models, detach the clutch cable bracket from the rear cylinder head and disconnect the cable from the clutch lifter arm (see Section 17), then remove the cable bracket from the engine **(see illustration)**.

15 Clearly label, then detach, all breather and vent hoses and/or tubes from the engine. On California models, detach the EVAP carburetor air vent control valve vent tube from the clip above the clutch lifter arm **(see illustration 5.14)** then remove the clip.

16 Disconnect the electrical connectors for the alternator and starter leads (see Chapter 9) and detach the alternator and starter wiring from the engine and frame and set it aside.

17 Disconnect the electrical leads for the

5.13 Remove the stud from the coolant pipe boss; use double nuts or a stud remover (shown)

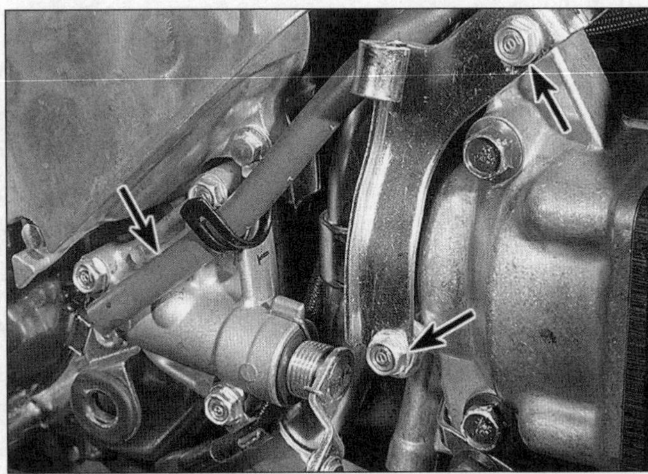

5.14 On cable clutch models, unbolt the cable bracket (right arrows); on California models, disengage the carburetor air vent control valve tube (left arrow) from the clamp

5.20 Disconnect the coolant hose (arrow) from the thermostat housing and each cylinder head cover

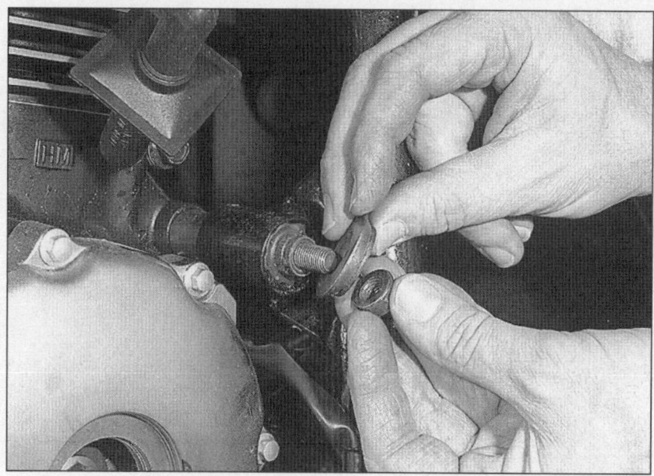
5.24a Remove the nut, metal washer and rubber washer from the right end of the front lower engine mounting bolt . . .

neutral switch and the oil pressure switch (see Chapter 9).

18 Disconnect the electrical connector(s) for the ignition pulse generator(s) and, on 1985 and 1986 models, the cam pulse generator (see Chapter 5). Detach the wiring from the engine and frame and set it aside.

19 Disconnect the horn leads and remove the horn (see Chapter 9).

20 Remove the radiator (see Chapter 3). Disconnect and remove the coolant hoses between the thermostat and the cylinder head covers **(see illustration)**.

21 Disconnect the hoses from the EVAP canister (see Chapter 4). The canister can remain attached to the sub-frame.

22 Place a floor jack or a special motorcycle lift beneath the engine. Be sure to place a block of wood between the jack and the engine to protect the aluminum crankcase. Raise the jack just enough to take the weight of the engine off the engine and sub-frame mounting bolts (you'll have to readjust the jack as the bolts are removed).

5.24b . . . remove the left sub-frame bolts (arrows) (upper arrow indicates left end of the front lower engine mounting bolt) . . .

23 On 1985 and 1986 models, remove the rear wheel (see Chapter 7) and the final drive unit (see Chapter 6).

24 Remove the nuts, washers, bolts and spacers from the engine sub-frame and remove the sub-frame **(see illustrations)**.

5.24c . . . remove the two rear sub-frame bolts (arrows) . . .

5.24d . . . remove the front sub-frame bolts (arrows) . . .

5.24e . . . and remove the sub-frame

5.24f After removing the sub-frame, remove the front lower engine mounting bolt and spacers (arrows)

5.25a Remove these two upper mounting bolts (arrows) . . .

5.25b . . . then remove the rubber insulators (upper arrows), these two upper front bracket bolts (arrows) and this bracket (engine removed for clarity)

25 Disengage the crankcase breather tube from the clamp above the front upper mounting nuts, then remove the two upper mounting bolts **(see illustration)**, the rubber insulators, the upper front bracket bolts and the upper front bracket **(see illustration)**.

26 Remove the rear upper and lower mounting nuts and the bracket bolt **(see illustration)** and knock out the upper and lower mounting bolts with a long drift punch.

27 Disengage the output driven gear shaft from the universal joint in the swingarm **(see illustration)**, then carefully lower the engine on the jack **(see illustration)**.

Warning: Do NOT try to lift the engine (it weighs over 200 pounds) by yourself! Lifting the engine without assistance, or dropping it on yourself, could cause a serious injury.

5.26 Remove the rear upper and lower mounting nuts and the bracket bolt (arrows) and knock out the upper and lower mounting bolts with a long drift punch

Installation

28 Installation is the reverse of removal. Note the following points:

a) Don't tighten any of the engine mounting bracket nuts and bolts until all of them have been installed.

b) Use new gaskets at all exhaust pipe connections.

c) Tighten the engine mounting bracket nuts and bolts and the sub-frame nuts and bolts securely. Don't forget to install

5.27a Disengage the output driven gear shaft from the universal joint in the swingarm . . .

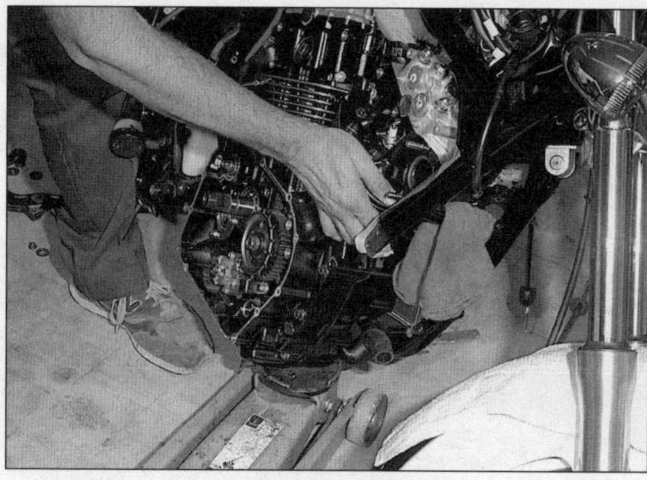

5.27b . . . then carefully lower the engine on the jack; DO NOT lift the engine without help

the spacers on the upper sub-frame bolt **(see illustration 5.24f)**, *one between the engine and the frame, on the left, and the other between the engine and the sub-frame, on the right.*

d) On models with a rear drum brake, adjust the rear brake pedal height and freeplay (see Chapter 1).

e) On models with a cable-actuated clutch, adjust the clutch cable freeplay (see Chapter 1).

f) Adjust the throttle cable freeplay (see Chapter 1).

g) Be sure to add engine oil and coolant (see Chapter 1) before starting the engine.

6 Engine disassembly and reassembly - general information

1 Before disassembling the engine, clean the exterior with a degreaser and rinse it with water. A clean engine will make the job easier and prevent the possibility of getting dirt into the internal areas of the engine.

2 In addition to the precision measuring tools mentioned earlier, you will need a torque wrench, a valve spring compressor, oil gallery brushes, a piston ring removal and installation tool, a piston ring compressor and a clutch holder tool (which is described in Section 16). Some new, clean engine oil of the correct grade and type, some engine assembly lube or moly-based grease, and a tube of RTV (silicone) sealant will also be required. Plastigage (type HPG-1) should be used for checking bearing oil clearances **(see illustrations)**.

3 An engine support stand made from short lengths of lumber bolted together will facilitate the disassembly and reassembly procedures **(see illustration)**. The perimeter of the mount should be just big enough to accommodate the crankcase when it's laid on its side for removal of the crankshaft and transmission components. If you have an automotive-type engine stand, an adapter plate can be made from a piece of plate, some angle iron and some nuts and bolts. The adapter plate can be attached to the

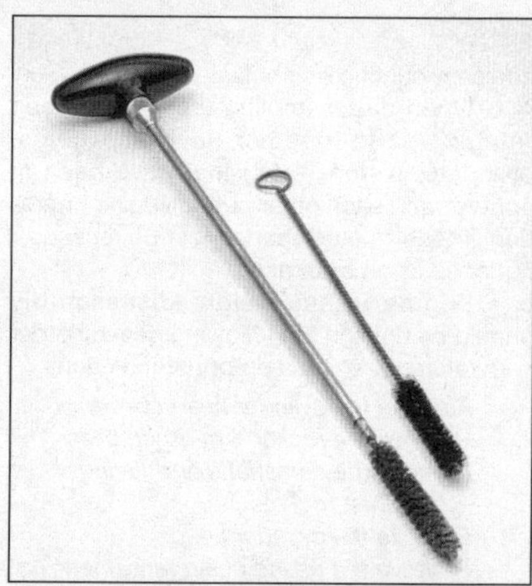

6.2a A selection of brushes is required for cleaning holes and passages in the engine components

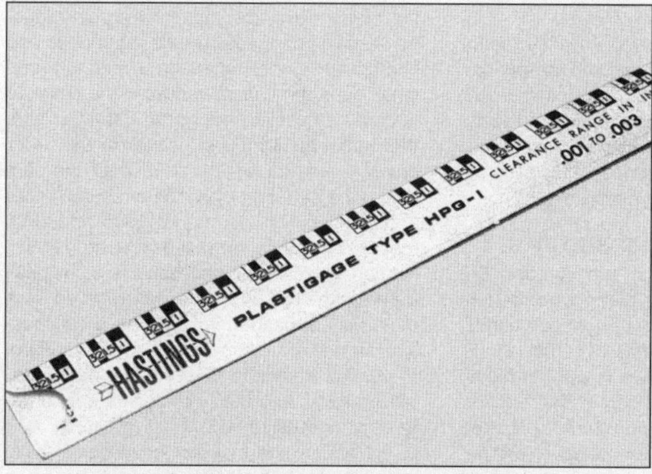

6.2b Type HPG-1 Plastigage is needed to check the connecting rod oil clearances

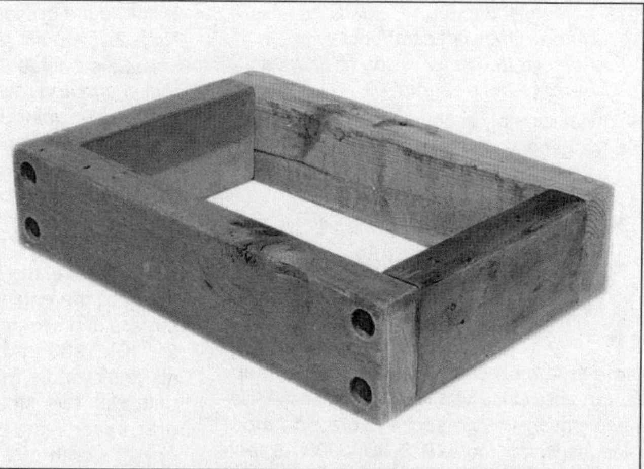

6.3 An engine stand can be made from short lengths of lumber and lag bolts or nails

7.3 Cylinder head cover nut and bolt locations (later model shown; early models have the same pattern) - the cast arrow marks on the cover indicate washer locations

7.4a Carefully lift up the cylinder head cover . . .

engine mounting bolt holes.

4 When disassembling the engine, keep "mated" parts together (including gears, cylinders, pistons, etc.) that have been in contact with each other during engine operation. These "mated" parts must be reused or replaced as an assembly.

5 Engine/transmission disassembly should be done in the following general order with reference to the appropriate Sections.

Remove the cylinder head covers
Remove the rocker arm assemblies
Remove the camshafts and timing chain sprockets
Remove the cylinder heads
Remove the timing chain tensioners
Remove the cylinders
Remove the pistons
Remove the flywheel and starter clutch assembly
Remove the clutch assembly
Remove the primary drive gear
Remove the gearshift mechanism
Separate the crankcase halves
Remove the crankshaft and connecting rods
Remove the shift cam/forks
Remove the transmission shafts/gears
Remove the oil pump

6 Reassembly is accomplished by reversing the general disassembly sequence.

7 Cylinder head cover and rocker arm assembly - removal, inspection and installation

Note 1: *All models are equipped with hydraulic tappets. Once you remove either cylinder head cover, you'll need a hydraulic tappet bleeder (Honda tool 07973-MJ00000) to bleed the tappets before the cover can be installed again. You'll also need a dial indicator (and suitable base) to measure the compression stroke of each tappet. The tappet bleeder tool is available at any Honda dealer; you can obtain a dial gauge at any well-stocked tool store that sells precision measuring tools. If you don't have these tools, have the tappets bled by a dealer service department before installing the cylinder head cover(s).*

Note 2: *If you are replacing the cylinder head cover, the cylinder head, a valve, valve guide, rocker arm and rocker arm shaft or camshaft, or if you're going to reface the valve seats, you will have to adjust the hydraulic tappets.*

Note 3: *The following procedure applies to the front and rear cylinder head covers.*

7.4b . . . and locate the dowels (A); remove the camshaft end plugs (B) and make sure the tappets (C) are in position

Removal and disassembly

1 Remove the engine (see Section 5), then put the engine on a clean work bench surface and secure it in an upright position.

2 On 1985 through 1996 VT1100C models, the cylinder head cover is a three-piece unit, with two smaller covers - the "rocker arm cover" and the "camshaft sprocket cover" - both of which are bolted to a third part, the "camshaft holder." This earlier cover is externally different in appearance from late-model covers, but it shares the same bolt pattern as the newer one-piece cover used on VT1100C2, VT1100T and 1997-on VT1100C models. Functionally, the two covers are similar. However, they differ significantly in design. The essential difference between the two types of covers is that, on the earlier style, the rocker arm cover must be unbolted to access the assist springs and shafts, while, on newer one-piece covers, small caps are unscrewed from the cover to access the assist springs and shafts. Also, the camshaft sprocket cover on the older cover makes it possible to inspect the cam chain, the cam sprocket, the chain tensioner and, on the rear cylinder on 1985 and 1986 models, the camshaft pulse generator. In this section, when it's not necessary to distinguish between the two, they're simply referred to as the "cylinder head cover." Where it is necessary to make a distinction between the two, the earlier design is referred to as a "three-piece cover" and the later design is referred to as a "one-piece cover."

3 Remove the cylinder head cover bolts and nuts **(see illustration)** and remove the coolant pipe from the cylinder head. On models with a three-piece cover, unbolt and

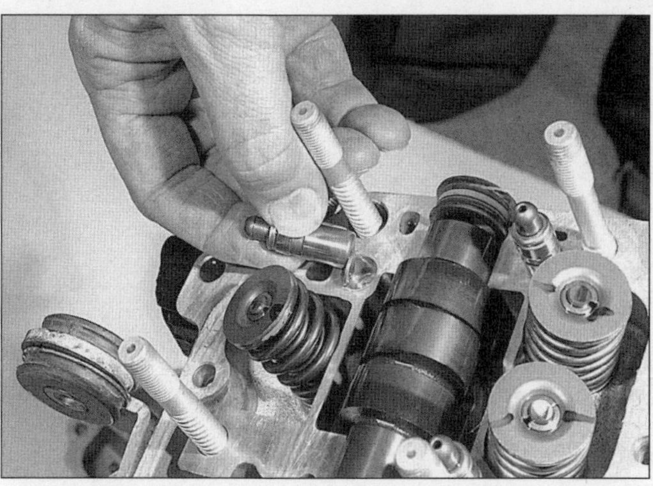
7.6a Label the tappets and shims and store them in sets; they must be returned to their original locations

7.6b Be sure to use the correct number of shims to adjust tappet clearance

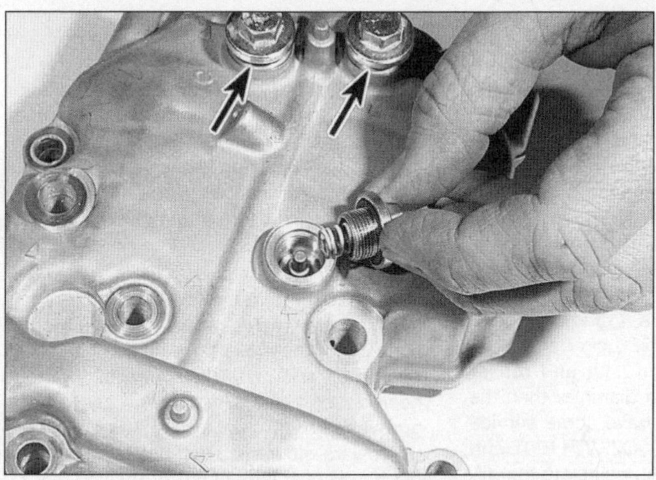
7.7a Unscrew the three assist shaft caps and springs, pull off the old O-rings and discard them . . .

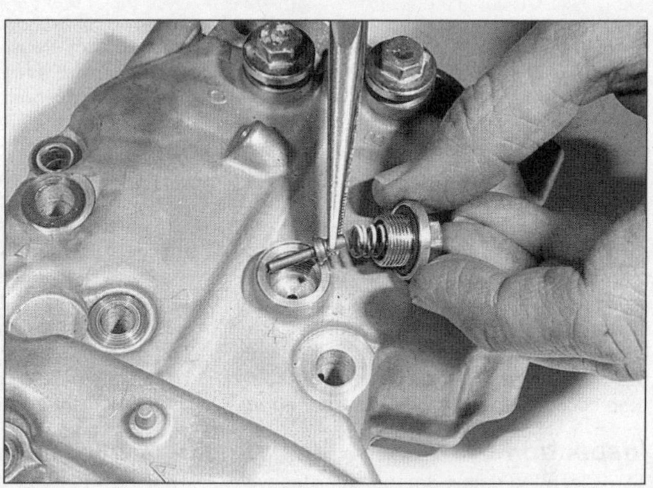
7.7b . . . and remove the assist shafts

carefully, so that the assist springs don't pop out, remove the rocker arm cover and remove the cover gasket. Remove the three assist springs, label them and store them in separate containers. If you're removing the rear cylinder head cover on a 1985 or 1986 model, remove the five cam chain cover bolts and the cam chain cover, then remove the camshaft pulse generator (see Chapter 5).

4 Remove the cylinder head cover from the cylinder head **(see illustration)**. The three hydraulic tappets and shims **(see illustration)** may stick to the cylinder head cover and come out of the head when the cover is lifted off; to prevent them from falling into the crankcase, tilt the engine to the right or left about 40 degrees so that the tappets can't fall down the cam chain tunnel. If a tappet does fall into the crankcase, locate it with a flashlight and fish it out immediately with a magnet.

5 Remove the dowel pins and the camshaft end plugs **(see illustration 7.4b)**. Discard the end plugs; reusing the old end plugs can cause leaks.

6 Remove the hydraulic tappets and shims **(see illustration)**. Note that the tappets don't all have the same number of shims **(see illustration)**. Each tappet/shim set is a matched assembly, so keep each set together in a separate container and label it with respect to its location so that it can be reinstalled in the same hole in the head.

7 On models with a one-piece cover, remove the three assist shaft caps and springs from the cylinder head cover, then remove the three assist shafts **(see illustrations)**. Discard the old O-rings. Put each cap, spring and assist shaft set in a clearly labeled container to insure that it's installed in the same hole from which it was removed.

8 On models with a three-piece cover, screw a 6 mm bolt into the rocker arm shaft hole plug on the cam chain side of the cover and pull out the plug by pulling on the bolt. Remove the rocker arm shaft hole plug on the opposite side with a slotted screwdriver. Remove the assist shafts and store them in the three containers with their respective assist springs. On models with a one-piece cover, unscrew the three rocker arm shaft hole plugs **(see illustration)**. Discard the old plug O-rings.

7.8 Unscrew the three rocker arm shaft hole plugs; remove and discard the old O-rings

7.9 Pull out the exhaust rocker arm shaft with a pair of needle-nose pliers, or screw a 6 mm bolt into the threaded bore in the end of the shaft and pull it out

7.10a Using a magnet, pull out the outer intake rocker arm shaft

9 On models with a three-piece cover, screw a 6 mm bolt into the exhaust rocker arm shaft (on the cam chain side and pull the bolt to pull out the shaft. On models with a one-piece cover, grasp the end of the shaft firmly with a pair of needle-nose pliers, and pull out the shaft **(see illustration)**.

10 On models with a three-piece cover, remove the intake rocker arm shafts by tapping the cover with a plastic hammer. On models with a one-piece cover, pull out the intake rocker arm shafts with a magnet **(see illustration)**. If a shaft won't budge, gently tap it loose with a drift, an extension or some other tool of suitable length **(see illustration)**.

Inspection

11 Clean the rocker arm components with solvent and dry them off. Blow through the oil passages in the rocker arms with compressed air. Inspect the rocker arm slipper faces (the friction surfaces that ride on the cam lobes) for pits, spalling, score marks and rough spots. Check the rocker arm-to-shaft contact areas. Look for cracks in each rocker arm. If the slipper faces are damaged, the rocker arms and the shafts should be replaced as a set. If the slipper faces are worn or damaged, look closely at the corresponding cam lobes; they're probably also worn and they may be damaged.

12 Measure the inside diameter of each rocker arm, then measure the diameter of the rocker arm shafts in the area where each rocker arm rides. On 1985 through 1996 VT1100C models, there is no factory specified oil clearance, so if the rocker arm is no bigger than the specified limit and rocker arm shaft is no smaller in diameter than the specified limit, they still have some service life remaining. On VT1100C2, VT1100T and 1997-on VT1100C models, calculate the difference between the inside diameter of each rocker arm and the diameter of the shaft where it rides. The difference is the oil clearance. Compare your measurements with the oil clearance listed in this Chapter's Specifications. If the clearance is beyond the specified limits, replace the rocker arms and shafts as a set.

13 Inspect the assist springs and shafts for wear and damage. Measure the free length of each assist spring and compare your measurement to the spring free length listed in this Chapter's Specifications. If a spring is shorter than the specified free length, replace it.

Reassembly

14 Coat the slipper faces and the shaft bores of the rocker arms and the friction surfaces of the rocker arm shafts with clean engine oil and install them in the cylinder head cover. Make sure that the assist shaft grooves in the rocker arm shafts are facing up, toward the assist shaft holes in the cylinder head cover **(see illustration)**.

15 After all three rocker arms are installed in the cylinder head cover, hold each rocker arm and turn the rocker arm shaft with a screwdriver so that the rocker arm arms move in, toward the center of the cylinder head cover.

7.10b Push out the other intake rocker arm shaft with a punch, extension or other suitable tool

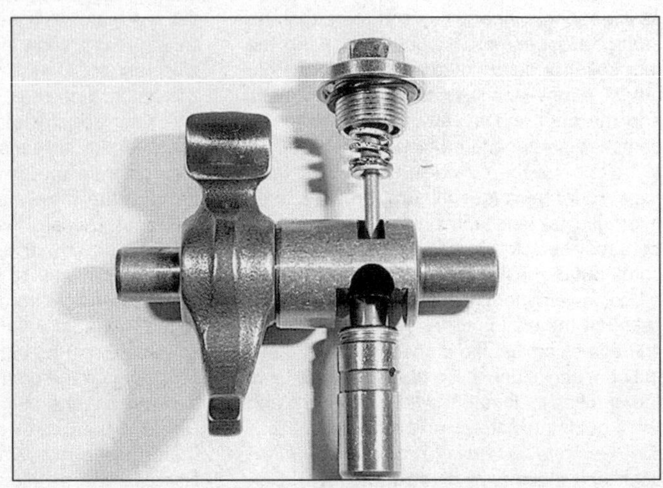

7.14 Here's how each assist shaft, rocker arm shaft and tappet fit together when installed (assembly removed from cylinder head cover for clarity)

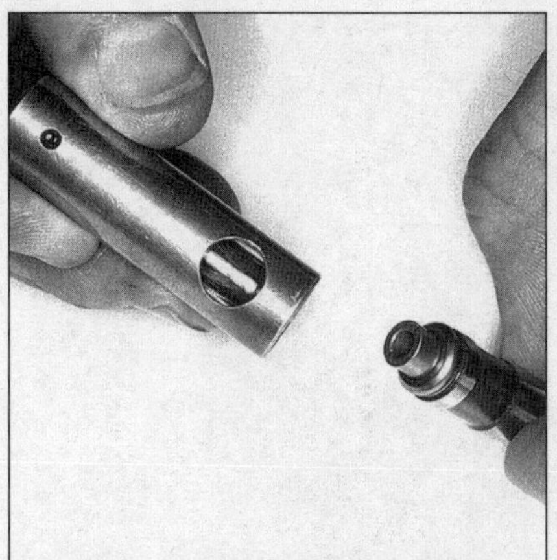

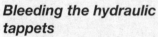

7.16 **Install the hydraulic tappet in the tappet bleeder, then immerse them in a container of kerosene and bleed the tappet of all air bubbles**

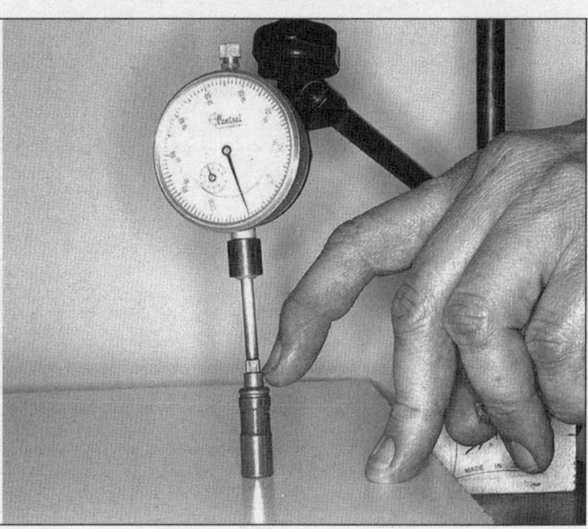

7.19 **To measure the stroke of a fully-bled hydraulic tappet, push down on it and measure the distance that it compresses with a dial indicator**

Bleeding the hydraulic tappets

16 Place each tappet inside the tappet bleeder **(see illustration)**.

17 Place the tappet and tappet bleeder in a container filled with kerosene. They must be standing on the bottom of the container in an upright, i.e. with the tappet in its "installed" position, inside the tappet bleeder.

18 Holding the tappet upright, smoothly "pump" the tappet bleeder until no air bubbles come out.

19 Remove the tappet bleeder. Remove the tappet from the kerosene, keeping it in an upright position, stand it upright on a clean workbench surface and try to compress the tappet by hand. You shouldn't be able to compress it more than 0.2 mm (0.008 inch). To measure the amount of compression, you will need a dial indicator and a suitable base **(see illustration)**.

20 Repeat this procedure for each of the three hydraulic tappets. Remember: don't mix up the tappets and shims; each tappet/shim assembly must be installed in the same hole it was in before removal.

21 Remember, if you're replacing the cylinder head cover, cylinder head, a valve, valve guide, a rocker arm/rocker arm shaft assembly or a camshaft, the hydraulic tappets must be adjusted with shims. Proceed to the next step. If you're not installing any new parts, proceed to Step 30.

Adjusting the hydraulic tappets

Note: *You'll need a dial gauge and a suitable base to adjust the hydraulic tappets. If you don't one, take the engine to a dealer and have the following procedure performed there.*

22 Coat the shims and tappets with clean engine oil and install them in the same holes they were in before they were removed.

23 Install the dowel pins.

24 Remove the timing hole cap **(see illustration 7.32a)**. Rotate the crankshaft clockwise and align the FT mark (front cylinder) or RT mark (rear cylinder) with the stationary index mark **(see illustration 7.32b or 7.32c)**. Verify that the cam lobes are facing down.

25 Install the cylinder head cover and install the 11 cylinder head cover bolts. Make sure that you install washers on the six bolts indicated by small arrows. Tighten the cover bolts to the torque listed in this Chapter's Specifications.

26 Install the assist shafts in their respective holes in the cylinder head cover.

27 Set up a dial gauge with its probe touching the top of an assist shaft, rotate the crankshaft clockwise a couple of revolutions and measure the stroke of the shaft. Using the accompanying table, determine the number of shims needed **(see illustration)**.

28 Measure the stroke of the other two assist shafts the same way and adjust them as necessary.

29 Remove the cylinder head cover and proceed to the next step.

Assist shaft stroke	Number of shims needed (each shim is 0.5 mm, or 0.02 inch, thick)
0 to 1.20 mm (0 to 0.047 inch)	0
1.20 to 1.50 mm (0.047 to 0.059 inch)	1
1.50 to 1.80 mm (0.059 to 0.070 inch)	2
1.80 to 2.10 mm (0.070 to 0.083 inch)	3
2.10 to 2.40 mm (0.083 to 0.094 inch)	4
2.40 to 2.70 mm (0.094 to 0.106 inch)	5

7.27 **Valve adjustment shim selection chart**

7.32a Remove the crankshaft timing hole cap from the right side of the engine

7.32b If you're aligning the front cylinder camshaft, align the FT marks with the stationary index mark

7.32c If you're aligning the rear cylinder camshaft, align the RT marks with the stationary index mark

7.35 The slots in the ends of the rocker shafts should be within the indicated angle from vertical; the slots in both intake shafts should be at approximately the same angle

Installation

***Caution:** If you haven't yet bled the hydraulic tappets, go back to Step 16 and do so now. If you're installing a new cylinder head cover, or if you replaced a cylinder head, valve stem, valve guide, rocker arm/rocker arm shaft assembly or camshaft, or refaced a valve seat, go back to Step 22 and adjust the tappets.*

30 Coat the shims and tappets with clean engine oil and install them in the same holes they were in before they were removed.

31 Install the dowel pins.

32 Remove the timing hole cap **(see illustration)**. Rotate the crankshaft in a clockwise direction and align the FT mark (front cylinder) or RT mark (rear cylinder) with the stationary index mark **(see illustrations)**. The cam lobes should now be facing down.

33 Coat the edges of a pair of new camshaft end plugs with liquid sealant and install both plugs.

34 Coat the mating surface of the cylinder head cover with liquid sealant, but avoid the immediate area surrounding each of the three hydraulic tappet holes. If sealant gets into a hydraulic tappet, it could cause the tappet to fail.

35 Coat the cam lobes liberally with clean engine oil. Install the cylinder head cover and press it securely against the mating surface of the cylinder head. Verify that the grooves in the ends of all three rocker arm shafts are within the indicated angle from vertical **(see illustration)**. Also, make sure that the two intake rocker arm shaft grooves are at the same angle. If any of the grooves is angled incorrectly, release pressure on the cylinder head cover and adjust the shaft(s) as necessary by rotating slightly with a screwdriver. Then push down on cylinder head cover again and recheck the angles of all three shaft grooves.

36 Install the cylinder head cover bolts (on models with a three-piece cover, don't install the rocker arm cover or camshaft sprocket covers yet). Make sure that the washers are installed with the bolts installed in holes marked with an arrow (there are six of them). Tighten the cylinder head cover bolts gradually and evenly (in at least three stages), in a criss-cross pattern, to the torque listed in this Chapter's Specifications.

37 Install the assist shafts into their holes in the cylinder head cover.

38 Install the assist springs onto the assist shafts. On models with a three-piece cover, install the springs on the shafts while twisting them so that the end of each spring seats firmly against the flange face, then install the rocker arm cover and tighten the rocker arm cover bolts to the torque listed in this Chapter's Specifications.

39 On models with a three-piece cover, install the camshaft pulse generator (see Chapter 5), then install the camshaft sprocket cover and tighten the bolts to the torque listed in this Chapter's Specifications.

40 On models with a one-piece cover, apply engine oil to the new O-rings, install the O-rings on the assist shaft caps, install the assist caps and tighten them to the torque listed in this Chapter's Specifications.

41 Apply engine oil to the new O-rings, install the O-rings, install the rocker arm shaft hole plugs and tighten them to the torque listed in this Chapter's Specifications.

42 Install the engine (see Section 5).

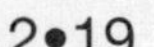

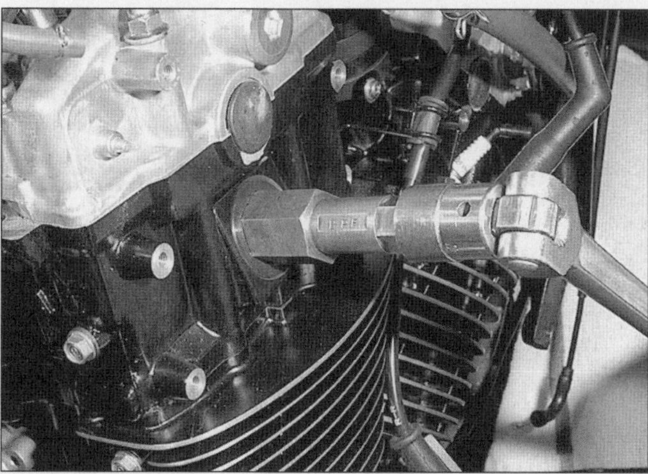
8.2 Using a 27 mm hex, unscrew the spark plug sleeve from cam chain side of the cylinder from which you are going to remove the camshaft

8.4 There's a thick wedge (A) and a thin wedge (B) at the upper end of the cam chain tensioner; measure how far the thick wedge projects above the top of the chain tensioner

8.5a Before removing the camshaft, pull up the thin wedge . . .

8.5b . . . and insert a paper clip through the hole in the wedge to keep it up

8 Camshaft and sprocket - removal, inspection and installation

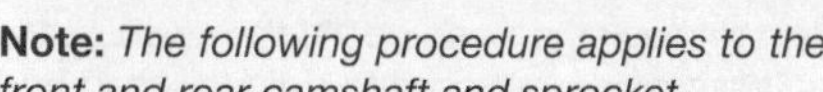

Note: *The following procedure applies to the front and rear camshaft and sprocket.*

Removal

1 Remove the engine (see Section 5).

2 Remove the spark plug sleeve from the cam chain side of the cylinder from which you're removing the camshaft **(see illustration)**. Discard the old O-rings from the sleeve.

3 Remove the cylinder head cover (see Section 7).

4 Before proceeding, determine cam chain wear as follows. There are two wedges, one behind the other, at the upper end of the cam chain tensioner: a thicker wedge adjacent to the chain and a thinner wedge next to the head **(see illustration)**. To determine whether the cam chain should be replaced, measure the height that the wedge near the chain projects above the top of the tensioner and compare your measurement to the maximum allowable height listed in this Chapter's Specifications. If the indicated height exceeds the specified maximum height, replace the cam chain (see Section 21).

5 Holding down the thicker cam chain tensioner wedge with a screwdriver, pull up the thinner cam chain tensioner wedge with a pair of pliers **(see illustration)** and insert a paper clip through the hole in the thinner wedge to keep it up **(see illustration)**.

6 Stuff rags into the cam chain tunnel to keep parts Remove the camshaft sprocket bolts **(see illustration)**. After removing the

8.6 Remove one camshaft sprocket bolt, then rotate the crankshaft clockwise for access to the other bolt

8.7a Pull the sprocket away from the camshaft flange, pull out the camshaft . . .

8.7b . . . remove the sprocket from the chain and secure the chain with a piece of wire

first bolt, rotate the crankshaft one full turn, which will rotate the camshaft 1/2 turn, to access the other bolt.

Caution: Do NOT let the camshaft sprocket bolts fall down the cam chain tunnel into the crankcase! If a bolt falls into the crankcase, retrieve it with a magnet.

7 Remove the camshaft and the camshaft sprocket **(see illustrations)**. Secure the cam chain with a piece of wire or string to prevent it from falling into the crankcase.

Caution: Do NOT rotate the crankshaft while either or both camshafts are removed.

Inspection

Note: *Before replacing camshafts because of damage, check with local machine shops specializing in motorcycle engine work. A machine shop might be able to weld, regrind and harden the cam lobes for less than the price of a new camshaft.*

8 Inspect the cam journal bearing surfaces in the camshaft holder (three-piece covers) or cylinder head cover, and in the cylinder head **(see illustration)**. Look for signs of "scoring" (scratches or grooves in the bearing surfaces) and "spalling" (a pitted appearance), both of which are usually caused by dirty or insufficient lubrication. If either holder is damaged or worn, replace it; if the cylinder head is worn or damaged, replace it (see Section 10).

8.8 Inspect the camshaft bearing surfaces (arrows) in the cylinder head cover (and their corresponding lower surfaces in the cylinder head) for scoring or spalling

9 Support the camshaft on V-blocks and measure the camshaft runout with a dial indicator and compare your measurement to the runout listed in this Chapter's Specifications.

10 Check the camshaft lobes for heat discoloration (blue appearance), score marks, chipped areas, flat spots and spalling **(see illustration)**. Measure the height of each lobe with a micrometer **(see illustration)** and compare the results to the minimum lobe height listed in this Chapter's Specifications. If damage is noted or wear is excessive, replace the camshaft.

11 Measure the camshaft bearing oil clearances. Clean the camshaft, the cam journal bearing surfaces in the cylinder head, and the cam journal bearing surfaces in the cam holder or cylinder head cover, with a clean lint-free cloth, then lay the cam in place in the cylinder head. Secure the cam by installing the cam sprocket and chain so the camshaft doesn't turn as the cam holder or cylinder head cover bolts are torqued.

12 Cut eight strips of Plastigage (type HPG-1) and lay one piece on each bearing journal, parallel with the camshaft centerline **(see illustration)**. Make sure that no oil hole in any journal is facing up; if Plastigage is laid across an oil hole, it will not produce an accurate representation of the actual clearance. Install the cam holder and the end holder in their proper positions and install the nut and bolts. Tighten the nut and bolts evenly in a criss-cross pattern until the specified torque is reached. While doing this, don't let the camshaft rotate.

13 Remove the cam holder or cylinder head cover bolts, a little at a time, and carefully lift off the cam holder or cylinder head cover.

14 To determine the oil clearance, compare the crushed Plastigage (at its widest point) on each journal to the scale printed on the Plastigage container **(see illustration)**. Compare the results to this Chapter's Specifications. If the oil clearance is greater than specified, measure the diameter of the cam bearing journal with a micrometer **(see illustration)**. If the journal diameter is less than the specified limit, replace the camshaft and recheck the clearance. If the clearance is still excessive, replace the cylinder head and holders.

15 Inspect the visible portion of the cam chain for obvious wear or damage. Except in cases of oil starvation, the chain wears very little. If the chain has stretched excessively, the tensioner cannot maintain correct chain tension; replace the chain (see Section 21).

16 Inspect the cam sprocket for wear, cracks and other damage. If any damage or wear is evident, replace the sprocket. If the sprocket is severely worn, the cam chain is probably worn too (see Section 21).

17 Using a flashlight, inspect the condition of the cam chain tensioner and the cam chain guide. If either of them looks worn or damaged, remove it for a better look (tensioner, see Section 9; guide, see Section 13).

8.10a Inspect the camshaft lobes for wear; here's a good example of damage that will require replacement or repair of the camshaft

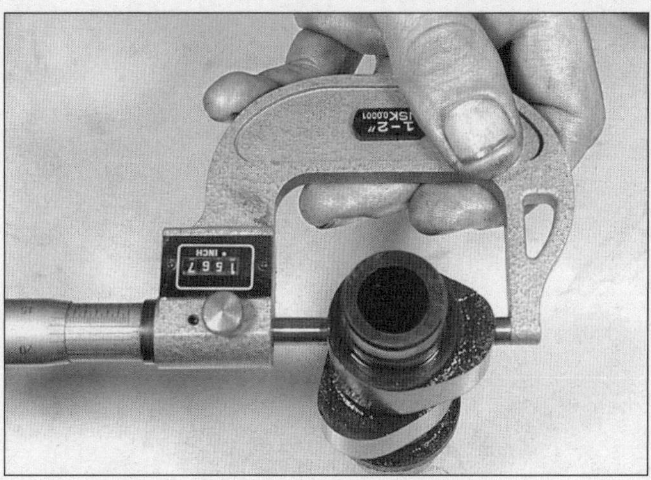

8.10b Measure the height of the cam lobes with a micrometer

Installation

Note: *If both the front and rear camshafts were removed, start with the front cylinder camshaft. Even if only one camshaft was removed, the other cylinder head cover must be removed and the position of the camshaft in that head verified.*

18 Lubricate the camshaft journal bearing surfaces in the cylinder head with engine oil.

Front cylinder camshaft

Rear cylinder camshaft not removed

19 If you did not remove the rear cylinder camshaft, remove the rear cylinder head cover and check the position of the camshaft before installing the front cylinder camshaft. If you did remove the rear cylinder camshaft, skip this part and proceed to Step 23.

20 Remove the timing hole cap **(see illustration 7.32a)**, turn the crankshaft clockwise and align the RT mark on the ignition pulse generator timing rotor with the stationary index mark on the right crankcase cover **(see illustration 7.32c)**, then note the position of the "R" mark on the rear cylinder camshaft flange.

8.12 Lay a strip of Plastigage across each camshaft bearing journal, parallel with the camshaft centerline and not across an oil hole

21 If the R mark on the rear cylinder camshaft flange is facing up, rotate the crankshaft clockwise 495 degrees (1-3/8 turns) and align the FT mark on the ignition pulse generator

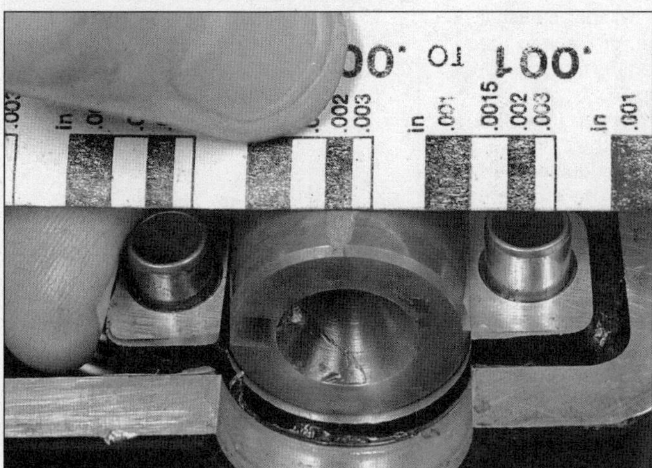

8.14a To calculate the clearance, compare the width of the crushed Plastigage to the scale printed on the Plastigage container

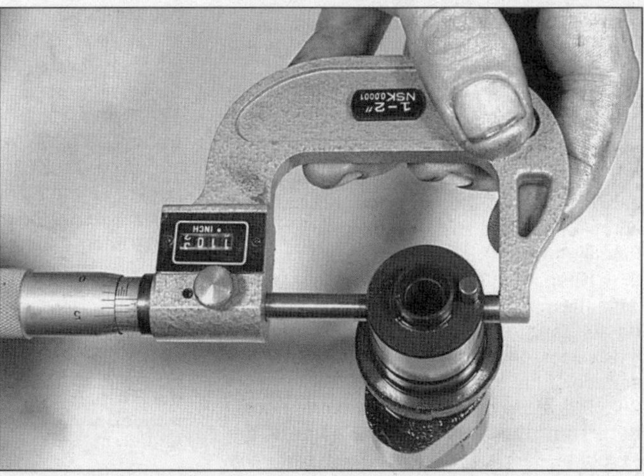

8.14b If any camshaft journal is less than the specified minimum diameter, replace the camshaft

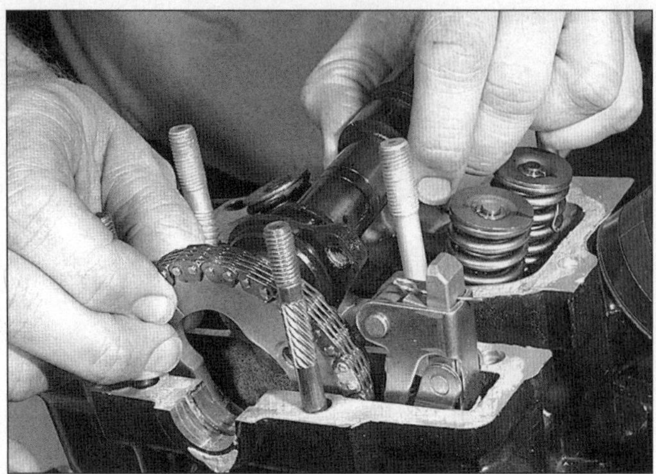

8.26 Insert the end of the camshaft through the sprocket, then place the camshaft in its bearings with the F mark on the camshaft's sprocket flange upward

8.30 The index marks on the sprocket must be aligned with the cylinder head gasket mating surface after the sprocket is bolted to the camshaft

rotor with the index mark on the crankcase, then proceed to Step 23 and install the front camshaft.

22 If the R mark on the rear cylinder camshaft flange is facing down, rotate the crankshaft clockwise 135 degrees (3/8-turn) and align the FT mark on the ignition pulse generator rotor with the index mark on the crankcase, then proceed to Step 23 and install the front camshaft.

Both camshafts removed

23 Remove the timing hole cap **(see illustration 7.32a)** and align the FT mark on the ignition pulse generator timing rotor with the index mark on the right crankcase cover **(see illustration 7.32b)**.

24 Place the cam sprocket in position and engage it with the cam chain without turning the crankshaft. Make sure the index lines on the sprocket are facing out and are aligned with the mating surface of the cylinder head.

25 Make sure you're installing the correct camshaft in the front cylinder head. The front and rear cylinder cams are not interchangeable. Look for the "F" (front cylinder camshaft) or "R" (rear cylinder camshaft) on the edge of the sprocket flange of each cam.

26 Keeping the sprocket teeth engaged with the cam chain, rotate the crankshaft clockwise until the elongated opening in the cam sprocket is vertical, or nearly vertical, then install the camshaft through the sprocket opening and onto the cylinder head **(see illustration)**.

27 Keeping the sprocket teeth engaged with the cam chain, rotate the crankshaft back (counterclockwise) and realign the index lines on the sprocket with the mating surface of the cylinder head.

28 Place the camshaft in its correct position, with the F mark on the edge of the sprocket flange facing up, then push the sprocket onto the camshaft.

29 Make one final check that everything is correctly aligned: the FT mark on the ignition pulse generator timing rotor should be aligned with the stationary index mark on the crankcase; the index marks on the sprocket should be aligned with the cylinder head mating surface; and the F mark on the camshaft sprocket flange should point upward.

30 If everything's correctly aligned, apply a thread locking agent to the sprocket bolts and install both bolts. Install, but don't torque, the first bolt, rotate the crankshaft clockwise and install, but don't torque, the second bolt, then go back and verify that the index marks on the sprocket are still aligned with the mating surface of the head **(see illustration)**. If the marks are correctly aligned, tighten the sprocket bolts to the torque listed in this Chapter's Specifications.

Rear cylinder camshaft

Front cylinder camshaft not removed

31 If you did not remove the front cylinder camshaft, remove the front cylinder head cover and check the position of the camshaft before installing the rear cylinder camshaft. If you did remove the front cylinder camshaft, and haven't installed it yet, go back to Step 23. If you have just installed the front cylinder camshaft, proceed to Step 36.

32 Remove the timing hole cap **(see illustration 7.32a)**, turn the crankshaft clockwise and align the FT mark on the ignition pulse generator timing rotor with the stationary index mark on the right crankcase cover **(see illustration 7.32b)**, then note the position of the "F" mark on the front cylinder camshaft flange.

33 If the F mark on the front cylinder camshaft flange is facing up, rotate the crankshaft clockwise 225 degrees (5/8-turn) and align the RT mark on the ignition pulse generator rotor with the index mark on the crankcase, then proceed to Step 35 and install the rear camshaft.

34 If the F mark on the rear cylinder camshaft flange is facing down, rotate the crankshaft clockwise 585 degrees (1-5/8 turn) and align the RT mark on the ignition pulse generator rotor with the index mark on the crankcase, then proceed to the next Step and install the rear camshaft.

Both camshafts removed

35 The rest of the rear cylinder camshaft installation procedure is identical to the procedure outlined in Steps 23 through 30 for the front cylinder camshaft, except that the camshaft identification mark that should be facing up is an R instead of an F.

Front or rear camshaft

36 Remove the paper clip from the thinner cam chain tensioner wedge.

37 Install the cylinder head cover (see Section 7).

38 Apply a light coat of oil to the O-ring grooves and the threads of the spark plug sleeve **(see illustration)**, install new O-rings in the grooves, install the sleeve in the cylinder head and tighten it to the torque listed in this Chapter's Specifications.

39 Install the engine (see Section 5).

8.38 Lightly oil the threads and O-ring grooves, install new O-rings (arrows) and tighten the sleeve to the specified torque

9.4 Remove the chain tensioner bolts (arrows); discard the old sealing washers . . .

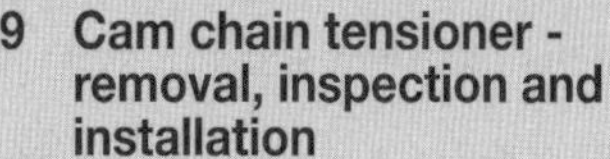

9 Cam chain tensioner - removal, inspection and installation

Note: *The following procedure applies to the front and rear cam chain tensioners.*

1 Remove the engine (see Section 5).

2 Remove the cylinder head cover (see Section 7).

3 Remove the camshaft and cam chain sprocket (see Section 8).

4 Remove the cam chain tensioner mounting bolts **(see illustration)** and discard the sealing washers.

5 Remove the cam chain tensioner **(see illustration)**.

6 Clean the chain tensioner in solvent and blow dry it with compressed air. Inspect the friction surface of the tensioner **(see illustration)** for wear and damage. If the friction surface is worn or damaged, replace the tensioner.

7 Install the chain tensioner. Make sure

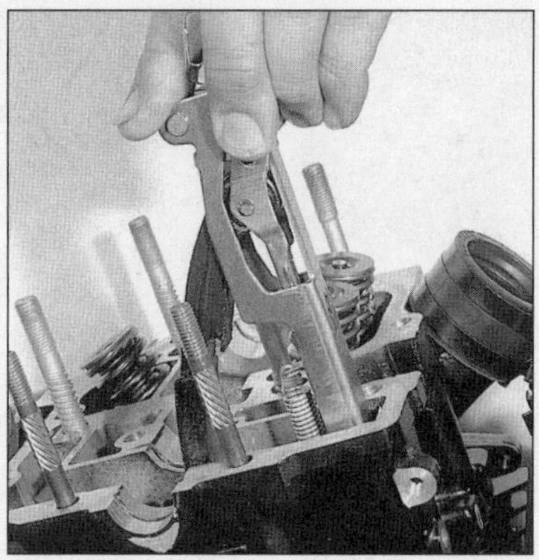

9.5 . . . and remove the chain tensioner from the cam chain tunnel

that the tensioner is correctly seated against its stop on the crankcase **(see illustration)**. Using new sealing washers, install the chain tensioner mounting bolts and tighten them to the torque listed in this Chapter's Specifications.

8 Install the camshaft and sprocket (see Section 8).

9 Install the cylinder head cover (see Section 7).

10 Install the engine (see Section 5).

10 Cylinder head - removal and installation

Note: *The following procedure applies to the front and rear cylinder heads.*

Removal

1 Remove the engine (see Section 5).

2 Remove the cylinder head cover (see Section 7).

3 Remove the camshaft and cam chain sprocket (see Section 8). Secure the chain so it can't fall into the crankcase.

4 Remove the cam chain tensioner (see Section 9).

5 Remove the cylinder head fins **(see illustration)**.

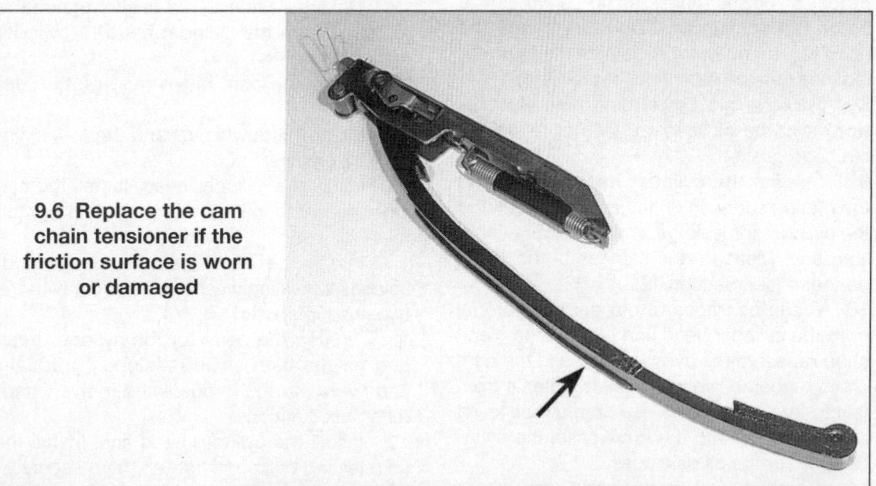

9.6 Replace the cam chain tensioner if the friction surface is worn or damaged

9.7 The tensioner (right arrow) and chain guide (left arrow) rest in pockets in the crankcase

10.5 Remove the Allen bolts (four on the cam chain side; three on the other side) to detach the fins from the cylinder head

10.6 To detach the cylinder head from the cylinder, remove these two bolts (upper arrows) and pry at the pry points (lower arrow); there's a pry point on each side of the head

10.7 Try to remove the cylinder head with your hands; if it's stuck, tap it loose with a small plastic or rubber mallet

6 Loosen the two remaining cylinder head bolts **(see illustration)**. Remove the bolts.

7 Lift the cylinder head off the studs **(see illustration)**. If it's stuck, tap it gently with a rubber or plastic mallet, being careful not to break the cooling fins. Don't try to pry the head loose anywhere except at the two prying lugs (one on each side of the head).

8 Remove the dowel pins **(see illustration)** and the old gasket. Do not reuse the old head gasket.

9 Inspect the cylinder head gasket and the mating surfaces on the cylinder head and the cylinder for leakage, which could indicate warpage. Measure the flatness of the cylinder head (see Section 12).

10 Clean all traces of old gasket material from the cylinder head and block. Stuff clean shop rags into the cylinder bore and the cam chain tunnel to prevent gasket material from falling into the engine. Be careful not to let any debris fall into the crankcase, the cylinder bore or the oil passages.

11 Remove and inspect the cam chain guide (see Section 13).

12 Loosen the hose clamp screw and remove the carburetor insulator from the head.

10.8 These are the dowel locations (arrows); in this case, one dowel came off with the cylinder head

Installation

13 Make sure that all old gasket material is removed from the cylinder head-to-cylinder mating surfaces.

14 Install the cam chain guide (see Section 13).

15 Install the dowel pins and the new cylinder head gasket.

16 Install the cylinder head. Install the cylinder head mounting bolts and hand tighten them.

17 Install the cam chain tensioner and, using new sealing washers, secure it with the two retaining bolts.

18 Tighten the bolts for the cylinder head and for the cam chain tensioner, gradually and evenly, to the torque listed in this Chapter's Specifications.

19 Install the cylinder head fins. Install the fin retaining bolts and tighten them securely.

20 Install the cam chain tensioner (see Section 9).

21 Install the camshaft and sprocket (see Section 8).

22 Install the cylinder head cover (see Section 7).

23 Install the carburetor insulator on the head and tighten the hose clamp screw securely. Make sure the positioning pins on the clamps are aligned with their respective slots on the insulator (see Chapter 4). Tighten the clamp screws securely.

24 Install the engine (see Section 5).

11 Valves/valve seats/valve guides - servicing

1 Because of the complex nature of this job and the special tools and equipment required, servicing of the valves, the valve seats and the valve guides (commonly known as a valve job) is best left to a professional.

2 The home mechanic can, however, remove and disassemble the head, do the initial cleaning and inspection, then reassemble and deliver the head to a dealer service department or properly equipped motorcycle repair shop for the actual valve servicing.

3 The dealer service department will remove the valves and springs, recondition or replace the valves and valve seats, replace the valve guides, check and, if necessary, replace the valve springs, spring retainers and keepers, install new valve seals and reassemble the valve components.

4 After the valve job has been performed, the head will be in like-new condition. When the head is returned, be sure to clean it again very thoroughly before installation on the engine to remove any metal particles or abrasive grit that may still be present from the valve service operations. Use compressed air, if available, to blow out all the holes and passages.

12.7a Compress the valve springs with a spring compressor until the keepers are exposed, remove the keepers, release the spring compressor . . .

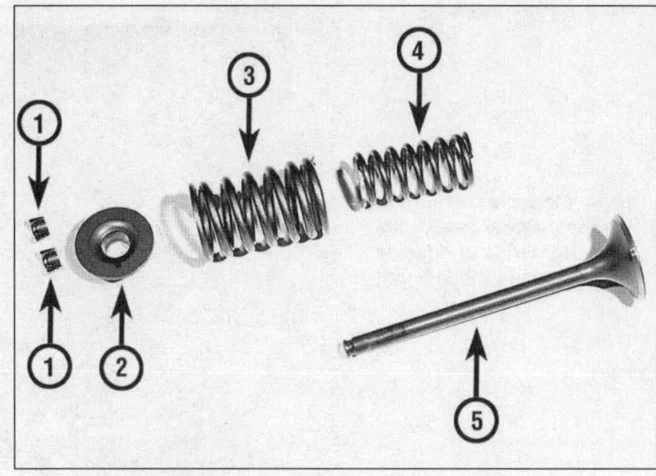

12.7b . . . and remove the valve springs

1 Keepers
2 Spring retainer
3 Outer spring
4 Inner spring
5 Valve

12 Cylinder head and valves - disassembly, inspection and reassembly

Note: *If the bearing surfaces in the cylinder head are damaged, a shop might be able to repair them. A new cylinder head is expensive, so explore your options before discarding the old head.*

1 Valve servicing and valve guide replacement should be done by a dealer service department or motorcycle repair shop (see Section 11). However, disassembly, cleaning and inspection of the cylinder head and valves can be done at home, with the right tools.

2 To disassemble the valve components safely, a valve spring compressor is absolutely necessary. If you don't own a valve spring compressor, you should be able to rent one at a local tool rental yard. If you're unable to obtain a valve spring compressor, leave the following procedure to a dealer service department or motorcycle repair shop.

Disassembly

3 Remove the cylinder head (see Section 10).

4 Before the valves are removed, scrape away any traces of gasket material from the head gasket sealing surface. Work slowly and do not nick or gouge the soft aluminum of the head. Gasket removing solvents, which work very well, are available at most motorcycle shops and auto parts stores.

5 Carefully scrape all carbon deposits out of the combustion chamber area. A hand held wire brush or a piece of fine emery cloth can be used once the majority of deposits have been scraped away. Do not use a wire brush mounted in a drill motor, or one with extremely stiff bristles, as the head material is soft and may be eroded away or scratched by the wire brush.

6 Label three plastic bags, one for each valve spring/valve assembly, so it can be installed in the same valve guide from which it's removed.

7 Compress each valve spring assembly with a spring compressor and remove the keepers **(see illustration)**. Do not compress the spring any more than is absolutely necessary. If the keepers stick to the groove in the valve stem, use a magnet or a pair of tweezers to pull them off. Carefully release the valve spring compressor and remove the retainer and the springs **(see illustration)**. Push on the valve stem, pull on the valve head and remove the valve from the head. If the valve binds in the guide, push it back into the head and deburr the area around the keeper groove with a very fine file or whetstone, then pull it out and remove the valve stem seal **(see illustration)** and discard it (never reuse the old seals).

8 Remove the lower spring seat and store it with the other valve spring parts.

9 Repeat the previous two Steps for the other two valves. Be sure to keep the parts for each valve assembly in separate plastic bags so they won't be mixed up.

10 Clean the cylinder head with solvent and dry it thoroughly. Compressed air will speed the drying process and ensure that all holes and recessed areas are clean.

11 Clean all of the valve springs, keepers, retainers and spring seats with solvent and dry them thoroughly. Do one valve assembly at a time to keep the original parts together.

12 Scrape off any deposits that may have formed on the valve, then use a motorized wire brush to remove deposits from the valve heads and stems. Again, make sure the valves do not get mixed up.

Inspection

13 Inspect the head very carefully for cracks and other damage. If cracks are found, a new head will be required. Inspect the cam bearing surfaces for wear and evidence of seizure. Check the camshaft (see Section 8) and rocker arms (see Section 7) for wear.

12.7c If the valve binds in the guide, deburr the area above the keeper groove, then pull it out and remove the stem seal (arrow)

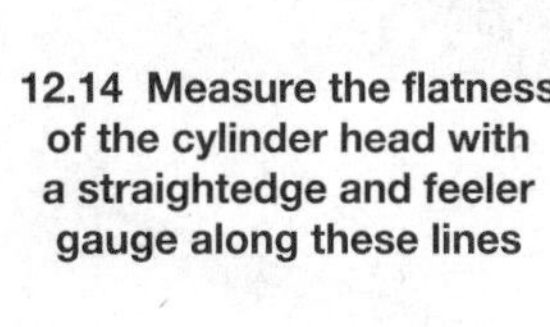
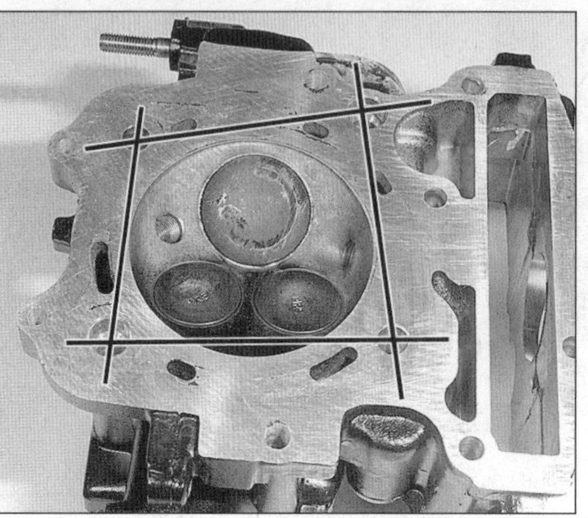

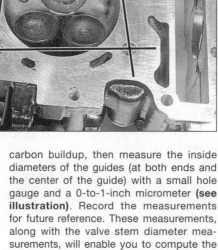

12.14 Measure the flatness of the cylinder head with a straightedge and feeler gauge along these lines

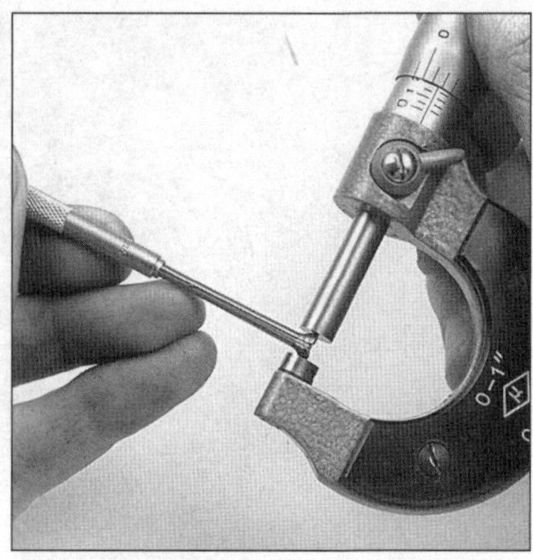

12.16 Measure the valve guide inside diameter with a small hole gauge, then measure the hole gauge with a micrometer

14 Using a precision straightedge and a feeler gauge, check the head gasket mating surface for warpage **(see illustration)**. Lay the straightedge between the head bolt holes, as shown, and try to slip a feeler gauge under it, on either side of the combustion chamber. The gauge should be the same thickness as the cylinder head warpage limit listed in this Chapter's Specifications. If the feeler gauge can be inserted between the head and the straightedge, the head is warped and must either be machined or, if warpage is excessive, replaced with a new one. Minor surface imperfections can be cleaned up by sanding on a surface plate in a figure-eight pattern with 400 or 600 grit wet or dry sandpaper. Be sure to rotate the head every few strokes to avoid removing material unevenly.

15 Examine the valve seats in each of the combustion chambers. If they are pitted, cracked or burned, the head will require valve service that's beyond the scope of the home mechanic. Measure the valve seat width and compare it to the seat width listed this Chapter's Specifications. If it is not within the specified range, or if it varies around its circumference, valve service work is required.

16 Clean the valve guides to remove any carbon buildup, then measure the inside diameters of the guides (at both ends and the center of the guide) with a small hole gauge and a 0-to-1-inch micrometer **(see illustration)**. Record the measurements for future reference. These measurements, along with the valve stem diameter measurements, will enable you to compute the valve stem-to-guide clearance. This clearance, when compared to the Specifications, will be one factor that will determine the extent of the valve service work required. The guides are measured at the ends and at the center to determine if they are worn in a bell-mouth pattern (more wear at the ends). If they are, guide replacement is an absolute must.

17 Carefully inspect each valve face for cracks, pits and burned spots. Check the valve stem and the keeper groove area for cracks **(see illustration)**. Rotate the valve and check for any obvious indication that it is bent. Check the end of the stem for pitting and excessive wear and make sure the bevel is the specified width. The presence of any of the above conditions indicates the need for valve servicing.

18 Measure the valve stem diameter **(see illustration)**. By subtracting the stem diameter from the valve guide diameter, the valve stem-to-guide clearance is obtained. If the stem-to-guide clearance is greater than listed in this Chapter's Specifications, the guides and valves will have to be replaced with new ones.

19 Check the end of each valve spring for wear and pitting. Measure the free length **(see illustration)** and compare it to this Chapter's Specifications. Any springs that are shorter than specified have sagged and should not be reused. Stand the spring on a flat surface and check it for squareness **(see illustration)**.

20 Check the spring retainers and keepers for obvious wear and cracks. Any questionable parts should not be reused, as extensive damage will occur in the event of failure during engine operation.

21 If the inspection indicates that no service work is required, the valve components can be reinstalled in the head.

Reassembly

22 Before installing the valves in the head, they should be lapped to ensure a positive

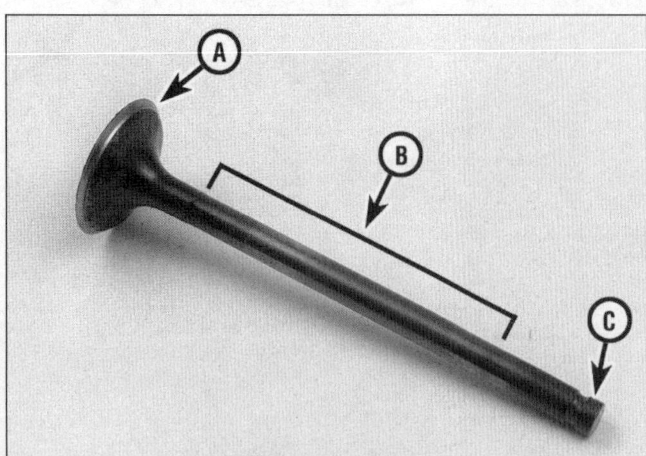

12.17 Check the valve face (A), stem (B) and keeper groove (C) for signs of wear and damage

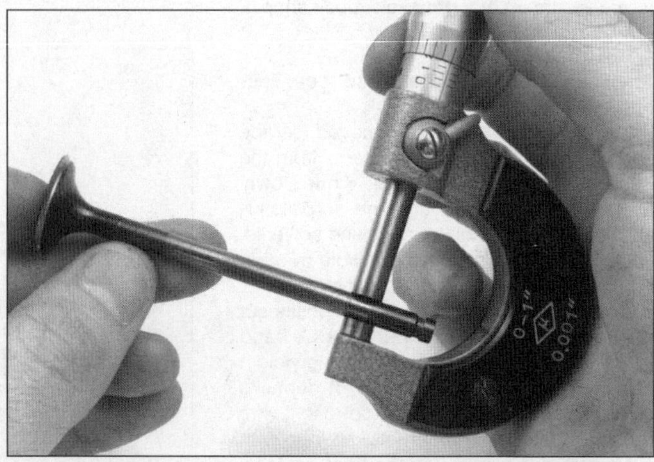

12.18 Measure the valve stem diameter with a micrometer

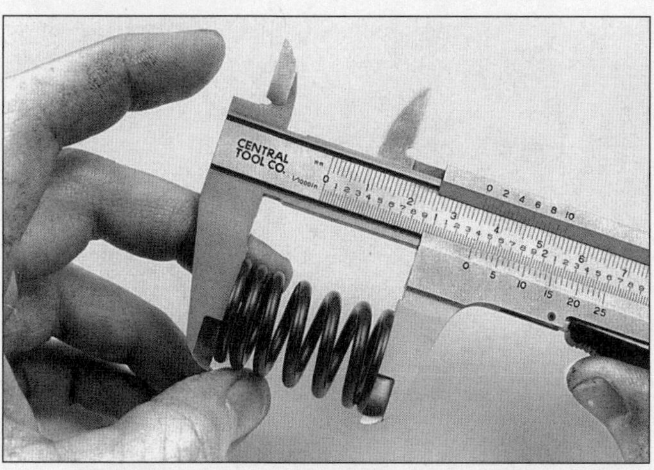

12.19a Measure the free length of the valve springs

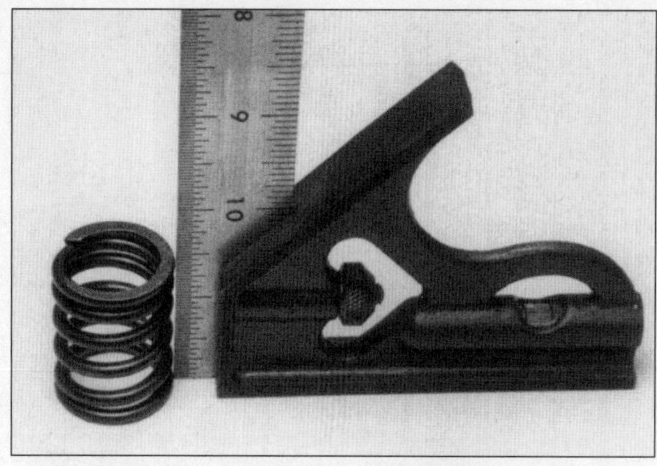

12.19b Check the valve springs for squareness

12.23 Apply the lapping compound very sparingly, in small dabs, to the valve face only

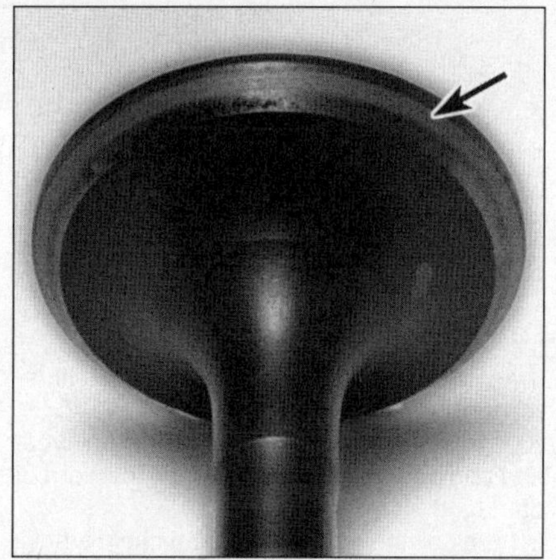

12.24 After lapping, the valve face should have a uniform, unbroken contact pattern (arrow)

12.28a A small dab of grease will hold the keepers in place on the valve while the spring is released

seal between the valves and seats. This procedure requires coarse and fine valve lapping compound (available at auto parts stores) and a valve lapping tool. If a lapping tool is not available, a piece of rubber or plastic hose can be slipped over the valve stem (after the valve has been installed in the guide) and used to turn the valve.

23 Apply a small amount of coarse lapping compound to the valve face **(see illustration)**, then slip the valve into the guide. **Note:** *Make sure the valve is installed in the correct guide and be careful not to get any lapping compound on the valve stem.*

24 Attach the lapping tool (or hose) to the valve and rotate the tool between the palms of your hands. Use a back-and-forth motion rather than a circular motion. Lift the valve off the seat and turn it at regular intervals to distribute the lapping compound properly. Continue the lapping procedure until the valve face and seat contact area is of uniform width and unbroken around the entire circumference of the valve face and seat **(see illustration)**.

25 Carefully remove the valve from the guide and wipe off all traces of lapping compound. Use solvent to clean the valve and wipe the seat area thoroughly with a solvent soaked cloth.

26 Repeat the procedure with fine valve lapping compound, then repeat the entire procedure for the remaining valves.

27 Lay the spring seats in place in the cylinder head, then install new valve stem seals on each of the guides **(see illustration 12.7c)**. Use an appropriate size deep socket to push the seals into place until they are properly seated. Don't twist or cock them, or they will not seal properly against the valve stems. Also, don't remove them again or they will be damaged.

28 Coat the valve stems with assembly lube or moly-based grease, then install one of them into its guide. Next, install the springs and retainers, compress the springs and install the keepers. **Note:** *Install the springs with the tightly wound coils at the bottom (next to the spring seat).* When compressing the springs with the valve spring compressor, depress them only as far as is absolutely necessary to slip the keepers into place. Apply a small amount of grease to the keepers **(see illustration)** *to help hold them in place as the pressure is released from the springs. Make certain that the keeper ridges are securely locked in the retaining groove in the valve stem* **(see illustration)**.

12.28b The small ridge near the top of each keeper locks the keeper into the groove in the valve stem (valve springs removed for clarity)

12.29 To fully seat the keepers in their grooves, tap each valve stem gently with a soft-face hammer

13.6 When installing the cam chain guide, make sure that the guide tabs are correctly seated in their grooves (arrow)

29 Support the cylinder head on blocks so the valves can't contact the workbench top, then very gently tap each of the valve stems with a soft-faced hammer **(see illustration)**. This will help seat the keepers in their grooves.

30 Once all of the valves have been installed in the head, check for proper valve sealing by pouring a small amount of solvent into each of the valve ports. If the solvent leaks past the valve(s) into the combustion chamber area, disassemble the valve(s) and repeat the lapping procedure, then reinstall the valve(s) and repeat the check. Repeat the procedure until a satisfactory seal is obtained.

13 Cam chain guide - removal, inspection and installation

Note: *The following procedure applies to the front and rear cam chain guides.*

1 Remove the engine (see Section 5).

2 Remove the cylinder head cover (see Section 7).

3 Remove the camshaft, sprocket and rocker arms (see Section 8).

4 Remove the cam chain tensioner (see Section 9).

5 Remove the cylinder head (see Section 10).

6 Remove the cam chain guide **(see illustration)**.

7 Inspect the cam chain guide for wear and damage. Replace the guide if it's worn or damaged.

8 Install the guide in the cam chain tunnel. Make sure that the guide mounting tabs are correctly seated in the grooves in the cylinder **(see illustration 13.6)** and the lower end of the guide is correctly seated against the lower guide stop in the crankcase **(see illustration 9.7)**.

9 Install the cylinder head (see Section 10).

10 Install the cam chain tensioner (see Section 9).

11 Install the camshaft, sprocket and rocker arms (see Section 8).

12 Install the cylinder head cover (see Section 7).

13 Install the engine (see Section 5).

14 Cylinder - removal, inspection and installation

Note: *The following procedure applies to the front and rear cylinders.*

Removal

1 Remove the engine (see Section 5).

2 Remove the cylinder head cover (see Section 7).

3 Remove the camshaft, sprocket and rocker arms (see Section 8).

4 Remove the cam chain tensioner (see Section 9).

5 Remove the cylinder head (see Section 10) and the cam chain guide (see Section 13).

14.6a To remove the coolant pipe collar (arrow), pull out the two retaining clips . . .

14.6b . . . and slide the collar away from the cylinder you're removing, until the coolant pipe and O-ring are exposed

14.7 If you're removing the rear cylinder, unbolt the coolant hose adapter (arrows) (one bolt hidden)

14.8a Lift the cylinder straight up off the studs

6 Coolant passes from the front cylinder to the rear cylinder through a pair of pipes, one on each cylinder, which are connected by a sliding collar locked into position by a pair of retaining clips. Remove the retaining clips **(see illustration)** and slide the collar away from the cylinder you're removing, far enough to expose the O-ring on the end of the coolant pipe **(see illustration)** for the cylinder head you're going to remove first (or the head you're removing, if you're only removing one head).

7 If you removing a rear cylinder, detach the coolant hose adapter **(see illustration)** from the rear side of the cylinder.

8 Lift the cylinder straight up to remove it **(see illustration)**. If it's stuck, tap around its perimeter with a soft-faced hammer, taking care not to break the cooling fins. Don't attempt to pry between the cylinder and the crankcase, as you will ruin the sealing surfaces. Remove the old base gasket and discard it. Note the location of the dowel pins **(see illustrations)**, then remove them. Be careful not to let the dowels drop into the engine.

14.8b Note the locations of the dowels (arrows), then remove them

9 Stuff clean shop towels into the cavity beneath the piston and carefully remove all traces of old gasket material from the mating surfaces of the cylinder and crankcase. Don't allow any gasket material to fall into the crankcase.

14.8c These are the dowel locations; they may come off with the cylinder or stay in the crankcase

14.8d Remove the base gasket (arrow); note the locations of the holes in the gasket so you can install it correctly

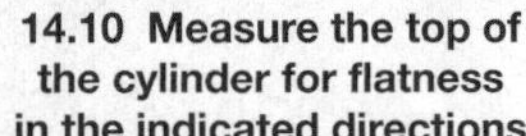
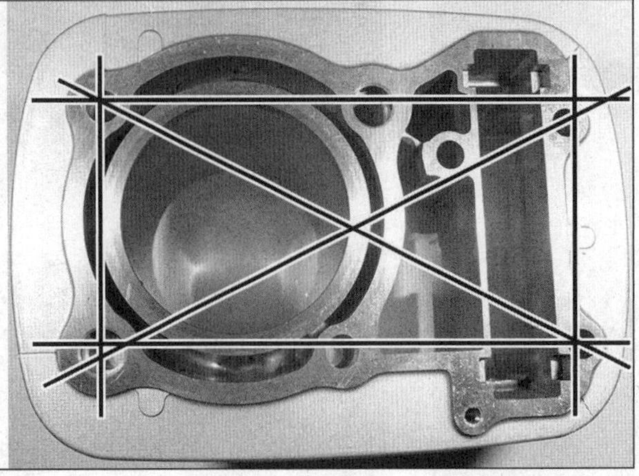

14.10 Measure the top of the cylinder for flatness in the indicated directions

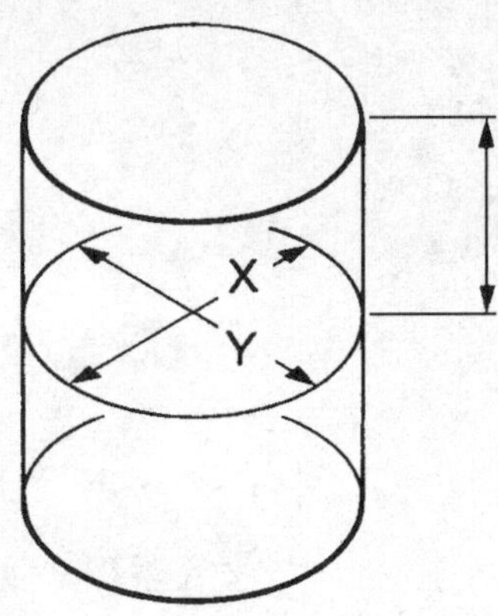

14.11 Measure the cylinder bore at the specified distance from the top of the cylinder; measure parallel to the crankshaft centerline, then at right angles to it

Inspection

Note: *If the following inspection indicates that a cylinder is warped, it can be resurfaced or replaced independently of the other cylinder. However, if a rebore is indicated for either cylinder, that cylinder will require an oversize piston, so BOTH cylinders must be rebored to accept the same size pistons, in order to maintain correct balance.*

10 Measure the top of the cylinder for flatness **(see illustration)** and compare your measurements to the allowable warpage listed in this Chapter's Specifications.

11 Inspect the cylinder wall thoroughly for scratches and score marks. Using a cylinder bore gauge or a telescoping snap-gauge and micrometer, measure the cylinder diameter. Make three pairs of measurements (six in all), parallel and perpendicular to the crankshaft axis, at the top, middle and bottom of the cylinder **(see illustration)**. First, determine cylinder bore diameter. Take the largest measurement and compare it to the cylinder bore diameter listed in this Chapter's Specifications. Next, determine whether the cylinder is round. Compare the readings in one direction to the readings in the other direction, subtract the smaller readings from the larger readings and compare any differences to the allowable out-of-round listed in this Chapter's Specifications. Finally, determine whether the cylinder is tapered. Compare the largest reading to the smallest reading in each direction, subtract the two and compare the difference to the allowable taper listed in this Chapter's Specifications. **Note:** *If you do not have access to a cylinder bore gauge or a three-inch telescoping snap-gauge and three-inch micrometer, have a dealer service department or motorcycle repair shop measure the cylinder(s).*

12 If the cylinder walls are worn, out-of-round or tapered beyond their specified limits, or badly scuffed or scored, have the cylinder rebored and honed by a dealer service department or a motorcycle repair shop. Remember, even if only one cylinder must be rebored, the other cylinder will also have to be rebored to the same diameter, so that both cylinders have the same oversize pistons, to maintain balance.

13 If the cylinder is in reasonably good condition and not worn beyond the limits, and if the piston-to-cylinder bore clearance (see Section 15) is still within the allowable range, then the cylinder does not have to be rebored; honing is all that is necessary.

14 To hone the cylinder, you will need the proper size flexible hone with fine stones, or a "bottle brush" type hone, plenty of light oil or honing oil, some shop towels and an electric drill motor. Hold the cylinder block in a vise (cushioned with soft jaws or wood blocks) when performing the honing operation. Mount the hone in the drill motor, compress the stones and slip the hone into the cylinder. Lubricate the cylinder thoroughly, turn on the drill and move the hone up and down in the cylinder at a pace which will produce a fine crosshatch pattern on the cylinder wall with the crosshatch lines intersecting at approximately a 60-degree angle **(see illustration)**. Be sure to use plenty of lubricant and do not take off any more material than is absolutely necessary to produce the desired effect. Do not withdraw the hone from the cylinder while it is running. Instead, shut off the drill and continue moving the hone up and down in the cylinder until it comes to a complete stop, then compress the stones and withdraw the hone. Wipe the oil out of the cylinder and repeat the procedure on the remaining cylinder. Remember, do not remove too much material from the cylinder wall. If you do not have the tools, or do not desire to perform the honing operation, a dealer service department or motorcycle repair shop will generally do it for a reasonable fee.

15 Wash the cylinders thoroughly with warm soapy water to remove all traces of the abrasive grit produced during the honing operation. Be sure to run a brush through the bolt holes and flush them with running water. After rinsing, dry the cylinders thoroughly and apply a coat of light, rust-preventative oil to all machined surfaces.

Installation

16 Lubricate the cylinder bore and piston with plenty of clean engine oil.

17 Place a new cylinder base gasket on the crankcase. Make sure the two dowel pins are in position **(see illustration 14.8b)**.

18 Attach a piston ring compressor to the piston and compress the piston rings. You can also use a large hose clamp; just make

14.14 Move the hone rapidly up-and-down without stopping

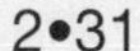

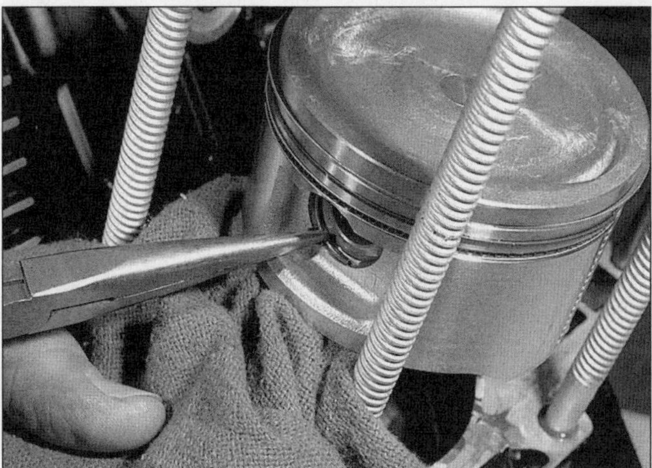

15.3 Wear eye protection when pulling out the circlips; they can pop out of the piston with sufficient force to cause eye injury

15.4a Pull out the pin and detach the piston; the IN mark (arrow) must face the carburetor side of the engine on installation

sure it doesn't scratch the piston and don't tighten it too much.

19 Install the cylinder over the piston and carefully lower it down until the piston crown fits into the cylinder liner. While doing this, pull the camshaft chain up, using a hooked tool or a piece of coat hanger. Also keep an eye on the cam chain guide to make sure it doesn't wedge against the cylinder. Push down on the cylinder, making sure the piston doesn't get cocked sideways, until the bottom of the cylinder liner slides down past the piston rings. A wood or plastic hammer handle can be used to gently tap the cylinder down, but don't use too much force or the piston will be damaged.

20 Remove the piston ring compressor or hose clamp, being careful not to scratch the piston.

21 Install a new O-ring on the coolant pipe, then lubricate the O-ring with coolant to allow the collar to slide over it without damaging it. Position the collar in the middle (covering the O-rings of both coolant pipes) and install the retaining clips.

22 If you're installing the front cylinder, install a new O-ring in the groove inside the coolant hose adapter, install the adapter and tighten the adapter bolts securely. If the coolant hose was detached from the adapter, reattach the hose and tighten the hose clamp securely.

23 Install the cam chain guide (see Section 13).

24 Install the cylinder head (see Section 10).

25 Install the cam chain tensioner (see Section 9).

26 Install the camshaft, sprocket and rocker arms (see Section 8).

27 Install the cylinder head cover (see Section 7).

28 Install the engine (see Section 5).

15 Pistons and oil jets - removal, inspection and installation

Note: *The following procedure applies to the front and rear pistons.*

1 The pistons are attached to the connecting rods with piston pins that are a slip fit in the pistons and rods.

2 Before removing the pistons from the rods, stuff a clean shop towel into each crankcase hole, around the connecting rods. This will prevent the circlips from falling into the crankcase if they are inadvertently dropped.

Removal

3 Using a sharp scribe, scratch the location of each piston (front or rear cylinder) into its crown (or use a felt pen if the piston is clean enough). Each piston should also have an IN mark on its crown; this mark faces the intake side of the cylinder when the piston is installed. If not, scribe an arrow into the piston crown before removal. Support the first piston, grasp the circlip with a pointed tool or needle-nose pliers **(see illustration)** and remove it from the groove.

4 Push the piston pin out from the opposite end to free the piston from the rod, then pull it out **(see illustration)**; if it's too slippery, jam a pair of needle-nose pliers into the pin and pull it out. You may have to deburr the area around the groove for the circlip to allow the pin to slide out (use a triangular file for this procedure). If the pin won't come out, remove the other circlip. Fabricate a piston pin removal tool from threaded stock, nuts, washers and a piece of pipe **(see illustration)**.

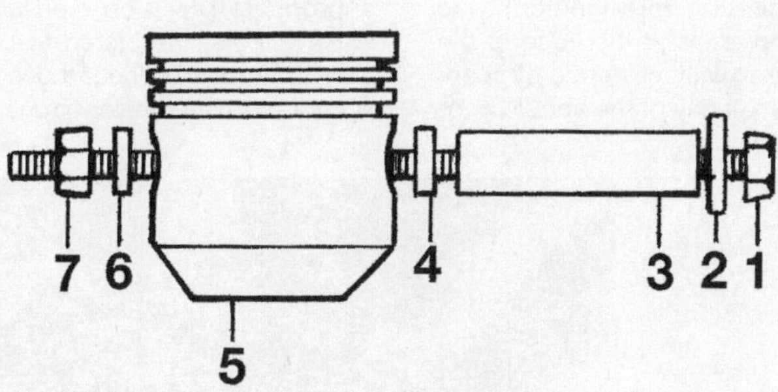

15.4b The piston pins should come out with hand pressure - if they don't, this removal tool can be fabricated from readily available parts

1 *Bolt*
2 *Washer*
3 *Pipe (A)*
4 *Padding (A)*
5 *Piston*
6 *Washer (B)*
7 *Nut (B)*
A *Large enough for piston pin to fit inside*
B *Small enough to fit through piston pin bore*

15.5 Pull the oil jet straight up; blow out the oil passage in the jet and use a new O-ring on installation

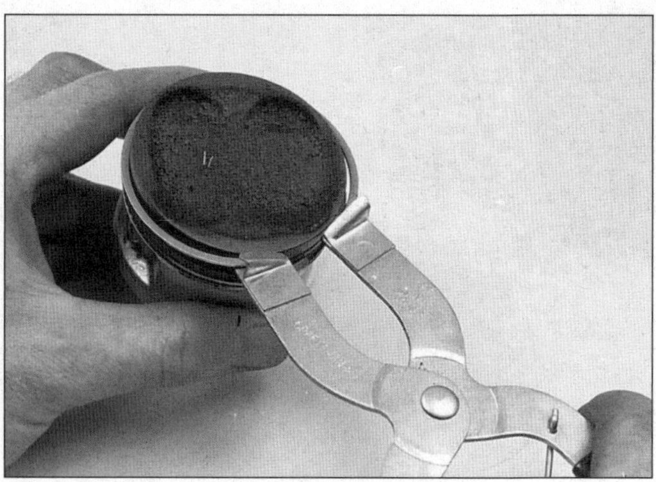

15.6 Remove the piston rings with a ring removal and installation tool

5 Remove the oil jet **(see illustration)**. Pull it straight up and discard the old O-ring.

Inspection

6 Using a piston ring installation tool, carefully remove the rings from the pistons **(see illustration)**. Do not nick or gouge the pistons in the process.

7 Clean the piston thoroughly. Scrape all traces of carbon from the top of the piston. A hand-held wire brush or a piece of fine emery cloth can be used once most of the deposits have been scraped away. Do not, under any circumstances, use a wire brush mounted in a drill motor to remove deposits from the piston; the piston material is soft and will be eroded away by the wire brush.

8 Use a piston ring groove cleaning tool to remove any carbon deposits from the ring grooves. If a tool is not available, a piece broken off the old ring will do the job. Be very careful to remove only the carbon deposits. Do not remove any metal and do not nick or gouge the sides of the ring grooves.

9 Once the deposits have been removed, clean the pistons with solvent and dry them thoroughly. Make sure the oil return holes below the oil ring grooves are clear.

10 If the pistons are not damaged or worn excessively and if the cylinders are not rebored, new pistons will not be necessary. Normal piston wear appears as even, vertical wear on the thrust surfaces of the piston and slight looseness of the top ring in its groove. New piston rings, on the other hand, should always be used when an engine is rebuilt.

11 Carefully inspect each piston for cracks around the skirt, at the pin bosses and at the ring lands **(see illustration)**.

12 Look for scoring and scuffing on the thrust faces of the skirt, holes in the piston crown and burned areas at the edge of the crown. If the skirt is scored or scuffed, the engine may have been suffering from overheating and/or abnormal combustion, which caused excessively high operating temperatures. The oil pump should be checked thoroughly. A hole in the piston crown, an extreme to be sure, is an indication that abnormal combustion (pre-ignition) was occurring. Burned areas at the edge of the piston crown are usually evidence of spark knock (detonation). If any of the above problems exist, the causes must be corrected or the damage will occur again.

13 Measure the piston ring-to-groove clearance by laying a new piston ring in the ring groove and slipping a feeler gauge in beside it **(see illustration)**. Check the clearance at three or four locations around the groove. Be sure to use the correct ring for each groove; they are different. If the clearance is greater than specified, new pistons will have to be used when the engine is reassembled.

14 Check the piston-to-bore clearance by measuring the cylinder bore (see Section 14) and the piston diameter. Make sure that the pistons and cylinders are correctly matched. Measure the piston across the skirt on the thrust faces at a 90-degree angle to the piston pin, at the distance from the bottom of the skirt listed in this Chapter's Specifications **(see illustration)**. Subtract the piston diameter from the bore diameter to obtain the clearance. If it is greater than specified, the cylinders will have to be rebored and new oversized pistons and rings installed. If the appropriate precision measuring tools are not available, the piston-to-cylinder clearances can be obtained, though not quite as accurately, using feeler gauge stock. Feeler

15.11 Check the piston pin bore and the piston skirt for wear, and make sure the internal holes are clear (arrows)

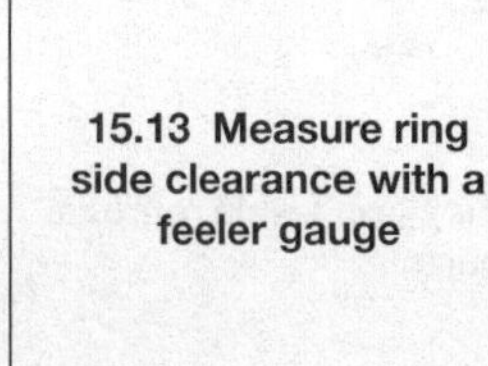

15.13 Measure ring side clearance with a feeler gauge

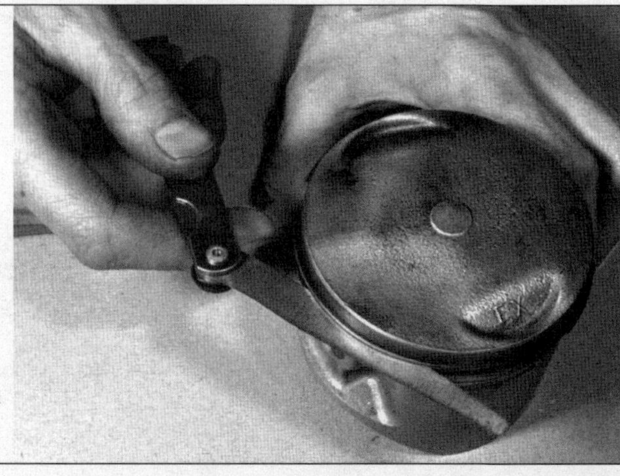

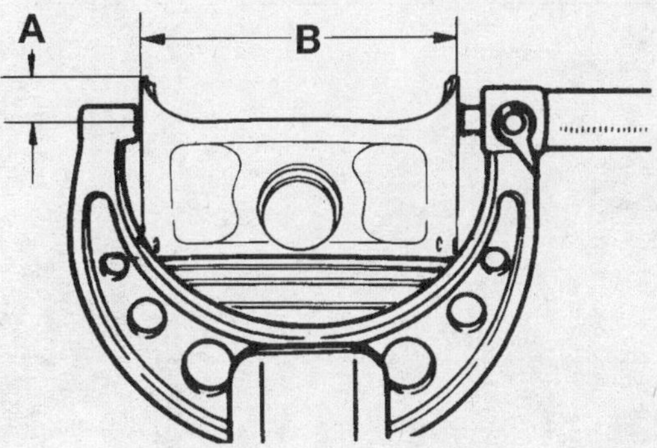

15.14 Measure the piston diameter with a micrometer

A Specified distance from bottom of piston
B Piston diameter

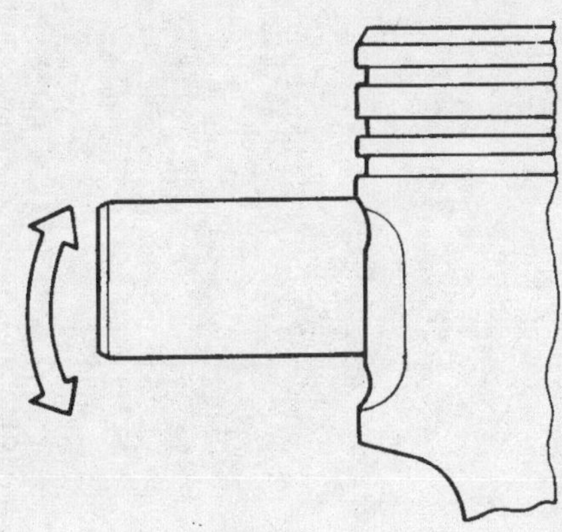

15.15 Slip the pin into the piston and try to wiggle it back-and-forth; if it's loose, replace the piston and pin

gauge stock comes in 12-inch lengths and various thicknesses and is generally available at auto parts stores. To check the clearance, select a feeler gauge of the same thickness as the piston clearance listed in this Chapter's Specifications and slip it into the cylinder along with the appropriate piston. The cylinder should be upside down and the piston must be positioned exactly as it normally would be. Place the feeler gauge between the piston and cylinder on one of the thrust faces (90-degrees to the piston pin bore). The piston should slip through the cylinder (with the feeler gauge in place) with moderate pressure. If it falls through, or slides through easily, the clearance is excessive and a new piston will be required. If the piston binds at the lower end of the cylinder and is loose toward the top, the cylinder is tapered, and if tight spots are encountered as the feeler gauge is placed at different points around the cylinder, the cylinder is out-of-round. Repeat the procedure for the remaining pistons and cylinders. Be sure to have the cylinders and pistons checked by a dealer service department or a motorcycle repair shop to confirm your findings before purchasing new parts.

15 Apply clean engine oil to the pin, insert it into the piston and check for freeplay by rocking the pin back-and-forth **(see illustration)**. If the pin is loose, new pistons and pins must be installed. For a more precise assessment of piston/piston pin wear, measure the diameter of the piston pin and compare your measurement to the piston pin diameter listed in this Chapter's Specifications. Replace the pin if it's excessively worn. Next, measure the inside diameter of the piston pin holes in the piston, subtract the diameter of the piston pin and compare your measurement to the piston pin-to-piston clearance listed in this Chapter's Specifications. If the clearance exceeds the specified maximum, replace the piston and/or the piston pin (depending on whether the pin diameter is acceptable). Finally, measure the inside diameter of the small end of the connecting rod, subtract the diameter of the piston pin and compare your measurement to the piston pin-to-connecting rod clearance listed in this Chapter's Specifications. If the clearance exceeds the specified maximum, replace the piston pin and/or the connecting rod (depending on whether the pin diameter is acceptable).

16 Install the rings on the piston (see Section 16).

Installation

17 Install a new O-ring on the oil jet and install the oil jet by pushing it firmly back into the crankcase until it's fully seated.

18 Install the piston with the IN mark pointing toward the intake side of the cylinder **(see illustration 15.3a)**. Lubricate the pins and the rod bores with clean engine oil. Install new circlips in the grooves in the inner sides of the pistons (don't reuse the old circlips). Push the pins into position from the opposite side and install new circlips. Compress the circlips only enough for them to fit in the piston. Make sure the circlips are correctly seated in the grooves **(see illustrations)**.

15.18a Slip the circlip into its bore with its gap away from the piston cutout . . .

15.18b . . . and push the circlip all the way into its groove; make sure it's securely seated

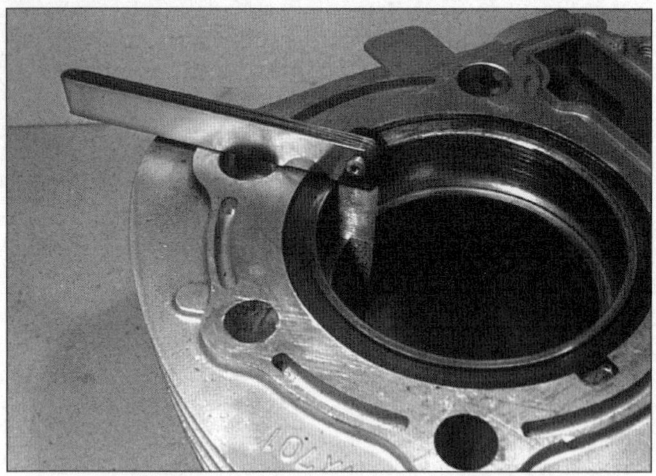

16.3 Measure ring end gap with a feeler gauge

16.5 If the end gap is too small, clamp a file in a vise and file the ring ends (from the outside in only) to enlarge the gap slightly

16 Piston rings - installation

1 Before installing the new piston rings, the ring end gaps must be checked.

2 Lay out the pistons and the new ring sets so the rings will be matched with the same piston and cylinder during the end gap measurement procedure and engine assembly.

3 Insert the top (No. 1) ring into the bottom of the first cylinder and square it up with the cylinder walls by pushing it in with the top of the piston **(see illustration)**. The ring should be about one inch above the bottom edge of the cylinder. To measure the end gap, slip a feeler gauge between the ends of the ring and compare the measurement to this Chapter's Specifications.

4 If the gap is larger or smaller than specified, double check to make sure that you have the correct rings before proceeding.

5 If the gap is too small, it must be enlarged or the ring ends may come in contact with each other during engine operation, which can cause serious damage. The end gap can be increased by filing the ring ends very carefully with a fine file **(see illustration)**. When performing this operation, file only from the outside in.

6 Excess end gap is not critical unless it is greater than 0.040-inch (1 mm). Again, double check to make sure you have the correct rings for your engine.

7 Repeat the procedure for each ring that will be installed in the first cylinder and for each ring in the remaining cylinder. Remember to keep the rings, pistons and cylinders matched up.

8 Once the ring end gaps have been checked/corrected, the rings can be installed on the pistons.

9 The oil control ring (lowest on the piston) is installed first. It is composed of three separate components. Slip the expander into the groove, then install the upper side rail **(see illustrations)**. Do not use a piston ring installation tool on the oil ring side rails as they may be damaged. Instead, place one end of the side rail into the groove between the spacer expander and the ring land. Hold it firmly in place and slide a finger around the piston while pushing the rail into the groove. Next, install the lower side rail in the same manner.

10 After the three oil ring components have been installed, check to make sure that both the upper and lower side rails can be turned smoothly in the ring groove.

11 Install the second (middle) ring next **(see illustration)**. Do not mix the top and middle rings. They can be identified by their profiles **(see illustration)**, as well as the fact that the top ring is thinner than the middle ring.

12 To avoid breaking the ring, use a piston ring installation tool and make sure that the identification mark is facing up **(see illustration)**. Fit the ring into the middle groove on the piston. Do not expand the ring any more than is necessary to slide it into place.

16.9a Install the oil ring expander first

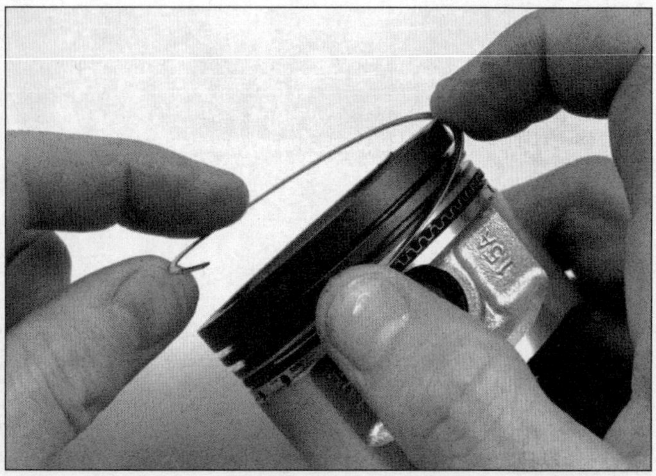

16.9b Installing an oil ring side rail - don't use a ring installation tool to do this

16.11a Install the middle ring with its identification mark up

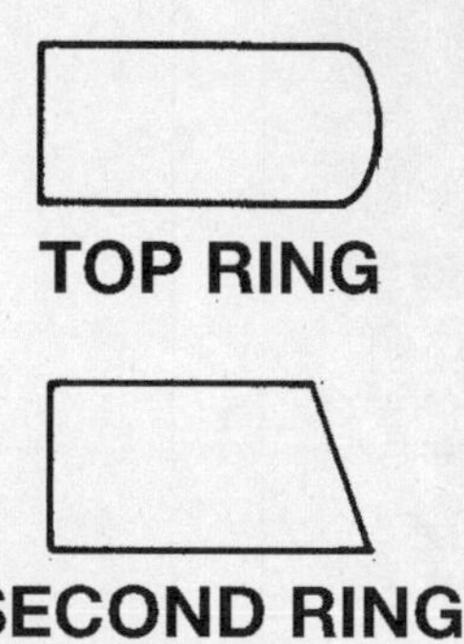

16.11b The top and middle rings can be identified by their profiles

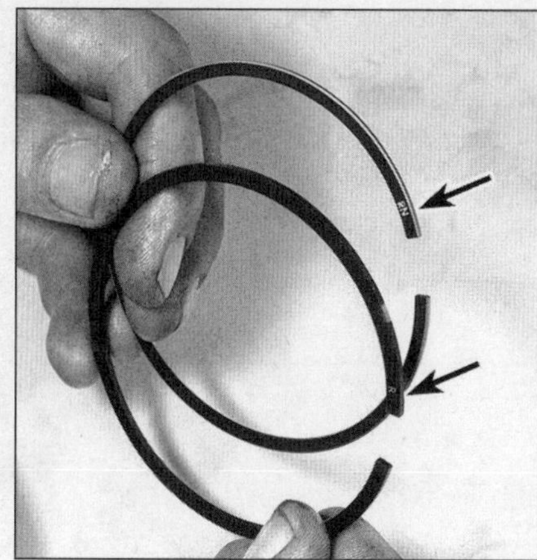

16.12 The top and middle rings have identification marks (arrows); these must be up when the rings are installed

13 Finally, install the top ring in the same manner. Make sure the identifying mark is facing up.

14 Repeat the procedure for the remaining piston and rings. Be very careful not to confuse the top and second rings.

15 Once the rings have been properly installed, stagger the end gaps, including those of the oil ring side rails **(see illustration)**.

17 Clutch release system - bleeding, removal and installation

Hydraulic system (1985 through 1996 VT1100C models)

1 These models use a hydraulic release system consisting of a master cylinder on the handlebar and a slave (release) cylinder on the left side of the engine.

Bleeding the hydraulic release system

2 Turn the handlebar so that the clutch master cylinder reservoir is as level as possible.

3 Remove the reservoir cover screws, then remove the cover, set plate and diaphragm from the reservoir.

Caution: Put some shop rags around the master cylinder to protect plastic and painted parts from damage (clutch fluid will ruin these surfaces).

Top up the master cylinder with fluid to the upper level line cast into the master cylinder.

4 Remove the crankcase left rear cover (see Section 10 in Chapter 1).

5 Remove the cap from the bleeder valve on the clutch slave cylinder, place a box wrench on the bleeder valve nut and connect a clear vinyl bleeder hose to the bleeder valve. Immerse the other end of the bleeder hose in a container of clean clutch fluid.

6 Pump the clutch lever several times and watch the bubbles rising from the bleed holes in the bottom of the master cylinder reservoir. When the bubbles stop, hold in the clutch lever and tap on the master cylinder body several times to free any air bubbles that might be stuck to the sides of the fluid line or the master cylinder bore.

7 Pump the lever several times and hold it in, then crack the bleeder valve nut open just enough to allow fluid and any air bubbles in the system to escape, then tighten the bleeder valve nut. Slowly release the clutch lever, wait several seconds, then repeat: Pump the lever several times, hold it in, crack the bleeder valve, etc. Continue this process until no more air bubbles come out at the bleeder valve. Keep an eye on the fluid level in the master cylinder reservoir and top it up as necessary.

8 When you're done, remove the bleeder hose, tighten the bleeder valve to the torque listed in this Chapter's Specifications, install the crankcase left rear cover, top up the master cylinder reservoir, install the diaphragm, set plate and cover and tighten the cover screws securely.

Master cylinder removal

9 Unscrew the rear view mirror from the master cylinder.

10 Disconnect the electrical lead from the clutch switch underneath the master cylinder.

11 Drain the hydraulic release system: Turn the handlebar so that the clutch master cylinder reservoir is as level as possible. Remove the reservoir cover screws, then remove the cover, set plate and diaphragm from the reservoir. Remove the crankcase left rear cover (see Section 10 in Chapter 1) and connect a bleeder hose to the bleeder valve on the clutch slave cylinder. Loosen the bleeder valve and pump the clutch lever. Continue doing so until no more fluid comes out of the bleeder valve. The system is now essentially empty.

12 Unscrew the banjo fitting from the master cylinder and disconnect the clutch hydraulic fluid hose from the master cylinder. Discard the old banjo bolt sealing washers.

13 Remove the master cylinder clamp bolts and clamp and remove the master cylinder from the handlebar.

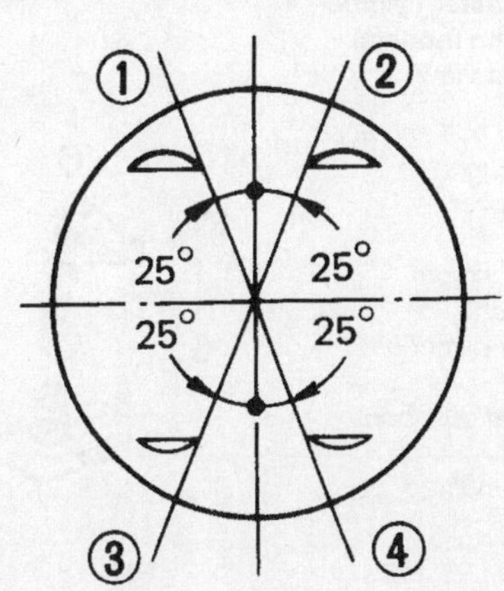

16.15 Arrange the ring gaps like this

1 Top compression ring
2 Oil ring lower rail
3 Oil ring upper rail
4 Second compression ring

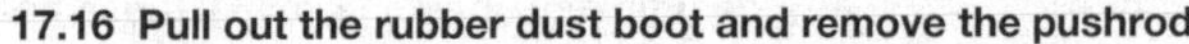

17.16 Pull out the rubber dust boot and remove the pushrod

17.17 Remove the snap-ring from its groove in the bore

Master cylinder overhaul

14 Remove the clutch switch (see Chapter 9).

15 Remove the nut from the clutch lever pivot bolt, pull out the pivot bolt and remove the clutch lever.

16 Remove the pushrod and dust boot **(see illustration)**.

17 Remove the snap-ring **(see illustration)**. If the snap-ring sticks in its groove because of corrosion, push the piston into the bore, away from the snap-ring, with a Phillips screwdriver and try again. Tape the tip of the screwdriver to protect the piston.

18 Remove the washer, secondary cup/master piston, primary cup and spring **(see illustration)**. If a part sticks in the bore, blow low-pressure compressed air through the fluid line hole.

Warning: Do NOT point the open bore of the master cylinder at yourself when using compressed air to dislodge a stuck piston, which can shoot out with enough force to cause serious injury. Instead, point the piston bore toward a pile of shop rags inside a box and apply pressure sparingly.

19 Thoroughly clean all the components in clean brake fluid. Do NOT use a petroleum-based solvent.

20 Inspect the piston and master cylinder bore for corrosion, rust, scratches and any other damage. If the piston shows signs of any type of wear or damage, replace it, and both rubber cups, as a set. If the master cylinder bore has similar damage or wear, replace the master cylinder. Do NOT try to hone out an aluminum master cylinder bore!

21 Even if there is no obvious damage or wear, measure the inside diameter of the master cylinder piston bore with a small hole gauge and a one-inch micrometer and measure the outside diameter of the master piston. Compare your measurements to the dimensions listed in this Chapter's Specifi-

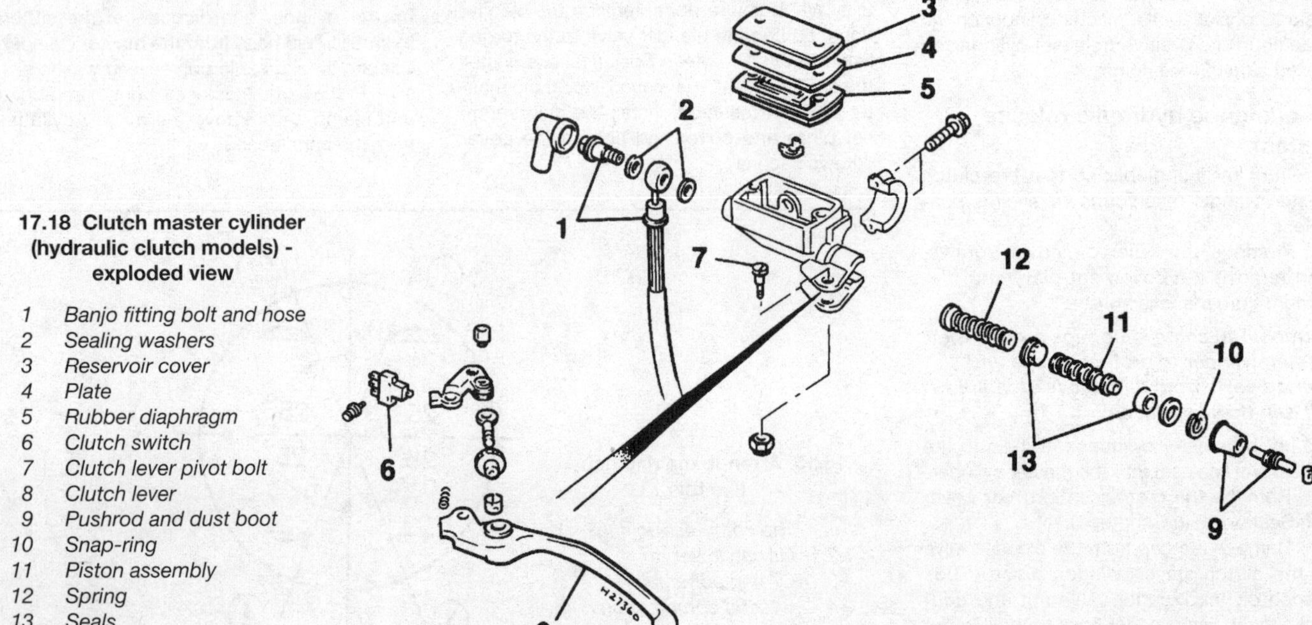

17.18 Clutch master cylinder (hydraulic clutch models) - exploded view

1 *Banjo fitting bolt and hose*
2 *Sealing washers*
3 *Reservoir cover*
4 *Plate*
5 *Rubber diaphragm*
6 *Clutch switch*
7 *Clutch lever pivot bolt*
8 *Clutch lever*
9 *Pushrod and dust boot*
10 *Snap-ring*
11 *Piston assembly*
12 *Spring*
13 *Seals*

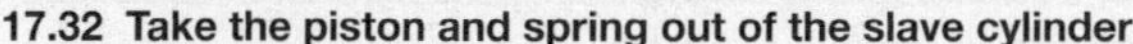
17.32 Take the piston and spring out of the slave cylinder

17.33 Replace the pushrod seal if it's damaged or worn

cations. If either part is outside the specified limit, replace it.

22 Reassembly is the reverse of disassembly. Dip all the parts in clean brake fluid, then install the spring (big end first), primary cup, master piston/secondary cup and washer.

23 Depress the piston/spring assembly and install the snap-ring. Make sure it's correctly seated in its groove inside the master cylinder bore. Install the rubber boot and pushrod.

24 Grease the clutch lever pivot bolt. Align the hole in the clutch lever with the holes in the clutch lever bracket and insert the pivot bolt. Install the pivot bolt nut and tighten it securely.

25 Install the clutch switch (see Chapter 9).

Master cylinder installation

26 Installation is the reverse of removal. Be sure to use new sealing washers when installing the clutch hose banjo bolt and tighten the banjo bolt to the torque listed in this Chapter's Specifications.

27 Before installing the crankcase left rear cover, bleed the hydraulic release system (see Steps 2 through 8).

Slave cylinder removal

28 Remove the crankcase left rear cover (see Section 10 in Chapter 1).

29 If you're planning to disassemble or replace the slave cylinder, drain the hydraulic release system (see Step 11). If you're simply detaching the slave cylinder from the engine to remove the engine or service something else, don't drain the system.

30 If you're going to disconnect the fluid hose, put some shop rags and a container under the slave cylinder to catch spilled fluid. Remove the fluid hose banjo bolt. Discard the old sealing washers. Put the end of the fluid hose in the container to catch any fluid still in the system.

31 Remove the slave cylinder mounting bolts and detach the slave cylinder from the engine.

Slave cylinder overhaul

32 Remove the piston and spring **(see illustration)**. If the piston sticks in the bore, blow low-pressure compressed air through the fluid line hole.

Warning: Do NOT point the open bore of the slave cylinder at yourself when using compressed air to dislodge a stuck piston, which can shoot out with enough force to cause serious injury. Instead, point the piston bore toward a pile of shop rags inside a box and apply pressure sparingly.

33 Remove the old pushrod seal from the piston **(see illustration)**.

34 Thoroughly clean all the components in clean brake fluid. Do NOT use a petroleum-based solvent.

35 Inspect the piston and slave cylinder bore for corrosion, rust, scratches and any other damage. If the piston shows signs of any type of wear or damage, replace it. If the slave cylinder bore has similar damage or wear, replace the slave cylinder. Do NOT try to hone out an aluminum slave cylinder bore!

36 Measure the inside diameter of the slave cylinder bore and the outside diameter of the piston and compare your measurements to the I.D. of the slave cylinder bore and the O.D. of the piston, respectively, listed in this Chapter's Specifications. If either part is outside the service limit, replace it.

37 Dip the parts in clean brake fluid, then install a new pushrod seal into the piston and install a new piston seal into the outer groove in the piston (the wide end of the piston seal faces in) **(see illustration)**.

38 Reassembly is the reverse of disassembly. Install the spring (big end first) in the piston bore, then install the piston with the pushrod seal facing out.

Slave cylinder installation

39 Installation is the reverse of removal. Be sure to use new sealing washers when installing the fluid hose banjo bolt. Tighten the banjo bolt to the torque listed in this Chapter's Specifications.

40 Before installing the crankcase left rear cover, bleed the hydraulic system (see Steps 2 through 8).

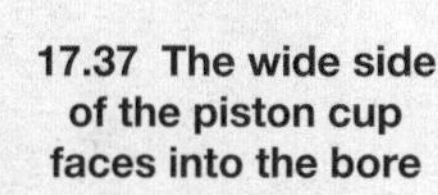
17.37 The wide side of the piston cup faces into the bore

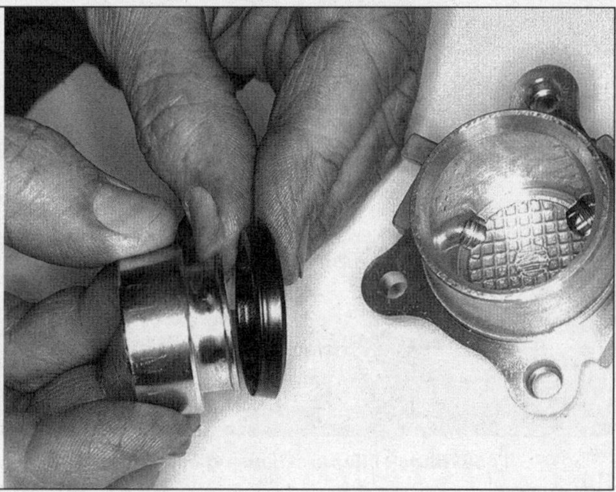

17.43 On models with a clutch cable, detach the cable bracket from the rear cylinder head

17.46 Push up the clutch lifter arm and disengage the clutch cable from the lifter arm clevis

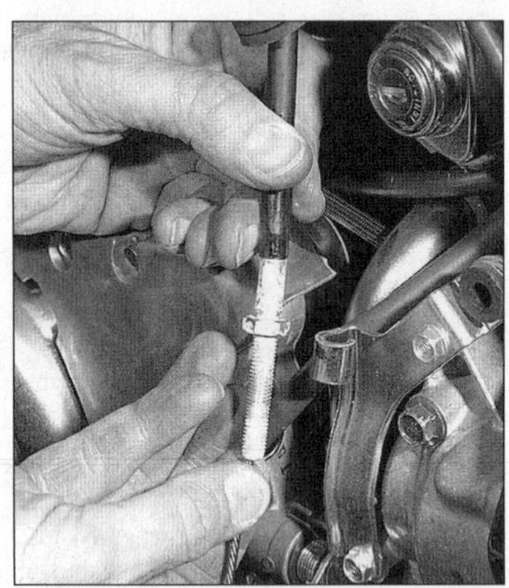
17.47 Loosen the cable locknut and adjuster nut and disengage the clutch cable from its bracket

Cable system (VT1100C2, VT1100T and 1997-on VT1100C models)

41 These models use a cable to operate the clutch. The cable release system consists of the clutch lever, the clutch cable and a clutch lifter arm at the engine end of the cable.

Cable removal and installation

42 Loosen the lockwheel and unscrew the adjuster from the clutch lever bracket **(see illustration 10.3 in Chapter 1)** and disengage the cable end plug from the lever.

43 Remove the clutch cable bracket from the rear cylinder head **(see illustration)**.

44 Remove the crankcase left rear cover (see Section 10 in Chapter 1).

45 Loosen the cable locknut and adjusting nut **(see illustration 10.8 in Chapter 1)**.

46 Push up the clutch lifter arm and disengage the clutch cable from the lifter arm clevis **(see illustration)**.

47 Disengage the clutch cable from the cable bracket **(see illustration)**.

48 Note the routing of the cable, then remove it.

49 Installation is the reverse of removal. Make sure that the cable is routed exactly the same as before and doesn't interfere with anything. There must be no kinks in the cable.

50 Be sure to adjust the cable when you're done (see Chapter 1).

Lifter arm removal

51 Disconnect the clutch cable from the lifter arm clevis (see Steps 44 through 46).

52 Remove the three lifter arm housing mounting bolts **(see illustration)**. On California models, detach the carburetor air vent control valve vent tube from the clamp above the upper bolt and, if necessary, loosen the clamp bolt and swing the clamp out of the way to provide clearance to remove the lifter arm housing.

53 Remove the lifter arm housing **(see illustration)**. Don't lose the dowel pin.

54 Remove the lifter rod **(see illustration)**.

17.52 Clutch lifter arm housing bolts (arrows)

17.53 Remove the lifter arm housing; don't lose the dowel (arrow)

17.54 Pull the lifter rod out of the crankcase

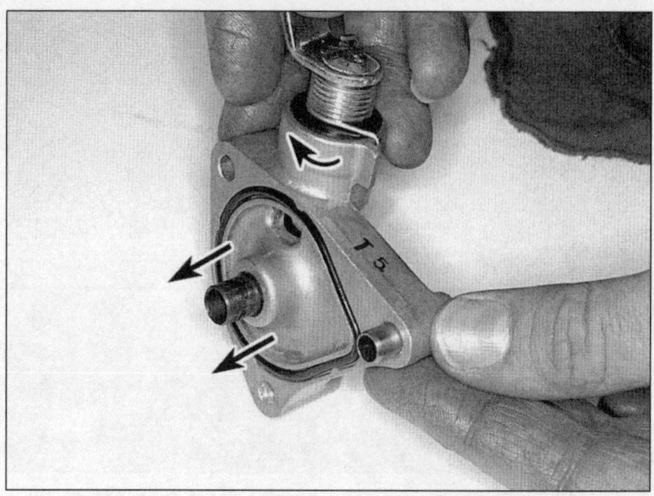

17.55 Rotate the lifter arm clockwise to expose the lifter piece, then remove the lifter piece

Lifter arm inspection

Note: *Unless it's been subjected to very severe conditions, the lifter arm shouldn't require any service. If it's stiff or frozen, disassemble, clean and inspect the lifter arm housing and replace any damaged or worn parts.*

55 Remove and discard the old O-ring, then rotate the lifter clockwise and remove the lifter piece **(see illustration)**.

56 Note how the end of the lifter arm return spring seats against the boss on the side of the housing, then pull the lifter arm out of the lifter arm housing **(see illustration)** and remove the washer.

57 Remove the lifter arm seal **(see illustration)** by prying it out with a small screwdriver.

58 Remove the lifter arm needle bearings.

59 Wash all the parts thoroughly in clean solvent and blow them dry with compressed air.

60 Inspect the condition of the lifter rod. Make sure that it's smooth and straight. To verify that the lifter rod is straight, roll it on a flat surface. If it doesn't roll smoothly, it's bent, and must be replaced.

61 Inspect the needle bearings. Make sure that they're not pitted or corroded or worn excessively. If they are, replace them.

62 Grease the needle bearings and install them in the housing.

63 Drive in a new lifter arm seal with a small socket.

64 Grease the lifter arm and install it in the housing. Make sure that the end of the return spring is firmly seated against the boss on the housing **(see illustration 17.56)**.

65 Lubricate the lifter rod with clean engine oil and install it.

66 Grease the lifter piece and install it in the housing with the solid end of the lifter piece facing in, toward the housing, and the open end facing out (the lifter rod seats in the open end of the lifter piece). Pushing the lifter piece into the housing, rotate the lifter arm clockwise to align the concave cutout in the lifter arm with the lifter piece. Verify that the two parts are correctly engaged by turning the arm clockwise and counterclockwise a few times. The lifter piece should retract into the housing when the arm is turned counterclockwise and protrude when the arm is turned clockwise.

67 Install a new O-ring in the groove in the housing.

68 Install the lifter arm housing, make sure the lifter rod seats correctly in the lifter piece, then install the housing mounting bolts. Tighten them gradually and evenly until they're snug, then tighten them to the torque listed in this Chapter's Specifications.

69 Reconnect the clutch cable to the lifter arm clevis (see above).

70 Adjust the clutch cable freeplay (see Chapter 1).

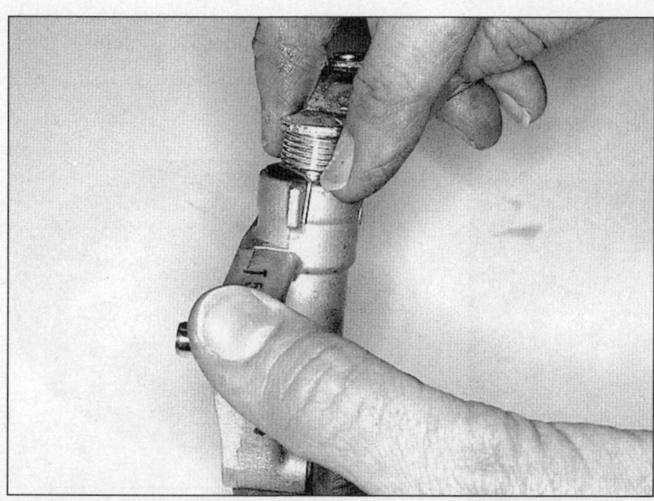

17.56 Note how the end of the return spring seats against this boss on the side of the housing, then pull the lifter arm, spring and washer out of the housing

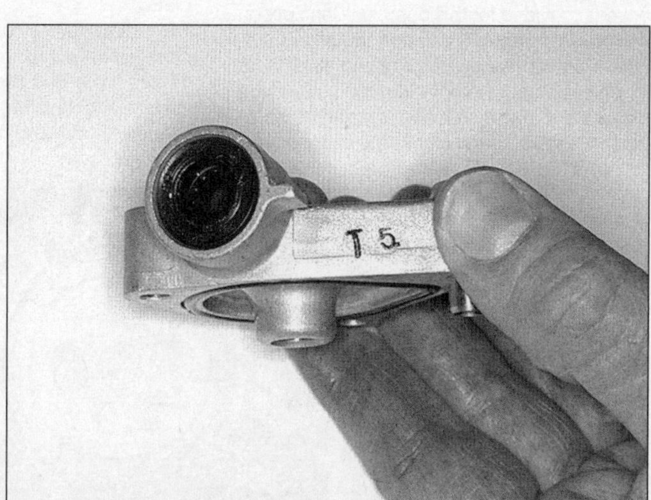

17.57 Pry the lifter arm seal out of the housing with a small screwdriver

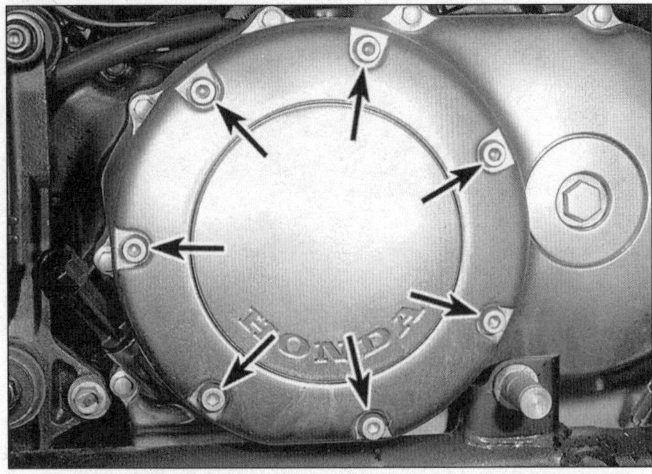

18.2a To remove any clutch component except the clutch housing, simply remove the seven clutch cover bolts (arrows) . . .

18.2b . . . and remove the clutch cover, gasket and three dowel pins (hydraulic clutch models) or two dowel pins (cable clutch models) (arrows)

18 Clutch - removal, inspection and installation

1 Support the bike on its sidestand and drain the engine oil (see Chapter 1).

2 If you're planning to remove any clutch component except the clutch housing, simply remove the seven clutch cover bolts and remove the clutch cover, gasket and dowel pins **(see illustrations)**. (On 1985 through 1996 VT1100C models, there are three dowel pins and an O-ring; on VT1100C, VT1100T and 1997-on VT1100C models, there are two dowel pins and no O-ring.)

3 If you're planning to remove the clutch housing, the right crankcase cover must also be removed. To get to all the crankcase cover bolts, the sub-frame must be removed (see Section 5). Then, remove the right crankcase cover bolts **(see illustration)**. If the cover is stuck, gently tap on one or more of the cover bosses provided for this purpose. Don't pry on the cover; prying will damage the gasket surface. Remove the dowel pins and store them in a plastic bag. Remove the old gasket and discard it. Carefully remove any gasket material that's stuck to the crankcase or the cover.

1985 through 1996 VT1100C models

Removal

4 Remove the snap-ring and the lifter plate, the bearing and the joint piece.

5 Put the transmission in first gear, apply the rear brake and remove the locknut. If the engine has been removed from the bike, hold the output drive shaft with a shaft holder (Honda tool 07923-6890101, or equivalent) instead of applying the brake.

6 Remove the lock washer, the spring set plate and the clutch spring.

7 Remove the clutch assembly from the clutch housing.

8 Remove the snap-ring and drive the joint piece out of the lifter plate bearing with a plastic hammer.

9 Remove the snap-ring and drive the lifter plate bearing out of the lifter plate.

10 Remove the snap-ring, the lifter spring and the clutch lifter from the clutch pressure plate.

11 Remove the clutch pressure plate, the clutch plates and the discs from the clutch center. Note that there are six friction discs and five steel plates. The outer (first and last) friction discs are different in appearance than the other four: The grooves cut into their friction surfaces are alternately wider and narrower. The other four friction discs have equal-width grooves, but their tabs (the "ears" that fit into the slots in the outer) have small semi-circular cutouts in them; the outer friction discs do not have these cutouts. Keep these differences between the friction discs in mind when installing the discs; they must be reinstalled exactly the same way.

12 Remove the clutch piston from the pressure plate.

13 Remove the clutch housing (see Step 51).

Inspection

14 Inspect the piston and the cylinder surface of the pressure plate for scoring or other damage.

15 Inspect the oil passages in the pressure plate for clogging.

16 Inspect the clutch piston for scoring or other damage.

17 Measure the height of the clutch diaphragm spring **(see illustration)** and compare your measurement to the spring mini-

18.3 To remove the clutch housing, remove the crankcase cover bolts (arrows) and the cover

18.17 On 1985 through 1996 models, measure the free height of the diaphragm spring

18.42 Remove the pressure plate bolts, gradually and evenly, in a criss-cross pattern, and remove the bolts and the springs

18.43 Remove the pressure plate

mum height listed in this Chapter's Specifications. If the spring is lower than the minimum allowable height, replace it.

18 The inspection procedure for the rest of the clutch assembly (friction discs, steel plates, clutch center, clutch housing, clutch housing guide, etc.) is similar to later models (see Steps through).

Installation

19 Install the clutch housing (see Step).

20 Install a new O-ring into the groove in the clutch piston.

21 Coat the O-ring with clean engine oil and install the clutch piston into the pressure plate.

22 Coat the clutch discs and plates with clean engine oil.

23 Install the six discs and plates with the grooves in the discs facing in the same direction as indicated on the clutch center. There are six friction discs and five steel plates; you should therefore start and end with the friction discs with the alternating wide and narrow grooves. The inner four friction discs have small semi-circular cutouts.

24 Install a new O-ring into the groove in the clutch center.

25 Coat the O-ring with clean engine oil and install the pressure plate, aligning the teeth with the grooves in the clutch center.

26 Install the clutch lifter.

27 Install the lifter spring with the concave side facing out and the secure it with the snap-ring.

28 If you have your own hydraulic press, drive a new bearing into the lifter plate. If you don't have a suitable press, have this job done by a machine shop.

29 Secure the bearing in the lifter plate with the snap-ring.

30 Blow compressed air through the oil passage in the joint piece, then install the joint piece in the bearing.

31 Install the snap-ring in the joint piece groove.

32 Install the clutch assembly in the clutch housing, aligning the splines of the clutch center and mainshaft, while aligning the teeth of the clutch discs with the slots in the clutch housing.

18.44 Remove the clutch lifter and pull out the lifter rod (arrow)

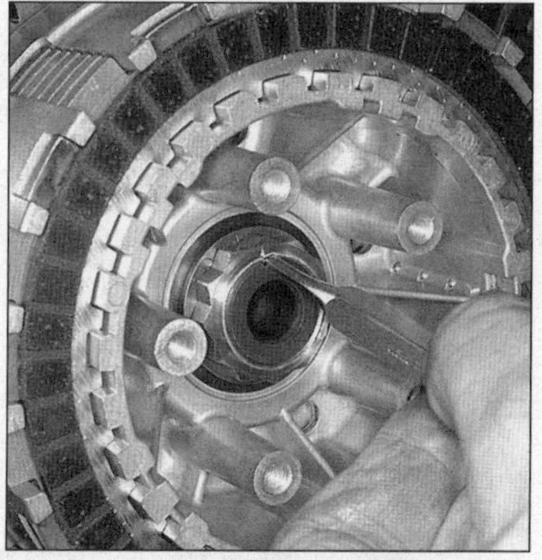

18.45 Unstake the clutch center locknut

33 Install the clutch spring and set plate and the lock washer.

34 Shift the transmission into first gear, apply the rear brake and install and tighten the locknut to the torque listed in this Chapter's Specifications. If the engine has been removed from the bike, hold the output drive shaft with a shaft holder (Honda tool 07923-6890101, or equivalent) instead of applying the brake.

35 Stake the locknut into the groove in the mainshaft.

36 Make sure that the mainshaft mating surface on the joint piece isn't scratched or scored, and make sure that the oil passage in the joint piece isn't clogged.

37 Install the clutch lifter plate with the bearing and the joint piece.

38 Make sure that the oil seal in the clutch cover is in good condition.

39 Remove the snap-ring and replace the oil seal with a new one if it's damaged or deteriorated.

40 Blow compressed air through the oil passage in the clutch cover.

VT1100C2, VT1100T and 1997-on VT1100C

Removal

41 If you're planning to remove the oil pump drive chain and sprockets (see Section 19) and/or the primary drive gear (see Section 20), put a penny between the clutch housing gear teeth and the primary drive gear teeth and loosen the primary drive gear bolt and/or the oil pump driven sprocket bolt.

42 Remove the clutch pressure plate bolts **(see illustration)**, gradually and evenly, in a crisscross pattern. Remove the clutch springs.

43 Remove the pressure plate **(see illustration)**.

44 Remove the clutch lifter **(see illustration)**. Pull out the lifter rod.

45 Unstake the clutch center locknut **(see illustration)**.

18.46a To loosen the clutch center locknut, immobilize the center with the special Honda clutch center holder . . .

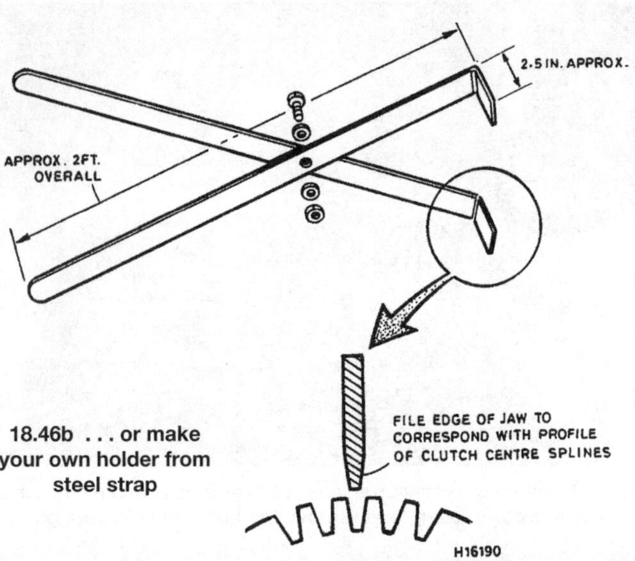

18.46b . . . or make your own holder from steel strap

18.46c A holding tool can also be made by bolting an old metal plate and friction disc together

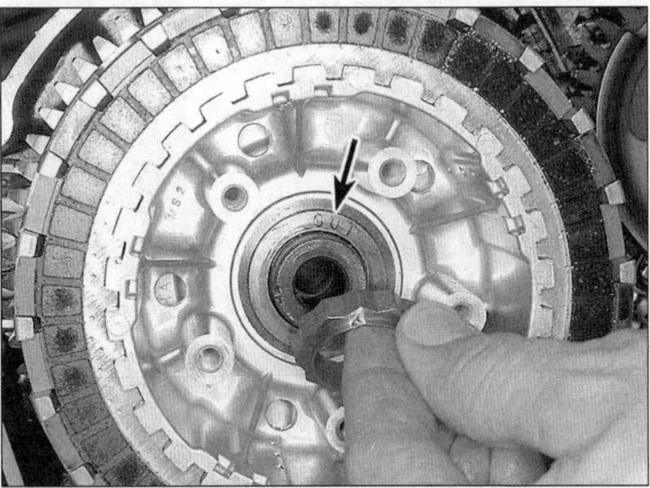
18.47 Remove the clutch center locknut and the washer; the OUT mark on the washer (arrow) faces away from the engine

18.48a Note how the tabs of the outermost friction disc fit into the shallow cutouts of the clutch housing (arrow) . . .

18.48b . . . then pull the clutch center and discs off as a unit

46 Using the factory clutch center holder tool **(see illustration)**, a suitable aftermarket tool **(see illustration)**, or a homemade tool **(see illustration)**, loosen the clutch center locknut.

47 Remove the clutch center locknut and the spring washer **(see illustration)**. Discard the old locknut and washer.

48 Before removing the "clutch pack" (the stack of friction discs and steel plates), take a moment to study how the discs are arranged: Note that the tabs of the outermost friction disc are not aligned with the tabs of the other friction discs, but are instead seated in their own cutouts in the clutch housing. With that firmly in mind, remove the clutch center, friction discs and steel plates as a single assembly **(see illustrations)**.

49 After separating the friction discs and steel plates from the center, note that they alternate **(see illustration)**, friction disc, steel plate, friction disc, etc. There are nine friction

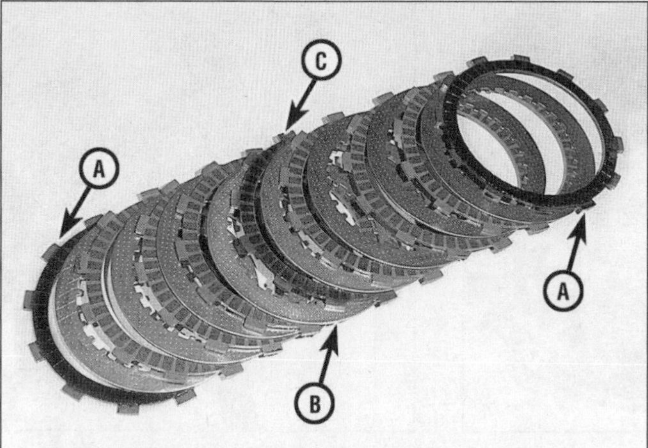

18.49 Clutch disc details

A *Innermost and outermost friction discs (black friction material)*
B *Steel plates (eight)*
C *Friction discs (seven; brown friction material)*

18.50 Remove the thrust washer

18.51a Insert and twist a screwdriver to pry the primary drive gear teeth into alignment . . .

18.51b . . . then slide off the clutch housing and slip the housing guide (arrow) off the mainshaft

discs (including the outermost friction disc discussed in the last step) and eight steel plates. Also note that the outermost and innermost friction discs are darker in color (they're black) than the other discs (which are brown). Also note that the friction pads on the black discs are closer together than the friction pads on the brown discs. These two black discs MUST be installed first and last.

50 Remove the clutch housing washer **(see illustration)**.

51 Insert a screwdriver into the teeth of the primary drive sub-gear, twist it to align the teeth of the (spring loaded) primary drive gear and sub-gear **(see illustration)**, and slip off the clutch housing **(see illustration)**.

52 Remove and inspect the oil pump drive chain and sprockets (see Section 19).

53 Remove the clutch housing guide **(see illustration 18.51b)** from the mainshaft.

54 Remove and inspect the primary drive gear (see Section 20).

Inspection

55 If the clutch lifter came out with the pressure plate, remove it from the pressure plate. Inspect the pressure plate bearing for wear and damage. Turn the bearing inner race with your finger; it should turn smoothly and quietly. Make sure that the bearing outer race fits tightly into the pressure plate. If the bearing is damaged or worn, replace the pressure plate and bearing. (The bearing can be replaced separately but it's a good idea to replace the pressure plate and bearing as a set to maintain a tight fit between the two.)

56 Measure the free length of the clutch springs **(see illustration)**. Replace the springs as a set if any one of them is not within the values listed in this Chapter's Specifications.

57 Examine the inner and outer splines on

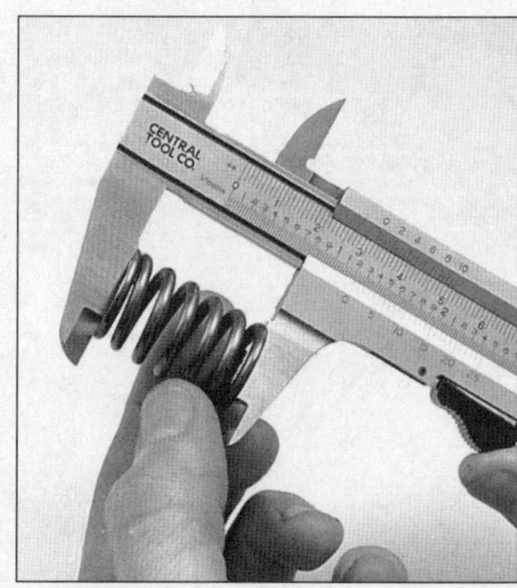

18.56 Measure the clutch spring free length

the clutch center **(see illustration)**. If any wear is evident, replace the clutch center.

58 If the lining material of the friction discs is burned or glazed, replace the friction discs. If the metal clutch plates are scored or discolored, replace them. Measure the thickness of each friction disc **(see illustration)** and compare your measurements to this Chapter's Specifications. If any are near the wear limit, replace the friction discs as a set.

59 Lay the metal plates, one at a time, on a perfectly flat surface (such as a piece of plate glass) and check for warpage by trying to slip a gauge between the flat surface and the plate **(see illustration)**. The feeler gauge should be the same thickness as the warpage limit listed in this Chapter's Specifications. Do this at several places around the plate's circumference. If the feeler gauge can be slipped under the plate, it is warped and should be replaced with a new one.

60 Check the tabs on the friction discs for excessive wear and mushroomed edges. They can be cleaned up with a file if the deformation is not severe.

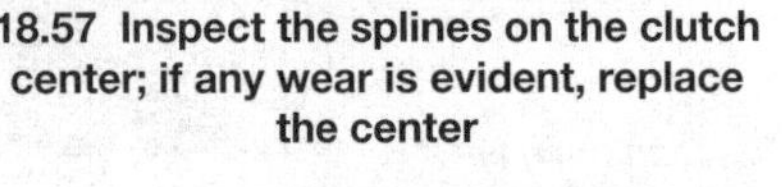

18.57 Inspect the splines on the clutch center; if any wear is evident, replace the center

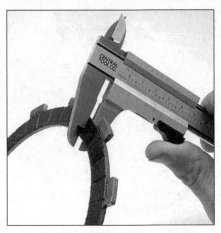

18.58 Measure the thickness of the friction discs

61 Check the edges of the slots in the clutch housing **(see illustration)** for indentations made by the friction plate tabs. If the indentations are deep they can prevent clutch release, so the housing should be replaced with a new one. If the indentations can be removed easily with a file, the life of the housing can be prolonged to an extent.

62 Check the primary driven gear teeth on the clutch housing **(see illustration)** for wear or damage. If the teeth are worn or damaged, replace the clutch housing. If the primary driven gear teeth are damaged, the primary drive gear teeth may also be damaged. Inspect the primary drive gear and, if necessary, replace it (see Section 20).

63 Inspect the needle bearing in the clutch housing hub. If the bushing or bearing is worn or damaged, have it replaced by a dealer or by a motorcycle machine shop.

64 Measure the inside and outside diameters of the clutch housing guide and compare your measurements to the dimensions listed in this Chapter's Specifications. If the guide is worn beyond either specified limit, replace it.

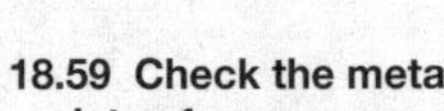

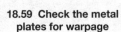

18.59 Check the metal plates for warpage

18.61 Inspect the clutch housing slots and bushing or bearing (arrows) for wear

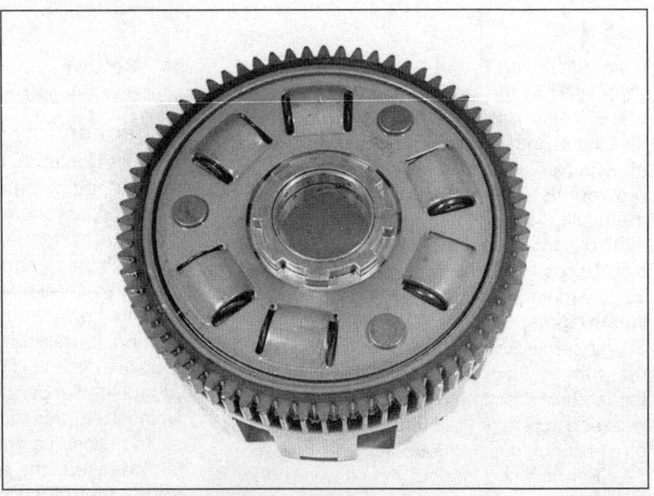

18.62 Inspect the primary driven gear teeth on the backside of the clutch housing; if the teeth are worn or damaged, replace the clutch housing

Installation

65 Lubricate the clutch housing guide with molybdenum disulfide grease and install the guide on the mainshaft.

66 Install the oil pump drive sprocket, chain and driven sprocket (see Section 19).

67 Install the primary drive gear (see Section 20).

68 Coat the clutch housing bearing surface with clean engine oil. Slip the clutch housing onto the guide, align the clutch housing hub with the oil pump drive sprocket **(see illustration)** and push the clutch housing onto the guide.

69 Coat the thrust washer with clean engine oil and install it on the mainshaft.

70 Coat the friction discs and the steel plates with engine oil and install them on the clutch center, alternating between friction discs and steel plates. Start with a black (or darker) friction disc, then install a steel plate, then another friction disc, etc., with another dark friction disc last.

71 Install the clutch pack assembly on the mainshaft. The tabs on all the clutch friction discs (except the outermost friction disc) should fit into the slots in the clutch housing (the tabs on the outer friction disc fit into their own cutouts between the slots) **(see illustration 18.47b)**.

72 On 2001 and later models (and 2000 and later VT1100C2 Shadow Sabre models), install the plain washer on the mainshaft. On all models, install the spring washer with the OUT mark facing away from the engine.

73 Apply clean engine oil to the threads and seating surface of a new clutch center locknut and thread the nut onto the mainshaft. Secure the clutch center with the holding tool and tighten the nut to the torque listed in this Chapter's Specifications. Stake the nut after tightening.

74 Coat the lifter rod with fresh engine oil and install it. Note that the ends of the rod are a different finish than the rest of the rod.

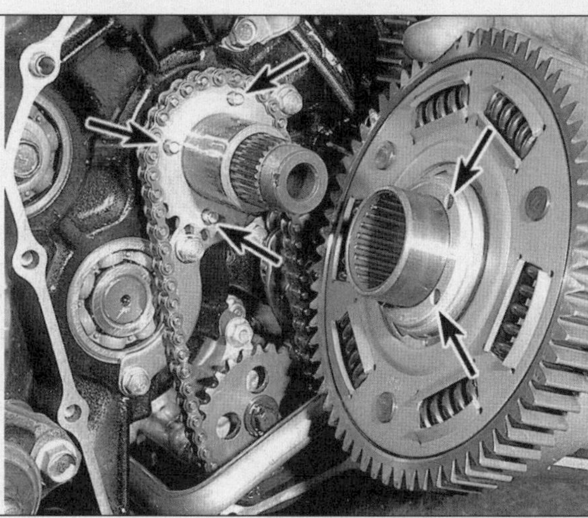

18.68 When installing the clutch housing, make sure the four holes in the housing hub mate with the four pins on the oil pump drive sprocket (arrows)

One end has a longer length of this different finish; that end goes in first, toward the lifter arm on the other side of the crankcase.

75 Install the lifter piece in the pressure plate bearing. Install the pressure plate; make sure that the lifter rod and lifter piece are correctly engaged. Install the pressure plate springs and the pressure plate bolts. Tighten the pressure plate bolts to the torque listed in this Chapter's Specifications.

All models

76 If the oil pump driven sprocket or primary drive gear was removed, put a penny between the primary drive gear teeth and the primary driven gear teeth and tighten the sprocket retaining bolt and/or primary drive gear bolt to the torque listed in this Chapter's Specifications.

77 Clean all traces of old gasket material from the right crankcase cover and its mating surface on the crankcase. Install a new gasket on the crankcase and install the dowel pins.

78 Install the right crankcase cover. Install the bolts **(see illustration 18.3)** finger tight, then tighten the bolts gradually, in stages, using a criss-criss pattern, until they're tight.

79 Install the clutch cover with a new gasket and the dowel pins (older clutch covers use three dowel pins and an O-ring; newer covers use two dowel pins, no O-rings). Tighten the clutch cover bolts to the torque listed in this Chapter's Specifications.

80 Fill the crankcase with the recommended type and amount of engine oil (see Chapter 1).

19 Oil pump drive chain and sprockets - removal, inspection and installation

Removal

1 Drain the oil, then remove the right crankcase cover (see Step 3 in Section 18).

2 Put a penny between the primary drive gear and the clutch housing driven gear **(see illustration)** and loosen the oil pump driven sprocket bolt **(see illustration)**.

3 Remove the clutch (see Section 18).

19.2a Wedge a penny between the gear teeth of the clutch housing and the primary drive gear (arrow) . . .

19.2b . . . then loosen the oil pump driven sprocket bolt (arrow)

19.4 Remove the oil pass pipe and discard the old O-ring on each end

19.5 Remove the oil pump driven sprocket bolt

4 Remove the oil pass pipe **(see illustration)**. Remove and discard the old pass pipe O-rings. Do not reuse the old O-rings.

5 Remove the oil pump driven sprocket bolt **(see illustration)**.

6 Remove the oil pump chain and sprockets **(see illustration)**. Slide off the clutch housing guide.

7 Remove the spacer washer **(see illustration)**.

Inspection

8 Inspect the drive chain rollers and side plates and the sprocket teeth for damage and wear. If the chain or either sprocket is damaged or worn, replace it. (It's a good idea to replace the sprockets and chain as a set.)

Installation

9 Lubricate and install the spacer washer on the mainshaft.

10 Install the drive sprocket, chain and driven sprocket as a set, with the four pins on the drive sprocket facing out, away from the engine, then slide the driven sprocket onto the oil pump. Install the driven sprocket retaining bolt and tighten it until the sprocket starts to turn.

11 Install the oil pass pipe. Use new O-rings.

12 Lubricate the clutch housing guide with clean engine oil, slide it onto the mainshaft and insert it into the inner diameter of the driven sprocket (the sprocket rides on the guide).

13 Install the clutch (see Section 18). When you're done installing the clutch, lock the primary drive gear and clutch housing driven gear the same way you did in Step 2 and tighten the driven sprocket retaining bolt to the torque listed in this Chapter's Specifications.

20 Primary drive gear - removal, inspection and installation

Removal

1 Drain the oil, then remove the right crankcase cover (see Step 3 in Section 18).

2 Put a penny between the primary drive gear and the clutch housing driven gear **(see illustration)** and loosen the primary drive gear bolt. **Note:** *To make removal of the primary gear easier, use a screwdriver to align the teeth of the primary gear and sub-gear* **(see illustration 18.51a)**. *To hold the teeth in the aligned position, thread a 6 mm Allen bolt into the threaded hole behind the elongated hole in the sub gear* **(see illustration 20.2)**.

3 Remove the ignition pulse generator(s) (see Chapter 5).

19.6 Remove the oil pump drive sprocket, chain and driven sprocket as a set, then slide the clutch housing guide off the mainshaft

19.7 Remove the spacer washer from behind the pump drive sprocket

20.2 Put a penny between the gears (A) and loosen the bolt (B); thread a 6 mm Allen bolt into the hole (C) to hold the primary gear and its sub-gear in alignment

20.5 Remove the pulse generator plate (1985 and 1986) or the rotor (all other models, shown); the wide spline (arrow) means the rotor can only be installed one way

4 Remove the primary drive gear bolt and washer.

5 Remove the pulse generator plate (1985 and 1986 models) or the ignition pulse generator timing rotor **(see illustration)**.

6 On VT1100C2, VT1100T and 1997-on VT1100C models, remove the sub-gear **(see illustration)**.

7 Remove the primary drive gear **(see illustration)**.

Inspection

8 Inspect the teeth of the primary drive gear and the sub-gear for wear and damage. If the teeth are worn or damaged, replace the primary drive gear.

9 Inspect the four primary drive gear springs for wear and damage. If anything is damaged or worn, replace it.

Installation

10 Install the primary drive gear with the wide groove in the gear hub aligned with the wide spline on the crankshaft **(see illustration 20.7)**. Make sure that the four springs are correctly seated in their cutouts in the gear.

11 On VT1100C2, VT1100T and 1997-on VT1100C models, install the sub-gear so that the elongated hole in the sub-gear is aligned with the threaded hole in the primary drive gear and the four tabs on the sub-gear are contacting the four springs in the primary drive gear.

12 Install the pulse generator plate (1985 and 1986 models) or ignition pulse generator timing rotor so that the wide notch in the plate or rotor is aligned with the wide spline on the crankshaft **(see illustration 20.5)**.

13 Install the primary drive gear bolt and washer. Using the penny again, lock the clutch and primary drive gear and tighten the primary drive gear bolt to the torque listed in this Chapter's Specifications.

20.6 Remove the sub-gear

20.7 Remove the primary drive gear; the wide spline (arrow) means the gear can only be installed one way

14 On 1985 and 1986, 1987 through 1990 and 1992 through 1996 VT1100C models, measure and, if necessary, adjust the air gap (see Chapter 5).

15 Install the right crankcase cover.

21 Cam chains and rear cam chain drive sprocket - removal, inspection and installation

Note: *This procedure applies to the front and rear cam chains and to the rear cam chain drive sprocket (the front cylinder cam chain drive sprocket is part of the crankshaft.)*

Removal

1 Remove the engine (see Section 5).

2 Remove the cylinder head cover (see Section 7).

3 Remove the camshaft, sprocket and rocker arms (see Section 8).

4 Remove the cam chain tensioner (see Section 9).

5 Remove the cylinder head (see Section 10).

6 Remove the chain guide (see Section 13).

7 If you're removing the front cylinder cam chain, remove the left crankcase cover and remove the alternator rotor and starter driven gear (see Chapter 9).

8 If you're removing the rear cylinder cam chain, remove the right crankcase cover and the clutch (see Section 18) and remove the primary drive gear (see Section 20).

9 If you're removing the rear cylinder cam chain, loosen the cam chain tensioner set plate bolt and swing the set plate out of the way.

10 Remove the cam chain from the drive sprocket and pull it up through the cam chain tunnel.

21.12a The drive sprocket for the front cylinder cam chain is part of the crankshaft; if it's worn or damaged, replace the crankshaft

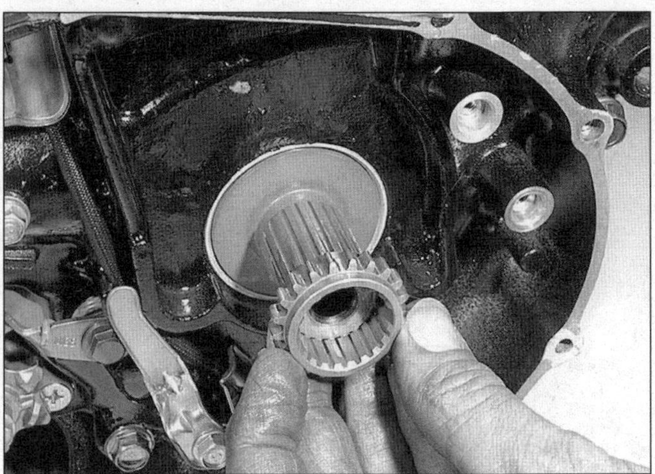

21.12b The drive sprocket for the rear cylinder crankshaft cam chain is removable; if it's worn or damaged, replace it

Inspection

11 Clean the cam chain in solvent and dry it with compressed air. Inspect the rollers and side plates for wear. Replace the chain if it's worn or damaged.

12 If the cam chain is worn, inspect the drive sprocket on the crankshaft **(see illustrations)** and the driven sprocket on the camshaft (see Section 8). If the drive sprocket for the front cylinder cam chain is worn, replace the crankshaft; if the drive sprocket for the rear cylinder cam is worn, replace the sprocket.

Installation

13 If you removed the drive sprocket for the rear cam chain, install it on the crankshaft.

14 Drop the cam chain through the cam chain tunnel and install it on the drive sprocket at the crank. Wire up the cam chain so it can't fall back into the crankcase and install the parts and components removed.

15 If you're installing the front cylinder cam chain, install the alternator rotor and the left crankcase cover (see Chapter 9).

16 If you're installing the rear cylinder cam chain, install the primary drive gear (see Section 20) and the clutch and the right crankcase cover (see Section 18).

17 Install the chain guide (see Section 13).

18 Install the cylinder head (see Section 10).

19 Install the cam chain tensioner (see Section 9).

20 Install the camshaft, sprocket and rocker arm assembly (see Section 8).

21 Install the cylinder head cover (see Section 7).

22 Install the engine (see Section 5).

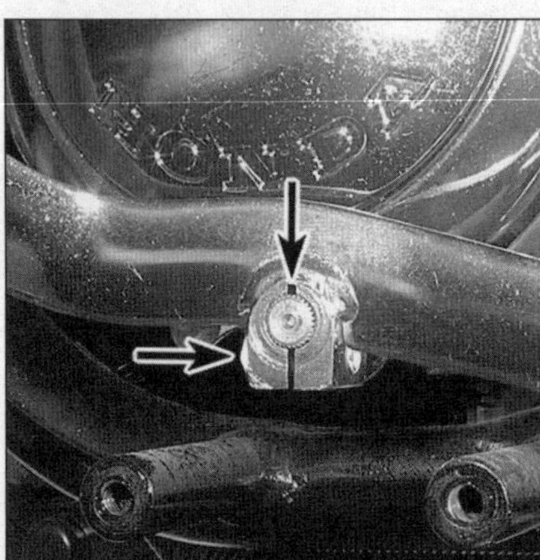

22.3 Mark the lever and spindle (upper arrow) to ensure correct installation, then remove the pinch bolt (lower arrow) and pull the lever off

22 Gearshift linkage - removal, inspection and installation

Removal

1 Put the transmission in Neutral.

2 Remove the left footpeg bracket and/or shift linkage as follows, depending on the model.

3 On all models, look for the index marks on the gearshift arm or the gearshift pedal, and on the end of the gearshift spindle **(see illustration)**. These marks must be aligned when the gearshift arm or the gearshift pedal is reinstalled on the gearshift spindle. If you can't find any marks, make your own punch marks to ensure correct realignment during installation.

4 On 1985 and 1986 models, remove the two footpeg bracket bolts, remove the gearshift arm pinch bolt, slide the gearshift arm off the gearshift spindle and remove the gearshift arm, shift rod, gearshift pedal and footpeg bracket as a single assembly.

5 On all (except 1985 and 1986) VT1100C models, the gearshift pedal and footpeg bracket are installed ahead of the left crankcase cover, so it's not necessary to remove them in order to remove the left crankcase cover. On these models, simply remove the gearshift arm pinch bolt, slide the gearshift arm off the gearshift spindle and let it hang out of the way. If you want to inspect or service the gearshift pedal or shift rod, simply unbolt the footpeg bracket from the frame and remove the footpeg, bracket, gearshift pedal, shift rod and gearshift arm as a single assembly.

6 On VT1100C2 and VT1100T models, there is no shift rod; the gearshift arm is attached directly to the gearshift spindle. Simply remove the footpeg and bracket (see Chapter 8), then remove the gearshift pedal from the gearshift spindle.

7 Remove the left crankcase cover (see Chapter 9).

8 Remove the gearshift spindle access plug **(see illustration)**. Removing this plug provides a "window" into the bottom of the crankcase so that you will be able to reinstall the right half of the two-part gearshift spindle assembly correctly (the left half of the gearshift spindle assembly cannot be removed until the crankcase halves are separated).

9 Remove the right crankcase cover and the clutch housing (see Section 18).

10 Remove the oil pass pipe, the oil pump drive chain and the sprockets (see Section 19).

11 Pull the right gearshift spindle out of the crankcase **(see illustration)**.

12 Remove the cam plate bolt **(see illustration)**. Pivot the stopper arm out of the way and remove the cam plate.

13 Remove the drum center and dowel pin **(see illustration)**.

14 Remove the stopper arm bolt, washers, stopper arm and spring **(see illustration)**.

22.8 Remove the gearshift spindle access plug

22.11 Pull the right gearshift spindle straight out of the crankcase

22.12 Unbolt the cam plate; note how the stopper arm return spring is hooked onto the edge of the arm (arrow)

22.13 Here's how the cam plate and drum center fit together on the end of the shift drum:

1 *Cam plate*
2 *Hole for dowel pin*
3 *Drum center*
4 *Hole for dowel pin*
5 *Dowel pin*

Inspection

External gearshift linkage (VT1100C models)

15 The shift rod is connected to the gearshift pedal and the gearshift arm by Heim joints (spherical bearings). To disconnect the shift rod from the pedal and arm, simply pry off the Heim joints with a screwdriver. Unbolt the gearshift pedal from the footpeg bracket, then remove the pedal, seals and bushing from the bracket.

16 Wipe off all grease and dirt and inspect the dust seals and the bushing for wear and damage. If any of these parts are worn or damaged, replace them. Inspect the shift rod. Make sure that the rod is straight; if it's bent, replace it. Inspect the Heim joints; if the dust seals are damaged, replace the Heim joints. To replace a Heim joint, simply back off the locknut, count the number of threads exposed and unscrew the Heim joint from the shift rod. When screwing on a new Heim joint, make sure that the same number of threads are showing. Tighten the locknut securely.

17 Lubricate the bushing and the dust seal lips with multipurpose grease and reassemble the shift pedal assembly. Tighten the shift pedal bolt securely. Reconnect the shift pedal to the shift arm with the shift rod. Tighten the locknuts securely.

22.14 Remove the stopper arm bolt, washers, stopper arm and return spring

Internal gearshift mechanism

18 Inspect the gearshift spindle and return spring **(see illustration)**. If the spindle is damaged, replace the gearshift spindle assembly. If the spring is fatigued, replace it.

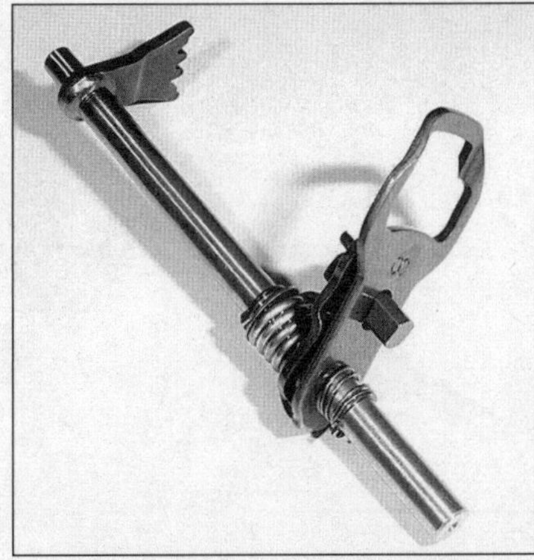

22.18 Inspect the right gearshift spindle assembly for wear and damage; pay particular attention to all friction surfaces

22.21 When reassembling the shift mechanism, make sure that the stopper arm spring (arrow) is hooked onto the arm before tightening the stopper arm bolt

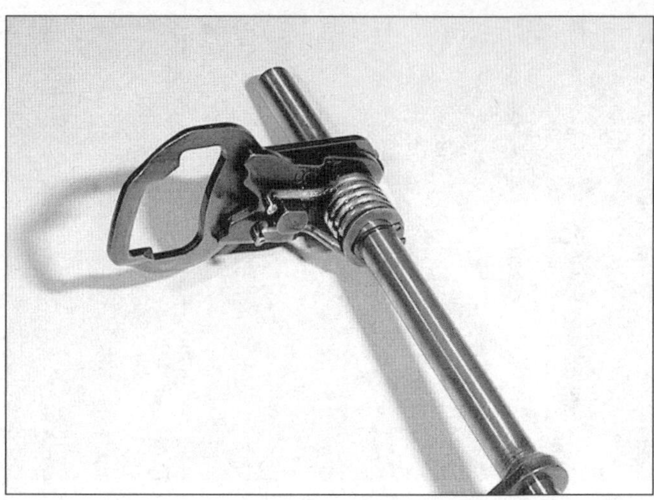
22.24a Before installing the right gearshift spindle, make sure that the ends of the return spring are positioned on either side of this lug, as shown

19 Inspect the stopper arm and spring. If the stopper arm is worn where it contacts the cam plate, replace the stopper arm. If the spring is distorted, replace it.

Installation

20 Install the dowel pin in the shift drum. Make sure the positioning hole in the drum center is aligned with the dowel pin in the shift drum and install the drum center.

21 Install the stopper arm, washer (between the arm and the spring), the return spring and the bolt **(see illustration 22.14)**. Hand tighten the stopper arm bolt, hook the return spring onto the stopper arm **(see illustration)** and tighten the stopper arm bolt to the torque listed in this Chapter's Specifications.

22 Pivot the stopper arm out of the way, align the hole in the cam plate with the dowel pin in the drum center and install the cam plate. Apply a thread locking agent to the threads of the cam plate bolt, install the bolt and tighten it securely.

23 Make sure that the cam plate is in the Neutral position. You can verify this by turning the rear wheel (if the engine is installed) or by turning the output shaft of the output gear (if the engine is removed). If not, click it into Neutral before proceeding.

24 Make sure that the ends of the right gearshift spindle return spring are positioned correctly **(see illustration)**. Install the right gearshift spindle assembly. Mesh the teeth on the right spindle with the left spindle teeth and make sure that the left end of the right gearshift spindle seats into its bore in the left crankcase half **(see illustrations)**.

25 This is how the shift mechanism should look when you're done **(see illustration)**. Rotate the left gearshift spindle and verify that the shift mechanism operates correctly.

26 Install the oil pump drive chain and sprockets and the oil pass pipe (see Section 19).

27 Install the clutch housing and the right crankcase cover and (see Section 18).

28 Install a new O-ring on the gearshift spindle access plug and install the gearshift spindle access plug.

29 Install the left crankcase cover (see Chapter 9).

30 On 1985 and 1986 models, install the two footpeg bracket bolts and tighten them securely. Align the punch marks on the gearshift arm and the spindle, slide the arm onto the spindle, install the arm pinch bolt and tighten it securely.

31 On all (except 1985 and 1986) VT1100C models, install the gearshift pedal and footpeg bracket, if removed. Align the punch

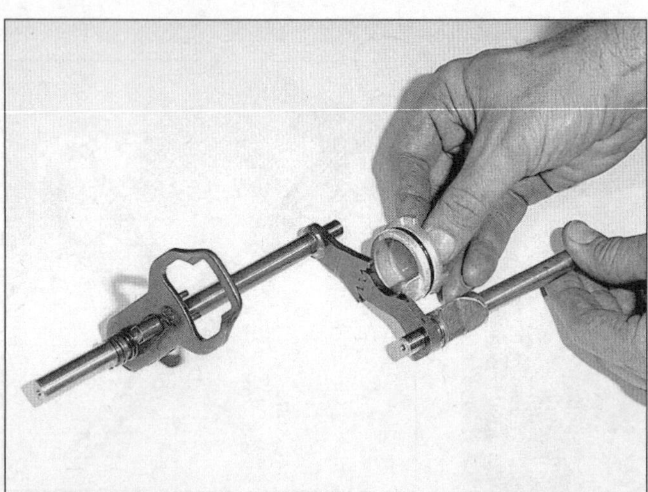
22.24b This is how the right gearshift spindle and the left gearshift spindle look when they're correctly engaged (gearshift spindle assembly removed from engine for clarity)

22.24c Make sure that the teeth of the right gearshift spindle are meshed with the teeth of the left gearshift spindle as shown

22.25 This is how the shift mechanism should look when it's reassembled

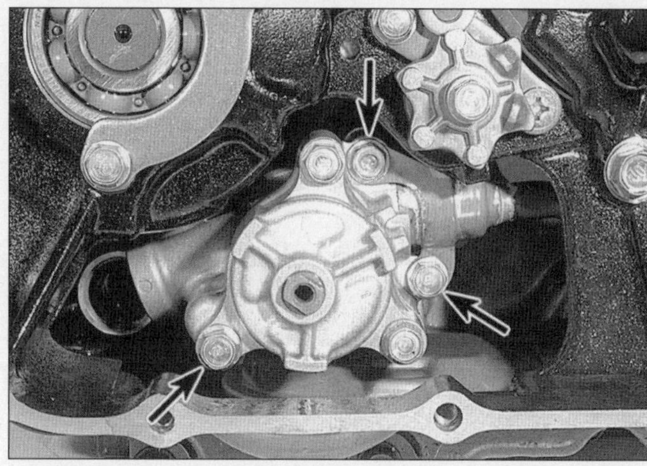

23.3 To detach the oil pump from the crankcase and from the oil pressure relief pipe, remove these three bolts (arrows); don't remove the other two bolts until the pump has been removed from the engine

marks on the gearshift arm and the spindle, slide the arm onto the spindle, install the arm pinch bolt and tighten it securely.

32 On VT1100C2 and VT1100T models, align the punch marks on the gearshift pedal and the gearshift spindle, install the gearshift pedal on the gearshift spindle, install the pinch bolt and tighten it securely. Install the footpeg and bracket, install the footpeg bracket mounting bolts and tighten them securely.

23 Oil pump - removal, inspection and installation

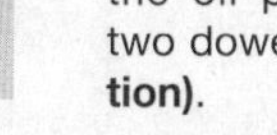

Removal

1 Remove the right crankcase cover and the clutch assembly (see Section 18).

2 Remove the gearshift mechanism (see Section 22).

3 Remove the three oil pump mounting bolts **(see illustration)** and detach the pump from the crankcase.

4 The oil pressure relief pipe is attached to the side of the oil pump that faces forward (on your right as you look through the access hole). The relief pipe actually fits over the oil pressure relief valve, which is installed in the forward side of the pump. Using a pair of needle-nose pliers, wiggle the oil pressure relief pipe loose from the oil pressure relief valve **(see illustration)**.

5 Remove the oil pump, then remove the oil pressure relief pipe. Remove the two dowel pins and the O-ring **(see illustration)**.

Disassembly

6 Remove the oil strainer and the old O-ring from the pump **(see illustration)**.

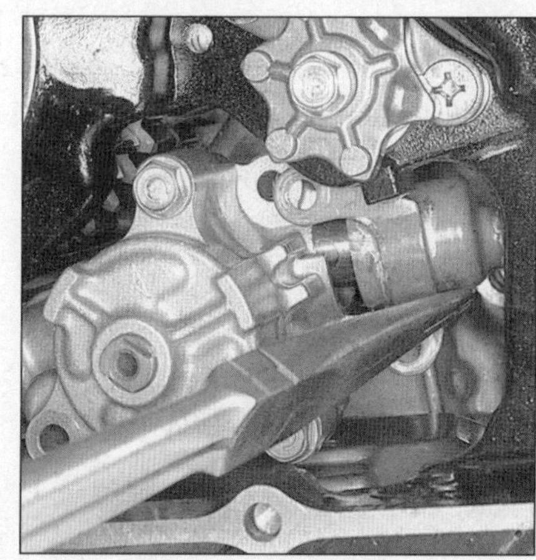

23.4 Wiggle the pipe off the oil pump's pressure relief valve with a pair of needle-nose pliers so the pump will fit through the access hole

23.5 Locate the two dowels (arrows), which may stay in the pump or the crankcase; use a new O-ring on the large dowel

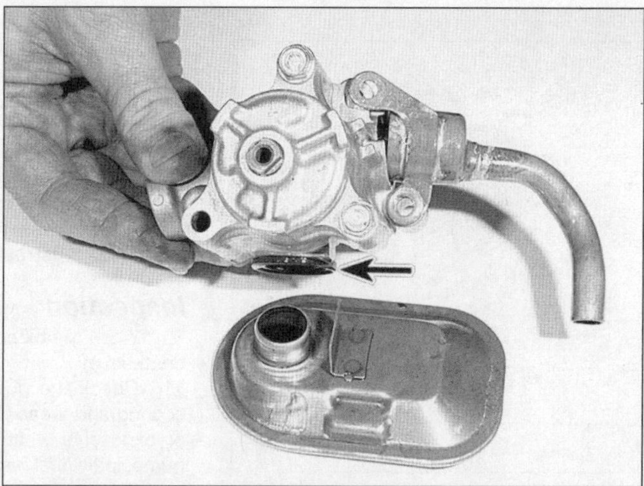

23.6 Remove the oil strainer from the pump and discard the old O-ring (arrow)

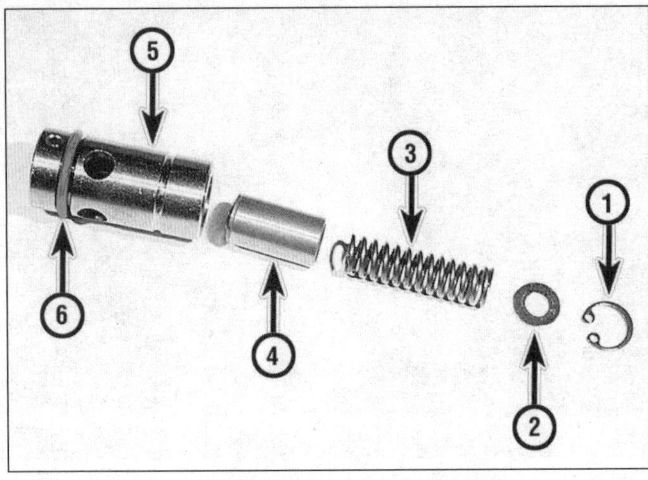

23.7 Oil pressure relief valve details

1 *Snap-ring*
2 *Washer*
3 *Spring*
4 *Piston*
5 *Oil pressure relief valve*
6 *O-ring*

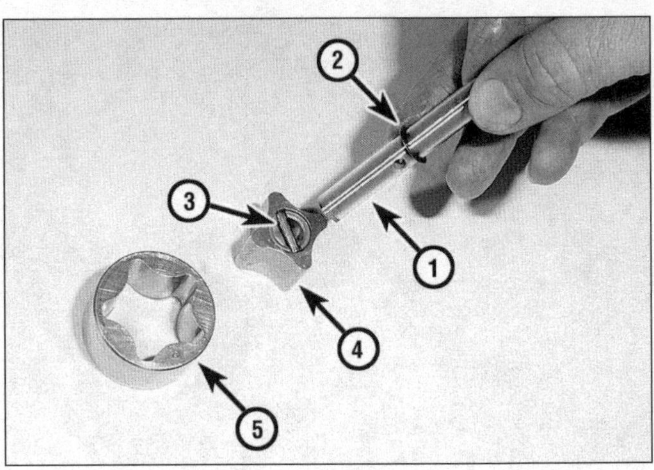

23.9 Oil pump details

1 *Oil pump driveshaft*
2 *Spacer washer*
3 *Drive pin (goes through hole in driveshaft and seats in groove in inner rotor)*
4 *Inner rotor*
5 *Outer rotor*

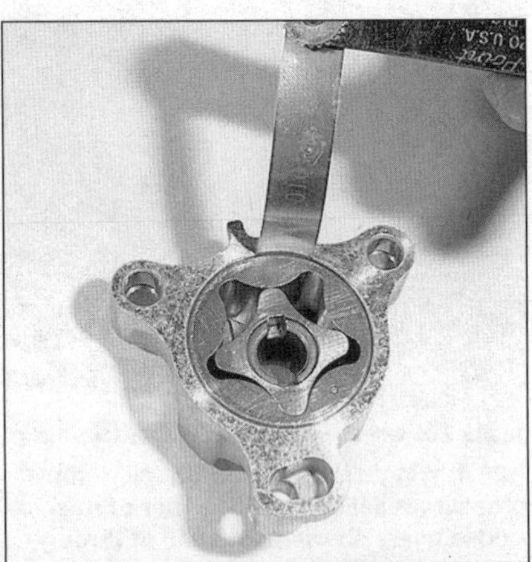

23.12a Measure the clearance between the outer rotor and pump body

23.12b Measure the clearance between the inner and outer rotors

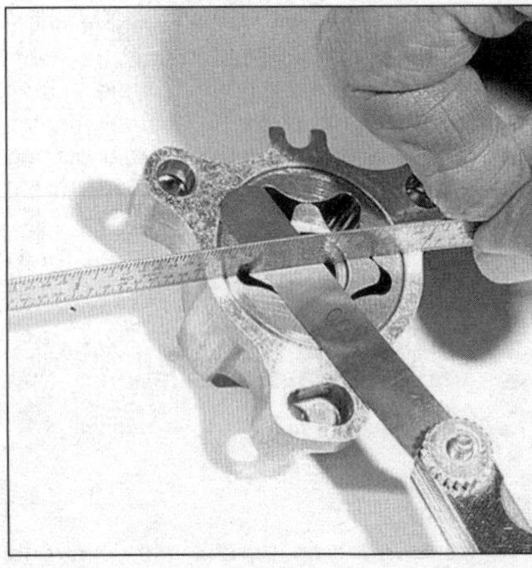

23.12c Measure the clearance between rotors and the cover

23.15 Install the outer rotor with the punch mark (arrow) facing out (toward the cover)

7 Remove the oil pressure relief valve from the oil pump, remove the snap-ring, and disassemble the oil pressure relief valve **(see illustration)**.

8 Remove the pump cover bolts, lift off the cover and remove the two dowel pins.

9 Remove the rotor shaft, the spacer washer, the drive pin and the outer and inner rotors **(see illustration)**.

Inspection

10 Wash the oil pump parts in solvent and dry them off.

11 Check the pump body and rotors for scoring and wear. If any damage or uneven or excessive wear is evident, replace the pump; individual parts aren't available. (If you are rebuilding the engine, it's a good idea to install a new oil pump anyway.)

12 Measure the clearance between the inner and outer rotors and between the outer rotor and housing **(see illustrations)**. Replace the pump if the clearance is excessive.

13 Inspect the piston and the bore of the relief valve for scoring or other damage. Inspect the spring for fatigue. If any of the relief valve parts are worn or damaged, replace the oil pump.

Reassembly

14 If the pump is good, make sure all the parts are spotlessly clean, then lubricate everything with clean engine oil or assembly lube.

15 Install the inner and outer rotors in the pump body. Make sure the outer rotor is installed with the punch mark facing out, toward the cover **(see illustration)**.

16 Install the driveshaft in the inner rotor.

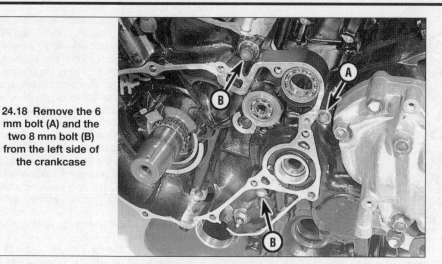

24.18 Remove the 6 mm bolt (A) and the two 8 mm bolt (B) from the left side of the crankcase

Make sure that the pin is centered in the driveshaft so it will align with the slot in the inner rotor.

17 Slide the washer onto the driveshaft and push it into the groove in the center of the inner rotor. The washer must be flush with the outer face of the inner rotor.

18 Install the pump cover and tighten the cover bolts to the torque listed in this Chapter's Specifications.

19 Install the piston, spring and washer in the pressure relief valve and secure them with the snap-ring. Using a new O-ring, install the pressure relief valve in the pump body.

20 Using a new O-ring, install the strainer in the pump body.

Installation

21 Make sure the dowels and O-ring are in position **(see illustration 23.5)**.

22 Rotate the oil pump driveshaft so that the lug on the end of the shaft is horizontal and rotate the water pump driveshaft so that the slot is horizontal. Angle the oil pump so that the oil pressure relief valve points toward the left crankcase, then insert it through the access hole into the crankcase, insert the oil pressure relief pipe through the hole, slide the relief pipe onto the pressure relief valve, then rotate the pump back to its installed position and push it into place. Make sure that the lug on the oil pump driveshaft engages with the slot in the water pump driveshaft, then rotate the pump slightly as necessary to align the bolt holes in the pump with the threaded bolt holes in the crankcase.

23 Install the oil pump mounting bolts and tighten them to the torque listed in this Chapter's Specifications.

24 Installation is otherwise the reverse of removal.

24 Crankcase - disassembly and reassembly

1 To examine and repair or replace the oil pump, the crankshaft, the connecting rods, the crankshaft bearings, the transmission or the output gear assembly, the crankshaft must be split into two halves.

Disassembly

2 Remove the engine from the frame (see Section 5).

3 Remove the cylinder head covers (see Section 7).

4 Remove the camshafts, sprockets and rocker arms (see Section 8).

5 Remove the cam chain tensioners (see Section 9).

6 Remove the cylinder heads (see Section 10).

7 Remove the cam chain guides (see Section 13).

8 Remove the cylinders (see Section 14).

9 Remove the pistons (see Section 15).

10 Remove the left crankcase cover and the alternator (see Chapter 9). Remove all electrical harnesses from the left side of the engine.

11 Remove the right crankcase cover and the clutch assembly (see Section 18).

12 Remove the oil pass pipe, the oil pump drive chain and the oil pump drive and driven sprockets (see Section 19).

13 Remove the ignition pulse generator(s) (see Chapter 5).

14 Remove the primary drive gear (see Section 20).

15 Remove the cam chains (see Section 21).

16 Remove the gearshift mechanism (see Section 22).

17 Remove the oil pump and strainer (see Section 23).

18 Remove the three bolts from the left crankcase half **(see illustration)**. There are two 8 mm bolts and one 6 mm bolt. Note the locations of the 8 mm bolts and the 6 mm bolt so that you don't switch them during reassembly.

19 Turn the engine over on its other side. Hold the output driven gear with a Honda shaft holder (07923-6890101), or a suitable equivalent, and loosen the output drive gear shaft bolt **(see illustrations)**. Remove the bolt and washer.

24.19a If you're going to remove the output gear, hold its driven gear shaft with Honda's special holder (07923-6890101) or a similar tool . . .

24.19b . . . and remove the output drive gear shaft bolt from the right side of the crankcase

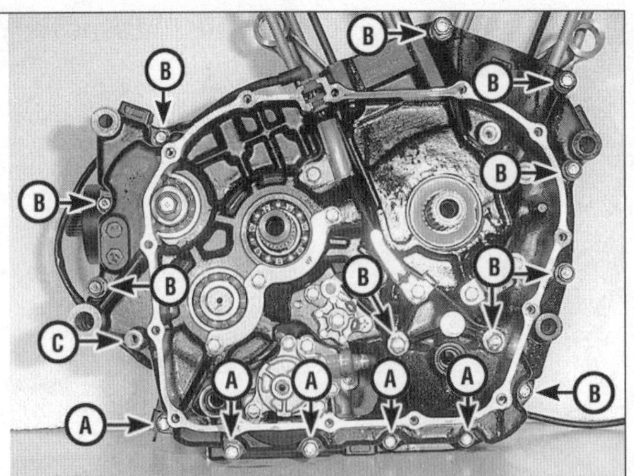

24.20a Right crankcase bolts

A 6 mm bolts
B 8 mm bolts
C 8 mm bolt (1985 through 1994) or 10 mm bolt (1995-on)

20 Remove the bolts from the right crankcase half **(see illustration)**. Working in a criss-cross pattern, loosen the bolts gradually and evenly. There are five 6 mm bolts and eleven 8 mm bolts (1985 through 1994 models) or ten 8 mm bolts and one 10 mm bolt (1995 and later models **(see illustration)**. Note the locations of the different size bolts so that you don't mix them up during reassembly.

21 If you're replacing the transmission and/ or shift drum bearings, remove the bearing set plate bolts and screw **(see illustration)**.

22 With the engine lying on its left crankcase half, carefully separate the crankcase halves by prying gently and evenly at the pry points around the crankcase seam **(see illustrations)**. Using a soft hammer, tap alternately on the transmission shafts and the engine mounting bosses. If the halves won't separate easily, double check to make sure that all fasteners have been removed. Don't pry against the crankcase mating surfaces or they'll leak.

23 Remove the dowels and O-rings **(see illustration)** from the right crankcase half. If any dowels are missing from the right crankcase half, look in the left crankcase half. If a dowel is missing from both crankcase halves, it has probably fallen into one or the other crankcase half. Find it now. Store the dowels in a plastic bag.

24 Remove all traces of sealant from the crankcase mating surfaces.

25 Refer to Sections 25 through 30 for information on servicing the internal components of the crankcase.

Reassembly

26 Make sure the crankshaft, transmission shafts and output drive gear are correctly installed in the upper crankcase half (see Sections 25, 28, 29 and 30, respectively).

24.20b . . . this 10 mm bolt on 1995 and later models is threaded to receive a stud

24.21 To remove the transmission and shift drum bearings, remove the set plate bolts and screw (arrows); note the UP mark on the double set plate

24.22a There are only two places that you can pry the crankcase halves apart: this is one . . .

24.22b . . . and this is the other; do NOT try to pry apart the cases anywhere else or you'll damage the mating surfaces

24.22c Once the seal between the case halves is broken, carefully pull them apart

24.23 As soon as you get the cases separated, remove these three dowel pins (arrows); remove the O-ring from the center dowel and discard it

27 Pour some engine oil over the transmission gears, the crankshaft main bearings and the shift drum. Also pour oil into the exposed internal oil passages. Don't get any oil on the crankcase mating surfaces.

28 Make sure the dowels are in place; install a new O-ring at the indicated location **(see illustration 24.23)**.

29 Apply a thin, even bead of sealant to the crankcase mating surfaces.

Caution: Don't apply an excessive amount of sealant. And make sure that no sealant is applied to oil passages.

30 Carefully assemble the crankcase halves over the dowels.

Caution: The crankcase halves should fit together completely without being forced. If they're slightly apart, DO NOT force them together by tightening the crankcase bolts.

31 Install the bearing set plates, bolts and screw, if removed **(see illustration 24.21)**. Tighten the bearing set plate bolts and screw to the torque listed in this Chapter's Specifications.

32 Install the right crankcase bolts in their holes **(see illustrations 24.20a and 24.20b)**. Make sure you don't install a 6 mm bolt in an 8 mm hole, or vice versa. Tighten the bolts gradually and evenly, in a criss-cross fashion, to the torque listed in this Chapter's Specifications. **Note:** *There are different torque settings for the 8 mm bolts and the 6 mm bolts.*

33 Install the output drive gear shaft bolt and washer **(see illustrations 24.19a and 24.19b)**. Hold the output driven gear with a Honda shaft holder (07923-6890101), or a suitable equivalent, and tighten the output drive gear shaft bolt to the torque listed in this Chapter's Specifications.

34 Turn the engine over and install the left crankcase bolts in their holes **(see illustration 24.18)**. Make sure you don't install a 6 mm bolt in an 8 mm hole, or vice versa. Tighten the bolts gradually and evenly, in a criss-cross fashion, to the torque listed in this Chapter's Specifications. **Note:** *There are different torque settings for the different size bolts.*

35 Turn the crankshaft, the mainshaft and the countershaft to make sure they turn freely. If they don't, stop and find out why before continuing; you may have made a mistake during assembly. If necessary, disassemble the crankcases again. Don't just put the engine back in the bike, hoping the problem will go away by itself.

36 The remainder of assembly is the reverse of disassembly.

25 Crankcase components - inspection and servicing

1 After the crankcases have been separated and the crankshaft, the shift drum and forks, the transmission shafts and the output gear have been removed, the crankcases should be cleaned thoroughly with new solvent and dried with compressed air.

2 Remove both oil jets **(see illustration 15.5)**. All oil passages should be blown out with compressed air.

3 All traces of old gasket sealant should be removed from the mating surfaces. Minor damage to the mating surfaces can be cleaned up with a fine sharpening stone or grindstone.

Caution: Be very careful not to nick or gouge the crankcase mating surfaces or leaks will result. Check both crankcase halves very carefully for cracks and other damage.

4 If any damage is found that can't be repaired, replace the crankcase halves as a set.

26 Main and connecting rod bearings - general note

1 Even though main and connecting rod bearings are generally replaced with new ones during the engine overhaul, the old bearings should be retained for close examination as they may reveal valuable information about the condition of the engine.

2 Bearing failure occurs mainly because of lack of lubrication, the presence of dirt or other foreign particles, overloading the engine and/or corrosion. Regardless of the cause of bearing failure, it must be corrected before the engine is reassembled to prevent it from happening again.

3 When examining the bearings, remove the rod bearings from the connecting rods and caps and lay them out on a clean surface in the same general position as their location on the crankshaft journals. This will enable you to match any noted bearing problems with the corresponding side of the crankshaft journal. The main bearings are pressed into the crankcase halves and are only removed if they need to be replaced.

4 Dirt and other foreign particles get into the engine in a variety of ways. It may be left in the engine during assembly or it may pass through filters or breathers. It may get into the oil and from there into the bearings. Metal chips from machining operations and normal engine wear are often present. Abrasives are sometimes left in engine components after reconditioning operations such as cylinder honing, especially when parts are not thoroughly cleaned using the proper cleaning methods. Whatever the source, these foreign objects often end up imbedded in the soft bearing material and are easily recognized. Large particles will not imbed in the bearing and will score or gouge the bearing and journal. The best prevention for this cause of

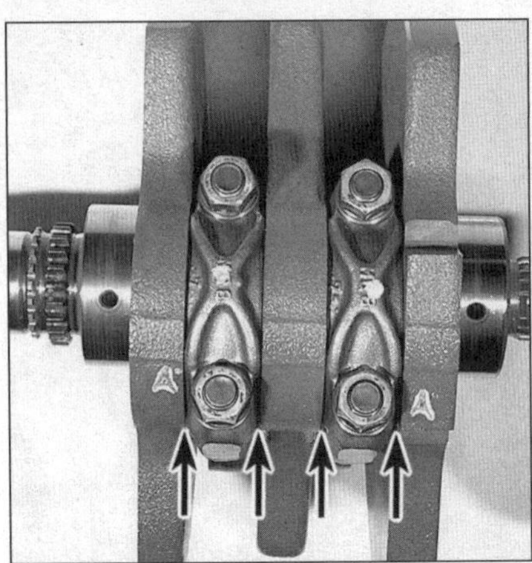

27.3 Measure the side clearance (arrows) between the rods and the crankshaft weights

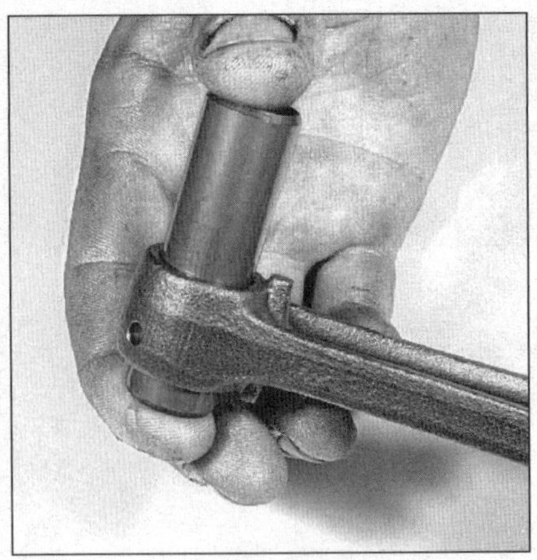

27.7 Slip the piston pin into the rod and rock it back-and-forth to check for looseness

bearing failure is to clean all parts thoroughly and keep everything spotlessly clean during engine reassembly. Frequent and regular oil and filter changes are also recommended.

5 Lack of lubrication or lubrication breakdown has a number of interrelated causes. Excessive heat (which thins the oil), overloading (which squeezes the oil from the bearing face) and oil leakage or throw off (from excessive bearing clearances, worn oil pump or high engine speeds) all contribute to lubrication breakdown. Blocked oil passages will also starve a bearing and destroy it. When lack of lubrication is the cause of bearing failure, the bearing material is wiped or extruded from the steel backing of the bearing. Temperatures may increase to the point where the steel backing and the journal turn blue from overheating.

6 Riding habits can have a definite effect on bearing life. Full throttle low speed operation, or lugging the engine, puts very high loads on bearings, which tend to squeeze out the oil film. These loads cause the bearings to flex, which produces fine cracks in the bearing face (fatigue failure). Eventually the bearing material will loosen in pieces and tear away from the steel backing. Short trip driving leads to corrosion of bearings, as insufficient engine heat is produced to drive off the condensed water and corrosive gases produced. These products collect in the engine oil, forming acid and sludge. As the oil is carried to the engine bearings, the acid attacks and corrodes the bearing material.

7 Incorrect bearing installation during engine assembly will lead to bearing failure as well. Tight fitting bearings which leave insufficient bearing oil clearances result in oil starvation. Dirt or foreign particles trapped behind a bearing insert result in high spots on the bearing which lead to failure.

8 To avoid bearing problems, clean all parts thoroughly before reassembly, double check all bearing clearance measurements and lubricate the new bearings with engine assembly lube or moly-based grease during installation.

27 Connecting rods and bearings - removal, inspection and installation

Removal

1 Separate the crankcase halves (see Section 24).

2 Lift the crankshaft out, together with the connecting rods, and set them on a clean surface.

3 Before removing the connecting rods from the crankshaft, measure the connecting rod side clearance. Insert a feeler gauge between each side of the big end of each connecting rod and the crankshaft **(see illustration)** and compare your measurements to the side clearance listed in this Chapter's Specifications. If the side clearance between either rod and the crank is greater than the specified side clearance, replace that rod.

4 Using a center punch or a laundry marker pen with indelible ink, mark the position of each rod and cap, relative to its position on the crankshaft (left or right) to ensure that the same rod removed from each crankpin will be reinstalled on the same crankpin.

5 Unscrew the bearing cap nuts, separate the cap from the rod, then detach the rod from the crankshaft. If a rod cap is stuck, tap on the ends of the rod bolts with a soft-faced hammer to free it.

6 Roll the bearing inserts sideways to separate them from the rods and caps. Keep them in order so they can be reinstalled in their original locations. Wash the parts in solvent and dry them with compressed air, if available.

Inspection

7 Inspect the connecting rods for cracks and other obvious damage. Lubricate the piston pin for each rod, install it in the proper rod and check for play **(see illustration)**. If it wobbles, measure the outside diameter of the piston pin, the inside diameter of the connecting rod, and the inside diameter of the pin bore in the piston (see Section 15). Replace the piston (see Section 15), the pin and/or the connecting rod (see Step 20) as necessary.

8 Examine the connecting rod bearing inserts. If they are scored, badly scuffed or appear to have seized, new bearings must be installed. Always replace the bearings in the connecting rods as a set. If they are badly damaged, check the corresponding crankshaft journal. Evidence of extreme heat, such as discoloration, indicates lubrication failure. Be sure to inspect the oil pump and pressure relief valve (see Section 23) as well as all oil holes and passages before reassembling the engine.

9 Have the rods checked for twist and bending at a dealer service department or other motorcycle repair shop. If a rod must be replaced, refer to Step 20.

10 If the bearings and journals appear to be in good condition, check the oil clearances as described in the following steps.

11 Start with the rod for one cylinder. Wipe the bearing inserts and the connecting rod and cap clean, using a lint-free cloth.

12 Install the bearing inserts in the connecting rod and cap. Make sure the tab on the bearing engages with the notch in the rod or cap **(see illustration)**.

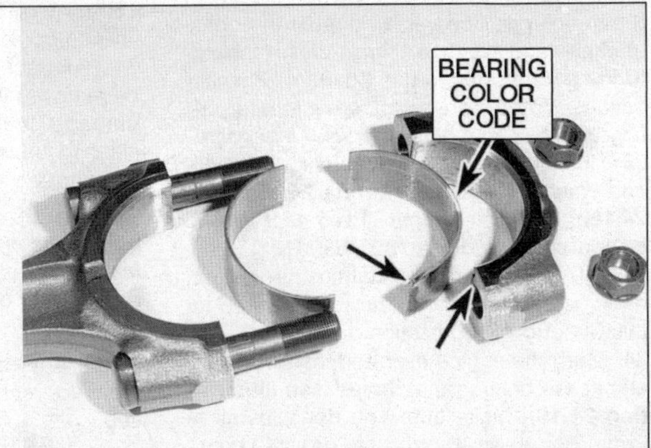

27.12 Position the tab (arrow) on the bearing in the notch (arrow) in the rod or cap; the strip of color on the edge of each insert is the color code for bearing replacement

27.13 Lay a strip of Plastigage on the journal, parallel to the crankshaft centerline

27.15 Place the Plastigage scale next to the flattened Plastigage to measure the bearing clearance

27.17 If the bearing clearance exceeds the limit in this Chapter's Specifications, measure the diameter of the connecting rod journal with a micrometer

13 Wipe off the connecting rod journal with a lint-free cloth. Lay a strip of Plastigage (type HPG-1) across the top of the journal, parallel with the journal axis **(see illustration).**

14 Referring to the marks you made prior to disassembly, position the connecting rod on the correct journal, then install the rod cap and nuts. Tighten the nuts to the torque listed in this Chapter's Specifications, but don't allow the connecting rod to rotate at all.

15 Unscrew the nuts and remove the connecting rod and cap from the journal, being very careful not to disturb the Plastigage. Compare the width of the crushed Plastigage to the scale printed in the Plastigage envelope to determine the bearing oil clearance **(see illustration).**

16 If the clearance is within the range listed in this Chapter's Specifications and the bearings are in perfect condition, they can be reused. If the clearance is greater than the wear limit, replace the bearing inserts with new inserts that have the same color code, then check the clearance once again. Always replace all of the inserts at the same time.

17 If the clearance is greater than the maximum clearance listed in this Chapter's Specifications, measure the diameter of the connecting rod journal with a micrometer **(see illustration).** To determine whether the journal is out-of-round, measure the diameter at a number of points around the journal's circumference. Take the measurement at each end of the journal to determine if the journal is tapered.

18 If any journal is tapered or out-of-round or bearing clearance is beyond the maximum listed in this Chapter's Specifications (with new bearings), replace the crankshaft (see Section 28).

Connecting rod bearing selection

19 Each connecting rod has a "1" or "2" stamped on it **(see illustration)**; this is the code for the connecting rod inside diameter. Next to that, on the crank weight, is an "A" or a B"; this is the code for the crankpin outside diameter. The bearings are color-coded pink, yellow or green. To determine the correct bearing color, match the connecting rod I.D. code (left column) to the crankpin O.D. code (upper row) and note the corresponding color code **(see illustration).** For example, a code 2 on the connecting rod and an A code on the crank weight would indicate a yellow color-coded rod bearing. The color codes are painted on the edges of the bearings **(see illustration 27.12).**

27.19a The number on each rod and the letters on the crankshaft weight are used to select the rod bearing inserts; the letter on each rod indicates the rod's weight grade

Crankpin O.D. code	Code "A" 47.982 to 47.990 mm (1.8891 to 1.8894 inches)	Code "B" 47.974 to 47.982 mm (1.8887 to 1.8891 inches)
Connecting rod I.D. code	Bearing color code	Bearing color code
Code "1" 51.000 to 51.008 mm (2.0079 to 2.0082 inches)	Pink 1.487 to 1.491 mm (0.0585 to 0.0587 inch)	Yellow 1.491 to 1.495 mm (0.0587 to 0.0589 inch)
Code "2" 51.008 to 51.016 mm (2.0082 to 2.0085 inches)	Yellow 1.491 to 1.495 mm (0.0587 to 0.0589 inch)	Green 1.495 to 1.499 mm (0.0589 to 0.0590 inch)

27.19b Connecting rod bearing selection chart

Rear connecting rod weight code	A	B	C	D	E
Front connecting rod weight code					
A	X	X			
B	X	X	X		
C		X	X	X	
D			X	X	X
E				X	X

27.20 Connecting rod weight selection chart

Connecting rod weight selection

20 If a connecting rod must be replaced, make sure you select a new rod with the same weight code as the rod being replaced. Each connecting rod has an A, B, C, D or E stamped on the side of the rod **(see illustration 27.19a)**. This is the connecting rod weight code. Only rods of certain weights can be used together. Using the accompanying table, cross-reference the weight code of the connecting rod being replaced to the weight code of the other rod **(see illustration)**.

Installation

21 Wipe off the bearing inserts, connecting rods and caps. Install the inserts into the rods and caps, using your hands only, making sure the tabs on the inserts engage with the notches in the rods and caps **(see illustration 27.12)**. When all the inserts are installed, lubricate them with engine assembly lube or moly-based grease. Don't get any lubricant on the mating surfaces of the rod or cap.

22 Install each connecting rod on the correct journal, referring to the marks you made prior to disassembly. Make sure that the connecting rod code number stamped on the side of the rod across the rod/cap seam fits together perfectly when the rod and cap are assembled **(see illustration)**. If it doesn't, the wrong cap is on the rod. Fix this problem before proceeding.

23 When you're sure the rods are positioned correctly, lubricate the threads of the rod bolts and the surfaces of the nuts with molybdenum disulfide grease and tighten the nuts to the torque listed in this Chapter's Specifications. Snug both rod cap nuts evenly, then gradually and evenly tighten them to the specified torque in several steps.

24 Turn the rods on the crankshaft. If either of them feels tight, tap on the bottom of the connecting rod caps with a hammer - this should relieve stress and free them up. If it doesn't, recheck the bearing clearance.

25 As a final step, recheck the connecting rod side clearances (see Step 3). If the clearances aren't correct, find out why before proceeding with engine assembly.

28 Crankshaft and main bearings - removal, inspection and installation

Crankshaft removal

1 Separate the crankcase halves (see Section 24).

2 Lift out the crankshaft and connecting rods and set the assembly on a clean surface.

3 Mark, remove and inspect the connecting rods and rod bearings (see Section 27).

Inspection

4 Clean the crankshaft with solvent, using a rifle-cleaning brush to scrub out the oil passages. Dry off the crank with compressed air. Inspect the main and connecting rod journals for uneven wear, scoring and pits. Rub a copper coin across the journal several times - if a journal picks up copper from the coin, it's too rough. Replace the crankshaft.

5 Inspect the teeth of the front cylinder cam chain drive sprocket on the left end of the crankshaft. If the sprocket teeth are damaged or worn, replace the crankshaft. If there's sprocket wear or damage, inspect the cam chains too (see Section 21). Inspect the rest of the crankshaft for cracks and other damage. Have it magnafluxed by a dealer service department or motorcycle machine shop; magnafluxing will reveal any hidden cracks.

6 Set the crankshaft on V-blocks and measure the crank runout at the bearing surfaces with a dial indicator **(see illustration)**. Compare your measurement with the runout listed in this Chapter's Specifications. If the runout exceeds the limit, replace the crank.

27.22 If the upper and lower halves of the number stamped on the rod and cap don't fit together perfectly, the wrong cap is on the rod (or the cap is on backwards)

28.6 Place the crankshaft in V-blocks or a holding fixture and check for runout with a dial indicator

28.7a Measure journal diameter with a micrometer

28.7b Measure main bearing diameter with a hole gauge, then measure the gauge with a micrometer

Main bearing selection

7 Measure the diameter of the main bearing journals with a micrometer **(see illustration)**. Measure the inside diameter of the main bearings with a telescoping gauge **(see illustration)** and micrometer. The difference between these two measurements is the bearing clearance. It should be within the range listed in this Chapter's Specifications.

8 If the clearance is greater than the service limit listed in this Chapter's Specifications, Honda specifies replacing the crankcase. Before going to this extreme, however, check with a machine shop or qualified motorcycle repair shop to see whether you can have new bearings pressed into the case halves **(see illustration)**.

9 The main journal outside diameter code number, a "1" or a "2," is stamped on the crankshaft weights **(see illustration 27.19a)**.

10 To determine what size main bearings you need, cross reference the crankcase main bearing I.D. code (stamped into the crankcase) with the crankshaft main journal O.D. code (**see illustration**). You'll need this information to buy new crankcase halves.

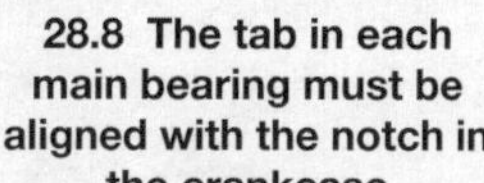

28.8 The tab in each main bearing must be aligned with the notch in the crankcase

Crankshaft main journal O.D. code	Code "1"	Code "2"
Crankcase I.D. code		
Code "A"	X	
Code "B"		X

28.10 Crankcase bearing diameter selection chart

Installation

11 Install the connecting rods on the crankshaft (see Section 27).

12 Lubricate the main bearings with engine assembly lube or moly-based grease.

13 Carefully lower the crankshaft/connecting rod assembly into the left crankcase half. Align the connecting rods with the cylinders.

14 Assemble the crankcase halves (see Section 24), then make sure the crankshaft and the transmission shafts turn freely. If they don't, stop and find out why before continuing; you may have made a mistake during assembly. If necessary, separate the crankcase halves again. Don't just put the engine back in the bike, hoping the problem will go away by itself.

29 Transmission - removal, inspection and installation

Removal

1 Remove the engine (see Section 5) and separate the crankcase halves (see Section 24).

2 On 1985 through 1996 VT1100C models, remove the mainshaft, countershaft, shift fork shaft and shift drum as a single assembly.

29.3a Firmly grasp the end of the shift fork shaft and carefully pull it out of the case and shift forks

29.3b Remove the first shift fork

29.3c Remove the M5 gear and the M5 spline bushing (arrow) from the mainshaft

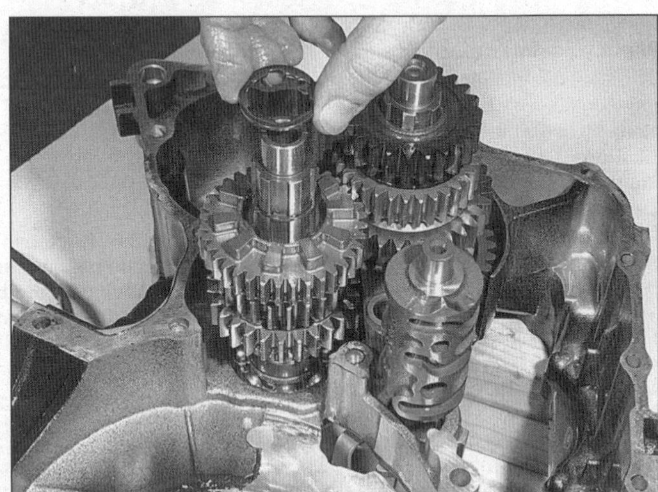

29.3d Remove the spline washer from the mainshaft

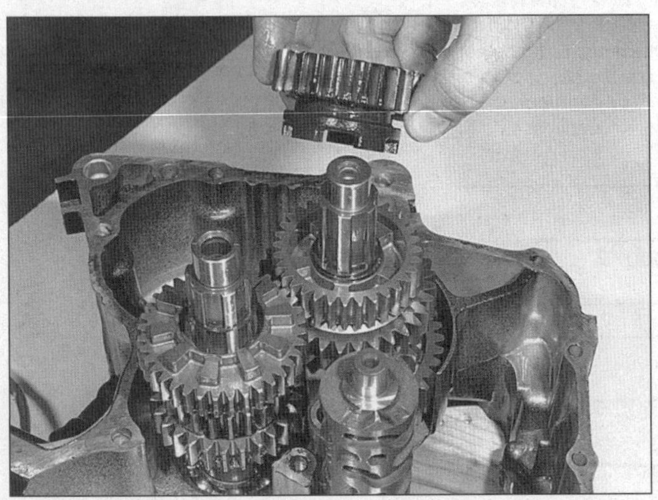

29.3e Remove the C5 gear from the countershaft

29.3f Remove the other shift forks

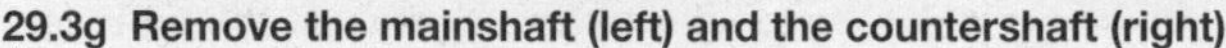

29.3g Remove the mainshaft (left) and the countershaft (right)

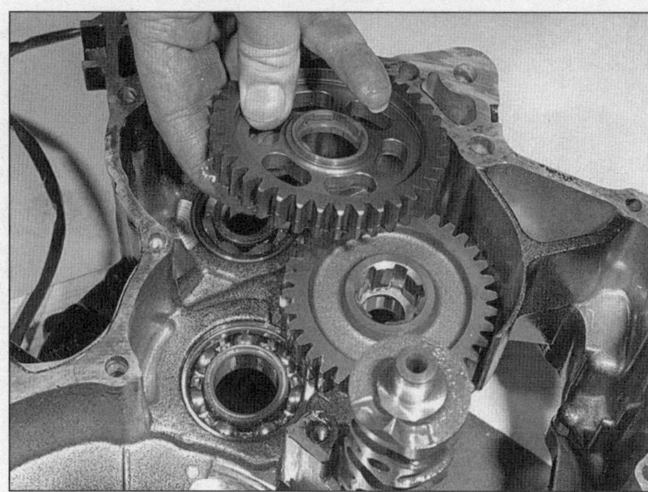

29.3h Remove the C1 gear

3 On VT1100C2, VT1100T and 1997-on VT1100C models, remove the shift forks and transmission in the indicated sequence **(see illustrations)**.

Inspection

4 Thoroughly wash the transmission components in clean solvent and dry them off with compressed air.

Shift drum, shift forks and shift fork shaft

5 Inspect the shift drum for evidence of insufficient lubrication and inspect the edges of the grooves in the shift drum for excessive wear. If the drum is worn or damaged, replace it. Measure the diameter of the left shift drum journal and compare your measurement to the journal diameter listed in this Chapter's Specifications. If it's smaller than the limit, replace the shift drum.

6 Inspect the shift forks for distortion and wear, especially the fork tips **(see illustration)**. If they're discolored or severely worn they are probably bent. If damage or wear is evident, check the shift fork groove in the corresponding sliding gear as well. Inspect the guide pins too. If the fork tips or the guide pins are worn or damaged, replace the forks. Measure the inside diameter of the shift fork shaft bore and the fork tip thickness of both forks and compare your measurements to the dimensions listed in this Chapter's Specifications. If the shift fork shaft bore is bigger than the limit or the tips are thinner than the limit, replace the shift fork(s).

7 Inspect the shift fork shaft for excessive wear, evidence of poor lubrication and straightness (roll it on a flat surface). See if the shift forks slide freely and smoothly on the shaft. Measure the diameter of the shaft and compare your measurement to the shift fork shaft diameter listed in this Chapter's Specifications.

29.3i Remove the final drive gear

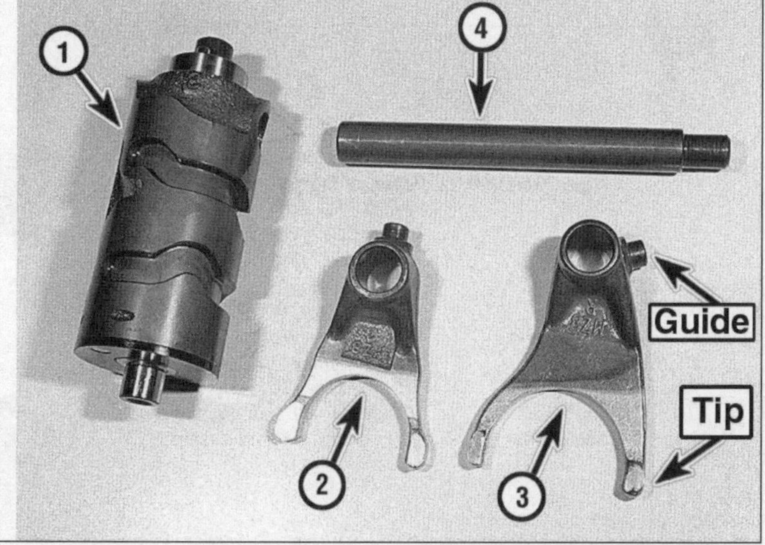

29.6 Inspect the grooves in the shift drum and the tips and pin guides of the shift forks (four-speed shown; five-speeds have another shift fork)

1 *Shift drum*
2 *Shift fork*
3 *Shift fork*
4 *Shift forkshaft*

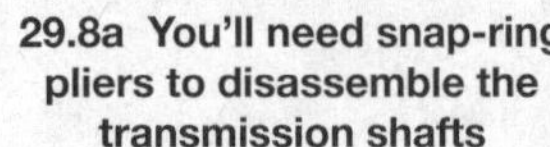
29.8a You'll need snap-ring pliers to disassemble the transmission shafts

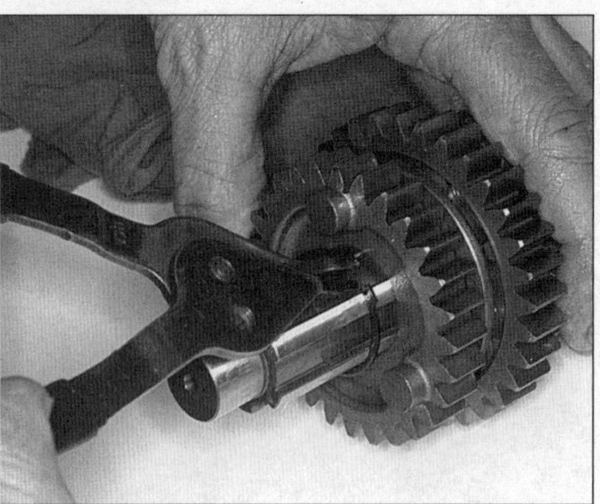

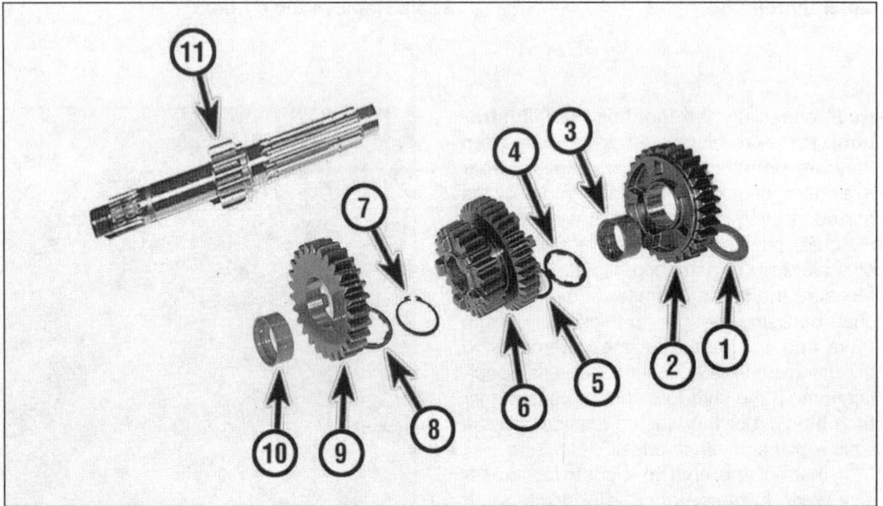

29.8b Lay out the mainshaft parts in the exact order in which they're disassembled

1 *Thrust washer*
2 *M5 gear*
3 *M5 spline bushing*
4 *Spline washer*
5 *Snap-ring*
6 *M2/M4 gear*
7 *Snap-ring*
8 *Spline washer*
9 *M3 gear*
10 *M3 gear bushing*
11 *Mainshaft*

Countershaft and mainshaft

8 Disassemble the transmission shafts. You'll need snap-ring pliers to remove some of the parts from the shafts **(see illustration)**. It's a good idea to discard all old snap-rings and install new ones when reassembling the transmission. Carefully study each part before removing it from the shaft; if the two sides of a part are not the same, make sure you know which side faces which way before removing that part. There are various ways to do this. One way to ensure that the parts retain their correct relationship to one another is to "stack" them on a long dowel, extension, etc. or to "thread" them on a piece of wire, as they're removed. If you're still in doubt, label the bigger parts to indicate which side faces left or right. Once you're confident that you know how the transmission goes back together, carefully lay out the parts in the order in which they were removed **(see illustrations)**.

9 Inspect the gears. Check the gear dogs, gear dog holes and gear teeth for cracks, excessive wear and other obvious damage. If a gear is obviously worn or damaged, replace it, and replace its corresponding gear on the other shaft too. Measure the inside diameter of each gear and compare your measurements to the inside diameters for the various gears listed in this Chapter's Specifications. If the inside diameter of a gear is excessive, replace the gear.

10 Inspect the gear bushings. Check the surface of the inner diameter of each bushing for scoring or heat discoloration or signs of poor lubrication. If a gear or bushing is obviously damaged or worn, replace it. Measure the inside and outside diameters of each bushing and compare your measurements to the I.D. and O.D. dimensions for the bushings listed in this Chapter's Specifications.

11 Inspect the mainshaft and countershaft. Check the splines and sliding surfaces for wear and damage. If either shaft is worn or damaged, replace it. Measure the diameter of each shaft at the gear and bushing sliding surfaces. Compare your measure-

29.8c Lay out the countershaft parts in the exact order in which they're disassembled

1 *C5 gear*
2 *Snap-ring*
3 *Spline washer*
4 *C4 gear*
5 *C4 gear bushing*
6 *Thrust washer*
7 *Final drive gear*
8 *C1 gear*
9 *C1 spline bushing*
10 *Spline washer*
11 *Snap-ring*
12 *C3 gear**
13 *Snap-ring*
14 *Spline washer*
15 *C2 gear*
16 *C2 gear bushing*

**On some ACE models, the C3 gear has six shift dogs*

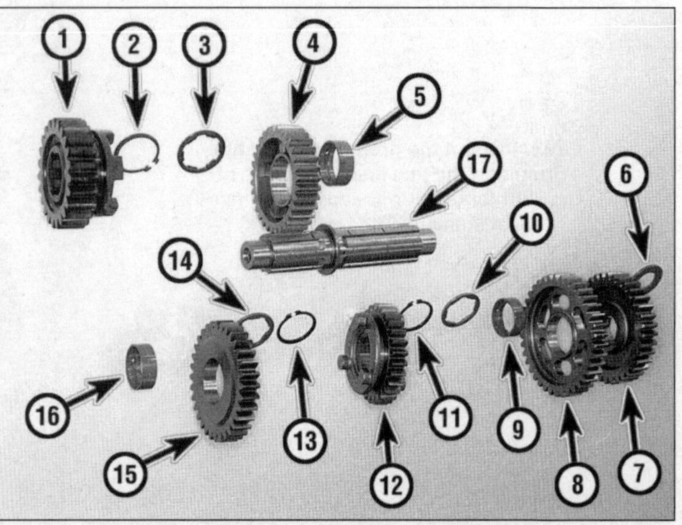

29.14a In the left half of the crankcase, inspect the mainshaft bearing (1) and the countershaft bearing (2)

29.14b In the right half of the crankcase, inspect the mainshaft bearing (1), the output gear shaft bearing (2), the countershaft bearing (3) and the shift drum bearing (4)

ments to the mainshaft and countershaft diameters listed in this Chapter's Specifications. If either shaft is worn below the limit, replace it.

12 To calculate the gear-to-mainshaft clearance, subtract the shaft diameter from the inside diameter of each gear. Compare your measurements to the gear-to-shaft clearances listed in this Chapter's Specifications. If the clearance is excessive, replace the gear and/or the shaft, depending on which part is causing the excessive clearance. Calculate the bushing-to-shaft clearances the same way and replace the bushing(s) and/or shaft accordingly.

13 Repeat Step 12 for the gear-to-countershaft clearance.

14 Inspect the bearings for the shift drum and the transmission shafts **(see illustrations)**. Make sure they rotate smoothly and quietly. If they're rough or noisy or loose, press them out of the cases and press in new bearings, or have them replaced at a dealer service department or motorcycle machine shop.

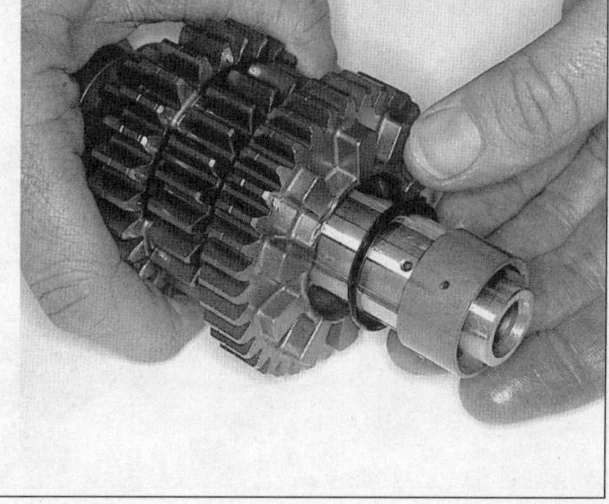

29.15 When reassembling the countershaft and mainshaft, make sure that the oil hole in each spline bushing is aligned with its corresponding oil hole in the shaft

15 Reassembly is the reverse of disassembly. Make sure that the oil holes on the spline bushings are aligned with the oil holes in the shafts **(see illustration)**.

16 When you're done this is how the two assembled shafts should look **(see illustration)**.

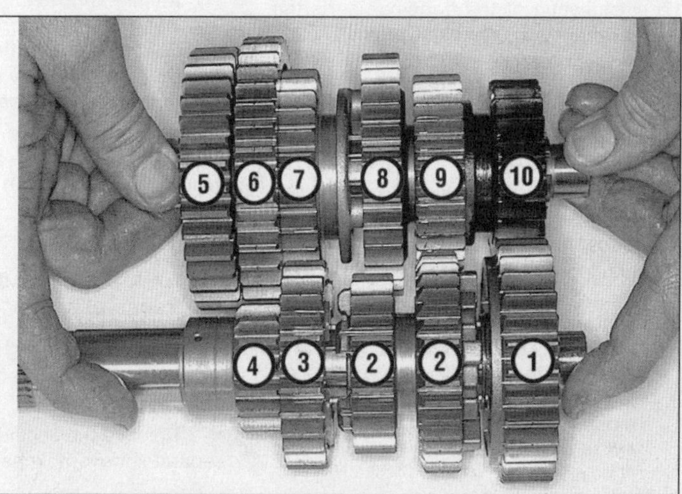

29.16 The assembled mainshaft and countershaft

1	*M5 gear*	6	*C1 gear*
2	*M2/M4 gear*	7	*C3 gear*
3	*M3 gear*	8	*C2 gear*
4	*M1 gear*	9	*C4 gear*
5	*Final drive gear*	10	*C5 gear*

29.17a The five-speed shift forks fit on their shaft like this; the letters R and C identify the right and center forks

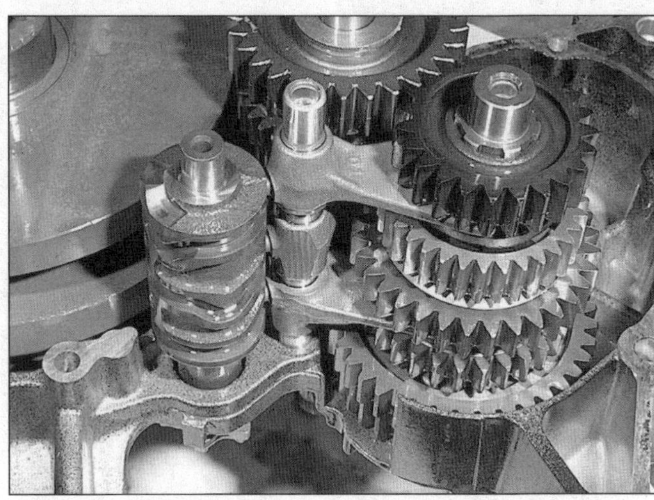

29.17b On five-speeds, the "R" fork fits into the collar between the C3 gear and the C2 gear on the countershaft, the "L" fork fits into the collar between C4 and C5 . . .

29.17c . . . and the "C" fork fits between the M2 and M4 gears on the mainshaft

29.17d Don't forget to install the end washer on the left end of the mainshaft (you should also have an end washer on the right end of the countershaft)

Installation

17 Installation of the transmission is the reverse of removal **(see illustrations)**, noting the following points:

a) *Lubricate all parts with engine oil before installing them.*
b) *Don't forget the washer on the right end of the countershaft.*
c) *Use the letters on the forks to position them correctly. On four-speed transmissions, the forks are identified by a "C" (center) or an "R" (right), starting from the left side of the engine. The letters face the right side of the engine when installed. On five-speeds, there is a third fork, but it is not identified by a letter* **(see illustration 29.17b)**. *On these models, this third fork is installed to the left of the other two forks (also labeled "C" and "R").*
d) *Engage the guide pin on each shift fork with the groove in the shift drum as you insert the shift fork shaft through the forks* **(see illustrations)**.
e) *Don't forget the washer on the left end of the mainshaft* **(see illustration)**.

18 After reassembling the case halves (see Section 24), make sure that both shafts turn freely and the shift drum and shift forks function correctly.

30 Output gear assembly - removal and installation

Removal

1 Remove the engine (see Section 5) and separate the crankcase halves (see Section 24).

2 Remove the output gear, bushing and thrust washer from the right crankcase **(see illustration)**.

3 Before the output gear assembly can be unbolted from the left half of the crankcase, the damper cam and spring must be removed from the output drive gear shaft. A special spring compressor (Honda 07964-ME90000) is needed to remove the snap-ring from the output drive gear shaft. At the time of publication, this tool was not available in the USA. Take the left half of the crankcase to a Honda dealer and have the service department remove the snap-ring from the output drive gear shaft.

4 Remove the damper cam and spring from the output drive gear shaft **(see illustration)**.

5 Remove the three output gear assembly retaining bolts **(see illustration)**.

30.2 Remove the bushing, output gear and thrust washer (arrow)

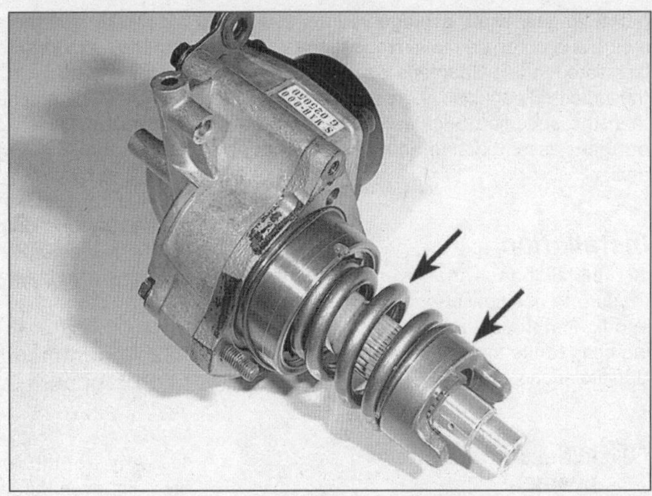

30.4 After the snap-ring has been removed, remove the damper cam and spring (arrows) from the output drive gear shaft (output gear assembly removed for clarity)

6 Remove the oil orifice and O-rings **(see illustration)**. Remove and discard the old O-rings.

Inspection

7 Inspect the condition of the teeth and the gear dog holes on the output gear. If they're damaged or excessively worn, replace the output gear. Measure the inside diameter of the output gear and compare your measurement to the output gear I.D. listed in this Chapter's Specifications. If the indicated I.D. exceeds the I.D. limit, replace the output gear.

8 Inspect the bushing and replace it if it's worn or damaged. Inspect the bushing I.D. and O.D. and compare your measurements to the bushing I.D. and O.D. If either measurement exceeds the I.D. or O.D. limit, replace the bushing.

9 Measure the diameter of the friction surface of the output drive gear shaft and compare your measurement to the output drive gear shaft diameter listed in this Chapter's Specifications. If the indicated diameter of the shaft is smaller than the shaft diameter limit, have a Honda dealer disassemble the output gear assembly and install a new shaft.

10 Measure the free length of the spring and compare your measurement to the spring free length listed in this Chapter's Specifications. If the spring free length is less than the specified limit, replace the spring.

11 Place the output gear assembly in a bench vise. Using a dial indicator and a suitable base, set the dial indicator next to the output gear assembly with the probe touching the output drive gear shaft **(see illustration)**. Using the shaft holder (Honda 07923-6890101) or a suitable equivalent, rotate the output driven gear shaft back and forth and measure the amount of backlash. Make this measurement at three locations on the out-

30.5 To detach the output gear assembly from the left crankcase half, remove these three bolts (arrows)

30.6 Remove the oil orifice and discard the old O-rings

30.11 Use a dial indicator to measure the output gear backlash

put drive gear shaft, average your measurements and compare the average to the backlash listed in this Chapter's Specifications. If the indicated backlash is greater than or less than the specified backlash, have the output gear assembly overhauled by a Honda dealer.

Installation

12 Installation is the reverse of removal. Be sure to use new O-rings on the oil orifice and tighten the output gear assembly retaining bolts to the torque listed in this Chapter's Specifications.

31 Initial start-up after overhaul

1 Make sure the engine oil level is correct, then remove the spark plugs from the engine. Place the engine kill switch in the Off position and unplug the primary (low tension) wires from the coils.

2 Turn on the key switch and crank the engine over with the starter several times to build up oil pressure. Reinstall the spark plugs, connect the wires and turn the switch to On.

3 Make sure there is fuel in the tank, then turn the fuel tap to the On position and operate the choke.

4 Start the engine and allow it to run at a moderately fast idle until it reaches operating temperature.

5 Check carefully for oil leaks and make sure the transmission and controls, especially the brakes, function properly before road testing the machine. Refer to Section 32 for the recommended break-in procedure.

32 Recommended break-in procedure

1 Any rebuilt engine needs time to break-in, even if parts have been installed in their original locations. For this reason, treat the machine gently for the first few miles to make sure oil has circulated throughout the engine and any new parts installed have started to seat.

2 Even greater care is necessary if the engine has been rebored or a new crankshaft has been installed. In the case of a rebore, the engine will have to be broken in as if the machine were new. This means greater use of the transmission and a restraining hand on the throttle until at least 500 miles have been covered. There's no point in keeping to any set speed limit - the main idea is to keep from lugging the engine and to gradually increase performance until the 500 mile mark is reached. These recommendations can be lessened to an extent when only a new crankshaft is installed. Experience is the best guide, since it's easy to tell when an engine is running freely. The following recommendations can be used as a guide:

a) *0 to 90 miles (0 to 150 km): Keep engine speed below 3,000 rpm. Turn off the engine after each hour of operation and let it cool for 5 to 10 minutes. Vary the engine speed and don't use full throttle.*
b) *90 to 300 miles (150 to 500 km): Don't run the engine for long periods above 4,000 rpm. Rev the engine freely through the gears, but don't use full throttle.*
c) *300 to 600 miles (500 to 1000 km): Don't use full throttle for prolonged periods and don't cruise at speeds above 5,000 rpm.*
d) *At 600 miles (1,000 km): Change the engine oil and filter. Full throttle can be used after this point.*

3 If a lubrication failure is suspected, stop the engine immediately and try to find the cause. If an engine is run without oil, even for a short period of time, severe damage will occur.

Chapter 3
Cooling system

Contents

Degrees of difficulty

Easy, suitable for novice with little experience	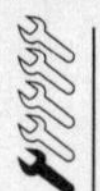	**Fairly easy,** suitable for beginner with some experience		**Fairly difficult,** suitable for competent DIY mechanic		**Difficult,** suitable for experienced DIY mechanic	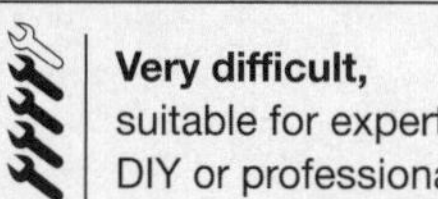	**Very difficult,** suitable for expert DIY or professional	

Specifications

General

Coolant type	See Chapter 1
Mixture ratio	See Chapter 1
Radiator cap pressure rating	
1985 through 1993 VT1100C	73.5 to 103 kPa (0.75 to 1.05 kg/cm², 10.7 to 14.9 psi)
1994 through 1996 VT1100C	93 to 123 kPa (0.95 to 1.25 kg/cm², 13.5 to 17.8 psi)
VT1100C2, VT1100T and 1997-on VT1100C	108 to 137 kPa (1.1 to 1.4 kg/cm², 16 to 20 psi)

General (continued)

Thermostatic fan switch	
Starts to open circuit at	93 to 97 degrees C (199 to 207 degrees F)
Starts to close circuit at	98 to 102 degrees C (208 to 216 degrees F)
Coolant temperature sensor resistance	
1985 and 1986	
At 60 degrees C (140 degrees F)	104.1 ohms
At 122 degrees C (252 degrees F)	15.3 ohms
1987 through 1996 VT1100C	
At 50 degrees C (122 degrees F)	130 to 180 ohms
At 100 degrees C (212 degrees F)	25 to 30 ohms
VT1100C2, VT1100T, 1997-on VT1100C	
At 80 degrees C (176 degrees F)	45 to 57 ohms
At 120 degrees C (248 degrees F)	14 to 18 ohms

Thermostat rating

Valve opening temperature	80 to 84-degrees C (176 to 183-degrees F)
Valve fully open at	95-degrees C (203-degrees F)
Valve travel (when fully open)	Not less than 8 mm (5/16-inch)

Torque specifications

Coolant temperature sensor	9 Nm (78 in-lbs)
Thermostatic fan switch	18 Nm (156 in-lbs)
Water pump cover bolts	13 Nm (108 in-lbs)
Water pump hold-down bolts	13 Nm (108 in-lbs)

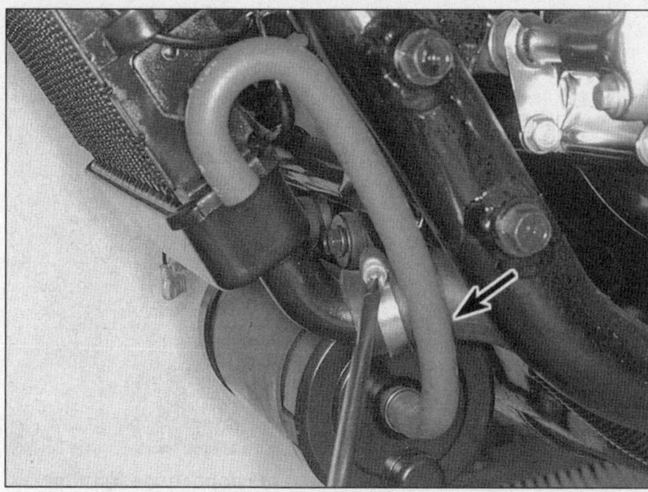

3.2 Loosen the lower radiator hose clamp, pull off the hose and drain the coolant into a pan; on California models, detach the EVAP canister vent hose (arrow)

3.4 Open up the clamps (arrows) on the right side of the radiator; detach any electrical wiring (and the EVAP hose on California models)

1 General information

The models covered by this manual are liquid-cooled. The liquid-cooling system uses a water/antifreeze mixture to carry away excess heat produced during the combustion process. The cylinders are surrounded by water jackets, through which the coolant is circulated by the water pump. The water pump is mounted on the left side of the crankcase and is driven by the oil pump shaft. Coolant is pumped through a flexible hose into the front cylinder. There, it flows through the water jacket surrounding the front cylinder. Some coolant exits through a smaller diameter pipe in the head and goes to the thermostat housing; the rest exits the front cylinder through a connecting pipe to the rear cylinder, where it again flows through the rear cylinder water jacket, exits the rear cylinder through another pipe and flows through a flexible hose to the thermostat housing. From the thermostat housing, coolant flows down into the radiator (which is mounted behind the front wheel, on the front of the frame, to take advantage of maximum air flow), where it is cooled by the passing air, through another hose and back to the water pump, where the cycle is repeated.

An electric fan, mounted behind the radiator and automatically controlled by a thermostatic switch, provides a flow of cooling air through the radiator when the coolant temperature exceeds an upper threshold.

The coolant temperature sending unit, threaded into the thermostat housing, senses the temperature of the coolant and turns on the coolant temperature warning light on the instrument cluster when the coolant temperature reaches a dangerous level.

The entire system is sealed and pressurized. The pressure is controlled by a valve which is part of the radiator cap. Pressurizing the coolant raises its boiling point, which prevents premature boiling of the coolant. An overflow hose directs coolant from the radiator to the reservoir tank when the radiator cap valve is opened by expanding coolant. The coolant is automatically siphoned back to the radiator as the engine cools.

Many cooling system inspection and service procedures are considered part of routine maintenance and are included in Chapter 1.

Warning 1: Do not allow antifreeze to come in contact with your skin or painted surfaces of the vehicle. Rinse off spills immediately with plenty of water. Antifreeze is highly toxic if ingested. Never leave antifreeze lying around in an open container or in puddles on the floor; children and pets are attracted by its sweet smell and may drink it. Check with local authorities about disposing of used antifreeze. Many communities have collection centers which will see that antifreeze is disposed of safely.

Warning 2: Do not remove the radiator cap when the engine and radiator are hot. Scalding hot coolant and steam may be blown out under pressure, which could cause serious injury. To open the radiator cap, remove the cover located between the fuel tank and the steering head on the right side of the bike. When the engine has cooled, place a thick rag, like a towel, over the radiator cap; slowly rotate the cap counterclockwise to the first stop. This procedure allows any residual pressure to escape. When the steam has stopped escaping, press down on the cap while turning counterclockwise and remove it.

2 Radiator cap - check

If problems such as overheating and loss of coolant occur, check the entire system as described in Chapter 1. The radiator cap opening pressure should be checked by a dealer service department or service station equipped with the special tester required to do the job. If the cap is defective, replace it.

3 Radiator - removal and installation

Warning: The engine must be completely cool before beginning this procedure.

1 Set the bike on its side stand. Disconnect the cable from the negative terminal of the battery.

2 Place a drain pan under the lower radiator hose, loosen the hose clamp screw **(see illustration)**, pull off the hose and drain the coolant. On California models, detach the EVAP canister vent hose from the radiator.

3 Remove the fuel tank (see Chapter 4) and the left steering head cover (see Chapter 8).

4 Follow the wiring harness from the fan motor to the two-pin black electrical connector on the left side, just behind the steering head. On all models, the wires on both sides of this connector are blue/black and green. Unplug the connector and carefully disentangle the fan motor harness so it doesn't snag other wiring when the radiator is removed. Also, if applicable, detach the wires for the horn and rear brake light switch and, on California models, the EVAP hose, from the right side of the radiator **(see illustration)**.

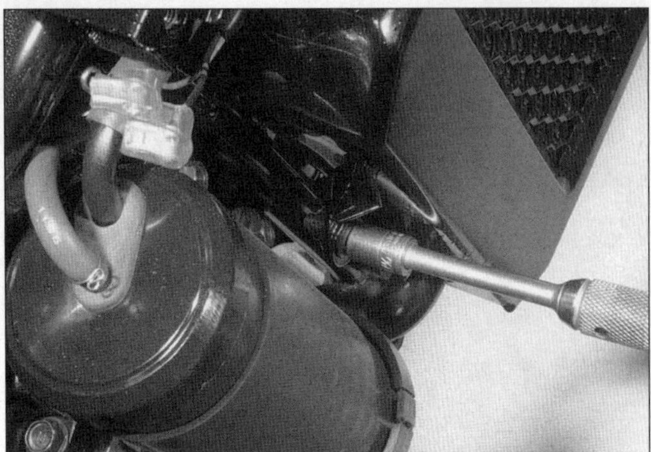

3.6 Remove the single radiator cover bolt (shown); on 1987 through 1996 VT1100C models, remove the two lower radiator mounting bolts (not shown)

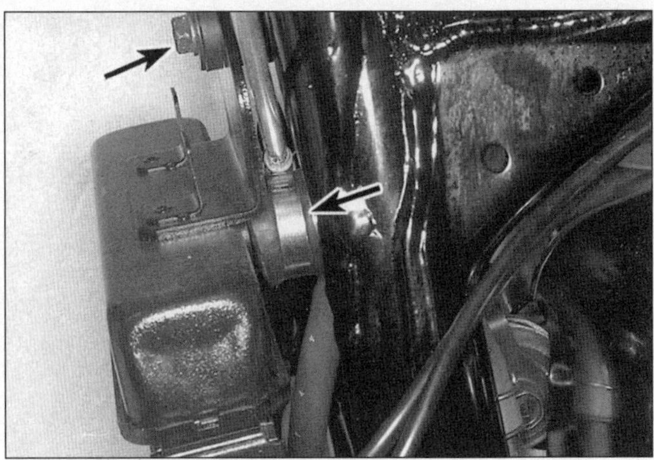

3.7 Loosen the clamp and detach the upper hose from the radiator, then remove the upper mounting bolt (arrows)

5 On 1985 and 1986 models, remove the upper radiator bolt.

6 On 1987 through 1996 VT1100C models, remove the two lower radiator mounting bolts. On all models, remove the single radiator cover mounting bolt **(see illustration)**.

7 Loosen the hose clamp on the upper radiator hose and detach the hose **(see illustration)**.

8 Remove the upper radiator mounting bolt **(see illustration 3.7)**.

9 Lift up the radiator and disengage the two rubber insulators on the lower edges of the radiator from the insulator brackets on the frame.

10 Remove the radiator.

11 If the radiator is to be repaired or replaced, remove the insulators and remove the fan assembly and the thermostatic fan switch (see Section 4).

12 Carefully inspect the radiator for signs of leaks and any other damage. If repairs are necessary, take the radiator to a reputable radiator repair shop. If the radiator is clogged, or if large amounts of rust or scale have formed, the repair shop will also do a thorough cleaning job.

13 Make sure the spaces between the cooling tubes and fins are clear. If necessary, use compressed air or running water to remove anything that may be clogging them. If the fins are bent or flattened, straighten them very carefully with a small screwdriver.

14 Inspect the radiator hoses for cracks, tears and other damage. Be sure to replace the hoses if they are damaged or deteriorated.

15 Installation is the reverse of removal.

16 Refill the cooling system with the recommended coolant (see Chapter 1).

4 Cooling fan and thermostatic fan switch - check and replacement

Check

1 If the engine is overheating and the cooling fan isn't coming on, remove the right side cover (see Chapter 8) and check the 10A fan motor fuse (see Chapter 9). If the fuse is blown, check the fan motor circuit for a short to ground (see the *Wiring diagrams* at the end of this book). If the fuse is good, locate the fan switch at the rear of the radiator **(see illustration)**. Warm up the engine, turn the ignition switch to OFF, unplug the electrical connector from the fan switch, ground the connector with a jumper wire, turn the ignition switch to ON and note whether the fan motor comes on. If the fan motor comes on, the fan switch is defective. If the fan motor still doesn't come on, inspect the wiring and the connectors (see *Wiring diagrams*), then check the fan motor itself.

2 To check the fan motor, remove the fuel tank (see Chapter 4), remove the steering head covers (see Chapter 8), unplug the two-wire black electrical connector (see Step 4 in Section 3) and, using a pair of jumper wires connected to the battery terminals, apply battery voltage to the fan-motor side of the connector. If the fan doesn't come on, replace the fan motor. If it does come on, the problem is in the wiring on the switch side of the connector, or the fan switch itself is defective.

3 To check the fan switch, remove the switch (see Step 10), suspend it in a pan of water, heat the water and, using a cooking thermometer and an ohmmeter, test the switch as shown **(see illustration)**.

4.1 The thermostatic fan switch (A) and fan motor bracket bolts (B); one bolt secures a ground wire and some models have four bolts

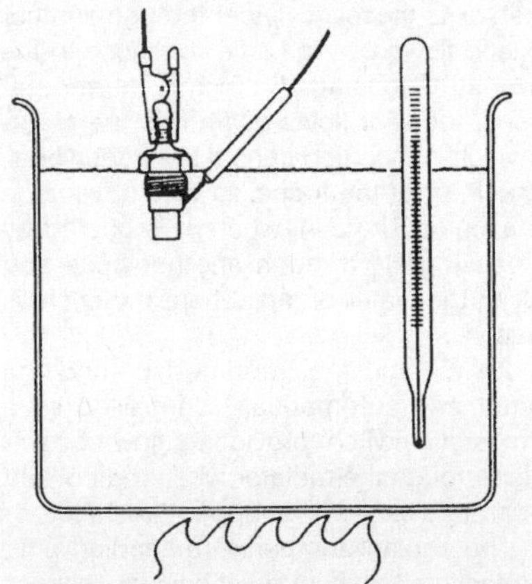

4.3 Heat the thermostatic fan switch in water with a thermometer and, using an ohmmeter, note the temperatures at which the switch closes and opens

4.7 To detach the fan from the fan motor shaft, remove this nut (center arrow); to detach the fan motor from the bracket, remove these three nuts (arrows)

Warning: Antifreeze is poisonous. Don't use a cooking pan.

Note the temperature at which the switch closes the circuit and compare this to the temperature listed in this Chapter's Specifications. If the switch doesn't perform as described, replace it.

Replacement

Fan motor

Warning: The engine must be completely cool before beginning this procedure.

4 Disconnect the cable from the negative terminal of the battery.

5 Remove the radiator (see Section 3).

6 On 1985 through 1996 VT1100C models, remove the four bolts securing the fan bracket to the radiator; on VT1100C2, VT1100T and 1997-on VT1100C models, remove the three bolts securing the fan bracket to the radiator **(see illustration 4.1)**. Note how the harnesses for the fan motor and fan switch are routed and how they're clamped to the fan bracket and to the radiator; they must be correctly rerouted before the radiator is installed. Separate the fan and bracket from the radiator.

7 Remove the nut that retains the fan to the motor shaft **(see illustration)** and remove the fan blade assembly from the motor.

8 Remove the three nuts that secure the fan motor to the bracket **(see illustration 4.7)** and detach the motor from the bracket.

9 Installation is the reverse of the removal procedure.

Thermostatic fan switch

Warning: The engine must be completely cool before beginning this procedure.

10 Remove the radiator (see Section 3).

11 Make sure there's a new O-ring on the new switch.

12 Remove the old switch.

13 Screw in the new switch and tighten it to the torque listed in this Chapter's Specifications.

14 Plug the electrical connector into the switch.

15 Install the radiator (see Section 3).

16 Check and, if necessary, add coolant to the system (see Chapter 1).

5 Coolant temperature warning system - check and component replacement

Note: *Before troubleshooting the coolant temperature warning system, make sure that the coolant is at the correct level (see Chapter 1) and there are no leaks in the system.*

Check

Coolant temperature gauge (1985 and 1986 models)

1 These models are equipped with a coolant temperature gauge. If the needle on the gauge is not indicating any temperature even when the engine is warmed up to its normal operating temperature, remove the fuel tank (see Chapter 4) and the steering head covers (see Chapter 8).

2 Disconnect the blue/green wire from the coolant temperature sensor, ground it, turn the ignition switch to On and verify that the coolant temperature gauge needle goes all the way to the right (to H).

3 If the gauge needle now goes to H, but hasn't been indicating any temperature recently, remove and check the temperature sensor (Step 34).

4 If the needle doesn't go to H when the blue/green wire to the temperature sensor is grounded, replace the gauge (see Chapter 9).

Coolant temperature indicator warning light (all other models)

5 These models are equipped with a coolant temperature warning light in the speedometer. The light comes on if the engine coolant exceeds its normal operating temperature. The system consists of the coolant temperature sensor (on the thermostat housing) that turns on the warning light; the microprocessor (inside the speedometer) that monitors the circuit between the sensor and the light (and switches the light off as long as the sensor and circuit are good); and the light itself. If any of the components is defective, you will not know that the engine is overheating. So, if the light either fails to come on, or comes on but won't go off, check the system immediately.

1987 through 1996 VT1100C models

Note: *Refer to the Wiring Diagrams at the end of Chapter 9.*

6 Turn the ignition key to the ON position and watch the coolant temperature warning light. It should come on for a few seconds, then go off. This verifies that the coolant temperature warning system is operating correctly.

7 If the coolant temperature warning light doesn't come on momentarily when the ignition key is turned to ON, or if it stays on all the time, check the system as follows.

8 First, remove the speedometer assembly (see Chapter 9), pull out the temperature indicator bulb and see if it's bad. If it's bad, install a new bulb and recheck. (Do not install the speedometer until you have completed the following tests, which require access to some of the wires connected to the speedometer.)

9 If the temperature warning light still fails to come on, turn the ignition switch to ON and measure the voltage between the connector terminals for the black/brown (positive) and green/black (negative) wires. There should be battery voltage.

10 If there is voltage, go to Step 12.

11 If there is no voltage, check the wiring harness for an open or short circuit, or for a loose connection. Once you have tracked down and repaired the problem, proceed to the next Step.

12 With the ignition switch turned to ON, measure the voltage between the connector terminals for the black/brown (positive) and the green/white (negative) wires. There should be battery voltage for a few seconds, then no voltage.

13 If there is battery voltage for a few seconds, then the voltage is cut off, the temperature indicator warning light microprocessor (inside the speedometer) is working satisfactorily. Remove and check the coolant temperature sensor (Step 34).

14 If there is no battery voltage at all, the coolant temperature indicator microprocessor is defective. Replace the speedometer (see Chapter 9) and recheck. (The microprocessor is inside the speedometer and cannot be replaced separately.)

15 If there is *continuous* battery voltage, *i.e.* it isn't cut off after a few seconds, either the coolant temperature sensor is shorted *or* the microprocessor for the coolant temperature indicator is shorted or defective. Start with the sensor and verify that it is okay (see Step 34).

16 If the sensor is okay, but there is still continuous battery voltage between the

black/brown and green/white wire connectors, the microprocessor is defective. Replace the speedometer (see Chapter 9).

VT1100C2, VT1100T and 1997-on VT1100C models

Note: *Refer to the Wiring Diagrams at the end of Chapter 9.*

17 Lower the sidestand and turn the ignition switch to ON.

18 Turn the ignition key to the ON position. The sidestand indicator light and the oil pressure indicator light should come on. If the coolant temperature indicator light also comes on, go to Step 29.

19 If the sidestand indicator and oil pressure indicator don't come on, remove the speedometer assembly, separate the speedometer from its metal case and, with the ignition switch turned to ON, check for battery voltage between the orange and green/black terminals.

20 If there is no voltage, either there is an open circuit in the orange or black/brown wire between the six-pin connector at the speedometer and the fuse box, or there's a loose or corroded contact at one of the connectors:

- *a) The speedometer six-pin connector*
- *b) The black nine-pin connector for the speedometer (inside the connector box, under the fuel tank, above the ignition coils)*
- *c) The white six-pin fuse box connector (under the seat)*

21 If there is battery voltage, proceed to the next Step.

22 If the sidestand indicator and oil pressure indicator DO come on, remove the fuel tank (see Chapter 4) and the steering head covers (see Chapter 8).

23 Disconnect the electrical connector from the coolant temperature sensor and ground the connector terminal with a jumper wire.

24 Turn the ignition switch to ON and watch the coolant temperature warning light. It should come on for a few seconds, then go off. This verifies that the coolant temperature warning system is operating correctly. If the circuit is normal, remove and check the coolant temperature sensor (Step 34).

25 If the coolant temperature indicator light does not come on, remove the speedometer assembly (see Chapter 9) and separate the speedometer from its metal case.

26 Ground the blue/green terminal of the speedometer six-pin connector, turn the ignition switch to ON and watch the coolant temperature indicator light again.

27 If the coolant temperature indicator light doesn't come on, replace the speedometer.

28 If the coolant temperature indicator light comes on, there is an open circuit in the blue/red wire between the speedometer six-pin connector and the coolant temperature sensor, or there is a loose or corroded contact in the speedometer six-pin connector, or in the black nine-pin connector inside the connector box.

29 If the indicator light doesn't go off with the ignition switch turned to ON, remove the fuel tank (see Chapter 4) and disconnect the electrical lead from the coolant temperature sensor.

30 Remove the speedometer (see Chapter 9), separate it from its metal case and unplug the six-pin connector.

31 Check for continuity between the green/blue wire at the six-pin connector and ground.

32 If there is continuity, there is a short in the green/blue wire.

33 If there is no continuity, remove and check the coolant temperature sensor (next Step). If the sensor is okay, replace the speedometer.

Coolant temperature sensor

34 Drain the coolant (see Chapter 1).

35 Remove the fuel tank (see Chapter 4).

36 Disconnect the electrical lead from the coolant temperature sensor (it's mounted in the thermostat housing).

37 Remove the coolant temperature sensor (see Step 11).

38 Suspend the temperature sensor in a pan of water, heat the water and, using a cooking thermometer and an ohmmeter, test the sensor **(see illustration 4.3)**.

Warning: Antifreeze is poisonous. Don't use a cooking pan.

Note the temperature at which the resistance changes and compare your observations to the sensor resistance listed in this Chapter's Specifications. If the sensor doesn't operate as specified, replace it.

Replacement

Coolant temperature sensor

Warning: The engine must be completely cool before beginning this procedure.

39 Drain the coolant (see Chapter 1).

40 Remove the fuel tank (see Chapter 4) and the steering head covers (see Chapter 8).

41 Disconnect the electrical lead from the coolant temperature sensor.

42 Prepare the new coolant temperature sensor by wrapping the threads with Teflon tape or by coating the threads with RTV sealant.

43 Unscrew the coolant temperature sensor from the thermostat housing.

44 Install the new sensor and tighten it to the torque listed in this Chapter's Specifications.

45 Reconnect the electrical connector to the sensor.

46 Refill the cooling system (see Chapter 1).

47 Install the fuel tank and steering head covers.

Speedometer

48 Refer to Chapter 9.

6 Thermostat - removal, check and installation

Removal

Warning: The engine must be completely cool before beginning this procedure.

1 If the thermostat is functioning correctly, the engine should warm up quickly, within a few minutes (unless the temperature is cold), and should not overheat (indicated by the coolant temperature warning light coming on). If the engine does not reach normal operating temperature quickly, or if it overheats, the thermostat should be removed, checked and, if necessary, replaced.

2 Remove the fuel tank (see Chapter 4) and the steering head covers (see Chapter 8).

3 On 1985 and 1986 models, remove the upper radiator mounting bolt and disconnect the upper radiator hose from the radiator.

4 On all models (except 1985 and 1986), remove the connector box above the ignition coils and remove the ignition coils (see Chapter 5).

5 Drain the cooling system (see Chapter 1).

6 Detach the siphon tube **(see illustration)** from the radiator filler neck.

7 On 1985 and 1986 models, remove the thermostat housing bracket bolt. On 1987 through 1996 VT1100C models, remove the bolt that secures the filler neck flange to the filler neck bracket. (On these earlier models, it is not absolutely necessary to remove the two bolts that secure the filler neck flange to the thermostat housing cover.)

8 On VT1100C2, VT1100T and 1997-on VT1100C models, remove the two bolts that secure the filler neck flange to the thermostat housing cover. Separate the filler neck flange from the housing cover and discard the old O-ring.

9 Remove the thermostat housing cover bolts and remove the cover. On some models, there may be a ground lead attached to one of the bolts. Don't forget which bolts it's attached to.

10 Note how the thermostat is oriented in the thermostat housing, then remove it from the housing and discard the old O-ring.

Check

11 Remove any coolant deposits, then visually check the thermostat for corrosion, cracks and other damage. If it was open when it was removed, it is defective. Check the O-ring for cracks and other damage.

12 To check the thermostat's operation, submerge it in a container of water along with a thermometer **(see illustration)**.

Warning: Antifreeze is poisonous. Don't use a cooking pan.

6.6 Back off the wire retainer and detach the siphon tube from the radiator filler neck

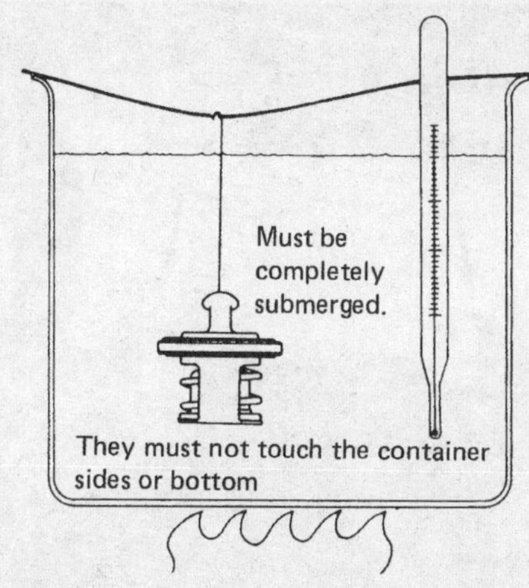
Must be completely submerged.
They must not touch the container sides or bottom
6.12 Heat the thermostat in water with a thermometer and note the temperatures when the thermostat begins to open and opens fully

The thermostat should be suspended so it does not touch the container.

13 Gradually heat the water in the container with a hot plate or stove and check the temperature when the thermostat first starts to open. Continue heating the water and check the temperature when the thermostat is fully open.

14 Compare your results to the specified thermostat opening temperature range listed in this Chapter's Specifications.

15 If the thermostat does not open as described, replace it.

Installation

16 Install the thermostat into the housing, spring end first. On 1985 through 1996 VT1100C models, make sure that the rib on the thermostat is aligned with the slot in the thermostat housing. On VT1100C2 models, make sure that the hole in the thermostat is aligned with the sealing bolt on the side of the thermostat housing; on VT1100T and 1997-on VT1100C models, make sure that the hole in the thermostat is oriented toward the front end of the bike. On all models, make sure that the flange of the thermostat fits into the groove in the thermostat housing so that the thermostat flange is flush with the mating surface of the housing.

17 Install a new O-ring in the groove in the thermostat housing cover.

18 Place the cover on the housing, install the cover screws and tighten them securely. If there was a ground lead attached to the one of the cover bolts, don't forget to reattach it.

19 On VT1100C2, VT1100T and 1997-on VT1100C models, install a new O-ring on the filler neck flange. Attach the filler neck flange to the thermostat housing cover, install the flange-to-cover bolts and tighten them securely.

20 On 1987 through 1996 VT1100C models, reattach the filler neck flange to the mounting bracket and tighten the bolt securely.

21 On 1985 and 1986 models, reattach the thermostat housing to the mounting bracket and tighten the bolt securely.

22 Reattach the siphon tube to the radiator filler neck. If the wire retainer is fatigued, replace it with a new retainer or with a hose clamp.

23 On 1985 and 1986 models, reattach the upper radiator hose to the radiator, install the upper radiator mounting bolt and tighten it securely.

24 Install the steering head covers (see Chapter 8) and the fuel tank (see Chapter 4).

25 Fill the cooling system with the recommended coolant (see Chapter 1).

7 Thermostat housing - removal and installation

Warning: The engine must be completely cool before beginning this procedure.

1 Remove the fuel tank (see Chapter 4) and the steering head covers (see Chapter 8).

2 On 1985 and 1986 models, remove the upper radiator mounting bolt and disconnect the upper radiator hose from the radiator.

3 On all models (except 1985 and 1986), remove the connector box above the ignition coils and remove the ignition coils (see Chapter 5).

4 Drain the cooling system (see Chapter 1).

5 Detach the siphon tube from the radiator filler neck **(see illustration 6.6)**.

6 On 1985 and 1986 models, remove the thermostat housing bracket bolt. On 1987 through 1996 VT1100C models, remove the bolt that secures the filler neck flange to the filler neck bracket.

7 Remove the two bolts that secure the filler neck flange to the thermostat housing cover. Separate the filler neck flange from the housing cover and discard the old O-ring.

8 Unplug the electrical lead from the coolant temperature sensor at the thermostat housing.

9 Loosen the hose clamps and detach all hoses from the thermostat housing.

10 Remove the thermostat housing.

11 Installation is the reverse of removal.

12 Fill the cooling system with the recommended coolant (see Chapter 1).

8 Coolant reservoir - removal and installation

1 The coolant reservoir is located behind the engine and in front of the swingarm.

2 Drain the cooling system (see Chapter 1).

3 Remove the swingarm (see Chapter 6).

4 Remove the filler neck retaining bolt **(see illustration)**, remove the right side cover (see Chapter 8), slide back the wire retainer and detach the filler neck from the filler hose.

8.4 Remove the filler neck bolt (upper arrow), slide back the hose retainer (lower arrow) and pull the filler neck loose

8.5 Disconnect the reservoir siphon tube and lower bolt (arrows), then remove the upper bolt (not shown), pull down the reservoir and disconnect the breather tube

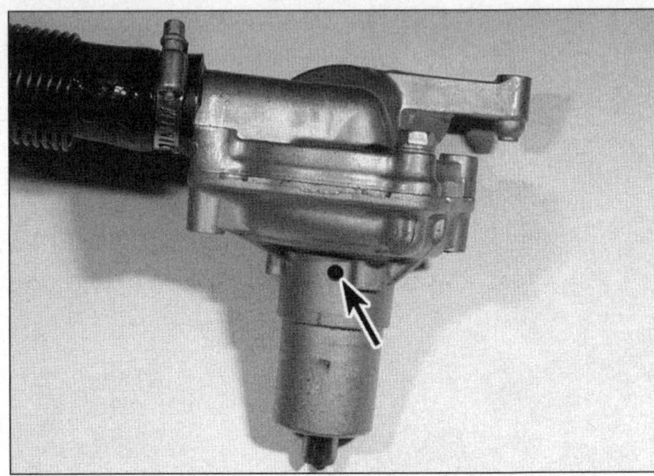

9.1 If coolant is leaking from the weep hole (arrow), the mechanical seal has failed; replace the water pump

5 Place a container under the reservoir to catch spilled coolant. Detach the siphon tube **(see illustration)**.

6 Remove the upper and lower reservoir mounting bolts **(see illustration 8.5)**.

7 Pull the reservoir down and detach the breather tube.

8 To remove the reservoir, pull it out of the frame to the rear.

9 Installation is the reverse of removal. Be sure to fill the cooling system when you're done (see Chapter 1).

9 Water pump - check, removal and installation

Check

1 Inspect the area around the water pump for coolant leaks. Try to determine whether the leak is simply the result of a loose hose clamp or deteriorated hose, or whether it's leaking from a damaged pump cover O-ring or from the "weep hole" (coolant drainage passage) in the underside of the pump body **(see illustration)**.

2 If the leak appears to be caused by a loose hose clamp, tighten the clamp, clean up the area, ride the bike and verify that the leak has been fixed. If the leak appears to be caused by a damaged hose, drain the coolant (see Chapter 1) and replace the hose. If the pump is leaking from a bad cover O-ring, replace the O-ring. If the pump is leaking from the weep hole, replace the pump.

3 If there is any sign of *oil* in the area around the water pump, the pump housing O-ring may be damaged. Remove the pump and replace the pump housing O-ring.

Removal, inspection and O-ring replacement

Note: *The water pump on these models can't be overhauled; if it's leaking, it must be replaced.*

4 Remove the engine (see Chapter 2).

5 On all models, loosen the hose clamp and pull off the hose that connects the pump's metal outlet pipe to the rear cylinder **(see illustration)**. On 1985 through 1996 VT1100C models, this metal outlet pipe has a one-into-two junction: one pipe is connected to a hose leading to the rear cylinder, as on later models; the other pipe runs along the left side of the crankcase and is connected to the front cylinder by another hose. On these models, loosen the hose clamps, detach the both front and rear hoses from their respective pipes, then remove the bolt from the bracket that attaches the front cylinder pipe to the crankcase.

6 Remove the pump and cover retaining bolts **(see illustration)** and remove the pump cover.

7 Try to wiggle the water pump impeller back-and-forth and in-and-out. If you can feel movement, the water pump must be replaced.

8 Inspect the impeller blades for corrosion. If they are heavily corroded, replace the

9.5 Disconnect the water pump hose (arrow) from the pipe (on 1985 through 1996 models, disconnect the front cylinder's water pump hose as well) . . .

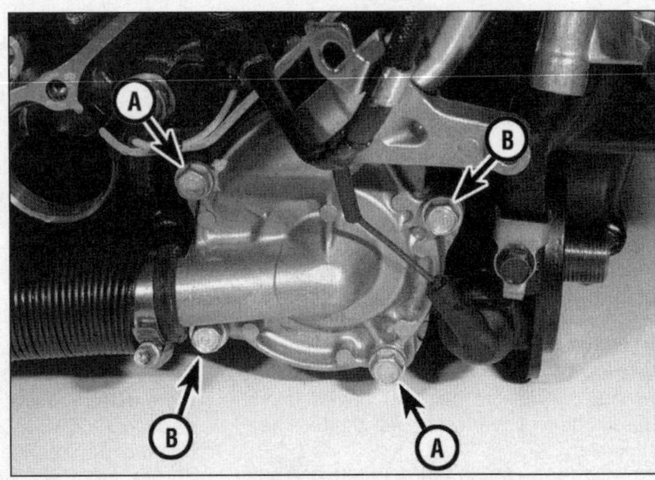

9.6 . . . remove the pump cover bolts (A) and the mounting bolts (B) . . .

9.9 . . . and pull out the pump; replace the O-ring (arrow) with a new one

9.10 Replace the pump if the impeller is heavily corroded; use a new O-ring on the cover

water pump and flush the system thoroughly (it would also be a good idea to check the internal condition of the radiator).

9 To remove the pump, simply pull it out **(see illustration)**. Remove and discard the old O-ring.

10 Install a new O-ring in the pump cover **(see illustration)**; even if you're planning to reuse the same pump, remove the old O-ring and install a new one.

11 Install the pump cover and the pump cover bolts **(see illustration)** and tighten the cover bolts to the torque listed in this Chapter's Specifications.

12 Remove the metal outlet pipe from the pump cover **(see illustration)**. Remove and discard the old pipe O-ring. Install a new O-ring and protect it with a little oil, then install the metal outlet pipe in the cover.

Installation

13 Before installing the pump, smear a little engine oil on the pump housing O-ring.

14 The water pump is driven off the left end of the oil pump shaft. Make sure the slot in the pump shaft is engaged properly with the ridge on the end of the oil pump shaft **(see illustration)**.

15 Reattach the coolant hose(s) to the metal outlet pipe and tighten the hose clamps securely. On 1985 through 1996 VT1100C models, reattach the front cylinder pipe bracket to the crankcase and tighten the bolt securely.

16 Install the engine (see Chapter 2).

17 Fill the cooling system with the recommended coolant (see Chapter 1), ride the bike and check for leaks.

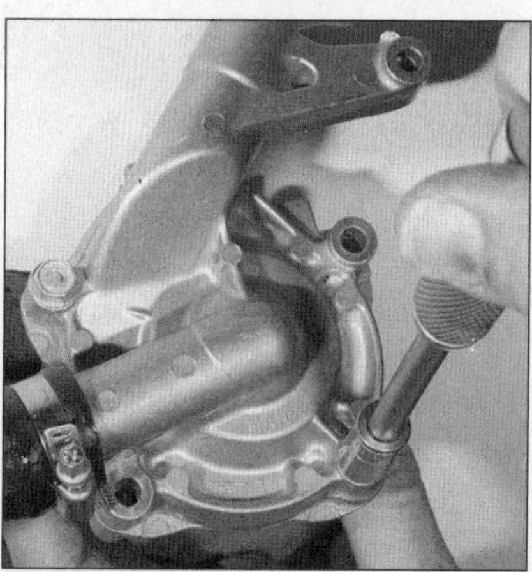

9.11 Install the cover and the cover bolts (the two holes without bolts are the holes for the pump bolts)

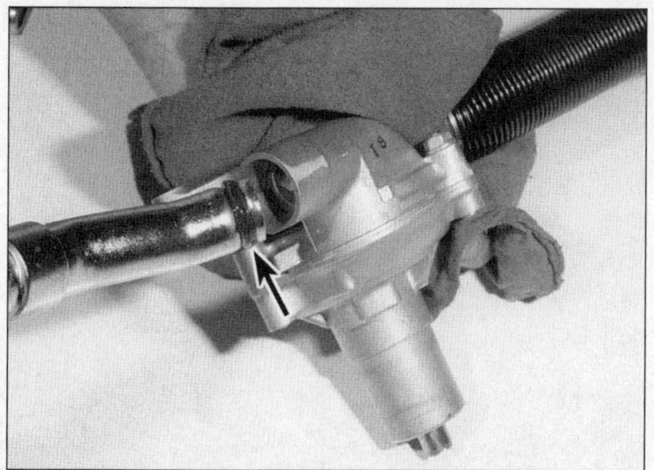

9.12 Install a new O-ring on the outlet pipe (arrow)

9.14 When installing the water pump, align the slot on the end of the water pump shaft with the ridge on the end of the oil pump shaft (arrows)

Notes

Chapter 4
Fuel and exhaust systems

Contents

Degrees of difficulty

Easy, suitable for novice with little experience 

Fairly easy, suitable for beginner with some experience 

Fairly difficult, suitable for competent DIY mechanic

Difficult, suitable for experienced DIY mechanic

Very difficult, suitable for expert DIY or professional 

Specifications

Carburetors

Type	
1985	VD7DA (VD7EA)
1986	VD7DC (VD7FA)
1987	
49-State	VDGAA
California	VDGAB
1988 through 1996 VT1100C	
49-State	VDGAB
California	VDGBB

Carburetors (continued)

Type (continued)	
VT1100C2 Shadow ACE (1995 through 1999)	
49-state	VDKBA
California	VDKCA
Canada	VDK2A
VT1100C22 Shadow Sabre (2000 and later)	
49-state and Canada	
2000 through 2005	VDKED
2006 and later	VDKEK
California	
2000 through 2003	VDKEE
2004 and later	VDKEJ
1997 through 2003 VT1100C	
49-state and Canada	VDKHA
California	VDKJA
2004 and 2005 VT1100C	
49-state and Canada	VDKHB
California	VDKHC
2006 and 2007 VT1100C	
49-state and Canada	VDKJB
California	VDKHC
VT1100T	
49-State/Canada	VDKFA
California	VDKJA
Float level	
1985	9.0 mm (0.38 inch)
1986 on (all models)	9.2 mm (0.36 inch)
Main jet	
1985	
Front	148
Rear	145
1986	140
1987	158
1988 through 1996 VT1100C	165
1997 through 2003 VT1100C	178
2004 and later VT1100C	
Front	178
Rear	185
VT1100C2	
Front	180
Rear	185
VT1100C3	
1998 through 2000	
Front	180
Rear	185
2001 and later	
Front	175
Rear	180
Slow jet (except 1985 and 1986)	42
Pilot screw	
Initial opening	
1985	3 turns out
1986	2-1/4 turns out
1987 and 1988	3 turns out
1989 through 1996 VT1100C	2-3/4 turns out
VT1100C2	
1995 through 1999	1-1/2 turns out
2000 and later	2-1/2 turns out
VT1100C3	2-1/2 turns out
1997-on VT1100C	2 turns out
VT1100T	2-1/2 turns out
High altitude adjustment	1/2 turn in

Fuel pump

Discharge volume (minimum)	
1985 and 1986	650 cc (22 ounces) per minute
1987 through 1993	700 cc (24 ounces) per minute
1994 through 1996 VT1100C	800 cc (27 ounces) per minute
VT1100C2	
1995	650 cc (22 ounces) per minute
1996 on	800 cc (27 ounces) per minute
VT1100T and 1997-on VT1100C	800 cc (27 ounces) per minute

Torque specifications

Exhaust pipe-to-cylinder head mounting nuts	
VT1100C	25 Nm (18 ft-lbs)
VT1100C2, VT1100T	23 Nm (17 ft-lbs)

1 General information

The fuel system consists of the fuel tank (and, on 1985 and 1986 models, the auxiliary fuel tank, under the seat), the fuel valve, the fuel pump, the fuel filter, the carburetors, the hoses connecting these components, and the accelerator cables.

All motorcycles covered in this manual use Keihin constant-velocity carburetors with butterfly-type throttle valves. For cold starting, an enrichment circuit is actuated by a choke lever mounted on the handlebar.

The exhaust system routes the exhaust gases through a pair of exhaust pipes and mufflers.

Some of the fuel system service procedures are included in Chapter 1 as routine maintenance items.

2 Fuel tank - removal and installation

Warning: Gasoline (petrol) is extremely flammable, so take extra precautions when you work on any part of the fuel system. Don't smoke or allow open flames or bare light bulbs near the work area, and don't work in a garage where a gas-type appliance (such as a water heater or clothes dryer) is present. If you spill any fuel on your skin, rinse it off immediately with soap and water. When you perform any kind of work on the fuel system, wear safety glasses and have a fire extinguisher suitable for class B fires (flammable liquids) on hand.

1 Support the bike securely so it can't be knocked over during this procedure.

2 Remove the seat (see Chapter 8).

1985 and 1986 models

Note: *These models have two fuel tanks - a conventional main fuel tank, and an in-the-frame auxiliary fuel tank located behind the engine, under the seat.*

Main fuel tank

3 Remove the left side cover (see Chapter 8).

4 Turn off the fuel valve. Disconnect the fuel inlet line from the fuel pump, turn on the fuel valve and drain the main fuel tank into a clean container.

5 Remove the four fuel tank cover bolts, lift up the cover, unplug the electrical connectors from the fuel gauge and the coolant temperature gauge and remove the cover.

6 Remove the two front and single rear fuel tank mounting bolts.

2.25 Remove the front fuel tank mounting bolt (arrow) and collar; replace the rubber insulator if it's damaged

2.26 Remove the rear fuel tank mounting bolt (arrow) and washer; replace the rubber insulator if it's damaged

7 Disconnect the fuel hose from the auxiliary fuel tank and plug the auxiliary fuel tank pipe with a rubber plug.
8 Raise the main fuel tank, disconnect the fuel tank breather tubes and remove the tank.
9 Installation is the reverse of removal. After the tank is installed and everything is hooked up, check for leaks before riding.

Auxiliary fuel tank

10 Remove the main fuel tank (see Steps 3 through 8).
11 Remove the rear wheel (see Chapter 7).
12 Remove the rear fender (see Chapter 8).
13 Unplug the electrical connectors from the fuel tank sending unit.
14 Turn off the fuel valve and remove the fuel valve knob.
15 Remove the voltage regulator/rectifier from its bracket (see Chapter 9).
16 Disconnect the fuel inlet pipe from the fuel pump.
17 Remove the nut from the fuel filter bracket and detach the bracket from the auxiliary fuel tank.
18 Disconnect the auxiliary fuel tank outlet hose from the fuel filter.
19 Remove the battery (see Chapter 9).
20 Remove the spark unit and the battery holder.
21 Remove the auxiliary fuel tank mounting bolt.
22 Move the auxiliary fuel tank to the rear and remove it from the frame.
23 Installation is the reverse of removal. Make sure that the tank mounting stays are correctly seated on the rubber insulators.

All other models

24 Turn the fuel valve to OFF.
25 Remove the front fuel tank mounting bolt and collar **(see illustration)**. Remove and inspect the rubber grommet. If it's cracked, torn or deteriorated, replace it.
26 Remove the rear tank mounting bolt **(see illustration)** and washer. Remove and inspect the rubber insulator bushing. If it's cracked, torn or deteriorated, replace it.
27 Hold a pan under the fittings to catch drained fuel, lift up the tank and disconnect the fuel hose from the fuel tap and, on California models, the breather tube from the right side of the tank **(see illustrations)**.
28 Remove the tank from the bike.

Warning: Pour the drained fuel into a safe fuel storage container. Don't leave it in the drain pan.

29 If you're going to have the tank professionally cleaned, or if you're going to replace it, unscrew the fuel valve nut and remove the fuel valve, the O-ring and the strainer. Discard the old O-ring.
30 Clean the fuel strainer screen thoroughly and inspect it. If the strainer is clogged, torn or otherwise damaged, replace it.
31 Install the strainer, a new O-ring and the fuel valve in the tank and tighten the fuel valve nut securely.

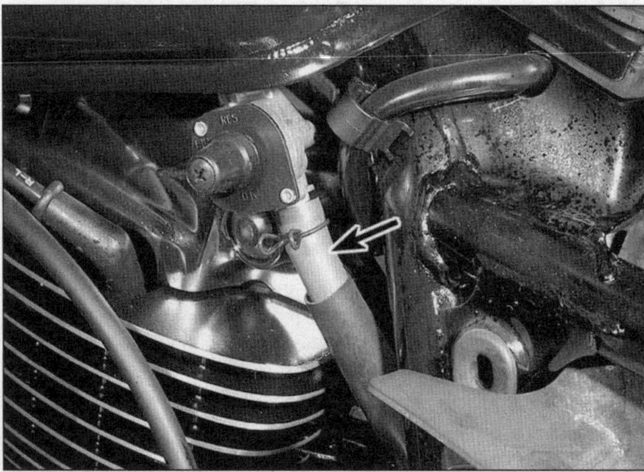
2.27a Lift the tank slightly, release the fuel hose clip and detach the hose (arrow) from the fuel valve

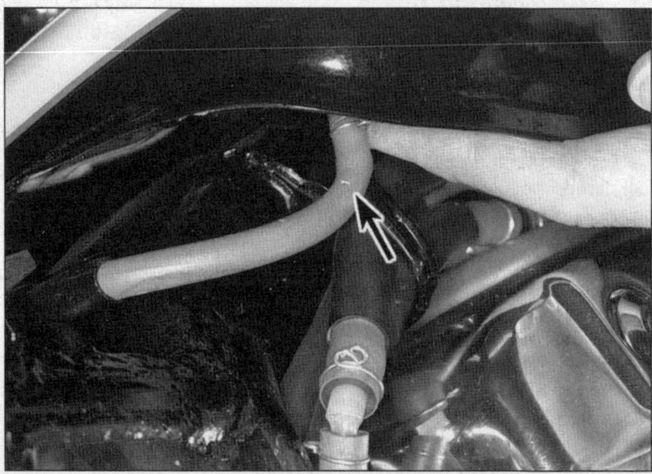
2.27b On California models, detach the breather hose from the right side of the tank

4.1 The crankcase breather separator (arrow) is mounted next to the air cleaner duct

4.3 These two hoses are connected to the crankcase breather separator

32 Before installing the tank, inspect the fuel hoses and the rubber tank insulators on the frame. If the hoses or insulators are cracked, hardened, or otherwise deteriorated, replace them.
33 Installation is the reverse of removal. Make sure the tank is correctly seated on the rubber insulators and make sure it doesn't pinch any control cables or wire harnesses.

3 Fuel tank - cleaning and repair

1 All repairs to the fuel tank should be carried out by a professional who has experience in this critical and potentially dangerous work. Even after cleaning and flushing of the fuel system, explosive fumes can remain and ignite during repair of the tank.
2 If the fuel tank is removed from the vehicle, it should not be placed in an area where sparks or open flames could ignite the fumes coming out of the tank. Be especially careful inside garages where a natural gas-type appliance is located, because the pilot light could cause an explosion.

4 Crankcase emission control system - description, check and component replacement

Description

1 The closed crankcase emission control system prevents crankcase emissions from escaping into the atmosphere by routing blow-by gas from the rear cylinder head through a hose into the crankcase breather separator **(see illustration)**. Blow-by gas is routed from the separator through another hose to the air cleaner housing, where it's mixed with fresh intake air. Finally, the blow-by is drawn into the intake ducts, through the carburetors and into the combustion chamber, where it is burned.

Check

2 Inspect the condition of the crankcase breather separator **(see illustration 4.1)**. If it's cracked, deteriorated or otherwise damaged, replace it.
3 Inspect the condition of the system hoses **(see illustration)**. Make sure that there are no cuts or tears in the hoses and all connections are tight. If the hoses are worn or damaged, replace them.
4 Inspect the left crankcase cover breather pipe adapter **(see illustration)** and the area around it for oil leaks. If there are any , replace the O-ring as described below.

Component replacement

Crankcase breather separator

5 Disconnect the upper breather hose that goes to the air cleaner housing from the breather separator and remove the separator hold-down screw **(see illustration)**.
6 Lift up the separator and disconnect the lower breather hose from the separator (the hose goes to the T-fitting for the front and rear crankcase breather hoses).
7 Installation is the reverse of removal.

Left crankcase cover breather pipe adapter O-ring

8 Remove the breather pipe adapter bolts **(see illustration 4.4)**.

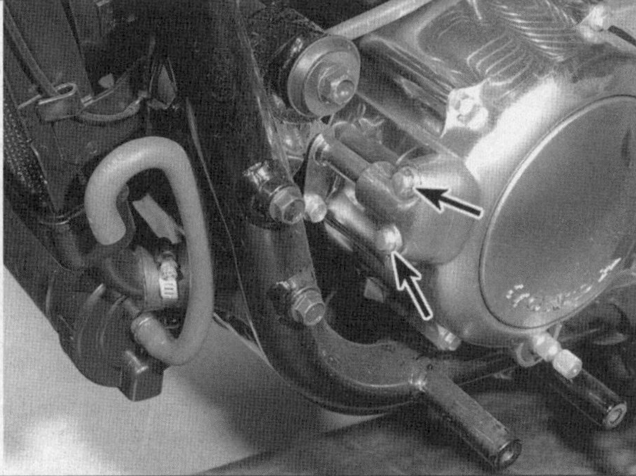

4.4 These bolts (arrows) secure the breather hose adapter to the left crankcase cover

4.5 Remove the breather separator retaining screw, disconnect the upper hose, lift up the separator and disconnect the lower hose

4.9a Detach the adapter from the left crankcase cover, slide the retainer (arrow) back and pull the pipe out of the breather hose

4.9b Remove the adapter dowel pins (arrows) and put them in a container

9 Detach the adapter from the left crankcase cover and remove the dowels **(see illustrations)**. Put the dowels in a container so you don't lose them.

10 Slide back the wire retainer and detach the pipe from the breather hose **(see illustration 4.9a)**.

11 Pull the pipe out of the adapter **(see illustration)** and either remove the old O-ring from the pipe, or dig it out of the adapter (it could be on the pipe or stuck inside the adapter).

12 Lubricate the new O-ring with clean oil and install it on the pipe.

13 Push the pipe back into the adapter.

14 Installation is the reverse of removal. Don't forget to install the dowel pins. Tighten the adapter bolts securely. If the wire retainer that secures the hose breather hose to the pipe is fatigued, replace it with a new retainer or a hose clamp.

Breather hoses

15 If you're replacing any of the three hoses, carefully note how they're routed before removing them and route the new hose(s) exactly the same way.

5 Evaporative emission control system (California models) - description, check and component replacement

Description

Note: *The first step in familiarizing yourself with the specific system configuration on your machine is to refer to the vacuum hose routing diagram on the inside of the left side cover.*

1 On California models, an evaporative emission control (EVAP) system captures raw hydrocarbon vapors from the carburetor float bowls and the fuel tank when the engine is not running. The vapors are stored in a canister located below the radiator **(see illustration)**. When the engine is started, these vapors are routed from the canister into the combustion chambers and burned.

2 The EVAP system is controlled by the carburetor air vent (CAV) control valve **(see illustration)** and the purge control valve. When the engine is started, both valves are opened by intake vacuum. Vacuum from the front intake opens the carburetor air vent valve, venting the carburetor float bowls through the air vent valve to the canister; vacuum from the rear intake opens the purge control valve, drawing vapors from the canister through the purge control valve into the intakes. When the engine is turned off, intake vacuum is cut, closing the valves. The principal components of the EVAP system have

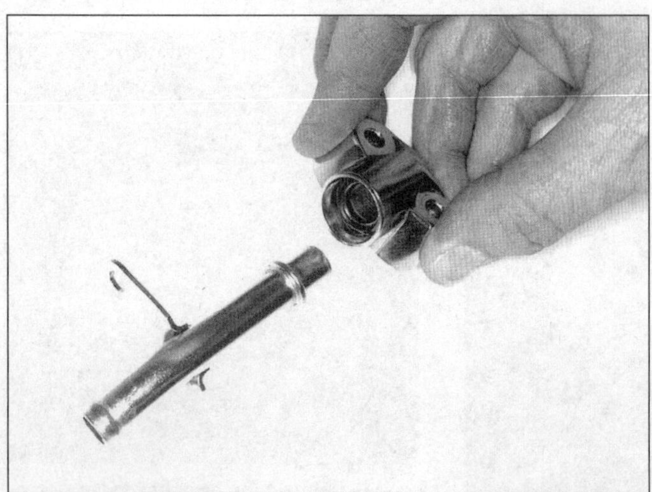
4.11 Pull the pipe out of the adapter and replace the O-ring

5.1 The EVAP canister is located below the radiator; make sure that all hoses are in good condition and are securely attached to the canister

5.2 The carburetor air vent control valve is located on the right side of the carburetors; the forward hose (right arrow) goes to the vacuum port for the right carburetor and the upper hose (left arrow) goes to the three-way joint pipe between the carburetors

5.8 This hose (arrow) vents the air vent control valve to the atmosphere

changed little since 1986. If you're inspecting or servicing the EVAP system on a 1985 model, it has a purge control valve but it doesn't have a "vacuum air control valve" (Honda's original name for what since 1994 has been referred to as the "carburetor air vent control valve," which is the terminology used here); the vacuum air control valve/carburetor air vent control valve was added in 1986.

3 When the fuel inside the carburetor float bowls heats up, vapors from the float bowls are pushed into the canister. When fuel inside the fuel tank heats up, vapors from the fuel tank are pushed into the canister. These vapors are stored in the canister until the next time the engine is started.

4 Periodically, inspect the hoses connecting the canister, the carburetor air vent control valve and the purge control valve and the carburetors (refer to the vacuum hose routing diagram inside the left side cover).

Check and component replacement

5 Remove the fuel tank (see Section 2).

6 Remove the left side cover (see Chapter 8) and refer to the vacuum hose routing diagram on the inside of the cover for the following inspection and component tests.

7 Make sure that all the hose connections are tight, the hoses are in good condition and none of the hoses are kinked. If any of the hoses are torn, frayed or otherwise deteriorated, replace them.

Carburetor air vent control valve

Note: *You will need a vacuum pump/gauge and a pressure pump/gauge to do the following test. If you don't have these tools, have the carburetor air vent control valve checked by a dealer service department.*

8 Mark the four hoses attached to the carburetor air vent control valve to ensure correct reassembly, then disconnect the upper hoses **(see illustration 5.2)** and lower hoses **(see illustration)** from the carburetor air vent control valve and remove the valve.

9 Connect a hand-held vacuum pump/gauge to the valve port **(see illustration)** for the hose which goes to a vacuum port on the right carburetor (front cylinder). Apply 250 mm Hg (9.8 in-Hg) and verify that the valve holds vacuum. If it doesn't, replace the valve.

10 Connect the vacuum pump/gauge to the air vent port on top of the valve, apply 250 mm Hg (9.8 in-Hg) and verify that the valve holds vacuum. If it doesn't, replace the valve.

11 Reconnect the vacuum pump/gauge to the port for hose that goes to the right carburetor vacuum port and connect a *hand-operated* (no compressed air!) pressure pump/gauge to the air vent port. Apply 250 mm Hg (9.8 in-Hg) vacuum to the lower port, pump some air into the air vent port and verify that air exits from the port for the hose which goes to the air vent joint pipe between the carburetors. If it doesn't, replace the valve.

12 If the carburetor air vent control valve fails to perform as described, replace it. Make sure that the hoses are reattached to the valve as indicated by the vacuum hose routing diagram label on the left side cover. Install the left side cover and the fuel tank.

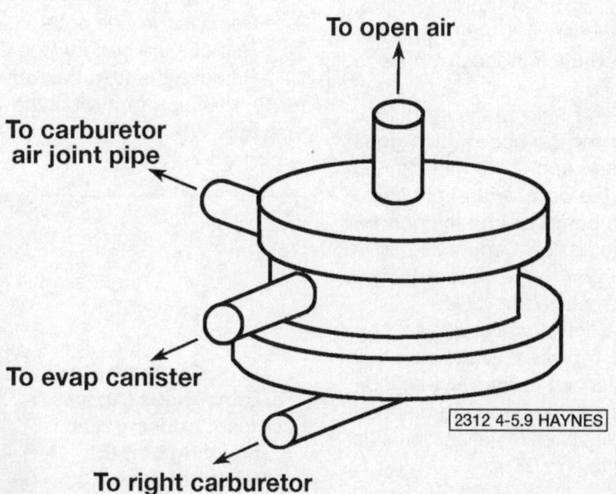

5.9 Carburetor air vent control valve (California models)

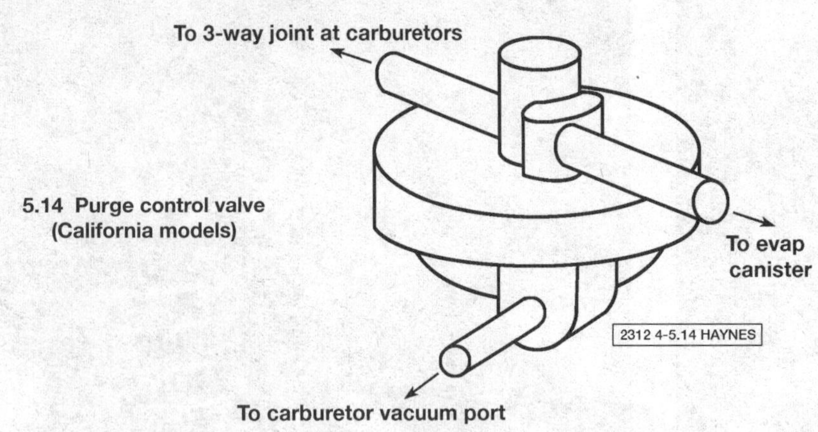

5.14 Purge control valve (California models)

5.19 To detach the EVAP canister, disconnect the hoses at each end and remove the mounting bolts (arrows)

Purge control valve

Note: *You will need a vacuum pump/gauge and a pressure pump/gauge to do the following tests. If you don't have these tools, have the purge control valve checked by a dealer service department.*

13 The purge control valve is located in the extreme forward area between the front cylinder head and the radiator, on the right side, directly below the cooling system pressure cap and behind a frame gusset. Mark the three hoses attached to the purge control valve to ensure correct reassembly, then disconnect all three hoses from the purge control valve and remove the valve.

14 Connect a hand-held vacuum pump/gauge to the output port **(see illustration)** for the hose which goes to the three-way joint and then to the carburetors. Apply 250 mm Hg (9.8 in-Hg) vacuum and verify that the valve holds this vacuum. If it doesn't, replace the valve.

15 Disconnect the vacuum pump from the output port and connect it to the port for the hose which goes to the vacuum port of the left carburetor (rear cylinder). Apply 250 mm Hg (9.8 in-Hg) vacuum and verify that the valve holds the vacuum. If it doesn't, replace the valve.

16 Connect a hand-held pressure pump/gauge to the port for the hose which goes to the EVAP canister. Apply 250 mm Hg (9.8 in-Hg) vacuum to the port for the rear cylinder carburetor and pump air into the port for the canister. Air should flow through the valve and out the output port to the three-way joint hose. If it doesn't, replace the valve.

17 If the purge control valve fails to perform as described, replace it. Make sure that the hoses are reattached to the valve as indicated by the vacuum hose routing diagram label on the left side cover. Install the left side cover and the fuel tank.

EVAP canister

18 Detach the hoses from both ends of the canister **(see illustration 5.1)**.

19 Remove the canister mounting bolts and remove the canister **(see illustration)**.

20 Installation is the reverse of removal.

6 Air cleaner housing - removal and installation

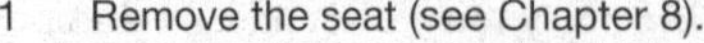

1 Remove the seat (see Chapter 8).

2 Remove the main fuel tank (1985 and 1986 models) or the fuel tank (see Section 2).

1985 and 1986 models

3 Unhook the rubber cover from the air cleaner housing.

4 Detach the electrical harness for the fuel and coolant temperature gauges from the clamp on the housing.

5 Remove the three air cleaner housing mounting bolts.

6 Lift the housing slightly, slide back the wire retainers for breather hose and drain tube and detach both from the air cleaner housing.

7 Remove the air cleaner housing.

8 Installation is the reverse of removal.

1987 and later models

9 Remove the side covers (see Chapter 8).

10 Remove the battery (see Chapter 9).

11 Remove the fuse box cover (see Chapter 9), the fuse box retaining bolts and the fuse box.

12 Remove the ignition control module (see Chapter 5).

13 Detach the starter motor cable and ground cable from the battery holder.

14 Remove the battery holder (see Chapter 9).

15 On 1987 through 1996 VT1100C models, remove the rear fender (see Chapter 8).

16 On VT1100C2, VT1100T and 1997-on VT1100C models, remove the swingarm (see Chapter 6).

17 On 1987 through 1996 VT1100C models, remove the bolt that attaches the coolant reservoir filler neck to the air cleaner housing.

18 On 1987 through 1996 VT1100C models, remove the connector box cover and unplug the electrical connectors. On VT1100C2 models, detach the electrical connector bracket from the top of the air cleaner housing (see Section 13 in Chapter 1) and set the bracket and harnesses aside. If the bracket still interferes with the air cleaner, clearly label and unplug the connectors and disengage them from the bracket.

19 Detach the crankcase breather hose from the front right corner of the air cleaner assembly **(see illustration)**.

20 Remove the tool kit.

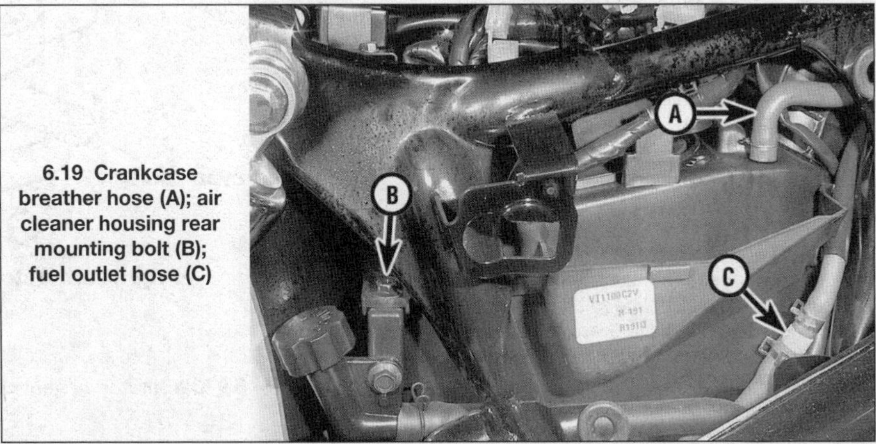

6.19 Crankcase breather hose (A); air cleaner housing rear mounting bolt (B); fuel outlet hose (C)

6.21 **Remove the plug from the air cleaner housing drain tube and pull the tube out of its guide**

6.22 **Disconnect the fuel pump wires (A) from the relay, disconnect the filter hoses (B) and pump hoses (C), then remove the air cleaner housing**

21 Disengage the lower end of the air cleaner housing drain tube from its guide on the frame **(see illustration)**.

22 Detach the fuel hoses from the fuel filter and fuel pump **(see illustration)**.

23 Remove the two front air cleaner housing mounting bolts and remove the single rear housing mounting bolt **(see illustration 6.19)**.

24 Loosen the clamp that secures the air intake duct to the air cleaner housing and disengage the duct from the air cleaner housing.

25 Remove the air cleaner housing.

26 Detach the fuel pump and fuel filter assembly from the underside of the air cleaner assembly (see Section 9).

27 Installation is the reverse of removal.

7 Air intake ducts - removal and installation

1 Remove the seat (see Chapter 8).

2 Remove the fuel tank (see Section 2).

3 Remove the crankcase breather separator (see Section 4).

4 Loosen the three clamp screws **(see illustration)** and remove the air intake ducts.

5 Installation is the reverse of removal.

8 Sub-air cleaner - removal and installation

Note: *This procedure applies only to VT1100T and 1997-on VT1100C models.*

1 Remove the seat (see Chapter 8).

2 Remove the fuel tank (see Section 2.

3 Remove the air intake ducts (see Section 7).

4 The sub-air cleaner is the small black box sandwiched between the upper frame crossmember and the carburetors. To remove the sub-air cleaner, simply detach the sub-air cleaner hoses from both carburetors and remove the sub-air cleaner assembly.

5 Installation is the reverse of removal.

9 Fuel pump system - check and component replacement

Warning: Gasoline (petrol) is extremely flammable, so take extra precautions when you work on any part of the fuel system. Don't smoke or allow open flames or bare light bulbs near the work area, and don't work in a garage where a gas-type appliance (such as a water heater or clothes dryer) is present. If you spill any fuel on your skin, rinse it off immediately with soap and water. When you perform any kind of work on the fuel system, wear safety glasses and have a fire extinguisher suitable for class B fires (flammable liquids) on hand.

System check

1985 and 1986 models

1 Remove the right side cover (see Chapter 8) and locate the fuel cut-off relay, right below the battery. The relay has three wires: black, blue, and black/blue.

2 Touch the positive probe of a voltmeter to the terminal for the black/blue wire and the negative probe to ground. Make sure the kill switch is on, then turn the ignition switch to ON and verify that there is no voltage.

3 Press the starter button momentarily and verify that there is continuous voltage.

4 If the relay fails either test, replace it.

All other models

5 Make sure that the ignition switch is off before proceeding.

6 On 1987 through 1993 models, remove the left side cover (see Chapter 8) and unplug the two fuel pump electrical connectors, a white three-pin connector (black, blue/yellow and black/yellow wires) and a single-pin connector (green wire).

7 On 1994 and later models, remove the seat (see Chapter 8), disconnect the fuel cut-off relay from its mounting stay and unplug the relay connector.

8 Turn the ignition switch to ON and check for voltage between the following terminals: On 1987 through 1993 models, check for voltage between the terminals for the black (positive) and green (negative) wires. On 1994 and later models, check for voltage between the terminal for the black (positive) wire and ground. On all models, there should be battery voltage with the ignition switch turned to ON.

9 If there is no voltage on a 1987 through 1993 model, check the circuit for a break in the wiring or a loose or corroded connection.

1994 and later models only

10 If there is no voltage on a 1994 or later model, check the black wire for a break or a loose or corroded connection.

7.4 **The air intake duct is secured by three clamps (right carburetor clamp shown)**

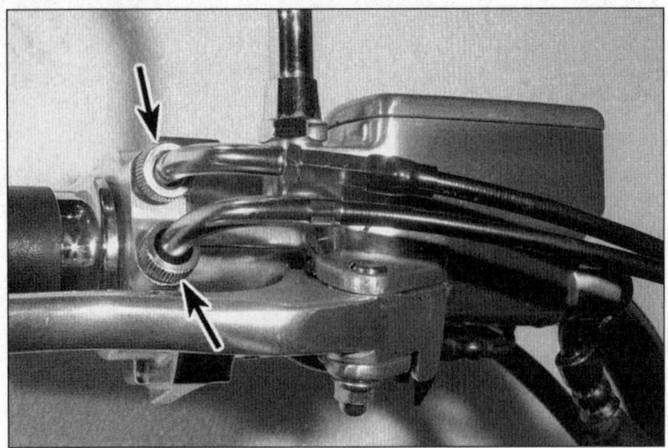

10.2 Before opening up the switch housing, loosen the throttle cable-to-switch housing locknuts (arrows)

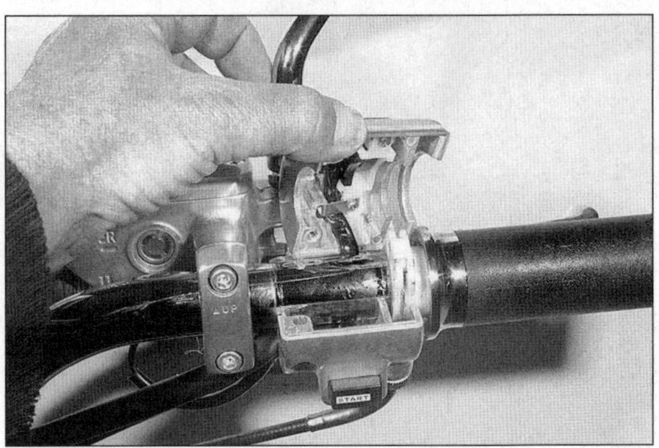

10.3a Remove the switch housing retaining screws from the underside of the lower half of the housing, then open up the switch housing

11 If there is voltage, check for continuity between the terminal for the black/blue wire and ground.
12 If there is continuity between the terminal for the black/blue wire and ground, replace the fuel cut-off relay.
13 If there is no continuity, short the relay connector terminals for the black and black/blue wires with a jumper wire, disconnect the black 2-pin fuel pump connector and, with the ignition switch turned to ON, check for battery voltage between the terminals for the black/blue and green wires.
14 If there is battery voltage, replace the fuel pump.
15 If there is no battery voltage, check for an open circuit or loose connection in the black/blue and green wires.

Fuel pump discharge volume check

16 The fuel pump system may check out okay but still deliver poor performance. If the engine lacks power or accelerates poorly, the fuel pump may be wearing out. Check the fuel pump discharge volume as follows.

1985 and 1986 models

17 Make sure that the ignition switch is off.
18 Remove the right side cover (see Chapter 8) and locate the fuel pump relay below the battery (it has three wires: black, blue, and black/blue). Unplug the connector for the fuel pump relay and short the terminals for the black and black/blue wires.
19 The fuel pump is mounted on the frame, right in front of the relay. Disconnect the fuel outlet hose from the pump, install a short section of hose in its place and put a graduated beaker under the other end of the hose.
20 Turn the ignition switch to ON and let fuel flow into the beaker for five seconds, then turn the ignition switch to OFF.
21 Multiply the amount in the beaker by 12 to determine the fuel pump discharge volume and compare your measurement to the discharge volume listed in this Chapter's Specifications.
22 If the fuel pump discharge volume is low, replace the pump.

All other models

23 On 1987 and later VT1100C models and on VT1100T models, remove the fuel tank mounting bolts (see Section 2) so that you can lift up the tank to get to the fuel hose from the T-joint between the carburetors.
24 On VT1100C2 models, remove the right side cover (see Chapter 8) and disconnect the fuel hose from the hose joint **(see illustration 6.19)**.
25 Put a graduated beaker under the outlet hose.
26 On 1987 through 1990, 1992 and 1993 models, short the terminals for the black/yellow and black wires with a jumper wire (the black/yellow wire terminates at the connector; its only purpose is for this test).
27 On 1994 and later models, short the terminals of the fuel cut-off relay connector for the black and black/blue wires with a jumper wire.
28 Turn the ignition switch to ON and allow fuel to flow into for five seconds, then turn the ignition switch to OFF. To determine the fuel pump discharge volume per minute, multiply by 12. Compare your measurement to the minimum fuel pump discharge volume listed in this Chapter's Specifications.
29 If the pump fails to deliver the minimum discharge volume, replace it.

Replacement

Fuel pump relay

30 On 1987 through 1993 models, remove the left side cover (see Chapter 8), remove the old relay and install a new one.
31 On 1994 and later models, remove the seat (see Chapter 8), remove the old relay and install a new one.

Fuel pump

32 On 1985 and 1986 models, the fuel pump is mounted on the frame on the right side of the bike. Simply unplug the electrical connector for the pump, disconnect the inlet and outlet hoses and detach the pump from its mounting bracket.
33 On all other models, the fuel pump and fuel filter are attached to the bottom of the air cleaner housing. Remove the air cleaner housing (see Section 6), then detach the fuel pump and filter from the air cleaner housing.
34 Installation is the reverse of removal.

10.3b Disengage the upper ends of both cables from the throttle grip pulley

10 Throttle cables and grip - removal, installation and adjustment

Removal

1 Loosen the throttle cable adjuster (see Section 9 in Chapter 1).
2 Back off the throttle cable-to-switch housing locknuts **(see illustration)**.
3 Remove the handlebar switch retaining screws. Separate the halves of the handlebar switch and detach the throttle cables from the throttle grip pulley **(see illustrations)**.

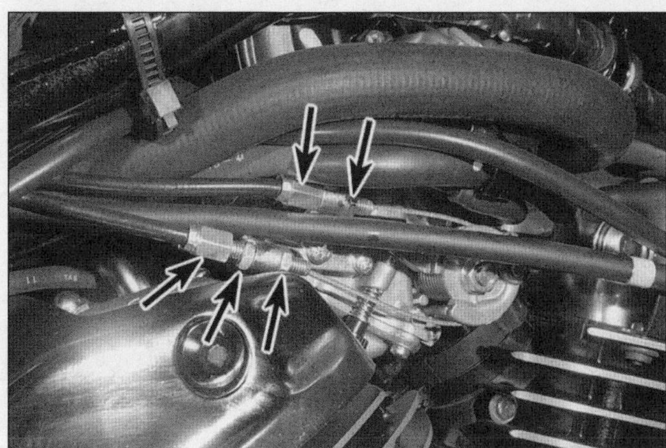

10.4 Loosen the cable adjusters and locknuts (arrows) . . .

10.5 Remove the accelerator cable bracket screws (arrows) and the bracket

4 On 1985 and 1986 models, remove the throttle linkage cover screws and remove the cover. On all models, loosen the cable adjusters and locknuts **(see illustration)**.

5 Remove the throttle cable bracket screws **(see illustration)** and detach the throttle cable bracket from the left carburetor. It's not absolutely necessary to detach the throttle cable bracket to replace the cable(s), but it's easier to disengage the cables from the bracket after it's detached.

6 Detach the throttle cables from the throttle pulley at the carburetors **(see illustration)**. Note how the cables are routed, then remove them.

7 Slide the throttle grip off the handlebar.

Installation

8 Clean the end of the handlebar and the inside of the throttle grip, apply a light coat of multi-purpose grease to both surfaces and install the grip on the handlebar. Verify that it turns freely and smoothly with no binding or rough spots.

9 Route the cables exactly the same way they were routed prior to removal. Make sure they don't interfere with other components and are not kinked or sharply angled.

10 Lubricate the ends of the accelerator and decelerator cables with multi-purpose grease and connect them to the throttle pulleys at the carburetors and at the throttle grip. Make sure that the cable ends are correctly engaged with the pulleys **(see illustration)**.

11 Install the throttle cable bracket. Tighten the screws securely.

Adjustment

12 Adjust the throttle cables (see Section 9 in Chapter 1).

13 Turn the handlebars back and forth to make sure the cables don't cause the steering to bind. With the engine idling, turn the handlebars back and forth and make sure idle speed doesn't change. If it does, find and fix the cause before riding the motorcycle.

11 Carburetor overhaul - general information

1 Poor engine performance, hesitation, hard starting, stalling, flooding and backfiring are all signs that major carburetor maintenance may be required.

2 Keep in mind that many so-called carburetor problems are really not carburetor problems at all, but engine mechanical problems or ignition system malfunctions. Try to verify that the carburetors need to be serviced before beginning a major overhaul.

3 Before assuming that a carburetor overhaul is required, inspect the fuel filter; the fuel lines; the crankcase emission control system hoses; the evaporative emission control system hoses (California models); all vacuum hoses; the hose clamps and connections for the air intake chamber and intake ducts; the air filter element; the sub-air cleaner element; the cylinder compression; the spark plugs; the carburetor synchronization; and the fuel pump.

4 Most carburetor problems are caused by dirt particles, varnish and other deposits which accumulate in, and eventually clog, fuel and air passages. Also, gaskets and O-rings shrink or deteriorate, causing fuel and air leaks which lead to poor performance.

5 A carburetor overhaul consists of disassembly, cleaning, reassembly and adjust-

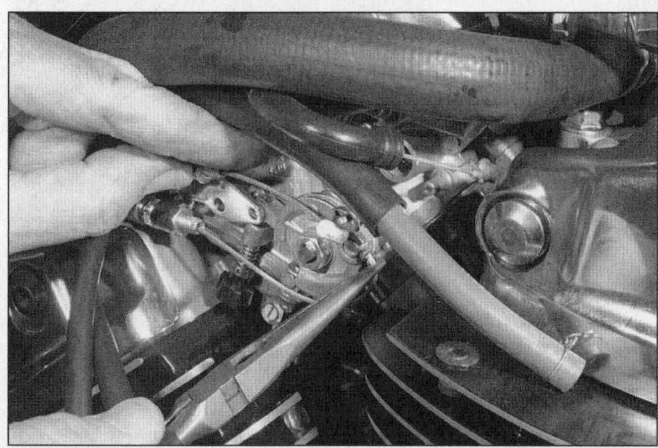

10.6 Disengage the ends of both cables from the throttle pulley

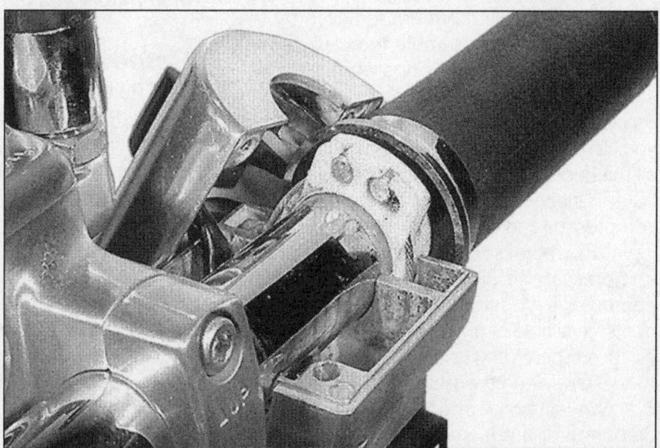

10.10 Make sure that the upper cable ends are correctly engaged with the throttle grip pulley

12.8 Disconnect the fuel hoses at the most convenient connections

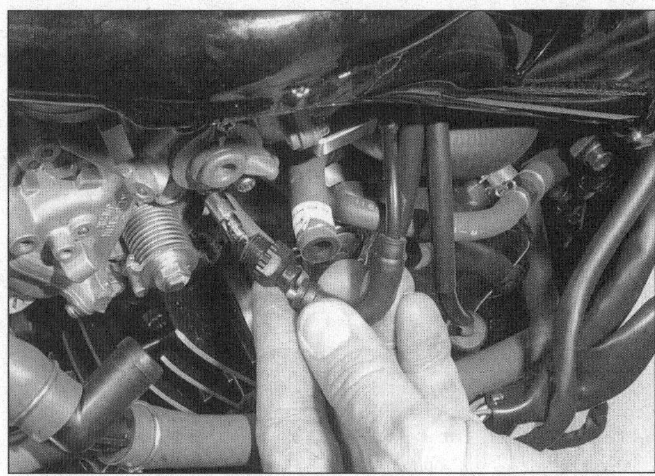

12.10a Unscrew the starting enrichment valve locknuts from each carburetor . . .

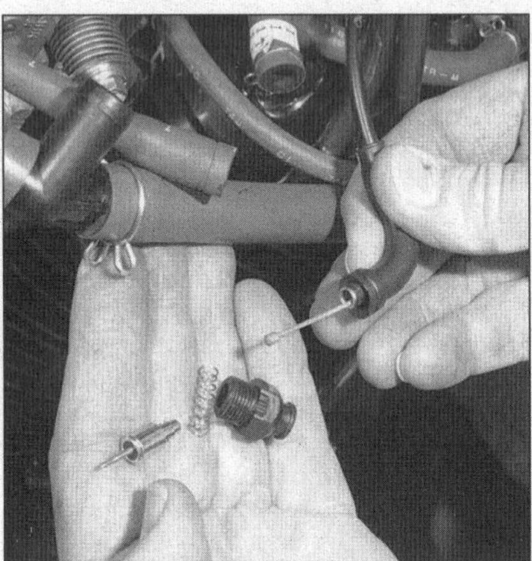

12.10b . . . and separate the SE valve, spring and locknut from each cable

ments. Completely disassemble both carburetors, clean all parts thoroughly with a carburetor cleaning solvent, then dry them with filtered, unlubricated, compressed air. Blow out the fuel and air passages with compressed air to force out any dirt that may have been loosened but not removed by the solvent. Finally, reassemble the carburetors, using new gaskets, O-rings and, if necessary, a new float valve and seat.

6 Before getting started, make sure that you have the correct carburetor rebuild kit with all the necessary O-rings and other parts, carburetor cleaner, some clean shop rags, an air compressor and a place to work. If you don't have a compressor, buy a couple of cans of compressed air (the type used for cleaning computer keyboards and electronic components, available at any office supply store).

7 Overhaul only one carburetor at a time to avoid mixing up parts.

8 We will show you how to separate the carburetors, but it isn't usually necessary to do so. Don't separate the carburetors unless one of the joints between them is leaking, or one of the carburetors must be replaced. The vacuum chamber, the air cut-off diaphragm, the float assembly and the jets can be serviced without separating the carburetors. Achieving correct synchronization can be tricky after disconnecting and reconnecting the carburetors.

12 Carburetors - removal and installation

Warning: Gasoline (petrol) is extremely flammable, so take extra precautions when you work on any part of the fuel system. Don't smoke or allow open flames or bare light bulbs near the work area, and don't work in a garage where a gas-type appliance (such as a water heater or clothes dryer) is present. If you spill any fuel on your skin, rinse it off immediately with soap and water. When you perform any kind of work on the fuel system, wear safety glasses and have an extinguisher suitable for class B fires (flammable liquids) on hand.

Removal

1 Remove the fuel tank (see Section 2).

2 If the carburetors are equipped with drain screws, remove the screws from both float bowls and drain the carburetors into a suitable container.

3 Remove the crankcase breather separator (see Section 4).

4 Remove the air cleaner housing (see Section 6).

5 Remove the air intake ducts (see Section 7).

6 On VT1100T and 1997-on VT1100C models, remove the sub-air cleaner element (see Section 8).

7 Detach all spark plug, clutch cable and hose clamps from the heads.

8 Disconnect the fuel hoses from the carburetors **(see illustration)**.

9 Detach the throttle cable bracket from the left carburetor and disengage the throttle cables from the pulley (see Section 10). Unless you're replacing the throttle cables, it's not necessary to detach them from the cable bracket; they can remain attached to the bracket.

10 Back off the choke cable nuts and disconnect the choke cables and starting enrichment valves from the carburetors **(see illustrations)**.

11 On California models, carefully study how the EVAP hoses are routed, mark them with adhesive labels or colored electrical tape, then detach them from the carburetors. Remove the carburetor air vent control valve (see Section 5), then detach the EVAP hose from the right (front cylinder) carburetor **(see illustration)**. Release the cable clamp and detach the EVAP hose from the left (rear cylinder) carburetor **(see illustrations)**.

12 Loosen the carburetor insulator clamp screws **(see illustration)** and carefully work the carburetors free from the insulators **(see**

12.11a With the air vent control valve out of the way, detach the EVAP hose (arrow) from the right (front cylinder) carburetor

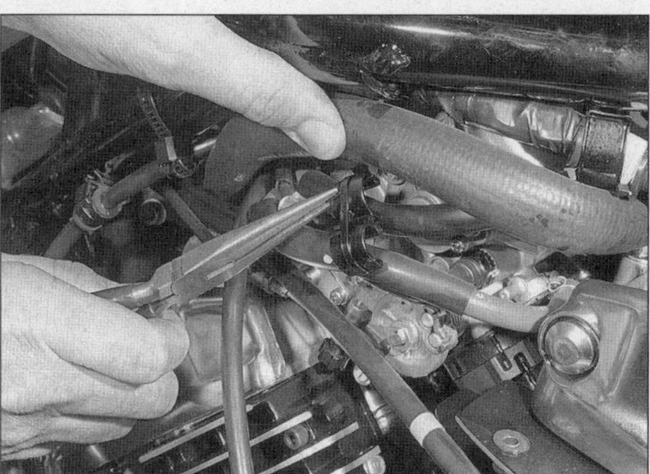

12.11b On the other side, disengage this clamp . . .

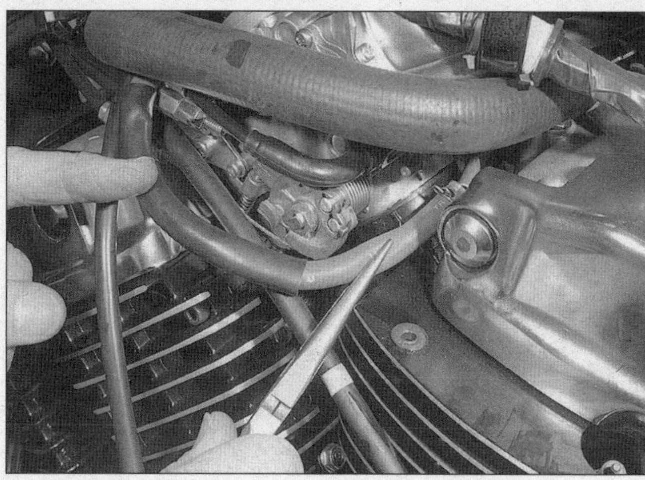

12.11c . . . and detach the EVAP hose from the left (rear cylinder) carburetor

illustration). Use a big screwdriver to pry them out, if necessary. Rotate the carburetors so that they're at a 90-degree angle to their installed position and lift them through the frame **(see illustrations)**. Detach any remaining EVAP hoses and remove the carburetors (again, be sure to label the hoses with adhesive labels or colored electrical tape).

13 After the carburetors have been removed, stuff clean rags into the insulators to prevent the entry of dirt or other objects.

14 Inspect the carburetor insulators. If they're cracked or brittle, replace them.

Installation

15 Place the carburetor assembly in position, reattach the EVAP hoses, then work the carburetors into the insulators, but don't tighten the insulator clamp screws yet.

16 Installation is basically the reverse of removal. After you have installed the starting enrichment valves, reattached the choke cables, connected the throttle cables, reattached the fuel lines and all vacuum hoses, carefully inspect the carburetors and the insulators for any emission or vacuum hoses that might have been accidentally knocked loose and reattach them.

12.12a Loosen both insulator clamp screws . . .

12.12b . . . separate the carburetors from the insulators (gently pry them loose if necessary) . . .

12.12c . . . rotate the carburetors so that they're positioned at a 90-degree angle to their installed position . . .

12.12d . . . and lift them through the frame

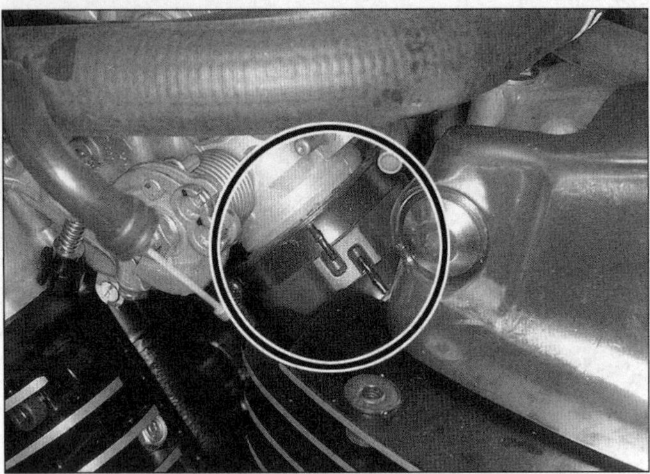

12.17 Before tightening the insulator clamp screws, be sure the pins on the clamps are aligned with the slots in the insulators

13.4 Loosen the synchronizing screw (right arrow) and the two carburetor attaching screws (arrow) (one screw shown; other screw on opposite side)

17 Make sure that both carburetors are seated securely in their insulators and the alignment pins on the clamps are aligned with the slots in the insulators **(see illustration)**, then tighten the clamp screws securely.

18 After the carburetors are installed and all cables, hoses, etc. are reattached, install the sub-air cleaner (VT1100T and 1997-on VT1100C models) and the air intake ducts. Install the fuel tank and the seat.

19 Adjust the throttle grip freeplay (see Chapter 1).

20 Check and, if necessary, adjust the idle speed and carburetor synchronization (see Chapter 1).

13 Carburetors - disassembly, inspection, cleaning and reassembly

Warning: Gasoline (petrol) is extremely flammable, so take extra precautions when you work on any part of the fuel system. Don't smoke or allow open flames or bare light bulbs near the work area, and don't work in a garage where a gas-type appliance (such as a water heater or clothes dryer) is present. If you spill any fuel on your skin, rinse it off immediately with soap and water. When you perform any kind of work on the fuel system, wear safety glasses and have a fire extinguisher suitable for class B type fires (flammable liquids) on hand.

Disassembly

Note: *Work on one carburetor at a time to avoid mixing up the parts, and to give you a "reference carburetor" to refer to if you can't remember how things go back together. As you disassemble each carburetor, store the parts for each sub-assembly in a clearly labeled plastic bag so you don't lose anything.*

1 Remove the carburetors (see Section 12).

2 Place the carburetors on a clean working surface.

3 It's not necessary to separate the carburetors in order to disassemble them. If you're simply rebuilding the carburetors, skip the following Steps and proceed to Step 6. If you are replacing a carburetor, proceed to the next Step.

4 Back off the synchronization adjusting screw and remove the two carburetor attaching screws **(see illustration)**.

5 Pull the two carburetors apart **(see illustration)**, remove the thrust spring and put it in a plastic bag so you don't lose it. Remove the air vent joint and remove the old O-rings from the ends of the joint and discard the O-rings.

6 Remove the float chamber cover screws **(see illustration)** and remove the float chamber cover.

7 Remove the float pivot pin **(see illustration)** and remove the float, the float valve and the float valve retainer.

8 Unscrew and remove the float valve seat, the main jet and the slow jet **(see illustration)**. Don't lose the washer for the float valve seat.

13.5 Pull the two carburetors apart and remove the thrust spring (arrow)

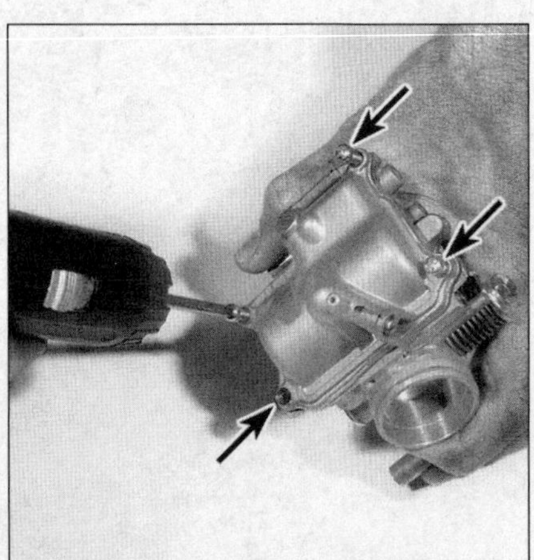

13.6 Remove the float chamber cover screws (arrows) and the cover

9 Center punch the plug for the pilot screw, then drill out the plug with a 4 mm (5/32-inch) drill bit **(see illustration)**. To protect the pilot screw from damage, use a drill stop set to prevent the drill bit from going deeper than 3 mm (1/8-inch). Make sure you don't damage the pilot screw.

10 Screw a self-tapping 4 mm screw (Honda 93903-35410, or equivalent) into the drilled-out plug, grasp the head of the self-tapping screw and pull out the plug **(see illustration)**.

11 Carefully counting the number of turns, screw in the pilot screw until it seats lightly.

Caution: Do NOT keep turning the pilot screw in after you feel it stop; this will damage the screw.

Jot down the number of turns it took to seat the screw; you'll need this number when reassembling the carburetor. Remove the pilot screw, the washer and the O-ring **(see illustrations)**.

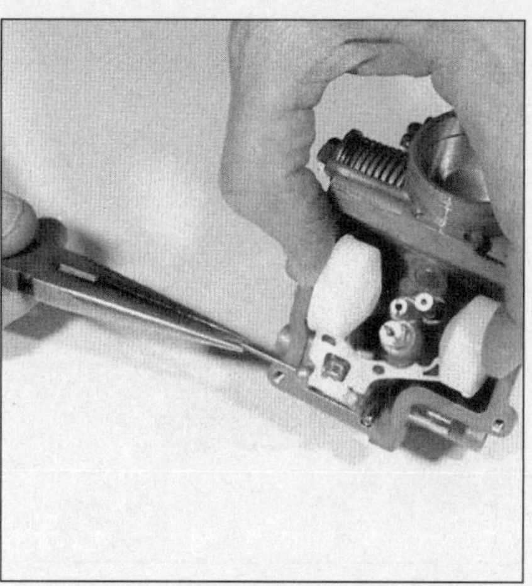

13.7 Pull out the float pivot pin and remove the float, needle valve and its retainer

13.8 Unscrew the float valve seat (1), the main jet (2) and the slow jet (3); don't lose the washer for the float valve seat

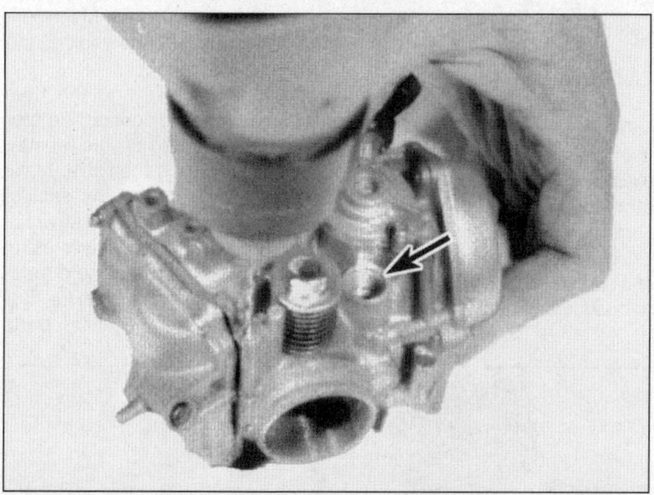

13.9 Drill out the pilot screw plug with a 5/32-inch drill bit; don't drill deeper than 1/8-inch or you may damage the pilot screw

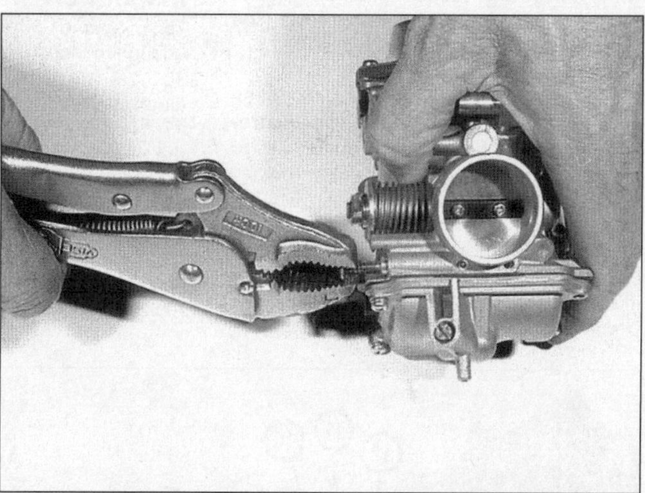

13.10 Thread a self-tapping screw into the drilled-out plug, then pull out the screw together with the plug

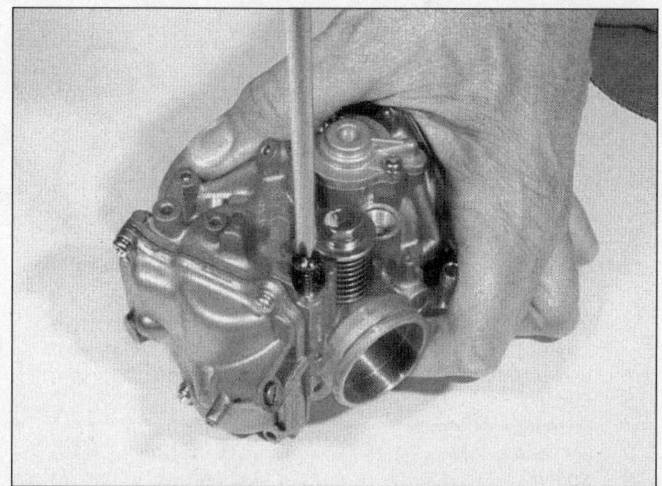

13.11a Carefully count the number of turns until the pilot screw seats lightly and write the number down

13.11b Remove the pilot screw, then remove the washer and the O-ring

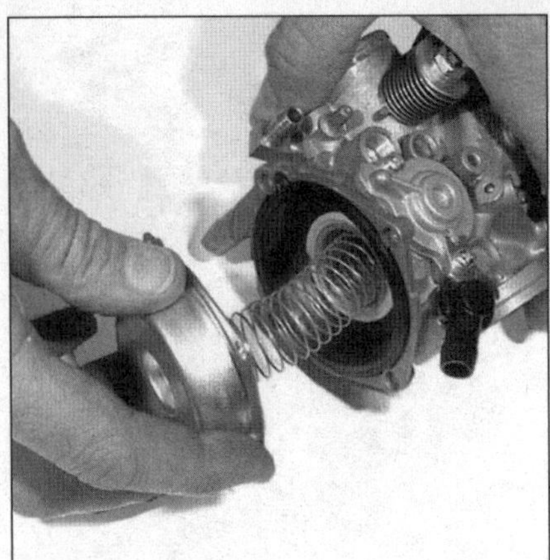

13.12 Remove the vacuum chamber cover screws, cover, spring and piston/diaphragm assembly

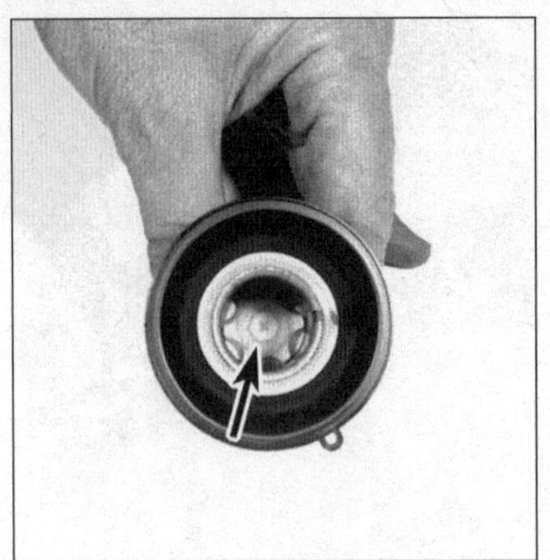

13.13 Push down on the jet needle holder with a Phillips screwdriver, turn it 1/4-turn counterclockwise, then remove the holder, spring and jet needle

13.14 Remove the air cut-off valve cover, spring and diaphragm; remove and discard the old U-ring

12 Remove the vacuum chamber screws and remove the vacuum chamber cover **(see illustration)**. Remove the spring and the piston/diaphragm assembly.

13 Using a Phillips screwdriver, push down on the jet needle holder **(see illustration)**, turn it counterclockwise 90 degrees to unlock it, and remove the jet needle holder, the spring and the jet needle.

14 Remove the air cut-off valve cover screws and remove the air cut-off valve cover, the spring and the diaphragm **(see illustration)**. Remove and discard the old U-ring.

Inspection

15 Clean or wipe off all the parts well enough to inspect them.

16 Lay out all the parts for inspection **(see illustrations)**.

17 Operate the throttle shaft to make sure the throttle butterfly valve opens and closes smoothly. If it doesn't, replace the carburetor.

18 Inspect the carburetor body, the float chamber cover and the vacuum chamber cover for cracks, distorted sealing surfaces and other damage. If either cover is damaged, replace it. If the carburetor body is damaged, you'll have to replace the entire carburetor.

19 Inspect the float for damage. Make sure it's not cracked or leaking (this is usually indicated by fuel inside the float).

20 Inspect the float valve and the float valve seat for scratches and scoring; if a pronounced groove has formed on the tapered portion of the valve, replace the valve. Make sure there are no deposits on the sealing surface of the valve or the valve seat which might prevent the valve from fully closing against the seat. Make sure that no deposits on the bore of the seat are blocking fuel flow through the seat. If any of these parts

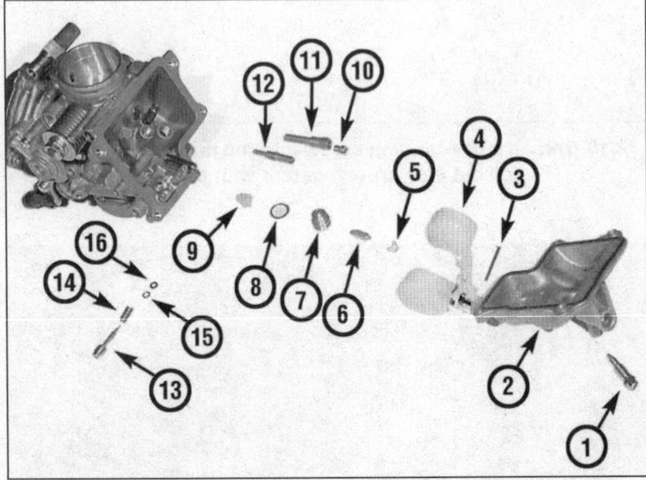

13.16a Float assembly, jets and pilot screw assembly

1 *Drain screw*
2 *Float chamber cover*
3 *Needle valve pin*
4 *Needle valve*
5 *Retainer*
6 *Needle valve*
7 *Needle valve seat*
8 *Needle valve seat washer*
9 *Needle valve seat filter*
10 *Main jet*
11 *Needle jet holder*
12 *Slow jet*
13 *Pilot screw*
14 *Spring*
15 *Washer*
16 *O-ring*

13.16b Vacuum chamber and air cut-off diaphragm assemblies

1 *Vacuum chamber cover screws*
2 *Vacuum chamber cover*
3 *Spring*
4 *Piston/diaphragm*
5 *Jet needle holder*
6 *Spring*
7 *Jet needle*
8 *Air cut-off diaphragm cover screw*
9 *Air cut-off diaphragm cover screw/bracket*
10 *Air cut-off diaphragm cover*
11 *Spring*
12 *Diaphragm*
13 *O-ring*
14 *Elbow fitting for sub-air cleaner hose*

13.30 Align the positioning tab on the edge of the diaphragm with the cavity in the carburetor body (arrow)

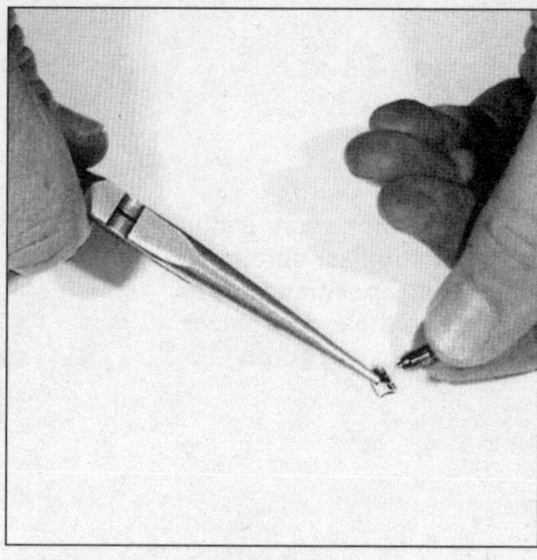

13.34a Reassemble the needle valve and retainer . . .

are damaged, replace them. There's a small filter in the seat; make sure it's not clogged or damaged.

21 Inspect the jets. Make sure that the passages through the jets are clean and free of deposits.

22 Inspect the tapered part of the pilot screw for wear and damage. Make sure the spring is in good shape. Replace any worn or damaged parts.

23 Inspect the spring for the vacuum piston; make sure it's not kinked or distorted. Inspect the vacuum chamber diaphragm for cracks, holes, tears and general deterioration (holding it up to a light will help to reveal problems of this nature). Inspect the surface of the vacuum chamber piston for scratches, scoring and excessive wear. Insert the piston in the piston bore in the carburetor body and note whether it moves up and down smoothly in the piston bore. If it doesn't move smoothly in the bore, replace the carburetor. Inspect the tip of the jet needle for excessive wear. Make sure it's not bent. A good way to check the jet needle for straightness is to roll it on a flat surface, such as a piece of glass. If the jet needle is damaged, replace it.

24 Inspect the spring for the air cut-off diaphragm; make sure it's in good shape. Inspect the air cut-off diaphragm for cracks, holes and tears. If it's damaged, replace it.

Cleaning

Caution: Use only a petroleum based solvent for carburetor cleaning. Don't use caustic cleaners.

25 Submerge the metal components in the solvent for about thirty minutes (or longer, if the directions recommend it).

26 After the carburetor has soaked long enough for the cleaner to loosen and dissolve most of the varnish and other deposits, use a brush to remove the stubborn deposits. Rinse it again, then dry it with compressed air. Blow out all of the fuel and air passages in the main body.

Caution: Never clean the jets or passages with a piece of wire or a drill bit, as they will be enlarged, causing the fuel and air metering rates to be upset.

27 Thoroughly wash the vacuum chamber diaphragm and the air cut-off valve diaphragm with soap and water, then rinse them off with clean water.

Reassembly

Note: *When reassembling the carburetors, be sure to use the new O-rings, gaskets and other parts supplied in the rebuild kit.*

28 Install a new U-ring with its flat side toward the carburetor. Install the air cut-off diaphragm, spring and cover. Tighten the cover screws securely.

29 Install the jet needle, spring, and jet needle holder in the vacuum piston. Push down on the jet needle holder and turn it clockwise 90 degrees to lock it into place.

30 Install the vacuum diaphragm/piston assembly in the piston bore. Make sure that the lip on the underside of the diaphragm is seated in the groove in the carburetor casting and the positioning tab on the edge of the diaphragm is aligned with the cavity in the groove **(see illustration)**.

31 Install the spring and the vacuum chamber cover. As you compress the spring, make sure you keep it straight. And don't pinch the diaphragm. Install the cover screws and tighten them securely.

32 Install the needle jet holder, main jet and slow jet.

Caution: Don't overtighten the jets. Because they're made of soft brass, it's easy to strip the threads.

33 Install the float valve seat/filter. Again, don't overtighten it.

34 Assemble the float valve, retainer and float **(see illustrations)**.

35 Place the float assembly in position and secure it with the float pin. Make sure that the float valve is correctly seated on the float valve seat and the float valve retainer is correctly engaged with the float **(see illustration)**.

36 Using a carburetor float level gauge (Honda special tool 07401-0010000), check

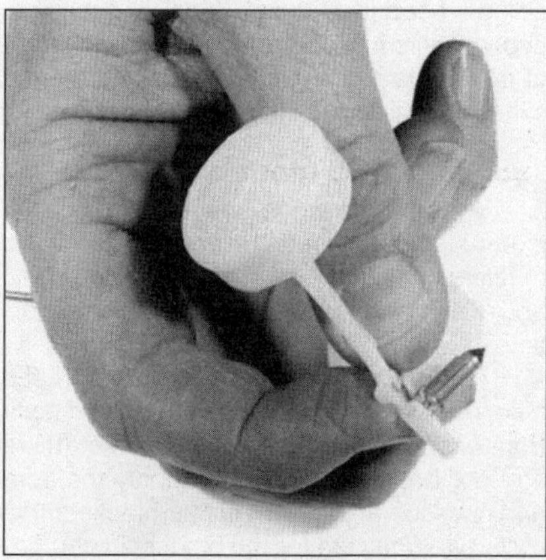

13.34b . . . and attach them to the float

13.35 Install the float and its pivot pin; make sure the needle valve is correctly seated and the needle valve retainer is correctly engaged with the float

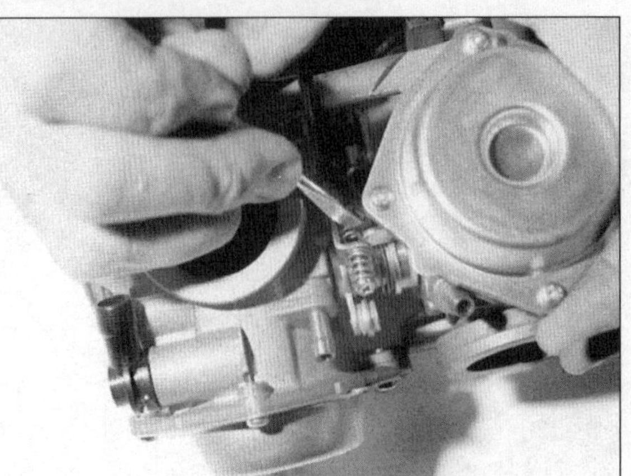

13.44 Make sure each synchronizer spring is correctly positioned, then tighten the synchronizer adjusting screw

the float level. Place the carburetor(s) on a bench with the float chamber on its side, so that the float is hanging from its pivot pin. Place the gauge so that it's perpendicular to the machined face of the float chamber and position it so that it's aligned with the main jet. Check the float level and compare your measurement to the float level listed in this Chapter's Specifications. If the float level is incorrect, replace the float assembly.

37 Install the float chamber cover with a new O-ring, install the cover screws and tighten them securely.

38 Install the pilot screw, return it to its original position in accordance with your notes and install a new sealing plug. If you're installing a new pilot screw, establish a baseline by setting it at the same position as the old pilot screw, then - after the carburetors are installed and synchronized - adjust it (see Section 14). Don't install a sealing plug at this time if you're using a new pilot screw.

39 Repeat Steps 6 through 38 for the other carburetor.

40 If you separated the carburetors, reattach them as follows. If not, go to Step 49.

41 Back off the synchronizer adjusting screw **(see illustration 13.4)** to remove spring tension.

42 Put new O-rings on the air vent joint and install the joint in one of the carburetors. Install the thrust spring **(see illustration 13.5)** between the throttle links.

43 Insert the other end of the air vent joint into its hole in the other carburetor and shove the carburetors together to seat the O-rings on both ends of the air vent joint. Reattach the carburetors with the two carburetor attaching screws **(see illustration 13.4)** and tighten the screws securely.

44 Make sure the synchronizer spring is correctly positioned **(see illustration)**, then tighten the synchronizer adjusting screw.

45 Open the throttle slightly by rotating the throttle valve, then release the throttle. It should close quickly and smoothly, without dragging.

46 Turn the throttle stop screw **(see illustration 17.3 in Chapter 1)** to align the throttle valve in the rear carburetor with the edge of the by-pass hole **(see illustration 13.11b)**.

47 Turn the synchronizer adjusting screw **(see illustration 13.4)** to align the throttle valve in the front carburetor with the edge of the by-pass hole.

48 Operate the throttle and verify that it operates smoothly and that both throttle valves are aligned with their respective by-pass holes.

49 Reattach all air and fuel hoses.

50 Install the carburetors (see Section 12).

51 Synchronize the carburetors (see Chapter 1).

14 Idle fuel/air mixture - adjustment

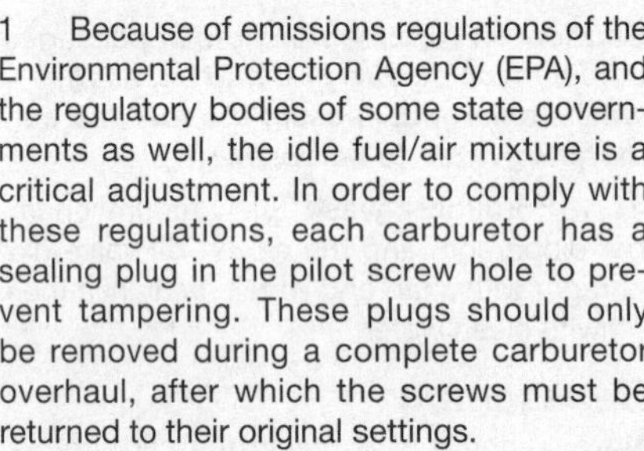

1 Because of emissions regulations of the Environmental Protection Agency (EPA), and the regulatory bodies of some state governments as well, the idle fuel/air mixture is a critical adjustment. In order to comply with these regulations, each carburetor has a sealing plug in the pilot screw hole to prevent tampering. These plugs should only be removed during a complete carburetor overhaul, after which the screws must be returned to their original settings.

2 If you replaced the pilot screws during a carburetor overhaul, adjust the idle fuel/air mixture as follows. Make sure that the carburetors are synchronized (see Chapter 1) before proceeding.

3 Remove each pilot screw plug, if necessary (see Steps 9 and 10 in Section 13).

4 Turn each pilot screw clockwise until it seats lightly, then back it out to the initial opening listed in this Chapter's Specifications.

Caution: Do NOT overtighten the pilot screw; overtightening it will damage it.

5 Start the engine and warm it up to its normal operating temperature.

6 Turn off the engine and hook up a tachometer in accordance with the manufacturer's instructions.

7 Start the engine and adjust the engine idle speed to the idle speed listed in the Chapter 1 Specifications with the throttle stop screw.

8 Back out each pilot screw 1/2-turn from its initial setting.

9 If the engine speed increases by 50 rpm or more, back out each pilot screw another 1/2 turn and continue doing so until the engine speed no longer increases.

10 Adjust the idle speed to the idle speed listed in the Chapter 1 Specifications with the throttle stop screw.

11 Turn in the pilot screw for the rear cylinder carburetor until the engine speed drops 50 rpm.

12 Back out the pilot screw for the rear cylinder carburetor to the final opening listed in this Chapter's Specifications.

13 Adjust the idle speed with the throttle stop screw.

14 Repeat Steps 11, 12 and 13 and adjust the pilot screw for the front cylinder carburetor.

15 Install new sealing plugs into the pilot screw holes with a 7 mm guide driver (on 1985 through 1996 VT1100C models, use Honda special tool 07942-8230000, or equivalent; on VT1100C, VT1100T and 1997-on VT1100C models, use Honda tool 07942-6570100, or equivalent). When each plug is fully seated, its surface is recessed 1 mm (1/32-inch).

16 If the engine runs extremely rough or blows black smoke at idle or continually stalls, and a carburetor overhaul, followed by the preceding adjustment, does not cure the problem, take the motorcycle to a Honda dealer service department, or a motorcycle repair shop, equipped with an exhaust gas analyzer. They will be able to correctly adjust the idle fuel/air mixture to achieve a smooth idle and restore low speed performance.

15 Exhaust system - removal and installation

Removal

Warning: Make sure the engine is cool before performing this procedure.

1 To detach the exhaust pipes from the cylinder heads, remove the four exhaust pipe flange nuts, two per flange, and any washers from the exhaust pipe mounting studs in each cylinder head **(see illustrations)**. Put the nuts and washers in a container. Pull the pipes out of the heads and remove and discard the old exhaust gaskets **(see illustration)**.

1985 and 1986 models

2 At the joints where the rear ends of the exhaust pipes meet the front ends of the mufflers, loosen the clamp bolts.

3 Pull the exhaust pipes out of the mufflers.

4 To detach the muffler assembly from the bike, remove the front and rear nuts and bolts from each passenger footpeg bracket (there are four bolts per bracket, but only the front and rear bolt are for the muffler brackets; the other two bolts are for the bracket itself).

5 Remove the muffler assembly.

15.1a To detach the front exhaust pipe from the front cylinder head, remove these two nuts (arrows) and washers

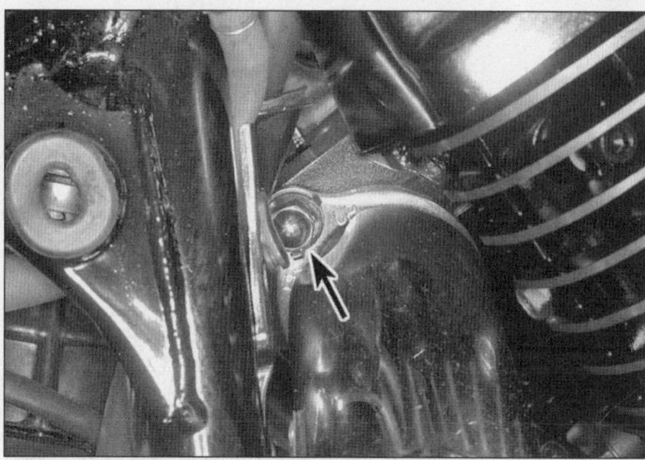

15.1b To detach the rear exhaust pipe from the rear cylinder head, remove the upper nut and washer (arrow) and the lower nut and washer

1987 through 1996 VT1100C models

6 Remove the two nuts that attach the lower muffler (front cylinder exhaust pipe) to the muffler bracket studs and pull the muffler off the studs.

7 Remove the exhaust system (the exhaust pipes and mufflers are a one-piece assembly).

VT1100C2 and 1997-on VT1100C models

8 There is a cover and a protector on each exhaust pipe. Unless you wish to replace one of them, or you plan to replace an exhaust pipe, it's not necessary to remove the cover or the protector in order to remove the exhaust system. However, this is a good time to inspect the length of each pipe for corrosion and other damage, particularly the part of each pipe concealed by the cover (especially if you live in a damp climate).

9 The cover and protector on the front exhaust pipe can be replaced without removing the exhaust system. To remove the cover, remove the single retaining bolt from the lower end of the cover, remove the clamp, pull the cover down to disengage its holders (straps welded to the upper inner edge of the cover) from the header flange tabs and remove it. To install the cover, align the two holders with the two retainer tabs on the header flange, push the cover on firmly, align the hole in the mounting bracket at the lower end of the cover with the threaded hole in the clamp and tighten the bolt securely.

10 Before removing the protector from the front exhaust pipe, be aware that it can NOT be reused. If you remove it, you replace it! To remove the protector, strike it firmly from the rear edge with a plastic hammer or mallet to break the locking tab on the underside of the protector. To install a new protector, place it in position and slide it firmly to the rear until the locking tab snaps into place. To verify that the protector is locked into place, try to move it forward.

11 Using a backup wrench, remove the two nuts and bolts from the lower muffler bracket **(see illustration)**. Using a backup wrench on VT1100C2 models, remove the Allen bolt located ahead of the two muffler bracket bolts **(see illustration)**.

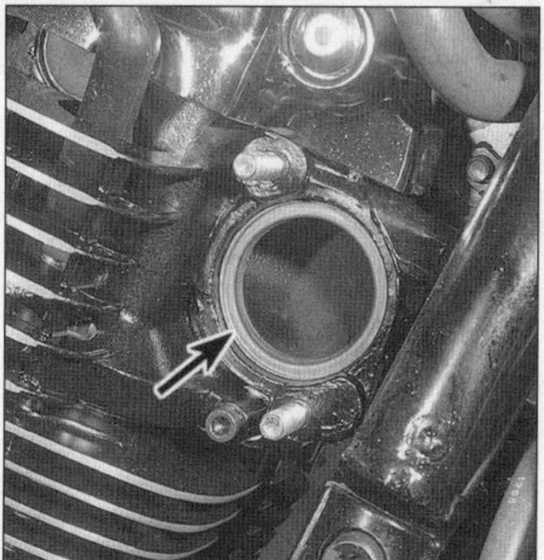

15.1c After detaching the exhaust pipes from the heads, carefully pry out the old gaskets arrow)

15.11a VT1100C2 and 1997-on VT1100C models use two exhaust system mounting bolts (left arrows); VT1100C2 models also use a third bolt (right arrow)

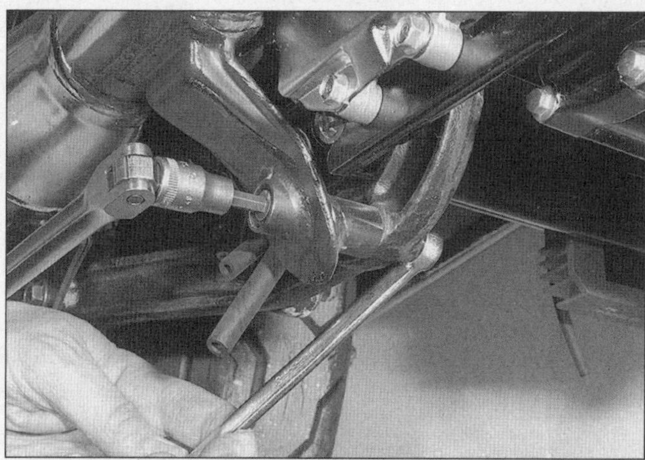

15.11b On VT1100C2 models, use a backup wrench to remove this Allen bolt and nut

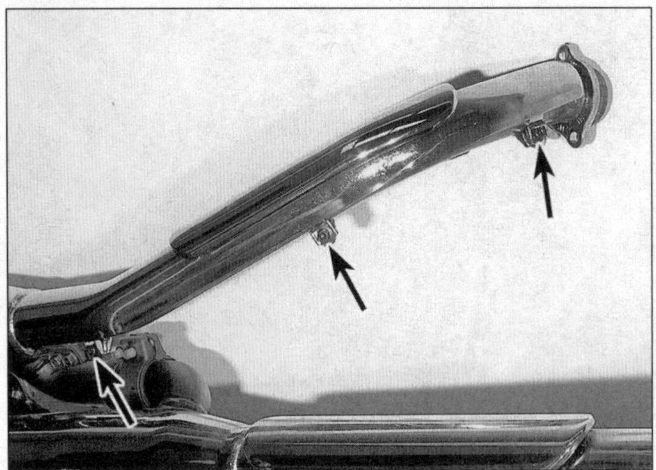

15.13 Here are the exhaust pipe cover Allen bolts on VT1100C2 and 1997-on VT1100C models

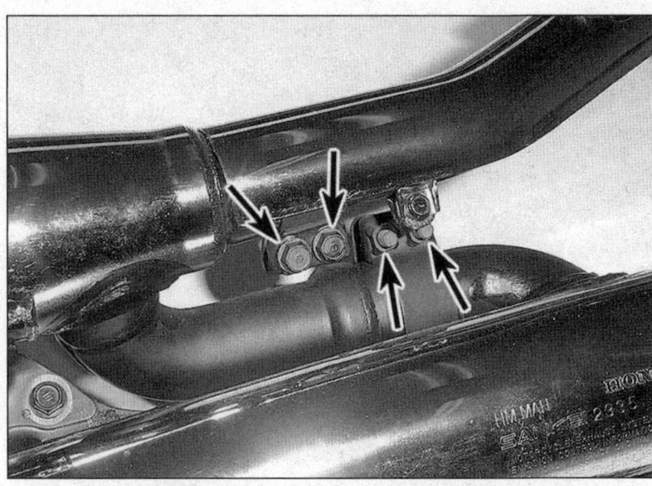

15.14 To separate the front and rear exhaust pipes, remove the two clamp bolts (lower arrows); to detach the rear muffler, remove the other two clamp bolts (upper arrows)

12 Remove the exhaust system as a single assembly.

13 To remove the rear exhaust pipe cover, simply remove the three Allen bolts **(see illustration)**. To remove the protector from the cover, remove the two retaining nuts.

14 If you're replacing a front exhaust pipe and muffler assembly, a rear exhaust pipe separate the two pipes by unbolting them at the crossover pipe **(see illustration)**. If you're replacing the muffler for the rear exhaust pipe, they can be separated by removing two more bolts. The front exhaust pipe, crossover pipe and muffler, however, are a single assembly; if one of these parts is damaged, the entire assembly must be replaced.

VT1100T models

15 These models have a two-into-one-into-two setup to provide adequate clearance for saddlebags. However, they utilize the same exhaust pipe cover and protector setup used by VT1100C2 and 1997-on VT1100C models. To replace the front exhaust pipe cover and/or protector, refer to Steps 8, 9 and 10.

16 Loosen the bolts for the clamps that attach the left and right mufflers to the exhaust pipe assembly.

17 Remove the two muffler bracket bolts from each muffler and remove the mufflers.

18 Remove the exhaust pipe assembly.

19 To replace the rear exhaust pipe and/or protector, refer to Step 13.

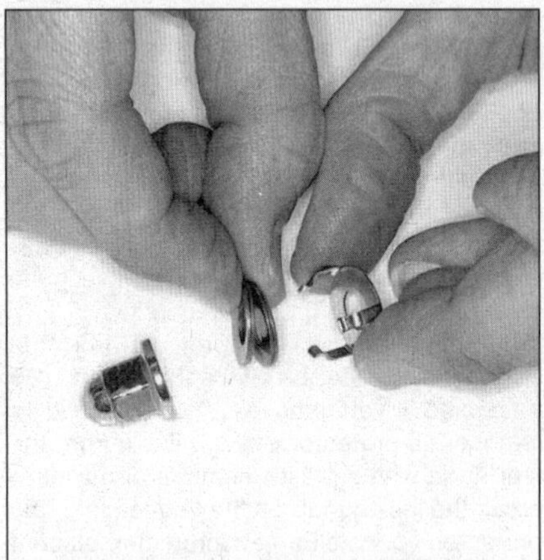

15.21a The exhaust pipe nuts on some later models must be installed with multiple washers; install the washers in the retainer . . .

15.21b . . . then push the nut into the retainer so that it looks like this

20 The mufflers on these models also have covers which can be replaced. To replace a muffler cover, remove the two cover bolts and straps. Installation is the reverse of removal.

Installation

21 Installation is the reverse of removal. Be sure to use new exhaust gaskets. On later models which use multiple washers and washer retainers, make sure that the exhaust pipe retainers, washers and nuts are assembled correctly before installing them (see illustrations). Tighten the exhaust pipe nuts to the torque listed in this Chapter's Specifications. Tighten all other fasteners securely.

Chapter 5
Ignition system

Contents

Degrees of difficulty

Easy, suitable for novice with little experience		**Fairly easy,** suitable for beginner with some experience		**Fairly difficult,** suitable for competent DIY mechanic		**Difficult,** suitable for experienced DIY mechanic		**Very difficult,** suitable for expert DIY or professional	

Specifications

Ignition coil

1985 and 1986	
Primary resistance	Approximately 2 ohms
Secondary resistance	20.6 to 27.4 k-ohms
1987 through 1996 VT1100C	
Primary resistance	2.2 to 2.6 ohms
Secondary resistance	
With plug wires attached	29 to 37 k-ohms
Without plug wires attached	20 to 26 k-ohms
VT1100C2	
Primary resistance	2.1 to 2.7 ohms
Secondary resistance	
With plug cap	24 to 32 k-ohms
Without plug cap	20 to 26 k-ohms
VT1100T and 1997-on VT1100C	
Primary peak voltage	100 volts minimum*

**Peak voltage tester (Honda 07HGJ-020100) required*

Ignition pulse generator(s) (1985 through 1996 VT110C only)

Coil resistance	
1985 through 1990	450 to 550 ohms
1992 through 1996 VT1100C	400 to 500 ohms
Air gap	
1985 and 1986	0.1 to 0.8 mm (0.004 to 0.031 inch)
1987 through 1996 VT1100C	0.30 to 0.70 mm (0.012 to 0.028 inch)

Camshaft pulse generator (1985 and 1986 only)

Coil resistance	570 to 690 ohms
Air gap	0.1 to 0.8 mm (0.004 to 0.031 inch)

Torque specifications

Cam pulse generator bolts (1985 and 1986)	25 to 29 Nm (18 to 21 ft-lbs)

1 General information

These motorcycles are equipped with a battery-operated, fully transistorized, breakerless ignition system. The system consists of the following components:

Spark units I and II (1985 and 1986 models)
Ignition control module (all other models)
Cam pulse generator, crank pulse generators and pulse generator plate (1985 and 1986 models)
Ignition pulse generator(s) and timing rotor (all other models)
Battery and fuse
Ignition coils
Spark plugs
Ignition (main) and engine kill (stop) switches
Primary and secondary circuit wiring

The crank pulse generators or ignition pulse generators are timing devices that signal the ignition control module to turn the primary voltage to the ignition coils on and off. 1985 and 1986 models are equipped with two crank pulse generators, one for each cylinder, and a cam pulse generator (a start-up timing device installed on the end of the rear cylinder camshaft). The cam pulse generator is used only on 1985 and 1986 models. 1987 through 1996 VT1100C models and 1995 and 1996 VT1100C2 models are equipped with two ignition pulse generators, one for each cylinder. VT1100T, VT1100C2 and 1997-on VT1100C models use one ignition pulse generator for both cylinders. Every time a tip of the timing rotor sweeps by the ignition pulse generator, the pulse generator produces a voltage signal to the spark units (1985 and 1986 models) or ignition control module (all other models). The spark unit or module switches primary voltage to the coils on and off in accordance with these signals from the pulse generator(s). With the exception of spark plug replacement, ignition system service is eliminated.

Ignition system components can be checked but they can't be repaired. If ignition system problems occur, the faulty component(s) must be replaced. Most electrical parts cannot be returned, so don't buy anything until you're sure that you have identified the problem.

2 Ignition system - check

***Warning:** Because of the very high voltage generated by the ignition system, extreme care should be taken when these checks are performed.*

1 If the ignition system is the suspected cause of poor engine performance or failure to start, a number of checks can be made to isolate the problem.

2 Make sure the engine kill switch is in the Run position.

Engine will not start

3 Disconnect one of the spark plug wires (there are two for each cylinder), connect the wire to a spare spark plug and lay the plug on the engine with the threads of the plug in contact with the engine. If necessary, hold the spark plug with an insulated tool. Crank the engine over and make sure a well-defined, blue spark occurs between the spark plug electrodes.

***Warning:** Don't remove one of the spark plugs from the engine to perform this check - atomized fuel being pumped out of the open spark plug hole could ignite, causing severe injury!*

4 If no spark occurs, repeat the same test on the *other* spark plug lead of the same coil.

5 If the plug sparks when the second lead is attached, then the first plug wire or cap is defective. Install a new wire and cap and retest.

6 If neither plug wire produces a spark on a 1985 through 1996 VT1100C or VT1100C2 model, check and, if necessary, replace the coil (see Section 3).

7 If neither plug wire produces a spark on a VT1100T or a 1997 or later VT1100C model, try swapping the coils (see Section 3). If the plug wires of the second coil produce a good spark, replace the first coil. No further testing of the ignition coil on these later models is possible without a special diagnostic tester. The coils must be checked by a Honda service department with the necessary diagnostic equipment.

2.16 A simple spark gap testing fixture can be made from a block of wood, a large alligator clip, two nails, a screw and a piece of wire

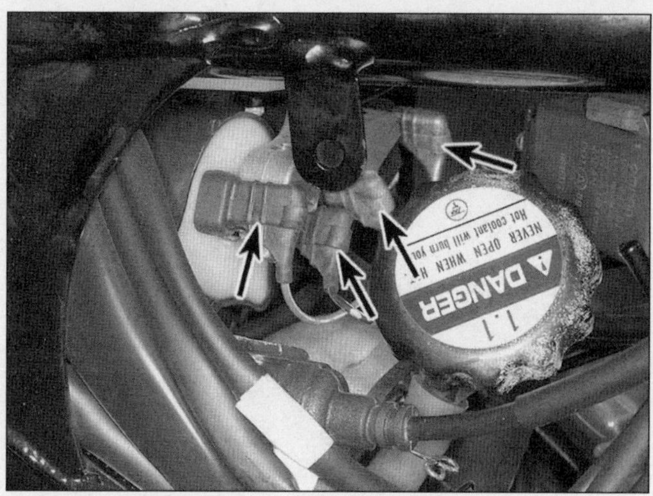

3.3a The primary terminals (arrows) for both coils are on the front ends of the coils

8 Repeat Steps 3 through 5 for the other ignition coil.

9 If both coils are operating satisfactorily, check the rest of the ignition system. Make sure that all electrical connectors are clean and tight. Check all wires for shorts, opens and incorrect installation.

10 Check the battery voltage with a voltmeter and - on models equipped with batteries having removable filler caps - check the specific gravity with a hydrometer (see Chapter 1). If the voltage is less than 12 volts or if the specific gravity is low, recharge the battery.

11 Check the ignition fuse and the fuse connections (see Chapter 9). If the fuse is blown, replace it; if the connections are loose or corroded, clean or repair them.

12 Check the ignition switch, engine kill switch, neutral switch and sidestand switch.

13 On 1985 through 1996 VT1100C models and on VT1100C2 models, check the ignition pulse generator resistance (see Section 4).

14 On VT1100T and 1997-on VT1100C models, the ignition pulse generator(s) cannot be tested without a special diagnostic tester. Have the pulse generator(s) checked by a Honda service department with the necessary diagnostic equipment.

Engine starts but misfires

15 If the engine starts but misfires, make the following checks before deciding that the ignition system is at fault.

16 The ignition system must be able to produce a spark across a six millimeter (1/4-inch) gap (minimum). A simple test fixture **(see illustration)** can be constructed to make sure the minimum spark gap can be jumped. Make sure the fixture electrodes are positioned six millimeters apart.

17 Connect one of the spark plug wires to the protruding test fixture electrode, then attach the fixture's alligator clip to a good engine ground.

18 Crank the engine over (it will probably start and run on the remaining cylinder) and see if well-defined, blue sparks occur between the test fixture electrodes. If the minimum spark gap test is positive, the ignition coil for that cylinder is functioning properly. Repeat the check on one of the spark plug wires connected to the other coil. If the spark will not jump the gap during either test, or if it is weak (orange colored), refer to Steps 3 through 8.

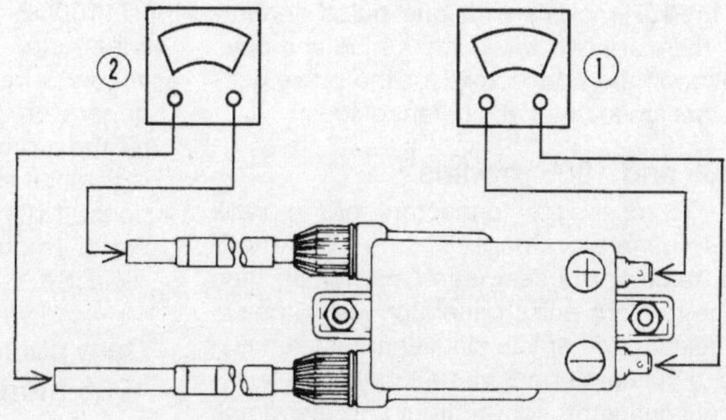

3.3b Ignition coil test (1985 through 1986 models)

1 *Primary resistance*
2 *Secondary resistance*

3 Ignition coils - check and replacement

Check

Note: *The following test applies to the ignition coils used on 1985 through 1996 VT1100C models and to VT1100C2 models. It does not apply to VT1100T and 1997 and later VT1100C models. To determine whether an ignition coil on one of these later models is defective, have it tested by a Honda dealer service department equipped with the necessary diagnostic equipment.*

1 To access the coils, remove the seat (see Chapter 8) and the fuel tank (see Chapter 4).

2 Inspect the coils for cracks and other damage. If either coil is obviously damaged, replace it. If the coils are undamaged, proceed to the next Step.

3 To check the primary resistance of a coil, unplug the electrical connectors from the primary terminals on the front ends of the coils **(see illustration)** and, using an ohmmeter, measure the resistance between these two terminals **(see illustration)**. Compare your measurement to the primary resistance listed in this Chapter's Specifications. If the indicated primary resistance is outside the specified range, replace the coil. If the primary resistance is within range, check the coil secondary resistance.

4 To check the coil secondary resistance, measure the resistance between the two spark plug leads and compare your measure-

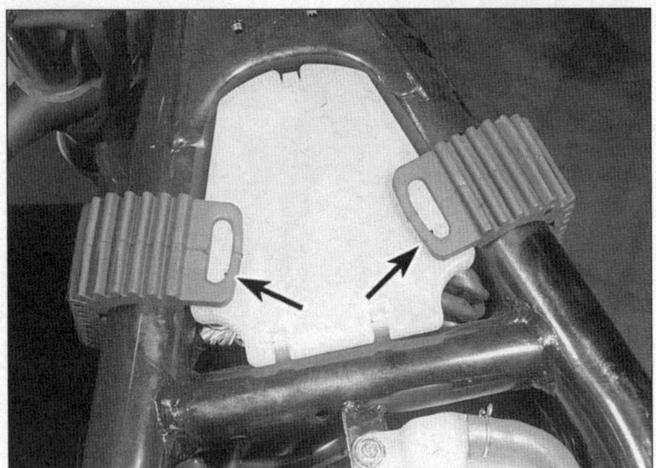

3.5a On all except 1985 and 1986 models, detach the hold-down straps (arrows) from the connector box cover, remove the cover . . .

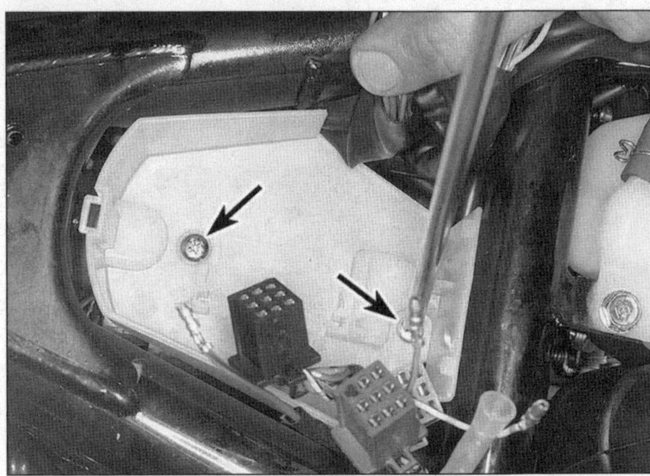

3.5b . . . label and disconnect the connectors inside the box, remove the box retaining screws (arrows) and remove the box

ment to the secondary resistance listed in this Chapter's Specifications. If the indicated secondary resistance is outside the specified range, unscrew the spark plug leads from the coil, measure the resistance between the two coil high tension terminals and compare your measurement to the secondary resistance listed in this Chapter's Specifications. If the indicated secondary resistance is now within the specified range, replace the spark plug high tension leads. If the indicated resistance is still not within the specified range, replace the coil.

Replacement

5 Remove the seat (see Chapter 8), the fuel tank (see Chapter 4) and, on all except 1985 and 1986 models, the connector box **(see illustrations)**.

6 Before detaching the coil, clearly label, then unplug, the primary electrical connectors **(see illustration 3.3a)**.

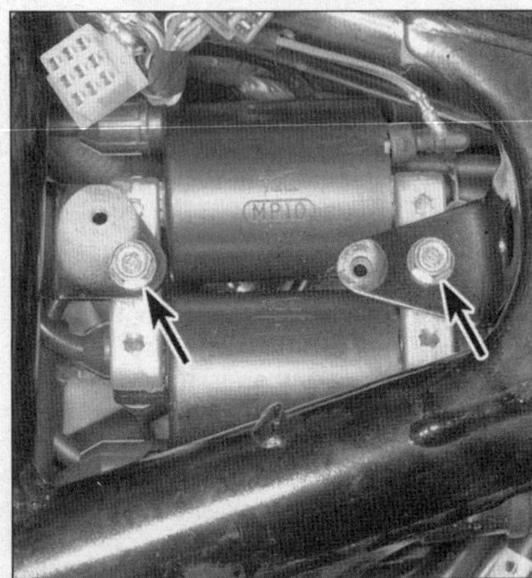

3.8 Disconnect the primary leads and remove the coil mounting bolts (arrows) (1987 and later models shown; 1985 and 1986 similar)

7 Detach the spark plug caps from the front cylinder plugs.

8 Remove the two coil mounting bolts **(see illustration)** and remove the coils. (On 1985 and 1986 models, the coils are also installed in the upper part of the frame, but farther back, above the rear cylinder head; they're also retained by two mounting bolts.)

9 Installation is the reverse of removal.

4 Ignition pulse generator(s) - check and replacement

Check

Note: *The following test applies to the pulse generators used on 1985 and 1986, 1987 through 1990 and 1992 through 1996 VT1100C models and to VT1100C2 models. It does not apply to VT1100T and 1997 and 1998 VT1100C models. In order to determine whether the ignition pulse generator on one of these latter models is defective, have it tested by a Honda dealer service department equipped with the necessary diagnostic equipment.*

1 The four wires for all models with two pulse generators are the same color: white/blue, blue, white/yellow and yellow. On VT1100C2 models with one pulse generator, there are two wires: white/blue and blue. However, the connectors for the pulse generators are located in different places.

1985 and 1986 models

2 To access the connectors for the crank pulse generators on 1985 and 1986 models, remove the seat (see Chapter 8), then trace the four pulse generator wires (they're bundled together in a single harness running along the right upper frame tube) to the electrical connectors for the front and rear crank pulse generators (one two-pin connector and two single connectors). The bigger connector is located at the right end of the connector bracket right in front of the rear fender; the two smaller connectors are located right below it.

1987 through 1996 VT1100C models

3 Remove the left side cover (see Chapter 8).

4 Trace the white/blue, blue, white/yellow and yellow wires to the white four-pin connector behind the ignition key switch. Unplug this connector.

VT1100C2 models

5 Remove the seat for access to the connector bracket (see Chapter 8).

6 On 1995 and 1996 models, trace the white/blue, blue, white/yellow and yellow wires to the white four-pin connector on the bracket next to the air intake (it's the third connector from the front on the bracket). On 1997 and later models, trace the white/blue and blue wires to the *black* four-pin connector **(see illustration)**.

All models

7 Measure the resistance between the white/blue and blue wire terminals for the front pulse generator (on 1997 and later VT1100C2 models, this is the only set of wires) and between the white/yellow and yellow wire terminals for the rear pulse generator. Compare your measurements to the crank or ignition pulse generator resistance listed in this Chapter's Specifications. If the resistance of either pulse generator is outside the specified resistance, replace it.

Cam pulse generator (1985 and 1986 models only)

8 These models also have a cam pulse generator. To test it, remove the fuel tank

4.6 The VT1100C2 ignition pulse generator connector (arrow) is on a bracket under the seat; the 1995 and 1996 connector is white and the 1997-on connector (shown) is black

4.12 Ignition pulse generator details

A Harness grommet
B Harness guide bolt
C Pulse generator bolts (all models)
D Pulse generator bolt locations (early models)

(see Chapter 4). Next to the ignition coils, trace the white/black and yellow/black wires to the electrical connector for the cam pulse generator. Unplug this connector and measure the resistance between the two wires (on the pulse generator side of the connector) and compare your measurement to the cam pulse generator resistance listed in this Chapter's Specifications. If the resistance of the cam pulse generator is outside the specified resistance, replace it.

Replacement

Crank or ignition pulse generator(s)

9 Remove the fuel tank (see Chapter 4) and the left steering head cover (see Chapter 8).
10 Unplug the white four-pin connector for the ignition pulse generator(s) (see Steps 2 through 6). Trace the wiring harness for the pulse generators down to the grommet on top of the right crankcase cover, note how the harness is routed, then detach it from the frame.
11 Remove the right crankcase cover (see "Clutch - removal and installation" in Chapter 2).
12 Unbolt the harness guide from the crankcase **(see illustration)**.
13 Remove the ignition pulse generator mounting bolts **(see illustration 4.12)**, pull the harness grommet out of the crankcase and remove the ignition pulse generator(s).
14 Install the ignition pulse generator and hand tighten the mounting bolts.
15 On 1985 through 1996 VT1100C models, measure the air gap with a feeler gauge and compare your measurement to the air gap listed in this Chapter's Specifications. Adjust the pulse generator(s) accordingly, then tighten the pulse generator mounting bolts securely.
16 Make sure that the weatherproofing grommet, where the pulse generator harness exits the engine through the hole in the crankcase, is correctly installed. Secure the harness to the crankcase with the harness guide and tighten the guide bolt securely.
17 Install the right crankcase cover (see "Clutch - removal and installation" in Chapter 2).
18 Route the wiring harness exactly the same way as before and plug in the electrical connector(s).
19 Install the seat or side cover (see Chapter 8).

Camshaft pulse generator (1985 and 1986 models)

20 Remove the engine (see Chapter 2).
21 Remove the rear cylinder camshaft sprocket cover (see Section 7 in Chapter 2).
22 Remove the camshaft pulse generator retaining bolts and remove the cam pulse generator.
23 Install the new camshaft pulse generator and the loosely tighten the retaining bolts.
24 Rotate the crankshaft and align the rotor tip with the pulse generator magnet.
25 Measure the air gap between the rotor tip and the pulse generator magnet with a feeler gauge and compare your measurement to the air gap listed in this Chapter's Specifications. Adjust the pulse generator accordingly, then tighten the pulse generator bolts securely.
26 Install the camshaft sprocket cover and tighten the cam sprocket cover bolts to the torque listed in the Chapter 2 Specifications.
27 Install the engine (see Chapter 2).

5 Timing rotor - removal and installation

The timing rotor is attached to the primary drive gear by the primary drive gear retaining bolt. It's removed and installed with the primary drive gear (see Chapter 2).

6 Ignition control module - check and replacement

Check

1 The ignition control module (or spark units I and II on 1985 and 1986 models) is diagnosed by a process of elimination. It should never even be *checked* until *after absolutely all other possible causes have been checked and eliminated*. Because a new module is expensive and cannot be returned, it's a good idea to have a Honda dealer test the old module before you buy a new unit.

Replacement

1985 and 1986 models

2 To remove either spark unit, remove the seat and right side cover (see Chapter 8).
3 Spark unit I (the larger unit) is nestled between the right side of the auxiliary fuel tank and the frame; spark unit II is located immediately behind the battery.
4 To remove either spark unit, unplug the electrical connector, disengage the spark unit from its retaining strap and remove it.
5 Installation is the reverse of removal.

6.8 The ignition control module on 1987 and later models (arrow) is located on the left side, behind the battery (removed for clarity)

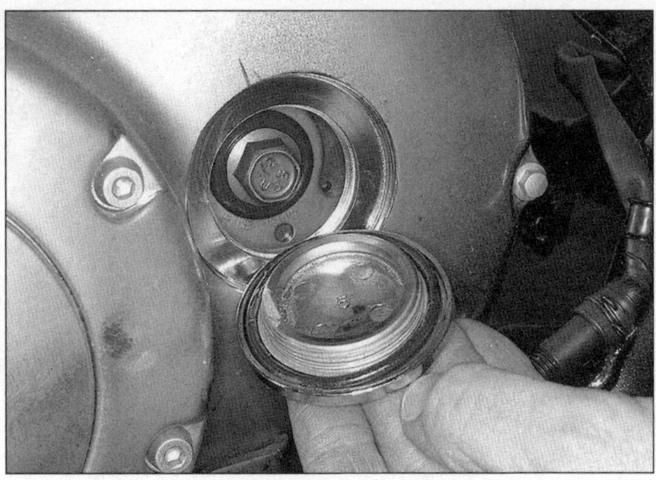

7.1 Remove the timing hole cap to expose the timing marks on the flywheel

All other models

6 Remove the left side cover (see Chapter 8).

7 Remove the battery (see Chapter 9).

8 Unplug the electrical connector(s) from the ignition control module **(see illustration)**.

9 Disengage the module from its rubber weather boot and remove it.

10 Installation is the reverse of removal.

7 Ignition timing - check

1 Remove the timing hole cap from the left side of the engine **(see illustration)**.

2 Hook up an inductive timing light in accordance with the manufacturer's instructions to one of the rear (No. 1 cylinder) spark plug wires.

3 Warm up the engine to its normal operating temperature.

4 With the engine at its normal idle speed (see Chapter 1), check the timing mark with the timing light. The ignition timing is correct if the firing (F) mark on the flywheel is aligned with the stationary index mark on the edge of the timing hole in the left crankcase cover **(see illustration)**.

5 Stop the engine, remove the inductive pickup from the rear cylinder spark plug wire and hook it up to one of the front cylinder (cylinder No. 2) spark plug wires.

6 Start the engine and allow it to return to its normal idle.

7 Check the timing for the front cylinder the same way (see Steps 4 and 5).

8 The ignition timing is not adjustable. If it's incorrect, either the ignition control module or an ignition pulse generator is defective. Have the system checked out by a Honda dealer with the necessary system diagnostic equipment.

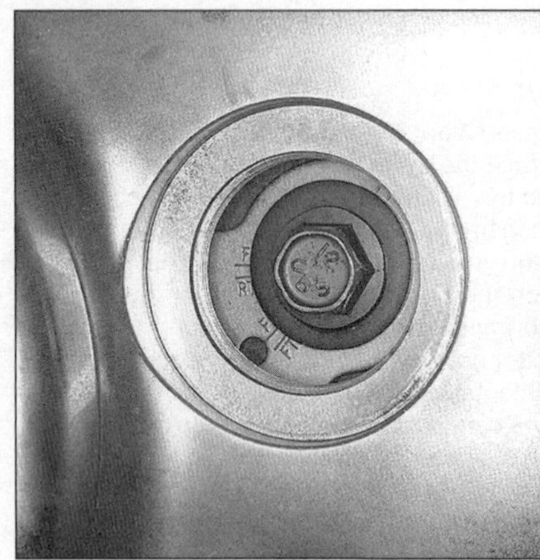

7.4 With the engine at idle, the firing (F) mark on the flywheel should be aligned with the stationary index mark on the bore of the timing plug hole

Chapter 6
Steering, suspension and final drive

Contents

Degrees of difficulty

Easy, suitable for novice with little experience 

Fairly easy, suitable for beginner with some experience 

Fairly difficult, suitable for competent DIY mechanic 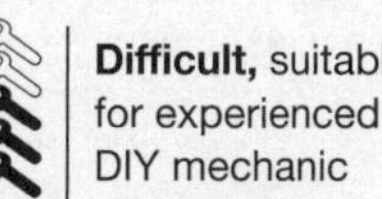

Difficult, suitable for experienced DIY mechanic 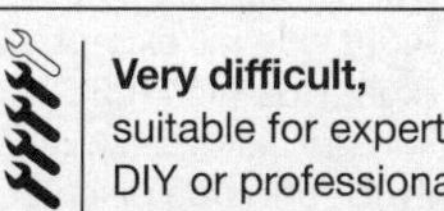

Very difficult, suitable for expert DIY or professional 

Specifications

Front fork

Fork air pressure (1985 and 1986 only)	0 to 6 psi
Spring free length	
VT1100C	
1985 and 1986	
Standard	455.7 mm (17.94 inches)
Limit	446.6 mm (17.58 inches)
1987 through 1990	
Standard	420.7 mm (16.56 inches)
Limit	412.3 mm (16.23 inches)
1992-on VT1100C	
Standard	459.4 mm (18.09 inches)
Limit	450.2 mm (17.72 inches)
VT1100C2	
1995 through 1997	
Standard	449.4 mm (17.69 inches)
Limit	440.4 mm (17.34 inches)
1998	
Standard	469.9 mm (18.50 inches)
Limit	460.5 mm (18.13 inches)
1999	
Standard	469.9 mm (18.50 inches)
Limit	460.5 mm (18.13 inches)
2000 and later	
Standard	331.4 mm (13.05 inches)
Limit	324.8 mm (12.79 inches)
VT1100C3	
Standard	429.9 mm (16.93 inches)
Limit	421.3 mm (16.59 inches)
VT1100T	
Standard	475.9 mm (18.74 inches)
Limit	466.4 mm (18.36 inches)

Front fork (continued)

Fork oil	
Type	Honda SS-8, or equivalent
Capacity	
VT1100C	
1985 and 1986	415 cc (14 ounces)
1987-on	449 cc (15.2 ounces)
VT1100C2	
1995 through 1998	482 cc (16.3 ounces)
1999	495 cc (16.7 ounces)
2000 and later	538 +/- 2.5 cc (18.2 +/- 0.08 ounces)
VT1100C3	488 +/- 2.5 cc (16.5 +/- 0.08 ounces)
VT1100T	497 cc (16.8 ounces)

Torque specifications

Front forks	
Fork caps	23 Nm (17 ft-lbs)
Fork damper rod bolts	22 Nm (16 ft-lbs)
Handlebar brackets	
Handlebar clamp-to-bracket bolts	30 Nm (22 ft-lbs)
Bracket-to-upper triple clamp nuts	27 Nm (20 ft-lbs)
Rear shock absorbers	
Upper mounting nuts or bolts	27 Nm (20 ft-lbs)
Lower mounting nuts or bolts	
1985 and 1986 (nuts)	35 Nm (26 ft-lbs)
1987 and later	
Left side	23 Nm (17 ft-lbs)
Right side (all except VT1100C3)	35 Nm (25 ft-lbs)
Right side (VT1100C3)	27 Nm (20 ft-lbs)
Steering stem nut	103 Nm (76 ft-lbs)
Triple clamp-to-fork tube pinch bolts	
Upper bolts	11 Nm (96 in-lbs)
Lower bolts	49 Nm (36 ft-lbs)
Swingarm	
Left pivot bolt	103 Nm (76 ft-lbs)
Right pivot bolt	18 Nm (156 in-lbs)
Right pivot locknut	113 Nm (83 ft-lbs)
Final drive-to-swingarm nuts	64 Nm (47 ft-lbs)

2.1 To get to the handlebar bracket bolts, pry out these four caps (arrows) with a small screwdriver

2.2 To remove the clutch lever bracket, remove these bolts (arrows)

1 General information

The front forks are a conventional coil-spring, hydraulically-damped telescopic type. The forks on 1985 and 1986 models are air-assisted and can be pressurized up to 6 psi. On all other models, the forks are designed to run at atmospheric pressure, *i.e.* they're not pressurized.

The rear suspension consists of two shock absorbers and a swingarm. The shocks on all models have spring preload adjusters which allow seven spring preload settings. Setting one is for light loads and/or good roads; setting seven is for heavy loads and/or bad roads. Setting two is the standard setting.

All models are equipped with a shaft drive system consisting of an output gear (see Chapter 2), a U-joint, a driveshaft and a final drive unit. The final drive unit, which houses a pinion gear and ring gear, cannot be serviced at home. If it's defective or excessively worn, remove it and have it rebuilt by a competent motorcycle machine shop or dealer service department, or obtain a new or good used unit.

2 Handlebar - removal and installation

1 If the handlebar is being removed only to service other components, such as the steering head or the fork tubes, simply pry out the caps from the handlebar brackets **(see illustration)**, remove the Allen bolts and the upper halves of the brackets, and set the handlebar aside. It isn't necessary to disconnect the brake hose, the clutch or throttle cables, or the wire harnesses for the handlebar switches, but it is a good idea to support the handlebar assembly with a piece of wire or rope, to avoid excessive strain on the brake hose, the cables and the harnesses. On 1985 and 1986 models, remove the handlebar cover (actually the fuse box), then remove the four bracket bolts.

2 If the handlebar itself is being replaced, do the following:

a) *Cut the cable ties (if equipped) that attach the cables to the handlebar.*
b) *Disconnect the electrical leads from the clutch switch.*
c) *Disconnect the clutch cable (see Chapter 2).*
d) *Remove the clutch lever bracket* **(see illustration)**, *the clutch lever pivot, and on models with hydraulic clutches, the clutch master cylinder reservoir.*
e) *Remove the switch housings (see Chapter 9).*
f) *Disconnect the throttle cables (see Chapter 4).*
g) *Remove the brake master cylinder (see Chapter 7).*
h) *Unbolt the handlebar (see Step 1).*

3 To remove the lower halves of the handlebar brackets from the upper triple clamp, remove the bracket nuts from the underside of the upper triple clamp and pull the brackets out of the triple clamp. Remove the rubber bushings.

4 Inspect the rubber bushings for cracks and distortion. If they're damaged or worn, replace them.

5 Inspect the handlebar for cracks and distortion and replace it if any damage is found.

6 Installation is the reverse of removal. Be sure to tighten the handlebar clamp-to-bracket bolts to the torque listed in this Chapter's Specifications.

3 Fork oil change

Note: *The following procedure applies to a routine fork oil change. If you are going to rebuild the forks, it's much easier to simply pour out the old fork oil after the forks have been removed from the bike.*

1 Support the bike securely so it can't be knocked over during this procedure. The front wheel must be raised off the ground using a hydraulic lift, a shop stand, a jack and wood support under the crankcase, axle stands, etc. Remove the front wheel (see Chapter 7).

2 On 1985 and 1986 models, remove the valve caps from the Schrader valves in the fork caps, depress each valve stem and bleed off any air in the forks.

3 Place a drain pan under the fork legs and remove the damper rod bolts **(see illus-**

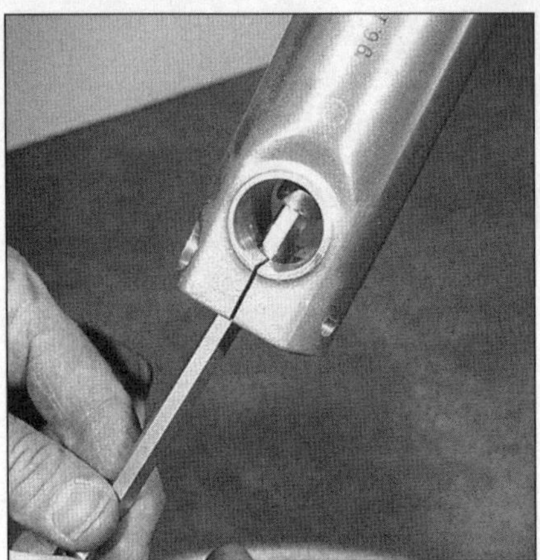

3.3a Unscrew the damper rod bolt from the lower end of the fork leg . . .

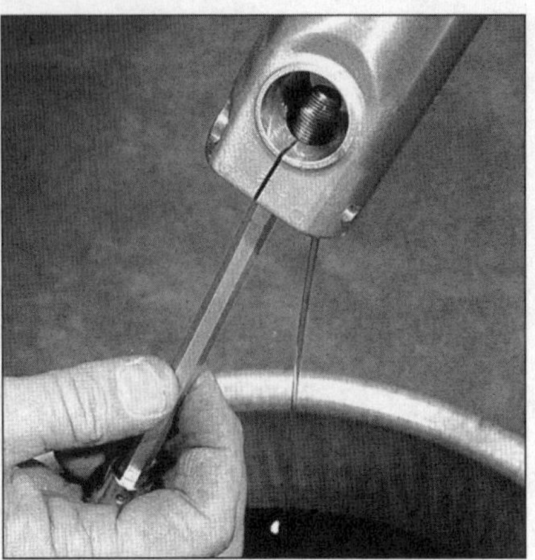

3.3b . . . remove the bolt, discard the sealing washer and drain the fork oil

3.4 Remove the fork cap

trations). Discard the old sealing washers. Damper rod bolts can be difficult to remove, because the damper rod turns with the bolt. If this happens, use an air wrench to back out the bolt. If you don't have air tools, have an assistant compress the fork while you loosen the damper rod bolt (compressing the fork makes it harder for the damper rod to turn with the bolt). If you still can't loosen the bolt, remove the fork (see Section 4), put it in a bench vise (be sure to protect the fork with brass or plastic jaw protectors) and, again, have an assistant compress the fork while you loosen the damper rod bolt (it's easier to compress the fork when it's in a bench vise than when it's on the bike).

4 Remove the fork caps **(see illustration)**.

5 After most of the oil has drained, alternate between *slowly* compressing and releasing the forks to pump out the remaining oil. Don't try to compress the forks too quickly or you will squirt oil everywhere!

6 Clean the threads of the damper rod bolts, and their threads in the damper rods, with solvent and dry them off with compressed air. Coat the threads of the bolts with non-permanent thread locking agent and install the bolts with new sealing washers, then tighten the bolts to the torque listed in this Chapter's Specifications.

7 Remove the fork springs from the forks.

8 Pour the type and amount of fork oil listed in this Chapter's Specifications into the fork tube through the opening at the top **(see illustration)**.

9 Measure the level of the oil in the fork with the fork fully compressed and without the spring in position **(see illustration)**. Compare it to the value listed in this Chapter's Specifications. Add or remove oil as necessary.

10 Install the springs with their more closely-wound coils at the top.

11 Install the fork caps and tighten them to the torque listed in this Chapter's Specifications.

12 The remainder of installation is the reverse of the removal steps.

3.8 Add the specified type and amount of fork oil (fork removed from bike for clarity; it's not necessary to remove the forks to add new fork oil)

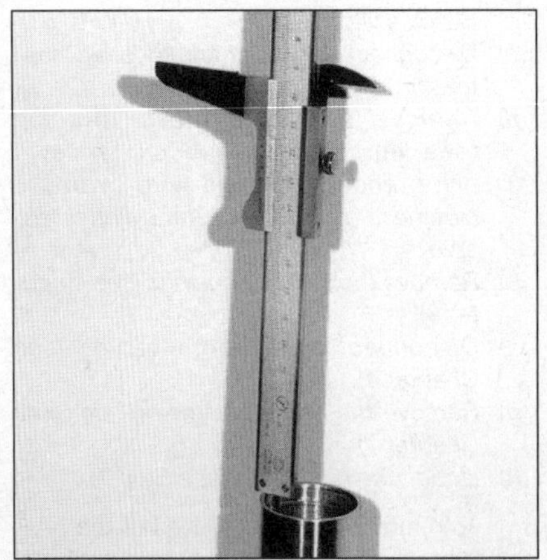

3.9 Measure the distance from the top of the fork tube to the fork oil (fork oil level) with the spring removed and the fork fully compressed

4 Forks - removal and installation

Removal

1 The front end of the bike must be off the ground for this procedure. Raise the bike on a hydraulic lift, shop stand, or some other suitable support. Make sure that whatever you use is strong enough to support the bike securely.

2 Remove the front wheel (see Chapter 7).

3 Remove the front fender (see Chapter 8).

4 Disconnect the brake hose clamp(s) and unbolt the brake caliper(s) (see Chapter 7). Hang the caliper(s) with a piece of wire or rope to protect the brake hose(s). This is a good time to inspect the caliper(s) and brake pads for wear (see Chapter 7).

5 On 1985 and 1986 models, remove the four bolt caps from the fork brace, remove the four Allen bolts and remove the fork brace. Don't lose the four small collars and bushings.

6 Note how the fork tubes protrude slightly above the top of the upper triple clamp. Mark this height with a permanent marker or measure it with a steel pocket ruler; the tube(s) must be reinstalled in exactly the same position (installing them higher or lower in the triple clamps will affect handling).

7 Either remove the turn signals (see Chapter 9) or loosen the turn signal clamp bolts enough to allow the tube to slide through them.

8 Loosen the fork upper and lower triple clamp bolt caps and bolts **(see illustration)**.

9 Using a twisting motion, pull the fork tube(s) out of the triple clamps.

4.8 To detach a fork tube from the triple clamps, remove each plug and fork tube pinch bolt (arrow) (upper triple clamp shown)

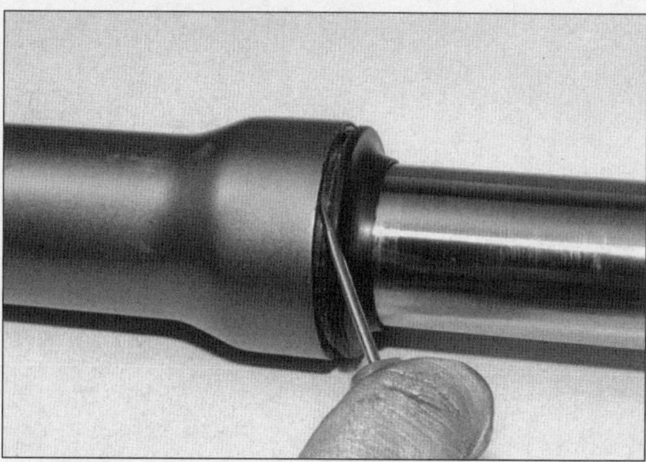

5.6 Pry the dust seal out of the fork slider with a small screwdriver and slide it out of the way; don't slide the seal over rough spots if you plan to reuse it

Installation

10 Installation is the reverse of removal. Tighten the upper and lower triple clamp bolts but don't torque them until the wheel is installed and the bike is on the ground.

11 After removing the bike from the lift, milk crate, etc., pump the front brake lever several times to bring the pads into contact with the disc.

12 Tighten the upper and lower triple clamp pinch bolts to the torque listed in this Chapter's Specifications.

5 Forks - disassembly, inspection and reassembly

Disassembly

Note: *Work on one fork leg at a time to avoid mixing up the parts.*

1 *Loosen* (do NOT remove), the damper rod bolts **(see illustration 3.3a)** and the fork tube caps **(see illustration 3.4)**.

2 Remove the forks (see Section 4).

3 Place a fork leg in a bench vise (clamp the vise jaws onto the slider; do not clamp onto the friction surface of the fork tube itself) and remove the fork cap and O-ring, the spacer, the spring seat and the fork spring. Discard the old fork cap O-ring.

4 Remove the fork from the bench vise and pour out the fork oil.

5 Place the fork leg back in the bench vise again. To finish disassembling the fork, you must remove the damper rod bolt (it's a large Allen bolt) from the bottom of the slider **(see illustration 3.3b)**. This bolt attaches the fork damper rod to the fork slider. When removing the Allen bolt, retrieve the old copper sealing washer and discard it. This washer must be replaced when the fork is reassembled. Sometimes, the damper rod bolt is so tight that the damper rod turns when you try to loosen the bolt. If this happens, try removing the bolt with an air tool, if you have it. If not, have an assistant push the inner fork tube firmly into the slider; compressing the fork spring is usually sufficient to lock the damper rod into place while the damper rod bolt is loosened. If that doesn't work, try compressing the fork spring *and* loosening the bolt with an air tool. And if that doesn't work? There are aftermarket tools designed to hold the damper rod; see your dealer parts department or an aftermarket motorcycle accessory shop. If you can't find a suitable special tool, have a dealer service department loosen the bolt.

6 Pry the dust seal from the fork slider **(see illustration)**.

7 Slide the dust seal up the fork tube and pry out the stopper ring **(see illustration)**.

8 To separate the fork tube from the slider, hold the slider and yank the tube upward repeatedly (like a slide hammer) until the seal, back-up ring and slider bushing pop loose from the slider **(see illustration)**. Remove the dust seal, stopper ring, seal and back-up ring from the fork tube. Discard the dust seal

5.7 Pry the stopper ring out of its groove in the fork slider; don't distort this ring any more than necessary

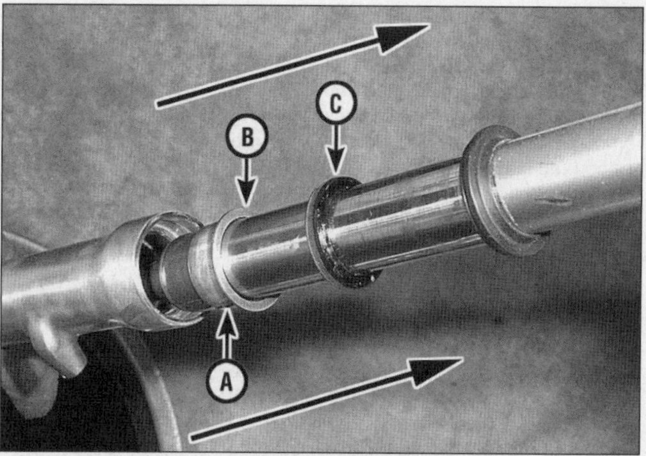

5.8 Yank the slider and fork tube apart a few times until they separate; the slider bushing (A), back-up ring (B) and oil seal (C) will pop out of the slider with the tube

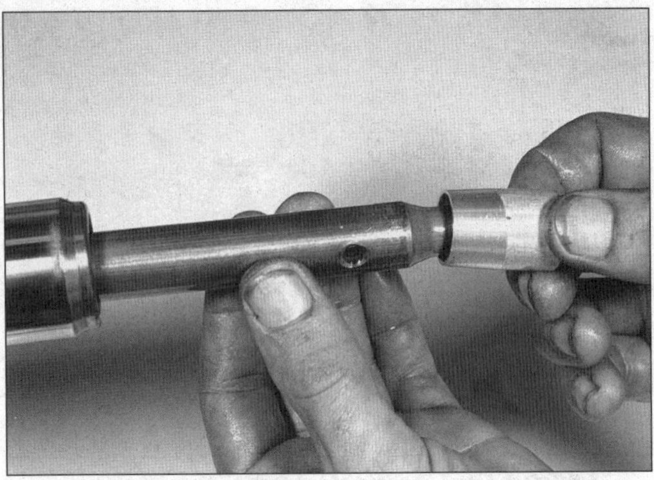

5.9a Remove the oil lock piece from the lower end of the damper rod (if it's still there; if not, it's probably in the bottom of the slider) . . .

5.9b . . . and remove the damper rod and rebound spring from the other (upper) end of the fork tube

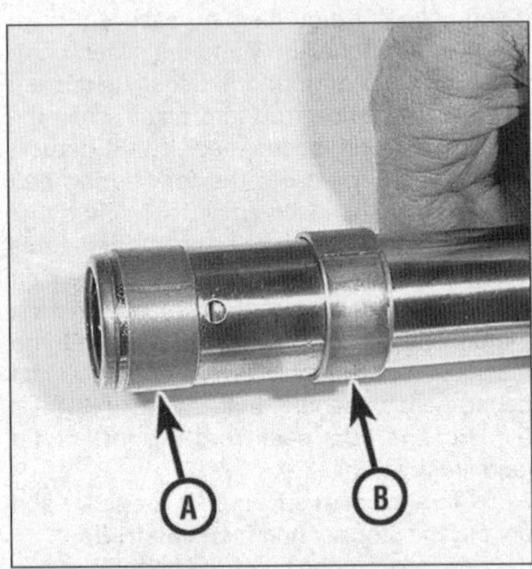

5.11a There are two bushings on the lower end of the fork tube; the smaller-diameter fork tube bushing (A) and the larger-diameter slider bushing (B)

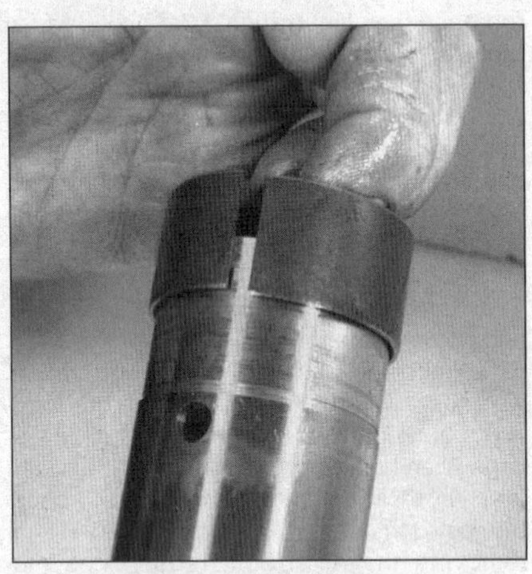

5.11b Pry the fork tube bushing apart at the slit just enough to slide it off . . .

5.11c . . . the slider bushing can now be removed by sliding it off

and fork seal. If the stopper ring is fatigued, replace it too.

9 Remove the oil lock piece from the fork damper rod **(see illustration)**. (If it's not there, see Step 10.) Invert the tube and remove the fork damper rod and rebound spring **(see illustration)**.

10 Invert the fork slider and retrieve the oil lock piece, the small conical-shaped plastic piece that fits around the lower end of the fork damper rod in the bottom of the slider.

11 There are two bushings at the lower end of the inner fork tube **(see illustration)**, the smaller-diameter fork tube bushing and the larger-diameter slider bushing. The fork tube bushing fits tightly around the end of the fork tube and is seated against a shoulder on the end of the tube, while the slider bushing slides freely up and down the fork tube and is seated against a shoulder inside the fork tube. You need not remove either bushing unless it appears worn or scratched. If it's necessary to replace the fork tube bushing (the lower bushing on the tube, the one that doesn't slide up and down), pry it apart at the slit and slide it off **(see illustration)**. To remove the slider bushing, simply slide it off the fork tube **(see illustration)**.

Inspection

12 Clean all parts in solvent and blow them dry with compressed air, if available. Lay out the parts for inspection **(see illustration)**.

13 Inspect the fork tube and slider, the bushings and the damper rod for score marks and scratches. Inspect the chrome surface of the fork tube for flaking and excessive wear. Look for dents in the tube. If the fork tube is damaged or worn, replace it.

14 Have the fork tube checked for runout at a dealer service department or other repair shop.

Warning: If the fork tube is bent, replace it; don't try to have it straightened.

15 Measure the overall length of the fork spring and check it for cracks and other damage. Compare the length to the minimum length listed in this Chapter's Specifications. If it's defective or sagged, replace both fork springs. Never replace only one spring.

Reassembly

16 Lightly lubricate all parts with clean fork oil as they're reassembled.

17 Install the new fork tube bushing, if the old bushing was removed. Do not pry open the bushing any more than necessary to install it. Be extremely careful not to damage the bushing friction surface. Make sure the bushing is seated at the bottom of the fork

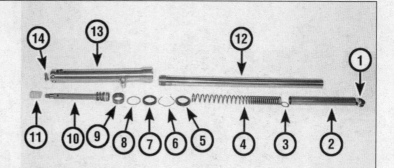

5.12 Front fork details

1 *Fork cap and O-ring*
2 *Spacer*
3 *Spring seat*
4 *Fork spring*
5 *Dust seal*
6 *Stopper ring*
7 *Fork seal*
8 *Back-up ring*
9 *Slider bushing*
10 *Damper rod and rebound spring*
11 *Lock piece*
12 *Fork tube and fork tube bushing*
13 *Fork slider*
14 *Damper rod bolt and sealing washer*

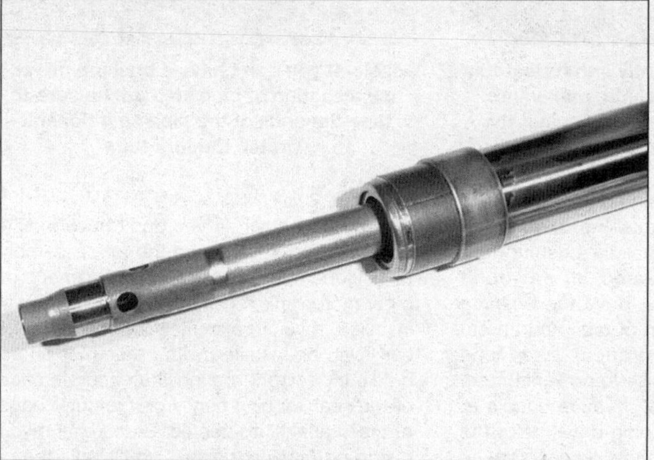

5.19 Put the rebound spring on the damper rod, then drop it into the fork tube so it protrudes from the lower end like this

5.20 Install the lock piece on the lower end of the damper rod

tube, against the shoulder.

18 Install the slider bushing on the fork tube.

19 Install the rebound spring on the damper rod. Install the damper rod into the fork tube, then let it slide slowly down until it protrudes from the bottom of the fork tube **(see illustration)**.

20 Install the oil lock piece over the end of the damper rod that protrudes from the fork tube **(see illustration)**.

21 Holding the fork slider upside down (so the lock piece doesn't fall off the lower end of the damper rod), insert the fork tube and damper rod into the slider.

22 Apply a non-permanent thread-locking agent to the damper rod bolt, then install the bolt and a new sealing washer **(see illustration)** and tighten it as much as you can. (Don't try to tighten to the torque listed in this Chapter's Specifications at this time unless you have a suitable tool for holding the damper rod.) If the bolt won't "catch," *i.e.* it won't tighten up, the damper rod is not correctly aligned with the bolt. Using a flashlight and a Phillips screwdriver with a taped tip, align the threaded bore in the lower end of the damper rod with the bore in the bottom of the slider.

23 Slide the back-up ring down the fork tube **(see illustration)**.

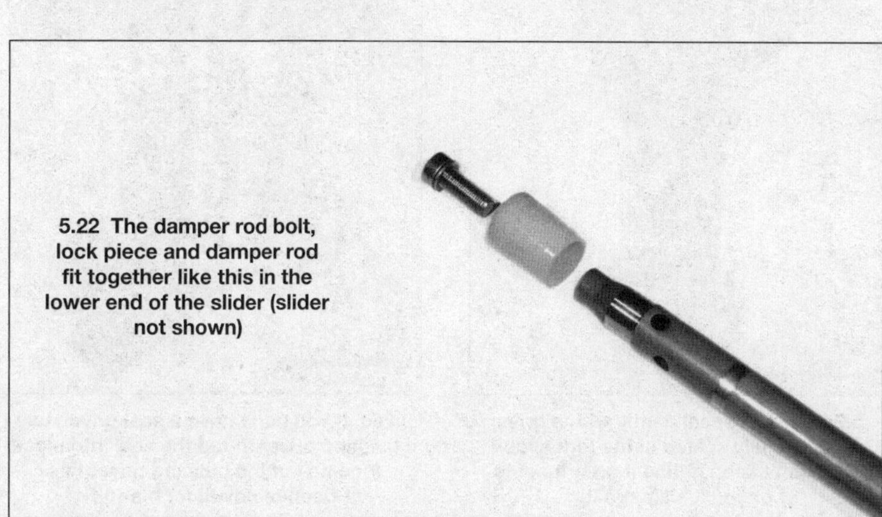

5.22 The damper rod bolt, lock piece and damper rod fit together like this in the lower end of the slider (slider not shown)

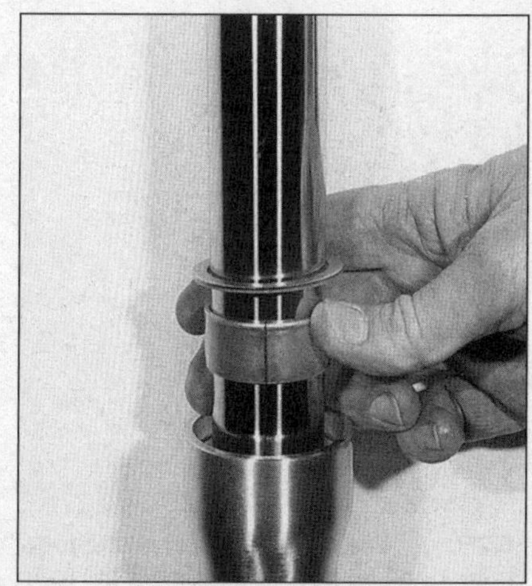

5.23 Install the back-up ring on the fork tube

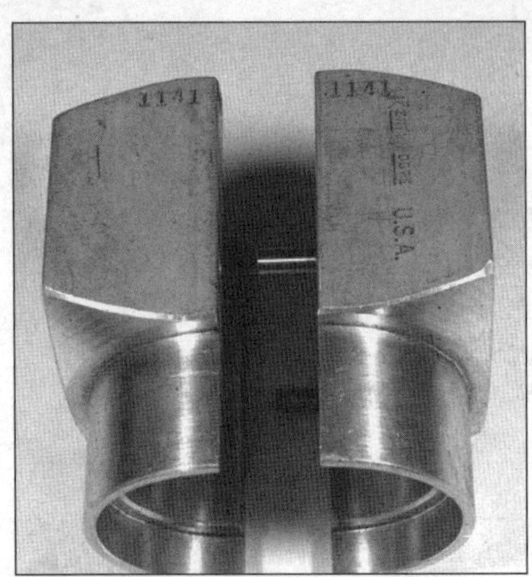

5.24a Using a split-type seal driver (this is a Kent-Moore, but any suitable equivalent will work) . . .

5.24b . . . tap down gently and repeatedly to seat the slider bushing; make sure the bushing is fully seated against the shoulder inside the slider

5.24c If you don't have a bushing driver, use a section of pipe instead; be sure to tape the ends of the pipe so it doesn't scratch the fork tube

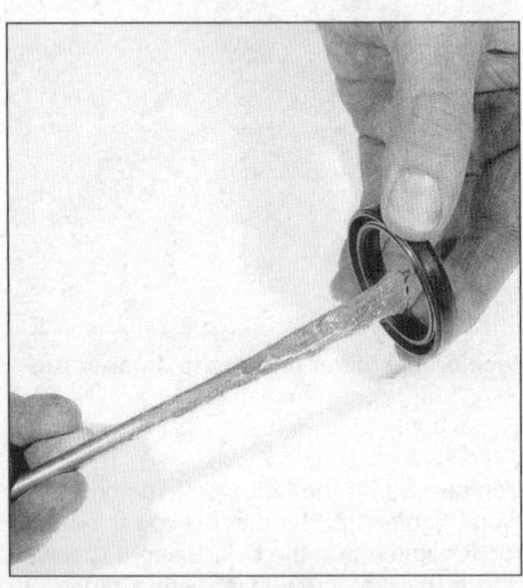

5.25a Coat the inner lip and the outer circumference of the new seal with grease or fork oil . . .

24 Using a suitable bushing driver **(see illustrations)**, drive the slider bushing into place until it's fully seated. If you don't have one of these tools, drive the bushing into place with a section of pipe and an old guide bushing **(see illustration)**. Wrap tape around the ends of the pipe to prevent it from scratching the fork tube. If you're unable to fabricate a suitable bushing driver, take the fork assembly to a Honda dealer service department or a motorcycle machine shop or repair shop to have the bushing installed.

25 Lubricate the lip and the outer circumference of the new oil seal with the fork oil listed in this Chapter's Specifications and slide the seal down the fork tube with the part number side of the seal facing up **(see illustrations)**. Drive the seal into place with a seal driver (or use the same tool used to drive in the slider bushing) **(see illustrations)** or make something that will do the job **(see illustration)**. Again, if you don't have a suitable tool for this job, take the fork assembly to a Honda dealer service department or other motorcycle repair shop to have the seal installed. If you're extremely careful, the seal can even be installed with a hammer and a drift punch. Work around the circumference of the seal, tapping gently on the outer edge of the seal until it's seated. Be careful! If you distort or damage the seal, you'll have to pry it out, which might mean disassembling the fork again (and taking it to a dealer!).

26 Install the stopper ring **(see illustration)**. Make sure the ring is correctly seated in its groove in the fork slider.

27 Install the dust seal and drive it into place with the same tool used to install the oil seal **(see illustration)**, or use the tool used to install the slider bushing driver. Make sure the dust seal is fully seated.

28 Add the recommended type and amount

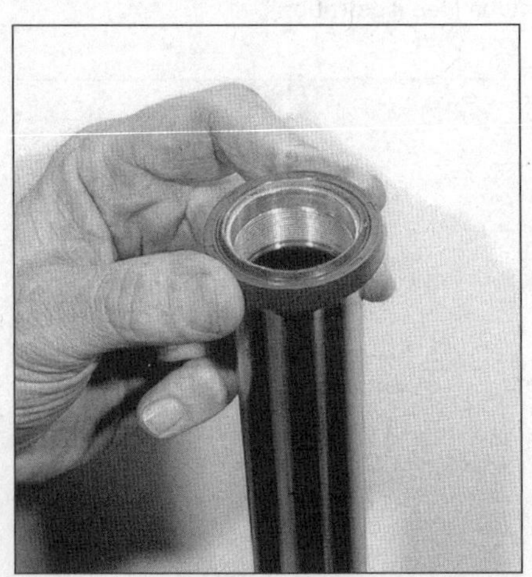

5.25b . . . and install the seal on the fork tube; don't let the upper edge of the fork tube damage the seal lip

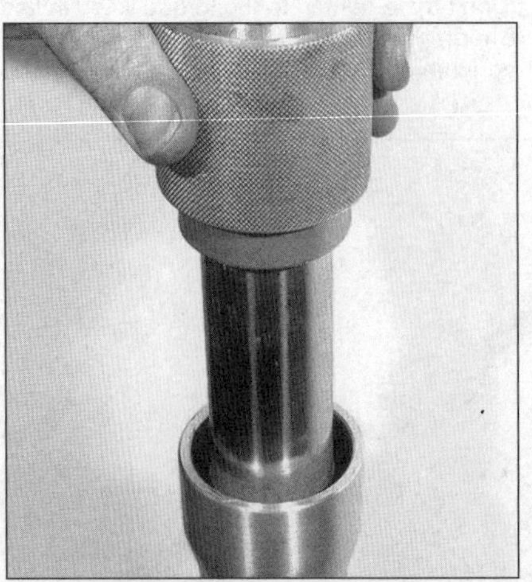

5.25c Tap the seal gently with a driver until it's fully seated in the fork slider (but don't keep hitting it after it seats or you'll damage it)

5.25d If you don't have a seal driver, use a bushing driver to tap the seal into place (one half of the bushing driver has been removed for clarity)

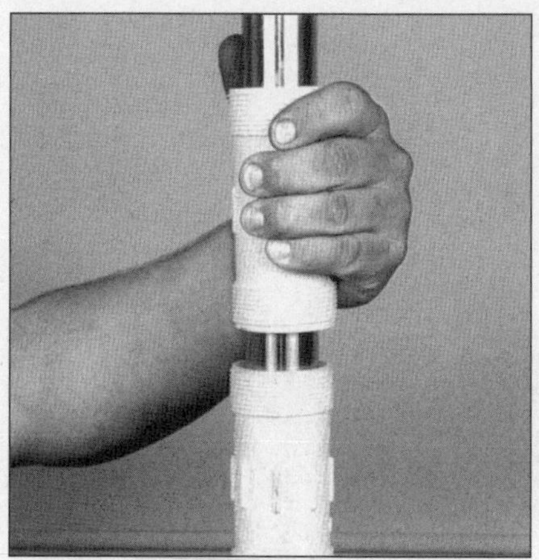

5.25e If you don't have the drivers, you can even drive the seal into place with PVC plumbing fittings; place one piece on top of the new seal and strike it with the other piece (like a slide hammer)

5.26 Compress the stopper ring and fit it securely into its groove in the fork slider (if the stopper doesn't "snap" into place, it's too fatigued to re-use)

5.27 Use any of the tools previously shown to drive the dust seal into place

6.4a Remove the steering stem nut . . .

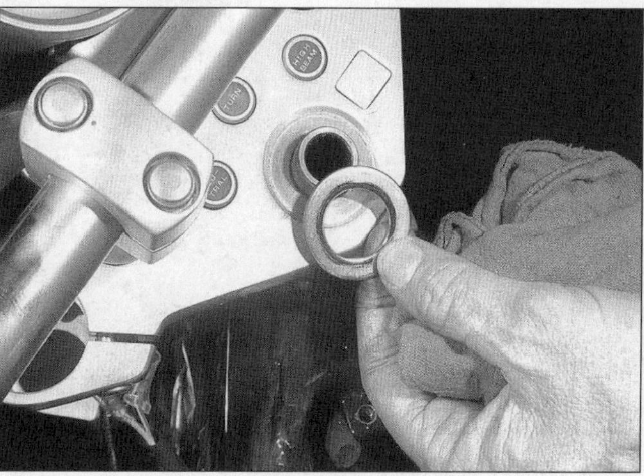

6.4b . . . and remove the washer

of fork oil (see Section 3).

29 Install the fork spring, with the closer-wound coils at the top.

30 Install the spring seat, the spacer and the fork cap. Use a new O-ring on the fork cap. Tighten the damper rod bolt to the torque listed in this Chapter's Specifications.

31 Install the fork assembly (see Section 4). If you won't be installing the fork right away, store it in an upright position.

32 Repeat this procedure for the other fork.

6 Steering stem and bearings - removal, inspection and installation

Removal

1 If the steering head bearing check/adjustment (see Chapter 1) does not remedy excessive play or roughness in the steering head bearings, the entire front end must be disassembled and the bearings and races replaced.

2 Remove the fuel tank (see Chapter 4) and the steering head covers (see Chapter 8).

3 Remove the front forks (see Section 4).

4 Remove the steering stem nut and washer **(see illustrations)**, then lift off the upper triple clamp (sometimes called the fork bridge or crown). Unless you plan to replace the upper triple clamp, it isn't necessary to remove the handlebars - just set the upper triple clamp aside with everything attached.

Caution: If any of the electrical harnesses for the handlebar switches are pulled tight, unplug them (see Chapter 9). It isn't necessary to disconnect the brake hydraulic hose, but make sure that the handlebar/triple clamp assembly is neither hanging by the hose or putting any strain on the hose.

If you are *replacing* the upper triple clamp, detach the brake hose clamp, if applicable, and remove any cable or wiring harness guides that are bolted to the triple clamp.

5 The locknut is secured by four lockwasher tabs. Straighten these tabs with a screwdriver **(see illustration)**.

6.5 Straighten the tabs on the lockwasher with a small screwdriver

6.6a Loosen the locknut with a ring nut wrench (also known as a C-spanner)

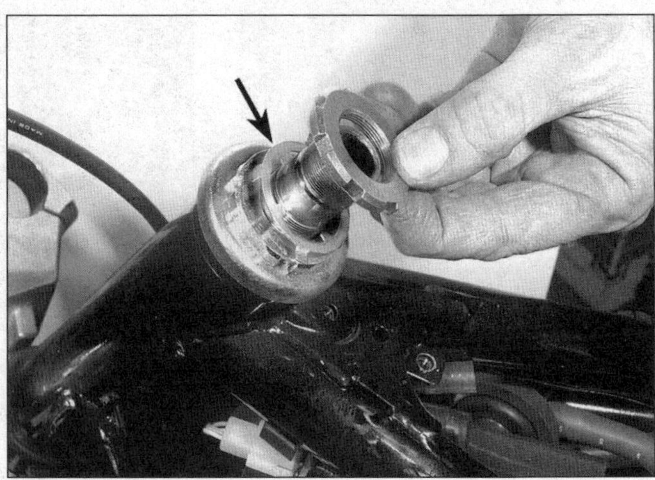
6.6b Remove the locknut and the lockwasher (arrow)

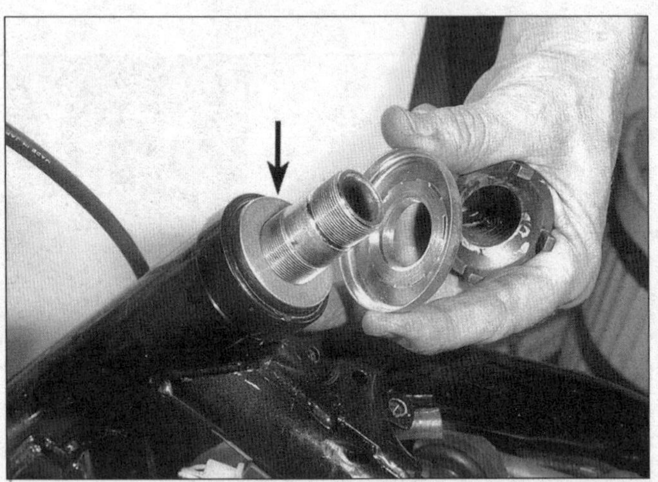
6.7 Remove the bearing adjustment nut and the upper bearing dust seal (arrow)

6.8 Remove the upper bearing inner race

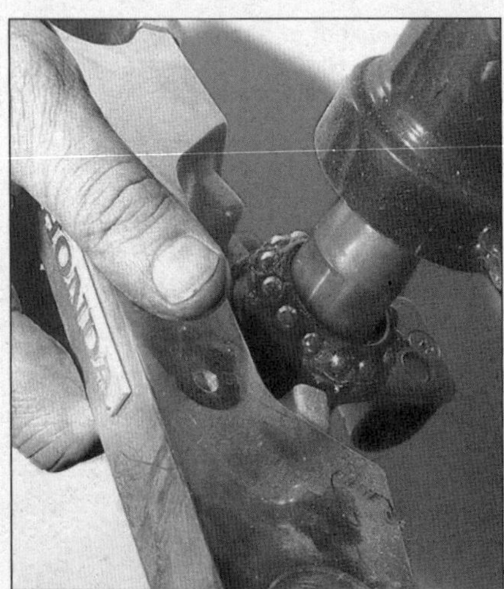
6.9 Carefully pull the steering stem/lower triple clamp assembly from the steering head

6 Using a ring nut wrench (also known as a C-spanner wrench), remove the locknut and the lockwasher **(see illustrations)**. There should be a suitable wrench in the bike's tool kit; if not, you can obtain one from a dealer or motorcycle accessory shop.

7 Remove the bearing locknut and the dust seal **(see illustration)**.

8 Remove the upper bearing inner race **(see illustration)** and remove the upper bearing assembly.

9 Pull down on the lower triple clamp and remove the steering stem/lower bearing/ lower triple clamp assembly **(see illustration)**. If it's stuck, gently tap on the top of the steering stem with a plastic mallet or a hammer and a wood block.

Inspection

10 Clean all the parts with solvent and dry them thoroughly, using compressed air, if available. Wipe the old grease out of the steering head and bearing races.

11 Examine the outer races in the steering head for cracks, dents, and pits. If even the slightest amount of wear or damage is evident, the races should be replaced.

12 To remove the outer races from the steering head, drive them out with a hammer and drift punch **(see illustrations)**. A slide hammer with the right internal-jaw puller will also work.

13 Since the outer races are an "interference-fit" in the frame, installation will be easier if the new races are left overnight in a refrigerator freezer. The frozen races will contract slightly, and slip into place in the frame with very little effort. When installing the races, tap them gently into place with a hammer and punch or a large socket **(see illustrations)**. Do not strike the bearing surface or the race will be damaged.

6.12a Insert a long punch or rod from below to tap out the upper bearing outer race . . .

6.12b . . . and from above to tap out the lower bearing outer race

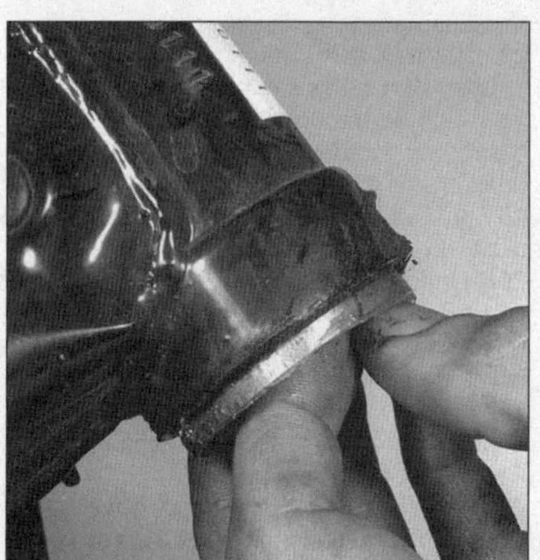

6.13a Position the lower bearing outer race in the steering head . . .

6.13b . . . and tap it into position with a socket slightly smaller in diameter than the race

6.13c Tap the upper bearing outer race into position with the same tools

14 Inspect the bearings **(see illustration)** for wear. Look for cracks, dents, and pits in the races and flat spots on the bearings. If either bearing assembly is damaged or worn, replace both the upper or lower steering head bearings as a set.

15 Inspect the lower bearing inner race (the one that's pressed onto the steering stem) for cracks, dents, and pits. If even the slightest amount of wear or damage is evident, replace the lower inner race. Examine the dust seal under the lower bearing; if it's damaged, replace it.

16 To remove the lower bearing inner race, use a bearing puller (available at tool rental yards, if you don't have one). A hammer and

6.13d . . . the upper bearing outer race should look like this when installed

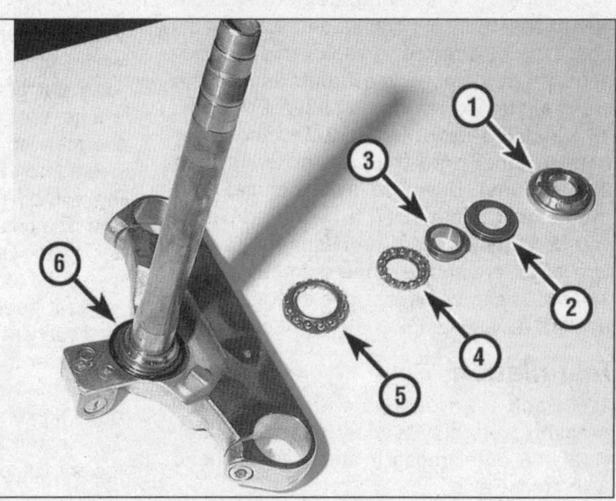

6.14 Steering stem/lower triple clamp details

1 *Bearing adjustment nut*
2 *Dust seal*
3 *Upper steering head bearing inner race*
4 *Upper steering head bearing assembly*
5 *Lower steering head bearing assembly*
6 *Lower steering head bearing inner race and dust seal*

6.16 Tap the seal and lower bearing inner race off the steering stem

6.18a Install a new seal with its concave side down . . .

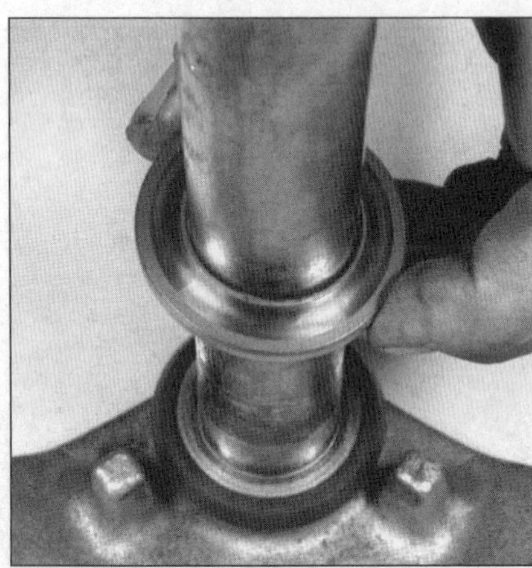
6.18b . . . then install the lower bearing inner race with its bearing surface facing up, and press the race onto the stem with a section of pipe (taped to protect the bearing surface)

7.2 Remove the upper and lower mounting bolts (arrows) and washers and pull the shock off the upper and lower mounting studs; DO NOT remove both shocks at once!

drift punch will also work **(see illustration)**. Don't remove this race unless it, or the dust seal, must be replaced. Removing the race will damage the dust seal, so replace the seal if the bearing is removed.

17 Inspect the steering stem/lower triple clamp assembly for cracks and other damage. Do not attempt to repair this component. If any damage is evident, replace the steering stem/lower triple clamp assembly.

18 Install a new dust seal and the lower bearing inner onto the steering stem **(see illustrations)**. Drive the lower bearing onto the steering stem using a bearing driver. If you don't have access to these tools, a section of pipe with the same diameter as the inner race can be used. Drive the bearing on until it's fully seated.

Installation

19 Pack the bearings with high-quality grease (preferably a moly-based grease). Coat the outer races in the steering head with grease also.

20 Install the lower steering head bearing assembly on the steering stem, then insert the steering stem/lower triple clamp into the lower end of the steering head. Install the upper bearing, inner race, dust seal and bearing adjustment nut. Using the spanner wrench (C-spanner), tighten the adjuster nut while moving the lower triple clamp back and forth. Continue to tighten the nut, 1/8-turn at a time, until all play has been removed from the steering head bearings. However, don't overtighten the adjustment nut, or the steering will be too firm and the new bearings and/or races will wear out prematurely.

21 Once all bearing play has been removed, install the lockwasher and the locknut, tightening it securely. Bend up the tabs on the lockwasher to secure the locknut, then install the upper triple clamp on the steering stem. Install the washer and steering stem nut but don't tighten it yet.

22 Install the fork tubes and tighten the lower triple clamp bolts to the torque listed in this Chapter's Specifications.

23 Tighten the steering stem nut to the torque listed in this Chapter's Specifications.

24 Tighten the upper triple clamp bolts to the torque listed in this Chapter's Specifications. Install the front wheel.

25 Install the handlebar assembly, if removed (see Section 2).

26 Check the alignment of the handlebars and the front wheel. If necessary, loosen the triple clamp bolts, have an assistant hold the front wheel, then turn the handlebars as to align them with the front wheel. Tighten the triple clamp bolts to the torque listed in this Chapter's Specifications.

27 Install the steering head covers (see Chapter 8) and fuel tank (see Chapter 4).

7 Rear shock absorbers - removal, inspection and installation

Warning: Do not attempt to disassemble these shock absorbers. They are nitrogen-charged under high pressure. Disassembly could result in serious injury.

Removal

1 The bike must be supported with the rear wheel off the ground for this procedure. Raise the bike on a hydraulic lift, shop stand, or some other suitable support. Make sure that whatever you use is strong enough to support the bike securely.

2 Remove the upper and lower mounting bolts and the washers from *one* shock absorber **(see illustration)**. Do NOT remove both shocks at the same time unless the swingarm is well supported.

Inspection

3 Inspect the shock for oil leaks and obvious external damage. Inspect the upper and

9.2 Loosen these four final drive-to-swingarm nuts (arrows) now, before removing the wheel and the shocks (fourth nut not visible in this photo)

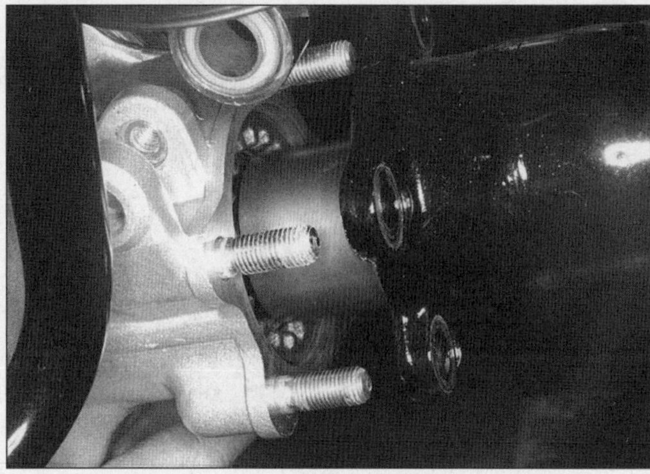

9.5 Pull the final drive unit to the rear; the driveshaft will come with it

lower mounting bolt bushings for cracks and excessive wear. If any damage is evident, replace the shock. It cannot be overhauled.

4 The shocks used on 1985 and 1986 models have external coil springs. The springs and shock absorbers on these units can be replaced separately, but a spring compressor tool is needed to do the job. If you don't have a spring compressor, take the shocks to a dealer or a motorcycle specialty shop and have the springs or shocks replaced there.

Installation

5 Install the shock absorber, install the washers and mounting bolts and tighten the bolts to the torque listed in this Chapter's Specifications.

6 Repeat Steps 2 and 3 for the other shock.

7 Remove the bike from its support.

8 Swingarm bearings - check

1 Remove the rear wheel (see Chapter 7).

2 Support the swingarm and remove the rear shock absorbers (see Section 7).

3 Grasp the rear of the swingarm with one hand and place your other hand at the junction of the swingarm and the frame. Try to move the rear of the swingarm from side-to-side. Any wear (play) in the bearings should be felt as movement between the swingarm and the frame at the front. The swingarm will actually be felt to move forward and backward at the front (not from side-to-side).

4 Move the swingarm up and down through its full travel. It should move freely, without any binding or rough spots. If it doesn't move up and down freely, either the swingarm pivot is too tight or the swingarm bearings and/or bushings are damaged.

5 If the swingarm has too much play or is stiff, remove the swingarm (see Section 10) and replace the swingarm bearings and/or bushings (see Section 11).

9 Final drive unit - removal and installation

1 Drain the final drive oil (see Chapter 1).

2 *Loosen*, but don't remove, the four final drive nuts **(see illustration)** while the swingarm is still braced by the axle and shock absorbers.

3 Remove the rear wheel (see Chapter 7).

4 Support the swingarm and remove the shock absorbers (see Section 7).

5 Remove the final drive mounting nuts **(see illustration 9.2)** and separate the final drive from the swingarm **(see illustration)**.

6 To remove the driveshaft from the final drive unit, slip the axle and spacer back into the final drive unit. Grasp the forward end of the driveshaft and wiggle it in a circle while pulling it away from the final drive unit. The stopper ring will provide some resistance, then the driveshaft should pull free of the final drive unit. Remove the spring, oil seal and stopper ring from the driveshaft.

Inspection

7 Look into the axle holes and check for obvious signs of wear or damage such as broken gear teeth **(see illustration)**. Also check the seals for signs of leakage. Slip the driveshaft into its splines (if it was removed) and turn the pinion by hand.

8 Final drive overhaul is a complicated procedure that requires several special tools, for which there are no readily available substitutes. If there's visible wear or damage, or if the differential rotation is rough or noisy, take it to a Honda dealer for disassembly and further inspection.

9 Check the coupling flange in the rear wheel for wear or damage **(see illustration)**. If necessary, remove the nuts and separate the flange from the wheel.

9.7 Inspect the final drive unit oil seal for leaks; make sure this spacer is in position before installing the wheel

9.9 Inspect the splines on the wheel hub coupling flange for damage

10.3 To detach the rear brake hose from the swingarm on models with a rear disc brake, remove these bolts (arrows)

10.8a Use this tool to loosen and tighten the swingarm pivot bolt locknut

10.8b Unscrew the locknut from the right pivot bolt

10.8c Use a 17 mm Allen bolt bit in a socket to hold the right pivot bolt while you turn the locknut, and to unscrew both pivot bolts

10.9 Remove the pivot bolts

10 Inspect the splines of the driveshaft for damage and wear. If they're damaged or worn, replace the driveshaft.

11 To remove the U-joint, remove the swingarm (see next Section).

12 Inspect the U-joint splines for wear and damage. Verify that the U-joint operates smoothly, without binding or noise. If the U-joint is damaged or worn, replace it.

Installation

13 Installation is the reverse of removal, with the following additions:

a) Install a new driveshaft oil seal if you removed the driveshaft from the final drive unit.

b) Install a new stopper ring.

c) On all models, lubricate the splines of the U-joint and the final drive unit with Honda Moly 60 grease or equivalent.

d) Install the final drive unit loosely. Do not tighten the final drive nuts to the torque listed in this Chapter's Specifications until after the rear axle is installed.

e) Check the final drive unit oil level (see Chapter 1).

10 Swingarm - removal and installation

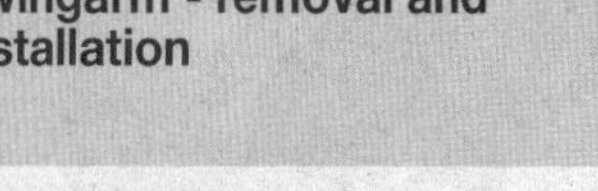

1 The bike must be supported with the rear wheel off the ground for this procedure. Raise the bike on a hydraulic lift, shop stand or some other suitable support. Make sure that whatever you use is strong enough to support the bike securely.

2 Remove the exhaust system (see Chapter 4).

3 On models with rear disc brakes, remove the brake hose clamps from the swingarm **(see illustration)**.

4 Remove the rear wheel (see Chapter 7).

5 Remove the rear shock absorbers (see Section 7).

6 Remove the final drive unit (see Section 9).

7 Pry out the left and right swingarm pivot caps.

8 Undo the locknut on the right pivot bolt, using Honda tool KS-HBA-08-469 or equivalent **(see illustrations)**. While you're undoing the locknut, hold the pivot bolt from turning with a 17 mm Allen bolt bit. These are available from tool stores.

9 Unscrew the swingarm pivot bolts with the 17 mm Allen bolt bit and remove both bolts **(see illustration)**.

10 Pull the swingarm back and remove it from the frame. The U-joint may bind a little on the output shaft splines, but it will come loose if you pull it firmly.

10.11 After pulling off the old U-joint dust boot, remove the U-joint from the swingarm

10.15 The universal joint splines must slide onto the splines on the output shaft (arrow)

11 Remove the old U-joint dust boot from the swingarm, then pull the U-joint out of the swingarm **(see illustration)**.

12 Check the pivot bearings in the swingarm for dryness or deterioration (See Section 11). Lubricate or replace them as necessary.

Installation

13 Lubricate the universal splines with moly-based grease. Make sure the universal joint dust boot is in place, then install the universal joint in the swingarm and push it onto the forward end of the driveshaft.

14 Place the swingarm in its installed position in the frame, but don't install the universal joint on the output shaft yet. Grease the tips of the pivot bolts and thread them into their holes, making sure the tips fit into the swingarm bearings. Don't tighten the pivot bolts yet.

15 Slide the universal joint forward onto the output shaft **(see illustration)**. If it hangs up on the output shaft splines, turn the rear end of the driveshaft back and forth while pushing forward until you feel the U-joint slide onto the output shaft splines.

16 **Note:** *The swingarm pivot bolts and locknut must be tightened in the specified sequence and to the correct torque settings.* Tighten the left pivot bolt to the torque listed in this Chapter's Specifications. Tighten the right pivot bolt after tightening the left pivot bolt. You may have noticed that the right pivot bolt's specified torque is much lower than that of the left pivot bolt. This is not a mistake. That is the way it is supposed to be.

17 Raise and lower the swingarm several times to seat the bearings, then retighten the right pivot bolt to its specified torque again.

18 Thread the locknut onto the right pivot bolt as far as you can with your fingers. Then place the special wrench on the locknut and install a torque wrench in the special wrench's square hole. Hold the pivot bolt with the 17 mm Allen bolt bit so it won't turn, then tighten the locknut to the torque listed in this Chapter's Specifications. **Note:** *The special wrench increases the torque applied to the nut, so the specified torque is less than the actual applied torque.*

19 The remainder of installation is the reverse of removal.

11 Swingarm bearings - replacement

1 The swingarm rides in a pair of tapered roller bearings.

2 Remove the swingarm from the motorcycle (see Section 10).

3 Pry out the seals and remove the bearings from the swingarm **(see illustrations)**.

4 Clean all the parts with solvent and dry them thoroughly, using compressed air, if available. If you do use compressed air, don't let the bearings spin as they're dried - it

11.3a Pry out the old grease seals from the swingarm with a seal removal tool or screwdriver

11.3b Remove the seal and bearing from each end of the swingarm pivot bore

could ruin them. Wipe the old grease out of the swingarm and bearing races.

5 Examine the bearing races **(see illustration)** for cracks, dents, and pits. If even the slightest amount of wear or damage is evident, the races should be replaced. If one race (or one bearing) needs to be replaced, replace both of the bearings, as well as their races and seals, as a set.

6 To remove the bearing races, drive them out of the swingarm with a hammer and long rod. A slide hammer with the proper internal-jaw puller will also work. Remove the internal grease retainers as well.

7 Since the races are an interference fit in the swingarm, installation will be easier if the new races are left overnight in a refrigerator. This will cause them to contract and slip into place in the frame with very little effort. When installing the races, tap them gently into place with a hammer and a bearing driver, punch or a large socket. Do not strike the bearing surface or the race will be damaged.

8 Check the bearings for wear. Look for cracks, dents, and pits in the rollers and flat spots on the bearings. Replace any defective parts with new ones. If a new bearing is required, replace both of them, and the bearing races and seals, as a set.

11.5 Replace the outer races and bearings as a set if either race is worn; don't forget to install the grease retainer (arrow) in each end

Chapter 7
Brakes, wheels and tires

Contents

Degrees of difficulty

Easy, suitable for novice with little experience 

Fairly easy, suitable for beginner with some experience 

Fairly difficult, suitable for competent DIY mechanic 

Difficult, suitable for experienced DIY mechanic

Very difficult, suitable for expert DIY or professional 

Specifications

Brakes

Brake fluid type	See Chapter 1
Brake disc thickness	
1985 through 1996 VT1100C (front only)	
Standard	4.5 to 5.2 mm (0.18 to 0.20 inch)
Minimum*	4.0 mm (0.16 inch)
VT1100C2, VT1100T and 1997-on VT1100C (front and rear)	
Standard	5.8 to 6.2 mm (0.23 to 0.24 inch)
Minimum*	5.0 mm (0.20 inch)
Disc runout limit	0.30 mm (0.012 inch)
Front brake pad minimum thickness	Replace when wear groove is exposed

Brakes (continued)

Rear brake drum inside diameter (VT1100C)	
Standard	180 mm (7.09 inches)
Maximum	181 mm (7.13 inches)
Rear brake shoe lining thickness (VT1100C)	
Standard	5.0 mm (0.20 inch)
Minimum	2.0 mm (0.08 inch)
Front master cylinder	
1985 and 1986	
Piston bore inside diameter service limit	15.93 mm (0.627 inch)
Piston outside diameter service limit	15.82 mm (0.623 inch)
1987 on	
Piston bore inside diameter service limit	12.75 mm (0.502 inch)
Piston outside diameter service limit	12.64 mm (0.498 inch)
Rear master cylinder (VT1100C2 and VT1100T)	
Piston bore inside diameter service limit	12.75 mm (0.502 inch)
Piston outside diameter service limit	12.64 mm (0.498 inch)
Pushrod adjustment	169 mm (6.7 inches)

**Refer to marks stamped into the disc (they supersede information printed here)*

Wheels and tires

Wheel runout	
Radial (up-and-down)	2.0 mm (0.08 inch)
Axial (side-to-side)	2.0 mm (0.08 inch)
Tire pressures	See Chapter 1
Tire sizes	
VT1100C	
1985 and 1986	
Front	110/90-18 61H
Rear	140/90-15 70 H
1987 on	
Front	110/90-19 62H
Rear	170/80-15 M/C 77H
VT1100C2	
Front	120/90-18 65H
Rear	170/80-15M/C 77H
VT1100T	
Front	130/80R-18 66H
Rear	170/70R-16 75H

Torque specifications

Front axle

1985 and 1986	
Axle holder bolts	27 to 33 Nm (0 to 24 ft-lbs)
Axle nut	55 to 65 Nm (40 to 47 ft-lbs)
1987 on	
Axle pinch bolts	22 Nm (16 ft-lbs)
Axle bolt	59 Nm (43 ft-lbs)

Front disc brake

Brake disc mounting bolts	
1985 and 1986	37 to 43 Nm (27 to 31 ft-lbs)
1987 through 1990	40 Nm (29 ft-lbs)
1992 on	42 Nm (31 ft-lbs)
Front brake caliper bracket mounting bolts	
1985 and 1986	30 to 40 Nm (22 to 29 ft-lbs)
1987 through 1993	35 Nm (25 ft-lbs)
1994 and later VT1100C	45 Nm (33 ft-lbs)
VT1100C2 and VT1100T	30 Nm (22 ft-lbs)
Brake caliper pin bolts	
1985 and 1986	
Upper bolt	25 to 30 Nm (18 to 22 ft-lbs)
Lower bolt	20 to 25 Nm (14 to 18 ft-lbs)
1987 through 1993	28 Nm (20 ft-lbs)
1994 on	
Pin bolt (upper bolt)	23 Nm (17 ft-lbs)
Bracket pin bolt (lower bolt)	13 Nm (108 in-lbs)

Brake pad pin retainer bolt	
1985 and 1986	8 to 13 Nm (72 to 108 in-lbs)
1987 through 1993	11 Nm (96 in-lbs)
1994 on	18 Nm (13 ft-lbs)
Brake hose banjo bolts (at caliper and master cylinder)	
1985 and 1986	25 to 35 Nm (18 to 25 ft-lbs)
1987 through 1993	30 Nm (22 ft-lbs)
1994 on	34 Nm (25 ft-lbs)
Brake lever pivot bolt nut	6 Nm (53 in-lbs)
Master cylinder clamp-to-handlebar bolts	12 Nm (108 in-lbs)

Rear axle

Axle pinch bolt	27 Nm (20 ft-lbs)
Rear axle nut	90 100 Nm (65 ft-lbs)

Rear drum brake (VT1100C)

Brake arm pinch bolt	26 Nm (20 ft-lbs)
Stopper arm-to-brake panel bolt	22 Nm (16 ft-lbs)
Brake pivot arm pinch bolt	26 Nm (20 ft-lbs)

Rear disc brake (VT1100C2 and VT1100T)

Brake caliper bolts	
Caliper-to-bracket bolt	23 Nm (17 ft-lbs)
Caliper pin bolt	27 Nm (20 ft-lbs)
Pad pin bolt	18 Nm (13 ft-lbs)
Caliper bracket stopper pin bolt	69 Nm (51 ft-lbs)
Brake hose banjo bolts (at caliper and master cylinder)	34 Nm (25 ft-lbs)
Master cylinder mounting bolts	12 Nm (108 in-lbs

2.3 Unscrew and remove the pad pin plug

2.4 Unscrew the pad pin

1 General information

The motorcycles covered in this Chapter are equipped with a hydraulic disc brake at the front and either a mechanical drum brake (VT1100C) or hydraulic disc brake (all others) at the rear. The front caliper is mounted on either the left or right fork leg, depending on model, but service procedures are the same for all front calipers. Some models are equipped with wire spoke wheels and tube-type tires; others are equipped with cast wheels and tubeless tires.

Caution: Disc brake components rarely require disassembly. Do not disassemble components unless absolutely necessary. If any hydraulic brake line connection in the system is loosened, the entire system should be disassembled, drained, cleaned and then properly filled and bled upon reassembly. Do not use solvents on internal brake components. Solvents will cause seals to swell and distort. Use only clean brake fluid, brake cleaner or alcohol for cleaning. Use care when working with brake fluid as it can injure your eyes and it will damage painted surfaces and plastic parts.

2 Brake pads - replacement

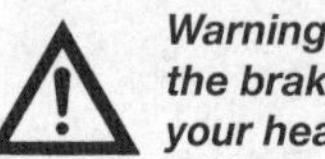

Warning: The dust created by the brake system is harmful to your health. Never blow it out with compressed air and don't inhale any of it. An approved filtering mask should be worn when working on the brakes.

1 Turn the handlebar so that the brake master cylinder is level, then remove the master cylinder reservoir cover, set plate and diaphragm (see Section 5).

2 Depress the caliper pistons by pushing the caliper in (toward the disc) with your thumbs. Watch the level of the brake fluid in the master cylinder reservoir; it will rise as you depress the caliper pistons. If it gets too close to the top, siphon off a little fluid from the reservoir. If you can't depress the pistons with thumb pressure, try using a C-clamp. If the pistons stick, remove the caliper and overhaul it (see Section 3).

Front brake pads

3 Remove the pad pin plug **(see illustration)**.

4 Remove the pad pin **(see illustration)**.

5 Remove the brake pads **(see illustration)**.

6 Remove the shims from the old pads (if they have shims).

7 Note whether the friction material on the pads has been worn down so that the wear grooves are exposed, or are about to be exposed. If so, replace the pads as a pair. If the pads are fouled with oil or are damaged, replace them.

8 Inspect the condition of the brake disc (see Section 4). If it needs to be machined or replaced, follow the procedure in that Section to remove it. If the disc is okay, deglaze it with sandpaper or emery cloth, using a swirling motion.

9 Inspect the condition of the pad retainer and the pad spring **(see illustration)**. If either of them is distorted or damaged, replace it. If you remove the retainer or the spring, make sure that the new part fits into the caliper exactly as shown. If either of these parts is incorrectly installed, the pads will not fit into the caliper correctly.

10 Install the shims (if equipped) on the new brake pads.

11 Install the pads in the caliper so that their upper ends rest against the pad retainer.

12 Push the pads against the pad spring, align the holes in the lower ends of the pads with the hole in the caliper, insert the pad pin **(see illustration)** and tighten it to the torque listed in this Chapter's Specifications.

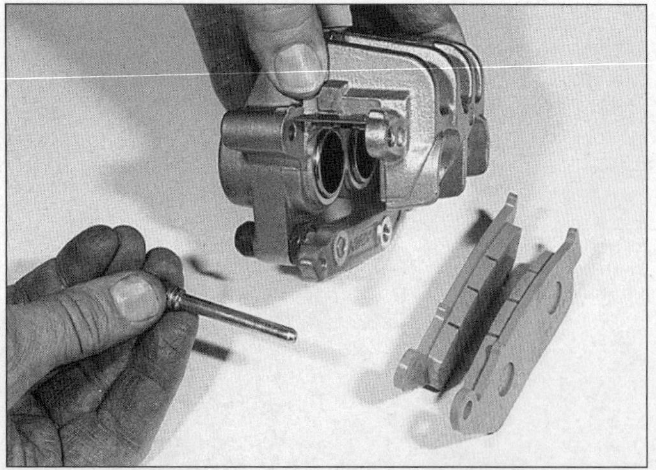

2.5 Pull out the pad pin plug and remove the brake pads; note how the pads are oriented to the caliper, with the holes for the pad pin at the bottom

2.9 Replace the pad retainer (left arrow) and the pad spring (right arrow) if either of them is damaged or worn

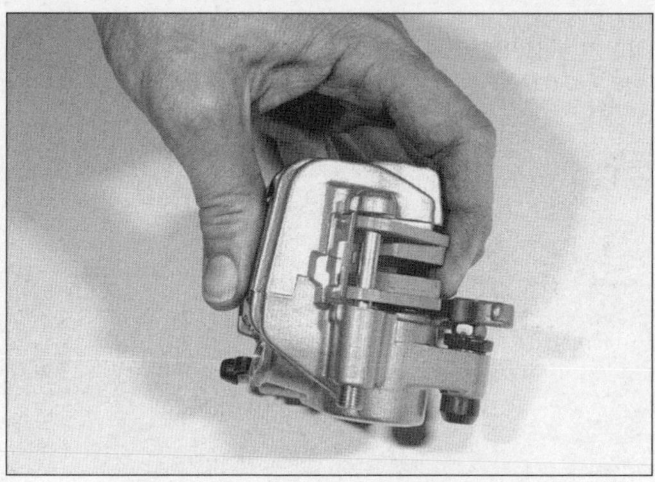

2.12 This is how the pads and the pad pin should look right before the pad pin is screwed into the caliper

2.14 Unscrew the pad pin plug and pin (upper arrow), remove the caliper bolt (lower arrow), swing the caliper up and pull out the pads

13 Install the pad pin plug and tighten it securely.

Rear brake pads

14 Remove the pad pin plug **(see illustration)** and loosen the pad pin.

15 Remove the caliper bracket bolt **(see illustration 2.14)**.

16 Swing the caliper up, remove the pad pin and remove the brake pads.

17 Inspect the brake pads, the brake disc, and the pad retainer and pad spring (see Steps 7, 8 and 9).

18 Install new pads and secure them with the pad pin.

19 Pivot the caliper back down and push the pads against the pad spring so that the ends of the pads are correctly engaged with the retainer on the caliper bracket.

20 Install the caliper bracket bolt and tighten it to the torque listed in this Chapter's Specifications.

21 Tighten the pad pin to the torque listed in this Chapter's Specifications.

22 Install the pad pin plug and tighten it securely.

Front and rear pads

23 Refill the master cylinder reservoir (see Chapter 1) and install the diaphragm and cover.

24 Operate the brake lever or brake pedal several times to bring the pads into contact with the disc. Check the operation of the brakes carefully before riding the motorcycle.

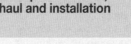

3 Brake caliper - removal, overhaul and installation

Warning: The dust created by the brake system is harmful to your health. Never blow it out with compressed air and don't inhale any of it. An approved filtering mask should be worn when working on the brakes. Do not, under any circumstances, use petroleum-based solvents to clean brake parts. Use brake cleaner or denatured alcohol only!

Removal

1 Remove the cover, set plate and diaphragm from the master cylinder and siphon out all of the old brake fluid.

2 Detach the brake hose from the fork slider. Disconnect the brake hose from the caliper **(see illustrations)**. Remove the brake hose banjo bolt and discard the sealing washers. Place the end of the hose in a container and operate the brake lever to pump out the rest of the brake fluid. After all the fluid has been expelled, wrap a clean shop rag tightly around the hose fitting to soak up any drips and prevent contamination.

3.2a To remove the front brake caliper, remove the banjo bolt (right arrow) and the mounting bolts (left arrows) - left-mounted caliper shown

3.2b To remove the rear brake caliper, remove the banjo bolt (upper arrow) and the mounting bolts (lower arrows)

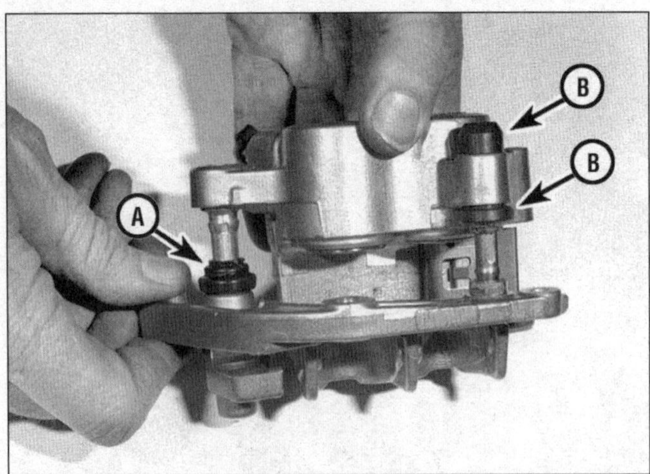

3.6 Pull the caliper and bracket apart; inspect the caliper pin dust boot (A) and the bracket pin boot (B) for cracks, tears and deterioration (front caliper shown)

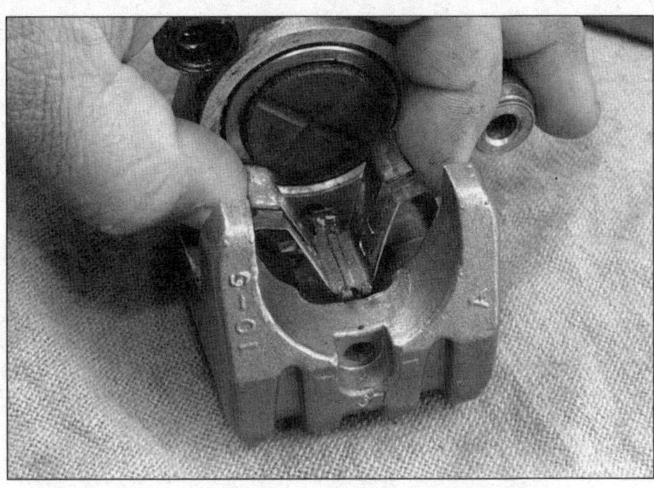

3.8 Remove the pad spring from the caliper and inspect it for cracks and fatigue (rear caliper shown)

3.11 After popping the pistons loose with compressed air, insert a pair of pliers inside each piston and pull them out of their bores (front caliper shown)

3 Remove the caliper bracket mounting bolts **(see illustration 3.2a or 3.2b)** and separate the caliper from the fork slider.

Overhaul

Note: *The accompanying illustrations depict a typical front caliper, which has two pistons. Rear calipers have only one dust seal, piston, piston seal, etc. but are otherwise similar to front calipers.*

4 Clean the exterior of the caliper with denatured alcohol or brake system cleaner.

5 Remove the brake pad pin and the brake pads (see Section 2).

6 If you're servicing a front caliper, separate the caliper bracket from the caliper **(see illustration)**.

7 On front calipers, remove the caliper pin dust boot and the pad retainer from the caliper bracket. Inspect the dust boot for cracks, tears and deterioration; replace it if it's damaged or worn. Make sure the retainer is neither bent nor damaged; if it is, replace it.

8 Remove the caliper bracket pin dust boot and the pad spring **(see illustration)** from the caliper. Inspect the boot for cracks, tears and deterioration; replace it if it's damaged or worn. Make sure the pad spring is neither bent nor damaged; if it is, replace it.

9 Place a few rags between the piston and the caliper frame to act as a cushion, lay the caliper on the work bench so that the pistons are facing down, toward the work bench surface, then use compressed air, directed into the fluid inlet, to remove the pistons. Use only small quick blasts of air to ease the pistons out of the bore. If a piston is blown out with too much force, it might be damaged.

Warning: Never place your fingers in front of the pistons in an attempt to catch or protect them when applying compressed air. Doing so could result in serious injury.

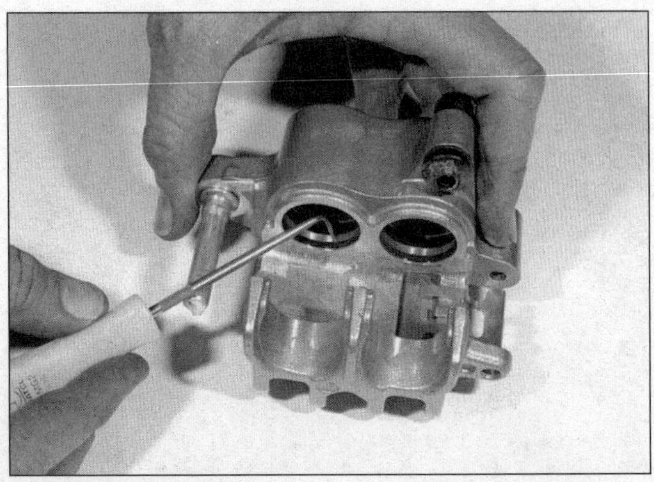

3.12a On front calipers, remove the dust (outer) seals and the piston (inner) seals from both bores; be careful not to scratch the bore surfaces

3.12b One way to protect the bore is to use a pencil to remove the seals (rear caliper shown)

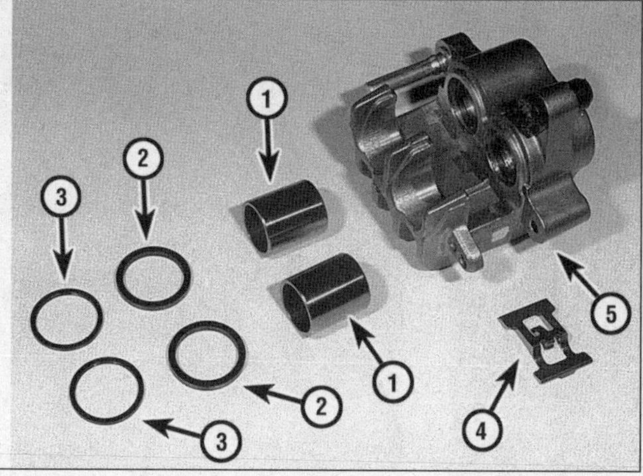

3.13 Front brake caliper assembly

1 *Pistons*
2 *Piston seal*
3 *Dust seal*
4 *Pad springs*
5 *Caliper*

10 If compressed air isn't available, reconnect the caliper to the brake hose and pump the brake lever until the piston is free. (You'll have to put brake fluid in the master cylinder reservoir and get most of the air out of the hose to use this method.)

11 Once the pistons are protruding from the caliper, remove them **(see illustration)**.

12 Using a wood or plastic tool, remove the dust seals and the piston seals **(see illustrations)**.

13 Clean the pistons and the piston bores with denatured alcohol, fresh brake fluid or brake system cleaner and dry them off with filtered, unlubricated compressed air. Inspect the surfaces of the pistons **(see illustration)** and the piston bores for nicks and burrs and loss of plating. If you find defects on the surface of either piston or piston bore, replace the caliper assembly (the pistons are matched to the caliper). If the caliper is in bad shape, inspect the master cylinder too.

14 Lubricate the new piston seals and dust seals with clean brake fluid and install them in their grooves in the caliper bore. Make sure they're not twisted and are fully and correctly seated.

15 Lubricate the pistons with clean brake fluid and install them into their bores in the caliper. Using your thumbs, push each piston all the way in **(see illustration)**; make sure it doesn't become cocked in the bore.

16 The caliper body should be able to slide in relation to its mounting bracket. If it was seized or operated stiffly prior to disassembly, inspect the slider pins on the caliper and the bracket for excessive wear. Minor blemishes can be cleaned up with crocus or emery cloth. If either pin shows signs of serious damage, replace it. The pins can be unscrewed from the bracket and caliper. If you remove either pin, be sure to tighten the new pin to the torque listed in this Chapter's Specifications. Coat the pins with high-temperature disc brake grease.

17 Reassemble the caliper and the caliper bracket. Make sure that the two parts slide smoothly in and out on the pins.

18 If the pad retainer or pad spring was removed, install it now **(see illustration 2.9)**.

19 Install the brake pads (see Section 2).

Installation

20 Install the caliper on the fork slider, install the caliper bracket mounting bolts and tighten them to the torque listed in this Chapter's Specifications.

21 Connect the brake hose to the caliper, using new sealing washers on each side of the banjo bolt.

22 Fill the master cylinder with the recommended brake fluid (see Chapter 1) and bleed the system (see Section 7). Check for leaks.

23 Check the operation of the brakes carefully before riding the motorcycle.

4 Brake disc - inspection, removal and installation

Inspection

1 Support the bike securely so it can't be knocked over during this procedure.

2 Visually inspect the surface of the disc for score marks and other damage. Light scratches are normal after use and won't affect brake operation, but deep grooves and heavy score marks will reduce braking efficiency and accelerate pad wear. If the disc is badly grooved it must be machined or replaced.

3 To check disc runout, mount a dial indicator to the fork leg with the plunger on the indicator touching the surface of the disc about 1/2-inch from the outer edge **(see illustration)**. Slowly turn the wheel and watch the indicator needle, comparing your reading with the limit listed in this Chapter's Specifications or stamped on the disc itself. If the runout is greater than allowed, replace the disc.

4 The disc must not be machined or allowed to wear down to a thickness less than the minimum allowable thickness, listed in this Chapter's Specifications. The thickness of the disc can be checked with

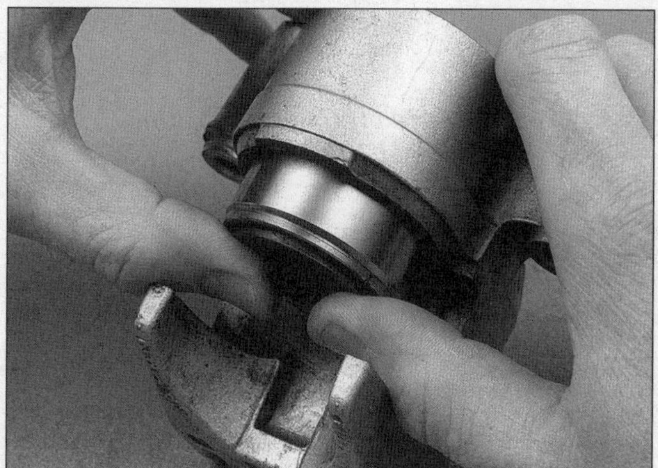

3.15 Bottom the piston in the caliper bore; make sure it goes in straight (rear caliper shown)

4.3 Set up a dial indicator as shown, with the probe touching the surface of the disc, and turn the wheel slowly to measure runout

4.4a Use a micrometer to measure the thickness of the disc at several points

4.4b If the minimum thickness stamped into the disc differs from the value listed in this Chapter's Specifications, use the information on the disc

a micrometer **(see illustration)**. If the thickness of the disc is less than the minimum allowable, it must be replaced. The minimum thickness is also stamped into the disc **(see illustration)**.

Removal

5 Remove the wheel (see Section 11 or 12).

6 Mark the relationship of the disc to the wheel, so it can be installed in the same position. Remove the bolts that retain the disc to the wheel hub **(see illustration)**. Loosen the bolts a little at a time, in a criss-cross pattern, to avoid distorting the disc. Once all the bolts are loose, take the disc off.

7 Take note of any paper shims that may be present where the disc mates to the hub. If there are any, mark their position and be sure to include them when installing the disc.

Installation

8 Position the disc on the wheel, aligning the previously applied match marks (if you're reinstalling the original disc). Make sure the arrow (stamped on the disc) marking the direction of rotation is pointing in the correct direction (the direction that the wheel rotates when the bike is moving forward).

9 Apply a non-hardening thread locking compound to the threads of the bolts. Install the bolts with new lockwashers, tightening them a little at a time, in a criss-cross pattern, until the torque listed in this Chapter's Specifications is reached. Clean off all grease from the brake disc using acetone or brake system cleaner.

10 Install the wheel (see Section 11 or 12).

11 Operate the brake lever several times to bring the pads into contact with the disc. Check the operation of the brakes carefully before riding the motorcycle.

4.6 To detach the disc from the wheel, remove the Allen bolts in a criss-cross fashion

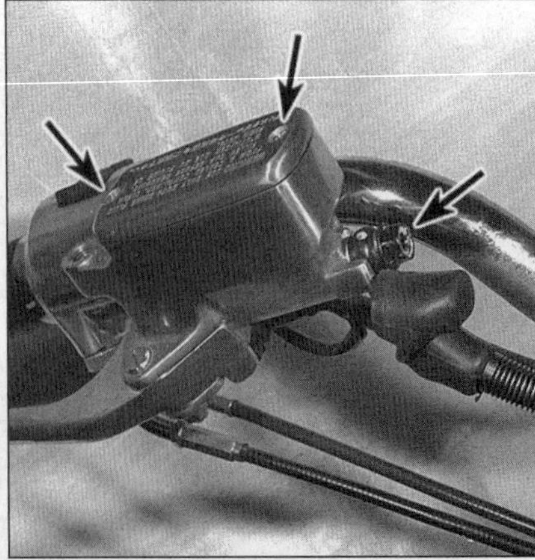

5.4 Master cylinder cover screws (left arrows) and brake hose banjo bolt (right arrow); use new sealing washers on the banjo fitting

5 Brake master cylinder - removal, overhaul and installation

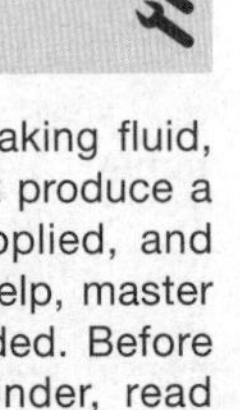

1 If the master cylinder is leaking fluid, or if the lever or pedal does not produce a firm feel when the brake is applied, and bleeding the brakes does not help, master cylinder overhaul is recommended. Before disassembling the master cylinder, read through the entire procedure and make sure that you have the correct rebuild kit. Also, you will need some new, clean brake fluid of the recommended type, some clean rags and internal snap-ring pliers. **Note:** *To prevent damage to the paint from spilled brake fluid, always cover the top cover or upper fuel tank when working on the master cylinder.*

2 ***Caution: Disassembly, overhaul and reassembly of the brake master cylinder must be done in a spotlessly clean work area to avoid contamination and possible failure of the brake hydraulic system components.***

Front master cylinder

Removal

3 Remove the rear view mirror.

4 Remove the reservoir cover retaining screws **(see illustration)**. Remove the reservoir, the set plate and the rubber diaphragm. Siphon as much brake fluid from the reservoir as you can to avoid spilling it on the bike.

5 Unplug the electrical connectors from the brake light switch (see Chapter 9).

6 Pull back the rubber dust boot, loosen the brake hose banjo bolt **(see illustration 5.4)** and separate the brake hose from the master cylinder. Wrap the end of the hose in a clean rag and suspend the hose in an upright position or bend it down carefully

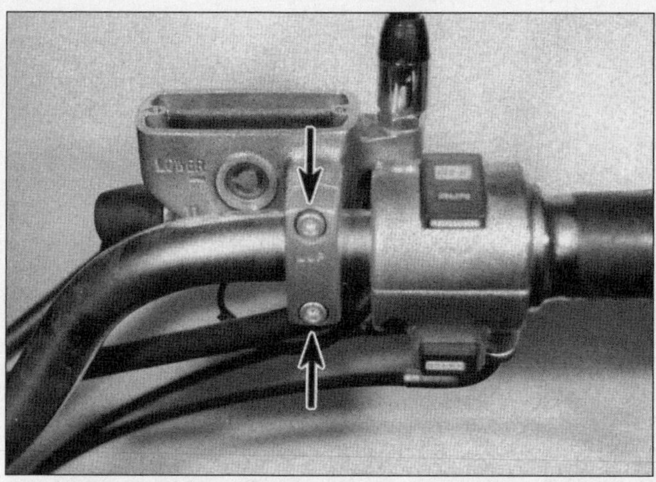

5.7 Master cylinder mounting bolts (arrows); the small arrow and the UP mark must point up when the master cylinder is installed

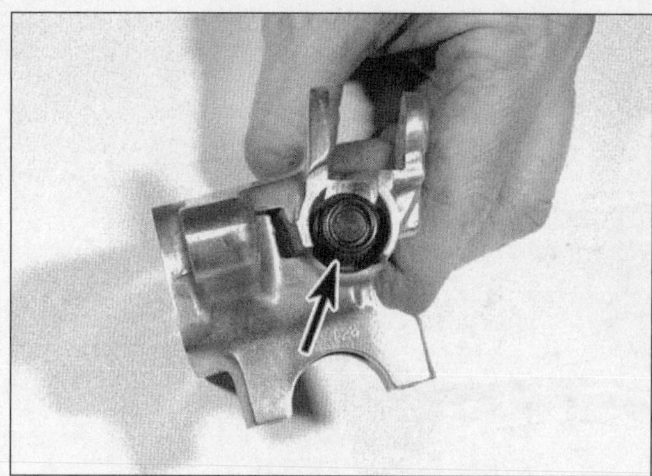

5.9a Remove the rubber dust boot (arrow) . . .

and place the open end in a clean container. The objective is to prevent excessive loss of brake fluid, fluid spills and system contamination.

7 Remove the master cylinder mounting bolts **(see illustration)** and separate the master cylinder from the handlebar.

Caution: Do not tip the master cylinder upside down or any brake fluid still in the reservoir will run out.

Overhaul

8 Remove the brake lever pivot bolt nut, remove the pivot bolt and remove the lever.

9 Carefully remove the rubber dust boot from the end of the piston **(see illustration)**. Using snap-ring pliers, remove the snap-ring **(see illustration)** and slide out the piston assembly and the spring.

10 Lay the parts out in the order in which they're removed to prevent confusion during reassembly **(see illustration)**.

11 Clean all of the parts with brake system cleaner (available at motorcycle dealerships and auto parts stores), isopropyl alcohol or clean brake fluid.

Caution: Do not, under any circumstances, use a petroleum-based solvent to clean brake parts.

If compressed air is available, use it to dry the parts thoroughly (make sure it's filtered and unlubricated). Check the master cylinder bore for corrosion, scratches, nicks and score marks. If damage is evident, the master cylinder must be replaced with a new one. If the master cylinder is in poor condition, then the calipers should be checked as well.

12 The dust seal, piston assembly and spring are included in the rebuild kit. Use all of the new parts, regardless of the apparent condition of the old ones.

13 Before reassembling the master cylinder, soak the piston and the rubber cup seals in clean brake fluid for ten or fifteen minutes. Lubricate the master cylinder bore with clean brake fluid, then carefully insert the piston and related parts in the reverse order of disassembly. Make sure the lips on the cup seals do not turn inside out when they are slipped into the bore.

14 Depress the piston, then install the snap-ring (make sure the snap-ring is prop-

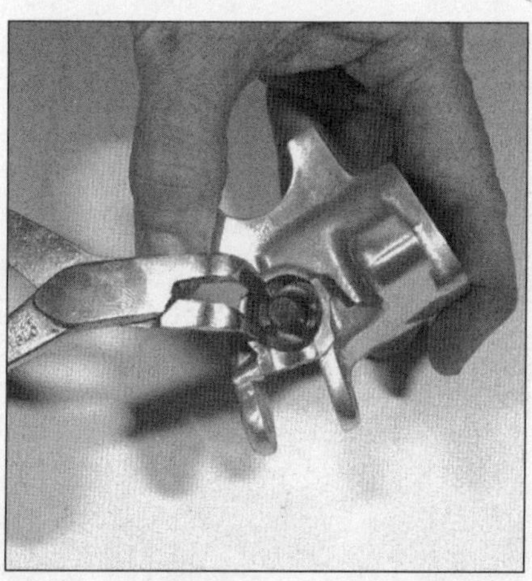

5.9b . . . and remove the snap-ring from the bore

5.10 Master cylinder details

1 *Reservoir cover*
2 *Set plate*
3 *Rubber diaphragm*
4 *Master cylinder body*
5 *Brake hose banjo bolt*
6 *Sealing washers*
7 *Master cylinder mounting bracket*
8 *Brake lever pivot bolt nut*
9 *Brake lever pivot bolt*
10 *Brake lever*
11 *Rubber dust boot*
12 *Snap-ring*
13 *Washer*
14 *Piston/spring assembly*
15 *Brake light switch mounting screw*
16 *Brake light switch*

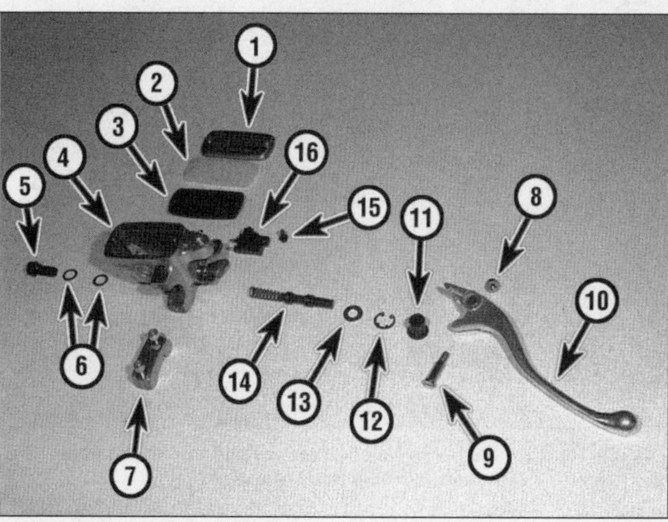

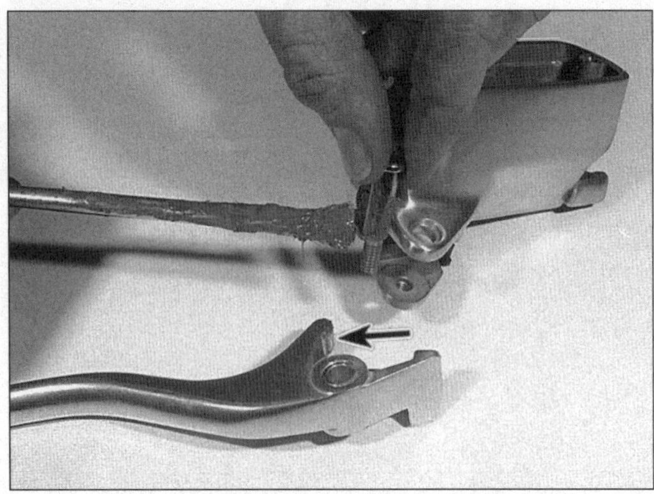

5.15 Lubricate the brake lever pivot and the part of the lever (arrow) that pushes against the piston

5.19a To reach the rear master cylinder reservoir, remove this bolt (arrow) . . .

5.19b . . . and remove the cover

erly seated in the groove). Install the rubber dust boot (make sure the lip is seated properly in the piston groove).

15 Lubricate the brake lever pivot bolt and the friction surface on the lever that pushes against the piston assembly **(see illustration)**.

Installation

16 Attach the master cylinder to the handlebar and tighten the bolts to the torque listed in this Chapter's Specifications.

17 Connect the brake hose to the master cylinder, using new sealing washers. Tighten the banjo bolt to the torque listed in this Chapter's Specifications.

18 Fill the master cylinder with the recommended brake fluid (see Chapter 1), then bleed the air from the system (see Section 7).

Rear master cylinder (VT1100C2 and VT1100T models)

Removal

19 Remove the master cylinder cover **(see illustrations)**, unscrew the reservoir cap and siphon the brake fluid from the rear master cylinder reservoir.

20 Remove the master cylinder mounting bolts and remove the shield **(see illustrations)**. Remove the brake hose banjo bolt. Discard the old sealing washers. Detach the reservoir hose from the master cylinder, either by sliding back the hose clamp and pulling the hose off the fitting or by removing the fitting screw. **Note:** *When the exhaust system is installed, the reservoir hose is a lot easier to detach by removing the screw.*

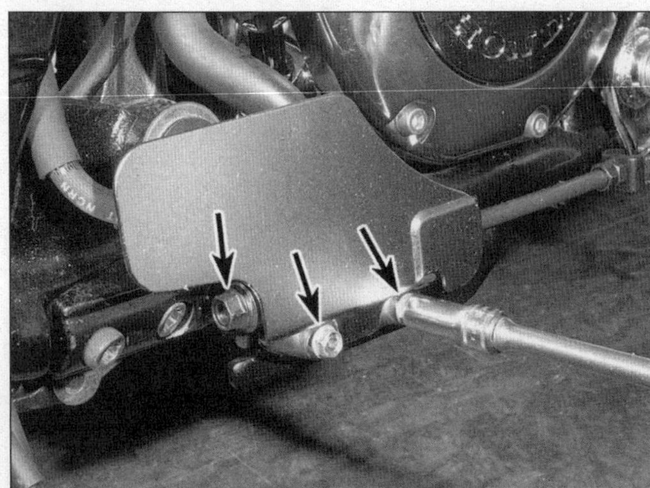

5.20a Remove the banjo bolt (left arrow) and the rear master cylinder mounting bolts (arrows) . . .

5.20b . . . remove the heat shield and disconnect the reservoir hose, either by sliding back the hose clamp or by removing this screw

5.21 Remove the cotter pin, pull out the clevis pin (arrow) and disengage the pushrod clevis from the brake pedal

21 Remove the cotter pin from the clevis pin **(see illustration 9.18)**, remove the clevis pin **(see illustration)** and disengage the pushrod clevis from the brake pedal.

Overhaul

Caution: Disassembly, overhaul and reassembly of the brake master cylinder must be done in a spotlessly clean work area to avoid contamination and possible failure of the brake hydraulic system components.

22 Pull the dust boot cover off the front end of the master cylinder and slide it forward on the pushrod. Remove the small end of the dust boot from its groove in the pushrod, detach the big end from the master cylinder and slide the dust boot forward.

23 Depress the pushrod and, using snap-ring pliers, remove the snap-ring. Remove the master piston and spring. Lay the parts out in the proper order to prevent confusion during reassembly.

24 Clean all of the parts with brake system cleaner (available at auto parts stores), isopropyl alcohol or clean brake fluid.

Caution: Do not, under any circumstances, use a petroleum-based solvent to clean brake parts.

If compressed air is available, use it to dry the parts thoroughly (make sure it's filtered and unlubricated). Check the master cylinder bore for corrosion, scratches, nicks and score marks. If damage is evident, the master cylinder must be replaced with a new one. If the master cylinder is in poor condition, then the caliper should be checked as well.

25 Inspect the bore of the master cylinder, piston and piston cups for wear, damage and deterioration. Measure the inside diameter of the master cylinder and the outside diameter of the piston and compare your measurements to the service limit for these components listed in this Chapter's Specifications. If either part is worn beyond the service limit, replace it.

26 Remove the old cup seals from the piston and spring and install the new ones. Make sure the lips face away from the pushrod end of the piston. If a new piston is included in the rebuild kit, use it regardless of the condition of the old one.

27 Before reassembling the master cylinder, soak the piston and the rubber cup seals in clean brake fluid for ten or fifteen minutes. Lubricate the master cylinder bore with clean brake fluid, then carefully insert the parts in the reverse order of disassembly. Make sure the lips on the cup seals do not turn inside out when they are slipped into the bore.

28 If you're installing a new dust boot cover and/or dust boot, back off the clevis locknut and adjustment nut and unscrew the clevis from the pushrod, tape the threads of the pushrod to protect the new rubber parts, slide the dust boot and dust boot cover onto the pushrod and install the clevis. Don't tighten the clevis adjustment nut and locknut yet; the clevis must be adjusted.

29 Lubricate the end of the pushrod with silicone grease designed for brake applications, and install the pushrod and stop washer into the cylinder bore. Depress the pushrod, then install the snap-ring (make sure the snap-ring is properly seated in the groove with the sharp edge facing out).

30 Install the rubber dust boot (make sure the small end is correctly seated in the groove in the pushrod). Install the dust boot cover and align the cut-out in the cover with the mounting boss of the master cylinder.

31 Screw the clevis onto the pushrod to set the distance from the center of the forward mounting bolt hole to the center of the clevis pin hole to the dimension listed in this Chapter's Specifications.

Installation

32 Position the master cylinder on the frame and secure it with the mounting bolts, but don't tighten the bolts yet.

33 Reattach the hose from the reservoir, if removed. If the hose joint was removed, install a new O-ring and tighten the screw securely.

34 Connect the master cylinder outlet hose with the banjo bolt, using new sealing washers on each side of the bolt. Hand tighten the banjo bolt.

35 Remove the master cylinder mounting bolts, install the heat shield, install the bolts and tighten them to the torque listed in this Chapter's Specifications.

36 Tighten the banjo bolt to the torque listed in this Chapter's Specifications.

37 Connect the clevis to the brake pedal, secure the clevis pin with a new cotter pin and install the retainer.

38 Fill the fluid reservoir with the specified fluid (see Chapter 1) and bleed the system following the procedure in Section 8. Install the cover.

39 Check the position of the brake pedal (see Chapter 1) and adjust it if necessary. Check the operation of the brakes carefully before riding the motorcycle.

6 Brake hose - inspection and replacement

Inspection

1 Once a week or, if the motorcycle is used less frequently, before every ride, check the condition of the brake hose(s).

2 Twist and flex the rubber hoses while looking for cracks, bulges and seeping fluid. Check extra carefully around the areas where the hoses connect with the banjo bolts, as these are common areas for hose failure.

3 Inspect the metal banjo fittings connected to the brake hoses. If the fittings are corroded, scratched or cracked, replace them.

Replacement

4 The brake hose has a banjo fitting on each end of the hose. Cover the surrounding area with plenty of rags and unscrew the union bolt on either end of the hose. Detach the hose from any clips that may be present and remove the hose.

5 Position the new hose, making sure it isn't twisted or otherwise strained, between the two components. Install the union bolts, using new sealing washers on both sides of the fittings, and tighten them to the torque listed in this Chapter's Specifications.

6 Flush the old brake fluid from the system, refill the system with the recommended fluid (see Chapter 1) and bleed the air from the system (see Section 7). Check the operation of the front brake carefully before riding the motorcycle.

7 Brake system bleeding

1 Bleeding the brake system removes all the air bubbles from the brake fluid reservoir(s), the lines and the brake caliper(s). Bleeding is necessary whenever a brake system hydraulic connection is loosened, when a component or hose is replaced, or when a master cylinder or caliper is overhauled. Leaks in the system may also allow air to enter, but leaking brake fluid will reveal their presence and warn you of the need for repair.

2 To bleed the brakes, you will need some new, clean brake fluid of the recommended type (see Chapter 1), a length of clear vinyl or plastic tubing, a small container partially filled with clean brake fluid, some rags and a wrench to fit the brake caliper bleeder valves.

3 Cover the fuel tank and any other painted surfaces near the reservoir to prevent damage in the event that brake fluid is spilled.

4 On the front brake, remove the reservoir cover screws and remove the cover, set plate

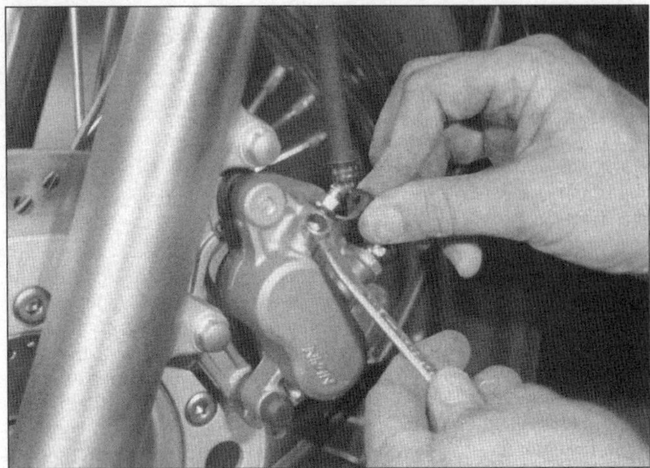

7.5a Remove the rubber dust boot from the bleed valve, place a box wrench over the bleed valve . . .

7.5b . . . then connect a length of clear plastic tubing to the valve and submerge the other end of the tubing in a jar of clean brake fluid

and diaphragm. On the rear brake, unscrew the reservoir cap. Slowly pump the brake lever or pedal a few times, until no air bubbles can be seen floating up from the bottom of the reservoir. Doing this bleeds the air from the master cylinder end of the line. Top up the reservoir with new fluid. Temporarily install the cover or cap, but don't tighten them; you may have to remove the cover or cap several times during the procedure.

5 Remove the rubber dust cover from the bleeder valve **(see illustration)** and slip a box wrench over the caliper bleed valve. Attach one end of the clear vinyl or plastic tubing to the bleed valve **(see illustration)** and submerge the other end in the brake fluid in the container.

6 Carefully pump the brake lever three or four times and hold it while opening the caliper bleeder valve. When the valve is opened, brake fluid will flow out of the caliper into the clear tubing and the lever will move toward the handlebar. Retighten the bleed valve, then release the brake lever gradually.

7 Repeat this procedure until no air bubbles are visible in the brake fluid leaving the caliper and the lever is firm when applied. **Note:** *Remember to add fluid to the reservoir as the level drops. Use only new, clean brake fluid of the recommended type. Never re-use the fluid lost during bleeding.*

8 Keep an eye on the fluid level in the reservoir, especially if there's a lot of air in the system. Every time you crack the bleed valve open, the fluid level in the reservoir drops a little. Do not allow the fluid level to drop below the lower mark during the bleeding process. If it drops too low, air will be drawn into the system and you'll have to do the whole procedure over. If the level looks low, uncover the reservoir and add some fluid.

9 When you're done, inspect the fluid level in the reservoir one more time, add some fluid if necessary, then install the diaphragm, set plate and reservoir cover and tighten the screws securely. Wipe up any spilled brake fluid and check the entire system for leaks. **Note:** *If bleeding is difficult, it may be necessary to let the brake fluid in the system stabilize for a few hours (it may be aerated). Repeat the bleeding procedure when the tiny bubbles in the system have settled out.*

8 Drum brake - removal, overhaul and installation

Drum brake

Removal and disassembly

1 Before you start, inspect the rear brake wear indicator (see Chapter 1). If the shoes are excessively worn, replace them.

8.2 Push the brake arm forward, unscrew the adjuster nut from the brake rod and disengage the rod from the clevis pin

8.3a To detach the stopper arm from the brake panel, remove the cotter pin . . .

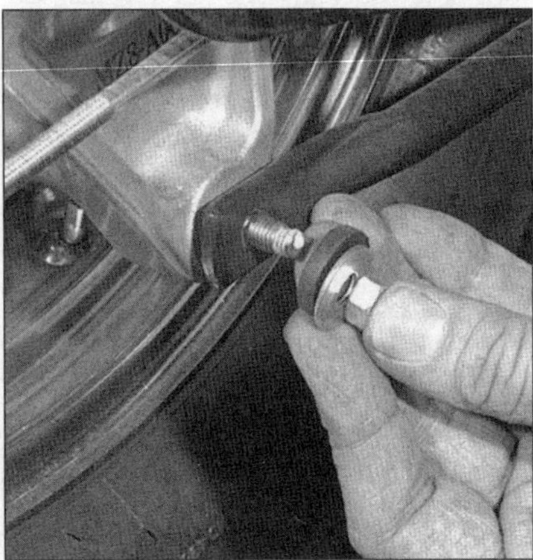

8.3b . . . remove the nut and the metal and rubber washers from the bolt, slide off the stopper arm and remove the bolt from the brake panel

8.5 Remove the brake panel from the wheel

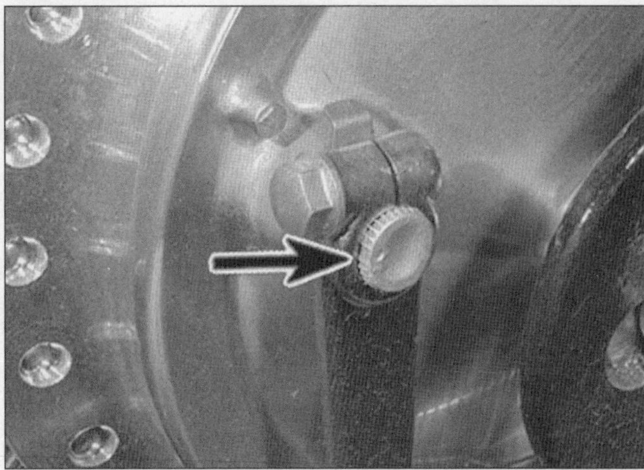

8.6a Remove the pinch bolt completely and slide the arm off the brake cam spindle; the punch mark on the spindle indicates the wide spline, used to align the arm when it's installed

2 Disconnect the brake rod from the brake arm **(see illustration)**. Store the adjuster nut, the clevis pin and the brake rod spring in a container so they won't be lost.

3 Disconnect the rear brake stopper arm **(see illustrations)**.

4 Remove the rear wheel (see Section 12).

5 Remove the brake panel from the wheel **(see illustration)**.

6 Remove the brake arm pinch bolt **(see illustration)** and remove the brake arm from the splined spindle end of the brake cam. Note the punch mark on the end of the brake cam spindle; this mark indicates the location of the wider spline on the spindle. This wider spline must be aligned with the corresponding wider spline on the brake arm when the arm is installed. Remove the indicator plate and the felt seal **(see illustrations)**. Pull the brake cam out of the brake panel.

7 Remove the cotter pins from the anchor pins **(see illustration)** and remove the set plate (the oblong-shaped spacer that fits over the ends of both anchor pins). To remove the shoes from the brake panel, spread them apart slightly to clear the ridges on the brake cam, then slide them up and off the anchor pins **(see illustration)**. Disengage the shoes and springs **(see illustration)**.

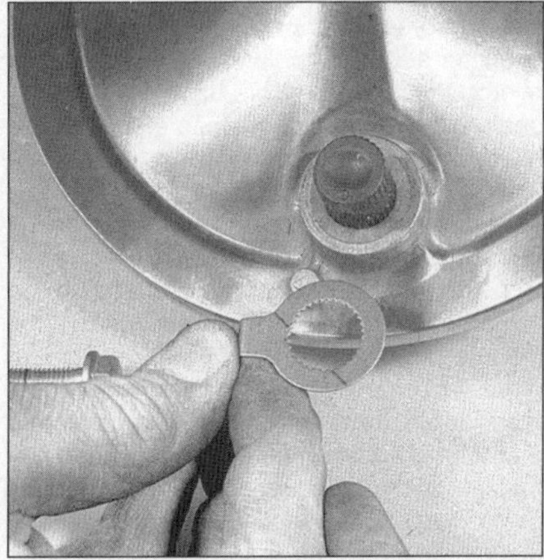

8.6b Remove the indicator plate from the brake cam spindle

8.6c Remove the felt seal from the brake cam spindle

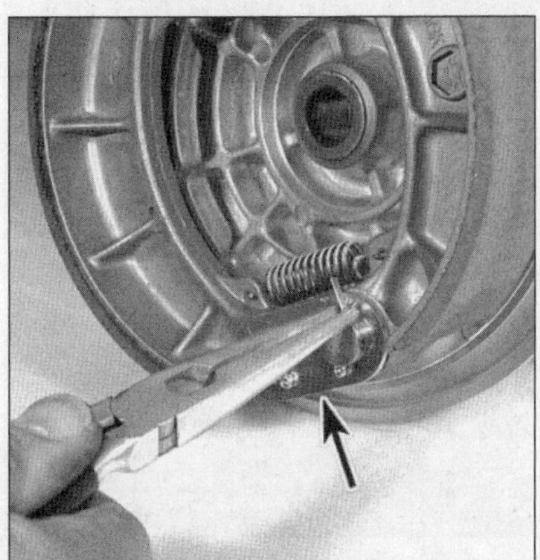

8.7a Remove the cotter pins from the anchor pins and remove the set plate (arrow)

8.7b Spread the upper ends of the shoes to clear the ridges on the brake cam and pull the shoes off

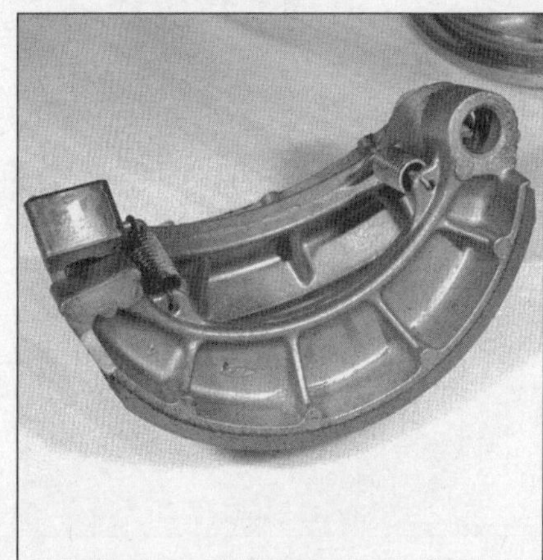

8.7c Disengage the brake shoes and springs

8.12 If maximum drum diameter cast into the hub differs from the limit in this Chapter's Specifications, use the number on the drum

8.14a When installing the brake shoes, make sure the upper ends of the shoes are correctly seated against the brake cam . . .

Inspection

8 Inspect the linings for wear, damage and signs of contamination from road dirt and water. If the linings are visibly defective, replace them.

9 Measure the thickness of the lining material (just the lining material, not the metal backing) and compare your measurements to the minimum thickness listed in this Chapter's Specifications. If the lining material is worn to less than the minimum, replace the shoes.

10 Inspect the ends of the shoes, where they contact the brake cam and where they slip over the anchor pins. If there's visible wear, replace the shoes.

11 Check the fit of the brake cam in the brake panel hole. If it feels loose, replace the brake cam or the panel, depending on which part is worn. Inspect the anchor pins for wear and damage. If the anchor pins are worn, replace the brake panel.

12 Inspect the brake drum (inside the wheel hub) for wear or damage. Measure the diameter at several points with a brake drum micrometer (or have this done by a Honda dealer). If the measurements are uneven (the brake drum is "out-of-round") or if there are scratches deep enough to snag a fingernail, have the drum turned by a dealer service department or a motorcycle machine shop to correct the surface. If the drum has to be turned beyond the wear limit to remove the defects, replace it. You'll find the maximum diameter of the drum cast into the wheel **(see illustration)**. If the specified maximum diameter on the wheel is different from the maximum diameter listed in this Chapter's Specifications, the specification on the wheel supersedes the value in the Specifications.

Reassembly and installation

13 Apply high-temperature brake grease to the ends of the springs, the brake cam and the anchor pins. Install the brake cam, the felt seal and the indicator plate. Install the brake arm. Make sure the punch marks on the brake arm and the brake cam spindle are aligned. Install the brake arm pinch bolt and tighten it securely.

14 Hook the springs to the shoes. Position the shoes over the brake panel, slide the lower ends of the shoes onto the ends of the anchor pins, spread the upper ends of the shoes apart far enough to clear the ridges on the brake cam, push the shoes down onto the anchor pins and release the upper ends of the shoes. Make sure the upper ends of the shoes fit correctly against the brake cam and the lower ends are fully seated on the anchor pins **(see illustrations)**. Install the set plate and install new cotter pins on the anchor pins **(see illustration)**.

15 Install the brake panel and brake shoe assembly in the wheel.

16 Install the wheel (see Section 12).

17 Reattach the brake rod to the brake arm

8.14b . . . and the lower ends are correctly seated against the shoulders at the lower ends of the anchor pins

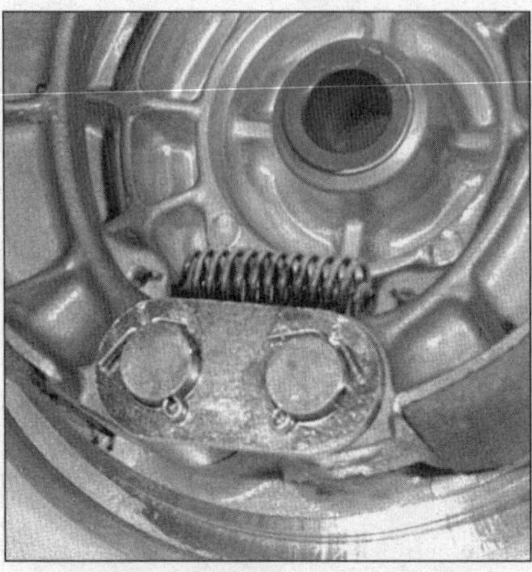

8.14c Once the shoes are correctly positioned on the brake panel, install the set plate and secure it with new cotter pins in the anchor pins

8.17 Install the spring on the brake rod, insert the rod in the clevis, push the brake arm forward and install the adjuster nut

9.4a Remove the cotter pin, pull out the clevis pin (arrow) and disconnect the middle brake rod from the brake pedal arm . . .

9.4b . . . and disconnect the other end of the middle brake rod from the brake shaft arm (arrow)

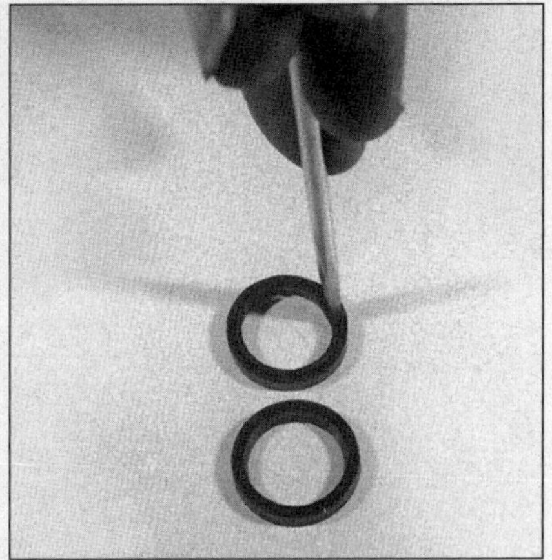
9.10 Install the dust seals with their open sides facing inward

clevis pin **(see illustration)** and install the adjuster nut.

18 Adjust the rear brake pedal freeplay (see Chapter 1).

19 Adjust the rear brake light switch (see Chapter 1).

9 Rear brake pedal and linkage - removal and installation

1985 and 1986 models

Note: *These models have no brake linkage. The brake pedal is attached directly to a pedal shaft that operates the brake rod.*

1 Look for a set of punch marks on the brake pedal and the pedal shaft. These marks must be aligned when the pedal is installed again. If there are no punch marks, make your own.

2 Loosen or remove the brake pedal pinch bolt and pull the pedal off the shaft.

3 Installation is the reverse of removal. Make sure the punch marks are aligned and tighten the pinch bolt securely.

1987 and later VT1100C models

Middle brake rod

4 Remove the cotter pins and clevis pins from both ends of the middle brake rod and disconnect the rod from the rear brake pedal and from the brake pivot arm **(see illustrations)**.

5 Installation is the reverse of removal. Use new cotter pins to secure the clevis pins.

Brake pedal

6 Disconnect the middle brake rod from the rear brake pedal (see Step 4).

7 Unbolt the right footpeg bracket from the frame.

8 Remove the footpeg bracket, the brake pedal, the pivot collar (bushing) and the dust seals from the footpeg bracket. Clean the parts thoroughly and dry them off for inspection. Clean out the pivot bore of the pedal (that fits over the pivot collar) with a cylindrical wire brush.

9 Inspect the pivot collar for scoring and other damage. If it's worn or damaged, replace it.

10 Inspect the dust seals **(see illustration)**. If they're torn, cracked or deteriorated, replace them.

11 Grease the collar **(see illustration)**. Make sure the surface of the bore in the pedal that fits over the collar is clean and free of debris and old grease.

12 Reassemble the collar, dust seals and brake pedal **(see illustration)**.

13 Installation is the reverse of removal.

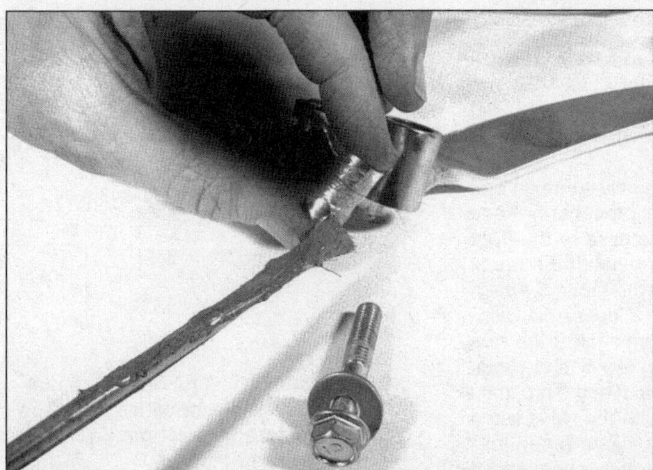
9.11 Grease the collar and the inside of the pivot bore in the pedal before reassembling

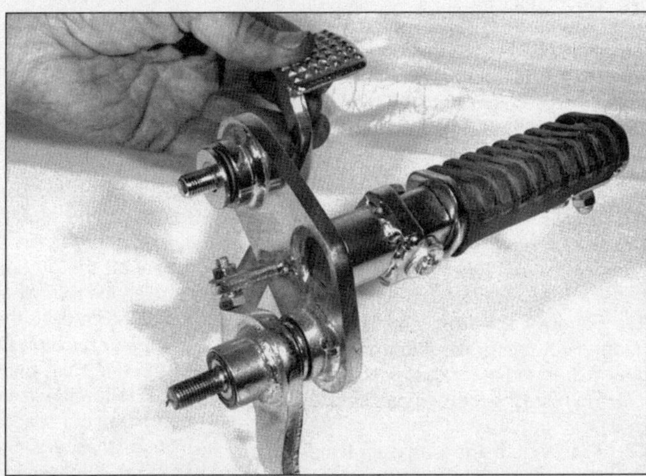
9.12 This is what the assembled footpeg bracket and rear brake pedal should look like when you're done

9.16 To detach the brake pedal from the pedal pivot shaft on a VT1100C2 or VT1100T, remove this snap-ring

9.18a After removing the footpeg bracket, disconnect the pedal return spring and the brake light switch return spring (arrows) . . .

9.18b . . . then slide the pedal brake pedal off the pivot shaft; unless you're replacing the pedal or the rear master cylinder, it's not necessary to disconnect the pushrod from the pedal

Tighten the footpeg bracket bolts securely.

14 Reconnect the middle brake rod to the brake pedal and install a new cotter pin in the clevis pin.

15 Check and, if necessary, adjust the rear brake pedal height and the rear brake light switch (see Chapter 1).

VT1100C2 and VT1100T models

Note: *The pushrod connecting the brake pedal to the rear brake master cylinder is part of the master cylinder (see Section 5).*

16 Remove the snap-ring from the brake pedal pivot shaft **(see illustration)**. Remove the washer and outer dust seal.

17 Remove the footpeg bracket (see Chapter 8).

18 Disconnect the pedal and brake light switch return springs **(see illustration)**. Remove the pedal **(see illustration)** and inner dust seal and disconnect the master cylinder pushrod from the pedal (see Section 5).

19 Wipe off the pedal pivot shaft and wipe out the pivot shaft bore of the brake pedal. Inspect both for any signs of corrosion or excessive wear. If the pedal shaft bore is corroded, clean it out with a cylindrical wire brush.

20 Inspect the dust seals **(see illustration 9.10)**. Discard them if they're worn or damaged.

21 Grease the pivot shaft, the pivot shaft bore and the dust seals. Install the inner and outer seals in the pivot shaft bore and install the pedal. Install the washer and the O-ring.

22 Reconnect the master cylinder pushrod if it was disconnected (see Section 5).

23 Hook up the brake light switch and pedal return springs.

24 Install the footpeg bracket (see Chapter 8).

10 Wheels - inspection and repair

1 Clean the wheels thoroughly to remove mud and dirt that may interfere with the inspection procedure or mask defects. Make a general check of the wheels and tires as described in Chapter 1.

2 Support the bike securely so it can't be knocked over during this procedure. Place a jack beneath the engine to raise the front wheel off the ground, or beneath the frame to raise the rear wheel off the ground. Attach a dial indicator to the fork slider or the swingarm and position the stem against the side of the rim. Spin the wheel slowly and check the side-to-side (axial) runout of the rim, then compare your readings with the value listed in this Chapter's Specifications **(see illustration)**. In order to accurately check radial runout with the dial indicator, the wheel would have to be removed from the machine and the tire removed from the wheel. With the axle clamped in a vise, the wheel can be rotated to check the runout.

3 An easier, though slightly less accurate, method is to attach a stiff wire pointer to the fork or the swingarm and position the end a fraction of an inch from the wheel (where the wheel and tire join). If the wheel is true, the distance from the pointer to the rim will be constant as the wheel is rotated. Repeat the procedure to check the runout of the rear wheel. **Note:** *If wheel runout is excessive, refer to the appropriate Section in this Chapter and check the wheel bearings very carefully before replacing the wheel or paying to have it trued.*

4 The wheels should also be visually

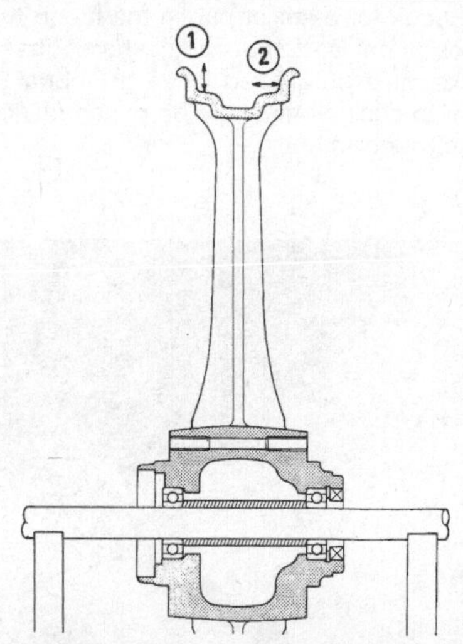

10.2 Measure wheel runout with a dial indicator, if available, or with a flat piece of metal and feeler gauge

1 *Radial (up-and-down) runout*
2 *Axial (side-to-side) runout*

10.5 **If a spoke is loose, tighten the spoke nipple with a poke wrench (available at any motorcycle dealership or accessory store)**

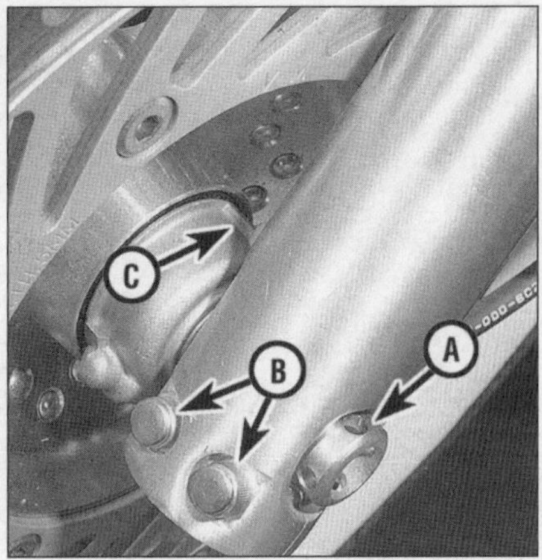

11.3a Left fork leg details

A *Axle*
B *Pinch bolt caps*
C *Speedometer drive unit lug*

11.3b Right fork leg pinch bolt caps (lower arrows) and axle bolt (upper arrow)

inspected for cracks, flat spots on the rim, bent spokes and other damage.

5 On models with spoke wheels, tap the spokes with a metal screwdriver blade or similar tool and listen to the sound. If the spoke makes a "clunk" or low-pitched sound, it's loose. Tighten the spoke **(see illustration)**.

6 If damage is evident, or if runout in either direction is excessive, the wheel will have to be trued or, if damage is severe, replaced with a new one.

11 Front wheel - removal and installation

Removal

1 Support the bike securely so it can't be knocked over during this procedure. Raise the front wheel off the ground by placing a floor jack, with a wood block on the jack head, under the engine.

2 Disconnect the speedometer cable from the speedometer gearbox (see Chapter 9).

3 On 1985 and 1986 models, loosen the axle holder bolts. On all other models, loosen the axle pinch bolts **(see illustrations)**. Unscrew the axle bolt from the right fork leg.

4 Support the wheel, then pull out the axle and carefully lower the wheel from the forks.

5 Remove the speedometer gearbox unit from the left side of the wheel and remove the collar from the right side **(see illustrations)**. Set the wheel aside.

Caution: Don't allow the wheel to rest on the brake disc - the disc could become warped. Set the wheel on wood blocks so the disc doesn't support the weight of the wheel.

Note: *Don't operate the front brake lever with the wheel removed.*

Inspection

6 Roll the axle on a flat surface such as a piece of plate glass. If it's bent, replace it. If the axle is corroded, remove the corrosion with fine emery cloth.

7 Inspect the wheel bearings (see Section 13).

Installation

8 Installation is the reverse of removal. Apply a thin coat of grease to the seal lip, then slide the axle into the hub. Slide the wheel into place. Make sure the lugs in the speedometer drive clutch line up with the notches in the speedometer drive unit **(see illustration)**. Make sure the protrusion on the speedometer drive unit rests against the back of the stop on the inner side of the left fork **(see illustration 11.3a)**.

9 Slip the axle into place, then tighten the axle bolt to the torque listed in this Chapter's Specifications. Tighten the axle pinch bolts

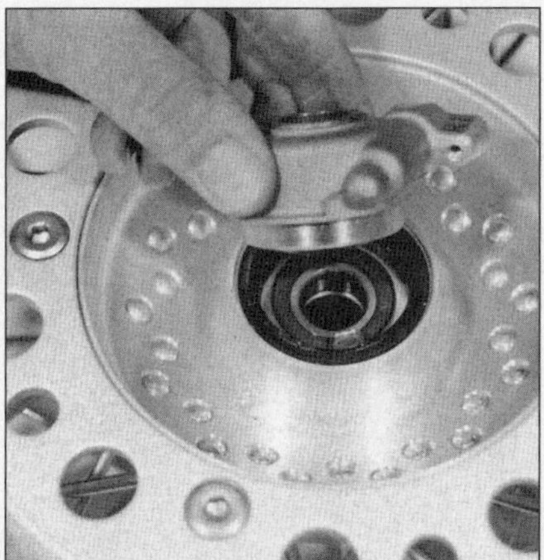

11.5a Remove the speedometer drive unit from the left side of the wheel . . .

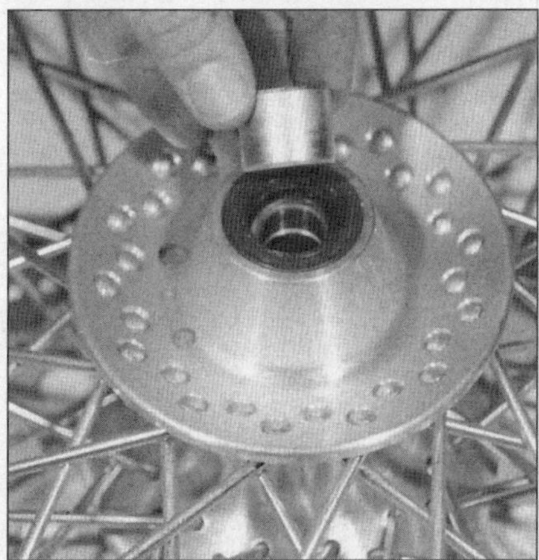

11.5b . . . and remove the collar from the right side

11.8 When installing the speedometer drive unit, make sure the tangs align with the slots

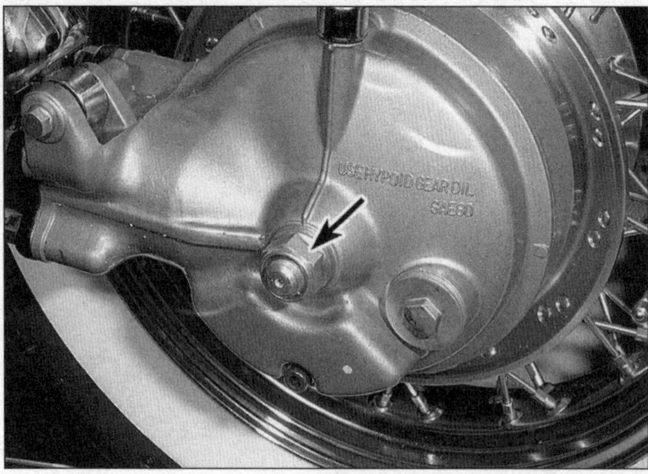

12.5 Hold the rear axle from the other side of the wheel with a hex bit and remove the axle nut (arrow)

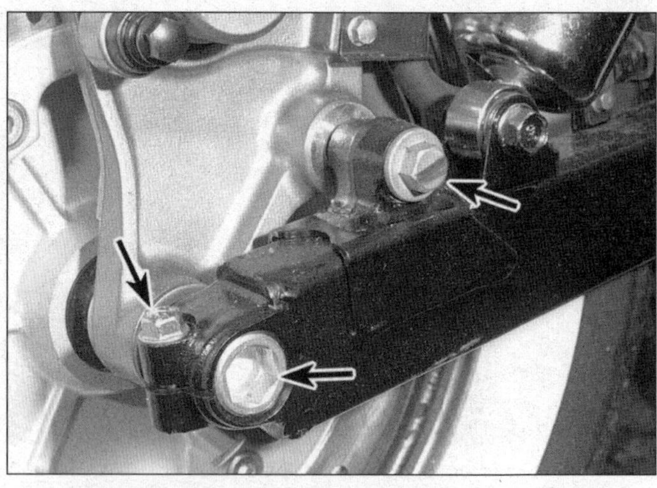

12.7 To detach the brake caliper bracket from the swingarm, remove the stopper pin bolt (right arrow), loosen the axle pinch bolt (left arrow) and pull out the axle (middle arrow)

to the torque listed in this Chapter's Specifications.

10 Apply the front brake, pump the forks up and down several times and check for binding and proper brake operation.

12 Rear wheel - removal and installation

Removal

1 Support the bike securely, with the rear wheel off the ground, during this procedure. 1985 and 1986 models have a center stand; other models will have to be raised with a jack, lift or hoist.

2 On 1987 through 1996 models, it's easier (but not absolutely necessary) to service the rear wheel with the exhaust system removed (see Chapter 4).

3 On VT1100T models, remove the mufflers (see Chapter 4) and the saddlebags (see Chapter 8).

4 On VT1100C2, VT1100T and 1997-on VT1100C models, it's easier (but not absolutely essential) to service the rear wheel with the rear fender removed (see Chapter 8).

5 Remove the axle nut **(see illustration)**.

6 On models with rear drum brakes, detach the brake rod from the brake arm and the stopper arm from the brake panel (see Section 8).

7 On models with rear disc brakes, remove the rear caliper stopper pin bolt **(see illustration)**.

8 Remove the axle pinch bolt **(see illustration 12.7)**.

9 Support the wheel, pull out the axle, lift up the caliper and caliper bracket, remove the thrust washer (goes between the caliper bracket and the swingarm), move the wheel to the right to disengage it from the final drive unit and remove the wheel. Remove the spacer collar from the right side of the wheel.

10 On models with rear drum brakes, remove the brake panel from the wheel (see Section 8).

11 Inspect the seals and the wheel bearings (see Section 13).

12 Before installing the wheel, check the axle for straightness by rolling it on a flat surface such as a piece of plate glass (if the axle is corroded, first remove the corrosion with fine emery cloth). If the axle is bent, replace it.

Installation

13 Installation is the reverse of removal. Apply a light coat of molybdenum disulfide grease to the splines on the final drive unit and the driven flange on the wheel hub. Tighten the axle nut, axle pinch bolt and brake fasteners to the torque listed in this Chapter's Specifications.

14 Adjust the rear brake pedal (see Chapter 1).

15 Carefully check the operation of the brake before riding the motorcycle.

13 Wheel bearings - inspection and maintenance

Note: *A common method of removing wheel bearings is to insert a drift from one side of the hub and drive out the opposite bearing. On these models, there is usually not enough room inside the hub for this method to work; the drift can't be positioned against the edge of the bearing. If you can't obtain or make the special tools shown in the illustrations, take the wheel to a dealer service department or other properly equipped shop for bearing replacement.*

1 Support the bike securely so it can't be knocked over during this procedure and remove the wheel. Remove the front wheel (see Section 11) or remove the rear wheel (see Section 12).

2 Set the wheel on blocks so as not to allow the weight of the wheel to rest on the brake disc or hub.

Front wheel bearings

3 From the left side of the wheel, remove the speedometer gearbox unit **(see illustration 11.5a)**, then pry out the grease seal **(see illustration)** and remove the speedometer gear retainer **(see illustration)**.

4 From the right side of the wheel, remove the collar **(see illustration 11.5b)**.

13.3a Pry out the left side seal from the front wheel with a seal removal tool

13.3b Remove the retainer for the speedometer gearbox unit

13.5a The slotted end of the remover head fits inside the bearing; the wedge of the remover shaft spreads the head and locks it to the bearing

13.5b Tap the slotted end of the remover head into the bearing

5 To remove the left side bearing, you'll need the Honda special tools (bearing remover head 07746-0050600 and bearing remover shaft 07746-0050100) or equivalents **(see illustrations)**. Place the slotted part of the remover head inside the bearing inner race. From the right side, place the wedge end of the shaft into the slot of the remover head. Tapping on the end of the shaft will drive it into the slot, which spreads the head and locks it to the bearing. Tapping some more will drive the remover head and the bearing out of the hub.

6 If you don't have these bearing remover tools, you can make your own equivalents from a large-diameter bolt (cut a lengthwise slot in the shaft with a hacksaw so it will work like the remover head) and a metal rod (grind a taper on one end so it will work like the remover shaft).

7 Turn the wheel over, pry out the right side grease seal, then remove the right side bearing the same way you removed the left one.

8 Clean the bearings with a high flash-point solvent (one which won't leave any residue) and blow them dry with compressed air (don't let the bearing spin as you dry them). Apply a few drops of oil to the bearing. Hold the outer race of the bearing and rotate the inner race - if the bearing doesn't turn smoothly, has rough spots or is noisy, replace it with a new one.

9 If the bearing checks out okay and will be re-used, wash it in solvent once again and dry it, then pack the bearing with high-quality bearing grease.

10 Thoroughly clean the hub area of the wheel. Install the left side bearing into the recess in the hub, with the marked or sealed side facing out. Using a bearing driver or a socket large enough to contact the outer race of the bearing, drive in the bearing until it's completely seated **(see illustration)**.

11 Install the speedometer gearbox retainer on top of the new bearing. Make sure the tangs on the retainer are aligned with the slots in the hub. Install a new left side grease seal with its closed side out. It should be possible to push the seal in with even finger pressure but, if necessary, use a seal driver, a large socket or a flat piece of wood to drive the seal into place.

12 Turn the wheel over and install the right side bearing as described in Step 10. Install a new right side seal as described in Step 11.

13 Install the speedometer gearbox unit, making sure the tangs on the speedometer gearbox are aligned with the slots in the retainer **(see illustration 11.8)**.

14 Clean off all grease from the brake disc using acetone or brake system cleaner.

15 Make sure the right side collar is in

13.5c From the other side of the wheel, install the wedge end of the bearing remover shaft in the remover head slot, then tap on the shaft to drive out the left side bearing

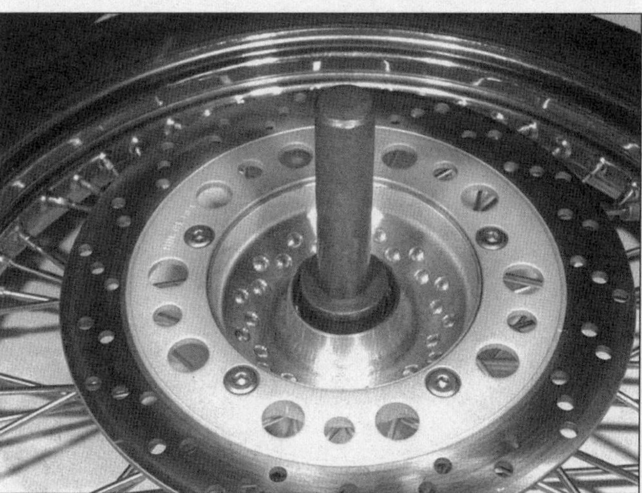

13.10 Install the new bearings with a seal driver, a large socket or a section of pipe, taped to protect the new bearing

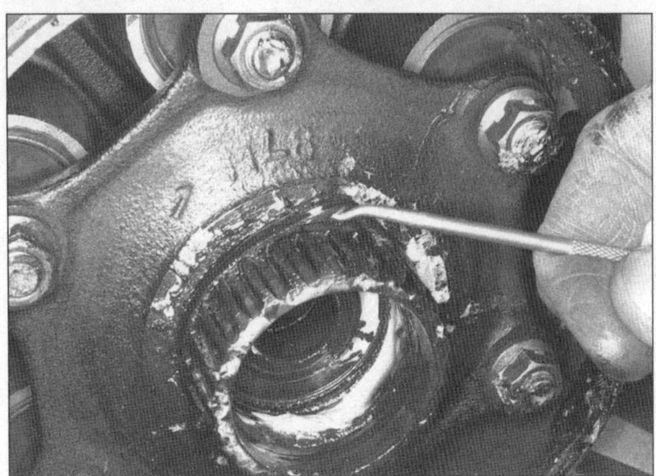

13.16a Remove the O-ring from the driven flange

13.16b Pry the driven flange out of the dampers

place **(see illustration 11.5b)** and install the wheel (see Section 11).

Rear wheel bearings

16 Remove the O-ring from the driven flange and remove the driven flange assembly **(see illustrations)**.

17 Remove the O-ring from the wheel hub.

18 On wheels with a rear disc, remove the damper holder plate bolts, align the arrow on the damper holder plate between the projections on the wheel by turning the holder plate and remove the plate.

19 Remove the rear wheel damper rubbers.

20 The rear wheel bearings are removed the same way as the front wheel bearings, in Steps 5 through 10 above **(see illustrations)**.

21 Reassembly of the rear wheel is the reverse of disassembly.

14 Tires - general information

1 Tires with tubes are used on spoked wheels; tubeless tires are used on cast wheels. Tube-type tires are generally easier to change than tubeless tires.

2 Before changing a tire yourself, check with your local dealership or repair shop to find out the labor charge for changing a tire. Although the procedure is not complicated, it is time-consuming, and for safety, it must be done correctly. For these reasons, it may be more practical to have the job done by a professional. Watching a trained technician do the job before attempting it yourself can provide valuable information.

3 The illustrations on the following page can be used to replace a tube-type tire in an emergency.

13.20a Install the 20 mm bearing remover head (07746-0050600, or equivalent) . . .

13.20b From the other side of the wheel, install the bearing remover shaft (07746-0050100, or equivalent) and drive out the left side bearing

13.20c Install the new bearings with a seal driver, a large socket or a section of pipe

TIRE CHANGING SEQUENCE - TUBED TIRES

1. Deflate tire. After pushing tire beads away from rim flanges push tire bead into well of rim at point opposite valve. Insert tire lever adjacent to valve and work bead over edge of rim.

2. Use two levers to work bead over edge of rim. Note use of rim protectors.

3. Remove inner tube from tire.

4. When first bead is clear, remove tire as shown.

5. When fitting, partially inflate inner tube and insert in tire.

6. Work first bead over rim and feed valve through hole in rim. Partially screw on retaining nut to hold valve in place.

7. Check that inner tube is positioned correctly and work second bead over rim using tire levers. Start at a point opposite valve.

8. Work final area of bead over rim while pushing valve inwards to ensure that inner tube is not trapped.

TIRE CHANGING SEQUENCE - TUBELESS TIRES

Deflate tire. After releasing beads, push tire bead into well of rim at point opposite valve. Insert lever next to valve and work bead over edge of rim.

Use two levers to work bead over edge of rim. Note use of rim protectors.

When first bead is clear, remove tire as shown.

Before installing, ensure that tire is suitable for wheel. Take note of any sidewall markings such as direction of rotation arrows.

Work first bead over the rim flange.

Use a tire lever to work the second bead over rim flange.

Chapter 8
Frame and bodywork

Contents

Degrees of difficulty

Easy, suitable for novice with little experience		**Fairly easy,** suitable for beginner with some experience		**Fairly difficult,** suitable for competent DIY mechanic		**Difficult,** suitable for experienced DIY mechanic		**Very difficult,** suitable for expert DIY or professional	

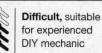

1 General information

The models covered in this manual use a steel frame of round-section tubing. The front fender is steel; the rear fender and side covers are plastic. VT1100T models are equipped with a windshield and saddlebags; both can be removed if necessary to service the bike.

2 Frame - inspection and repair

1 The frame should not require attention unless accident damage has occurred. In most cases, frame replacement is the only satisfactory remedy for such damage. A few frame specialists have the jigs and other equipment necessary for straightening the frame to the required standard of accuracy, but even then there is no simple way of assessing to what extent the frame may have been overstressed.

2 After the machine has accumulated a lot of miles, the frame should be examined closely for signs of cracking or splitting at the welded joints. Corrosion can also cause weakness at these joints. Loose engine mount bolts can cause elongation of the bolt holes or fracturing of the mounting tabs. Minor damage can often be repaired by welding, depending on the extent and nature of the damage.

3 Remember that a frame which is out of alignment will cause handling problems. If misalignment is suspected as the result of an accident, it will be necessary to strip the machine completely so the frame can be thoroughly checked.

3 Footpegs - removal and installation

1 The front footpegs are mounted on brackets bolted to the frame. On 1987 and later VT1100C models, the footpeg brackets also serve as the mounting brackets for the gearshift linkage on the left side (see Chapter 2) and the rear brake pedal linkage on the right side (see Chapter 7). The rear footpegs are mounted on brackets bolted to the frame.

2 To replace a footpeg, remove the cotter pin and the washer, pull out the clevis pin and separate the footpeg from the bracket. If the footpeg is spring-loaded, note how the spring is installed before removing the footpeg. Installation is the reverse of removal. Grease the footpeg clevis pin before installing it.

3.3a The left footpeg bracket is secured by two bolts (arrows) (VT1100C2 shown); on VT1100C models, the gearshift pedal is mounted on the back of the bracket

3.3b The right footpeg bracket is secured by two bolts (arrows) (VT1100C2 shown); on VT1100C models, the brake pedal is mounted on the back of the bracket

3 To replace a footpeg bracket, remove the bolts that secure the bracket to the frame **(see illustrations)**. If you're removing the left or right footpeg assembly on a 1987 or later VT1100C, detach the gearshift pedal from the back of the bracket (see "Gearshift linkage - removal, inspection and installation" in Chapter 2). If you're removing the right footpeg assembly on one of these models, detach the brake pedal from the back of the bracket (see "Rear brake pedal and linkage - removal and installation" in Chapter 7). Installation is the reverse of removal. Tighten the bracket bolts securely.

4 Sidestand - maintenance

1 The sidestand is attached to a bracket on the frame. A return spring **(see illustration)** anchored to a bracket on the frame ensures that the stand remains in the extended or retracted position.

2 Make sure the pivot bolt is tight and the return spring is not fatigued. An accident could occur if the stand extends while the machine is in motion, and damage to the machine could occur if the stand retracts while the machine is resting on the stand.

5 Sidestand - removal and installation

1 Support the bike securely so it can't be knocked over during this procedure.

2 Unhook the sidestand spring **(see illustration 4.1)**.

3 Remove the sidestand switch (see Chapter 9).

4 Remove the dust cap **(see illustration)**.

5 Remove the sidestand pivot bolt and nut.

6 Installation is the reverse of removal. Be sure to grease the pivot bolt and tighten the nut securely.

6 Seat - removal and installation

1 On 1985 and 1986 models, locate the two plugs behind the rear seat and remove them. Remove the two rear seat bolts and remove the rear seat. Remove the two bolts from the back of the front seat and remove the front seat.

2 On 1987 and later VT1100C models, remove the single cap nut (acorn nut) from behind the rear seat and remove the rear seat. Remove the two bolts from the back of the front seat and remove the front seat.

3 On VT1100C2 and VT1100T models, remove the cap nut from behind the rear seat, remove the two side bolts (one on each side)

4.1 Make sure the sidestand spring is in good condition and correctly installed

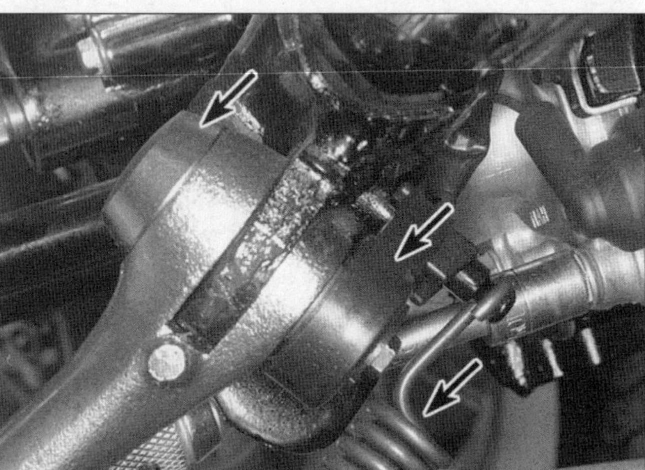

5.4 Remove the cap (left arrow), the return spring (right arrow), the sidestand switch (center arrow) and the sidestand nut and pivot bolt

6.3a To detach the seat on VT1100C2 and VT1100T models, remove this cap nut . . .

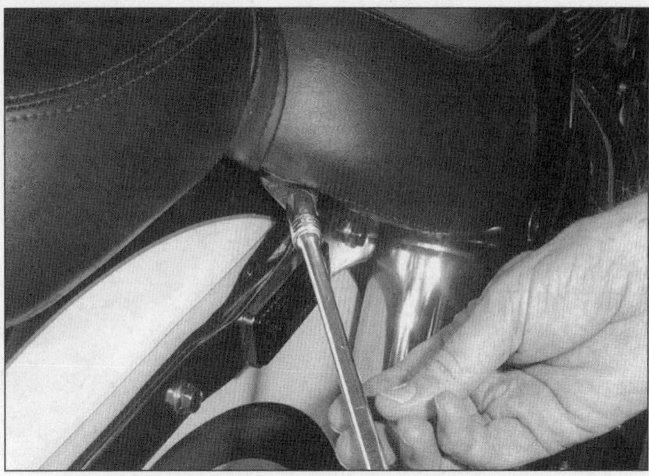

6.3b . . . and remove the two side bolts (one on each side)

(see illustrations) and remove the seat.

4 Installation is the reverse of removal. To install the seat, place it in position, then slide it forward. Make sure that the lug under the forward end of the seat (the front seat on dual-seat models) slides under the small crossmember on the frame. Some seats also have smaller lugs at the back that must be inserted under small frame crossmembers. Tighten all seat bolts securely.

7 Steering head covers - removal and installation

1 The steering head covers conceal and protect wiring harnesses and connectors in the area between the steering head and the fuel tank.

2 Remove the fuel tank (see Chapter 4).

3 The steering head covers on VT1100C models have interlocking fingers that wrap around the front of the front of the steering head and lock together. Near the rear edge of each cover is a locator pin that's pushed into a grommet in the gusset area of the frame. On these models, remove the retaining screw from the upper edge of either cover, pull the rear edge of the cover out of the grommet, swing the cover out and forward and disengage it from the other cover.

4 To remove either steering cover on VT1100C2 and VT1100T models, simply pop up the two trim clips **(see illustration)** and pull off the cover.

5 Installation is the reverse of removal. Make sure that neither cover half interferes with any wiring harnesses or connectors.

7.4 To remove a steering head cover from a VT1100C2 or VT1100T, pop up the two trim clips (arrows) and remove the cover

8 Side covers - removal and installation

1985 and 1986 models

1 To remove a side cover from a 1985 or 1986 model, grasp it firmly and pull it off, disengaging the mounting bosses on the side cover from their grommets on the frame. Installation is the reverse of removal. Place the cover in position so that the mounting bosses are aligned with their grommets on the frame and push the cover in until you feel the bosses pop through the grommets.

1987 and later VT1100C models

2 To remove the left side cover, remove the Allen bolt from the middle of the lower edge, then grasp the cover firmly and pull it off, disengaging the two upper mounting bosses from their grommets in the frame and the grommet in the cover from the ignition key switch. Installation is the reverse of removal. Place the cover in position so that the mounting bosses are aligned with their grommets on the frame and push the cover in until you feel the two upper bosses pop through the grommets and the ignition switch fits through the large grommet in the side cover. Install the Allen bolt and tighten it securely.

3 To remove the right side cover, insert the ignition key in the lock, turn the key 1/4-turn clockwise, pull the upper edge of the cover out to disengage the two upper locator pins from their grommets in the frame, then lift up the cover slightly to disengage the two tabs on the lower edge of the cover from their respective slots in the frame. Installation is the reverse of removal. Fit the tabs on the lower edge of the cover into their slots in the frame, then push in on the upper edge of the cover until you feel the mounting bosses pop into the grommets. Turn the locking key counterclockwise 1/4-turn.

4 These models have another cover on the right side; it's located below the right side cover. To remove it, remove the exhaust system (see Chapter 4), then remove the two cover bolts and disengage the tab on the forward edge of the cover from its mounting rubber. Installation is the reverse of removal.

VT1100C2 and VT1100T models

5 To remove the left side cover, grasp it firmly and disengage the three mounting bosses from their grommets on the frame

8.5 To remove the left side cover from a VT1100C2 or VT1100T, pull the mounting bosses (arrows) out of the grommets (arrows)

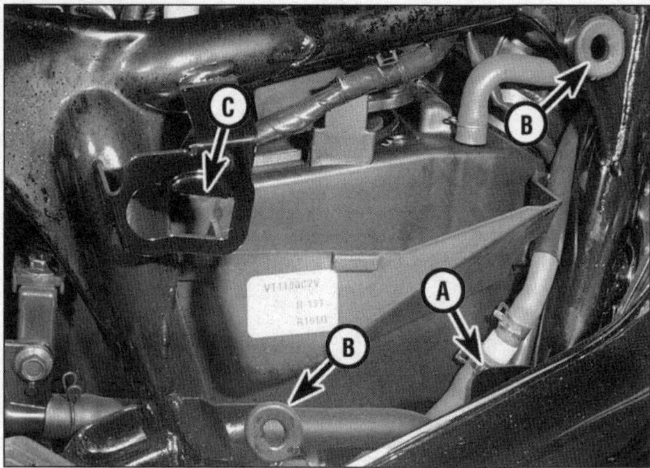

8.6 Right side cover mounting details (VT1100C2 and VT1100T)

A Bracket for rubber on bottom of cover
B Grommets
C Lock hole

(see illustration). Installation is the reverse of removal. Position the cover so that the mounting bosses are aligned with their grommets, then push in on the cover until you feel the mounting bosses pop into the grommets.

6 To remove the right side cover, insert the ignition key in the lock and turn it 1/4-turn clockwise 90, then pull off the cover, disengaging the two mounting bosses from their grommets. Installation is the reverse of removal. Place the rubber insulator on the bottom of the cover in its bracket on the frame **(see illustration)**, align the mounting bosses on the cover with their grommets, then push in the cover and pop the two bosses into their grommets. Turn the ignition key counterclockwise 1/4-turn and remove it.

9 Front fender - removal and installation

1 Detach any cable clamps or guides from the fender.

2 Remove the front wheel (see Chapter 7).

3 Unbolt the fender from the forks.

4 Installation is the reverse of the removal steps. Tighten the bolts securely. Don't forget to route the speedometer cable through the loop on the left side of the fender.

10 Saddlebags (VT1100C2 models) - removal and installation

Note: *This procedure applies to either saddlebag.*

1 Open the saddlebag.

2 Remove the four saddlebag mounting bolts, two in the inner wall and two in the bottom.

3 Remove the saddlebag.

4 Installation is the reverse of removal.

11 Rear fender - removal and installation

1 Remove the seat(s) (see Section 6).

2 Trace the brake light and taillight leads to the connectors inside the connector boot and unplug them.

VT1100C and VT1100T models

3 On VT1100C models, remove the four sissy bar retaining bolts and washers and remove the sissy bar assembly.

4 Remove the two 10 mm bolts, lower the rear fender and let it sit on the rear wheel.

5 Detach the white two-pin fuse box connector from the bracket on the fender and remove the fender.

6 Installation is the reverse of removal.

VT1100C2 models

7 Detach the white two-pin fuse box connector from the bracket on the fender.

8 Remove the six bolts and washers and remove the fender.

9 Installation is the reverse of removal.

12 Rear grab rails and fender stays - removal and installation

Note: *This procedure applies to either grab rail or fender stay.*

VT1100C and VT1100T models

1 Remove the seat(s) (see Section 6).

2 On VT1100T models, remove the saddlebags (see Section 10).

3 Remove the rear fender (see Section 11).

4 Remove the rear shock absorber (see Chapter 6).

5 On VT1100C models, locate the elec-

12.12 The VT1100C2 fender stays are secured by three bolts (arrows) and a fourth bolt (not shown) at the front end of the stay

trical connectors for the turn signal lights (they're inside the connector boot), unplug them and detach the turn signal wiring from the clamps on the frame.

6 Remove the 14 mm bolt and remove the fender stay.

7 To remove the turn signal assembly from the fender stay on VT1100C models, remove the grab rail bolt and nut, remove the grab rail, detach the turn signal harness from the clamps on the backside of the fender stay, then remove the nut, spacer plate and rear turn signal assembly.

8 Installation is the reverse of removal.

VT1100C2 models

9 Remove the seat (see Section 6).

10 Remove the rear shock absorber (see Chapter 6).

11 Locate the electrical connectors for the turn signal lights (they're inside the connector boot), unplug them and detach the turn signal wiring from the clamps on the frame.

12 Remove the two 8 mm bolts and washers and remove the 10 mm and 14 mm bolts **(see illustration)**.

13 Remove the fender stay.

14 If you're removing a left fender stay, remove the grab rail bolt and nut and remove the grab rail.

15 Detach the turn signal harness from the clamps on the fender stay, remove the turn signal assembly retaining nut and remove the turn signal assembly.

16 Installation is the reverse of removal.

13 Windshield (VT1100C2 models) - removal and installation

1 On the front side of the windshield, remove the two cap nuts right below the headlight.

2 On the back side of the windshield, remove the cap nut, collar and bolt from the bracket at the upper end of each fork tube.

3 Remove the windshield.

4 Installation is the reverse of removal.

Notes

Chapter 9
Electrical system

Contents

Degrees of difficulty

Easy, suitable for novice with little experience 	**Fairly easy,** suitable for beginner with some experience 	**Fairly difficult,** suitable for competent DIY mechanic 	**Difficult,** suitable for experienced DIY mechanic 	**Very difficult,** suitable for expert DIY or professional 

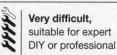

Specifications

Battery type

VT1100C	
1985 through 2000	12V, 16 Ah
2001 and later	12V, 12 Ah
VT1100T	12V, 16 Ah
VT1100C2	
1995 through 1999	12V, 16 Ah
2000 and later	12V, 12 Ah
VT1100C3	
1998 through 2000	12V, 16 Ah
2001 and later	12V, 12 Ah

Fuse specifications

Main fuse	30 amps
Fuse box	
1985 through 1993	Six 10-amp and one 15 amp
1994 on	Four 10-amp and one 15 amp

Bulb specifications

Headlight bulb	60/55W
Brake light/taillight bulbs	32/3 cp
Front turn signal/running light bulbs	32/3 cp
Rear turn signal bulbs	32 cp
License plate bulb	4 cp
Speedometer light bulb	
All except VT1100C3	3 watts
VT1100C3	1.7 watts
Indicator bulbs (turn signal, high beam, neutral)	3.4W

Charging system

Stator coil resistance	0.3 to 0.5 ohms
Charging system output	329 watts at 5,000 rpm
Regulated voltage output	14 to 14.8 volts at 5,000 rpm
Maximum current leakage	1 mA

Starter

Starter brush length	
1985 through 1993	
Standard	12.0 to 13.0 mm (0.47 to 0.51 inch)
Minimum	6.5 mm (0.26 inch)
1994 on	
Standard	12.5 mm (0.49 inch)
Minimum	6.5 mm (0.26 inch)
Starter driven gear outside diameter	
Standard	57.749 to 57.768 mm (2.2735 to 2.2743 inches)
Limit	57.639 mm (2.2692 inches)
Starter clutch housing inside diameter	
Standard	74.414 to 74.440 mm (2.9297 to 2.9307 inches)
Limit	74.50 mm (2.933 inches)

Torque specifications

Neutral switch	12 Nm (108 in-lbs)
Oil pressure switch	12 Nm (108 in-lbs)
Sidestand switch retaining bolt	10 Nm (84 in-lbs)
Flywheel (rotor) bolt	137 Nm (101 ft-lbs)
Left crankcase cover bolts	10 Nm (89 in-lbs)
Flywheel-to-starter clutch housing bolts	23 Nm (17 ft-lbs)

1 General information

The machines covered by this manual are equipped with a 12-volt electrical system. The charging system uses an alternator consisting of a flywheel (rotor) with permanent magnets that rotate around a stator coil of copper wire. The alternator produces alternating current, which is converted to direct current by the regulator/rectifier. The regulator/rectifier also controls the charging system output.

An electric starter mounted behind the rear cylinder is standard equipment. The starter has two brushes. The starting system includes the motor, the battery, the starter relay switch and the wiring harnesses and switches. When the engine kill switch and the ignition switch are both in the On position, the starter relay switch allows the starter motor to operate only if the transmission is in Neutral (Neutral switch on) or the clutch lever is pulled in (clutch switch on) and the sidestand is up (sidestand switch on). **Note:** *Keep in mind that electrical parts, once purchased, can't be returned. To avoid unnecessary expense, make very sure the faulty component has been positively identified before buying a replacement part.*

2 Electrical troubleshooting

A typical electrical circuit consists of an electrical component, the switches, relays, etc. related to that component and the wiring and connectors that hook the component to both the battery and the frame. To aid in locating a problem in any electrical circuit, complete wiring diagrams of each model are included at the end of this Chapter.

Before tackling any troublesome electrical circuit, first study the appropriate diagrams thoroughly to get a complete picture of what makes up that individual circuit. Trouble spots, for instance, can often be narrowed down by noting if other components related to that circuit are operating properly or not. If several components or circuits fail at one time, chances are the fault lies in the fuse or ground connection, as several circuits often are routed through the same fuse and ground connections.

Electrical problems often stem from simple causes, such as loose or corroded connections or a blown fuse. Prior to any electrical troubleshooting, always visually check the condition of the fuse, wires and connections in the problem circuit. Intermittent failures can be especially frustrating, since you can't always duplicate the failure when it's convenient to test. In such situations, a good practice is to clean all connections in the affected circuit, whether or not they appear to be good. All of the connections and wires should also be wiggled to check for looseness which can cause intermittent failure.

If testing instruments are going to be utilized, use the diagrams to plan where you will make the necessary connections in order to accurately pinpoint the trouble spot.

The basic tools needed for electrical troubleshooting include a test light or voltmeter, a continuity tester (which includes a bulb, battery and set of test leads) and a jumper wire, preferably with a circuit breaker incorporated, which can be used to bypass electrical components. Specific checks described later in this Chapter may also require an ohmmeter.

Voltage checks should be performed if a circuit is not functioning properly. Connect one lead of a test light or voltmeter to either the negative battery terminal or a known good ground. Connect the other lead to a connector in the circuit being tested, preferably nearest to the battery or fuse. If the bulb lights, voltage is reaching that point, which means the part of the circuit between that connector and the battery is problem-free. Continue checking the remainder of the circuit in the same manner. When you reach a point where no voltage is present, the problem lies between there and the last good test point. Most of the time the problem is due to a loose connection. Keep in mind that some circuits only receive voltage when the ignition key is in the On position.

One method of finding short circuits is to remove the fuse and connect a test light or voltmeter in its place to the fuse terminals. There should be no load in the circuit (it should be switched off). Move the wiring harness from side-to-side while watching the test light. If the bulb lights, there is a short to ground somewhere in that area, probably where insulation has rubbed off a wire. The same test can be performed on other components in the circuit, including the switch.

A ground check should be done to see if a component is grounded properly. Disconnect the battery and connect one lead of a self-powered test light (continuity tester) to a known good ground. Connect the other lead to the wire or ground connection being tested. If the bulb lights, the ground is good. If the bulb does not light, the ground is not good.

A continuity check is performed to see if a circuit, section of circuit or individual component is capable of passing electricity through it. Disconnect the battery and connect one lead of a self-powered test light (continuity tester) to one end of the circuit being tested and the other lead to the other end of the circuit. If the bulb lights, there is continuity, which means the circuit is passing electricity through it properly. Switches can be checked in the same way.

Remember that all electrical circuits are designed to conduct electricity from the battery, through the wires, switches, relays, etc. to the electrical component (light bulb, motor, etc.). From there it is directed to the frame (ground) where it is passed back to the battery. Electrical problems are basically an interruption in the flow of electricity from the battery or back to it.

3.4 To release the battery holder, remove this bolt (arrow)

3 Battery - removal, inspection, maintenance and installation

1 Most battery damage is caused by heat, vibration, and/or low electrolyte levels, so make sure the battery is securely mounted, check the electrolyte level frequently (if the battery is a conventional unit) and make sure the charging system is functioning properly.

2 Remove the left side cover (see Chapter 8).

3 Disconnect the battery cables from the battery terminals, negative cable (left terminal) first, then positive.

4 Remove the battery holder bolt **(see illustration)**.

5 Lift up the forward end of the battery slightly and detach the breather tube, then remove the battery.

6 Installation is the reverse of removal. Make sure the vent tube is correctly routed and is not kinked or pinched. Be sure to attach the positive cable first, then the negative one. Tighten the cables securely. Don't forget to put the protective cap back on the positive terminal.

Inspection and maintenance

7 Check the electrolyte level and specific gravity (see Chapter 1).

8 Look for sediment in the floor of the battery case. Sediment is the result of sulfation caused by low electrolyte levels. These deposits will cause internal short circuits, which can quickly discharge the battery. Look for cracks in the case and replace the battery if either of these conditions is found.

9 Check the battery terminals and cable ends for tightness and corrosion. If corrosion is evident, remove the cables from the battery and clean the terminals and cable ends with a wire brush or knife and emery paper.

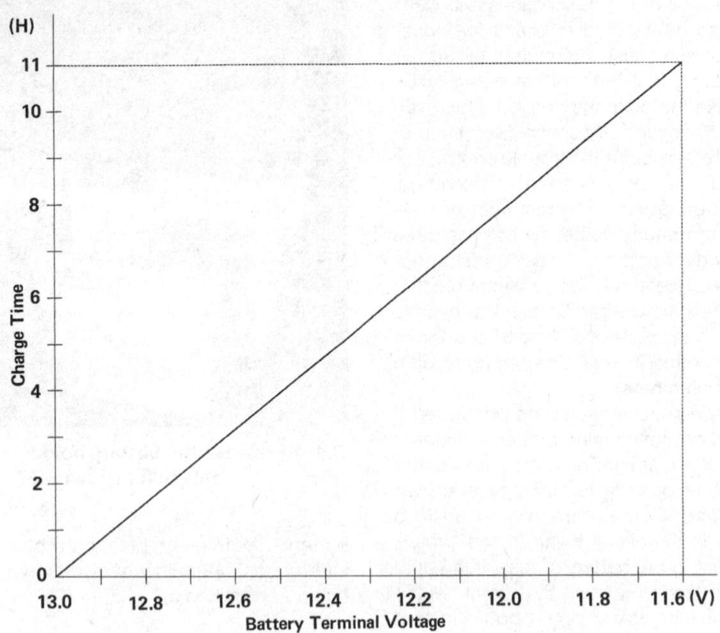

4.13 Battery charge-time table (maintenance-free batteries)

Reconnect the cables and apply a thin coat of petroleum jelly to the connections to slow further corrosion.

10 The battery case should be kept clean to prevent current leakage, which can discharge the battery over a period of time (especially when it sits unused). Wash the outside of the case with a solution of baking soda and water. Do not get any baking soda solution in the battery cells. Rinse the battery thoroughly, then dry it.

11 If acid has been spilled on the frame or battery box, neutralize it with the baking soda and water solution, dry it thoroughly, then touch up any damaged paint.

12 If the motorcycle sits unused for long periods of time, disconnect the cables from the battery terminals. Charge the battery about once a month (see Section 4).

4 Battery - charging

1 If the machine sits idle for extended periods or if the charging system malfunctions, the battery can be charged from an external source.

Conventional batteries

2 To charge the battery, you will need a charger of the correct rating, a hydrometer, a clean rag and a syringe for adding distilled water to the battery cells.

3 The maximum charging rate for any battery is 1/10 of the rated amp/hour capacity. As an example, the maximum charging rate for a 12 amp/hour battery would be 1.2 amps and the maximum charging rate for a 14 amp/hour battery would be 1.4 amps. If the battery is charged at a higher rate, it could be damaged.

4 Do not allow the battery to be subjected to a so-called quick charge (high rate of charge over a short period of time) unless you are prepared to buy a new battery. The heat of a quick charge will warp the plates inside the battery enough that they'll touch each other, causing an internal short.

5 When charging the battery, always remove it from the machine and be sure to check the electrolyte level before hooking up the charger. Add distilled water to any cells that are low.

6 Loosen the cell caps, hook up the battery charger leads (red to positive, black to negative), cover the top of the battery with a clean rag, then, and only then, plug in the battery charger.

Warning: The hydrogen gas escaping from a charging battery is explosive, so keep open flames and sparks well away from the area. If the hydrogen explodes, it will cause the battery to burst and spray extremely corrosive electrolyte.

7 Allow the battery to charge until the specific gravity is as specified (refer to Chapter 1 for specific gravity checking procedures). The charger must be unplugged and disconnected from the battery when making specific gravity checks. If the battery overheats or gases excessively, the charging rate is too high. Either disconnect the charger or lower the charging rate to prevent damage to the battery.

8 It's time for a new battery if:

a) One or more of the cells is significantly lower in specific gravity than the others after a long slow charge.
b) The battery as a whole doesn't seem to want to take a charge.
c) Battery voltage won't increase.
d) The electrolyte doesn't bubble.
e) The plates are white (indicating sulfation) or debris has accumulated in the bottom of a cell.
f) The plates or insulators are warped or buckled.

9 When the battery is fully charged, unplug the charger first, then disconnect the leads from the battery. Install the cell caps and wipe any electrolyte off the outside of the battery case.

Maintenance-free batteries

Note: *None of the models covered by this manual were originally equipped with maintenance-free batteries. However, if you or a previous owner have installed one in place of a conventional battery, use the following procedure to charge the battery.*

10 Charging maintenance-free batteries requires a digital voltmeter and a variable-voltage charger with a built-in ammeter.

11 When charging the battery, always remove it from the machine and be sure to check the electrolyte level by looking through the translucent battery case before hooking up the charger. If the electrolyte level is low, the battery must be discarded; never remove the sealing plug to add water.

12 Disconnect the battery cables (negative cable first), then connect a digital voltmeter between the battery terminals and measure the voltage.

13 If terminal voltage is 12.6 volts or higher, the battery is fully charged. If it's lower, recharge the battery. Refer to the accompanying illustration for charging rate and time **(see illustration)**.

14 A quick charge can be used in an emergency, provided the maximum charge rates and times are not exceeded (exceeding the maximum rate or time may ruin the battery). A quick charge should always be followed as soon as possible by a charge at the standard rate and time.

15 Hook up the battery charger leads (positive lead to battery positive terminal, negative lead to battery negative terminal), then, and only then, plug in the battery charger.

Warning: The hydrogen gas escaping from a charging battery is explosive, so keep open flames and sparks well away from the area. Also, the electrolyte is extremely corrosive and will damage anything it comes in contact with.

16 Start charging at a high voltage setting (no more than 25 volts) and watch the ammeter for about 5 minutes. If the charging current doesn't increase, replace the battery.

17 When the charging current increases

beyond the specified maximum, reduce the charging voltage to reduce the charging current to the rate listed in this Chapter's Specifications. Do this periodically as the battery charges.

18 Allow the battery to charge for the time specified by the battery manufacturer (it's sometimes printed on the battery). If the battery overheats or gases excessively, the charging rate is too high. Either disconnect the charger or lower the charging rate to prevent damage to the battery.

19 After the specified time, unplug the charger first, then disconnect the leads from the battery.

20 Wait 30 minutes, then measure voltage between the battery terminals. If it's 12.6 volts or higher, the battery is fully charged. If it's between 12.0 and 12.6 volts, charge the battery again (refer to this Chapter's Specifications and **illustration 4.13** for charge rate and time). If it's less than 12.0 volts, it's time for a new battery.

21 When the battery is fully charged, unplug the charger first, then disconnect the leads from the battery. Wipe off the outside of the battery case and install the battery in the bike.

5 Fuses - check and replacement

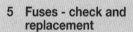

Note: *For the most up-to-date location and specification of all important fuses, always refer to your owner's manual. If there's a difference between the information below and the information in the owner's manual, use the owner's manual. It supersedes the information presented here.*

1 Most of the fuses are located in the fuse box. On 1985 and 1986 models, it's located under the handlebar cover; on 1987 and later models, it's behind the left side cover.

2 Remove the fuse cover screws **(see illustration)**. The fuse box houses six 10-amp fuses and one 15-amp fuse (1985 through 1993 models) or four 10-amp fuses and one 15-amp fuse (1994 and later models).

3 The main (30-amp) fuse is located above the battery on 1987 through 1996 VT1100C models, and on the starter relay on VT1100C2, VT1100T and 1997-on VT1100C models.

4 Other fuses are installed inline, usually near the electrical connector for each circuit device. These fuses are fairly easy to find when troubleshooting a circuit. For further help in locating inline fuses, refer to the wiring diagrams at the end of this Chapter.

5 If you have a test light, all of the fuses can be checked without removing them. Turn the ignition key to the On position, connect one end of the test light to a good ground, then probe each terminal on top of the fuse. If the fuse is good, there will be voltage available at both terminals. If the fuse is blown, there will only be voltage present at one of the terminals.

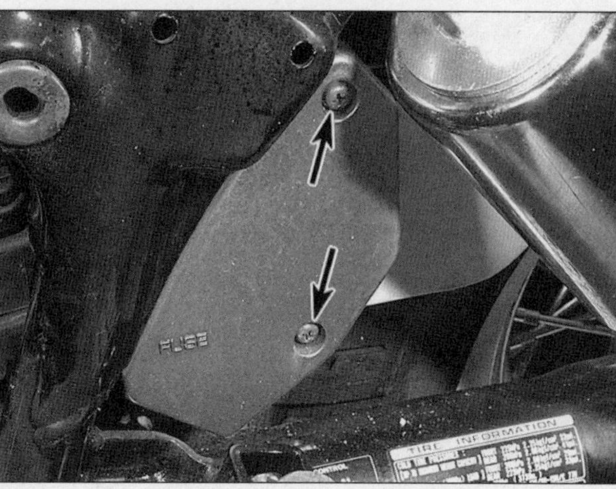

5.2 Remove the left side cover and these screws (arrows) to open the fuse box on 1987 and later models

6 The fuses can also be tested with an ohmmeter or self-powered test light. Remove the fuse and connect the tester to the ends of the fuse. If the ohmmeter shows continuity or the test lamp lights, the fuse is good. If the ohmmeter shows infinite resistance or the test lamp stays out, the fuse is blown.

7 The fuses can be removed and checked visually. If you can't pull the fuse out with your fingertips, use a pair of needle-nose pliers. A blown fuse is easily identified by a break in the element.

8 If a fuse blows, be sure to check the wiring harnesses very carefully for evidence of a short circuit. Look for bare wires and chafed, melted or burned insulation. If a fuse is replaced before the cause is located, the new fuse will blow immediately. Occasionally a fuse will blow or cause an open circuit for no obvious reason. Corrosion of the fuse ends and fuse block terminals may occur and cause poor fuse contact. If this happens, remove the corrosion with a wire brush or emery paper, then spray the fuse end and terminals with electrical contact cleaner.

9 Fuse ratings are listed in this Chapter's Specifications. Fuse ratings are also marked on the fuses themselves. Never, under any circumstances, use a higher rated fuse or bridge the fuse block terminals, as damage to the electrical system could result.

6 Lighting system - check

1 The battery provides power for operation of the headlight, taillight, brake light, license plate light, instrument and warning lights. If none of the lights operate, always check battery voltage before proceeding. Low battery voltage indicates either a faulty battery, low battery electrolyte level or a defective charging system. If the bike has a conventional battery, check the battery electrolyte level and the specific gravity (see Chapter 1). Inspect the battery; make sure it's fully charged (see Sections 3 and 4). Check the condition of the fuses and replace any blown fuses (see Section 5). Check the charging system (see Sections 28 and 29).

Headlight

2 If the headlight is out when the engine is running, check the fuse first with the key or switch On (see Section 5), then unplug the electrical connector for the headlight (see Section 7) and use jumper wires to connect the bulb directly to the battery terminals. If the light comes on, the problem lies in the wiring (see the wiring diagrams at the end of this Chapter).

Turn signal lights/brake light/ taillight/license plate light

3 If a light fails to work, check the bulb and the bulb terminal first, then check for battery voltage at the electrical connector. If voltage is present, check the ground circuit for an open or poor connection.

4 If no voltage is indicated, check the wiring between the taillight and the ignition switch, then check the switch.

Brake light switches

5 See Section 12 for the brake light switch checking procedure.

Instrument and indicator lights

6 If an instrument light fails to operate when the key switch is On, check the fuse (see Section 5) and the bulb (see Section 16). If the bulb and fuses are in good condition, check for battery voltage at the connector. If the turn signal indicator light fails to operate when the turn signal switch is in the LEFT or RIGHT position, or if the high-beam indicator light fails to operate when the dimmer switch is in the HI position, see Section 18. If the neutral indicator light fails to operate when the transmission in Neutral, see Section 20.

7.1 Headlight housing details

A Headlight cover screw (right side)
B Headlight adjusting screw (right side)
C Headlight assembly mounting bolts and nuts

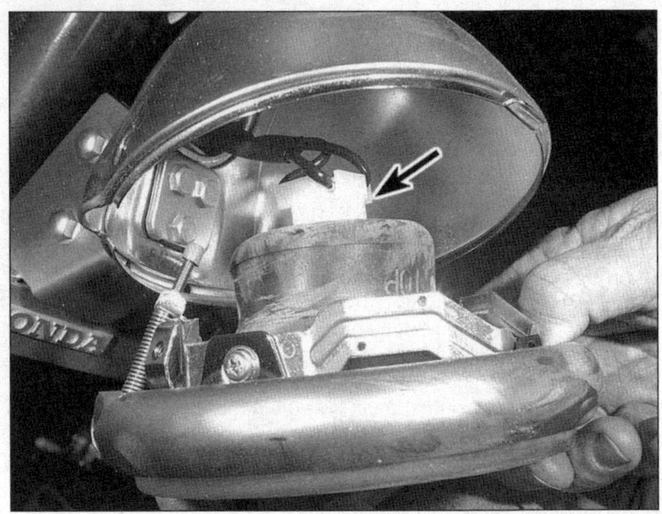

7.2 Tilt the cover out of the headlight assembly and disconnect the wiring connector

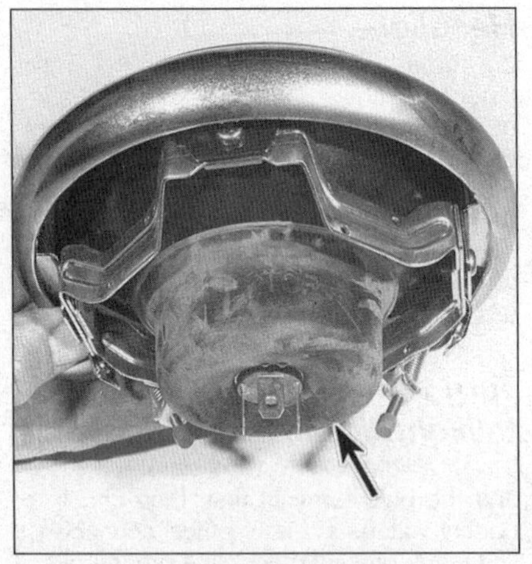

7.3 Remove the dust cover (arrow) from the headlight

7 Headlight bulb - replacement

Warning: If the bulb has just burned out, allow it to cool. It will be hot enough to burn your fingers.

1 Remove the headlight retaining screws **(see illustration)**.

2 Tilt the headlight forward out of the headlight housing and unplug the electrical connector **(see illustration)**.

3 Remove the dust cover **(see illustration)**.

4 Remove the bulb retainer **(see illustration)**.

5 Remove the bulb **(see illustration)**.

6 Installation is the reverse of removal. Be sure not to touch the bulb glass with your fingers - oil from your skin will cause the bulb to overheat and fail prematurely. If you do touch the bulb, wipe it off with a clean rag dampened with rubbing alcohol.

8 Headlight aim - check and adjustment

1 An improperly adjusted headlight may cause problems for oncoming traffic or provide poor, unsafe illumination of the road ahead. Before adjusting the headlight, be sure to consult with local traffic laws and regulations.

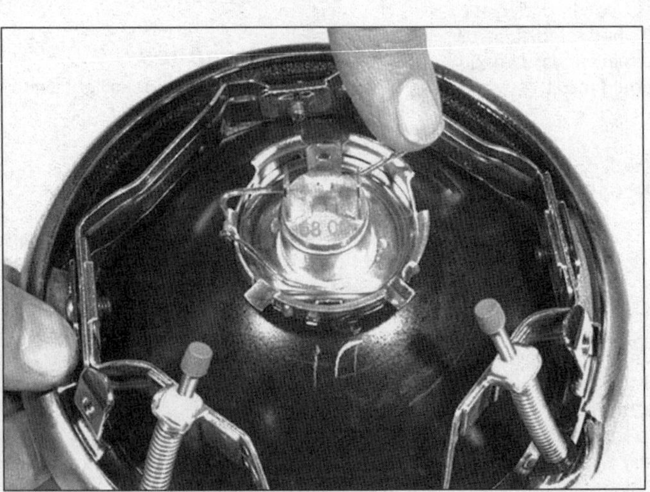

7.4 Remove the headlight bulb retainer

7.5 Lift out the bulb; don't touch the glass on the new bulb

8.3 The headlight adjusting screws are on either side of the headlight assembly (headlight removed for clarity; the screws can be adjusted from the front without removing the headlight)

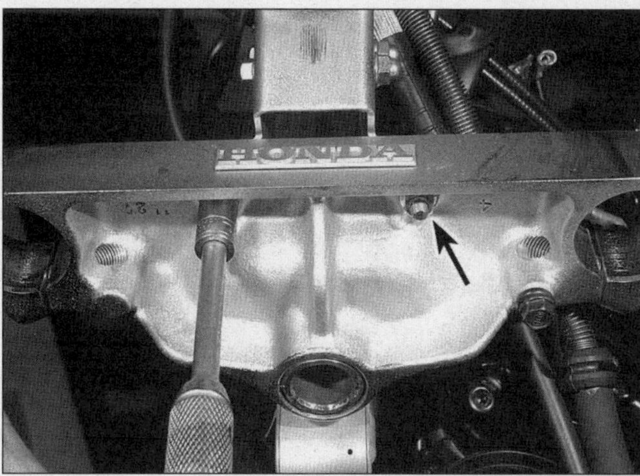

9.4 To detach the headlight housing bracket from the lower triple clamp, remove these two nuts (1987 and later models)

2 The headlight beam can be adjusted both vertically and horizontally. Before performing the adjustment, make sure the fuel tank is at least half full and have an assistant sit on the seat.

3 The adjusting screws are located in the lower edge of the headlight **(see illustration)**.

9 Headlight assembly - removal and installation

1 Remove the headlight (see Section 7).

2 Clearly label, then disconnect, all electrical connectors inside the headlight housing, then remove the wiring from the housing. Be careful not to cut any wires when pulling them through the holes in the housing.

3 On 1985 and 1986 models, remove the two Allen bolts from the headlight brackets and remove the headlight housing.

4 On 1987 and later models, the headlight housing bracket is attached to the lower triple clamp by two nuts **(see illustration)** which are located on the underside of the lower triple clamp. On 1997 and later VT1100C models, a small cover is bolted to the underside of the triple clamp. This cover must be removed to get to the headlight housing bracket nuts. Remove the two cover bolts and remove the cover; note that each cover bolt also secures a cable guide. On VT1100T models, the front windshield is attached to the headlight housing bracket; on these models, remove the two cap nuts below the headlight to detach the windshield from the headlight housing bracket.

5 Installation is the reverse of removal.

10 Turn signal, tail/brake light and license plate bulbs - replacement

Turn signal bulbs

1 To replace a turn signal bulb, remove the lens retaining screws **(see illustration)**.

2 Push the bulb in and turn it counterclockwise to remove it.

3 Check the socket terminals for corrosion and clean them if necessary. Line up the pins on the new bulb with the slots in the socket, push in and turn the bulb clockwise until it locks in place.

4 Position the lens on the housing and install the screws. Be careful not to overtighten them or the lens will crack.

Tail/brake light bulbs

5 Remove the lens screws **(see illustration)** and take the lens off.

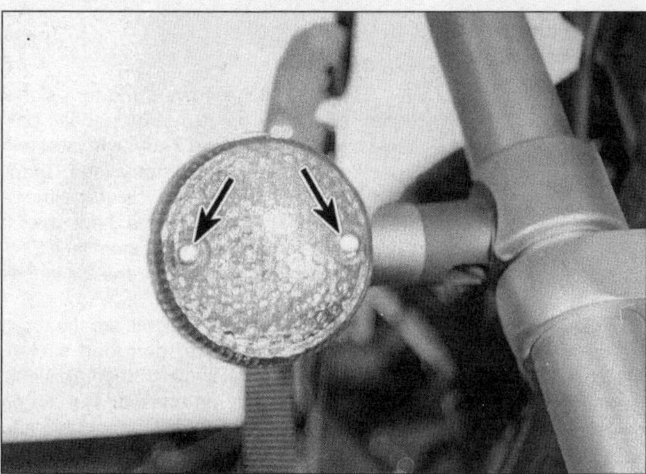

10.1 To detach a turn signal lens, remove these two retaining screws (arrows)

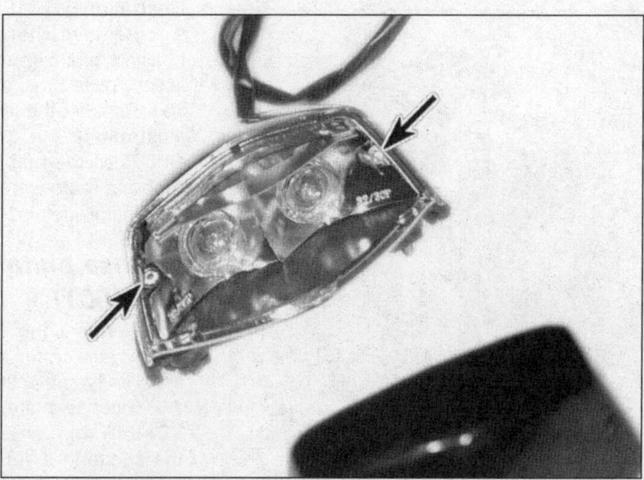

10.5 Remove the brake light lens screws (arrows) and take off the lens

10.8a To remove the license plate bracket from the rear fender on VT1100C2 models, remove these two bolts (arrows) . . .

10.8b . . . and remove this nut from the back

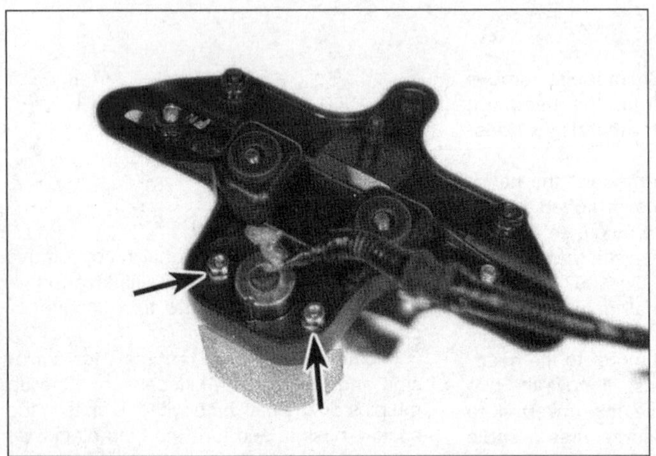

10.9 To detach the license plate lens and housing from the license plate bracket, remove these two retaining bolts (arrows)

10.10 Remove the license plate lens and housing from the license plate bracket

6 To remove a brake or taillight bulb, push the bulb in and turn it counterclockwise.
7 Install the bulb (see Steps 3 and 4).

10.11 To remove the license plate bulb, push it in and turn it counterclockwise; to install it, push it in and turn it clockwise

License plate light bulb (VT1100C2)

8 Remove the license plate bracket **(see illustrations)**.
9 Remove the two license plate lens/housing retaining bolts from the back of the license plate bracket **(see illustration)**.
10 Remove the lens and the housing **(see illustration)**.
11 Push the bulb in, turn it counterclockwise and remove it **(see illustration)**.
12 Installation is the reverse of removal.

License plate light bulb (VT1100T)

13 Remove the two turn signal bracket screws (one on the bottom of each turn signal stalk) and remove the turn signal assembly.
14 License plate bulb replacement on a VT1100T model is otherwise identical to the procedure for replacing the bulb on a VT1100C2 model. Refer to Steps 9, 10 and 11 above.
15 Installation is the reverse of removal.

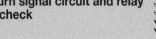

11 Turn signal circuit and relay - check

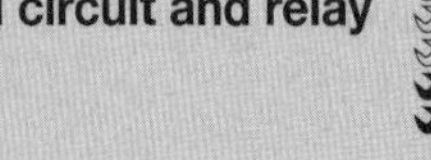

Circuit

1 Battery voltage powers the turn signal lights, so if they don't operate, check battery voltage first and the electrolyte level and specific gravity of the battery (see Chapter 1). Low battery voltage indicates either a defective battery (see Sections 3 and 4) or a malfunction in the charging system (see Sections 28 and 29). Also, check the fuses (see Section 5).
2 Most turn signal problems are the result of a burned out bulb or corroded socket. This is even more likely when the turn signal lights flash correctly on one side but not on the other. Check the turn signal bulbs and the sockets (see Section 10).
3 If the bulbs and sockets check out okay, check the turn signal relay.

12.5 Disconnect the two electrical leads from the front brake light switch

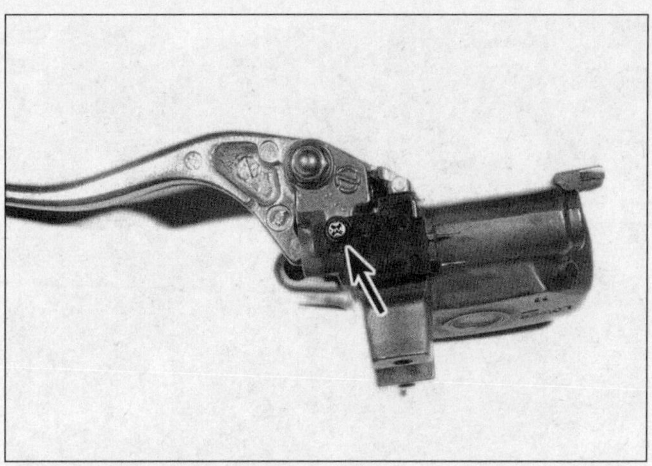

12.6 To detach the front brake light switch from the master cylinder, remove this retaining screw (arrow) (master cylinder removed from handlebar for clarity)

Turn signal relay

4 On 1985 and 1986 models, remove the right side cover (see Chapter 8). The turn signal relay is located above the battery and can be identified by its wire colors (refer to the wiring diagrams at the end of the Chapter).

5 On 1987 and later models, the turn signal relay is located on the left side of the bike, right behind the steering head. Remove the fuel tank (see Chapter 4) and the left steering head cover (see Chapter 8).

6 Locate the terminals of the turn signal relay connector for the white/green wire (fuse side of circuit) and the gray wire (switch side of circuit). Connect these terminals to each other with a jumper wire.

7 Turn the ignition switch to ON and operate the turn signal switch.

8 If the turn signal lights *don't* come on, check the turn signal switch for an open circuit (see Section 18). If the turn signal switch is okay, look for an open circuit in the gray wire or in the green/white wire.

9 If the turn signal lights *do* come on, check for continuity between the terminal for the green wire and the ground terminal at the connector. If there is no continuity, there is an open circuit in the green wire. If there is continuity, either there's a loose (intermittent) or poor contact in the turn signal relay connector, or the turn signal relay is defective.

12 Brake light switches - check and replacement

Circuit check

1 Before checking any electrical circuit, check the fuse (see Section 5).

2 If the fuse is okay, remove the fuel tank (see Chapter 4) and the left steering head cover (see Chapter 8). The switch connector is a white two-pin connector. Using a test light connected to a good ground, check for voltage at the brake light switch. If there's no voltage present, check the wire between the switch and the fuse box (see the wiring diagrams at the end of this Chapter).

3 If voltage is available, touch the probe of the test light to the other terminal of the switch, then pull the brake lever or depress the brake pedal - if the test light doesn't light up, replace the switch.

4 If the test light does light, check the wiring between the switch and the brake lights (see the wiring diagrams at the end of this Chapter).

Switch replacement

Front brake lever switch

5 Disconnect the two electrical leads from the switch **(see illustration)**.

6 Remove the switch retaining screw **(see illustration)**.

7 Installation is the reverse of removal. Make sure that the positioning pin on the switch is aligned with the hole in the master cylinder **(see illustration)**.

Rear brake pedal switch

8 On 1985 and 1986 models, the switch is located on the right side, behind the passenger footpeg bracket. On all other models, the switch **(see illustration)** is located up front,

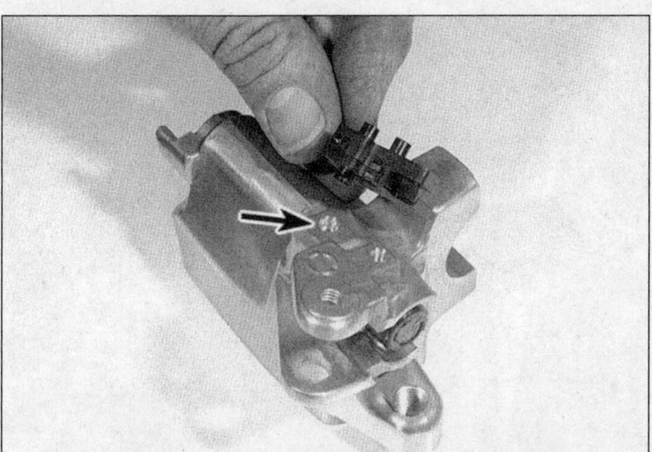

12.7 Be sure the front brake light switch positioning pin is aligned with the hole (arrow) in the master cylinder

12.8 The rear brake light switch on 1987 and later models is located up front, next to the rear brake pedal

12.10 Brake pedal switch return spring (left arrow) and locknut (right arrow) (1987-on shown; 1985 and 1986 similar)

13.2 To remove the connector box cover, disengage these two rubber straps from the cover tabs

next to the rear brake pedal. Aside from the different location, the switch used on 1985 and 1986 models is virtually identical to the switch shown here.

9 Unplug the switch electrical connector. On 1985 and 1986 models, the connector is located in a boot above and behind the switch, just ahead of the right rear shock absorber. On 1987 and later models, remove the fuel tank (see Chapter 4) and the left steering head cover (see Chapter 8). Follow the switch wire up the right frame tube, detach it from all frame clips, find the white two-pin connector inside the boot and unplug it. (Pay attention to the wire colors. There may be more than one white connector inside the boot.)

10 Unhook the switch return spring **(see illustration)**.

11 Back off the switch locknut and slide the switch out of its mounting bracket.

12 Installation is the reverse of removal.

13 Adjust the switch (see Chapter 1).

13 Turn signal assembly - removal and installation

Front turn signals

1 On 1985 and 1986 models, the front turn signal wires and connectors are inside the headlight housing. Remove the headlight (see Section 7).

2 On 1987 and later models, the front turn signal wires and connectors are inside the connector box, which is above the ignition coils. Remove the fuel tank (see Chapter 4). Remove the connector box cover **(see illustration)**.

3 On all models, the three left turn signal wires are green, orange and orange/white; the three right turn signal wires are green, light blue and light blue/white. Unplug the connectors for the turn signal(s) **(see illustration)**.

4 The turn signal assemblies are attached to the fork tubes by split clamps. To detach a turn signal assembly from the fork tube, remove the clamp pinch bolt, remove the stopper plate, separate the two halves of the clamp and remove the turn signal **(see illustrations)**.

5 Installation is the reverse of removal. Make sure that the stopper plate is correctly aligned (use the other turn signal assembly as a reference). Tighten the bolt securely.

Rear turn signals

6 On all models, the rear turn signal wires and connectors are located under the seat. Remove the seat (see Chapter 8).

7 Locate the electrical leads for the rear turn signals. On all models, the two left turn signal wires are green and orange; the two right turn signal wires are green and light blue. Unplug the leads for the turn signal you are removing.

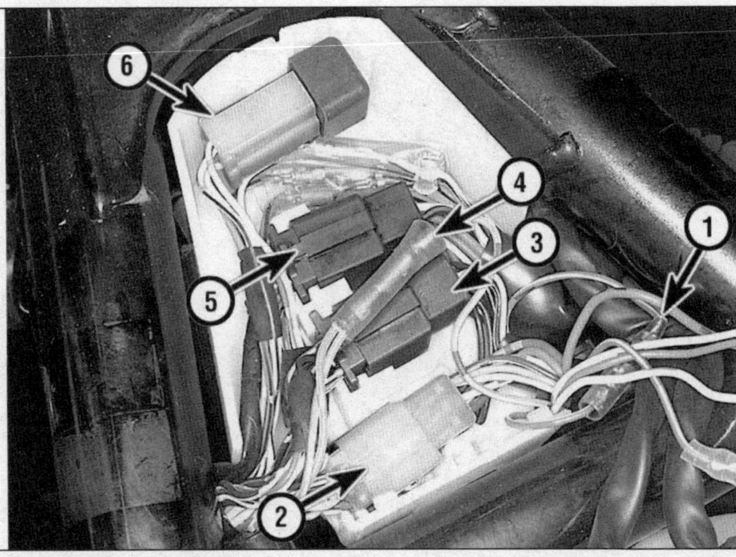

13.3 The connector box houses several important connectors (1997 VT1100C2 shown; other 1987 and later models similar)

1 *Turn signal connectors (some are already unplugged)*
2 *Left handlebar switch connector*
3 *Right handlebar switch connector*
4 *Clutch switch/sidestand switch*
5 *Speedometer assembly connector*
6 *Clutch diode(s) (the second diode, if equipped, is under the unit shown here)*

13.4a To detach a front turn signal assembly from the fork tube, remove this pinch bolt (arrow), separate the two halves of the clamp . . .

13.4b . . . and pull off the turn signal assembly

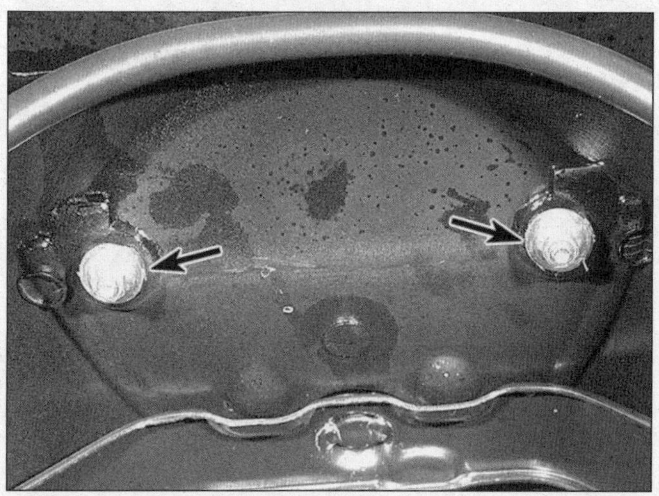

14.4a To detach the brake light/taillight assembly from the rear fender on VT1100C2 and VT1100T models, remove these two nuts (arrows) . . .

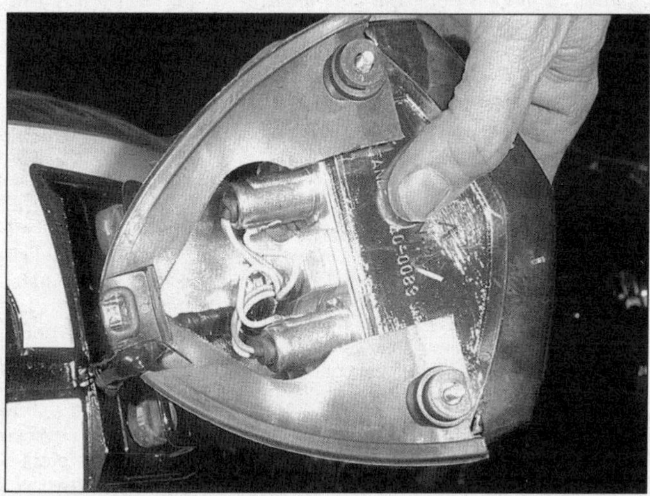

14.4b . . . pull the two studs out of the fender and carefully pull the wire harness through the hole in the fender

8 Trace the harness back to the turn signal, detach the harness from all clips and clamps on the frame and/or fender, then remove the turn signal assembly mounting nut from the fender stay and detach the turn signal stalk from the stay.

9 Installation is the reverse of removal.

14 Taillight assembly - removal and installation

1 Remove the seat (see Chapter 8).

2 The wires for the brake light and tail light are brown, green and green/yellow. Trace the wires to the electrical connector(s) in the dust boot under the seat and unplug the connector.

3 Trace the harness back to the brake light/taillight assembly and detach all clips and clamps.

4 From underneath the fender, remove the brake light/taillight assembly mounting nuts **(see illustration)** and remove the brake light/taillight assembly **(see illustration)** and pull out the harness.

5 Installation is the reverse of removal.

15 Instruments and speedometer cable - removal and installation

Speedometer cable

1 Unscrew the upper speedometer cable end from the speedometer **(see illustration)** and detach the cable from the speedometer.

2 Note how it's routed, then unscrew the speedometer cable from the speedometer

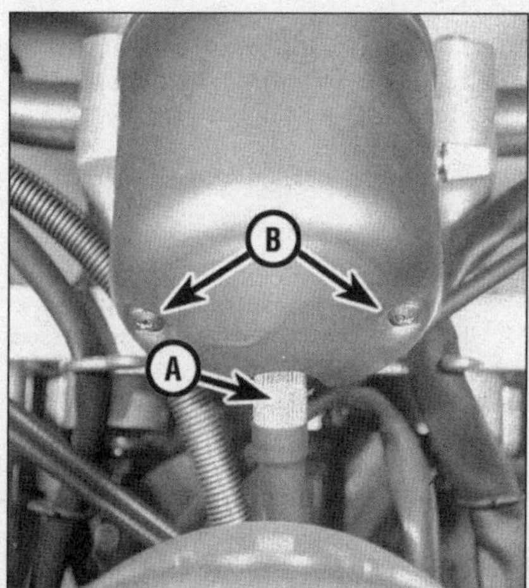

15.1 Speedometer cable knurled nut (A) and speedometer-to-housing screws (B)

15.2 To disconnect the lower end of the speedometer cable from the speedometer gearbox, remove this screw and pull out the cable

16.4a To replace the light bulb that illuminates the speedometer face, pull the bulb socket out of the speedometer assembly . . .

gearbox at the left front fork **(see illustration)**.

3 Installation is the reverse of removal.

Instruments

4 Disconnect the cable from the speedometer **(see illustration 15.1)**.

1985 and 1986 models (speedometer and tachometer assembly)

5 Remove the headlight (see Section 7).

6 Remove the headlight housing (see Section 9). Some of the instrument cluster electrical connectors are in the headlight housing and some are in the connector box below the headlight. Trace the wire harnesses down from the instrument cluster and unplug all electrical connectors.

7 Remove the two cap nuts from the underside of the cluster and remove the cluster.

8 To separate the indicator panel from the instrument cluster, remove the two bolts from the ends of the upper side of the indicator panel.

9 To separate the instruments from the cluster assembly, remove the bolt that attaches each instrument to the cluster assembly.

10 Installation is the reverse of removal.

1987 and later models (speedometer)

11 Remove the fuel tank (see Chapter 4).

12 Remove the connector box cover **(see illustration 13.2)**. Trace the speedometer assembly wire harness to the headlight and disconnect the nine-pin black connector for the following wires: brown/white, green, black/brown, green/blue, blue/red, light blue, orange, light green/red, blue, and a separate connector for the green/black wire, and, on VT1100C2 and VT1100T and 1997 and 1998 VT1100C models, a separate connector for the yellow/black wire.

13 On 1987 through 1990 and 1992 through 1996 VT1100C models, remove the three speedometer mounting cap nuts from the bracket on the forward side of the speedometer and remove the speedometer. To separate the speedometer unit from the chrome cover, remove the two cover screws and pull off the cover.

14 On VT1100C2, VT1100T and 1997 and 1998 VT1100C models, you will see two bolts facing up, just below and to either side of the speedometer. Do not attempt to turn these bolts; they have lugs on their shoulders that prevent them from turning. These two bolts are the studs for the two mounting nuts underneath. Remove the two nuts and washers and remove the speedometer unit. Remove the two special bolts. To separate the speedometer unit from the chrome cover, remove the two cover screws **(see illustration 15.1)**.

15 Installation is the reverse of removal. Be sure the speedometer cable and wiring harness are routed so that neither causes the steering to bind or interferes with other components.

16 Instrument and indicator lights - replacement

Instrument light bulb

1 The light bulb that illuminates the face of the speedometer can be replaced. The warning lights (oil pressure, sidestand and coolant temperature), also located inside the speedometer, cannot be replaced. They're light emitting diodes (LEDs). If one of the warning lights fails, replace the speedometer assembly.

2 Remove the speedometer and tachometer assembly (1985 and 1986 models) or the speedometer (1987 and later models) (see Section 15).

16.4b . . . then pull the bulb out of the socket

3 Remove the speedometer or tachometer cover screws **(see illustration 15.1)** and remove the cover.

4 Remove the bulb socket **(see illustration)**, then pull the bulb out of the socket **(see illustration)**. If the socket contacts are dirty or corroded, they should be scraped clean and sprayed with electrical contact cleaner before new bulbs are installed.

5 Carefully push the new bulb into position, then push the socket into the speedometer or tachometer.

6 Installation is otherwise the reverse of removal.

Indicator lights (1987 and later models)

7 The indicator lights (turn signal, neutral and high-beam) are located in a small panel below the speedometer.

8 Remove the speedometer (see Section 15.

9 To replace a blown indicator light bulb, pull out the socket for the bad bulb from underneath the indicator panel, pull out the

17.1 On VT1100C2, VT1100T and 1997-on VT1100C models, remove the battery holder to get to the ignition switch connector (also the neutral switch, oil pressure switch and sidestand switch connectors)

17.2 On VT1100C2, VT1100T and 1997-on VT1100C models, the ignition switch connector is white and has three pins (arrow); the single-pin connectors are for the oil pressure and neutral switches

bad bulb from the socket, install a new bulb in the socket and install the new bulb and socket into its receptacle in the indicator panel. Make sure it's firmly seated.

17 Ignition main (key) switch - check and replacement

Check

1 On 1985 and 1986 models, remove the headlight (see Section 7). On 1987 and later models, remove the left side cover (see Chapter 8), the battery (see Section 3) and the battery holder **(see illustration)**.

2 Trace the wiring harness from the ignition switch to the four-pin white connector **(see illustration)** and disconnect it. The ignition switch wires are red, red/black and blue/orange (the battery, ignition and fan motor wires, respectively). On 1985 through 1993 models, there's also a brown/white wire to this connector, and two more wires, brown and yellow/blue, lead to a black two-pin connector which must be disconnected (the extra wires on these models are for the Park position, which was eliminated after 1993).

3 Using an ohmmeter, check the continuity of the terminal pairs indicated in the following steps. Connect the ohmmeter to the *switch* side of the connector, not the wiring harness side.

4 In the OFF position, there should be no continuity between any of the wires.

5 In the ON position, there should be continuity between the red, red/blue and blue/orange wires (and, on 1985 through 1993 models, between the brown/white and brown wires).

6 In the PARK position, on 1985 through 1993 models, there should be continuity between the red and yellow/blue wires.

7 In the LOCK position (1985 and 1986 models only), there should be NO continuity between any of the terminals.

8 If the switch fails any of the tests, replace it.

Replacement

1985 and 1986 models

9 Remove the headlight (see Section 7).

10 Unplug the ignition switch electrical connectors.

11 Remove the ignition switch mounting bolts (underneath the triple clamp).

12 Installation is the reverse of removal.

1987 and later models

13 Disconnect the electrical connector(s), if you haven't already done so. Free the wiring harness from any clips or retainers.

14 If the ignition switch has a decorative cover, remove the cover screw **(see illustration)** and remove the cover.

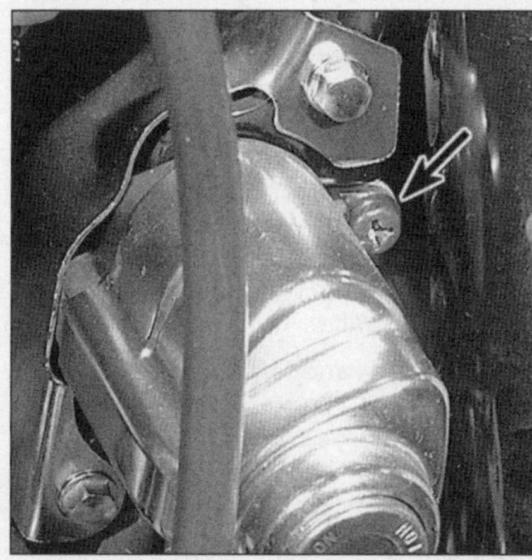
17.14 To remove the ignition switch cover (if equipped), remove this screw (arrow)

15 Remove the ignition switch mounting bolts **(see illustration)** and remove the ignition switch. Some models use Torx or Allen bolts; some later models use "break-off bolts" which must be drilled out and discarded.

16 Installation is the reverse of removal. If the switch was equipped with break-off bolts, obtain new break-off bolts (available at the dealer parts department). Tighten the bolts securely. If you're installing break-off bolts, tighten them until their heads snap off.

18 Handlebar switches - check

1 Most handlebar switch problems are caused by dirty or corroded contacts, or by worn or broken internal parts. If some part of a switch breaks, the switch assembly must be replaced. Individual parts are not available.

2 If a handlebar switch malfunctions, check it for continuity with an ohmmeter or a continuity test light. Be sure to disconnect the battery negative cable to prevent a short circuit, before making the checks.

3 On 1985 and 1986 models, remove the headlight (see Section 7). Remove the two cover screws from the junction box cover below the headlight, between the two horns, and remove the cover.

4 On 1987 and later models, remove the fuel tank (see Chapter 4) and the connector box cover **(see illustration 13.2)**.

5 Trace the wiring harness from the suspect switch and unplug the electrical connector(s) **(see illustration 13.3)**. On 1985 and 1986 models, trace the wire harness from each handlebar switch and disconnect the connector(s) in the headlight housing or in the junction box below the headlight. All 1987 and later models use nine-pin white connectors for the left handlebar switches. The left handlebar switch also has a pair of single-pin connectors for the horn leads. On

17.15 To detach the ignition switch, remove the two Torx bolts or drill out the break-off bolts (if equipped) (arrows)

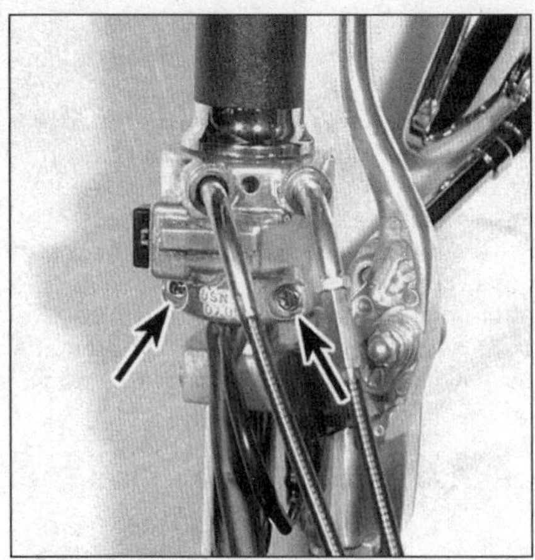

19.1a The handlebar switches are held together by screws (arrows); this is the throttle side . . .

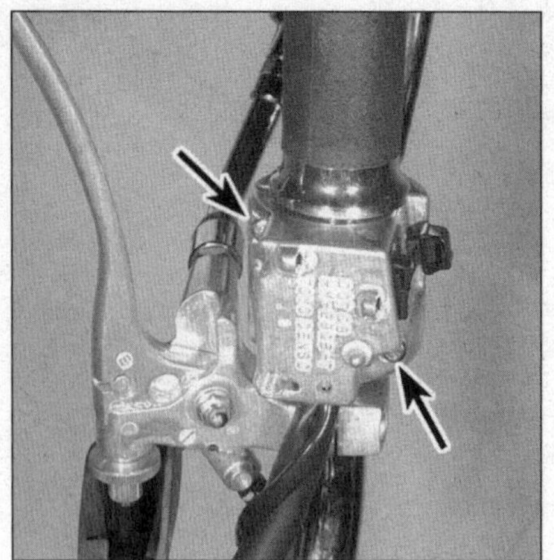

19.1b . . . the clutch side switches are also held together by screws (arrows)

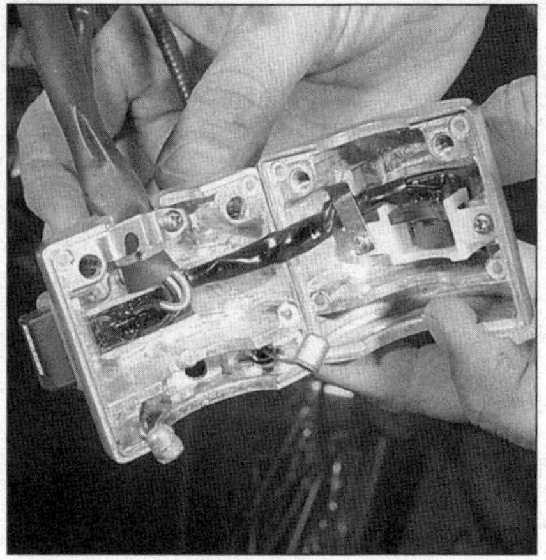

19.1c Separate the switch halves for access to the individual switches

1987 through 1990 and 1992 and 1993 models, the right switches have red connectors. On 1994 and later models, the right handlebar switches use brown connectors.

6 Using an ohmmeter, check the continuity of the terminal pairs indicated in the following steps. Connect the ohmmeter to the *switch* side of the connector, not the wiring harness side.

Left handlebar switches

7 The wire colors for the **left** handlebar switches are as follows:

- *a) The **dimmer switch** wires on all models are blue/white, blue and white.*
- *b) The **turn signal switch** wires on 1985 through 1996 VT1100C models are green, orange, light blue, brown/white, light blue/white and orange/white.*
- *c) The **turn signal switch** wires on VT1100C2, VT1100T and 1997-on VT1100C models are orange, green, light blue, brown/white, orange/white and light blue/white (they're the same colors, but the first two wire colors are switched, which is important to remember when making the following continuity tests).*
- *d) The **horn switch** wires on 1985 through 1996 VT1100C models are light green and white/green.*
- *e) The **horn switch** wires on VT1100C2 models are white/green and blue/white.*
- *f) The h**orn switch** wires on VT1100T and 1997-on VT1100C models are white/green and light green.*

Dimmer switch

8 LO position - continuity between blue/white and white.

9 HI position - continuity between blue/white and blue.

Turn signal switch

10 LEFT - continuity between green and orange, and between brown/white and light blue/white.

11 RIGHT - continuity between green and light blue, and between brown/white and orange/white.

Horn switch

1985 through 1996 VT1100C models

12 DEPRESSED - continuity between light green and white/green.

13 RELEASED - no continuity between light green and white/green.

VT1100C2, VT1100T and 1997-on VT1100C models

14 DEPRESSED - continuity between white/green and blue/white.

15 RELEASED - no continuity between white/green and blue/white.

Right handlebar switches

16 The wire colors for the **right** handlebar switches are as follows:

- *a) The **starter switch** wires on 1985 through 1993 models are black, yellow/red, black/red and blue/white.*
- *b) The **starter switch** wires on 1994 and later models are black/white, yellow/red, black/red and blue/white.*
- *c) The **kill switch** wires on 1985 through 1993 models are black and black/white.*
- *d) The **kill switch** wires on 1994 and later models are black/blue and black/white.*

Starter switch

1985 through 1993 models

17 DEPRESSED - continuity between black and yellow/red.

18 RELEASED - continuity between black/red and blue/white.

1994 and later models

19 DEPRESSED - continuity between black/white and yellow/red.

20 RELEASED - continuity between black/red and blue/white.

Kill switch

1985 through 1993 models

21 RUN - continuity between black and black/white.

22 OFF - no continuity between black and black/white.

All other models

23 RUN - continuity between black/blue and black/white.

24 OFF - no continuity between black/blue and black/white.

25 If any continuity check indicates a problem, remove the switch (see Section 19), spray the switch contacts with electrical contact cleaner, then retest. The contacts can also be scraped clean with a knife or polished with crocus cloth, if they're accessible. If the switch still fails to check out as described above, or if it's obviously damaged or broken, replace the switch.

19 Handlebar switches - removal and installation

1 The handlebar switches are composed of two halves that clamp around the bars. They are easily removed for cleaning or inspection by taking out the clamp screws and pulling the switch halves away from the handlebars **(see illustrations)**.

2 To completely remove the switches, the electrical connectors in the wiring harness must be unplugged as follows:

3 On 1985 and 1986 models, remove the headlight (see Section 7). Remove the two cover screws from the junction box cover below the headlight, between the two horns and remove the cover. Trace the wire harness from the handlebar switch(es) and unplug the connector(s).

4 On 1987 and later models, remove the fuel tank (see Chapter 4) and the connector box cover **(see illustration 13.2)**. Trace the wiring harness from the suspect switch and unplug the electrical connector(s) **(see illustration 13.3)**. All models use nine-pin white connectors for the left handlebar switches. The left handlebar switch also has a pair of

20.15 The neutral switch (arrow) is on the left side of the engine behind the flywheel; to remove it, disconnect the wire and unscrew the switch (but be ready for some oil to leak out!)

21.3 The oil pressure switch (A) and oil orifice bolt (B) are next to the oil filter mounting stud (C)

single-pin connectors for the horn leads. On 1987 through 1993 models, the right switches have red connectors. On 1994 and later models, the right handlebar switches use brown connectors.

5 When installing the switches, make sure the wiring harnesses are properly routed to avoid pinching or stretching the wires.

20 Neutral switch - check and replacement

Check

1 On 1985 through 1996 VT1100C models, remove the seat (see Chapter 8) and the fuel tank (see Chapter 4).

2 On 1985 and 1986 models, the neutral switch wire is light green/red and the connector is located in the bank of connectors under the seat, right in front of the rear fender. Turn the ignition key to ON and place the transmission in neutral. Backprobe the connector terminal with the positive probe of a voltmeter, touch the negative probe to ground and verify that there is voltage between the light green/red wire and ground. Put the transmission in each other gear and verify that there is no voltage between the light green/red wire and ground.

3 On 1987 through 1996 VT1100C models, remove the connector box cover **(see illustration 13.2)**. The neutral switch wire is light green/red; its connector is a terminal in the nine-pin black connector in the connector box **(see illustration 13.3)**. With the ignition key ON and the transmission in neutral, backprobe the connector terminal for the light green/red wire with the positive probe of a voltmeter and the black/brown wire (ground) with the negative probe and verify that there is voltage. Put the transmission in each of the other gears and verify that there is no voltage at the terminals for the light green/red and the black/brown wires.

4 On VT1100C2, VT1100T and 1997-on VT1100C models, remove the left side cover (see Chapter 8), the battery (see Section 3) and the battery holder **(see illustration 17.1)**. The neutral switch wire is light green with a red band around the end of the wire at the connector terminal **(see illustration 17.2)**. Turn the ignition key to ON, shift the transmission into neutral, backprobe the connector with the positive probe of a voltmeter, ground the other probe and verify that there is voltage between the light green/red wire and ground. Put the transmission in each other gear and verify that there is no voltage.

5 If the indicator light fails to come on, either the bulb or the switch is bad.

6 Remove and check the bulb (see Section 16). If it's bad, replace it.

7 Recheck the neutral switch circuit as described above.

8 If the indicator light still fails to come on, the switch is probably bad (although a short or open in the circuit is a possibility too). First, check the switch as follows:

9 On 1985 and 1986 models, unplug the electrical connector for the light green/red wire and put the transmission in neutral. Using an ohmmeter, verify that there is continuity between the light green/red wire and ground. Put the transmission in each other gear and verify that there is no continuity between the light green/red wire and ground.

10 On 1987 through 1996 VT1100C models, unplug the nine-pin black connector, put the transmission in neutral and verify that there is continuity between the terminals for the light green/red wire and the black/brown wire (ground). Put the transmission in each other gear and verify that there is no continuity between the terminals for the light green/red wire and the black/brown wire.

11 On VT1100C2, VT1100T and 1997-on VT1100C models, unplug the connector for the light green/red wire, shift the transmission into neutral and verify that there is continuity between the light green/red wire and ground. Put the transmission in each other gear and verify that there is no continuity.

12 If the neutral switch fails to operate as described, replace it (see below).

13 If the neutral switch checks out okay, inspect the neutral switch circuit for a short or open, repair it as necessary and retest.

Replacement

14 Remove the left crankcase cover (see Section 30).

15 Locate the neutral switch **(see illustration)**. Detach the electrical lead from the switch, then unscrew the switch. Some oil is going to come out when you unscrew the switch and remove it from the crankcase, so be prepared to catch it with a drain pan.

16 Apply thread sealant to the threads of the new switch and tighten it to the torque listed in this Chapter's Specifications.

17 Installation is otherwise the reverse of removal. Be sure to route the wire harness for the oil pressure switch and the neutral switch correctly so that it's not damaged by the drive chain.

21 Oil pressure switch - check and replacement

Check

1 When the ignition switch is turned to ON, the oil pressure warning light on the speedometer should come on. This verifies that the oil pressure switch and circuit are functioning normally.

2 If the oil pressure warning light doesn't come on when the ignition switch is turned to ON, remove the left crankcase cover (see Section 30).

3 Locate the oil pressure switch **(see illustration)**. Remove the dust boot, remove

22.2 The red, three-pin electrical connector (arrow) for the sidestand switch is located on the left side, in the boot with the ignition switch connector and the connectors for the neutral switch and oil pressure switch

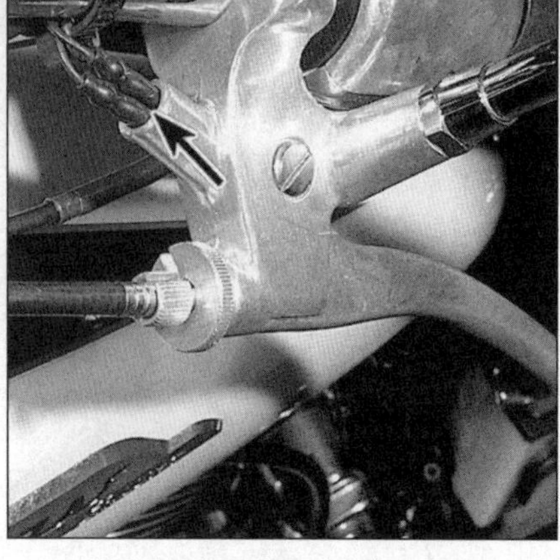

23.1 Unplug the clutch switch electrical connectors

24.1 To detach the horn, unplug the electrical connectors and remove the bracket bolt (arrows) (VT1100C2 shown)

the electrical lead retaining screw and detach the lead from the switch.

4 Short the switch lead to ground with a jumper wire. Turn the ignition switch to ON. The oil pressure warning indicator light should now come on.

5 If the oil pressure warning light still doesn't come on, check the 10A inline mini-fuse and check the switch circuit for a break or poor connection.

6 Start the engine and verify that the oil pressure warning light goes out.

7 If the oil pressure warning light doesn't go out, have the oil pressure checked by a Honda dealer service department. You can do this yourself if you have a mechanical oil pressure gauge with the correct threads to screw into the fitting for the oil pressure switch. Remove the oil pressure switch (see below), install the gauge in its place and run the engine.

8 If the oil pressure is normal, replace the oil pressure switch.

Replacement

9 Remove the left crankcase cover (see Section 30).

10 Unplug the electrical lead from the oil pressure switch **(see illustration 21.3)**.

11 Some oil is going to come out when you unscrew the switch, so be prepared to catch it with a drain pan.

12 Apply thread sealant to the threads of the new switch, install the switch and tighten it to the torque listed in this Chapter's Specifications.

13 Installation is otherwise the reverse of removal. Be sure to route the wire harness for the oil pressure switch and the neutral switch correctly before installing the left crankcase cover.

22 Sidestand switch - check and replacement

Note: *This procedure applies to VT1100C2, VT1100T and 1997-on VT1100C models.*

Check

1 Remove the left side cover (see Chapter 8), the battery (see Section 3) and the battery holder **(see illustration 17.1)**.

2 The wires in the sidestand switch circuit are green/white, yellow/black and green. The electrical connector is a red three-pin connector **(see illustration)**. Unplug the connector.

3 Connect the leads of an ohmmeter to the terminals for the indicated wire colors.

4 With the sidestand in the down position, there should be continuity between the terminals for the yellow/black and green wires.

5 With the sidestand in the up position, there should be continuity between the terminals for the green/white and green wires.

6 If the sidestand switch fails either of these tests, replace it.

Replacement

7 Disconnect the electrical connector for the sidestand switch, if you haven't already done so (see Steps 1 and 2).

8 Remove the sidestand switch bolt and remove the switch.

9 When installing the new sidestand switch, align the positioning pin on the switch with the hole in the sidestand and align the groove in the switch with the pin on the sidestand.

10 Install the sidestand switch retaining bolt and tighten it to the torque listed in this Chapter's Specifications.

11 Installation is otherwise the reverse of the removal procedure. Be sure to route the electrical lead correctly.

23 Clutch switch - check and replacement

Check

1 Disconnect the electrical connectors from the clutch switch **(see illustration)**.

2 Connect an ohmmeter to the terminals of the clutch switch. With the clutch lever pulled in, the ohmmeter should show continuity. With the lever out, the ohmmeter should show no continuity.

3 If the switch doesn't check out as described, replace it.

Replacement

4 Disconnect the electrical connectors from the clutch switch **(see illustration 23.1)**.

5 Remove the clutch switch.

6 Installation is the reverse of removal.

24 Horn - check and replacement

Check

1 On 1985 and 1986 models, there are two horns, located on the front forks below the headlight. On 1987 through 1996 VT1100C models, the horn is located on the left side of the engine (it's bolted to the rear cylinder). On VT1100C2, VT1100T and 1997-on VT1100C models, the horn is located at the lower right corner of the radiator **(see illustration)**.

2 Disconnect the electrical connectors from the horn(s). Using two jumper wires, apply battery voltage directly to the terminals on the horn. If the horn sounds,

check the switch (see Section 18) and the wiring between the switch and the horn (see the wiring diagrams at the end of this Chapter). The horn wiring harness is connected to the main harness at a black two-pin connector (same connector as the fan motor) behind the steering head. To get to it, remove the steering head covers (see Chapter 8).

3 If the horn doesn't sound, replace it.

Replacement

4 Disconnect the electrical connectors **(see illustration 24.1)**.

5 Unbolt the horn **(see illustration 24.1)**.

6 Installation is the reverse of removal.

25 Starter relay switch - check and replacement

Check

1 Make sure the battery is fully charged.

2 On 1985 and 1986 models, remove the right side cover (see Chapter 8); the starter relay switch is located right behind the battery. On 1987 through 1990 and 1992 through 1996 VT1100C models, remove the left side cover; the starter relay is located right in front of the battery. On VT1100C2, VT1100T and 1997-on VT1100C models, remove the seat; the starter relay **(see illustration)** is located at the left rear corner of the air cleaner housing, behind the connector bracket.

25.2 VT1100C2, VT1100T and 1997-on VT1100C models

A Starter relay switch
B Alternator connector (white three-pin)
C Regulator/rectifier connectors (white 2-pin and green 2-pin)

Warning: Make sure the transmission is in neutral for the following step.

3 Turn the ignition switch to ON and the engine kill switch to RUN. When you push the starter button, the starter relay switch should click.

4 If the starter relay switch doesn't click, unplug the starter relay switch connector(s) and check for continuity between the terminal for the green/red wire (on the harness side of the connector) and ground.

5 If there is continuity when the transmission is in Neutral or when the clutch is disengaged and the sidestand is up (sidestand switch closed), the ground circuit is okay (you will note a slight resistance in the circuit because of the clutch diode).

6 Reconnect the starter relay switch electrical connector, shift the transmission into Neutral and, using a voltmeter, measure the voltage between the terminal for the yellow/red wire (backprobe the connector) and ground. Battery voltage should be indicated when the starter button is pushed with the ignition switch ON.

7 Unplug the starter relay switch connector again, remove the cable attaching bolts and disconnect the cables from the relay. Using jumper wires, hook up the positive terminal of a 12-volt battery to the starter relay switch terminal for the yellow/red wire and hook up the negative terminal of the battery to the starter relay terminal for the green/red wire. Using an ohmmeter hooked up to the starter relay cable terminals, verify that there is continuity when the battery is connected to the relay. Disconnect the battery from the relay and verify that there is no continuity across the relay terminals.

8 If the starter relay switch fails any of these tests, replace it.

Replacement

9 Disconnect the cable from the negative terminal of the battery.

10 On 1985 and 1986 models, remove the right side cover (see Chapter 8); the starter relay switch is located right behind the battery. On 1987 through 1996 VT1100C models, remove the left side cover; the starter relay is located right in front of the battery. On VT1100C2, VT1100T and 1997-on VT1100C models, remove the seat; the starter relay **(see illustration 25.2)** is located at the left rear corner of the air cleaner housing, behind the connector bracket.

11 Unplug the starter relay switch connector(s).

12 Remove the cable attaching bolts and disconnect the cables from the starter relay switch.

13 Remove the starter relay switch.

14 Installation is the reverse of removal. Reconnect the negative battery cable after all the other electrical connections are made.

26 Clutch diode - check and replacement

1 Remove the fuel tank (see Chapter 4).

2 On 1985 and 1986 models, the clutch diode is located above the left end of the bank of connectors just ahead of the rear fender. The clutch diode on 1985 and 1986 models has two terminals; when the diode is lying flat (on its long side, not its edge), the horizontal terminal is the negative terminal and the other terminal is the positive terminal.

3 On 1987 and later models, remove the cover from the connector box **(see illustration 13.2)**. On 1987 models, there is one two-terminal diode (just like the one described in the previous Step for earlier models), in the forward end of the connector box. On 1988 through 1996 VT1100C models, and on VT1100C2 models, there are two diodes in the forward end of the connector box. One is a two-terminal type just like the ones used on earlier models. The other diode is a three-terminal design. On this type of diode, the two terminals parallel to one another are the positive terminals and the third terminal is the negative terminal. On VT1100T and 1997-on VT1100C models, there is one three-terminal diode.

4 The purpose of the clutch diode is to prevent reverse current from flowing from the neutral indicator to the clutch switch. A clutch diode allows current to flow from the negative terminal to the positive terminal(s), but it does not allow current the flow the other way. Think of the negative terminal as the "in" terminal; think of the positive terminal(s) as the "out" terminal(s).

5 Using an ohmmeter, verify that there is continuity between the negative terminal and the positive terminal(s) in one direction, but NOT in the other direction.

6 If the clutch diode fails to operate as described, replace it.

7 Installation is the reverse of removal.

27 Starter motor, drive gear and torque limiter - removal and installation

Starter motor

1 Disconnect the cable from the negative terminal of the battery.

2 Pull back the rubber cover, remove the

27.2 Remove this retaining nut (arrow) and detach the starter cable from the terminal on the starter motor

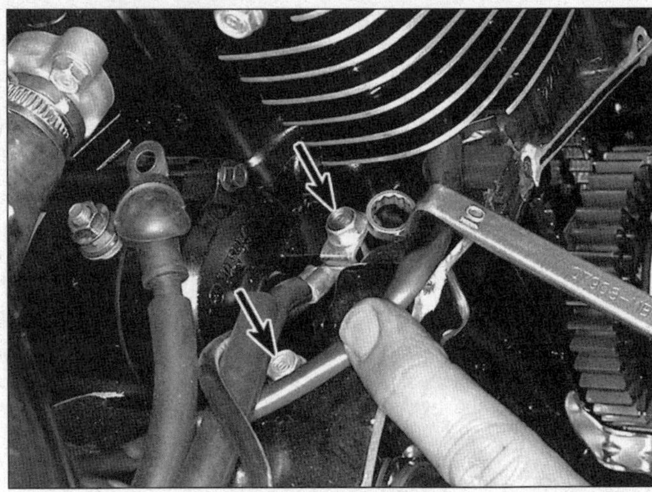

27.3 Remove the starter mounting bolts (arrows); don't forget to attach the ground cable with the front bolt when installing the starter)

nut retaining the starter cable to the starter and disconnect the cable **(see illustration)**.

3 Remove the starter mounting bolts and the ground strap **(see illustration)**.

4 Lift the end of the starter slightly and disengage the starter from the crankcase by pulling it out to the right **(see illustration)**.

5 Inspect the teeth on the starter pinion gear and on the reduction gear; make sure the gear teeth are neither chipped nor excessively worn. (With a flashlight, you can inspect the reduction gear teeth through the hole in the case for the starter.)

6 Apply a little engine oil to the O-ring. Installation is otherwise the reverse of removal. Tighten the starter mounting bolts to the torque listed in this Chapter's Specifications.

Starter drive gear and torque limiter

7 Remove the left crankcase rear cover (see "Clutch - check and adjustment" in Chapter 1).

8 On California models, detach the EVAP carburetor air vent (CAV) control valve hose from the clamp.

9 Remove the starter gear cover bolts and remove the cover **(see illustrations)**. Don't lose the clamp, if equipped, for the EVAP CAV control valve hose. Remove the gasket and the dowel pins; store the dowels in a plastic bag.

10 Remove the starter drive gear and the torque limiter.

11 Inspect the teeth on both gears for excessive wear and damage. If either gear is in bad condition, replace it.

12 Inspect the bearings in the cover. If they're noisy or stiff, have them replaced at a motorcycle machine shop or at a dealer service department.

13 Installation is the reverse of removal. Be sure to clean the gears well and lubricate the splines and gear teeth with a little assembly lube or oil. Also be sure to use a new gasket. Don't forget to install the dowel pins.

27.4 Lift the right end of the starter motor slightly and pull it out

28 Charging system testing - general information and precautions

1 If the performance of the charging system is suspect, the system as a whole should be checked first, followed by testing of the individual components (the alternator and the voltage regulator/rectifier). **Note:** *Before beginning the checks, make sure the battery is fully charged and that all system connections are clean and tight.*

2 Checking the output of the charging system and the performance of the various components within the charging system requires the use of special electrical test equipment. A voltmeter or a multimeter are the absolute minimum tools required. In addition, an ohmmeter is generally required for checking the remainder of the system.

3 When making the checks, follow the procedures carefully to prevent incorrect connections or short circuits, as irreparable damage to electrical system components may result if short circuits occur. Because of the special tools and expertise required, it is recommended that the job of checking the charging system be left to a dealer service department or a reputable motorcycle repair shop.

29 Charging system - check

Caution: Never disconnect the battery cables from the battery while the engine is running. If the battery is disconnected, the alternator and regulator/rectifier will be damaged.

27.9a Remove the starter gear cover bolts (arrows) . . .

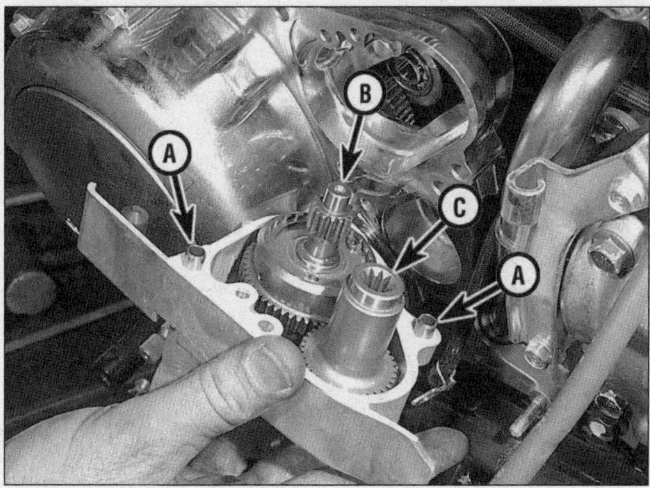

27.9b . . . and pull off the cover; remove the dowel pins (A), the torque limiter (B) and the drive gear (C)

1 To check the charging system output, you will need a voltmeter or a multimeter with a voltmeter function.
2 On 1985 and 1986 models, remove the right side cover; on all other models, remove the left side cover (see Chapter 8).
3 The battery must be fully charged (charge it from an external source if necessary) and the engine must be at normal operating temperature to obtain an accurate reading.

Regulated voltage output test

4 Attach the positive (red) voltmeter lead to the positive (+) battery terminal and the negative (black) lead to the battery negative (-) terminal. The voltmeter selector switch (if equipped) must be in a DC volt range greater than 15 volts.
5 Start the engine and allow it to warm up to its normal operating temperature. With the headlight on LOW beam and the engine running at the rpm indicated in this Chapter's Specifications, note the regulated voltage output of the charging system and compare your measurement to the regulated output listed in this Chapter's Specifications. Turn off the engine.
6 If the charging system fails to produce the specified regulated voltage output, there could be an open or a short circuit, or a loose, corroded or shorted connector, somewhere in the charging system wire harness; there could be an open or short in the alternator (see Section 30); or the voltage regulator/rectifier could be defective (see Section 31).
7 If the charging system produces a higher-than-specified voltage output, the regulator/rectifier is either poorly grounded or it's defective (see Section 31), or the battery is defective (see Section 3).
8 If the indicated regulated voltage output is within the specified range, but the battery is frequently discharged, this is an indication that the battery is probably worn out. But it's also possible that there's a current leak.

Current leakage test

9 To test for a current leak, disconnect the negative battery cable (see Section 3) and hook up a digital ammeter capable of readings in the milliampere range. Connect the positive probe of the ammeter to the battery negative cable and the negative probe to the battery negative terminal. With the ignition switch turned to OFF, note whether there is any current leakage. If there is, compare your reading to the permissible current leakage listed in this Chapter's Specifications.
10 If the indicated current leakage exceeds the specified allowable maximum, there's a short circuit that could be anywhere in the bike's electrical system. To locate the circuit where the short is occurring, unplug the harness electrical connectors one by one until the leak stops.
11 If the indicated current leakage is less than the specified allowable maximum, but the battery is frequently discharged, replace the battery (see Section 3).

30 Alternator - check and replacement

Check

1 On 1985 and 1986 models, remove the seats and the right side cover; on 1987 through 1996 VT1100C models, remove the right side cover; on VT1100C2, VT1100T and 1997-on models, remove the seat (see Chapter 8).
2 Trace the three-wire harness (all three wires are yellow on all models) from the alternator, on the left side of the engine, to the three-pin white electrical connector and disconnect the connector. On 1985 and 1986 models, the connector is located on the far left of the connector bank just in front of the rear fender. On 1987 through 1996 VT1100C models, the connector is located in the connector boot at the front of the air cleaner housing. On VT1100C2, VT1100T and 1997-on VT1100C models, the connector is located on the connector bracket on top of the air cleaner housing **(see illustration 25.2)**.
3 Using an ohmmeter, measure the resistance between each terminal and each of the other two terminals of the connector (on the alternator side of the connector, not the wiring harness side). Compare your measurements to the stator coil resistance listed in this Chapter's Specifications.
4 If the reading between any two terminals is outside the range listed in this Chapter's Specifications, replace the stator.
5 If the reading is within the Specifications, refer to the wiring diagrams at the end of the book and check the charging circuit for breaks or poor connections. If the wiring is good, check the voltage regulator/rectifier (see Section 31).

Replacement

Stator

6 On 1985 and 1986 models, remove the seats and the right side cover; on 1987 through 1996 VT1100C models, remove the right side cover; on VT1100C2, VT1100T and 1997-on models, remove the seat (see Chapter 8).
7 Trace the three-wire harness (all three wires are yellow on all models) from the alternator, on the left side of the engine, to the three-pin white electrical connector and disconnect the connector **(see illustration 25.2)**. Trace the wire harness down the frame and cut or remove any cable ties or clamps

30.10a Remove the left crankcase cover bolts (arrows) . . .

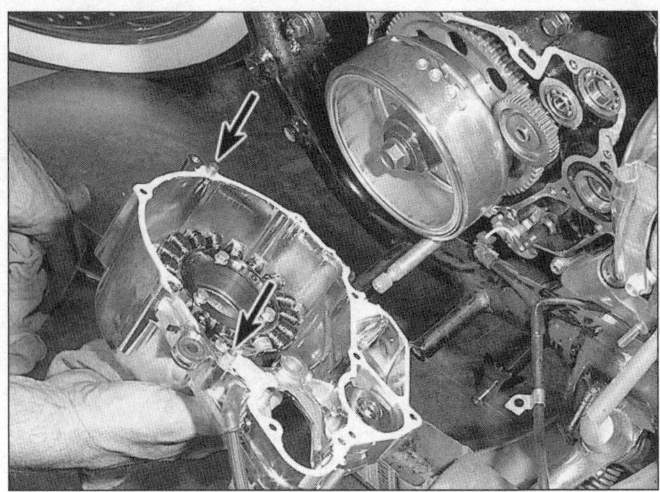
30.10b . . . pull off the cover (tap it loose if it's stuck) and locate the dowels (arrows)

securing it to the frame. Pay attention to how the harness is routed; it must be rerouted in exactly the same way when the stator is installed again.

8 On VT1100C2 and VT1100T models, remove the left footpeg bracket (see Chapter 8). On VT1100C models, remove the gearshift arm from the gearshift spindle; on VT1100C2 and VT1100T models, remove the gearshift pedal from the gearshift spindle (see "Gearshift linkage - removal, inspection and installation" in Chapter 2). Detach the left crankcase cover breather pipe adapter (see "Crankcase emission control system - description, check and component replacement" in Chapter 4).

9 Remove the starter gear cover, the starter drive gear and the starter torque limiter (see Section 27).

10 Loosen the left crankcase cover mounting bolts evenly in a criss-cross pattern and remove the cover **(see illustrations)**.

11 Remove the dowel pins, remove the stator wire harness clamp bolt, note how the wire harness is routed in the cover, disengage it from the cover and remove the stator retaining bolts **(see illustration)** and remove the stator assembly.

12 Clean all traces of old gasket sealer from the cover and its mating surface on the engine. Thoroughly clean the left engine cover with solvent and blow it dry with compressed air.

13 Install the stator in the cover, install the stator retaining bolts and tighten them securely. Route the stator wire harness exactly as before, seat the harness grommet firmly and secure the harness with the clamp. Tighten the clamp bolt securely.

14 Install the dowel pins. Position a new gasket over the dowels.

15 Make sure there are no metal particles or parts stuck to the rotor magnets, then install the cover and tighten the cover bolts evenly, in a criss-cross pattern, to the torque listed in this Chapter's Specifications. Route the wiring harness over the top of the crankcase to the frame, reattach it to the frame as before and plug in the electrical connector.

Flywheel (rotor)

16 Remove the left crankcase cover (see Steps 6 through 10).

17 Remove the starter reduction gear and shaft **(see illustration)**.

18 Install a flywheel holder tool (Honda 07725-0040000, or equivalent) to lock the flywheel in place. If you don't have a suitable flywheel holder tool, shift the transmission into gear and have an assistant apply the rear brake. Remove the rotor bolt and washer **(see illustration)**. **Note:** *The flywheel bolt is reverse thread; turn it clockwise to loosen it.*

30.11 Remove the old gasket, pull the wire harness grommet from the cover, unbolt the harness clamp and remove the three stator bolts (arrows)

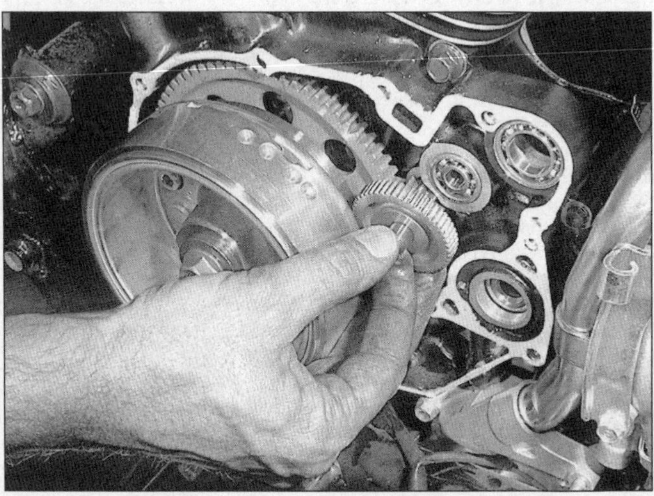
30.17 Remove the starter reduction gear and shaft

30.18 Hold the rotor and turn the bolt clockwise to remove it (it has reverse threads)

30.19 Use a tool like this one to separate the rotor from the crankshaft

19 Thread a rotor puller (Honda 07733-0020001, or 07933-3290001, or equivalent) into the rotor **(see illustration)**. Remove the rotor from the end of the crankshaft and take the Woodruff key out of its slot in the end of the crankshaft.

Caution: Don't try to remove the rotor without a proper puller. The flywheel can easily be damaged by makeshift tools. Aftermarket rotor pullers are inexpensive and readily available at motorcycle dealers and accessory shops.

20 Remove and inspect the starter clutch assembly, if necessary (see Section 32).

21 Installation is the reverse of removal. Be sure to reinstall the Woodruff key in the crankshaft.

Caution: Make sure no metal objects have stuck to the magnets inside the rotor.

Tighten the rotor bolt to the torque listed in this Chapter's Specifications.

31 Voltage regulator/rectifier - check and replacement

Check

1 The voltage regulator/rectifier **(see illustration)** is located below and behind the coolant reservoir. It's checked by process of elimination (when all other possible causes of the problem have been ruled out, the regulator/rectifier is assumed to be bad). Since electrical parts, including regulator/rectifiers, can't usually be returned once you buy them, it's a good idea to have your test results confirmed by a dealer service department or other qualified shop before buying a new part.

2 Remove the seat(s) (see Chapter 8).

3 The wires for the regulator/rectifier are red/white and green on all models. On 1985 and 1986 models, trace the wire harness from the regulator/rectifier up to the white six-pin connector, third connector from the left in the bank of connectors in front of the rear fender. On 1987 and later VT1100C models, and on VT1100T models, trace the wire harness from the regulator/rectifier to the connector boot on top of the air cleaner housing. These models use a 2-pin green and a 2-pin white connector. VT1100C2 models also use a 2-pin white connector and a 2-pin green connector, but they're located on the connector bracket **(see illustration 25.2)**.

4 Using a voltmeter, verify that there is voltage between the terminals for the red/white and green wires. There shouldn't be any voltage between them (if there is voltage between them, there is a short in the connector).

5 If there is no voltage between the terminals for the red/white and green wires, verify that there *is* voltage between the terminal for the red/white wire and ground. If there is, then you know that there is power to the regulator/rectifier. Finally, using an ohmmeter, verify that there is continuity between the terminal for the green wire and ground. If there is, then you know that the regulator/rectifier output line is good. By process of elimination, the voltage regulator/rectifier is probably bad.

Replacement

6 Trace the harness from the regulator/rectifier up to the connector(s) as described in Step 3.

7 Remove the regulator/rectifier mounting bolts **(see illustration 31.1)**.

8 Installation is the reverse of removal.

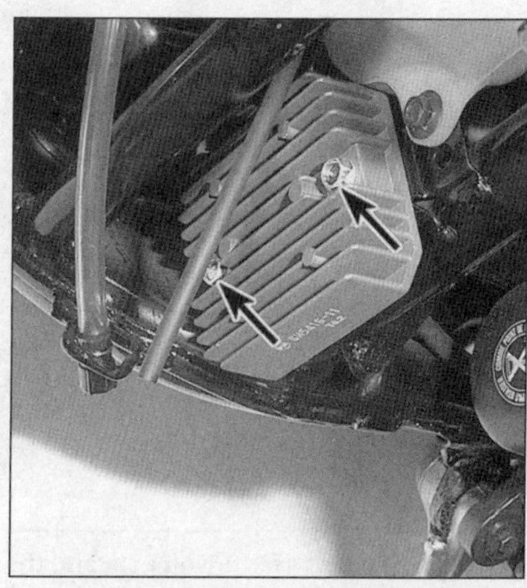

31.1 The voltage regulator/rectifier is located behind and below the coolant reservoir; to detach it, remove its bolts (arrows)

32 Starter clutch assembly - removal, inspection and installation

1 Remove the left crankcase rear cover (see "Clutch - check and adjustment" in Chapter 1). Remove the starter gear cover (see Section 27). Remove the left crankcase cover (see Section 30).

2 Remove the reduction gear and shaft **(see illustration 30.17)**. Inspect the reduction gear for wear and chipped teeth. Inspect the gear shaft for scoring and excessive wear. Replace any worn or damaged parts.

3 Remove the flywheel (see Section 30). Remove the needle bearing and the starter

32.3a Remove the starter driven gear needle bearing from the crankshaft

32.3b Remove the starter driven gear

32.4a If the starter driven gear and the flywheel have been separated, insert the starter driven gear hub into the starter clutch rollers

32.4b Hold the rotor and turn the gear; it should turn freely counterclockwise, but lock up when you try to turn it clockwise

32.6 To detach the starter clutch housing from the flywheel, remove these six Torx bolts

32.8 Inspect the one-way clutch and the starter clutch housing; if anything is damaged or excessively worn, replace the starter clutch

32.9 Compare the outside diameter of the starter driven gear hub to that listed in this Chapter's Specifications

32.12 With the needle bearing and Woodruff key in place, install the assembled flywheel/starter driven gear onto the crankshaft

reduction gear from the crankshaft **(see illustrations)**.

4 Holding the flywheel in one hand, with the flywheel facing down and the starter clutch facing toward you, verify that the starter clutch turns freely in a counterclockwise direction **(see illustrations)**, but not at all in a clockwise direction.

5 If the starter clutch turns in both directions, or will not turn in either direction, remove it from the flywheel and inspect the starter clutch assembly.

6 Remove the six Torx bolts from the flywheel **(see illustration)** and detach the starter clutch housing and one-way clutch from the flywheel.

7 Clean all parts thoroughly in clean solvent and blow them dry with compressed air.

8 Inspect the needle bearing, the one-way clutch sprag and the clutch housing for scoring or other signs of excessive wear **(see illustration)**. If anything is damaged or worn, replace the entire assembly.

9 Measure the inside diameter (I.D.) of the starter clutch housing (with the one-way clutch assembly removed) and the outside diameter (O.D.) of the starter driven gear hub **(see illustration)**. Compare your measurements to the starter clutch I.D. and starter driven gear O.D. listed in this Chapter's Specifications. If the starter clutch I.D. is greater than the specified I.D., replace the starter clutch. If the starter driven gear hub O.D. is less than the specified O.D., replace the starter gear.

10 Apply clean engine oil to the one-way clutch sprags and install the one-way clutch unit into the clutch housing. Install the housing with its flange toward the flywheel, install the six Torx bolts and tighten them to the torque listed in this Chapter's Specifications.

11 Lubricate the outer surface of the starter driven gear hub and install the gear into the starter clutch housing.

12 Install the flywheel and starter driven gear assembly on the crankshaft **(see illustration)**. Install the large washer, install the flywheel bolt and tighten it to the torque listed in this Chapter's Specifications.

13 The remainder of installation is the reverse of removal.

33 Wiring diagrams

Prior to troubleshooting a circuit, check the fuses to make sure they're in good condition. Make sure the battery is fully charged and check the cable connections.

When checking a circuit, make sure all connectors are clean, with no broken or loose terminals or wires. When unplugging a connector, don't pull on the wires - pull only on the connector housings themselves.

Notes

Wiring diagrams on the following pages

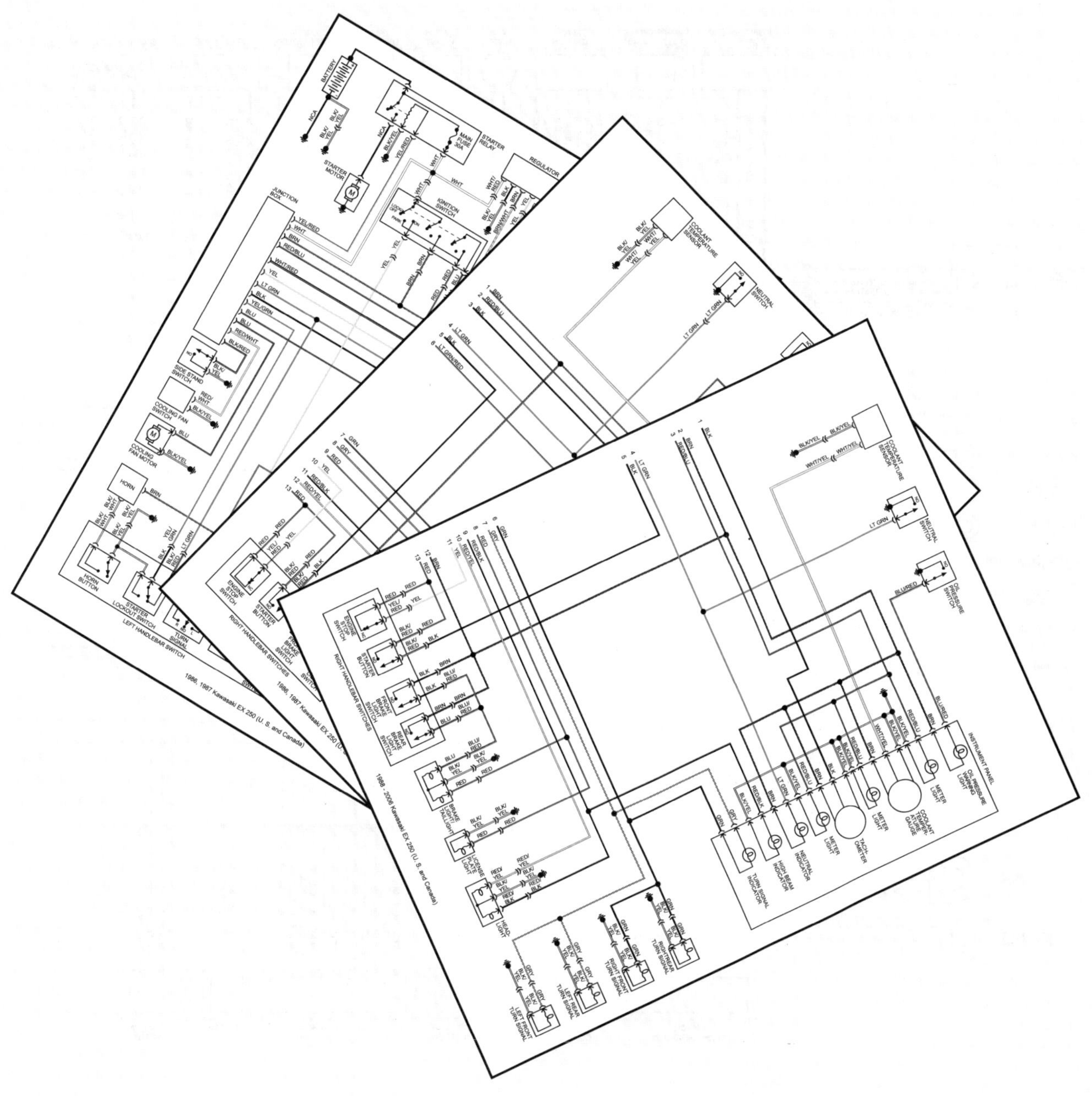

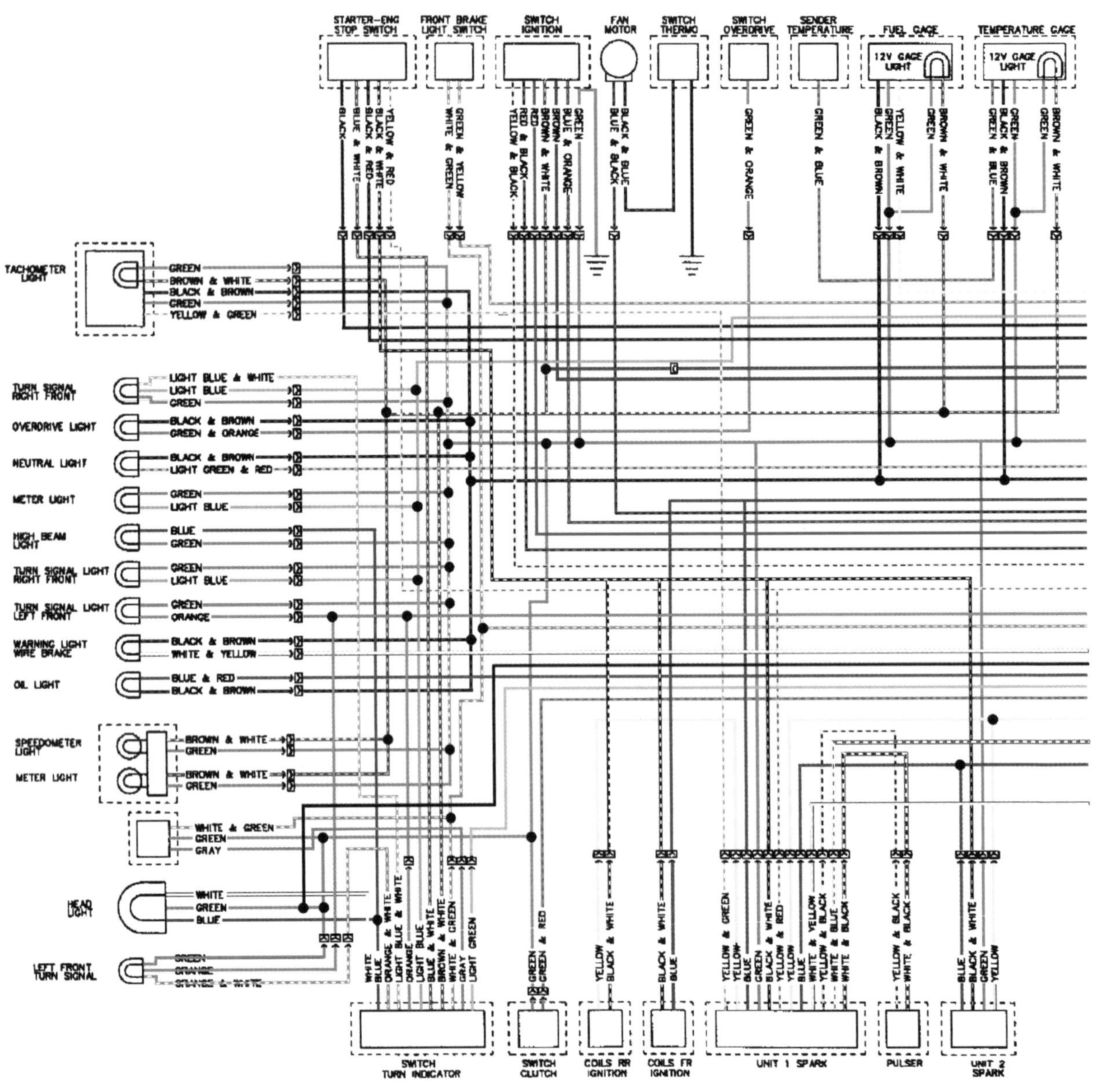

Honda VT1100 wiring diagram - 1985 and 1986 models (1 of 2)

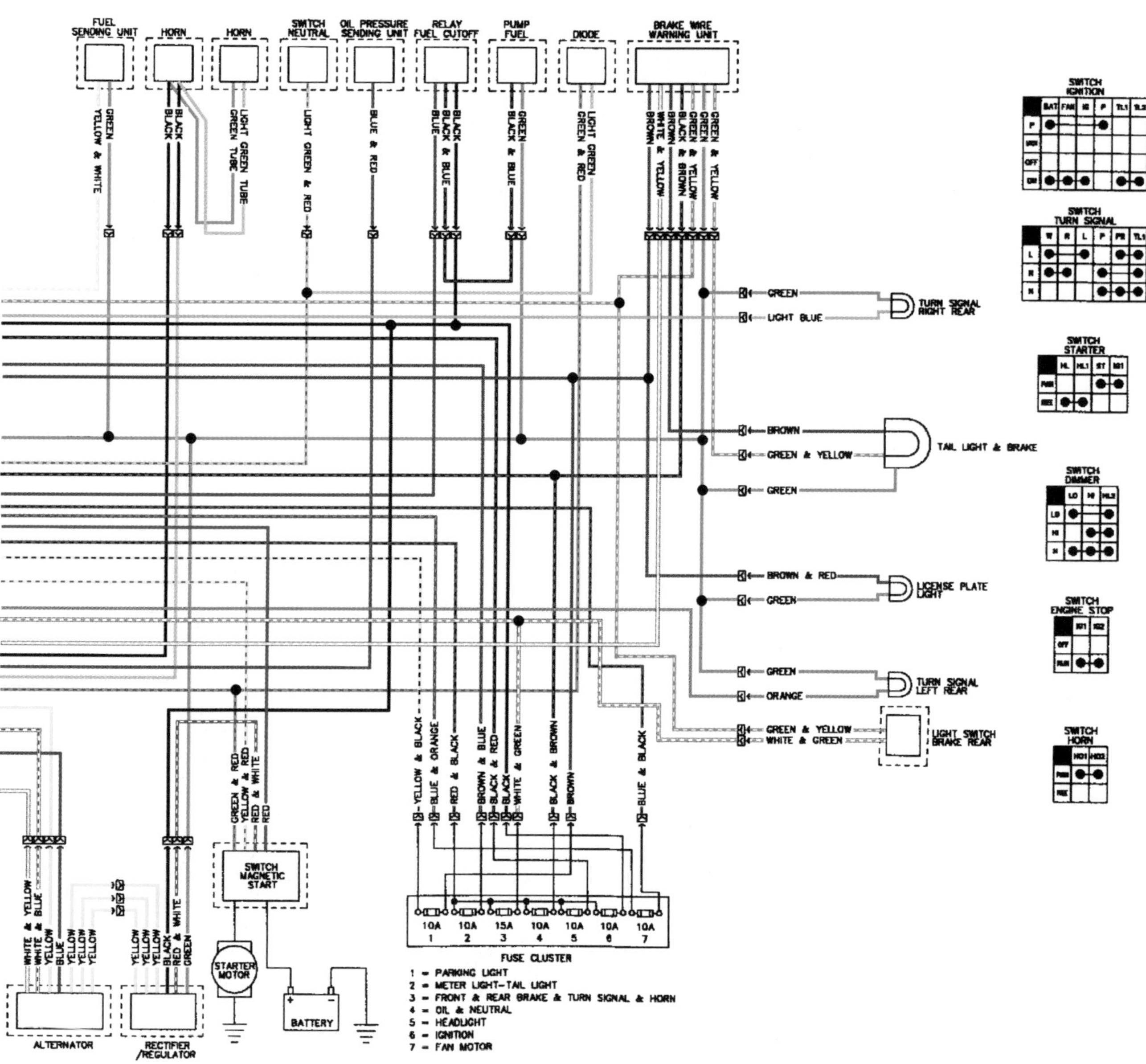

Honda VT1100 wiring diagram - 1985 and 1986 models (2 of 2)

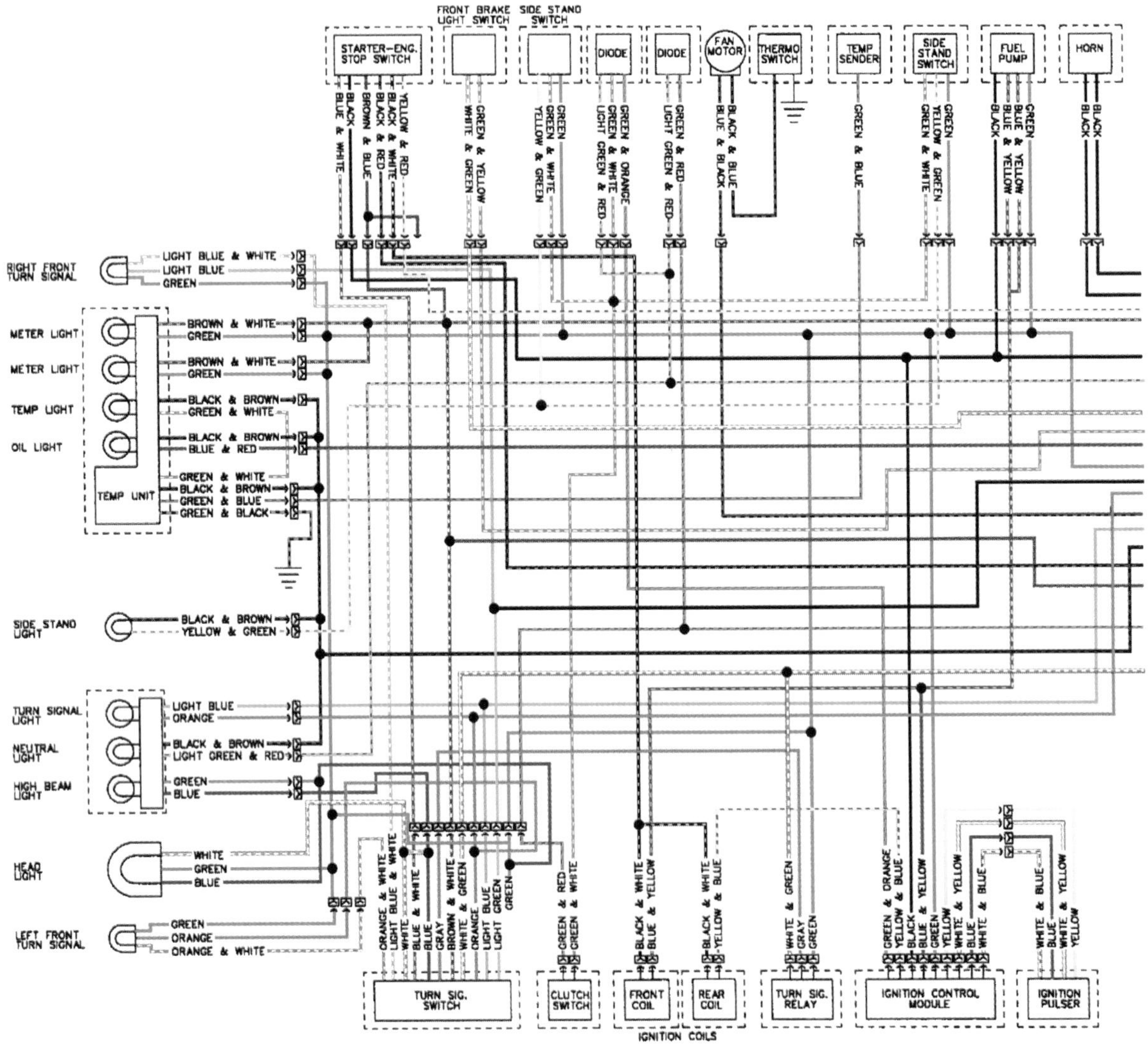

Honda VT1100 wiring diagram - 1987 through 1993 models (1 of 2)

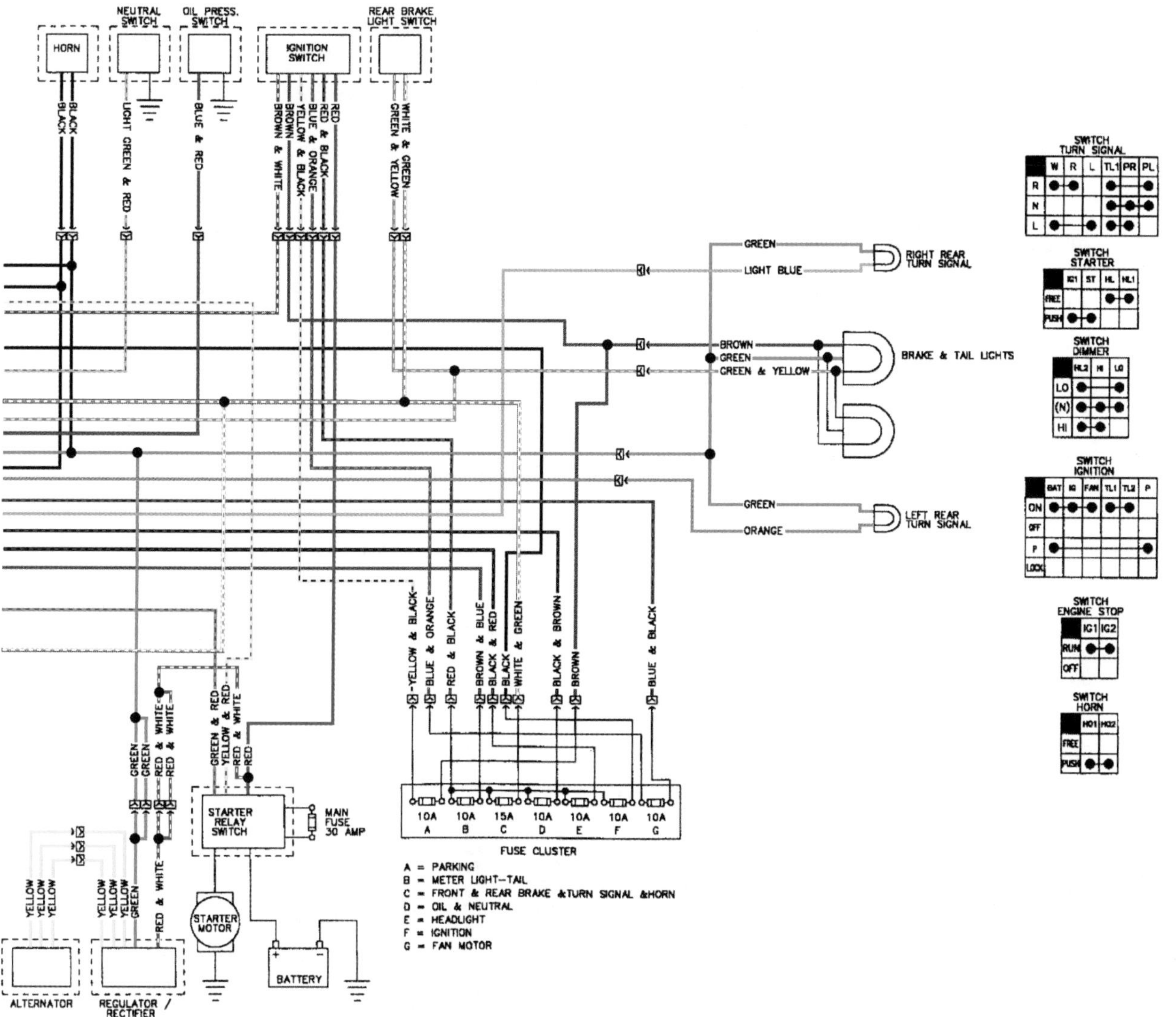

Honda VT1100 wiring diagram - 1987 through 1993 models (2 of 2)

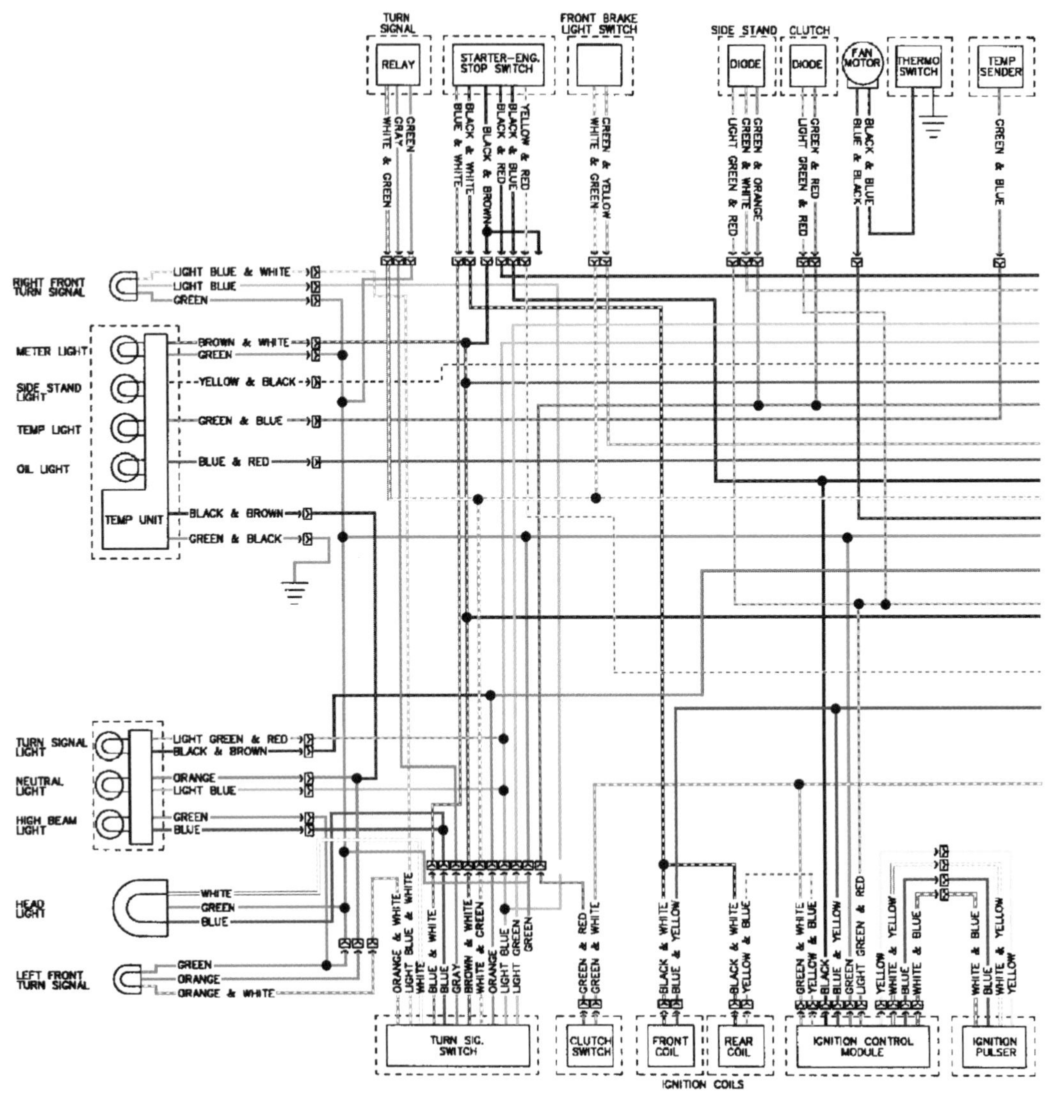

Honda VT1100 wiring diagram - 1994 and 1995 models (1 of 2)

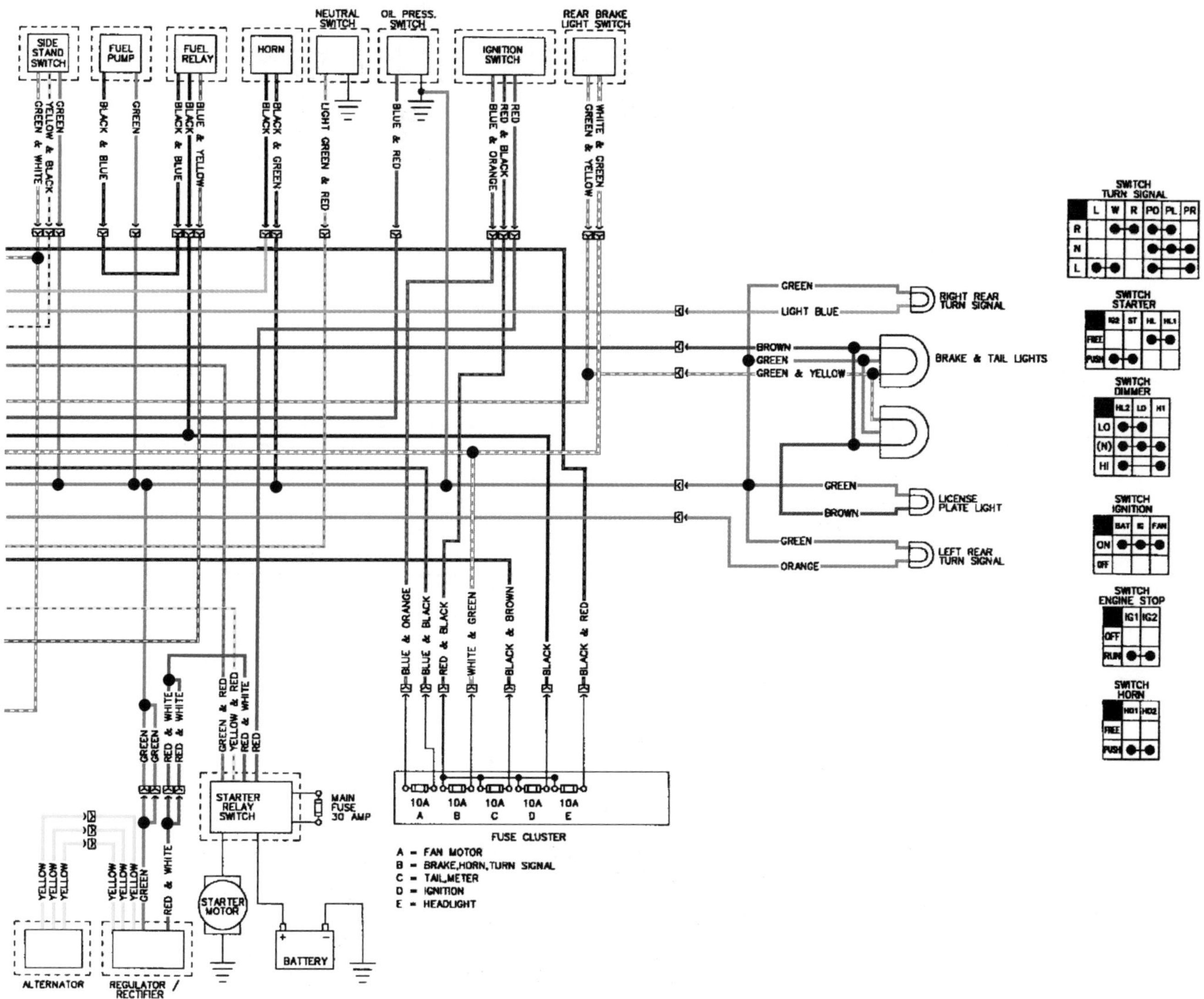

Honda VT1100 wiring diagram - 1994 and 1995 models (2 of 2)

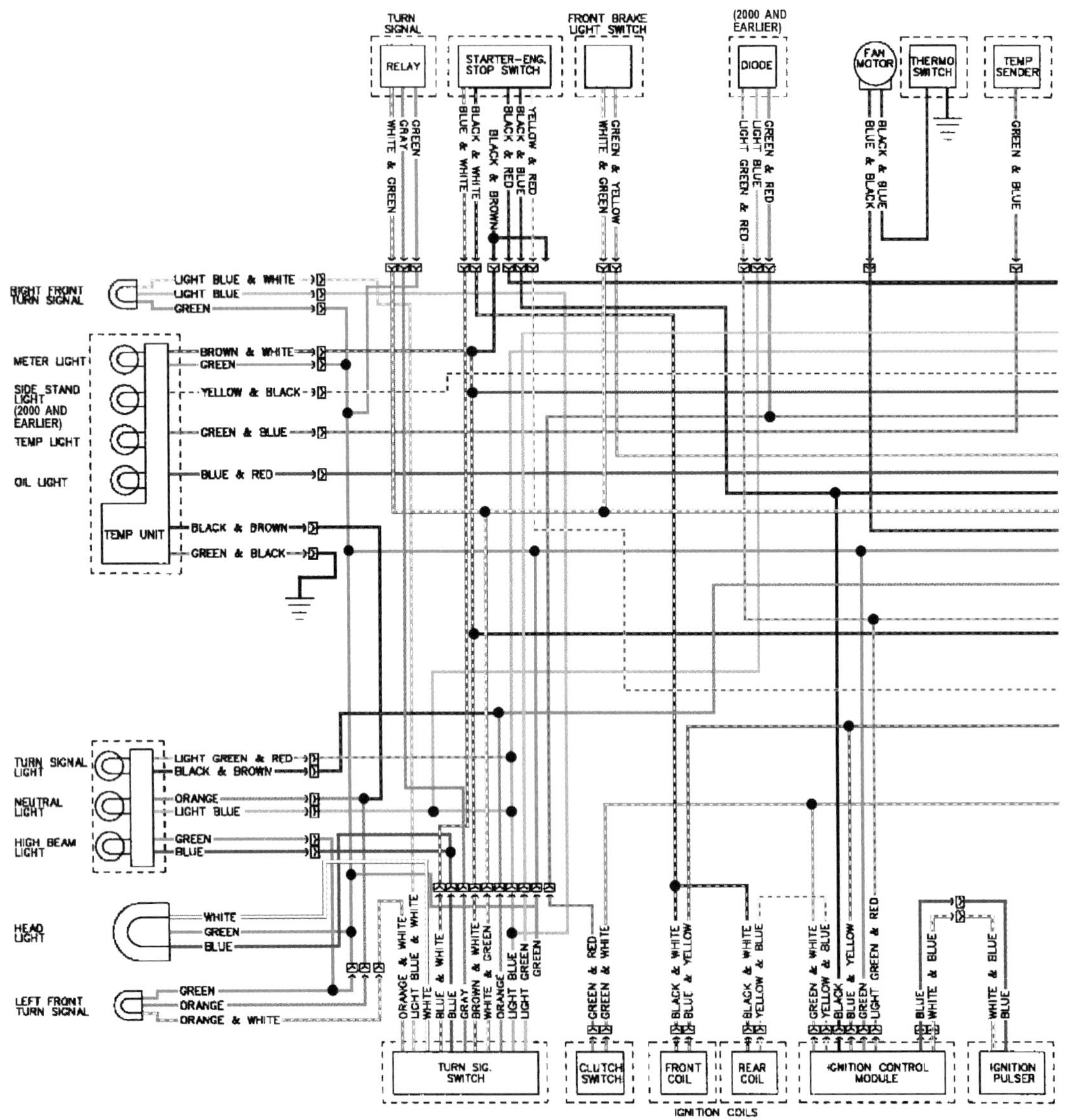

Honda VT1100 wiring diagram - 1996 and later models (1 of 2)

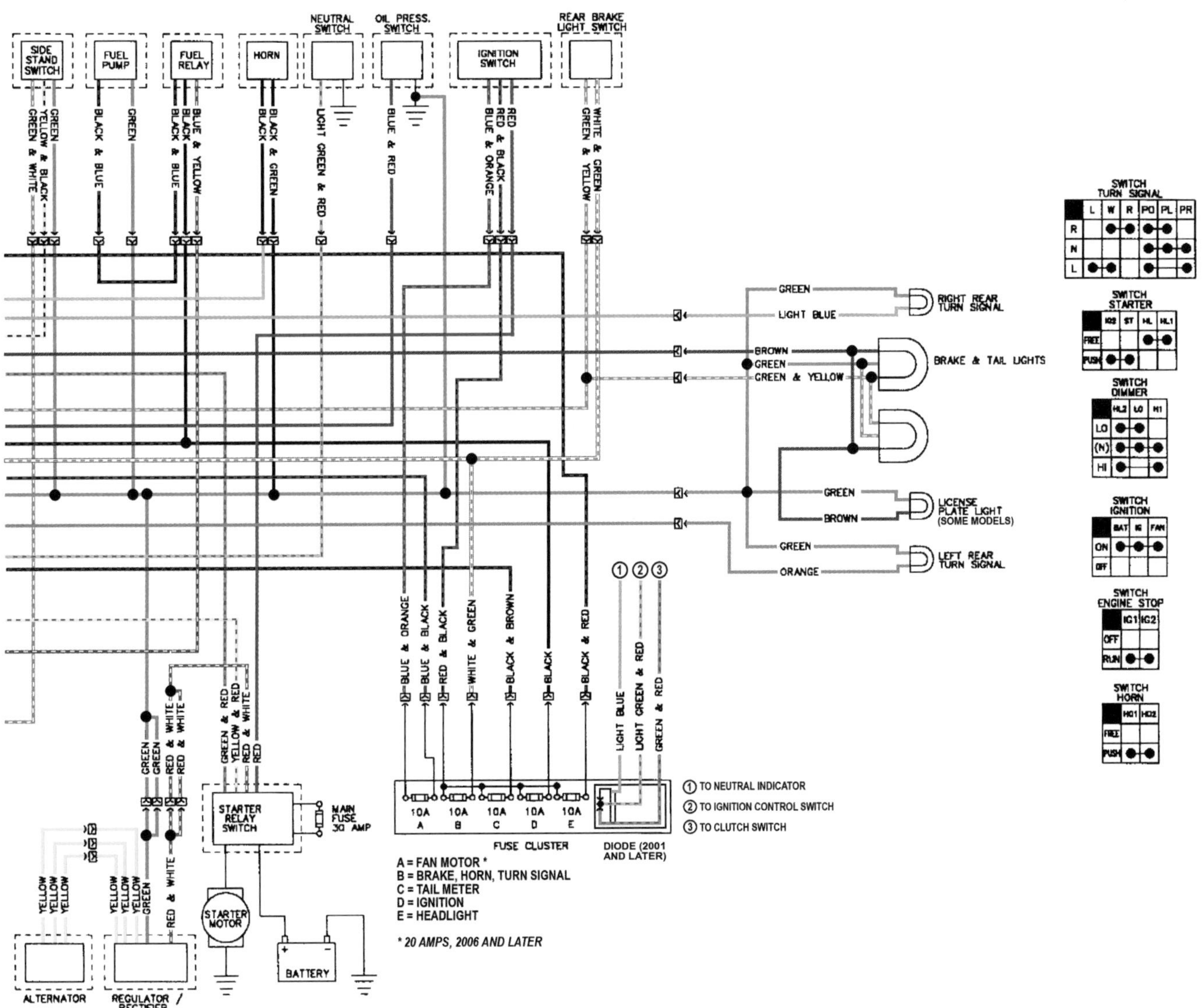

Honda VT1100 wiring diagram - 1996 and later models (2 of 2)

Notes

Dimensions and weights

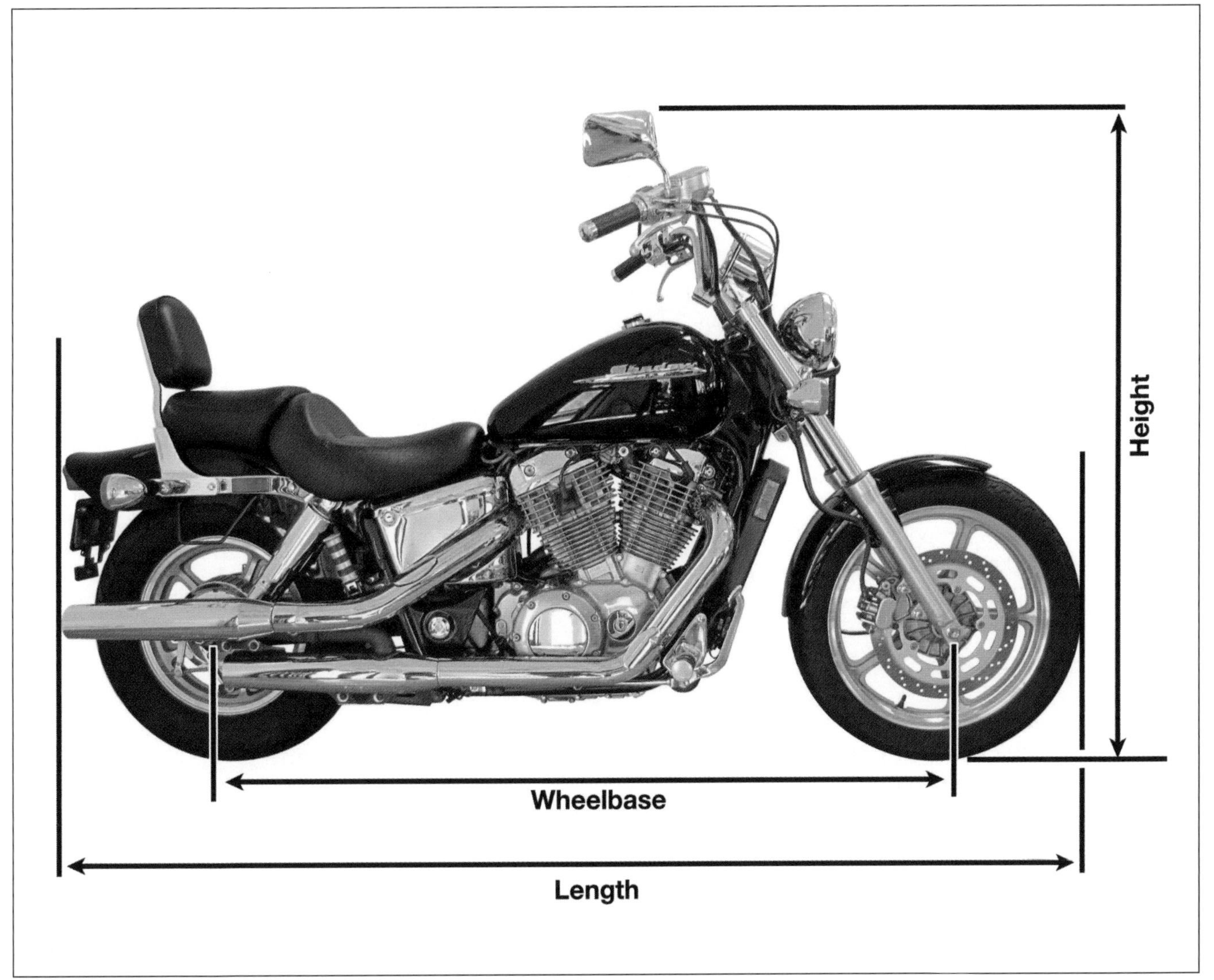

Frame and suspension

Wheelbase

VT1100C	
1985 and 1986	1610 mm (63.4 inches)
1987 through 1996	1651 mm (65.0 inches)
1997 and later	1650 mm (65.0 inches)
VT1100C2	
1995 through 1999	1650 mm (65.0 inches)
2000 and later	
49-state and Canada	1640 mm (64.57 inches)
California	1642 mm (64.64 inches)
VT1100C3	1680 mm (66.1 inches)
VT1100T	1655 mm (65.2 inches)

Overall length

VT1100C	
1985 and 1986	2325 mm (91.5 inches)
1987 through 1996	2376 mm (93.5 inches)
1997 and later	2480 mm (97.6 inches)
VT1100C2	
1995 through 1999	2435 mm (95.9 inches)
2000 and later	2490 mm (98.0 inches)
VT1100C3	2540 mm (100.0 inches)
VT1100T	2480 mm (97.6 inches)

Overall width

VT1100C	
1985 and 1986	810 mm (31.9 inches)
1987 through 1996	791 mm (31.1 inches)
1997 and later	880 mm (34.6 inches)
VT1100C2	
1995 through 1999	965 mm (38.0 inches)
2000 and later	920 mm (36.2 inches)
VT1100C3	975 mm (38.4 inches)
VT1100T	965 mm (38.0 inches)

Seat height

VT1100C	
1985 and 1986	750 mm (29.5 inches)
1987 through 1993	660 mm (25.9 inches)
1994 through 1996	690 mm (27.2 inches)
1997 and later	730 mm (28.7 inches)
VT1100C2	
1995 through 1999	700 mm (27.6 inches)
2000 and later	690 mm (27.2 inches)
VT1100C3	725 mm (28.5 inches)
VT1100T	730 mm (28.7 inches)

Weight

VT1100C	
1985 and 1986 (dry)	245 kg (540 lbs)
1987 through 1996 (dry)	242 kg (534 lbs)
1987 through 1996 (curb)	262 kg (578 lbs)
1997 and later (curb)	
49-state and Canada	270 kg (595 lbs)
California	271 kg (597 lbs)
VT1100C2 (curb)	
49-state and Canada	279 kg (615 lbs)
California	280 kg (617 lbs)
VT1100C3 (curb)	
49-state and Canada	299 kg (659 lbs)
California	300 kg (661 lbs)
VT1100T	
49-state and Canada	296 kg (653 lbs)
California	297 kg (655 lbs)
Front suspension	Telescopic fork
Rear suspension	Shock absorbers/coil springs
Front brake	Single hydraulic disc with 2-piston caliper
Rear brake	Mechanically-actuated drum brake or single hydraulic disc with single-piston caliper
Fuel capacity	
VT1100C	
1985 and 1986	15 liters (4.0 US gallons)
1987 through 1996	13 liters (3.44 US gallons)
1997 and later	15.8 liters (4.17 US gallons)
VT1100C2	15.8 liters (4.17 US gallons)
VT1100C3	16.0 liters (4.23 US gallons)
VT1100T	15.8 liters (4.17 US gallons)

Engine

Type	Liquid-cooled, 4-stroke, SOHC V-twin, three valves per cylinder
Displacement	1099 cc (67 cubic inches)
Compression ratio	
VT1100C	
1985 and 1986	9.0 to 1
1987 through 1996	8.5 to 1
1997 and later	8.0 to 1
VT1100C2, VT1100C3, VT1100T	8.0 to 1
Ignition system	Transistorized
Carburetor type	Two 36 mm Keihin CV
Transmission	
1987 through 1996 VT1100C	4-speed, constant mesh
All others	5-speed, constant mesh

Buying tools

A good set of tools is a fundamental requirement for servicing and repairing a motorcycle. Although there will be an initial expense in building up enough tools for servicing, this will soon be offset by the savings made by doing the job yourself. As experience and confidence grow, additional tools can be added to enable the repair and overhaul of the motorcycle. Many of the special tools are expensive and not often used so it may be preferable to rent them, or for a group of friends or motorcycle club to join in the purchase.

As a rule, it is better to buy more expensive, good quality tools. Cheaper tools are likely to wear out faster and need to be replaced more often, nullifying the original savings.

Warning: To avoid the risk of a poor quality tool breaking in use, causing injury or damage to the component being worked on, always aim to purchase tools which meet the relevant national safety standards.

The following lists of tools do not represent the manufacturer's service tools, but serve as a guide to help the owner decide which tools are needed for this level of work. In addition, items such as an electric drill, hacksaw, files, soldering iron and a workbench equipped with a vise, may be needed. Although not classed as tools, a selection of bolts, screws, nuts, washers and pieces of tubing always come in useful.

For more information about tools, refer to the Haynes *Motorcycle Workshop Practice Techbook* (Bk. No. 3470).

Manufacturer's service tools

Inevitably certain tasks require the use of a service tool. Where possible an alternative tool or method of approach is recommended, but sometimes there is no option if personal injury or damage to the component is to be avoided. Where required, service tools are referred to in the relevant procedure.

Service tools can usually only be purchased from a motorcycle dealer and are identified by a part number. Some of the commonly-used tools, such as rotor pullers, are available in aftermarket form from mail-order motorcycle tool and accessory suppliers.

Maintenance and minor repair tools

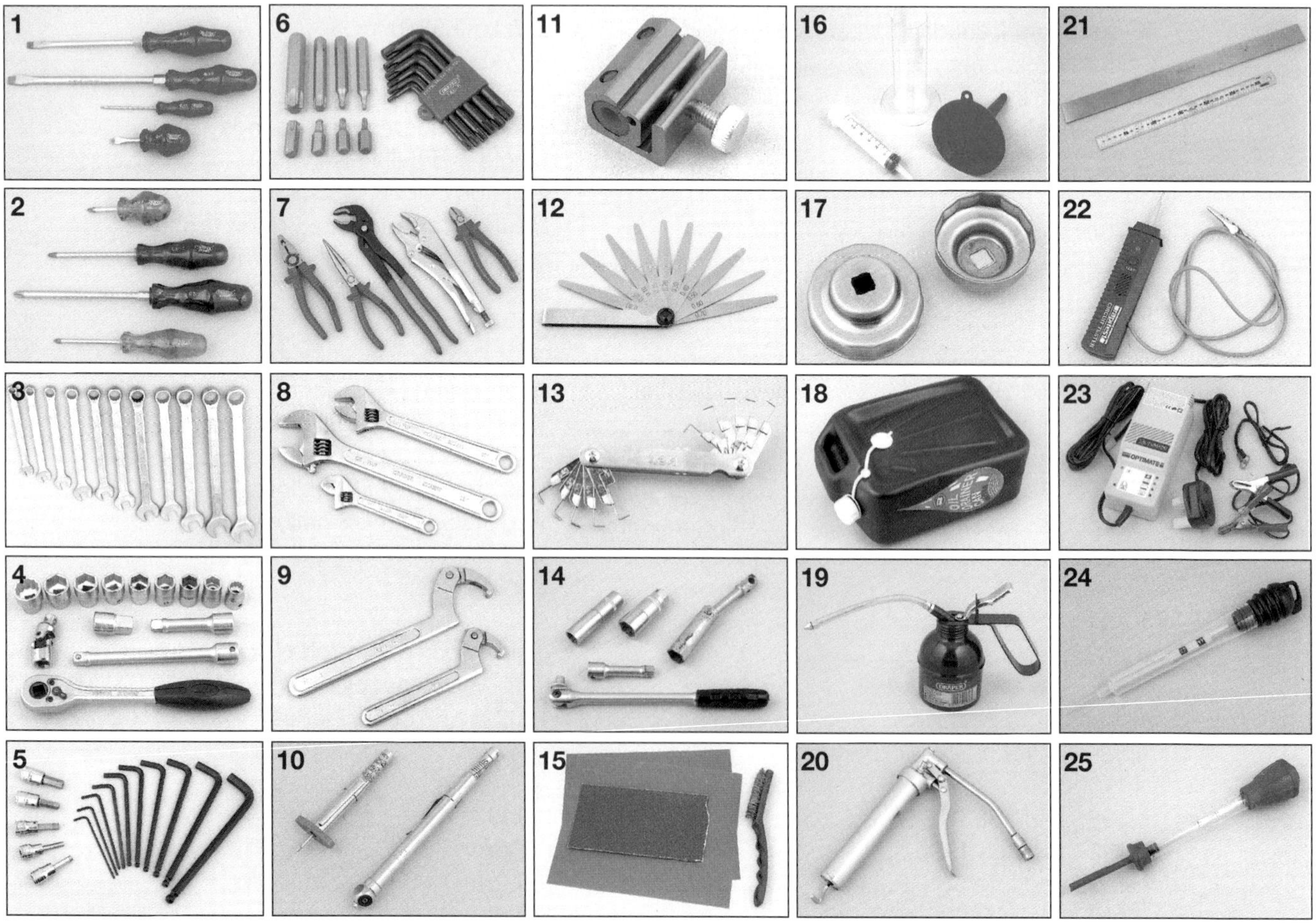

1 *Set of flat-bladed screwdrivers*
2 *Set of Phillips head screwdrivers*
3 *Combination open-end and box wrenches*
4 *Socket set (3/8 inch or 1/2 inch drive)*
5 *Set of Allen keys or bits*
6 *Set of Torx keys or bits*
7 *Pliers, cutters and self-locking grips (vise grips)*
8 *Adjustable wrenches*
9 *C-spanners*
10 *Tread depth gauge and tire pressure gauge*
11 *Cable oiler clamp*
12 *Feeler gauges*
13 *Spark plug gap measuring tool*
14 *Spark plug wrench or deep plug sockets*
15 *Wire brush and emery paper*
16 *Calibrated syringe, measuring cup and funnel*
17 *Oil filter adapters*
18 *Oil drainer can or tray*
19 *Pump type oil can*
20 *Grease gun*
21 *Straight-edge and steel rule*
22 *Continuity tester*
23 *Battery charger*
24 *Hydrometer (for battery specific gravity check)*
25 *Antifreeze tester (for liquid-cooled engines)*

Repair and overhaul tools

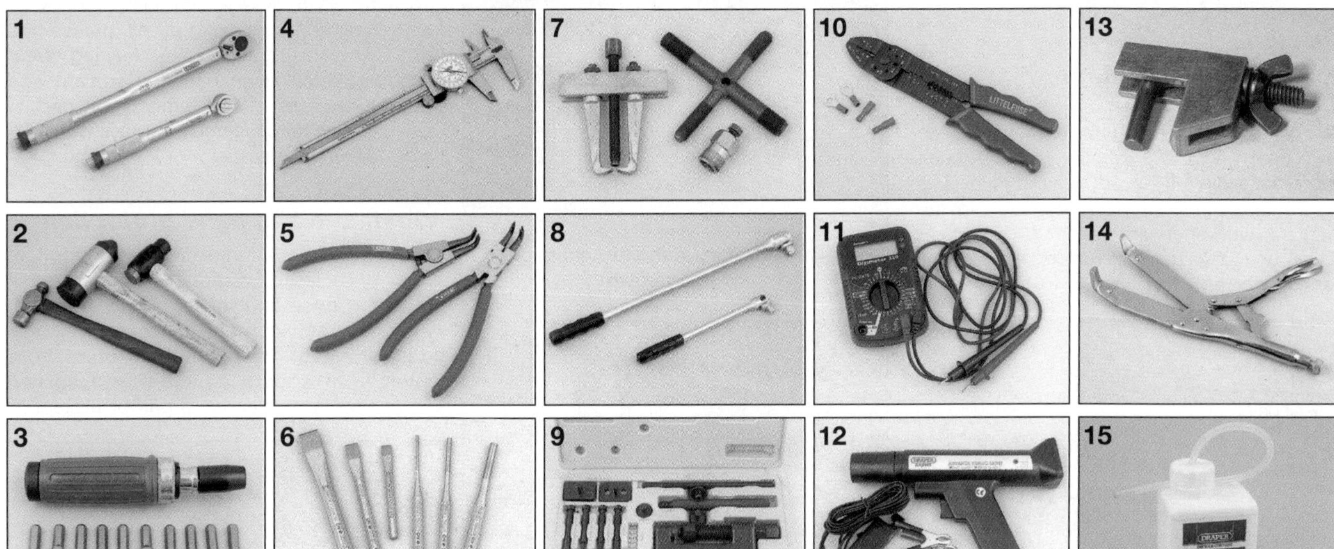
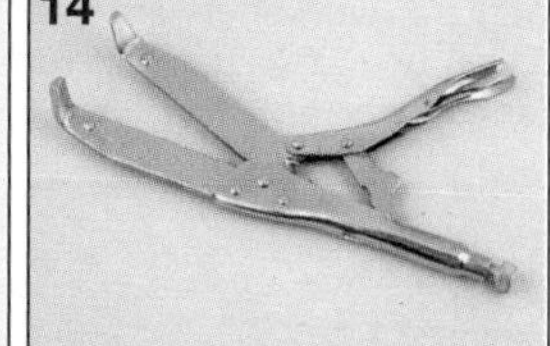

1 *Torque wrench (small and mid-ranges)*
2 *Conventional, plastic or soft-faced hammers*
3 *Impact driver set*
4 *Vernier caliper*
5 *Snap-ring pliers (internal and external, or combination)*
6 *Set of cold chisels and punches*
7 *Selection of pullers*
8 *Breaker bars*
9 *Chain breaking/ riveting tool set*
10 *Wire stripper and crimper tool*
11 *Multimeter (measures amps, volts and ohms)*
12 *Stroboscope (for dynamic timing checks)*
13 *Hose clamp (wingnut type shown)*
14 *Clutch holding tool*
15 *One-man brake/clutch bleeder kit*

Special tools

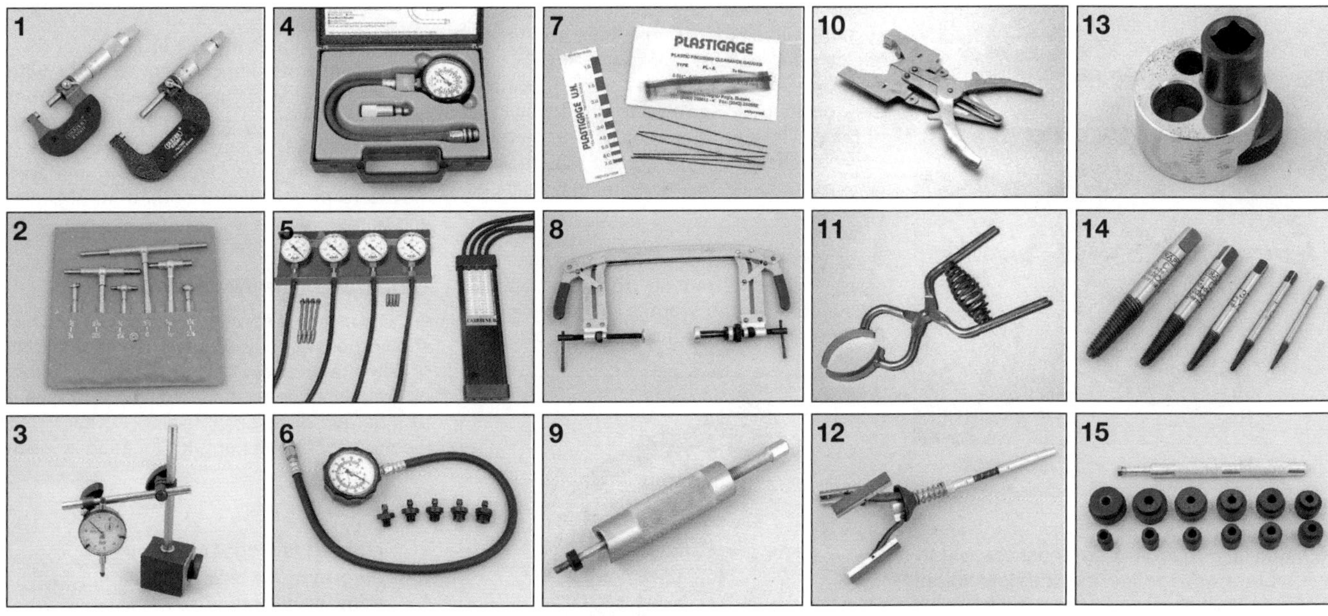

1 *Micrometers (external type)*
2 *Telescoping gauges*
3 *Dial gauge*
4 *Cylinder compression gauge*
5 *Vacuum gauges (left) or manometer (right)*
6 *Oil pressure gauge*
7 *Plastigage kit*
8 *Valve spring compressor (4-stroke engines)*
9 *Piston pin drawbolt tool*
10 *Piston ring removal and installation tool*
11 *Piston ring clamp*
12 *Cylinder bore hone (stone type shown)*
13 *Stud extractor*
14 *Screw extractor set*
15 *Bearing driver set*

1 Workshop equipment and facilities

The workbench

● Work is made much easier by raising the bike up on a ramp - components are much more accessible if raised to waist level. The hydraulic or pneumatic types seen in the dealer's workshop are a sound investment if you undertake a lot of repairs or overhauls **(see illustration 1.1)**.

1.1 Hydraulic motorcycle ramp

● If raised off ground level, the bike must be supported on the ramp to avoid it falling. Most ramps incorporate a front wheel locating clamp which can be adjusted to suit different diameter wheels. When tightening the clamp, take care not to mark the wheel rim or damage the tire - use wood blocks on each side to prevent this.

● Secure the bike to the ramp using tie-downs **(see illustration 1.2)**. If the bike has only a sidestand, and hence leans at a dangerous angle when raised, support the bike on an auxiliary stand.

1.2 Tie-downs are used around the passenger footrests to secure the bike

● Auxiliary (paddock) stands are widely available from mail order companies or motorcycle dealers and attach either to the wheel axle or swingarm pivot **(see illustration 1.3)**. If the motorcycle has a centerstand, you can support it under the crankcase to prevent it toppling while either wheel is removed **(see illustration 1.4)**.

1.3 This auxiliary stand attaches to the swingarm pivot

1.4 Always use a block of wood between the engine and jack head when supporting the engine in this way

Fumes and fire

● Refer to the Safety first! page at the beginning of the manual for full details. Make sure your workshop is equipped with a fire extinguisher suitable for fuel-related fires (Class B fire - flammable liquids) - it is not sufficient to have a water-filled extinguisher.

● Always ensure adequate ventilation is available. Unless an exhaust gas extraction system is available for use, ensure that the engine is run outside of the workshop.

● If working on the fuel system, make sure the workshop is ventilated to avoid a build-up of fumes. This applies equally to fume build-up when charging a battery. Do not smoke or allow anyone else to smoke in the workshop.

Fluids

● If you need to drain fuel from the tank, store it in an approved container marked as suitable for the storage of gasoline **(see illustration 1.5)**. Do not store fuel in glass jars or bottles.

1.5 Use an approved can only for storing gasoline

● Use proprietary engine degreasers or solvents which have a high flash-point, such as kerosene, for cleaning off oil, grease and dirt - never use gasoline for cleaning. Wear rubber gloves when handling solvent and engine degreaser. The fumes from certain solvents can be dangerous - always work in a well-ventilated area.

Dust, eye and hand protection

● Protect your lungs from inhalation of dust particles by wearing a filtering mask over the nose and mouth. Many frictional materials still contain asbestos which is dangerous to your health. Protect your eyes from spouts of liquid and sprung components by wearing a pair of protective goggles **(see illustration 1.6)**.

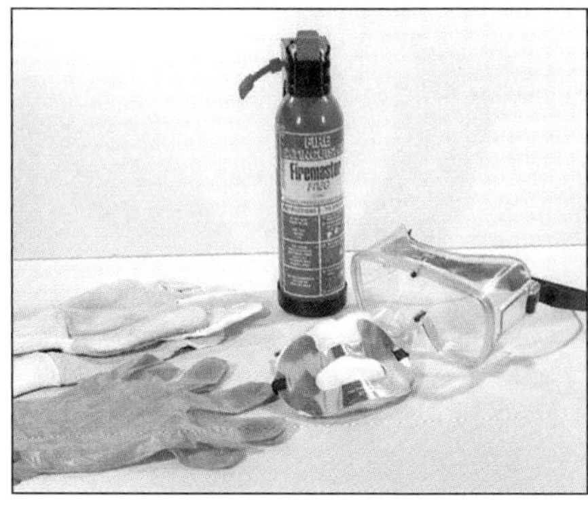

1.6 A fire extinguisher, goggles, mask and protective gloves should be at hand in the workshop

● Protect your hands from contact with solvents, fuel and oils by wearing rubber gloves. Alternatively apply a barrier cream to your hands before starting work. If handling hot components or fluids, wear suitable gloves to protect your hands from scalding and burns.

What to do with old fluids

● Old cleaning solvent, fuel, coolant and oils should not be poured down domestic drains or onto the ground. Package the fluid up in old oil containers, label it accordingly, and take it to a garage or disposal facility. Contact your local disposal company for location of such sites.

Note: It is illegal to dump oil down the drain. Check with your local auto parts store, disposal facility or environmental agency to see if they accept the oil for recycling.

2 Fasteners - screws, bolts and nuts

Fastener types and applications

Bolts and screws

● Fastener head types are either of hexagonal, Torx or splined design, with internal and external versions of each type **(see illustrations 2.1 and 2.2)**; splined head fasteners are not in common use on motorcycles. The conventional slotted or Phillips head design is used for certain screws. Bolt or screw length is always measured from the underside of the head to the end of the item **(see illustration 2.11)**.

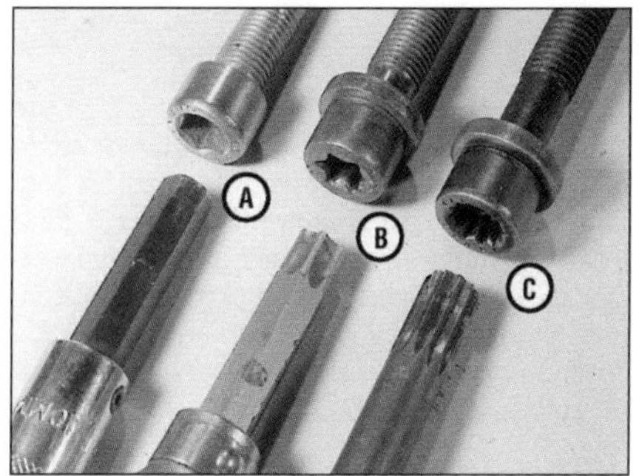

2.1 Internal hexagon/Allen (A), Torx (B) and splined (C) fasteners, with corresponding bits

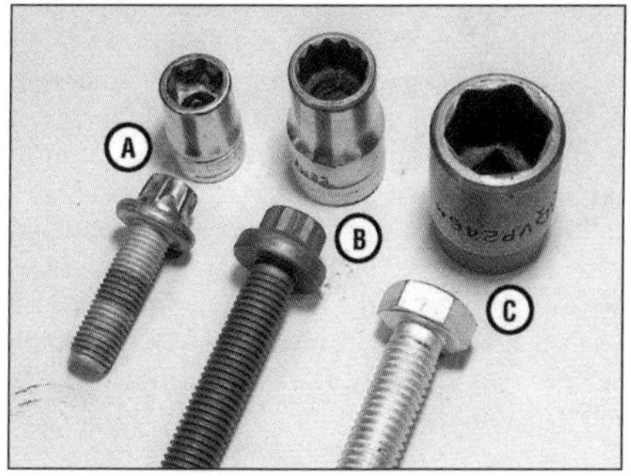

2.2 External Torx (A), splined (B) and hexagon (C) fasteners, with corresponding sockets

● Certain fasteners on the motorcycle have a tensile marking on their heads, the higher the marking the stronger the fastener. High tensile fasteners generally carry a 10 or higher marking. Never replace a high tensile fastener with one of a lower tensile strength.

Washers (see illustration 2.3)

● Plain washers are used between a fastener head and a component to prevent damage to the component or to spread the load when torque is applied. Plain washers can also be used as spacers or shims in certain assemblies. Copper or aluminum plain washers are often used as sealing washers on drain plugs.

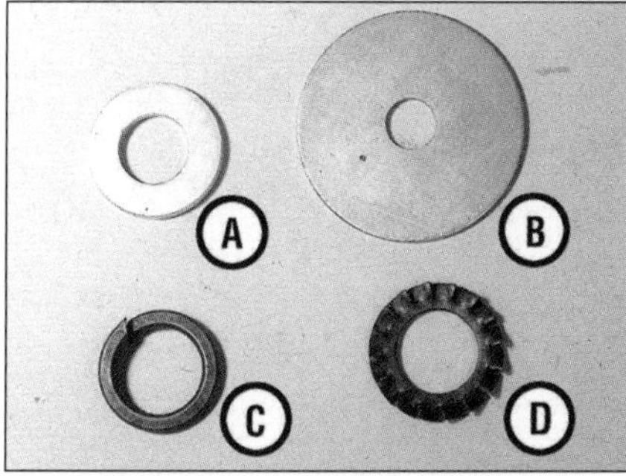

2.3 Plain washer (A), penny washer (B), spring washer (C) and serrated washer (D)

● The split-ring spring washer works by applying axial tension between the fastener head and component. If flattened, it is fatigued and must be replaced. If a plain (flat) washer is used on the fastener, position the spring washer between the fastener and the plain washer.

● Serrated star type washers dig into the fastener and component faces, preventing loosening. They are often used on electrical ground connections to the frame.

● Cone type washers (sometimes called Belleville) are conical and when tightened apply axial tension between the fastener head and component. They must be installed with the dished side against the component and often carry an OUTSIDE marking on their outer face. If flattened, they are fatigued and must be replaced.

● Tab washers are used to lock plain nuts or bolts on a shaft. A portion of the tab washer is bent up hard against one flat of the nut or bolt to prevent it loosening. Due to the tab washer being deformed in use, a new tab washer should be used every time it is removed.

● Wave washers are used to take up endfloat on a shaft. They provide light springing and prevent excessive side-to-side play of a component. Can be found on rocker arm shafts.

Nuts and cotter pins

● Conventional plain nuts are usually six-sided **(see illustration 2.4)**. They are sized by thread diameter and pitch. High tensile nuts carry a number on one end to denote their tensile strength.

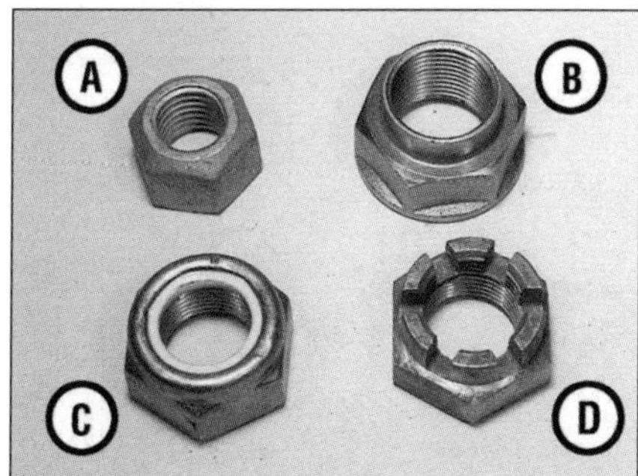

2.4 Plain nut (A), shouldered locknut (B), nylon insert nut (C) and castellated nut (D)

● Self-locking nuts either have a nylon insert, or two spring metal tabs, or a shoulder which is staked into a groove in the shaft - their advantage over conventional plain nuts is a resistance to loosening due to vibration. The nylon insert type can be used a number of times, but must be replaced when the friction of the nylon insert is reduced, i.e. when the nut spins freely on the shaft. The spring tab type can be reused unless the tabs are damaged. The shouldered type must be replaced every time it is removed.

● Cotter pins are used to lock a castellated nut to a shaft or to prevent loosening of a plain nut. Common applications are wheel axles and brake torque arms. Because the cotter pin arms are deformed to lock around the nut a new cotter pin must always be used on installation - always use the correct size cotter pin which will fit snugly in the shaft hole. Make sure the cotter pin arms are correctly located around the nut **(see illustrations 2.5 and 2.6)**.

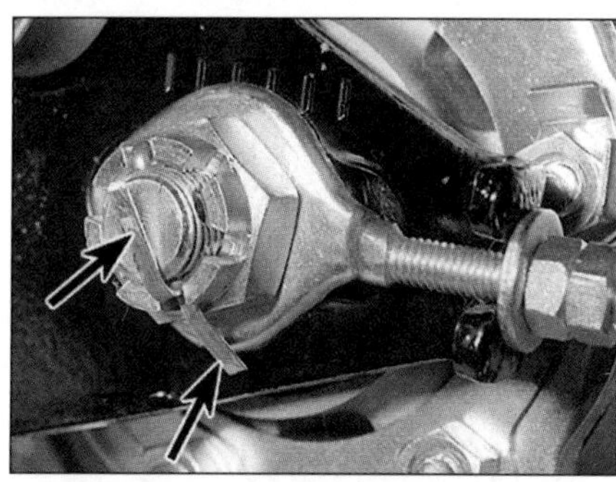

2.5 Bend cotter pin arms as shown (arrows) to secure a castellated nut

2.6 Bend cotter pin arms as shown to secure a plain nut

Caution: If the castellated nut slots do not align with the shaft hole after tightening to the torque setting, tighten the nut until the next slot aligns with the hole - never loosen the nut to align its slot.

● R-pins (shaped like the letter R), or slip pins as they are sometimes called, are sprung and can be reused if they are otherwise in good condition. Always install R-pins with their closed end facing forwards **(see illustration 2.7)**.

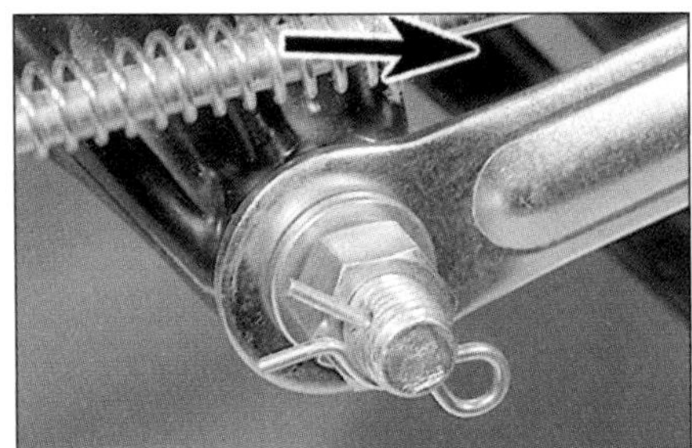

2.7 Correct fitting of R-pin. Arrow indicates forward direction

Snap-rings (see illustration 2.8)

● Snap-rings (sometimes called circlips) are used to retain components on a shaft or in a housing and have corresponding external or internal ears to permit removal. Parallel-sided (machined) snap-rings can be installed either way round in their groove, whereas stamped snap-rings (which have a chamfered edge on one face) must be installed with the chamfer facing away from the direction of thrust load **(see illustration 2.9)**.

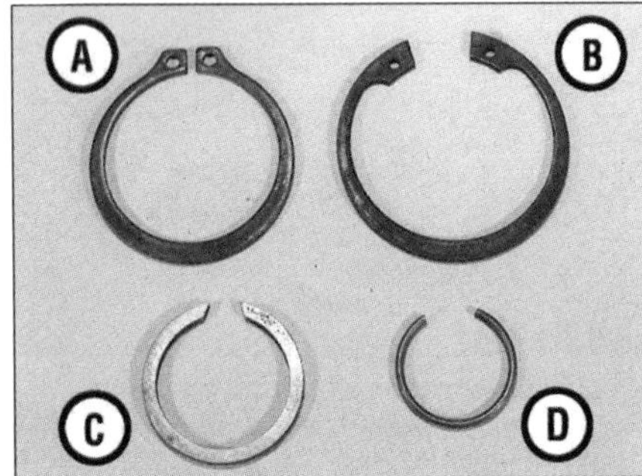

2.8 External stamped snap-ring (A), internal stamped snap-ring (B), machined snap-ring (C) and wire snap-ring (D)

● Always use snap-ring pliers to remove and install snap-rings; expand or compress them just enough to remove them. After installation, rotate the snap-ring in its groove to ensure it is securely seated. If installing a snap-ring on a splined shaft, always align its opening with a shaft channel to ensure the snap-ring ends are well supported and unlikely to catch **(see illustration 2.10)**.

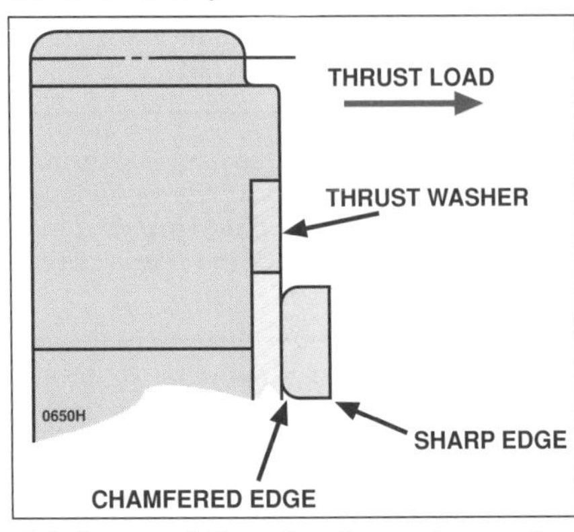

2.9 Correct fitting of a stamped snap-ring

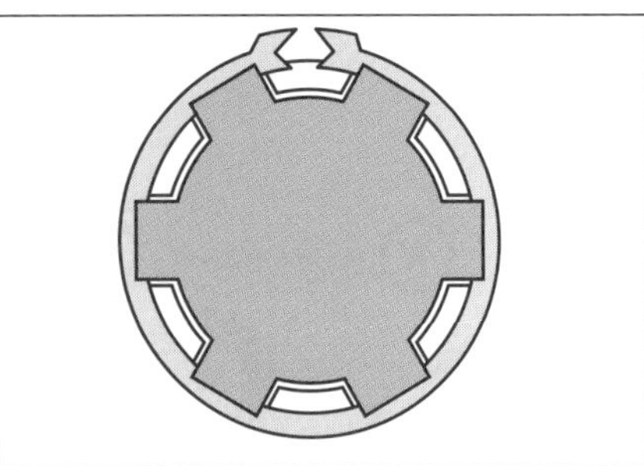

2.10 Align snap-ring opening with shaft channel

● Snap-rings can wear due to the thrust of components and become loose in their grooves, with the subsequent danger of becoming dislodged in operation. For this reason, replacement is advised every time a snap-ring is disturbed.

● Wire snap-rings are commonly used as piston pin retaining clips. If a removal tang is provided, long-nosed pliers can be used to dislodge them, otherwise careful use of a small flat-bladed screwdriver is necessary. Wire snap-rings should be replaced every time they are disturbed.

Thread diameter and pitch

● Diameter of a male thread (screw, bolt or stud) is the outside diameter of the threaded portion **(see illustration 2.11)**. Most motorcycle manufacturers use the ISO (International Standards Organization) metric system expressed in millimeters. For example, M6 refers to a 6 mm diameter thread. Sizing is the same for nuts, except that the thread diameter is measured across the valleys of the nut.

● Pitch is the distance between the peaks of the thread **(see illustration 2.11)**. It is expressed in millimeters, thus a common bolt size may be expressed as 6.0 x 1.0 mm (6 mm thread diameter and 1 mm pitch). Generally pitch increases in proportion to thread diameter, although there are always exceptions.

● Thread diameter and pitch are related for conventional fastener applications and the accompanying table can be used as a guide. Additionally, the AF (Across Flats), wrench or socket size dimension of the bolt or nut **(see illustration 2.11)** is linked to thread and pitch specification. Thread pitch can be measured with a thread gauge **(see illustration 2.12)**.

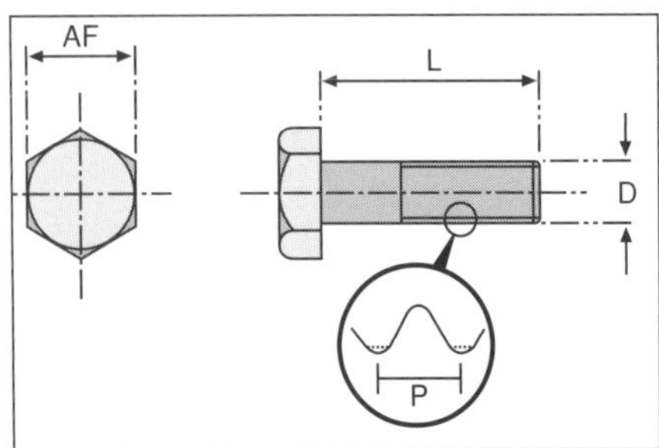

2.11 Fastener length (L), thread diameter (D), thread pitch (P) and head size (AF)

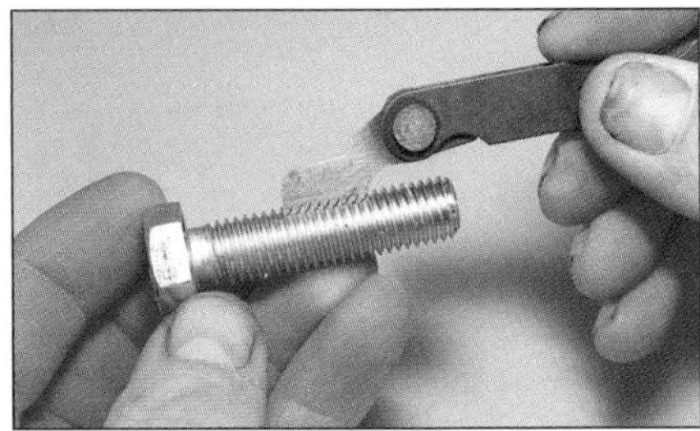

2.12 Using a thread gauge to measure pitch

AF size	Thread diameter x pitch (mm)
8 mm	M5 x 0.8
8 mm	M6 x 1.0
10 mm	M6 x 1.0
12 mm	M8 x 1.25
14 mm	M10 x 1.25
17 mm	M12 x 1.25

● The threads of most fasteners are of the right-hand type, ie they are turned clockwise to tighten and counterclockwise to loosen. The reverse situation applies to left-hand thread fasteners, which are turned counterclockwise to tighten and clockwise to loosen. Left-hand threads are used where rotation of a component might loosen a conventional right-hand thread fastener.

Seized fasteners

● Corrosion of external fasteners due to water or reaction between two dissimilar metals can occur over a period of time. It will build up sooner in wet conditions or in countries where salt is used on the roads during the winter. If a fastener is severely corroded it is likely that normal methods of removal will fail and result in its head being ruined. When you attempt removal, the fastener thread should be heard to crack free and unscrew easily - if it doesn't, stop there before damaging something.

● A smart tap on the head of the fastener will often succeed in breaking free corrosion which has occurred in the threads **(see illustration 2.13)**.

● An aerosol penetrating fluid (such as WD-40) applied the night beforehand may work its way down into the thread and ease removal. Depending on the location, you may be able to make up a modeling-clay well around the fastener head and fill it with penetrating fluid.

2.13 A sharp tap on the head of a fastener will often break free a corroded thread

● If you are working on an engine internal component, corrosion will most likely not be a problem due to the well lubricated environment. However, components can be very tight and an impact driver is a useful tool in freeing them **(see illustration 2.14)**.

2.14 Using an impact driver to free a fastener

● Where corrosion has occurred between dissimilar metals (e.g. steel and aluminum alloy), the application of heat to the fastener head will create a disproportionate expansion rate between the two metals and break the seizure caused by the corrosion. Whether heat can be applied depends on the location of the fastener - any surrounding components likely to be damaged must first be removed **(see illustration 2.15)**. Heat can be applied using a paint stripper heat gun or clothes iron, or by immersing the component in boiling water - wear protective gloves to prevent scalding or burns to the hands.

2.15 Using heat to free a seized fastener

● As a last resort, it is possible to use a hammer and cold chisel to work the fastener head unscrewed **(see illustration 2.16)**. This will damage the fastener, but more importantly extreme care must be taken not to damage the surrounding component.

Caution: Remember that the component being secured is generally of more value than the bolt, nut or screw - when the fastener is freed, do not unscrew it with force, instead work the fastener back and forth when resistance is felt to prevent thread damage.

2.16 Using a hammer and chisel to free a seized fastener

Broken fasteners and damaged heads

● If the shank of a broken bolt or screw is accessible you can grip it with self-locking grips. The knurled wheel type stud extractor tool or self-gripping stud puller tool is particularly useful for removing the long studs which screw into the cylinder mouth surface of the crankcase or bolts and screws from which the head has broken off **(see illustration 2.17)**. Studs can also be removed by locking two nuts together on the threaded end of the stud and using a wrench on the lower nut **(see illustration 2.18)**.

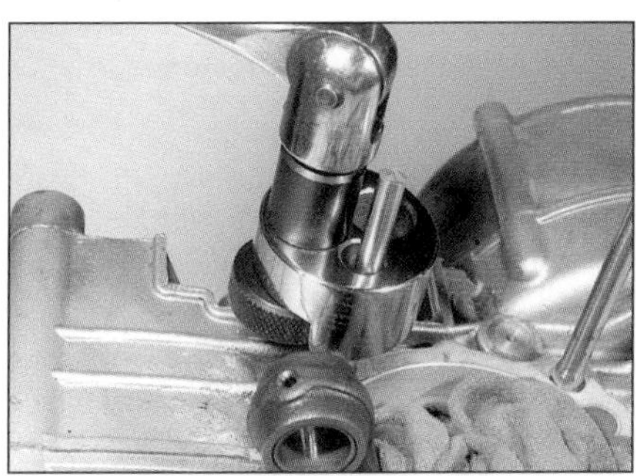

2.17 Using a stud extractor tool to remove a broken crankcase stud

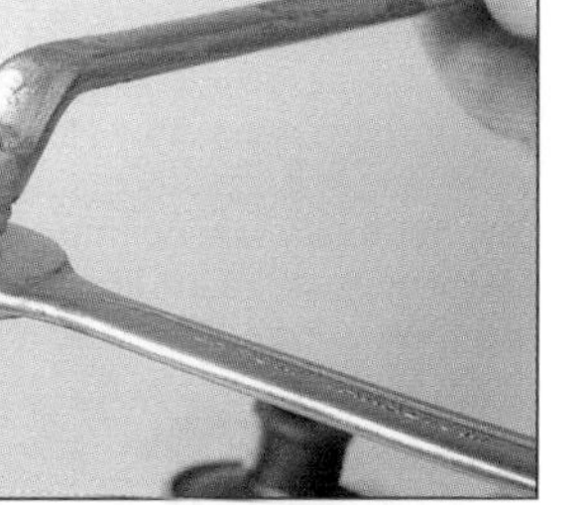

2.18 Two nuts can be locked together to unscrew a stud from a component

● A bolt or screw which has broken off below or level with the casing must be extracted using a screw extractor set. Centerpunch the fastener to centralize the drill bit, then drill a hole in the fastener **(see illustration 2.19)**. Select a drill bit which is approximately half

2.19 When using a screw extractor, first drill a hole in the fastener . . .

to three-quarters the diameter of the fastener and drill to a depth which will accommodate the extractor. Use the largest size extractor possible, but avoid leaving too small a wall thickness otherwise the extractor will merely force the fastener walls outwards wedging it in the casing thread.

● If a spiral type extractor is used, thread it counterclockwise into the fastener. As it is screwed in, it will grip the fastener and unscrew it from the casing **(see illustration 2.20)**.

2.20 . . . then thread the extractor counterclockwise into the fastener

● If a taper type extractor is used, tap it into the fastener so that it is firmly wedged in place. Unscrew the extractor (counter-clockwise) to draw the fastener out.

Warning: Stud extractors are very hard and may break off in the fastener if care is not taken - ask a machine shop about spark erosion if this happens.

● Alternatively, the broken bolt/screw can be drilled out and the hole retapped for an oversize bolt/screw or a diamond-section thread insert. It is essential that the drilling is carried out squarely and to the correct depth, otherwise the casing may be ruined - if in doubt, entrust the work to a machine shop.

● Bolts and nuts with rounded corners cause the correct size wrench or socket to slip when force is applied. Of the types of wrench/socket available always use a six-point type rather than an eight or twelve-point type - better grip

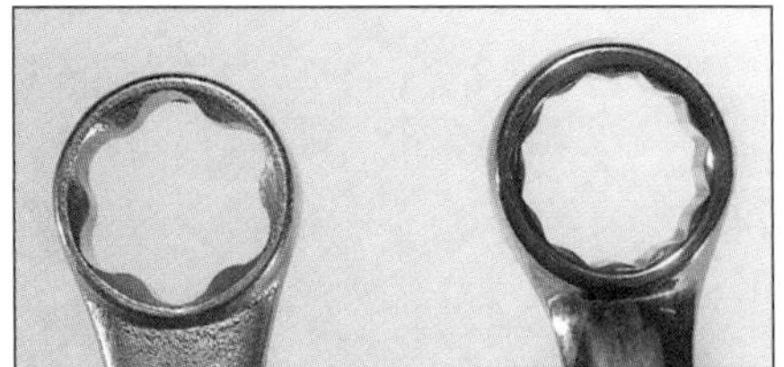
2.21 Comparison of surface drive box wrench (left) with 12-point type (right)

is obtained. Surface drive wrenches grip the middle of the hex flats, rather than the corners, and are thus good in cases of damaged heads **(see illustration 2.21)**.

● Slotted-head or Phillips-head screws are often damaged by the use of the wrong size screwdriver. Allen-head and Torx-head screws are much less likely to sustain damage. If enough of the screw head is exposed you can use a hacksaw to cut a slot in its head and then use a conventional flat-bladed screwdriver to remove it. Alternatively use a hammer and cold chisel to tap the head of the fastener around to loosen it. Always replace damaged fasteners with new ones, preferably Torx or Allen-head type.

A dab of valve grinding compound between the screw head and screw-driver tip will often give a good grip.

Thread repair

● Threads (particularly those in aluminum alloy components) can be damaged by overtightening, being assembled with dirt in the threads, or from a component working loose and vibrating. Eventually the thread will fail completely, and it will be impossible to tighten the fastener.

● If a thread is damaged or clogged with old locking compound it can be renovated with a thread repair tool (thread chaser) **(see illustrations 2.22 and 2.23);** special thread chasers are available for spark plug hole threads. The tool will not cut a new thread, but clean and true the original thread. Make sure that you use the correct diameter and pitch tool. Similarly, external threads can be cleaned up with a die or a thread restorer file **(see illustration 2.24)**.

2.22 A thread repair tool being used to correct an internal thread

2.23 A thread repair tool being used to correct an external thread

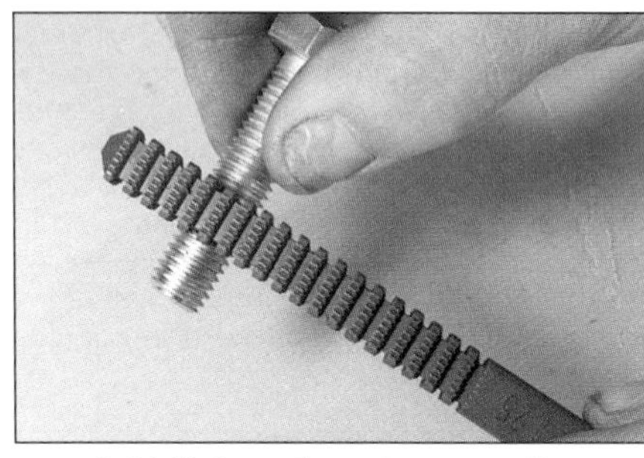
2.24 Using a thread restorer file

● It is possible to drill out the old thread and retap the component to the next thread size. This will work where there is enough surrounding material and a new bolt or screw can be obtained. Sometimes, however, this is not possible - such as where the bolt/screw passes through another component which must also be suitably modified, also in cases where a spark plug or oil drain plug cannot be obtained in a larger diameter thread size.

● The diamond-section thread insert (often known by its popular trade name of Heli-Coil) is a simple and effective method of replacing the thread and retaining the original size. A kit can be purchased which contains the tap, insert and installing tool **(see illustration 2.25)**. Drill out the damaged thread with the size drill specified **(see illustration 2.26)**. Carefully retap the thread **(see illustration 2.27)**. Install the insert on the installing tool and thread it slowly into place using a light downward pressure **(see illustrations 2.28 and 2.29)**. When positioned between a 1/4 and 1/2 turn below the surface withdraw the installing tool and use the break-off tool to press down on the tang, breaking it off **(see illustration 2.30)**.

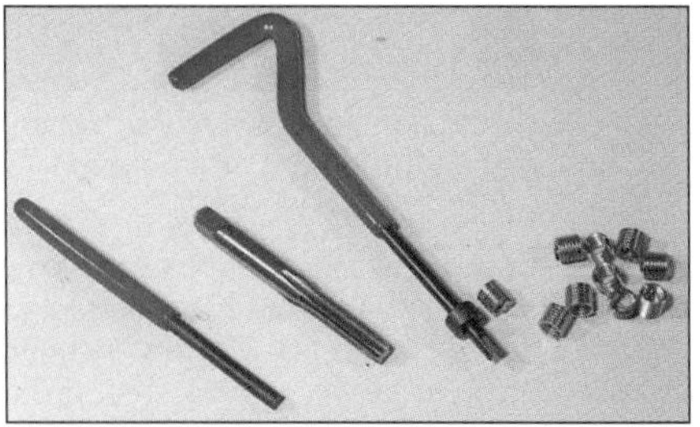
2.25 Obtain a thread insert kit to suit the thread diameter and pitch required

2.26 To install a thread insert, first drill out the original thread . . .

2.27 . . . tap a new thread . . .

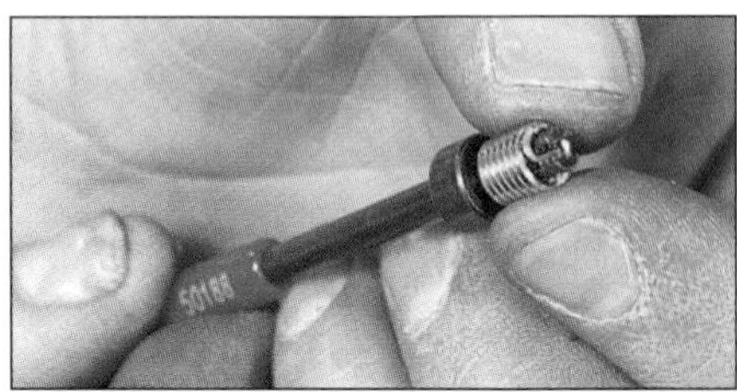
2.28 . . . fit insert on the installing tool . . .

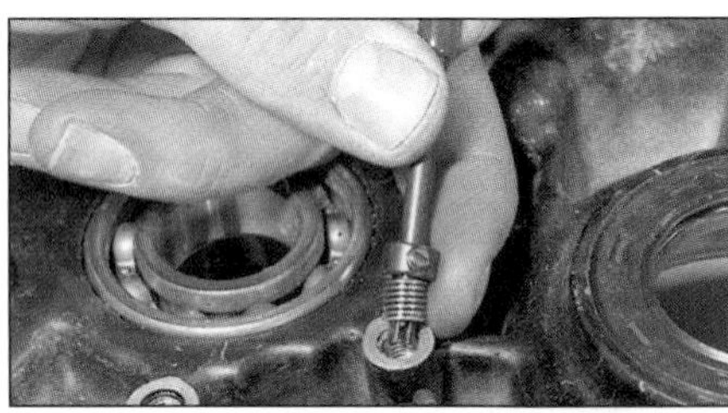
2.29 . . . and thread into the component . . .

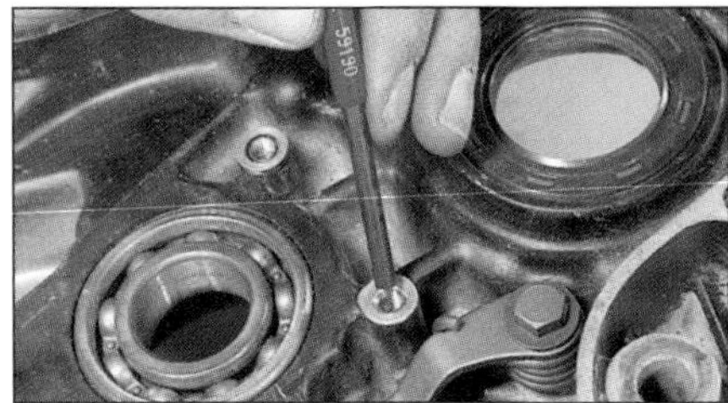
2.30 . . . break off the tang when complete

● There are epoxy thread repair kits on the market which can rebuild stripped internal threads, although this repair should not be used on high load-bearing components.

Thread locking and sealing compounds

● Locking compounds are used in locations where the fastener is prone to loosening due to vibration or on important safety-related items which might cause loss of control of the motorcycle if they fail. It is also used where important fasteners cannot be secured by other means such as lockwashers or cotter pins.

● Before applying locking compound, make sure that the threads (internal and external) are clean and dry with all old compound removed. Select a compound to suit the component being secured - a non-permanent general locking and sealing type is suitable for most applications, but a high strength type is needed for permanent fixing of studs in castings. Apply a drop or two of the compound to the first few threads of the fastener, then thread it into place and tighten to the specified torque. Do not apply excessive thread locking compound otherwise the thread may be damaged on subsequent removal.

● Certain fasteners are impregnated with a dry film type coating of locking compound on their threads. Always replace this type of fastener if disturbed.

● Anti-seize compounds, such as copper-based greases, can be applied to protect threads from seizure due to extreme heat and corrosion. A common instance is spark plug threads and exhaust system fasteners.

3 Measuring tools and gauges

Feeler gauges

● Feeler gauges (or blades) are used for measuring small gaps and clearances **(see illustration 3.1)**. They can also be used to measure endfloat (sideplay) of a component on a shaft where access is not possible with a dial gauge.

● Feeler gauge sets should be treated with care and not bent or damaged. They are etched with their size on one face. Keep them clean and very lightly oiled to prevent corrosion build-up.

3.1 Feeler gauges are used for measuring small gaps and clearances - thickness is marked on one face of gauge

● When measuring a clearance, select a gauge which is a light sliding fit between the two components. You may need to use two gauges together to measure the clearance accurately.

Micrometers

● A micrometer is a precision tool capable of measuring to 0.01 or 0.001 of a millimeter. It should always be stored in its case and not in the general toolbox. It must be kept clean and never dropped, otherwise its frame or measuring anvils could be distorted resulting in inaccurate readings.

● External micrometers are used for measuring outside diameters of components and have many more applications than internal micrometers. Micrometers are available in different size ranges, typically 0 to 25 mm, 25 to 50 mm, and upwards in 25 mm steps; some large micrometers have interchangeable anvils to allow a range of measurements to be taken. Generally the largest precision measurement you are likely to take on a motorcycle is the piston diameter.

● Internal micrometers (or bore micrometers) are used for measuring inside diameters, such as valve guides and cylinder bores. Telescoping gauges and small hole gauges are used in conjunction with an external micrometer, whereas the more expensive internal micrometers have their own measuring device.

External micrometer

Note: *The conventional analogue type instrument is described. Although much easier to read, digital micrometers are considerably more expensive.*

● Always check the calibration of the micrometer before use. With the anvils closed (0 to 25 mm type) or set over a test gauge

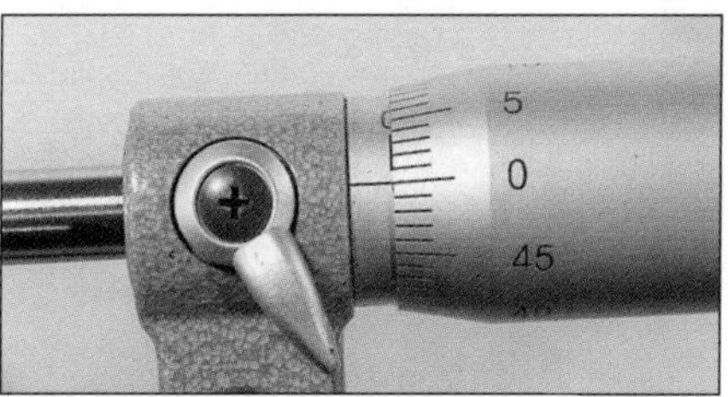

3.2 Check micrometer calibration before use

(for the larger types) the scale should read zero **(see illustration 3.2)**; make sure that the anvils (and test piece) are clean first. Any discrepancy can be adjusted by referring to the instructions supplied with the tool. Remember that the micrometer is a precision measuring tool - don't force the anvils closed, use the ratchet (4) on the end of the micrometer to close it. In this way, a measured force is always applied.

● To use, first make sure that the item being measured is clean. Place the anvil of the micrometer (1) against the item and use the thimble (2) to bring the spindle (3) lightly into contact with the other side of the item **(see illustration 3.3)**. Don't tighten the thimble down because this will damage the micrometer - instead use the ratchet (4) on the end of the micrometer. The ratchet mechanism applies a measured force preventing damage to the instrument.

● The micrometer is read by referring to the linear scale on the sleeve and the annular scale on the thimble. Read off the sleeve first to obtain the base measurement, then add the fine measurement from the thimble to obtain the overall reading. The linear scale on the sleeve represents the measuring range of the micrometer (eg 0 to 25 mm). The annular scale

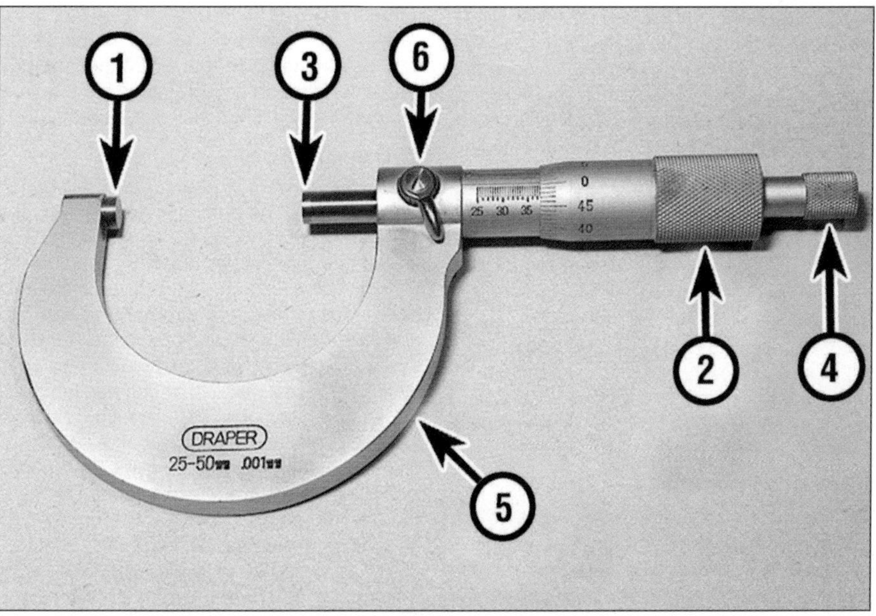

3.3 Micrometer component parts

1 Anvil
2 Thimble
3 Spindle
4 Ratchet
5 Frame
6 Locking lever

on the thimble will be in graduations of 0.01 mm (or as marked on the frame) - one full revolution of the thimble will move 0.5 mm on the linear scale. Take the reading where the datum line on the sleeve intersects the thimble's scale. Always position the eye directly above the scale otherwise an inaccurate reading will result.

In the example shown the item measures 2.95 mm **(see illustration 3.4)**:

Linear scale	2.00 mm
Linear scale	0.50 mm
Annular scale	0.45 mm
Total figure	**2.95 mm**

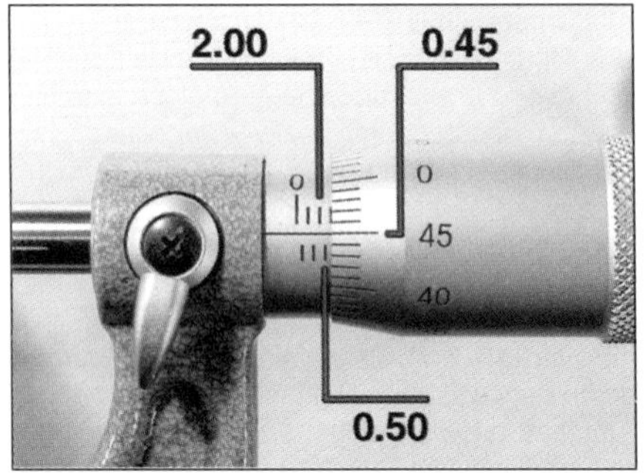

3.4 Micrometer reading of 2.95 mm

Most micrometers have a locking lever (6) on the frame to hold the setting in place, allowing the item to be removed from the micrometer.

● Some micrometers have a vernier scale on their sleeve, providing an even finer measurement to be taken, in 0.001 increments of a millimeter. Take the sleeve and thimble measurement as described above, then check which graduation on the vernier scale aligns with that of the annular scale on the thimble **Note:** *The eye must be perpendicular to the scale when taking the vernier reading - if necessary rotate the body of the micrometer to ensure this.* Multiply the vernier scale figure by 0.001 and add it to the base and fine measurement figures.

In the example shown the item measures 46.994 mm **(see illustrations 3.5 and 3.6)**:

Linear scale (base)	46.000 mm
Linear scale (base)	00.500 mm
Annular scale (fine)	00.490 mm
Vernier scale	00.004 mm
Total figure	**46.994 mm**

Internal micrometer

● Internal micrometers are available for measuring bore diameters, but are expensive and unlikely to be available for home use. It is suggested that a set of telescoping gauges and small hole gauges, both of which must be used with an external micrometer, will suffice for taking internal measurements on a motorcycle.

● Telescoping gauges can be used to measure internal diameters of components. Select a gauge with the correct size range, make sure its ends are clean and insert it into the bore. Expand the gauge, then lock its position and withdraw it from the bore **(see illustration 3.7)**. Measure across the gauge ends with a micrometer **(see illustration 3.8)**.

● Very small diameter bores (such as valve guides) are measured with a small hole gauge. Once adjusted to a slip-fit inside the component, its position is locked and the gauge withdrawn for measurement with a micrometer **(see illustrations 3.9 and 3.10)**.

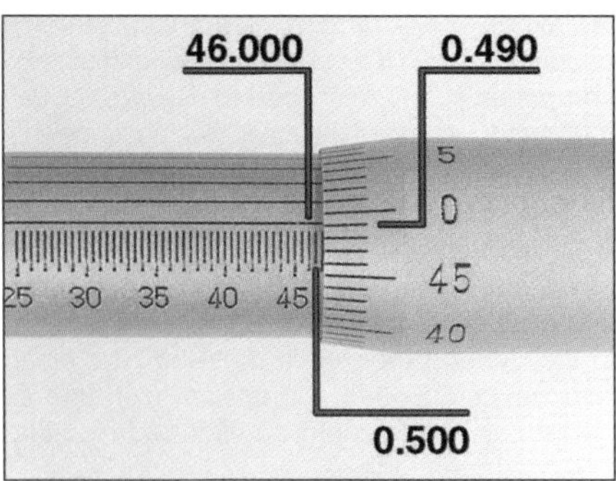

3.5 Micrometer reading of 46.99 mm on linear and annular scales . . .

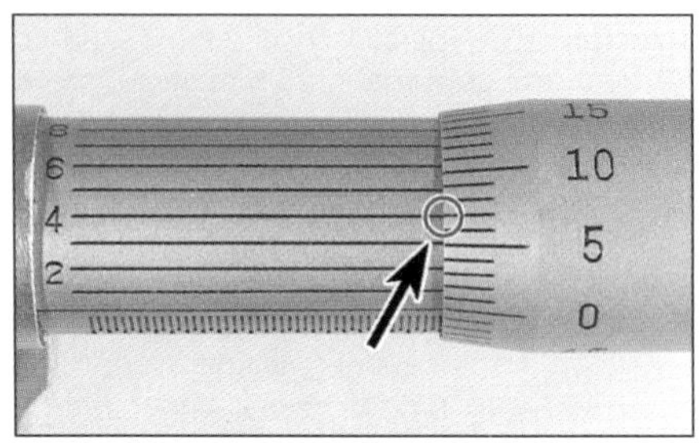

3.6 . . . and 0.004 mm on vernier scale

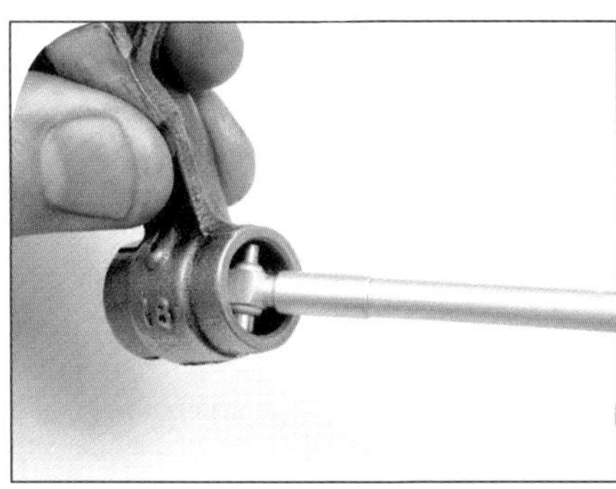

3.7 Expand the telescoping gauge in the bore, lock its position . . .

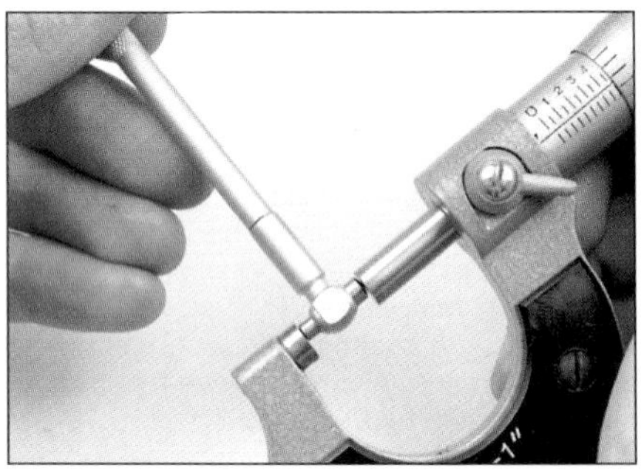

3.8 . . . then measure the gauge with a micrometer

3.9 Expand the small hole gauge in the bore, lock its position . . .

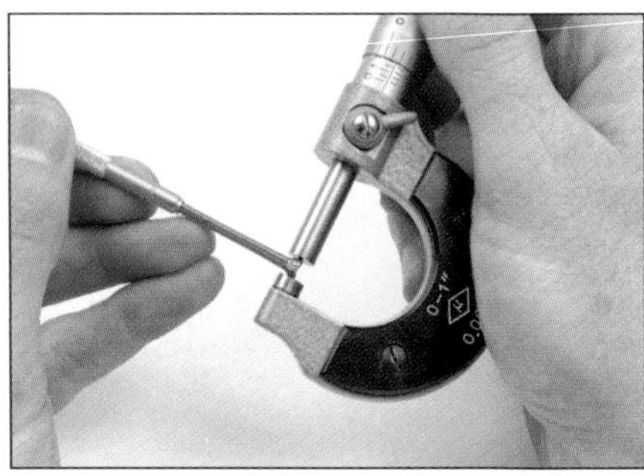

3.10 . . . then measure the gauge with a micrometer

Vernier caliper

Note: *The conventional linear and dial gauge type instruments are described. Digital types are easier to read, but are far more expensive.*

● The vernier caliper does not provide the precision of a micrometer, but is versatile in being able to measure internal and external diameters. Some types also incorporate a depth gauge. It is ideal for measuring clutch plate friction material and spring free lengths.

● To use the conventional linear scale vernier, loosen off the vernier clamp screws (1) and set its jaws over (2), or inside (3), the item to be measured **(see illustration 3.11)**. Slide the jaw into contact, using the thumb-wheel (4) for fine movement of the sliding scale (5) then tighten the clamp screws (1). Read off the main scale (6) where the zero on the sliding scale (5) intersects it, taking the whole number to the left of the zero; this provides the base measurement. View along the sliding scale and select the division which lines up exactly with any of the divisions on the main scale, noting that the divisions usually represents 0.02 of a millimeter. Add this fine measurement to the base measurement to obtain the total reading.

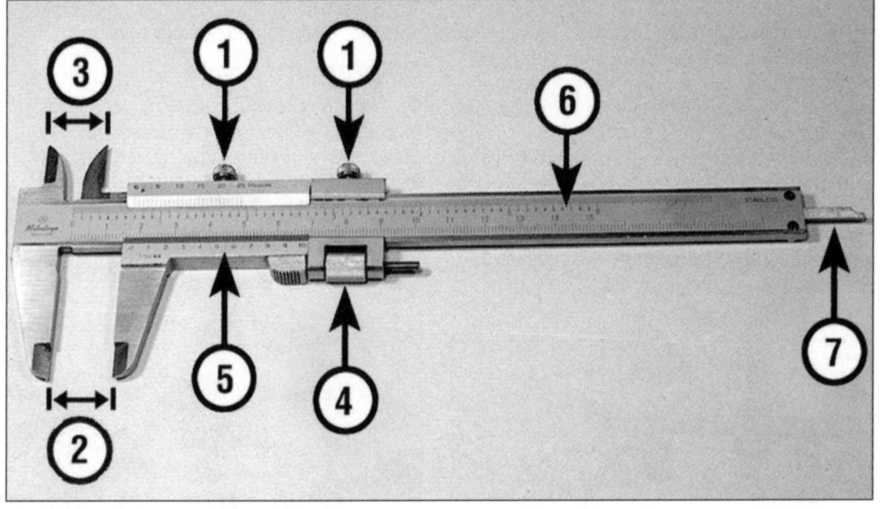

3.11 Vernier component parts (linear gauge)

1 *Clamp screws*
2 *External jaws*
3 *Internal jaws*
4 *Thumbwheel*
5 *Sliding scale*
6 *Main scale*
7 *Depth gauge*

In the example shown the item measures 55.92 mm **(see illustration 3.12)**:

Base measurement	55.00 mm
Fine measurement	00.92 mm
Total figure	**55.92 mm**

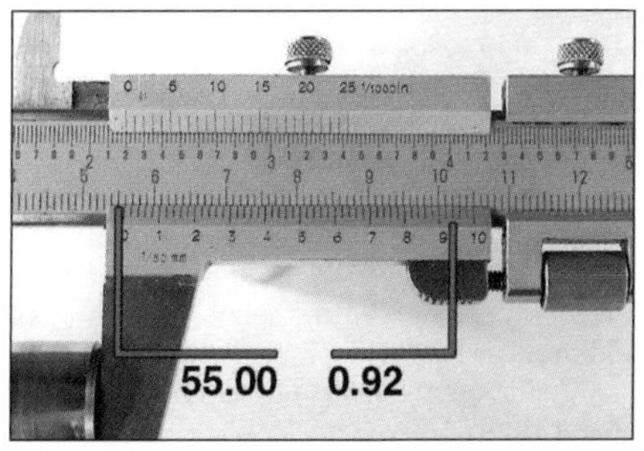

3.12 Vernier gauge reading of 55.92 mm

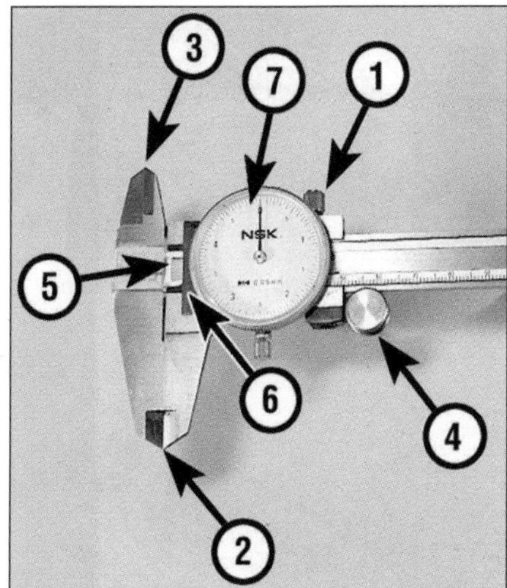

3.13 Vernier component parts (dial gauge)

1 *Clamp screw*
2 *External jaws*
3 *Internal jaws*
4 *Thumbwheel*
5 *Main scale*
6 *Sliding scale*
7 *Dial gauge*

● Some vernier calipers are equipped with a dial gauge for fine measurement. Before use, check that the jaws are clean, then close them fully and check that the dial gauge reads zero. If necessary adjust the gauge ring accordingly. Slacken the vernier clamp screw (1) and set its jaws over (2), or inside (3), the item to be measured **(see illustration 3.13)**. Slide the jaws into contact, using the thumbwheel (4) for fine movement. Read off the main scale (5) where the edge of the sliding scale (6) intersects it, taking the whole number to the left of the zero; this provides the base measurement. Read off the needle position on the dial gauge (7) scale to provide the fine measurement; each division represents 0.05 of a millimeter. Add this fine measurement to the base measurement to obtain the total reading.

In the example shown the item measures 55.95 mm **(see illustration 3.14)**:

Base measurement	55.00 mm
Fine measurement	00.95 mm
Total figure	**55.95 mm**

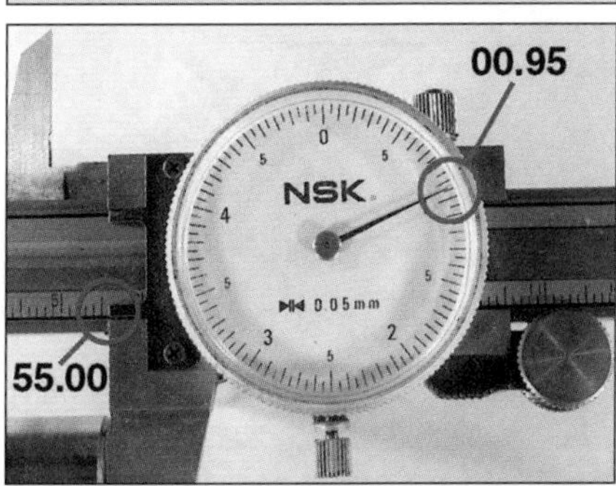

3.14 Vernier gauge reading of 55.95 mm

Plastigage

● Plastigage is a plastic material which can be compressed between two surfaces to measure the oil clearance between them. The width of the compressed Plastigage is measured against a calibrated scale to determine the clearance.

● Common uses of Plastigage are for measuring the clearance between crankshaft journal and main bearing inserts, between crankshaft journal and big-end bearing inserts, and between camshaft and bearing surfaces. The following example describes big-end oil clearance measurement.

● Handle the Plastigage material carefully to prevent distortion. Using a sharp knife, cut a length which corresponds with the width of the bearing being measured and place it carefully across the journal so that it is parallel with the shaft **(see illustration 3.15)**. Carefully install both bearing shells and the connecting rod. Without rotating the rod on the journal tighten its bolts or nuts (as applicable) to the specified torque. The connecting rod and bearings are then disassembled and the crushed Plastigage examined.

3.15 Plastigage placed across shaft journal

● Using the scale provided in the Plastigage kit, measure the width of the material to determine the oil clearance **(see illustration 3.16)**. Always remove all traces of Plastigage after use using your fingernails.

Caution: Arriving at the correct clearance demands that the assembly is torqued correctly, according to the settings and sequence (where applicable) provided by the motorcycle manufacturer.

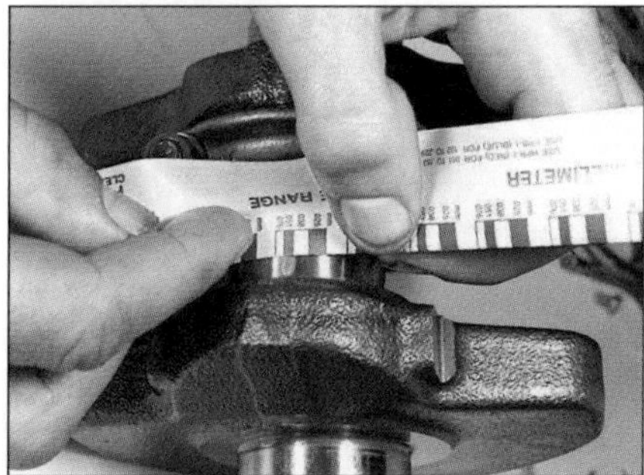

3.16 Measuring the width of the crushed Plastigage

Dial gauge or DTI (Dial Test Indicator)

● A dial gauge can be used to accurately measure small amounts of movement. Typical uses are measuring shaft runout or shaft endfloat (sideplay) and setting piston position for ignition timing on two-strokes. A dial gauge set usually comes with a range of different probes and adapters and mounting equipment.

● The gauge needle must point to zero when at rest. Rotate the ring around its periphery to zero the gauge.

● Check that the gauge is capable of reading the extent of movement in the work. Most gauges have a small dial set in the face which records whole millimeters of movement as well as the fine scale around the face periphery which is calibrated in 0.01 mm divisions. Read off the small dial first to obtain the base measurement, then add the measurement from the fine scale to obtain the total reading.

Base measurement	1.00 mm
Fine measurement	0.48 mm
Total figure	**1.48 mm**

3.17 Dial gauge reading of 1.48 mm

In the example shown the gauge reads 1.48 mm **(see illustration 3.17)**:

● If measuring shaft runout, the shaft must be supported in vee-blocks and the gauge mounted on a stand perpendicular to the shaft. Rest the tip of the gauge against the center of the shaft and rotate the shaft slowly while watching the gauge reading **(see illustration 3.18)**. Take several measurements along the length of the shaft and record the maximum gauge reading as the amount of runout in the shaft. **Note:** *The reading obtained will be total runout at that point - some manufacturers specify that the runout figure is halved to compare with their specified runout limit.*

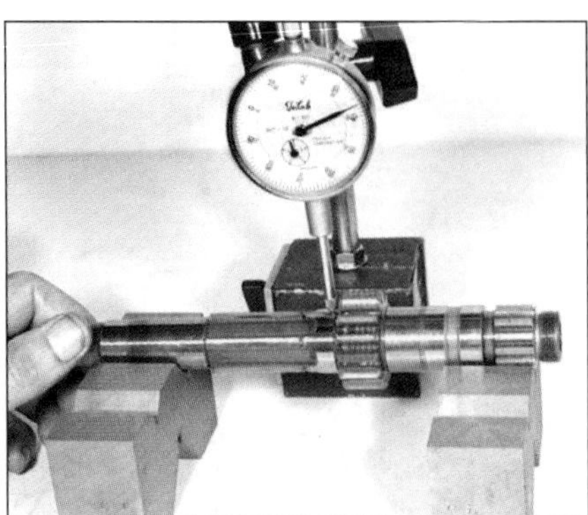

3.18 Using a dial gauge to measure shaft runout

● Endfloat (sideplay) measurement requires that the gauge is mounted securely to the surrounding component with its probe touching the end of the shaft. Using hand pressure, push and pull on the shaft noting the maximum endfloat recorded on the gauge **(see illustration 3.19)**.

3.19 Using a dial gauge to measure shaft endfloat

● A dial gauge with suitable adapters can be used to determine piston position BTDC on two-stroke engines for the purposes of ignition timing. The gauge, adapter and suitable length probe are installed in the place of the spark plug and the gauge zeroed at TDC. If the piston position is specified as 1.14 mm BTDC, rotate the engine back to 2.00 mm BTDC, then slowly forwards to 1.14 mm BTDC.

Cylinder compression gauges

● A compression gauge is used for measuring cylinder compression. Either the rubber-cone type or the threaded adapter type can be used. The latter is preferred to ensure a perfect seal against the cylinder head. A 0 to 300 psi (0 to 20 Bar) type gauge (for gasoline engines) will be suitable for motorcycles.

● The spark plug is removed and the gauge either held hard against the cylinder head (cone type) or the gauge adapter screwed into the cylinder head (threaded type) **(see illustration 3.20)**. Cylinder compression is measured with the engine turning over, but not running - carry out the compression test as described in *Troubleshooting Equipment*. The gauge will hold the reading until manually released.

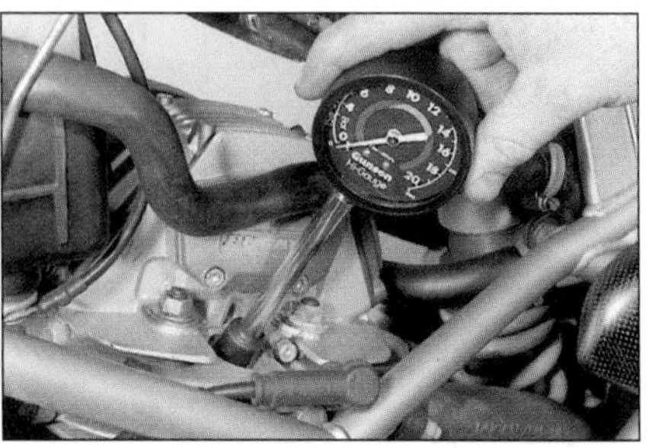

3.20 Using a rubber-cone type cylinder compression gauge

Oil pressure gauge

● An oil pressure gauge is used for measuring engine oil pressure. Most gauges come with a set of adapters to fit the thread of the take-off point **(see illustration 3.21)**. If the take-off point specified by the motorcycle manufacturer is an external oil pipe union, make sure that the specified replacement union is used to prevent oil starvation.

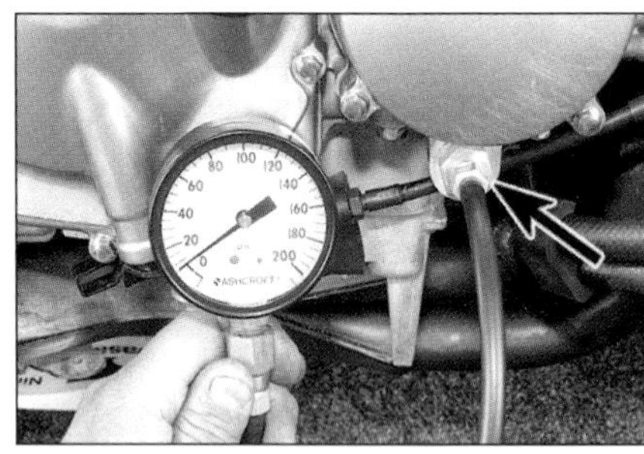

3.21 Oil pressure gauge and take-off point adapter (arrow)

● Oil pressure is measured with the engine running (at a specific rpm) and often the manufacturer will specify pressure limits for a cold and hot engine.

Straight-edge and surface plate

● If checking the gasket face of a component for warpage, place a steel rule or precision straight-edge across the gasket face and measure any gap between the straight-edge and component with feeler gauges **(see illustration 3.22)**. Check diagonally across the component and between mounting holes **(see illustration 3.23)**.

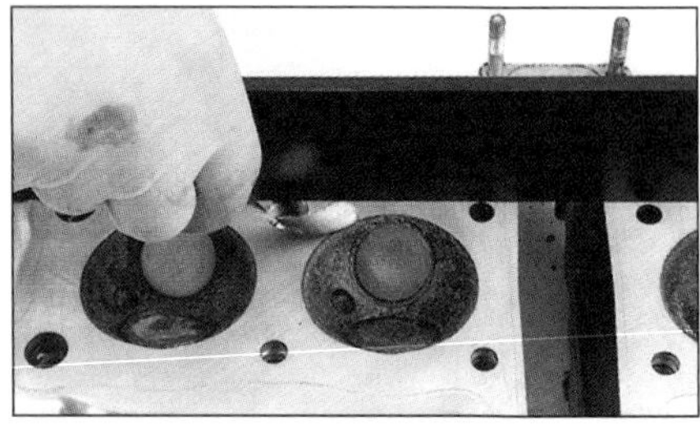

3.22 Use a straight-edge and feeler gauges to check for warpage

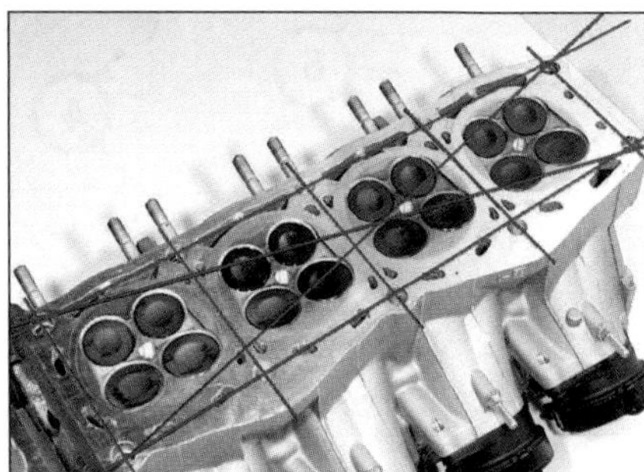

3.23 Check for warpage in these directions

● Checking individual components for warpage, such as clutch plain (metal) plates, requires a perfectly flat plate or piece of plate glass and feeler gauges.

4 Torque and leverage

What is torque?

● Torque describes the twisting force around a shaft. The amount of torque applied is determined by the distance from the center of the shaft to the end of the lever and the amount of force being applied to the end of the lever; distance multiplied by force equals torque.

● The manufacturer applies a measured torque to a bolt or nut to ensure that it will not loosen in use and to hold two components securely together without movement in the joint. The actual torque setting depends on the thread size, bolt or nut material and the composition of the components being held.

● Too little torque may cause the fastener to loosen due to vibration, whereas too much torque will distort the joint faces of the component or cause the fastener to shear off. Always stick to the specified torque setting.

Using a torque wrench

● Check the calibration of the torque wrench and make sure it has a suitable range for the job. Torque wrenches are available in Nm (Newton-meters), kgf m (kilograms-force meter), lbf ft (pounds-feet), lbf in (inch-pounds). Do not confuse lbf ft with lbf in.

● Adjust the tool to the desired torque on the scale **(see illustration 4.1)**. If your torque wrench is not calibrated in the units specified, carefully convert the figure (see *Conversion Factors*). A manufacturer sometimes gives a torque setting as a range (8 to 10 Nm) rather than a single figure - in this case set the tool midway between the two settings. The same torque may be expressed as 9 Nm ± 1 Nm. Some torque wrenches have a method of locking the setting so that it isn't inadvertently altered during use.

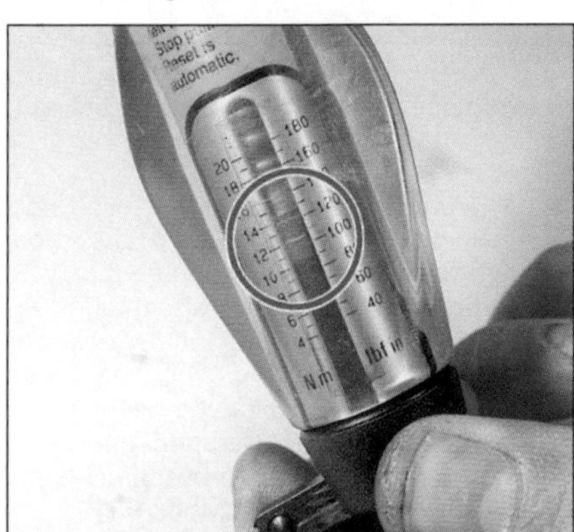

4.1 Set the torque wrench index mark to the setting required, in this case 12 Nm

● Install the bolts/nuts in their correct location and secure them lightly. Their threads must be clean and free of any old locking compound. Unless specified the threads and flange should be dry - oiled threads are necessary in certain circumstances and the manufacturer will take this into account in the specified torque figure. Similarly, the manufacturer may also specify the application of thread-locking compound.

● Tighten the fasteners in the specified sequence until the torque wrench clicks, indicating that the torque setting has been reached. Apply the torque again to double-check the setting. Where different thread diameter fasteners secure the component, as a rule tighten the larger diameter ones first.

● When the torque wrench has been finished with, release the lock (where applicable) and fully back off its setting to zero - do not leave the torque wrench tensioned. Also, do not use a torque wrench for loosening a fastener.

Angle-tightening

● Manufacturers often specify a figure in degrees for final tightening of a fastener. This usually follows tightening to a specific torque setting.

● A degree disc can be set and attached to the socket **(see illustration 4.2)** or a protractor can be used to mark the angle of movement on the bolt/nut head and the surrounding casting **(see illustration 4.3)**.

4.2 Angle tightening can be accomplished with a torque-angle gauge . . .

4.3 . . . or by marking the angle on the surrounding component

Loosening sequences

● Where more than one bolt/nut secures a component, loosen each fastener evenly a little at a time. In this way, not all the stress of the joint is held by one fastener and the components are not likely to distort.

● If a tightening sequence is provided, work in the REVERSE of this, but if not, work from the outside in, in a criss-cross sequence **(see illustration 4.4)**.

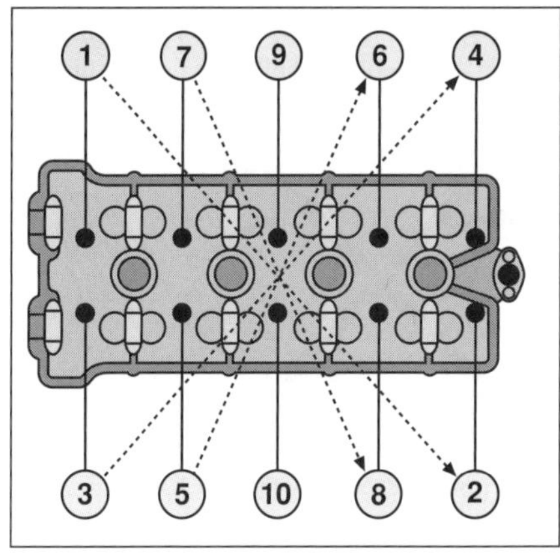

4.4 When loosening, work from the outside inwards

Tightening sequences

● If a component is held by more than one fastener it is important that the retaining bolts/nuts are tightened evenly to prevent uneven stress build-up and distortion of sealing faces. This is especially important on high-compression joints such as the cylinder head.

● A sequence is usually provided by the manufacturer, either in a diagram or actually marked in the casting. If not, always start in the center and work outwards in a criss-cross pattern **(see illustration 4.5)**. Start off by securing all bolts/nuts finger-tight, then set the torque wrench and tighten each fastener by a small amount in sequence until the final torque is reached. By following this practice,

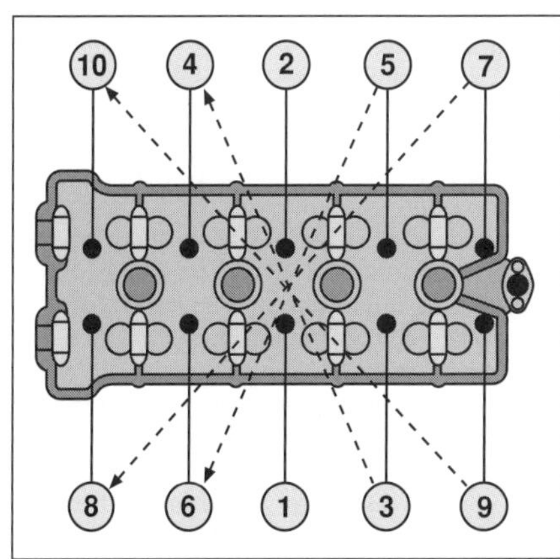

4.5 When tightening, work from the inside outwards

the joint will be held evenly and will not be distorted. Important joints, such as the cylinder head and big-end fasteners often have two- or three-stage torque settings.

Applying leverage

● Use tools at the correct angle. Position a socket or wrench on the bolt/nut so that you pull it towards you when loosening. If this can't be done, push the wrench without curling your fingers around it **(see illustration 4.6)** - the wrench may slip or the fastener loosen suddenly, resulting in your fingers being crushed against a component.

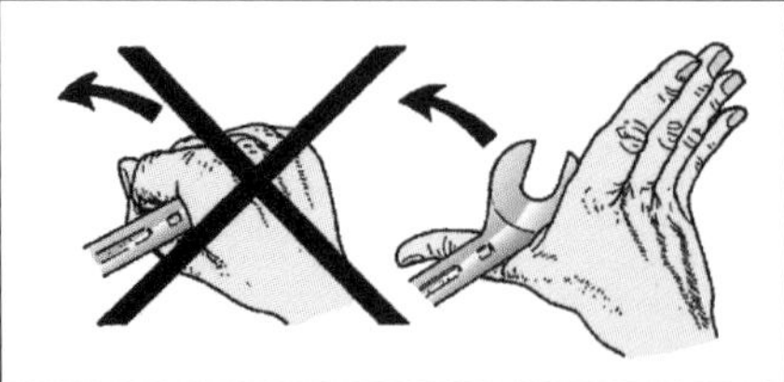

4.6 If you can't pull on the wrench to loosen a fastener, push with your hand open

● Additional leverage is gained by extending the length of the lever. The best way to do this is to use a breaker bar instead of the regular length tool, or to slip a length of tubing over the end of the wrench or socket.

● If additional leverage will not work, the fastener head is either damaged or firmly corroded in place (see *Fasteners*).

5 Bearings

Bearing removal and installation

Drivers and sockets

● Before removing a bearing, always inspect the casing to see which way it must be driven out - some casings will have retaining plates or a cast step. Also check for any identifying markings on the bearing and, if installed to a certain depth, measure this at this stage. Some roller bearings are sealed on one side - take note of the original installed position.

● Bearings can be driven out of a casing using a bearing driver tool (with the correct size head) or a socket of the correct diameter. Select the driver head or socket so that it contacts the outer race of the bearing, not the balls/rollers or inner race. Always support the casing around the bearing housing with wood blocks, otherwise there is a risk of fracture. The bearing is driven out with a few blows on the driver or socket from a heavy mallet. Unless access is severely restricted (as with wheel bearings), a pin-punch is not recommended unless it is moved around the bearing to keep it square in its housing.

● The same equipment can be used to install bearings. Make sure the bearing housing is supported on wood blocks and line up the bearing in its housing. Install the bearing as noted on removal - generally they are installed with their marked side facing outwards. Tap the bearing squarely into its housing using a driver or socket which bears only on the bearing's outer race - contact with the bearing balls/rollers or inner race will destroy it **(see illustrations 5.1 and 5.2)**.

● Check that the bearing inner race and balls/rollers rotate freely.

5.1 Using a bearing driver against the bearing's outer race

5.2 Using a large socket against the bearing's outer race

Pullers and slide-hammers

● Where a bearing is pressed on a shaft a puller will be required to extract it **(see illustration 5.3).** Make sure that the puller clamp or legs fit securely behind the bearing and are unlikely to slip out. If pulling a bearing off a gear shaft for example, you may have to locate the puller behind a gear pinion if there is no access to the race and draw the gear pinion off the shaft as well **(see illustration 5.4)**.

5.3 This bearing puller clamps behind the bearing and pressure is applied to the shaft end to draw the bearing off

Caution: Ensure that the puller's center bolt locates securely against the end of the shaft and will not slip when pressure is applied. Also ensure that puller does not damage the shaft end.

5.4 Where no access is available to the rear of the bearing, it is sometimes possible to draw off the adjacent component

● Operate the puller so that its center bolt exerts pressure on the shaft end and draws the bearing off the shaft.

● When installing the bearing on the shaft, tap only on the bearing's inner race - contact with the balls/rollers or outer race will destroy the bearing. Use a socket or length of tubing as a drift which fits over the shaft end **(see illustration 5.5)**.

5.5 When installing a bearing on a shaft use a piece of tubing which bears only on the bearing's inner race

● Where a bearing locates in a blind hole in a casing, it cannot be driven or pulled out as described above. A slide-hammer with knife-edged bearing puller attachment will be required. The puller attachment passes through the bearing and when tightened expands to fit firmly behind the bearing **(see illustration 5.6)**. By operating the slide-hammer part of the tool the bearing is jarred out of its housing **(see illustration 5.7)**.

● It is possible, if the bearing is of reasonable weight, for it to drop out of its housing if the casing is heated as described opposite. If

5.6 Expand the bearing puller so that it locks behind the bearing . . .

5.7 . . . attach the slide hammer to the bearing puller

this method is attempted, first prepare a work surface which will enable the casing to be tapped face down to help dislodge the bearing - a wood surface is ideal since it will not damage the casing's gasket surface. Wearing protective gloves, tap the heated casing several times against the work surface to dislodge the bearing under its own weight **(see illustration 5.8)**.

5.8 Tapping a casing face down on wood blocks can often dislodge a bearing

● Bearings can be installed in blind holes using the driver or socket method described above.

Drawbolts

● Where a bearing or bushing is set in the eye of a component, such as a suspension linkage arm or connecting rod small-end, removal by drift may damage the component. Furthermore, a rubber bushing in a shock absorber eye cannot successfully be driven out of position. If access is available to a hydraulic press, the task is straightforward. If not, a drawbolt can be fabricated to extract the bearing or bushing.

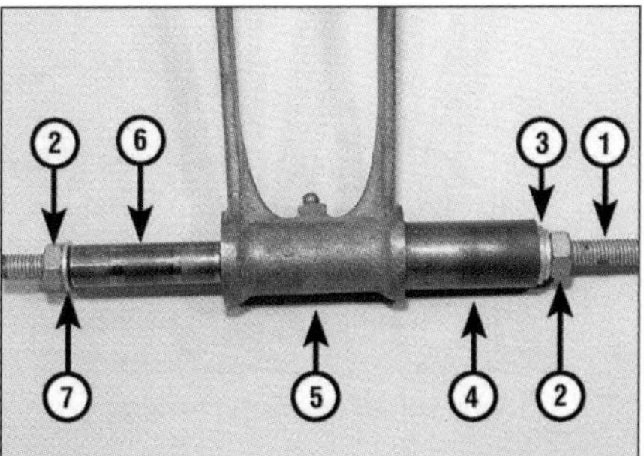

5.9 Drawbolt component parts assembled on a suspension arm

1. *Bolt or length of threaded bar*
2. *Nuts*
3. *Washer (external diameter greater than tubing internal diameter)*
4. *Tubing (internal diameter sufficient to accommodate bearing)*
5. *Suspension arm with bearing*
6. *Tubing (external diameter slightly smaller than bearing)*
7. *Washer (external diameter slightly smaller than bearing)*

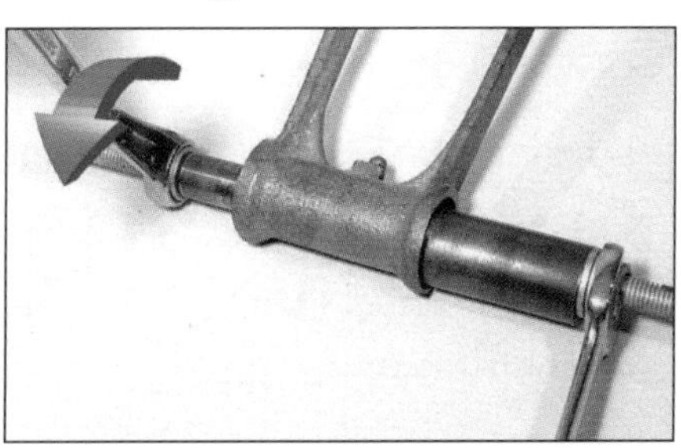

5.10 Drawing the bearing out of the suspension arm

● To extract the bearing/bushing you will need a long bolt with nut (or piece of threaded bar with two nuts), a piece of tubing which has an internal diameter larger than the bearing/bushing, another piece of tubing which has an external diameter slightly smaller than the bearing/bushing, and a selection of washers **(see illustrations 5.9 and 5.10)**. Note that the pieces of tubing must be of the same length, or longer, than the bearing/bushing.

● The same kit (without the pieces of tubing) can be used to draw the new bearing/bushing back into place **(see illustration 5.11)**.

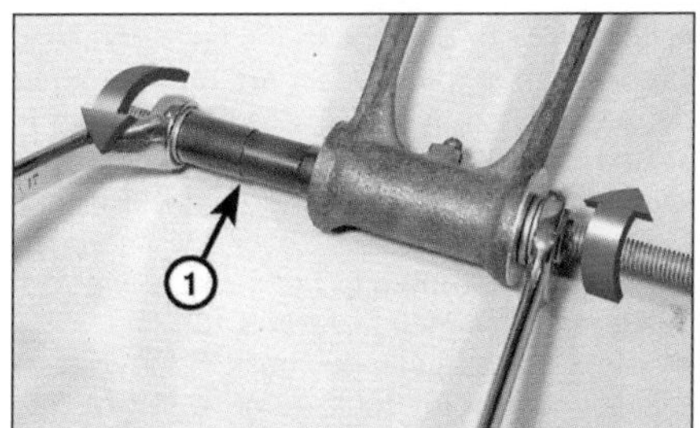

5.11 Installing a new bearing (1) in the suspension arm

Temperature change

● If the bearing's outer race is a tight fit in the casing, the aluminum casing can be heated to release its grip on the bearing. Aluminum will expand at a greater rate than the steel bearing outer race. There are several ways to do this, but avoid any localized extreme heat (such as a blow torch) - aluminum alloy has a low melting point.

● Approved methods of heating a casing are using a domestic oven (heated to 100°C/200°F) or immersing the casing in boiling water **(see illustration 5.12)**. Low temperature range localized heat sources such as a paint stripper heat gun or clothes iron can also be used **(see illustration 5.13)**. Alternatively, soak a rag in boiling water, wring it out and wrap it around the bearing housing.

Warning: All of these methods require care in use to prevent scalding and burns to the hands. Wear protective gloves when handling hot components.

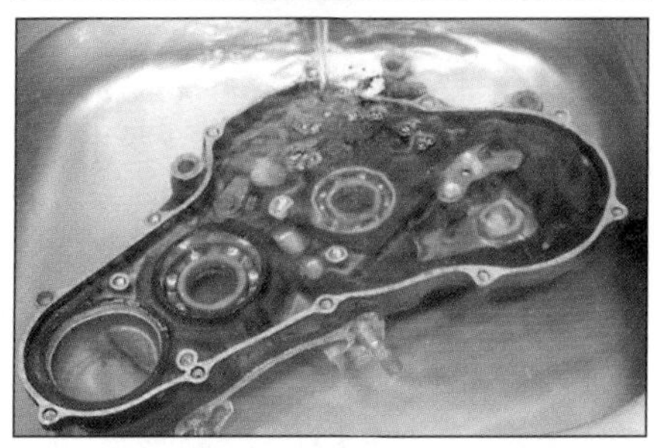

5.12 A casing can be immersed in a sink of boiling water to aid bearing removal

5.13 Using a localized heat source to aid bearing removal

● If heating the whole casing note that plastic components, such as the neutral switch, may suffer - remove them beforehand.

● After heating, remove the bearing as described above. You may find that the expansion is sufficient for the bearing to fall out of the casing under its own weight or with a light tap on the driver or socket.

● If necessary, the casing can be heated to aid bearing installation, and this is sometimes the recommended procedure if the motorcycle manufacturer has designed the housing and bearing fit with this intention.

● Installation of bearings can be eased by placing them in a freezer the night before installation. The steel bearing will contract slightly, allowing easy insertion in its housing. This is often useful when installing steering head outer races in the frame.

Bearing types and markings

● Plain shell bearings, ball bearings, needle roller bearings and tapered roller bearings will all be found on motorcycles **(see illustrations 5.14 and 5.15)**. The ball and roller types are usually caged between an inner and outer race, but uncaged variations may be found.

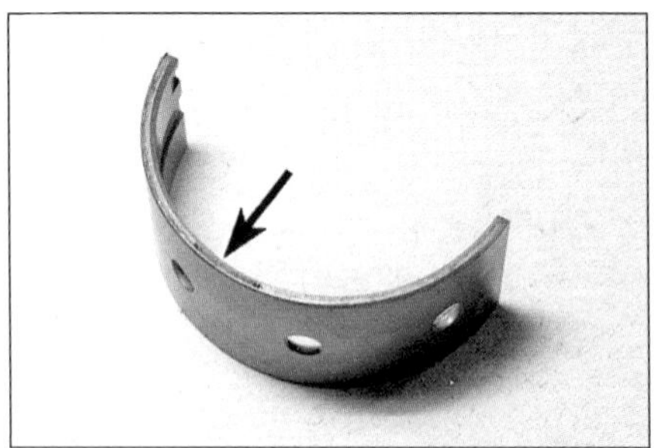

5.14 Shell bearings are either plain or grooved. They are usually identified by color code (arrow)

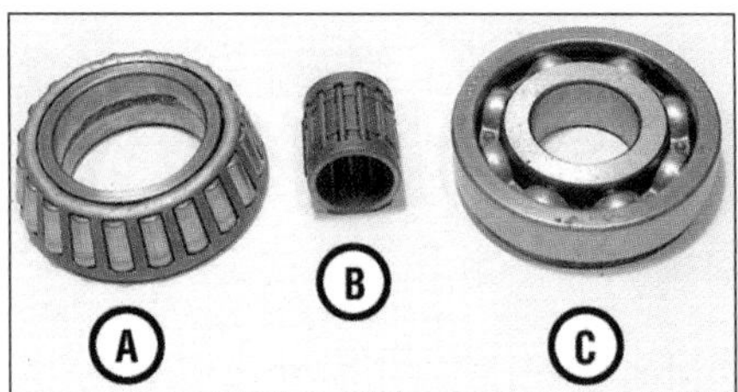

5.15 Tapered roller bearing (A), needle roller bearing (B) and ball journal bearing (C)

● Shell bearings (often called inserts) are usually found at the crankshaft main and connecting rod big-end where they are good at coping with high loads. They are made of a phosphor-bronze material and are impregnated with self-lubricating properties.

● Ball bearings and needle roller bearings consist of a steel inner and outer race with the balls or rollers between the races. They require constant lubrication by oil or grease and are good at coping with axial loads. Taper roller bearings consist of rollers set in a tapered cage set on the inner race; the outer race is separate. They are good at coping with axial loads and prevent movement along the shaft - a typical application is in the steering head.

● Bearing manufacturers produce bearings to ISO size standards and stamp one face of the bearing to indicate its internal and external diameter, load capacity and type **(see illustration 5.16)**.

● Metal bushings are usually of phosphor-bronze material. Rubber bushings are used in suspension mounting eyes. Fiber bushings have also been used in suspension pivots.

5.16 Typical bearing marking

Bearing troubleshooting

● If a bearing outer race has spun in its housing, the housing material will be damaged. You can use a bearing locking compound to bond the outer race in place if damage is not too severe.

● Shell bearings will fail due to damage of their working surface, as a result of lack of lubrication, corrosion or abrasive particles in the oil **(see illustration 5.17)**. Small particles of dirt in the oil may embed in the bearing material whereas larger particles will score the bearing and shaft journal. If a number of short journeys are made, insufficient heat will be generated to drive off condensation which has built up on the bearings.

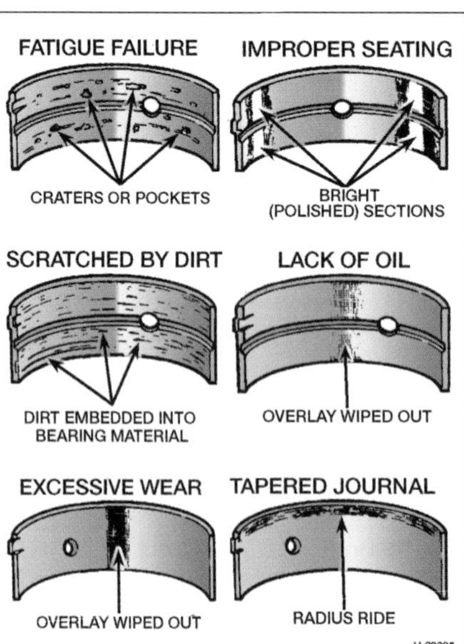

5.17 Typical bearing failures

● Ball and roller bearings will fail due to lack of lubrication or damage to the balls or rollers. Tapered-roller bearings can be damaged by overloading them. Unless the bearing is sealed on both sides, wash it in kerosene to remove all old grease then allow it to dry. Make a visual inspection looking to dented balls or rollers, damaged cages and worn or pitted races **(see illustration 5.18)**.

● A ball bearing can be checked for wear by listening to it when spun. Apply a film of light oil to the bearing and hold it close to the ear - hold the outer race with one hand and spin the

5.18 Example of ball journal bearing with damaged balls and cages

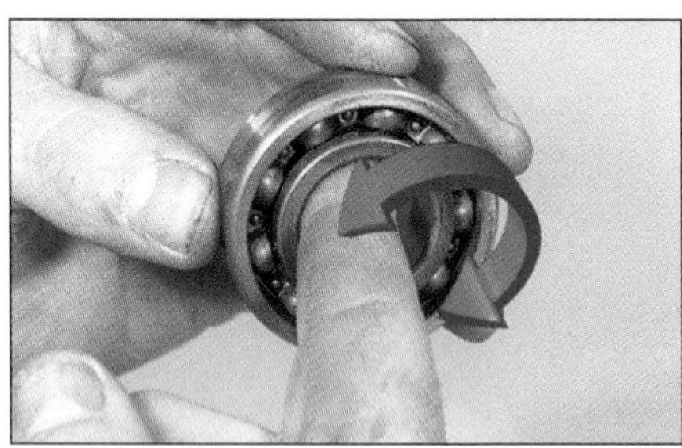

5.19 Hold outer race and listen to inner race when spun

inner race with the other hand **(see illustration 5.19)**. The bearing should be almost silent when spun; if it grates or rattles it is worn.

6 Oil seals

Oil seal removal and installation

● Oil seals should be replaced every time a component is dismantled. This is because the seal lips will become set to the sealing surface and will not necessarily reseal.

● Oil seals can be pried out of position using a large flat-bladed screwdriver **(see illustration 6.1)**. In the case of crankcase seals, check first that the seal is not lipped on the inside, preventing its removal with the crankcases joined.

6.1 Pry out oil seals with a large flat-bladed screwdriver

● New seals are usually installed with their marked face (containing the seal reference code) outwards and the spring side towards the fluid being retained. In certain cases, such as a two-stroke engine crankshaft seal, a double lipped seal may be used due to there being fluid or gas on each side of the joint.

● Use a bearing driver or socket which bears only on the outer hard edge of the seal to install it in the casing - tapping on the inner edge will damage the sealing lip.

Oil seal types and markings

● Oil seals are usually of the single-lipped type. Double-lipped seals are found where a liquid or gas is on both sides of the joint.

● Oil seals can harden and lose their sealing ability if the motorcycle has been in storage for a long period - replacement is the only solution.

● Oil seal manufacturers also conform to the ISO markings for seal size - these are molded into the outer face of the seal **(see illustration 6.2)**.

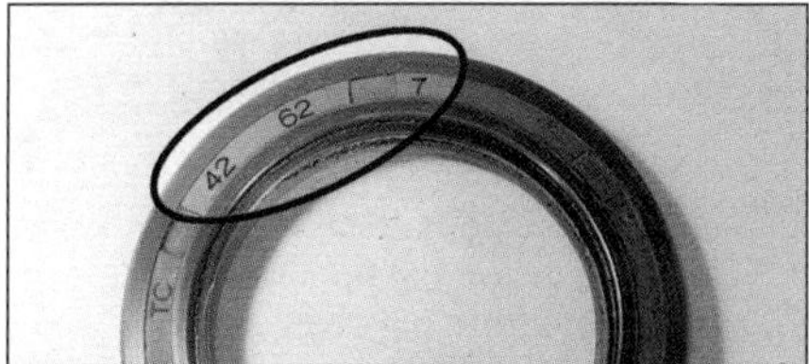

6.2 These oil seal markings indicate inside diameter, outside diameter and seal thickness

7 Gaskets and sealants

Types of gasket and sealant

● Gaskets are used to seal the mating surfaces between components and keep lubricants, fluids, vacuum or pressure contained within the assembly. Aluminum gaskets are sometimes found at the cylinder joints, but most gaskets are paper-based. If the mating surfaces of the components being joined are undamaged the gasket can be installed dry, although a dab of sealant or grease will be useful to hold it in place during assembly.

● RTV (Room Temperature Vulcanizing) silicone rubber sealants cure when exposed to moisture in the atmosphere. These sealants are good at filling pits or irregular gasket faces, but will tend to be forced out of the joint under very high torque. They can be used to replace a paper gasket, but first make sure that the width of the paper gasket is not essential to the shimming of internal components. RTV sealants should not be used on components containing gasoline.

● Non-hardening, semi-hardening and hard setting liquid gasket compounds can be used with a gasket or between a metal-to-metal joint. Select the sealant to suit the application: universal non-hardening sealant can be used on virtually all joints; semi-hardening on joint faces which are rough or damaged; hard setting sealant on joints which require a permanent bond and are subjected to high temperature and pressure. **Note:** *Check first if the paper gasket has a bead of sealant impregnated in its surface before applying additional sealant.*

● When choosing a sealant, make sure it is suitable for the application, particularly if being applied in a high-temperature area or in the vicinity of fuel. Certain manufacturers produce sealants in either clear, silver or black colors to match the finish of the engine. This has a particular application on motorcycles where much of the engine is exposed.

● Do not over-apply sealant. That which is squeezed out on the outside of the joint can be wiped off, whereas an excess of sealant on the inside can break off and clog oilways.

Breaking a sealed joint

● Age, heat, pressure and the use of hard setting sealant can cause two components to stick together so tightly that they are difficult to separate using finger pressure alone. Do not resort to using levers unless there is a pry point provided for this purpose **(see illustration 7.1)** or else the gasket surfaces will be damaged.

● Use a soft-faced hammer **(see illustration 7.2)** or a wood block and conventional hammer to strike the component near the mating surface. Avoid hammering against cast extremities since they may break off. If this method fails, try using a wood wedge between the two components.

Caution: If the joint will not separate, double-check that you have removed all the fasteners.

7.1 If a pry point is provided, apply gentle pressure with a flat-bladed screwdriver

7.2 Tap around the joint with a soft-faced mallet if necessary - don't strike cooling fins

Removal of old gasket and sealant

● Paper gaskets will most likely come away complete, leaving only a few traces stuck on the sealing faces of the components. It is imperative that all traces are removed to ensure correct sealing of the new gasket.

● Very carefully scrape all traces of gasket away making sure that the sealing surfaces are not gouged or scored by the scraper **(see illustrations 7.3, 7.4 and 7.5)**. Stubborn deposits can be removed by spraying with an aerosol gasket remover. Final preparation of

Most components have one or two hollow locating dowels between the two gasket faces. If a dowel cannot be removed, do not resort to gripping it with pliers - it will almost certainly be distorted. Install a close-fitting socket or Phillips screwdriver into the dowel and then grip the outer edge of the dowel to free it.

7.3 Paper gaskets can be scraped off with a gasket scraper tool . . .

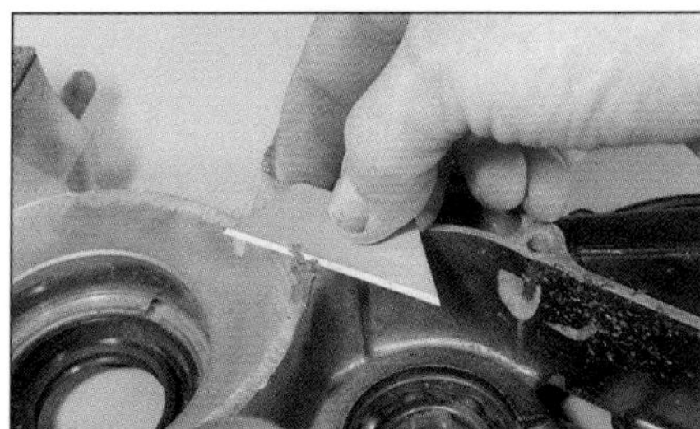

7.4 . . . a knife blade . . .

7.5 . . . or a household scraper

7.6 Fine abrasive paper is wrapped around a flat file to clean up the gasket face

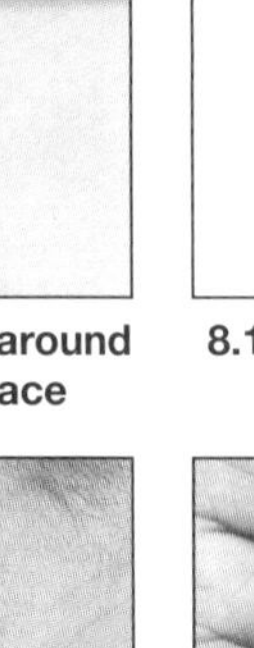

7.7 A kitchen scourer can be used on stubborn deposits

the gasket surface can be made with very fine abrasive paper or a plastic kitchen scourer **(see illustrations 7.6 and 7.7)**.

- Old sealant can be scraped or peeled off components, depending on the type originally used. Note that gasket removal compounds are available to avoid scraping the components clean; make sure the gasket remover suits the type of sealant used.

8 Chains

Breaking and joining final drive chains

- Drive chains for all but small bikes are continuous and do not have a clip-type connecting link. The chain must be broken using a chain breaker tool and the new chain securely riveted together using a new soft rivet-type link. Never use a clip-type connecting link instead of a rivet-type link, except in an emergency. Various chain breaking and riveting tools are available, either as separate tools or combined as illustrated in the accompanying photographs - read the instructions supplied with the tool carefully.

> ***Warning: The need to rivet the new link pins correctly cannot be overstressed - loss of control of the motorcycle is very likely to result if the chain breaks in use.***

- Rotate the chain and look for the soft link. The soft link pins look like they have been deeply center-punched instead of peened over like all the other pins **(see illustration 8.9)** and its sideplate may be a different color. Position the soft link midway between the sprockets and assemble the chain breaker tool over one of the soft link pins **(see illustration 8.1)**. Operate the tool to push the pin out through the chain **(see illustration 8.2)**. On an O-ring chain, remove the O-rings **(see illustration 8.3)**. Carry out the same procedure on the other soft link pin.

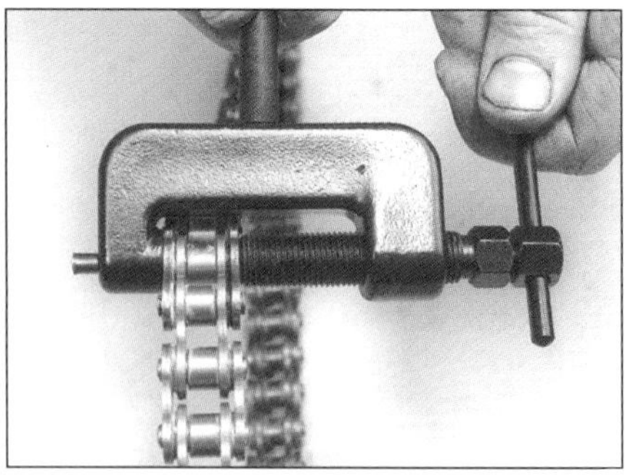

8.1 Tighten the chain breaker to push the pin out of the link . . .

8.2 . . . withdraw the pin, remove the tool . . .

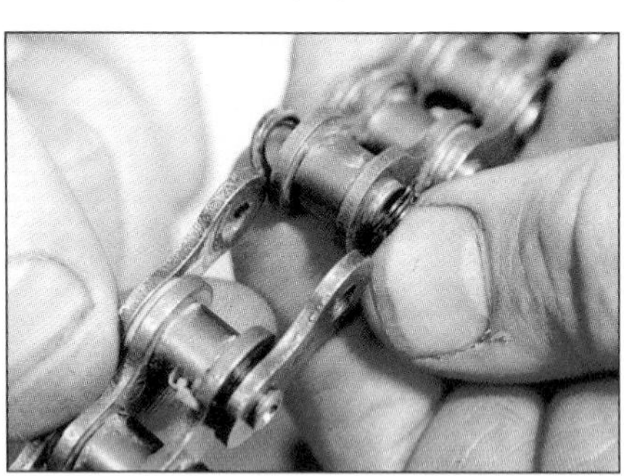

8.3 . . . and separate the chain link

> ***Caution: Certain soft link pins (particularly on the larger chains) may require their ends to be filed or ground off before they can be pressed out using the tool.***

- Check that you have the correct size and strength (standard or heavy duty) new soft link - do not reuse the old link. Look for the size marking on the chain sideplates **(see illustration 8.10)**.
- Position the chain ends so that they are engaged over the rear sprocket. On an O-ring chain, install a new O-ring over each pin of the link and insert the link through the two chain ends **(see illustration 8.4)**. Install a new O-ring over the end of each pin, followed by the sideplate (with the chain manufacturer's marking facing outwards) **(see illustrations 8.5 and 8.6)**. On an unsealed chain, insert the link through the two chain ends, then install the sideplate with the chain manufacturer's marking facing outwards.
- Note that it may not be possible to install the sideplate using finger pressure alone. If using a joining tool, assemble it so that the plates of the tool clamp the link and press the sideplate over the pins **(see illustration 8.7)**. Otherwise, use two small sockets placed over

8.4 Insert the new soft link, with O-rings, through the chain ends . . .

8.5 . . . install the O-rings over the pin ends . . .

8.6 . . . followed by the sideplate

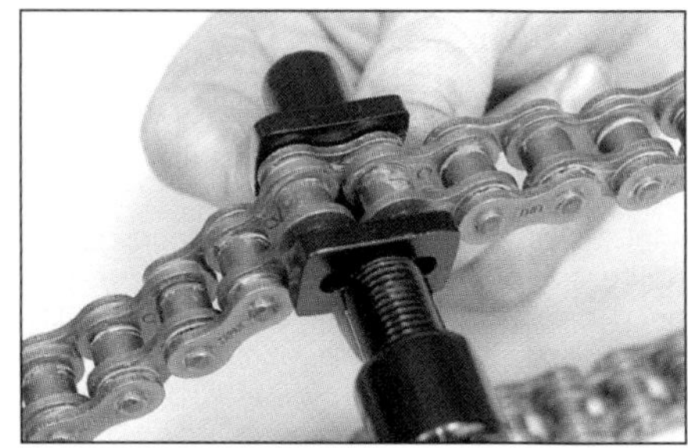

8.7 Push the sideplate into position using a clamp

8.8 Assemble the chain riveting tool over one pin at a time and tighten it fully

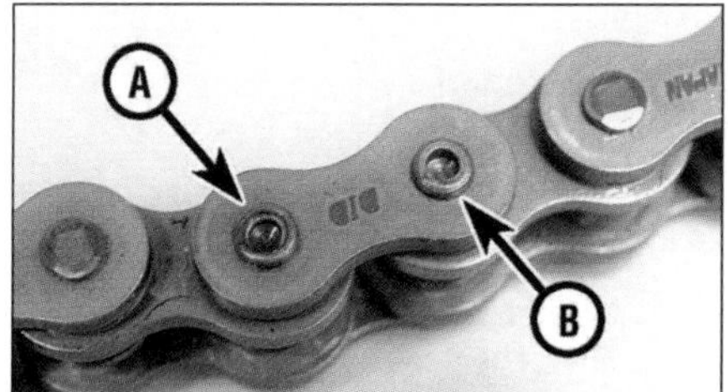

8.9 Pin end correctly riveted (A), pin end unriveted (B)

the rivet ends and two pieces of the wood between a C-clamp. Operate the clamp to press the sideplate over the pins.

● Assemble the joining tool over one pin (following the manufacturer's instructions) and tighten the tool down to spread the pin end securely **(see illustrations 8.8 and 8.9)**. Do the same on the other pin.

Warning: Check that the pin ends are secure and that there is no danger of the sideplate coming loose. If the pin ends are cracked the soft link must be replaced.

Final drive chain sizing

● Chains are sized using a three digit number, followed by a suffix to denote the chain type **(see illustration 8.10)**. Chain type is either standard or heavy duty (thicker sideplates), and also unsealed or O-ring/X-ring type.

● The first digit of the number relates to the pitch of the chain, ie the distance from the center of one pin to the center of the next pin **(see illustration 8.11)**. Pitch is expressed in eighths of an inch, as follows:

8.10 Typical chain size and type marking

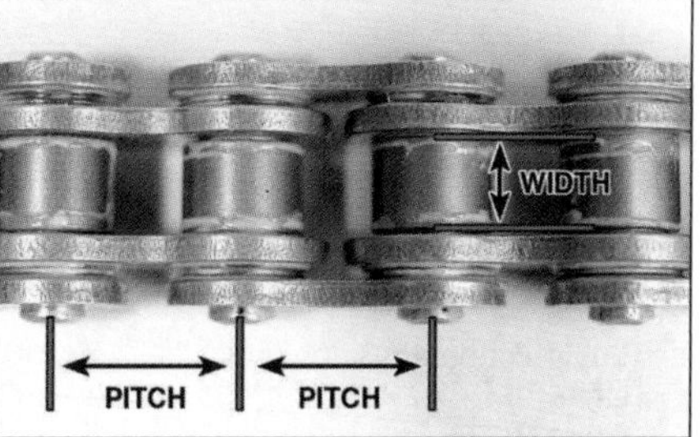

8.11 Chain dimensions

Sizes commencing with a 4 (for example 428) have a pitch of 1/2 inch (12.7 mm)

Sizes commencing with a 5 (for example 520) have a pitch of 5/8 inch (15.9 mm)

Sizes commencing with a 6 (for example 630) have a pitch of 3/4 inch (19.1 mm)

● The second and third digits of the chain size relate to the width of the rollers, for example the 525 shown has 5/16 inch (7.94 mm) rollers **(see illustration 8.11)**.

9 Hoses

Clamping to prevent flow

● Small-bore flexible hoses can be clamped to prevent fluid flow while a component is worked on. Whichever method is used, ensure that the hose material is not permanently distorted or damaged by the clamp.

a) A brake hose clamp available from auto parts stores **(see illustration 9.1)**.

b) A wingnut type hose clamp **(see illustration 9.2)**.

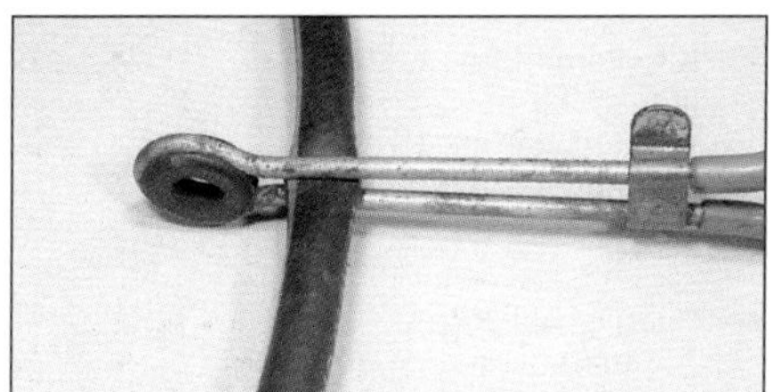

9.1 Hoses can be clamped with an automotive brake hose clamp . . .

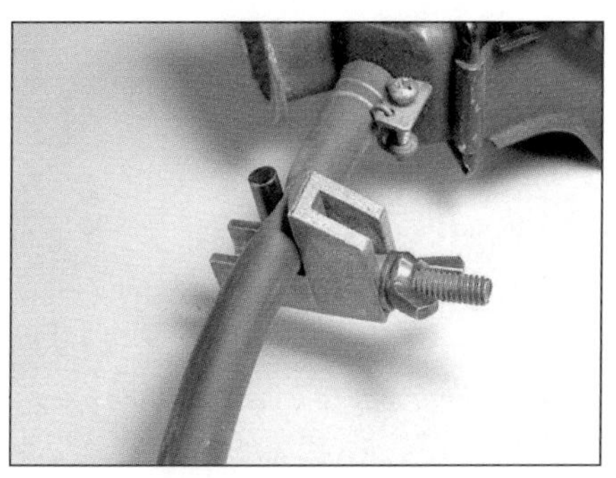

9.2 . . . a wingnut type hose clamp . . .

c) Two sockets placed on each side of the hose and held with straight-jawed self-locking pliers **(see illustration 9.3)**.

d) Thick card stock on each side of the hose held between straight-jawed self-locking pliers **(see illustration 9.4)**.

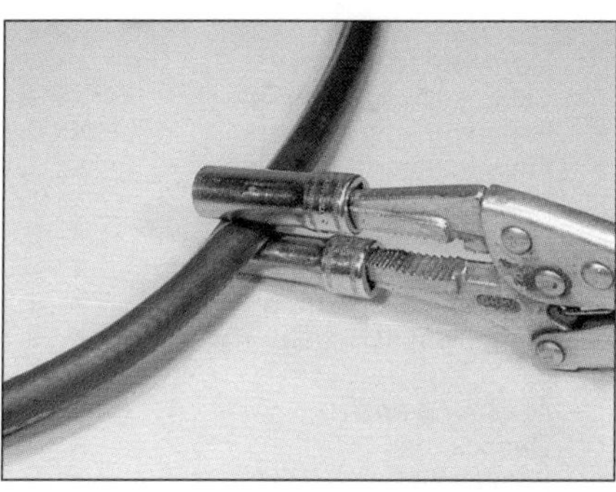

9.3 . . . two sockets and a pair of self-locking grips . . .

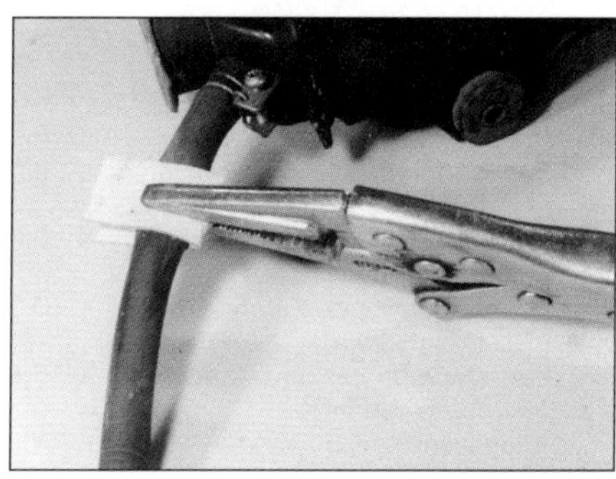

9.4 . . . or thick card and self-locking grips

Freeing and fitting hoses

● Always make sure the hose clamp is moved well clear of the hose end. Grip the hose with your hand and rotate it while pulling it off the union. If the hose has hardened due to age and will not move, slit it with a sharp knife and peel its ends off the union **(see illustration 9.5)**.

● Resist the temptation to use grease or soap on the unions to aid installation; although it helps the hose slip over the union it will equally aid the escape of fluid from the joint. It is preferable to soften the hose ends in hot water and wet the inside surface of the hose with water or a fluid which will evaporate.

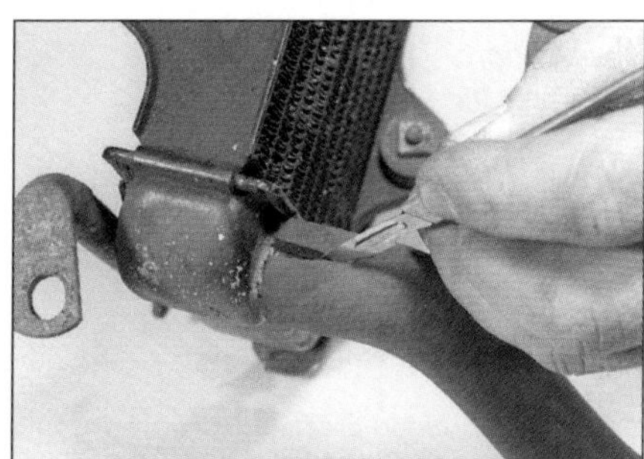

9.5 Cutting a coolant hose free with a sharp knife

Conversion Factors

Length (distance)					
Inches (in)	X 25.4	= Millimeters (mm)	X 0.0394	= Inches (in)
Feet (ft)	X 0.305	= Meters (m)	X 3.281	= Feet (ft)
Miles	X 1.609	= Kilometers (km)	X 0.621	= Miles
Volume (capacity)				
Cubic inches (cu in; in^3)	X 16.387	= Cubic centimeters (cc; cm^3)	X 0.061	= Cubic inches (cu in; in^3)
Imperial pints (Imp pt)	X 0.568	= Liters (l)	X 1.76	= Imperial pints (Imp pt)
Imperial quarts (Imp qt)	X 1.137	= Liters (l)	X 0.88	= Imperial quarts (Imp qt)
Imperial quarts (Imp qt)	X 1.201	= US quarts (US qt)	X 0.833	= Imperial quarts (Imp qt)
US quarts (US qt)	X 0.946	= Liters (l)	X 1.057	= US quarts (US qt)
Imperial gallons (Imp gal)	X 4.546	= Liters (l)	X 0.22	= Imperial gallons (Imp gal)
Imperial gallons (Imp gal)	X 1.201	= US gallons (US gal)	X 0.833	= Imperial gallons (Imp gal)
US gallons (US gal)	X 3.785	= Liters (l)	X 0.264	= US gallons (US gal)
Mass (weight)				
Ounces (oz)	X 28.35	= Grams (g)	X 0.035	= Ounces (oz)
Pounds (lb)	X 0.454	= Kilograms (kg)	X 2.205	= Pounds (lb)
Force				
Ounces-force (ozf; oz)	X 0.278	= Newtons (N)	X 3.6	= Ounces-force (ozf; oz)
Pounds-force (lbf; lb)	X 4.448	= Newtons (N)	X 0.225	= Pounds-force (lbf; lb)
Newtons (N)	X 0.1	= Kilograms-force (kgf; kg)	X 9.81	= Newtons (N)
Pressure				
Pounds-force per square inch (psi; lbf/in^2; lb/in^2)	X 0.070	= Kilograms-force per square centimeter (kgf/cm^2; kg/cm^2)	X 14.223	= Pounds-force per square inch (psi; lbf/in^2; lb/in^2)
Pounds-force per square inch (psi; lbf/in^2; lb/in^2)	X 0.068	= Atmospheres (atm)	X 14.696	= Pounds-force per square inch (psi; lbf/in^2; lb/in^2)
Pounds-force per square inch (psi; lbf/in^2; lb/in^2)	X 0.069	= Bars	X 14.5	= Pounds-force per square inch (psi; lbf/in^2; lb/in^2)
Pounds-force per square inch (psi; lbf/in^2; lb/in^2)	X 6.895	= Kilopascals (kPa)	X 0.145	= Pounds-force per square inch (psi; lbf/in^2; lb/in^2)
Kilopascals (kPa)	X 0.01	= Kilograms-force per square centimeter (kgf/cm^2; kg/cm^2)	X 98.1	= Kilopascals (kPa)
Torque (moment of force)				
Pounds-force inches (lbf in; lb in)	X 1.152	= Kilograms-force centimeter (kgf cm; kg cm)	X 0.868	= Pounds-force inches (lbf in; lb in)
Pounds-force inches (lbf in; lb in)	X 0.113	= Newton meters (Nm)	X 8.85	= Pounds-force inches (lbf in; lb in)
Pounds-force inches (lbf in; lb in)	X 0.083	= Pounds-force feet (lbf ft; lb ft)	X 12	= Pounds-force inches (lbf in; lb in)
Pounds-force feet (lbf ft; lb ft)	X 0.138	= Kilograms-force meters (kgf m; kg m)	X 7.233	= Pounds-force feet (lbf ft; lb ft)
Pounds-force feet (lbf ft; lb ft)	X 1.356	= Newton meters (Nm)	X 0.738	= Pounds-force feet (lbf ft; lb ft)
Newton meters (Nm)	X 0.102	= Kilograms-force meters (kgf m; kg m)	X 9.804	= Newton meters (Nm)
Vacuum				
Inches mercury (in. Hg)	X 3.377	= Kilopascals (kPa)	X 0.2961	= Inches mercury
Inches mercury (in. Hg)	X 25.4	= Millimeters mercury (mm Hg)	X 0.0394	= Inches mercury
Power				
Horsepower (hp)	X 745.7	= Watts (W)	X 0.0013	= Horsepower (hp)
Velocity (speed)				
Miles per hour (miles/hr; mph)	X 1.609	= Kilometers per hour (km/hr; kph)	X 0.621	= Miles per hour (miles/hr; mph)
Fuel consumption*				
Miles per gallon, Imperial (mpg)	X 0.354	= Kilometers per liter (km/l)	X 2.825	= Miles per gallon, Imperial (mpg)
Miles per gallon, US (mpg)	X 0.425	= Kilometers per liter (km/l)	X 2.352	= Miles per gallon, US (mpg)

Temperature

Degrees Fahrenheit = (°C x 1.8) + 32

Degrees Celsius (Degrees Centigrade; °C) = (°F - 32) x 0.56

****It is common practice to convert from miles per gallon (mpg) to liters/100 kilometers (l/100km), where mpg (Imperial) x l/100 km = 282 and mpg (US) x l/100 km = 235***

A number of chemicals and lubricants are available for use in motorcycle maintenance and repair. They include a wide variety of products ranging from cleaning solvents and degreasers to lubricants and protective sprays for rubber, plastic and vinyl.

• **Contact point/spark plug cleaner** is a solvent used to clean oily film and dirt from points, grim from electrical connectors and oil deposits from spark plugs. It is oil free and leaves no residue. It can also be used to remove gum and varnish from carburetor jets and other orifices.

• **Carburetor cleaner** is similar to contact point/spark plug cleaner but it usually has a stronger solvent and may leave a slight oily residue. It is not recommended for cleaning electrical components or connections.

• **Brake system cleaner** is used to remove brake dust, grease and brake fluid from the brake system, where clean surfaces are absolutely necessary. It leaves no residue and often eliminates brake squeal caused by contaminants.

• **Silicone-based lubricants** are used to protect rubber parts such as hoses and grommets, and are used as lubricants for hinges and locks.

• **Multi-purpose grease** is an all purpose lubricant used wherever grease is more practical than a liquid lubricant such as oil. Some multi-purpose grease is colored white and specially formulated to be more resistant to water than ordinary grease.

• **Gear oil** (sometimes called gear lube) is a specially designed oil used in transmissions and final drive units, as well as other areas where high friction, high temperature lubrication is required. It is available in a number of viscosities (weights) for various applications.

• **Motor oil** is the lubricant formulated for use in engines. It normally contains a wide variety of additives to prevent corrosion and reduce foaming and wear. Motor oil comes in various weights (viscosity ratings) from 0 to 50. The recommended weight of the oil depends on the season, temperature and the demands on the engine. Light oil is used in cold climates and under light load conditions. Heavy oil is used in hot climates and where high loads are encountered. Multi-viscosity oils are designed to have characteristics of both light and heavy oils and are available in a number of weights from 0W-20 to 20W-50.

• **Gasoline additives** perform several functions, depending on their chemical makeup. They usually contain solvents that help dissolve gum and varnish that build up on carburetor and inlet parts. They also serve to break down carbon deposits that form on the inside surfaces of the combustion chambers. Some additives contain upper cylinder lubricants for valves and piston rings.

• **Brake and clutch fluid** is a specially formulated hydraulic fluid that can withstand the heat and pressure encountered in break/clutch systems. Care must be taken that this fluid does not come in contact with painted surfaces or plastics. An opened container should always be resealed to prevent contamination by water or dirt.

• **Chain lubricants** are formulated especially for use on motorcycle final drive chains. A good chain lube should adhere well and have good penetrating qualities to be effective as a lubricant inside the chain and on the side plates, pins and rollers. Most chain lubes are either the foaming type or quick drying type and are usually marketed as sprays. Take care to use a lubricant marked as being suitable for O-ring chains.

• **Degreasers** are heavy duty solvents used to remove grease and grime that may accumulate on the engine and frame components. They can be sprayed or brushed on and, depending on the type, are rinsed with either water or solvent.

• **Solvents** are used alone or in combination with degreasers to clean parts and assemblies during repair and overhaul. The home mechanic should use only solvents that are non-flammable and that do not produce irritating fumes.

• **Gasket sealing compounds** may be used in conjunction with gaskets, to improve their sealing capabilities, or alone, to seal metal-to-metal joints. Many gasket sealers can withstand extreme heat, some are impervious to gasoline and lubricants, while others are capable of filling and sealing large cavities. Depending on the intended use, gasket sealers either dry hard or stay relatively soft and pliable. They are usually applied by hand, with a brush or are sprayed on the gasket sealing surfaces.

• **Thread locking compound** is an adhesive locking compound that prevents threaded fasteners from loosening because of vibration. It is available in a variety of types for different applications.

• **Moisture dispersants** are usually sprays that can be used to dry out electrical components such as the fuse block and wiring connectors. Some types an also be used as treatment for rubber and as a lubricant for hinges, cables and locks.

• **Waxes and polishes** are used to help protect painted and plated surfaces from the weather. Different types of pain may require the use of different types of wax polish. Some polishes utilize a chemical or abrasive cleaner to help remove the top layer of oxidized (dull) paint on older vehicles. In recent years, many non-wax polishes (that contain a wide variety of chemicals such as polymers and silicones) have been introduced. These non-wax polishes are usually easier to apply and last longer than conventional waxes and polishes.

Preparing for storage

Before you start

If repairs or an overhaul is needed, see that this is carried out now rather than left until you want to ride the bike again.

Give the bike a good wash and scrub all dirt from its underside. Make sure the bike dries completely before preparing for storage.

Engine

- Remove the spark plug(s) and lubricate the cylinder bores with approximately a teaspoon of motor oil using a spout-type oil can **(see illustration 1)**. Reinstall the spark plug(s). Crank the engine over a couple of times to coat the piston rings and bores with oil. If the bike has a kickstart, use this to turn the engine over. If not, flick the kill switch to the OFF position and crank the engine over on the starter **(see illustration 2)**. If the nature of the ignition system prevents the starter operating with the kill switch in the OFF position, remove the spark plugs and fit them back in their caps; ensure that the plugs are grounded against the cylinder head when the starter is operated **(see illustration 3)**.

Warning: It is important that the plugs are grounded away from the spark plug holes otherwise there is a risk of atomized fuel from the cylinders igniting.

On a single cylinder four-stroke engine, you can seal the combustion chamber completely by positioning the piston at TDC on the compression stroke.

- Drain the carburetor(s) otherwise there is a risk of jets becoming blocked by gum deposits from the fuel **(see illustration 4)**.

- If the bike is going into long-term storage, consider adding a fuel stabilizer to the fuel in the tank. If the tank is drained completely, corrosion of its internal surfaces may occur if left unprotected for a long period. The tank can be treated with a rust preventative especially for this purpose. Alternatively, remove the tank and pour half a liter of motor oil into it, install the filler cap and shake the tank to coat its internals with oil before draining off the excess. The same effect can also be achieved by spraying WD40 or a similar water-dispersant around the inside of the tank via its flexible nozzle.

- Make sure the cooling system contains the correct mix of antifreeze. Antifreeze also contains important corrosion inhibitors.

- The air intakes and exhaust can be sealed off by covering or plugging the openings. Ensure that you do not seal in any condensation; run the engine until it is hot, then switch off and allow to cool. Tape a

Squirt a drop of motor oil into each cylinder

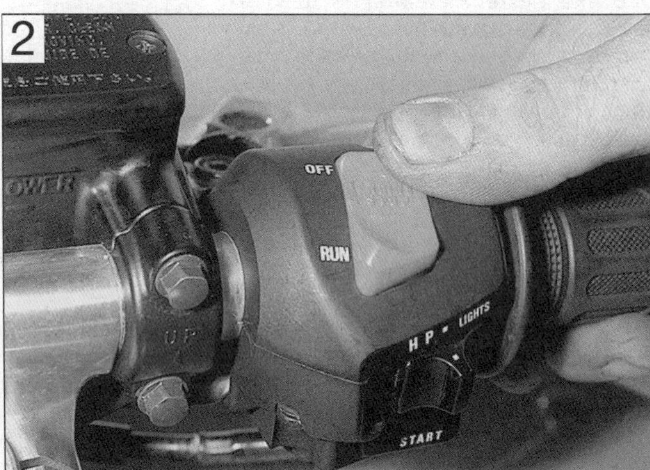

Flick the kill switch to OFF . . .

. . . and ensure that the metal bodies of the plugs (arrows) are grounded against the cylinder head

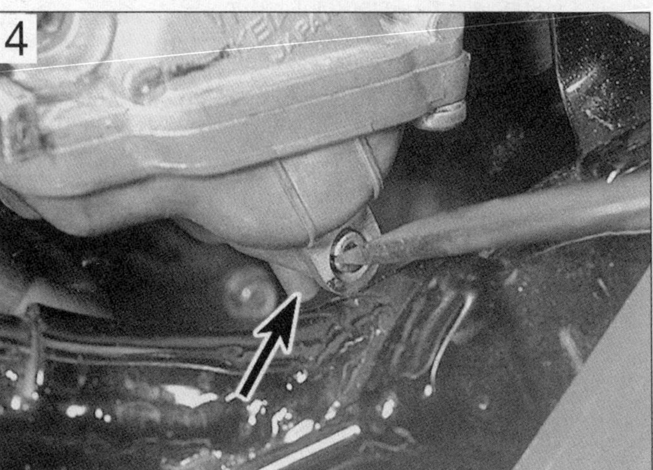

Connect a hose to the carburetor float chamber drain stub (arrow) and unscrew the drain screw

Exhausts can be sealed off with a plastic bag

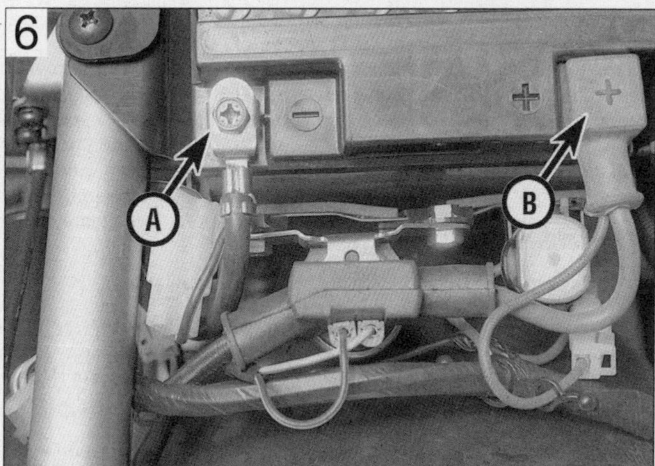

Disconnect the negative lead (A) first, followed by the positive lead (B)

piece of thick plastic over the silencer end(s) **(see illustration 5)**. Note that some advocate pouring a tablespoon of motor oil into the silencer(s) before sealing them off.

Battery

- Remove it from the bike - in extreme cases of cold the battery may freeze and crack its case **(see illustration 6)**.
- Check the electrolyte level and top up if necessary (conventional refillable batteries). Clean the terminals.
- Store the battery off the motorcycle and away from any sources of fire. Position a wooden block under the battery if it is to sit on the ground.
- Give the battery a trickle charge for a few hours every month **(see illustration 7)**.

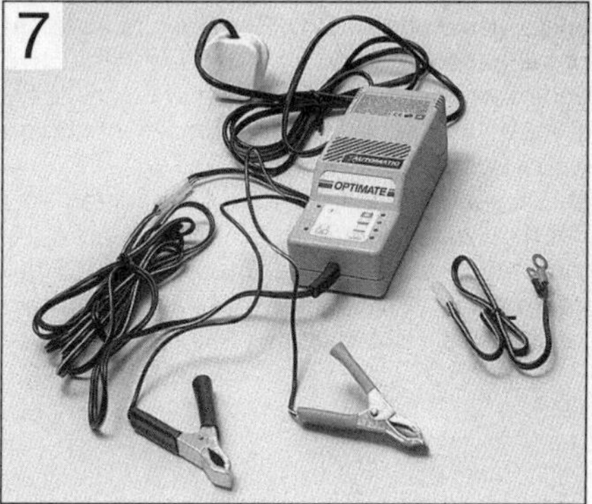

Use a suitable battery charger - this kit also assesses battery condition

Tires

- Place the bike on its centerstand or an auxiliary stand which will support the motorcycle in an upright position. Position wood blocks under the tires to keep them off the ground and to provide insulation from damp. If the bike is being put into long-term storage, ideally both tires should be off the ground; not only will this protect the tires, but will also ensure that no load is placed on the steering head or wheel bearings.
- Deflate each tire by 5 to 10 psi, no more or the beads may unseat from the rim, making subsequent inflation difficult on tubeless tires.

Pivots and controls

- Lubricate all lever, pedal, stand and footrest pivot points. If grease nipples are fitted to the rear suspension components, apply lubricant to the pivots.
- Lubricate all control cables.

Cycle components

- Apply a wax protectant to all painted and plastic components. Wipe off any excess, but don't polish to a shine. Where fitted, clean the screen with soap and water.
- Coat metal parts with Vaseline (petroleum jelly). When applying this to the fork tubes, do not compress the forks otherwise the seals will rot from contact with the Vaseline.
- Apply a vinyl cleaner to the seat.

Storage conditions

- Aim to store the bike in a shed or garage which does not leak and is free from damp.
- Drape an old blanket or bedspread over the bike to protect it from dust and direct contact with sunlight (which will fade paint). Beware of tight-fitting plastic covers which may allow condensation to form and settle on the bike.

Getting back on the road

Engine and transmission

- Change the oil and replace the oil filter. If this was done prior to storage, check that the oil hasn't emulsified - a thick whitish substance which occurs through condensation.
- Remove the spark plugs. Using a spout-type oil can, squirt a few drops of oil into the cylinder(s). This will provide initial lubrication as the piston rings and bores comes back into contact. Service the spark plugs, or buy new ones, and install them in the engine.
- Check that the clutch isn't stuck on. The plates can stick together if left standing for some time, preventing clutch operation. Engage a gear and try rocking the bike back and forth with the clutch lever held against the handlebar. If this doesn't work on cable-operated clutches, hold the clutch lever back against the handlebar with a strong rubber band or cable tie for a couple of hours **(see illustration 8)**.
- If the air intakes or silencer end(s) were blocked off, remove the plug or cover used.
- If the fuel tank was coated with a rust

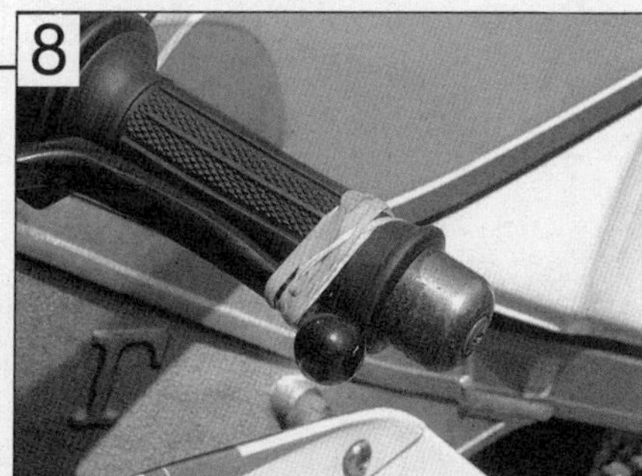
Hold the clutch lever back against the handlebar with rubber bands or a cable tie

preventative, oil or a stabilizer added to the fuel, drain and flush the tank and dispose of the fuel sensibly. If no action was taken with the fuel tank prior to storage, it is advised that the old fuel is disposed of since it will go bad over a period of time. Refill the fuel tank with fresh fuel.

Frame and running gear

- Oil all pivot points and cables.
- Check the tire pressures. They will definitely need inflating if pressures were reduced for storage.
- Lubricate the final drive chain (where applicable).
- Remove any protective coating applied to the fork tubes (stanchions) since this may well destroy the fork seals. If the fork tubes weren't protected and have picked up rust spots, remove them with very fine abrasive paper and refinish with metal polish.
- Check that both brakes operate correctly. Apply each brake hard and check that it's not possible to move the motorcycle forwards, then check that the brake frees off again once released. Brake caliper pistons can stick due to corrosion around the piston head, or on the sliding caliper types, due to corrosion of the slider pins. If the brake doesn't free after repeated operation, take the caliper off for examination. Similarly drum brakes can stick due to a seized operating cam, cable or rod linkage.
- If the motorcycle has been in long-term storage, replace the brake fluid and clutch fluid (where applicable).
- Depending on where the bike has been stored, the wiring, cables and hoses may have been nibbled by rodents. Make a visual check and investigate disturbed wiring loom tape.

Battery

- If the battery has been previously removed and given top up charges it can simply be reconnected. Remember to connect the positive cable first and the negative cable last.
- On conventional refillable batteries, if the battery has not received any attention, remove it from the motorcycle and check its electrolyte level. Top up if necessary then charge the battery. If the battery fails to hold a charge and a visual check show heavy white sulfation of the plates, the battery is probably defective and must be replaced. This is particularly likely if the battery is old. Confirm battery condition with a specific gravity check.
- On sealed (MF) batteries, if the battery has not received any attention, remove it from the motorcycle and charge it according to the information on the battery case - if the battery fails to hold a charge it must be replaced.

Starting procedure

- If a kickstart is fitted, turn the engine over a couple of times with the ignition OFF to distribute oil around the engine. If no kickstart is fitted, flick the engine kill switch OFF and the ignition ON and crank the engine over a couple of times to work oil around the upper cylinder components. If the nature of the ignition system is such that the starter won't work with the kill switch OFF, remove the spark plugs, fit them back into their caps and ground their bodies on the cylinder head. Reinstall the spark plugs afterwards.
- Switch the kill switch to RUN, operate the choke and start the engine. If the engine won't start don't continue cranking the engine - not only will this flatten the battery, but the starter motor will overheat. Switch the ignition off and try again later. If the engine refuses to start, go through the troubleshooting procedures in this manual. **Note:** *If the bike has been in storage for a long time, old fuel or a carburetor blockage may be the problem. Gum deposits in carburetors can block jets - if a carburetor cleaner doesn't prove successful the carburetors must be dismantled for cleaning.*
- Once the engine has started, check that the lights, turn signals and horn work properly.
- Treat the bike gently for the first ride and check all fluid levels on completion. Settle the bike back into the maintenance schedule.

This Section provides an easy reference-guide to the more common faults that are likely to afflict your machine. Obviously, the opportunities are almost limitless for faults to occur as a result of obscure failures, and to try and cover all eventualities would require a book. Indeed, a number have been written on the subject.

Successful troubleshooting is not a mysterious 'black art' but the application of a bit of knowledge combined with a systematic and logical approach to the problem. Approach any troubleshooting by first accurately identifying the symptom and then checking through the list of possible causes, starting with the simplest or most obvious and progressing in stages to the most complex. Take nothing for granted, but above all apply liberal quantities of common sense.

The main symptom of a fault is given in the text as a major heading below which are listed the various systems or areas which may contain the fault. Details of each possible cause for a fault and the remedial action to be taken are given. Further information should be sought in the relevant Chapter.

1 Engine doesn't start or is difficult to start

Starter motor doesn't rotate

- ☐ Engine kill switch OFF.
- ☐ Fuse blown. Check main fuse and starter circuit fuse (Chapter 9).
- ☐ Battery voltage low. Check and recharge battery (Chapter 9).
- ☐ Starter motor defective. Make sure the wiring to the starter is secure. Make sure the starter relay clicks when the start button is pushed. If the relay clicks, then the fault is in the wiring or motor.
- ☐ Starter relay faulty. Check it according to the procedure in Chapter 9.
- ☐ Starter switch not contacting. The contacts could be wet, corroded or dirty. Disassemble and clean the switch (Chapter 9).
- ☐ Wiring open or shorted. Check all wiring connections and harnesses to make sure that they are dry, tight and not corroded. Also check for broken or frayed wires that can cause a short to ground (see wiring diagram, Chapter 9).
- ☐ Ignition (main) switch defective. Check the switch according to the procedure in Chapter 9. Replace the switch with a new one if it is defective.
- ☐ Engine kill switch defective. Check for wet, dirty or corroded contacts. Clean or replace the switch as necessary (Chapter 9).
- ☐ Faulty neutral, side stand or clutch switch. Check the wiring to each switch and the switch itself according to the procedures in Chapter 9.

Starter motor rotates but engine does not turn over

- ☐ Starter motor clutch defective. Inspect and repair or replace (Chapter 2).
- ☐ Damaged idler or starter gears. Inspect and replace the damaged parts (Chapter 2).

Starter works but engine won't turn over (seized)

- ☐ Seized engine caused by one or more internally damaged components. Failure due to wear, abuse or lack of lubrication. Damage can include seized valves, followers/rocker arms, camshafts, pistons, crankshaft, connecting rod bearings, or transmission gears or bearings. Refer to Chapter 2 for engine disassembly.

No fuel flow

- ☐ No fuel in tank.
- ☐ Fuel tank breather hose obstructed.
- ☐ Fuel filter is blocked (see Chapter 1).

Engine flooded

- ☐ Starting technique incorrect. Under normal circumstances the machine should start with little or no throttle. When the engine is cold, the choke should be operated and the engine started without opening the throttle. When the engine is at operating temperature, only a very slight amount of throttle should be necessary.

No spark or weak spark

- ☐ Ignition switch OFF.
- ☐ Engine kill switch turned to the OFF position.
- ☐ Battery voltage low. Check and recharge the battery as necessary (Chapter 9).
- ☐ Spark plugs dirty, defective or worn out. Locate reason for fouled plugs using spark plug condition chart and follow the plug maintenance procedures (Chapter 1).
- ☐ Spark plug caps or secondary (HT) wiring faulty. Check condition. Replace either or both components if cracks or deterioration are evident (Chapter 5).
- ☐ Spark plug caps not making good contact. Make sure that the plug caps fit snugly over the plug ends.
- ☐ Ignition HT coils defective. Check the coils, referring to Chapter 5.
- ☐ IC igniter unit defective. Refer to Chapter 5 for details.
- ☐ Pick-up coil defective. Check the unit, referring to Chapter 5 for details.
- ☐ Ignition or kill switch shorted. This is usually caused by water, corrosion, damage or excessive wear. The switches can be disassembled and cleaned with electrical contact cleaner. If cleaning does not help, replace the switches (Chapter 9).
- ☐ Wiring shorted or broken between:

  a) Ignition (main) switch and engine kill switch (or blown fuse)
  b) IC igniter unit and engine kill switch
  c) IC igniter unit and ignition HT coils
  d) Ignition HT coils and spark plugs
  e) IC igniter unit and ignition pick-up coil.

- ☐ Make sure that all wiring connections are clean, dry and tight. Look for chafed and broken wires (Chapters 5 and 9).

Compression low

- ☐ Spark plugs loose. Remove the plugs and inspect their threads. Reinstall and tighten to the specified torque (Chapter 1).
- ☐ Cylinder head not sufficiently tightened down. If the cylinder head is suspected of being loose, then there's a chance that the gasket or head is damaged if the problem has persisted for any length of time. The head bolts should be tightened to the proper torque in the correct sequence (Chapter 2).
- ☐ Improper valve clearance. This means that the valve is not closing completely and compression pressure is leaking past the valve. Check and adjust the valve clearances (Chapter 1).
- ☐ Cylinder and/or piston worn. Excessive wear will cause compression pressure to leak past the rings. This is usually accompanied by worn rings as well. A top-end overhaul is necessary (Chapter 2).
- ☐ Piston rings worn, weak, broken, or sticking. Broken or sticking piston rings usually indicate a lubrication or fuelling problem that causes excess carbon deposits or seizures to form on the pistons and rings. Top-end overhaul is necessary (Chapter 2).
- ☐ Piston ring-to-groove clearance excessive. This is caused by excessive wear of the piston ring lands. Piston replacement is necessary (Chapter 2).
- ☐ Cylinder head gasket damaged. If a head is allowed to become loose, or if excessive carbon build-up on the piston crown and combustion chamber causes extremely high compression, the head gasket may leak. Retorquing the head is not always sufficient to restore the seal, so gasket replacement is necessary (Chapter 2).
- ☐ Cylinder head warped. This is caused by overheating or improperly tightened head bolts. Machine shop resurfacing or head replacement is necessary (Chapter 2).
- ☐ Valve spring broken or weak. Caused by component failure or wear; the springs must be replaced (Chapter 2).
- ☐ Valve not seating properly. This is caused by a bent valve (from over-revving or improper valve adjustment), burned valve or seat (improper fuelling) or an accumulation of carbon deposits on the seat (from fuelling or lubrication problems). The valves must be cleaned and/or replaced and the seats serviced if possible (Chapter 2).

1 Engine doesn't start or is difficult to start (continued)

Stalls after starting

- ☐ Improper choke action (carbureted models). Make sure the choke linkage shaft is getting a full stroke and staying in the out position (Chapter 4).
- ☐ Ignition malfunction. See Chapter 5.
- ☐ Carburetor or fuel injection malfunction. See Chapter 4.
- ☐ Fuel contaminated. The fuel can be contaminated with either dirt or water, or can change chemically if the machine is allowed to sit for several months or more. Drain the tank (Chapter 4).
- ☐ Intake air leak. Check for loose intake manifold retaining clips and damaged/disconnected vacuum hoses (Chapter 4).
- ☐ Engine idle speed incorrect. Turn idle adjusting screw until the engine idles at the specified rpm (Chapter 1).

Rough idle

- ☐ Ignition malfunction. See Chapter 5.
- ☐ Idle speed incorrect. See Chapter 1.
- ☐ Carburetors not synchronized (twin carburetor models). Adjust them with vacuum gauge or manometer set as described in Chapter 4.
- ☐ Carburetor or fuel injection malfunction. See Chapter 4.
- ☐ Fuel contaminated. The fuel can be contaminated with either dirt or water, or can change chemically if the machine is allowed to sit for several months or more. Drain the tank (Chapter 4).
- ☐ Intake air leak. Check for loose intake manifold retaining clips and damaged/disconnected vacuum hoses. Replace the intake ducts if they are split or deteriorated (Chapter 4).
- ☐ Air filter clogged. Replace the air filter element (Chapter 1).

2 Poor running at low speeds

Spark weak

- ☐ Battery voltage low. Check and recharge battery (Chapter 9).
- ☐ Spark plugs fouled, defective or worn out. Refer to Chapter 1 for spark plug maintenance.
- ☐ Spark plug cap or HT wiring defective. Refer to Chapters 1 and 5 for details on the ignition system.
- ☐ Spark plug caps not making contact.
- ☐ Incorrect spark plugs. Wrong type, heat range or cap configuration. Check and install correct plugs listed in Chapter 1.
- ☐ IC igniter unit or ECM faulty. See Chapter 5.
- ☐ Pick-up coil defective. See Chapter 5.
- ☐ Ignition coils defective. See Chapter 5.

Fuel/air mixture incorrect

- ☐ Pilot screws incorrectly set (Chapter 4)
- ☐ Pilot jet or air passage blocked. Remove and overhaul the carburetors (Chapter 4).
- ☐ Air filter clogged, poorly sealed or missing (Chapter 1).
- ☐ Air filter housing poorly sealed. Look for cracks, holes or loose clamps and replace or repair defective parts.
- ☐ Fuel tank breather hose obstructed.
- ☐ Intake air leak. Check for loose intake manifold retaining clips and damaged/disconnected vacuum hoses. Replace the intake ducts if they are split or deteriorated (Chapter 4).

Compression low

- ☐ Spark plugs loose. Remove the plugs and inspect their threads. Reinstall and tighten to the specified torque (Chapter 1).
- ☐ Cylinder head not sufficiently tightened down. If the cylinder head is suspected of being loose, then there's a chance that the gasket and head are damaged if the problem has persisted for any length of time. The head bolts should be tightened to the proper torque in the correct sequence (Chapter 2).
- ☐ Improper valve clearance. This means that the valve is not closing completely and compression pressure is leaking past the valve. Check and adjust the valve clearances (Chapter 1).
- ☐ Cylinder and/or piston worn. Excessive wear will cause compression pressure to leak past the rings. This is usually accompanied by worn rings as well. A top-end overhaul is necessary (Chapter 2).
- ☐ Piston rings worn, weak, broken, or sticking. Broken or sticking piston rings usually indicate a lubrication or fuelling problem that causes excess carbon deposits or seizures to form on the pistons and rings. Top-end overhaul is necessary (Chapter 2).
- ☐ Piston ring-to-groove clearance excessive. This is caused by excessive wear of the piston ring lands. Piston replacement is necessary (Chapter 2).
- ☐ Cylinder head gasket damaged. If a head is allowed to become loose, or if excessive carbon build-up on the piston crown and combustion chamber causes extremely high compression, the head gasket may leak. Retorquing the head is not always sufficient to restore the seal, so gasket replacement is necessary (Chapter 2).
- ☐ Cylinder head warped. This is caused by overheating or improperly tightened head bolts. Machine shop resurfacing or head replacement is necessary (Chapter 2).
- ☐ Valve spring broken or weak. Caused by component failure or wear; the springs must be replaced (Chapter 2).
- ☐ Valve not seating properly. This is caused by a bent valve (from over-revving or improper valve adjustment), burned valve or seat (improper fuelling) or an accumulation of carbon deposits on the seat (from fuelling, lubrication problems). The valves must be cleaned and/or replaced and the seats serviced if possible (Chapter 2).

Poor acceleration

- ☐ Fuel system fault. Remove and overhaul the carburetors or check the fuel injection system (Chapter 4).
- ☐ Engine oil viscosity too high. Using a heavier oil than that recommended in Chapter 1 can damage the oil pump or lubrication system and cause drag on the engine.
- ☐ Brakes dragging. Usually caused by debris which has entered the brake piston seals, or from a warped disc or drum or bent axle. Repair as necessary (Chapter 7).

3 Poor running or no power at high speed

Firing incorrect

- ☐ Air filter restricted. Clean or replace filter (Chapter 1).
- ☐ Spark plugs fouled, defective or worn out. See Chapter 1 for spark plug maintenance.
- ☐ Spark plug caps or HT wiring defective. See Chapters 1 and 5 for details of the ignition system.
- ☐ Spark plug caps not in good contact. See Chapter 5.
- ☐ Incorrect spark plugs. Wrong type, heat range or cap configuration. Check and install correct plugs listed in Chapter 1.
- ☐ IC igniter unit or ECM defective. See Chapter 5.
- ☐ Pick-up coil defective. See Chapter 5.
- ☐ Ignition coils defective. See Chapter 5.

Fuel/air mixture incorrect

- ☐ Fuel system fault. Remove and overhaul the carburetors or check the fuel injection system (Chapter 4).
- ☐ Air filter clogged, poorly sealed, or missing (Chapter 1).
- ☐ Air filter housing poorly sealed. Look for cracks, holes or loose clamps, and replace or repair defective parts.
- ☐ Fuel tank breather hose obstructed.
- ☐ Intake air leak. Check for loose intake manifold retaining clips and damaged/disconnected vacuum hoses. Replace the intake ducts if they are split or deteriorated (Chapter 4).

Compression low

- ☐ Spark plugs loose. Remove the plugs and inspect their threads. Reinstall and tighten to the specified torque (Chapter 1).
- ☐ Cylinder head not sufficiently tightened down. If the cylinder head is suspected of being loose, then there's a chance that the gasket and head are damaged if the problem has persisted for any length of time. The head bolts should be tightened to the proper torque in the correct sequence (Chapter 2).
- ☐ Improper valve clearance. This means that the valve is not closing completely and compression pressure is leaking past the valve. Check and adjust the valve clearances (Chapter 1).
- ☐ Cylinder and/or piston worn. Excessive wear will cause compression pressure to leak past the rings. This is usually accompanied by worn rings as well. A top-end overhaul is necessary (Chapter 2).
- ☐ Piston rings worn, weak, broken, or sticking. Broken or sticking piston rings usually indicate a lubrication or fueling problem that causes excess carbon deposits or seizures to form on the pistons and rings. Top-end overhaul is necessary (Chapter 2).
- ☐ Piston ring-to-groove clearance excessive. This is caused by excessive wear of the piston ring lands. Piston replacement is necessary (Chapter 2).
- ☐ Cylinder head gasket damaged. If a head is allowed to become loose, or if excessive carbon build-up on the piston crown and combustion chamber causes extremely high compression, the head gasket may leak. Retorquing the head is not always sufficient to restore the seal, so gasket replacement is necessary (Chapter 2).
- ☐ Cylinder head warped. This is caused by overheating or improperly tightened head bolts. Machine shop resurfacing or head replacement is necessary (Chapter 2).
- ☐ Valve spring broken or weak. Caused by component failure or wear; the springs must be replaced (Chapter 2).
- ☐ Valve not seating properly. This is caused by a bent valve (from over-revving or improper valve adjustment), burned valve or seat (improper fuelling) or an accumulation of carbon deposits on the seat (from fuelling or lubrication problems). The valves must be cleaned and/or replaced and the seats serviced if possible (Chapter 2).

Knocking or pinging

- ☐ Carbon build-up in combustion chamber. Use of a fuel additive that will dissolve the adhesive bonding the carbon particles to the crown and chamber is the easiest way to remove the build-up. Otherwise, the cylinder head will have to be removed and decarbonized (Chapter 2).
- ☐ Incorrect or poor quality fuel. Old or improper grades of fuel can cause detonation. This causes the piston to rattle, thus the knocking or pinging sound. Drain old fuel and always use the recommended fuel grade.
- ☐ Spark plug heat range incorrect. Uncontrolled detonation indicates the plug heat range is too hot. The plug in effect becomes a glow plug, raising cylinder temperatures. Install the proper heat range plug (Chapter 1).
- ☐ Improper air/fuel mixture. This will cause the cylinders to run hot, which leads to detonation. An intake air leak can cause this imbalance. See Chapter 4.

Miscellaneous causes

- ☐ Throttle valve doesn't open fully. Adjust the throttle grip freeplay (Chapter 1).
- ☐ Clutch slipping. May be caused by loose or worn clutch components. Refer to Chapter 2 for clutch overhaul procedures.
- ☐ Engine oil viscosity too high. Using a heavier oil than the one recommended in Chapter 1 can damage the oil pump or lubrication system and cause drag on the engine.
- ☐ Brakes dragging. Usually caused by debris which has entered the brake piston seals, or from a warped disc, out-of-round drum or bent axle. Repair as necessary.

4 Overheating

Engine overheats

- ☐ Coolant level low. Check and add coolant (Chapter 1).
- ☐ Leak in cooling system. Check cooling system hoses and radiator for leaks and other damage. Repair or replace parts as necessary (Chapter 3).
- ☐ Thermostat sticking open or closed. Check and replace as described in Chapter 3.
- ☐ Faulty pressure cap. Remove the cap and have it pressure tested (Chapter 3).
- ☐ Coolant passages clogged. Have the entire system drained and flushed, then refill with fresh coolant.
- ☐ Water pump defective. Remove the pump and check the components (Chapter 3).
- ☐ Clogged radiator fins. Clean them by blowing compressed air through the fins from the backside.
- ☐ Cooling fan or fan switch fault (Chapter 3).

Firing incorrect

- ☐ Spark plugs fouled, defective or worn out. See Chapter 1 for spark plug maintenance.
- ☐ Incorrect spark plugs.
- ☐ IC igniter unit or ECM defective. See Chapter 5.
- ☐ Pick-up coil faulty. See Chapter 5.
- ☐ Faulty ignition coils. See Chapter 5.

Fuel/air mixture incorrect

- ☐ Fuel system fault. Remove and overhaul the carburetors or check the fuel injection system (Chapter 4).
- ☐ Air filter clogged, poorly sealed, or missing (Chapter 1).
- ☐ Air filter housing poorly sealed. Look for cracks, holes or loose clamps, and replace or repair defective parts.
- ☐ Fuel tank breather hose obstructed.
- ☐ Intake air leak. Check for loose intake manifold retaining clips and damaged/disconnected vacuum hoses. Replace the intake manifold(s) if they are split or deteriorated (Chapter 4).

Compression too high

- ☐ Carbon build-up in combustion chamber. Use of a fuel additive that will dissolve the adhesive bonding the carbon particles to the piston crown and chamber is the easiest way to remove the build-up. Otherwise, the cylinder head will have to be removed and decarbonized (Chapter 2).
- ☐ Improperly machined head surface or installation of incorrect gasket during engine assembly.

Engine load excessive

- ☐ Clutch slipping. Can be caused by damaged, loose or worn clutch components. Refer to Chapter 2 for overhaul procedures.
- ☐ Engine oil level too high. The addition of too much oil will cause pressurization of the crankcase and inefficient engine operation. Check Specifications and drain to proper level (Chapter 1).
- ☐ Engine oil viscosity too high. Using a heavier oil than the one recommended in Chapter 1 can damage the oil pump or lubrication system as well as cause drag on the engine.
- ☐ Brakes dragging. Usually caused by debris which has entered the brake piston seals, or from a warped disc or drum or bent axle. Repair as necessary.

Lubrication inadequate

- ☐ Engine oil level too low. Friction caused by intermittent lack of lubrication or from oil that is overworked can cause overheating. The oil provides a definite cooling function in the engine. Check the oil level (Chapter 1).
- ☐ Poor quality engine oil or incorrect viscosity or type. Oil is rated not only according to viscosity but also according to type. Some oils are not rated high enough for use in this engine. Check the Specifications section and change to the correct oil (Chapter 1).

Miscellaneous causes

- ☐ Modification to exhaust system. Most aftermarket exhaust systems cause the engine to run leaner, which makes it run hotter.

5 Clutch problems

Clutch slipping

- ☐ Clutch cable freeplay incorrectly adjusted (cable clutch models) (Chapter 1).
- ☐ Friction plates worn or warped. Overhaul the clutch assembly (Chapter 2).
- ☐ Plain plates warped (Chapter 2).
- ☐ Clutch springs broken or weak. Old or heat-damaged (from slipping clutch) springs should be replaced with new ones (Chapter 2).
- ☐ Clutch pushrod bent. Check and, if necessary, replace (Chapter 2).
- ☐ Clutch center or housing unevenly worn. This causes improper engagement of the plates. Replace the damaged or worn parts (Chapter 2).
- ☐ Wrong type of oil used. Make sure oil with anti-friction additives (such as molybdenum disulfide) is *NOT* used in an engine/transmission with a wet clutch.

Clutch not disengaging completely

- ☐ Clutch cable freeplay incorrectly adjusted (Chapter 1).
- ☐ Air in clutch hydraulic system (hydraulic clutch models). Bleed the system (Chapter 2).
- ☐ Worn master or slave cylinder (hydraulic clutch models). Inspect and repair or replace as necessary (Chapter 2).
- ☐ Clutch plates warped or damaged. This will cause clutch drag, which in turn will cause the machine to creep. Overhaul the clutch assembly (Chapter 2).
- ☐ Clutch spring tension uneven. Usually caused by a sagged or broken spring. Check and replace the springs as a set (Chapter 2).
- ☐ Engine oil deteriorated. Old, thin, worn out oil will not provide proper lubrication for the plates, causing the clutch to drag. Replace the oil and filter (Chapter 1).
- ☐ Engine oil viscosity too high. Using a heavier oil than recommended in Chapter 1 can cause the plates to stick together, putting a drag on the engine. Change to the correct weight oil (Chapter 1).
- ☐ Clutch housing bearing seized. Lack of lubrication, severe wear or damage can cause the bearing to seize on the input shaft. Overhaul of the clutch, and perhaps transmission, may be necessary to repair the damage (Chapter 2).
- ☐ Loose clutch center nut. Causes housing and center misalignment putting a drag on the engine. Engagement adjustment continually varies. Overhaul the clutch assembly (Chapter 2).

6 Gearchanging problems

Doesn't go into gear or lever doesn't return

- ☐ Clutch not disengaging. See Section 5.
- ☐ Shift fork(s) bent or seized. Often caused by dropping the machine or from lack of lubrication. Overhaul the transmission (Chapter 2).
- ☐ Gear(s) stuck on shaft. Most often caused by a lack of lubrication or excessive wear in transmission bearings and bushings. Overhaul the transmission (Chapter 2).
- ☐ Gear shift drum binding. Caused by lubrication failure or excessive wear. Replace the drum and bearing (Chapter 2).
- ☐ Gear shift lever pawl spring weak or broken (Chapter 2).
- ☐ Gear shift lever broken. Splines stripped out of lever or shaft, caused by allowing the lever to get loose or from dropping the machine. Replace necessary parts (Chapter 2).
- ☐ Gear shift mechanism stopper arm broken or worn. Full engagement and rotary movement of shift drum results. Replace the arm (Chapter 2).
- ☐ Stopper arm spring broken. Allows arm to float, causing sporadic shift operation. Replace spring (Chapter 2).

Jumps out of gear

- ☐ Shift fork(s) worn. Overhaul the transmission (Chapter 2).
- ☐ Gear groove(s) worn. Overhaul the transmission (Chapter 2).
- ☐ Gear dogs or dog slots worn or damaged. The gears should be inspected and replaced. No attempt should be made to service the worn parts.

Overselects

- ☐ Stopper arm spring weak or broken (Chapter 2).
- ☐ Return spring post broken or distorted (Chapter 2).

7 Abnormal engine noise

Knocking or pinging

- ☐ Carbon build-up in combustion chamber. Use of a fuel additive that will dissolve the adhesive bonding the carbon particles to the piston crown and chamber is the easiest way to remove the build-up. Otherwise, the cylinder head will have to be removed and decarbonized (Chapter 2).
- ☐ Incorrect or poor quality fuel. Old or improper fuel can cause detonation. This causes the pistons to rattle, thus the knocking or pinging sound. Drain the old fuel and always use the recommended grade fuel (Chapter 4).
- ☐ Spark plug heat range incorrect. Uncontrolled detonation indicates that the plug heat range is too hot. The plug in effect becomes a glow plug, raising cylinder temperatures. Install the proper heat range plug (Chapter 1).
- ☐ Improper air/fuel mixture. This will cause the cylinders to run hot and lead to detonation. Blocked carburetor jets or an air leak can cause this imbalance. See Chapter 4.

Piston slap or rattling

- ☐ Cylinder-to-piston clearance excessive. Caused by improper assembly. Inspect and overhaul top-end parts (Chapter 2).
- ☐ Connecting rod bent. Caused by over-revving, trying to start a badly flooded engine or from ingesting a foreign object into the combustion chamber. Replace the damaged parts (Chapter 2).
- ☐ Piston pin or piston pin bore worn or seized from wear or lack of lubrication. Replace damaged parts (Chapter 2).
- ☐ Piston ring(s) worn, broken or sticking. Overhaul the top-end (Chapter 2).
- ☐ Piston seizure damage. Usually from lack of lubrication or overheating. Replace the pistons and cylinders, as necessary (Chapter 2).
- ☐ Connecting rod bearing clearance excessive. Caused by excessive wear or lack of lubrication. Replace worn parts.

Valve noise

- ☐ Incorrect valve clearances. Adjust the clearances by referring to Chapter 1.
- ☐ Valve spring broken or weak. Check and replace weak valve springs (Chapter 2).
- ☐ Camshaft or cylinder head worn or damaged. Lack of lubrication at high rpm is usually the cause of damage. Insufficient oil or failure to change the oil at the recommended intervals are the chief causes. Since there are no replaceable bearings in the head, the head itself will have to be replaced if there is excessive wear or damage (Chapter 2).

Other noise

- ☐ Cylinder head gasket leaking.
- ☐ Exhaust pipe leaking at cylinder head connection. Caused by improper fit of pipe(s) or loose exhaust nuts. All exhaust fasteners should be tightened evenly and carefully. Failure to do this will lead to a leak.
- ☐ Crankshaft runout excessive. Caused by a bent crankshaft (from over-revving) or damage from an upper cylinder component failure. Can also be attributed to dropping the machine on either of the crankshaft ends.
- ☐ Engine mounting bolts loose. Tighten all engine mount bolts (Chapter 2).
- ☐ Crankshaft bearings worn (Chapter 2).
- ☐ Cam chain, tensioner or guides worn. Replace according to the procedure in Chapter 2.

8 Abnormal driveline noise

Clutch noise

- ☐ Clutch outer drum/friction plate clearance excessive (Chapter 2).
- ☐ Loose or damaged clutch pressure plate and/or bolts (Chapter 2).

Transmission noise

- ☐ Bearings worn. Also includes the possibility that the shafts are worn. Overhaul the transmission (Chapter 2).
- ☐ Gears worn or chipped (Chapter 2).
- ☐ Metal chips jammed in gear teeth. Probably pieces from a broken clutch, gear or shift mechanism that were picked up by the gears. This will cause early bearing failure (Chapter 2).
- ☐ Engine oil level too low. Causes a howl from transmission. Also affects engine power and clutch operation (Chapter 1).

Final drive noise

- ☐ Chain or drive belt not adjusted properly (Chapter 1).
- ☐ Front or rear sprocket loose. Tighten fasteners (Chapter 6).
- ☐ Sprockets worn. Replace sprockets (Chapter 6).
- ☐ Rear sprocket warped. Replace sprockets (Chapter 6).
- ☐ Differential worn or damaged. Have it repaired or replace it (Chapter 7).

9 Abnormal frame and suspension noise

Front end noise

- ☐ Low fluid level or improper viscosity oil in forks. This can sound like spurting and is usually accompanied by irregular fork action (Chapter 6).
- ☐ Spring weak or broken. Makes a clicking or scraping sound. Fork oil, when drained, will have a lot of metal particles in it (Chapter 6).
- ☐ Steering head bearings loose or damaged. Clicks when braking. Check and adjust or replace as necessary (Chapters 1 and 6).
- ☐ Triple clamps loose. Make sure all clamp bolts are tightened to the specified torque (Chapter 6).
- ☐ Fork tube bent. Good possibility if machine has been dropped. Replace tube with a new one (Chapter 6).
- ☐ Front axle bolt or axle pinch bolts loose. Tighten them to the specified torque (Chapter 7).
- ☐ Loose or worn wheel bearings. Check and replace as needed (Chapter 7).

Shock absorber noise

- ☐ Fluid level incorrect. Indicates a leak caused by defective seal. Shock will be covered with oil. Replace shock or seek advice on repair from a dealer (Chapter 6).
- ☐ Defective shock absorber with internal damage. This is in the body of the shock and can't be remedied. The shock must be replaced with a new one (Chapter 6).
- ☐ Bent or damaged shock body. Replace the shock with a new one (Chapter 6).
- ☐ Loose or worn suspension linkage components (EX250 models). Check and replace as necessary (Chapter 6).

Brake noise

- ☐ Squeal caused by dust on brake pads. Usually found in combination with glazed pads. Clean using brake cleaning solvent (Chapter 7).
- ☐ Contamination of brake pads. Oil, brake fluid or dirt causing brake to chatter or squeal. Clean or replace pads (Chapter 7).
- ☐ Pads glazed. Caused by excessive heat from prolonged use or from contamination. Do not use sandpaper/emery cloth or any other abrasive to roughen the pad surfaces as abrasives will stay in the pad material and damage the disc. A very fine flat file can be used, but pad replacement is suggested as a cure (Chapter 7).
- ☐ Disc warped. Can cause a chattering, clicking or intermittent squeal. Usually accompanied by a pulsating lever and uneven braking. Replace the disc (Chapter 7).
- ☐ Loose or worn wheel bearings. Check and replace as needed (Chapter 7).

10 Oil pressure warning light comes on

Engine lubrication system

- ☐ Engine oil pump defective, blocked oil strainer screen or failed relief valve. Carry out oil pressure check (Chapter 1).
- ☐ Engine oil level low. Inspect for leak or other problem causing low oil level and add recommended oil (Chapter 1).
- ☐ Engine oil viscosity too low. Very old, thin oil or an improper weight of oil used in the engine. Change to correct oil (Chapter 1).
- ☐ Camshaft or journals worn. Excessive wear causing drop in oil pressure. Replace cam and/or cylinder head. Abnormal wear could be caused by oil starvation at high rpm from low oil level or improper weight or type of oil (Chapter 1).
- ☐ Crankshaft and/or bearings worn. Same problems as above. Check and replace crankshaft and/or bearings (Chapter 2).

Electrical system

- ☐ Oil pressure switch defective. Check the switch according to the procedure in Chapter 9. Replace it if it is defective.
- ☐ Oil pressure indicator light circuit defective. Check for pinched, shorted, disconnected or damaged wiring (Chapter 9).

11 Excessive exhaust smoke

White smoke

- ☐ Piston oil ring worn. The ring may be broken or damaged, causing oil from the crankcase to be pulled past the piston into the combustion chamber. Replace the rings with new ones (Chapter 2).
- ☐ Cylinders worn, cracked, or scored. Caused by overheating or oil starvation. Install a new cylinder block (Chapter 2).
- ☐ Valve oil seal damaged or worn. Replace oil seals with new ones (Chapter 2).
- ☐ Valve guide worn. Perform a complete valve job (Chapter 2).
- ☐ Engine oil level too high, which causes the oil to be forced past the rings. Drain oil to the proper level (Chapter 1).
- ☐ Head gasket broken between oil return and cylinder. Causes oil to be pulled into the combustion chamber. Replace the head gasket and check the head for warpage (Chapter 2).
- ☐ Abnormal crankcase pressurization, which forces oil past the rings. Clogged breather is usually the cause.

Black smoke

- ☐ Air filter clogged. Clean or replace the element (Chapter 1).
- ☐ Carburetor flooding. Remove and overhaul the carburetor(s) (Chapter 4).
- ☐ Main jet too large. Remove and overhaul the carburetor(s) (Chapter 4).
- ☐ Choke cable stuck (Chapter 4).
- ☐ Fuel level too high. Check the fuel level (Chapter 4).
- ☐ Fuel injector problem (Chapter 4).

12 Poor handling or stability

Handlebar hard to turn

- ☐ Steering head bearing adjuster nut too tight. Check adjustment as described in Chapter 1.
- ☐ Bearings damaged. Roughness can be felt as the bars are turned from side-to-side. Replace bearings and races (Chapter 6).
- ☐ Races dented or worn. Denting results from wear in only one position (e.g., straight ahead), from a collision or hitting a pothole or from dropping the machine. Replace races and bearings (Chapter 6).
- ☐ Steering stem lubrication inadequate. Causes are grease getting hard from age or being washed out by high pressure car washes. Disassemble steering head and repack bearings (Chapter 6).
- ☐ Steering stem bent. Caused by a collision, hitting a pothole or by dropping the machine. Replace damaged part. Don't try to straighten the steering stem (Chapter 6).
- ☐ Front tire air pressure too low (Chapter 1).

Handlebar shakes or vibrates excessively

- ☐ Tires worn or out of balance (Chapter 7).
- ☐ Swingarm bearings worn. Replace worn bearings (Chapter 6).
- ☐ Wheel rim(s) warped or damaged. Inspect wheels for runout (Chapter 7).
- ☐ Spokes loose (see Chapter 1).
- ☐ Wheel bearings worn. Worn front or rear wheel bearings can cause poor tracking. Worn front bearings will cause wobble (Chapter 7).
- ☐ Handlebar clamp bolts loose (Chapter 6).
- ☐ Fork yoke bolts loose. Tighten them to the specified torque (Chapter 6).
- ☐ Engine mounting bolts loose. Will cause excessive vibration with increased engine rpm (Chapter 2).

Handlebar pulls to one side

- ☐ Frame bent. Definitely suspect this if the machine has been dropped. May or may not be accompanied by cracking near the bend. Replace the frame (Chapter 8).
- ☐ Wheels out of alignment. Caused by improper location of axle spacers or from bent steering stem or frame (Chapters 6 and 8).
- ☐ Swingarm bent or twisted. Caused by age (metal fatigue) or impact damage. Replace the arm (Chapter 6).
- ☐ Steering stem bent. Caused by impact damage or by dropping the motorcycle. Replace the steering stem (Chapter 6).
- ☐ Fork tube bent. Disassemble the forks and replace the damaged parts (Chapter 6).
- ☐ Fork oil level uneven. Check and add or drain as necessary (Chapter 1).

Poor shock absorbing qualities

Too hard:

a) Fork oil level excessive (Chapter 1).
b) Fork oil viscosity too high. Use a lighter oil (see the Specifications in Chapter 1).
c) Fork tube bent. Causes a harsh, sticking feeling (Chapter 6).
d) Shock shaft or body bent or damaged (Chapter 6).
e) Fork internal damage (Chapter 6).
f) Shock internal damage.
g) Tire pressure too high (Chapter 1).

Too soft:

a) Fork or shock oil insufficient and/or leaking (Chapter 1).
b) Fork oil level too low (Chapter 6).
c) Fork oil viscosity too light (Chapter 6).
d) Fork springs weak or broken (Chapter 6).
e) Shock internal damage or leakage (Chapter 6).

13 Braking problems

Brakes are spongy, don't hold

- ☐ Air in brake line. Caused by inattention to master cylinder fluid level or by leakage. Locate problem and bleed brakes (Chapter 7).
- ☐ Pad or disc worn (Chapters 1 and 7).
- ☐ Brake fluid leak. See paragraph 1.
- ☐ Contaminated pads. Caused by contamination with oil, grease, brake fluid, etc. Clean or replace pads. Clean disc thoroughly with brake cleaner (Chapter 7).
- ☐ Brake fluid deteriorated. Fluid is old or contaminated. Drain system, replenish with new fluid and bleed the system (Chapter 7).
- ☐ Master cylinder internal parts worn or damaged causing fluid to bypass (Chapter 7).
- ☐ Master cylinder bore scratched by foreign material or broken spring. Repair or replace master cylinder (Chapter 7).
- ☐ Disc warped. Replace disc (Chapter 7).

Brake lever or pedal pulsates

- ☐ Disc warped. Replace disc (Chapter 7).
- ☐ Axle bent. Replace axle (Chapter 7).
- ☐ Brake caliper bolts loose (Chapter 7).
- ☐ Wheel warped or otherwise damaged (Chapter 7).
- ☐ Wheel bearings damaged or worn (Chapter 7).
- ☐ Brake drum out of round. Replace brake drum.

Brakes drag

- ☐ Master cylinder piston seized. Caused by wear or damage to piston or cylinder bore (Chapter 7).
- ☐ Lever binding. Check pivot and lubricate (Chapter 7).
- ☐ Brake caliper piston seized in bore. Caused by wear or ingestion of dirt past deteriorated seal (Chapter 7).
- ☐ Brake caliper mounting bracket pins corroded. Clean off corrosion and lubricate (Chapter 7).
- ☐ Brake pad or shoe damaged. Material separated from backing plate. Usually caused by faulty manufacturing process or from contact with chemicals. Replace pads or shoes (Chapter 7).
- ☐ Pads improperly installed (Chapter 7).
- ☐ Drum brake springs weak. Replace springs

14 Electrical problems

Battery dead or weak

- ☐ Battery faulty. Caused by sulfated plates which are shorted through sedimentation. Also, broken battery terminal making only occasional contact (Chapter 9).
- ☐ Battery cables making poor contact (Chapter 9).
- ☐ Load excessive. Caused by addition of high wattage lights or other electrical accessories.
- ☐ Ignition (main) switch defective. Switch either grounds internally or fails to shut off system. Replace the switch (Chapter 9).
- ☐ Regulator/rectifier defective (Chapter 9).
- ☐ Alternator stator coil open or shorted (Chapter 9).
- ☐ Wiring faulty. Wiring grounded or connections loose in ignition, charging or lighting circuits (Chapter 9).

Battery overcharged

- ☐ Regulator/rectifier defective. Overcharging is noticed when battery gets excessively warm (Chapter 9).
- ☐ Battery defective. Replace battery with a new one (Chapter 9).
- ☐ Battery amperage too low, wrong type or size. Install manufacturer's specified amp-hour battery to handle charging load (Chapter 9).

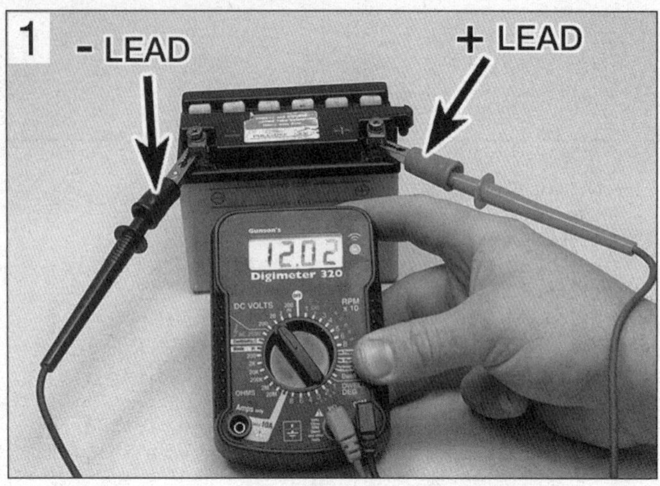

Measuring open-circuit battery voltage

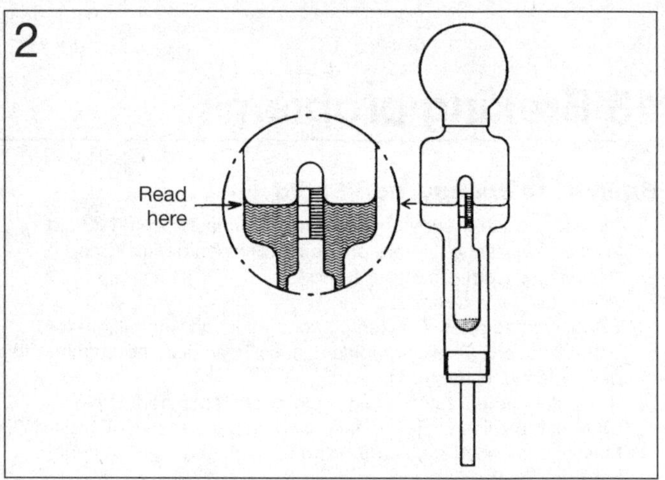

Float-type hydrometer for measuring battery specific gravity

Checking engine compression

- Low compression will result in exhaust smoke, heavy oil consumption, poor starting and poor performance. A compression test will provide useful information about an engine's condition and if performed regularly, can give warning of trouble before any other symptoms become apparent.
- A compression gauge will be required, along with an adapter to suit the spark plug hole thread size. Note that the screw-in type gauge/adapter set up is preferable to the rubber cone type.
- Compression testing procedures for the motorcycles covered in this manual are described in Chapter 1.

Checking battery open-circuit voltage

Warning: The gases produced by the battery are explosive - never smoke or create any sparks in the vicinity of the battery. Never allow the electrolyte to contact your skin or clothing - if it does, wash it off and seek immediate medical attention.

- Before any electrical fault is investigated the battery should be checked.
- You'll need a dc voltmeter or multimeter to check battery voltage. Check that the leads are inserted in the correct terminals on the meter, red lead to positive (+), black lead to negative (-). Incorrect connections can damage the meter.
- A sound, fully-charged 12 volt battery should produce between 12.3 and 12.6 volts across its terminals (12.8 volts for a maintenance-free battery). On machines with a 6 volt battery, voltage should be between 6.1 and 6.3 volts.

1 Set a multimeter to the 0 to 20 volts dc range and connect its probes across the battery terminals. Connect the meter's positive (+) probe, usually red, to the battery positive (+) terminal, followed by the meter's negative (-) probe, usually black, to the battery negative terminal (-) **(see illustration 1)**.

2 If battery voltage is low (below 10 volts on a 12 volt battery or below 4 volts on a six volt battery), charge the battery and test the voltage again. If the battery repeatedly goes flat, investigate the motorcycle's charging system.

Checking battery specific gravity (SG)

Warning: The gases produced by the battery are explosive - never smoke or create any sparks in the vicinity of the battery. Never allow the electrolyte to contact your skin or clothing - if it does, wash it off and seek immediate medical attention.

- The specific gravity check gives an indication of a battery's state of charge.
- A hydrometer is used for measuring specific gravity. Make sure you purchase one which has a small enough hose to insert in the aperture of a motorcycle battery.
- Specific gravity is simply a measure of the electrolyte's density compared with that of water. Water has an SG of 1.000 and fully-charged battery electrolyte is about 26% heavier, at 1.260.
- Specific gravity checks are not possible on maintenance-free batteries. Testing the open-circuit voltage is the only means of determining their state of charge.

1 To measure SG, remove the battery from the motorcycle and remove the first cell cap. Draw some electrolyte into the hydrometer and note the reading **(see illustration 2)**. Return the electrolyte to the cell and install the cap.

2 The reading should be in the region of 1.260 to 1.280. If SG is below 1.200 the battery needs charging. Note that SG will vary with temperature; it should be measured at 20°C (68°F). Add 0.007 to the reading for every 10°C above 20°C, and subtract 0.007 from the reading for every 10°C below 20°C. Add 0.004 to the reading for every 10°F above 68°F, and subtract 0.004 from the reading for every 10°F below 68°F.

3 When the check is complete, rinse the hydrometer thoroughly with clean water.

Checking for continuity

- The term continuity describes the uninterrupted flow of electricity through an electrical circuit. A continuity check will determine whether an **open-circuit** situation exists.
- Continuity can be checked with an ohmmeter, multimeter, continuity tester or battery and bulb test circuit **(see illustrations 3, 4 and 5)**.
- All of these instruments are self-powered by a battery, therefore the checks are made with the ignition OFF.
- As a safety precaution, always disconnect the battery negative (-) lead before making checks, particularly if ignition switch checks are being made.
- If using a meter, select the appropriate

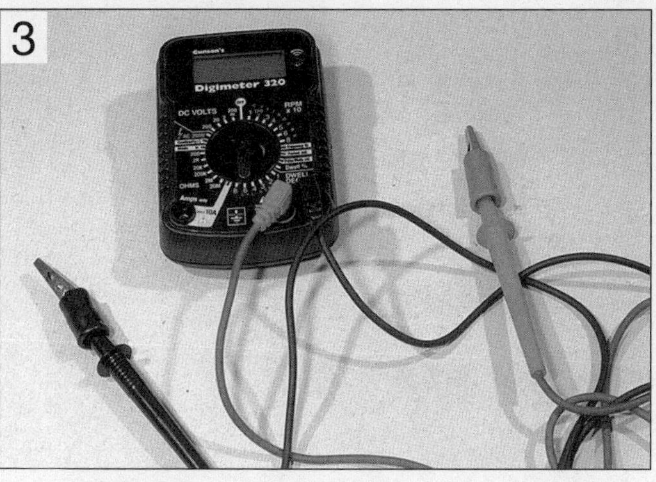

Digital multimeter can be used for all electrical tests

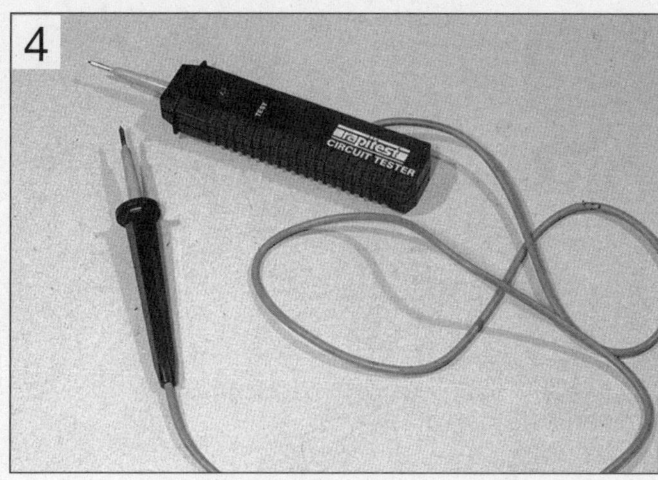

Battery-powered continuity tester

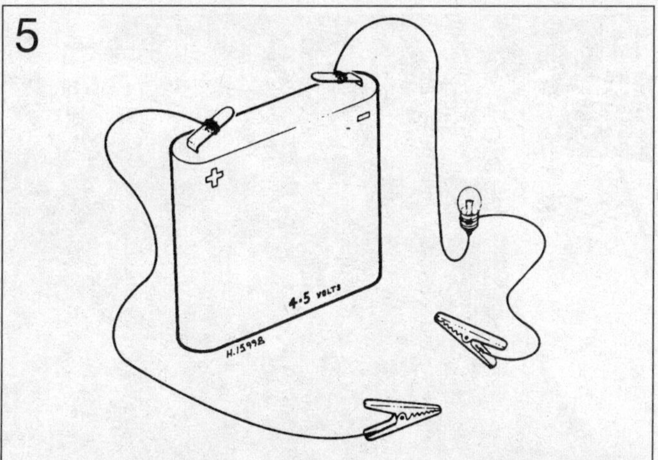

Battery and bulb test circuit

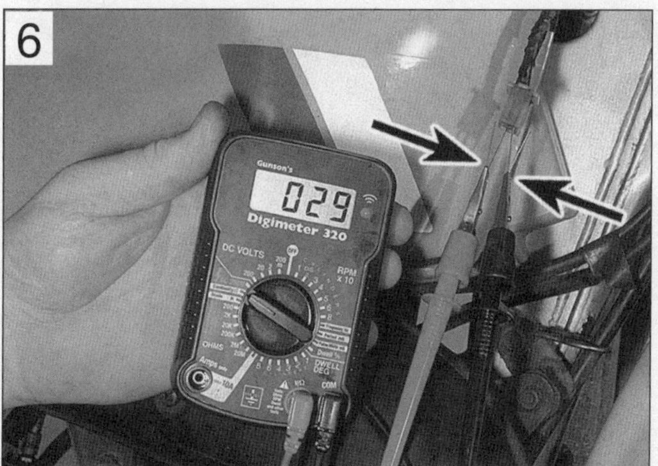

Continuity check of front brake light switch using a meter - note cotter pins used to access connector terminals

ohms scale and check that the meter reads infinity (∞). Touch the meter probes together and check that meter reads zero; where necessary adjust the meter so that it reads zero.

● After using a meter, always switch it OFF to conserve its battery.

Switch checks

1 If a switch is at fault, trace its wiring up to the wiring connectors. Separate the wire connectors and inspect them for security and condition. A build-up of dirt or corrosion here will most likely be the cause of the problem - clean up and apply a water dispersant such as WD40.

2 If using a test meter, set the meter to the ohms x 10 scale and connect its probes across the wires from the switch **(see illustration 6)**. Simple ON/OFF type switches, such as brake light switches, only have two wires whereas combination switches, like the ignition switch, have many internal links. Study the wiring diagram to ensure that you are connecting across the correct pair of wires. Continuity (low or no measurable resistance - 0 ohms) should be indicated with the switch ON and no continuity (high resistance) with it OFF.

3 Note that the polarity of the test probes doesn't matter for continuity checks, although care should be taken to follow specific test procedures if a diode or solid-state component is being checked.

4 A continuity tester or battery and bulb circuit can be used in the same way. Connect its probes as described above **(see illustration 7)**. The light should come on to indicate continuity in the ON switch position, but should extinguish in the OFF position.

Wiring checks

● Many electrical faults are caused by damaged wiring, often due to incorrect routing or chaffing on frame components.

● Loose, wet or corroded wire connectors can also be the cause of electrical problems, especially in exposed locations.

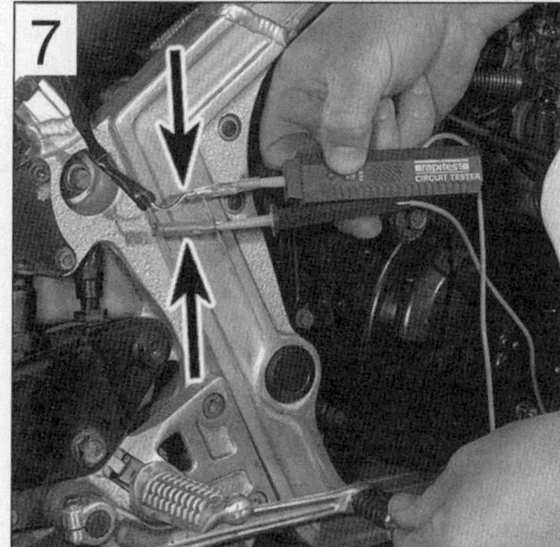

Continuity check of rear brake light switch using a continuity tester

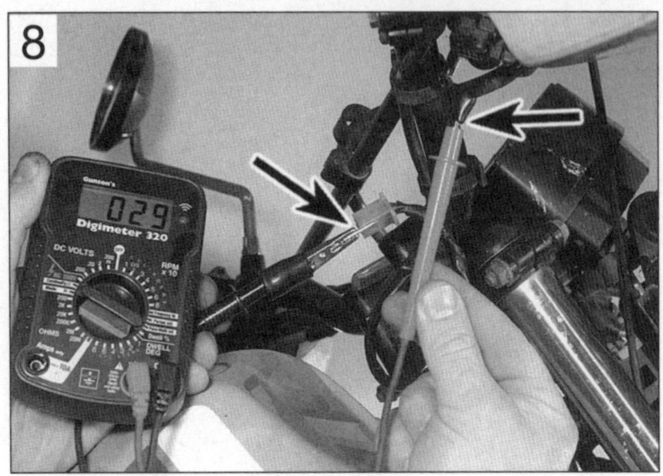

Continuity check of front brake light switch sub-harness

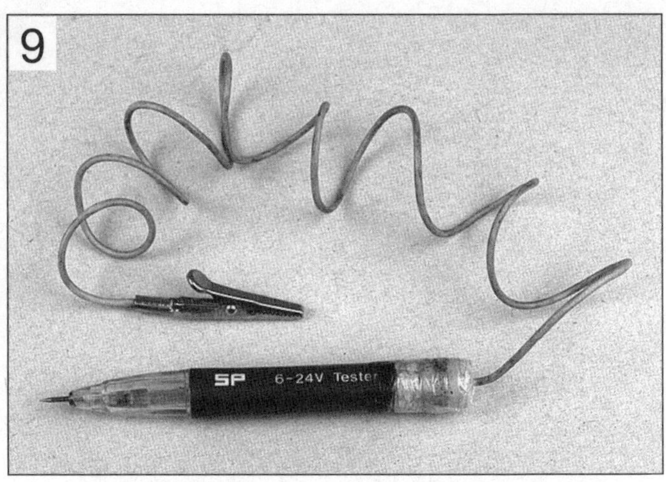

A simple test light can be used for voltage checks

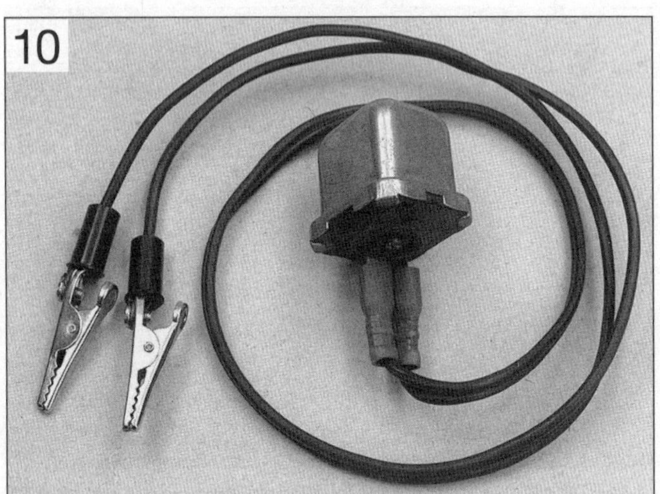

A buzzer is useful for voltage checks

Checking for voltage at the rear brake light power supply wire using a meter . . .

1 A continuity check can be made on a single length of wire by disconnecting it at each end and connecting a meter or continuity tester across both ends of the wire **(see illustration 8)**.

2 Continuity (low or no resistance - 0 ohms) should be indicated if the wire is good. If no continuity (high resistance) is shown, suspect a broken wire.

Checking for voltage

● A voltage check can determine whether current is reaching a component.

● Voltage can be checked with a dc voltmeter, multimeter set on the dc volts scale, test light or buzzer **(see illustrations 9 and 10)**. A meter has the advantage of being able to measure actual voltage.

● When using a meter, check that its leads are inserted in the correct terminals on the meter, red to positive (+), black to negative (-). Incorrect connections can damage the meter.

● A voltmeter (or multimeter set to the dc volts scale) should always be connected in parallel (across the load). Connecting it in series will destroy the meter.

● Voltage checks are made with the ignition ON.

1 First identify the relevant wiring circuit by referring to the wiring diagram at the end of this manual. If other electrical components share the same power supply (ie are fed from the same fuse), take note whether they are working correctly - this is useful information in deciding where to start checking the circuit.

2 If using a meter, check first that the meter leads are plugged into the correct terminals on the meter (see above). Set the meter to the dc volts function, at a range suitable for the battery voltage. Connect the meter red probe (+) to the power supply wire and the black probe to a good metal ground on the motor-cycle's frame or directly to the battery negative (-) terminal **(see illustration 11)**. Battery voltage should be shown on the meter with the ignition switched ON.

3 If using a test light or buzzer, connect its positive (+) probe to the power supply terminal and its negative (-) probe to a good ground on the motorcycle's frame or directly to the battery negative (-) terminal **(see illustration 12)**. With the ignition ON, the test light should illuminate or the buzzer sound.

4 If no voltage is indicated, work back towards the fuse continuing to check for voltage. When you reach a point where there is voltage, you know the problem lies between that point and your last check point.

Checking the ground

● Ground connections are made either

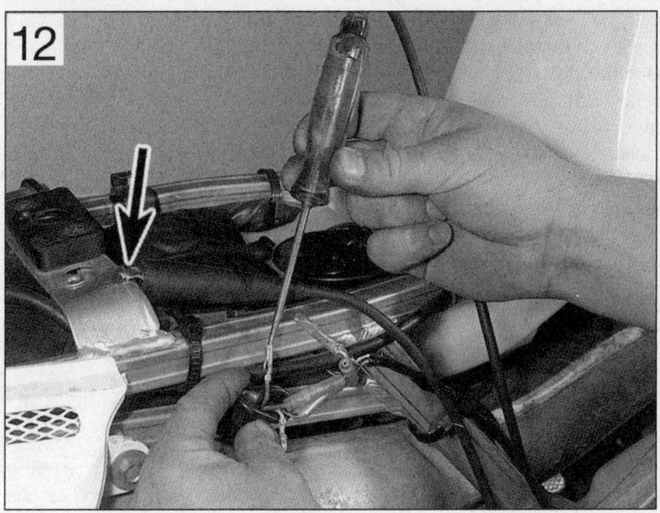

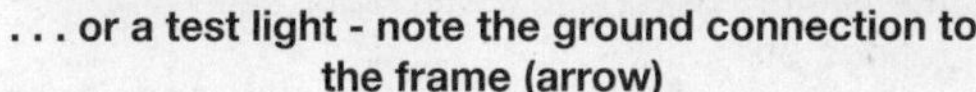
. . . or a test light - note the ground connection to the frame (arrow)

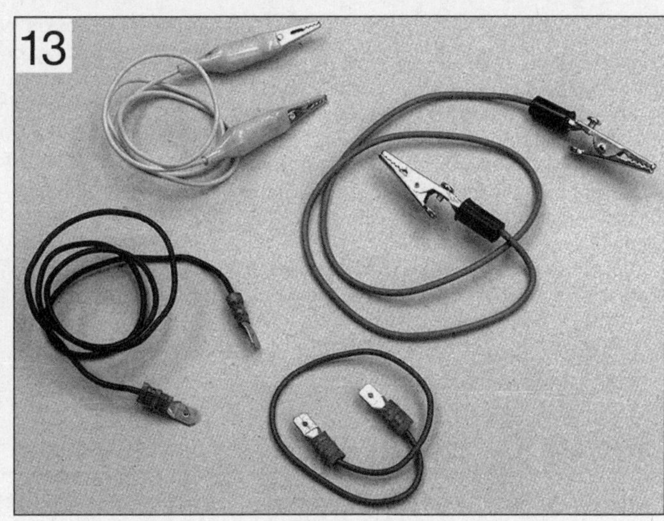

A selection of jumper wires for making ground checks

directly to the engine or frame (such as sensors, neutral switch etc. which only have a positive feed) or by a separate wire into the ground circuit of the wiring harness. Alternatively a short ground wire is sometimes run directly from the component to the motor-cycle's frame.

- Corrosion is often the cause of a poor ground connection.
- If total failure is experienced, check the security of the main ground lead from the negative (-) terminal of the battery and also the main ground point on the wiring harness. If corroded, dismantle the connection and clean all surfaces back to bare metal.

1 To check the ground on a component, use an insulated jumper wire to temporarily bypass its ground connection **(see illustration 13)**. Connect one end of the jumper wire between the ground terminal or metal body of the component and the other end to the motorcycle's frame.

2 If the circuit works with the jumper wire installed, the original ground circuit is faulty. Check the wiring for open-circuits or poor connections. Clean up direct ground connections, removing all traces of corrosion and remake the joint. Apply petroleum jelly to the joint to prevent future corrosion.

Tracing a short-circuit

- A short-circuit occurs where current shorts to ground bypassing the circuit components. This usually results in a blown fuse.
- A short-circuit is most likely to occur where the insulation has worn through due to wiring chafing on a component, allowing a direct path to ground on the frame.

1 Remove any body panels necessary to access the circuit wiring.

2 Check that all electrical switches in the circuit are OFF, then remove the circuit fuse and connect a test light, buzzer or voltmeter (set to the dc scale) across the fuse terminals. No voltage should be shown.

3 Move the wiring from side to side while observing the test light or meter. When the test light comes on, buzzer sounds or meter shows voltage, you have found the cause of the short. It will usually shown up as damaged or burned insulation.

4 Note that the same test can be performed on each component in the circuit, even the switch.

Introduction

In less time than it takes to read this introduction, a thief could steal your motorcycle. Returning only to find your bike has gone is one of the worst feelings in the world. Even if the motorcycle is insured against theft, once you've got over the initial shock, you will have the inconvenience of dealing with the police and your insurance company.

The motorcycle is an easy target for the professional thief and the joyrider alike and the official figures on motorcycle theft make for depressing reading; on average a motor-cycle is stolen every 16 minutes in the UK!

Motorcycle thefts fall into two categories, those stolen 'to order' and those taken by opportunists. The thief stealing to order will be on the look out for a specific make and model and will go to extraordinary lengths to obtain that motorcycle. The opportunist thief on the other hand will look for easy targets which can be stolen with the minimum of effort and risk.

While it is never going to be possible to make your machine 100% secure, it is estimated that around half of all stolen motorcycles are taken by opportunist thieves. Remember that the opportunist thief is always on the look out for the easy option: if there are two similar motorcycles parked side-by-side, they will target the one with the lowest level of security. By taking a few precautions, you can reduce the chances of your motorcycle being stolen.

Security equipment

There are many specialized motorcycle security devices available and the following text summarizes their applications and their good and bad points.

Once you have decided on the type of security equipment which best suits your needs, we recommended that you read one of the many equipment tests regularly carried out by the motorcycle press. These tests compare the products from all the major manufacturers and give impartial ratings on their effectiveness, value-for-money and ease of use.

Ensure the lock and chain you buy is of good quality and long enough to shackle your bike to a solid object

No one item of security equipment can provide complete protection. It is highly recommended that two or more of the items described below are combined to increase the security of your motorcycle (a lock and chain plus an alarm system is just about ideal). The more security measures fitted to the bike, the less likely it is to be stolen.

Lock and chain

Pros: *Very flexible to use; can be used to secure the motorcycle to almost any immovable object. On some locks and chains, the lock can be used on its own as a disc lock (see below).*

Cons: *Can be very heavy and awkward to carry on the motorcycle, although some types will be supplied with a carry bag which can be strapped to the pillion seat.*

- Heavy-duty chains and locks are an excellent security measure **(see illustration 1)**. Whenever the motorcycle is parked, use the lock and chain to secure the machine to a solid, immovable object such as a post or railings. This will prevent the machine from being ridden away or being lifted into the back of a van.

- When fitting the chain, always ensure the chain is routed around the motorcycle frame or swingarm **(see illustrations 2 and 3)**. Never merely pass the chain around one of the wheel rims; a thief may unbolt the wheel and lift the rest of the machine into a van, leaving you with just the wheel! Try to avoid having excess chain free, thus making it difficult to use cutting tools, and keep the chain and lock off the ground to prevent thieves attacking it with a cold chisel. Position the lock so that its lock barrel is facing downwards; this will make it harder for the thief to attack the lock mechanism.

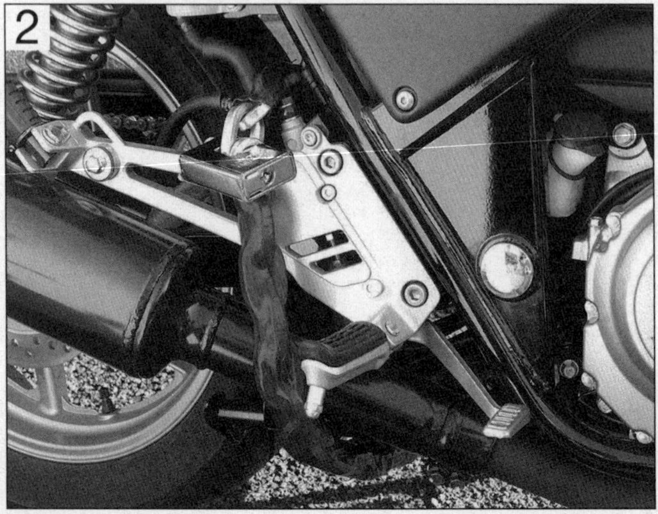

Pass the chain through the bike's frame, rather than just through a wheel . . .

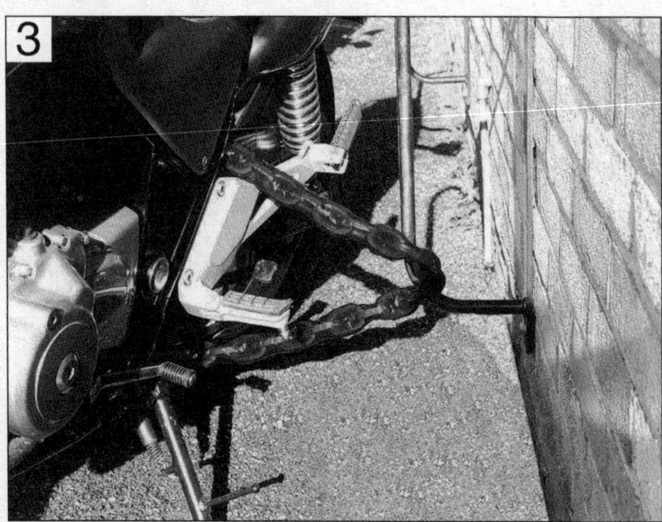

. . . and loop it around a solid object

U-locks

Pros: *Highly effective deterrent which can be used to secure the bike to a post or railings. Most U-locks come with a carrier which allows the lock to be easily carried on the bike.*

Cons: *Not as flexible to use as a lock and chain.*

● These are solid locks which are similar in use to a lock and chain. U-locks are lighter than a lock and chain but not so flexible to use. The length and shape of the lock shackle limit the objects to which the bike can be secured **(see illustration 4)**.

U-locks can be used to secure the bike to a solid object - ensure you purchase one which is long enough

Disc locks

Pros: *Small, light and very easy to carry; most can be stored underneath the seat.*

Cons: *Does not prevent the motorcycle being lifted into a van. Can be very embarrassing if you forget to remove the lock before attempting to ride off!*

A typical disc lock attached through one of the holes in the disc

● Disc locks are designed to be attached to the front brake disc. The lock passes through one of the holes in the disc and prevents the wheel rotating by jamming against the fork/brake caliper **(see illustration 5)**. Some are equipped with an alarm siren which sounds if the disc lock is moved; this not only acts as a theft deterrent but also as a handy reminder if you try to move the bike with the lock still fitted.

● Combining the disc lock with a length of cable which can be looped around a post or railings provides an additional measure of security **(see illustration 6)**.

Alarms and immobilisers

Pros: *Once installed it is completely hassle-free to use. If the system is 'Thatcham' or 'Sold Secure-approved', insurance companies may give you a discount.*

Cons: *Can be expensive to buy and complex to install. No system will prevent the motorcycle from being lifted into a van and taken away.*

● Electronic alarms and immobilizers are available to suit a variety of budgets. There are three different types of system available: pure alarms, pure immobilizers, and the more expensive systems which are combined alarm/immobilizers **(see illustration 7)**.

● An alarm system is designed to emit an audible warning if the motorcycle is being tampered with.

● An immobilizer prevents the motorcycle being started and ridden away by disabling its electrical systems.

● When purchasing an alarm/immobilizer system, check the cost of installing the system unless you are able to do it yourself. If the motorcycle is not used regularly, another consideration is the current drain of the system. All alarm/immobilizer systems are powered by the motorcycle's battery; purchasing a system with a very low current drain could prevent the battery losing its charge while the motorcycle is not being used.

A disc lock combined with a security cable provides additional protection

A typical alarm/immobilizer system

Indelible markings can be applied to most areas of the bike – always apply the manufacturer's sticker to warn off thieves

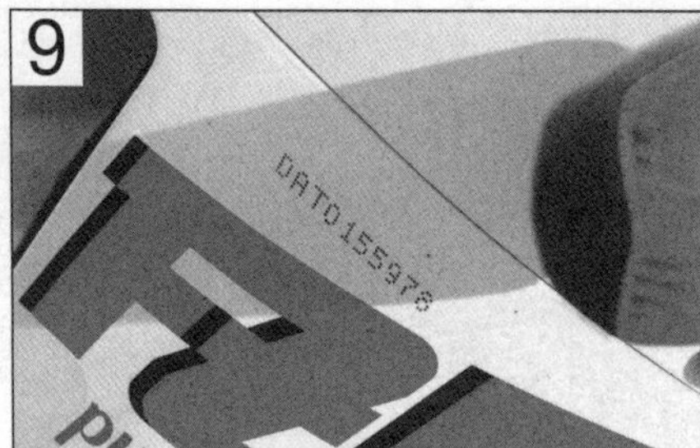

Chemically-etched code numbers can be applied to main body panels . . .

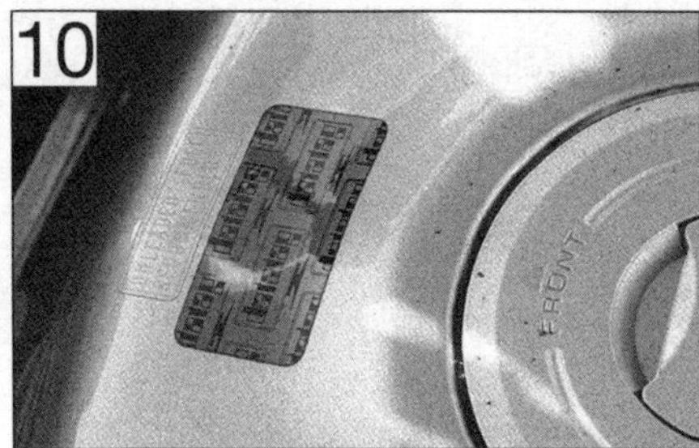

. . . again, always ensure that the kit manufacturer's sticker is applied in a prominent position

Security marking kits

Pros: *Very cheap and effective deterrent. Many insurance companies will give you a discount on your insurance premium if a recognized security marking kit is used on your motorcycle.*

Cons: *Does not prevent the motorcycle being stolen by joyriders.*

● There are many different types of security marking kits available. The idea is to mark as many parts of the motorcycle as possible with a unique security number **(see illustrations 8, 9 and 10)**. A form will be included with the kit to register your personal details and those of the motorcycle with the kit manufacturer. This register is made available to the police to help them trace the rightful owner of any motorcycle or components which they recover should all other forms of identification have been removed. Always apply the warning stickers provided with the kit to deter thieves.

Ground anchors, wheel clamps and security posts

Pros: *An excellent form of security which will deter all but the most determined of thieves.*

Cons: *Awkward to install and can be expensive.*

● While the motorcycle is at home, it is a good idea to attach it securely to the floor or a solid wall, even if it is kept in a securely locked garage. Various types of ground anchors, security posts and wheel clamps are available for this purpose **(see illustration 11)**. These security devices are either bolted to a solid concrete or brick structure or can be cemented into the ground.

Permanent ground anchors provide an excellent level of security when the bike is at home

Security at home

A high percentage of motorcycle thefts are from the owner's home. Here are some things to consider whenever your motorcycle is at home:

✔ Where possible, always keep the motorcycle in a securely locked garage. Never rely solely on the standard lock on the garage door, these are usual hopelessly inadequate. Fit an additional locking mechanism to the door and consider having the garage alarmed. A security light, activated by a movement sensor, is also a good investment.

✔ Always secure the motorcycle to the ground or a wall, even if it is inside a securely locked garage.

✔ Do not regularly leave the motorcycle outside your home, try to keep it out of sight wherever possible. If a garage is not available, fit a motorcycle cover over the bike to disguise its true identity.

✔ It is not uncommon for thieves to follow a motorcyclist home to find out where the bike is kept. They will then return at a later date. Be aware of this whenever you are returning home on your motorcycle. If you suspect you are being followed, do not return home, instead ride to a garage or shop and stop as a precaution.

✔ When selling a motorcycle, do not provide your home address or the location where the bike is normally kept. Arrange to meet the buyer at a location away from your home. Thieves have been known to pose as potential buyers to find out where motorcycles are kept and then return later to steal them.

Security away from the home

As well as fitting security equipment to your motorcycle here are a few general rules to follow whenever you park your motorcycle.

✔ Park in a busy, public place.

✔ Use car parks which incorporate security features, such as CCTV.

✔ At night, park in a well-lit area, preferably directly underneath a street light.

✔ Engage the steering lock.

✔ Secure the motorcycle to a solid, immovable object such as a post or railings with an additional lock. If this is not possible, secure the bike to a friend's motorcycle. Some public parking places provide security loops for motorcycles.

✔ Never leave your helmet or luggage attached to the motorcycle. Take them with you at all times.

A

ABS (Anti-lock braking system) A system, usually electronically controlled, that senses incipient wheel lockup during braking and relieves hydraulic pressure at wheel which is about to skid.

Aftermarket Components suitable for the motorcycle, but not produced by the motorcycle manufacturer.

Allen key A hexagonal wrench which fits into a recessed hexagonal hole.

Alternating current (ac) Current produced by an alternator. Requires converting to direct current by a rectifier for charging purposes.

Alternator Converts mechanical energy from the engine into electrical energy to charge the battery and power the electrical system.

Ampere (amp) A unit of measurement for the flow of electrical current. Current = Volts ÷ Ohms.

Ampere-hour (Ah) Measure of battery capacity.

Angle-tightening A torque expressed in degrees. Often follows a conventional tightening torque for cylinder head or main bearing fasteners **(see illustration)**.

Angle-tightening cylinder head bolts

Antifreeze A substance (usually ethylene glycol) mixed with water, and added to the cooling system, to prevent freezing of the coolant in winter. Antifreeze also contains chemicals to inhibit corrosion and the formation of rust and other deposits that would tend to clog the radiator and coolant passages and reduce cooling efficiency.

Anti-dive System attached to the fork lower leg (slider) to prevent fork dive when braking hard.

Anti-seize compound A coating that reduces the risk of seizing on fasteners that are subjected to high temperatures, such as exhaust clamp bolts and nuts.

API American Petroleum Institute. A quality standard for 4-stroke motor oils.

Asbestos A natural fibrous mineral with great heat resistance, commonly used in the composition of brake friction materials. Asbestos is a health hazard and the dust created by brake systems should never be inhaled or ingested.

ATF Automatic Transmission Fluid. Often used in front forks.

ATU Automatic Timing Unit. Mechanical device for advancing the ignition timing on early engines.

ATV All Terrain Vehicle. Often called a Quad.

Axial play Side-to-side movement.

Axle A shaft on which a wheel revolves. Also known as a spindle.

B

Backlash The amount of movement between meshed components when one component is held still. Usually applies to gear teeth.

Ball bearing A bearing consisting of a hardened inner and outer race with hardened steel balls between the two races.

Bearings Used between two working surfaces to prevent wear of the components and a build-up of heat. Four types of bearing are commonly used on motorcycles: plain shell bearings, ball bearings, tapered roller bearings and needle roller bearings.

Bevel gears Used to turn the drive through 90°. Typical applications are shaft final drive and camshaft drive **(see illustration)**.

BHP Brake Horsepower. The British measurement for engine power output. Power output is now usually expressed in kilowatts (kW).

Bevel gears are used to turn the drive through 90°

Bias-belted tire Similar construction to radial tire, but with outer belt running at an angle to the wheel rim.

Big-end bearing The bearing in the end of the connecting rod that's attached to the crankshaft.

Bleeding The process of removing air from a hydraulic system via a bleed nipple or bleed screw.

Bottom-end A description of an engine's crankcase components and all components contained therein.

BTDC Before Top Dead Center in terms of piston position. Ignition timing is often expressed in terms of degrees or millimeters BTDC.

Bush A cylindrical metal or rubber component used between two moving parts.

Burr Rough edge left on a component after machining or as a result of excessive wear.

C

Cam chain The chain which takes drive from the crankshaft to the camshaft(s).

Canister The main component in an evaporative emission control system (California market only); contains activated charcoal granules to trap vapors from the fuel system rather than allowing them to vent to the atmosphere.

Castellated Resembling the parapets along the top of a castle wall. For example, a castellated wheel axle or spindle nut.

Catalytic converter A device in the exhaust system of some machines which

Cush drive rubber segments dampen out transmission shocks

converts certain pollutants in the exhaust gases into less harmful substances.

Charging system Description of the components which charge the battery, ie the alternator, rectifer and regulator.

Clearance The amount of space between two parts. For example, between a piston and a cylinder, between a bearing and a journal, etc.

Coil spring A spiral of elastic steel found in various sizes throughout a vehicle, for example as a springing medium in the suspension and in the valve train.

Compression Reduction in volume, and increase in pressure and temperature, of a gas, caused by squeezing it into a smaller space.

Compression damping Controls the speed the suspension compresses when hitting a bump.

Compression ratio The relationship between cylinder volume when the piston is at top dead center and cylinder volume when the piston is at bottom dead center.

Continuity The uninterrupted path in the flow of electricity. Little or no measurable resistance.

Continuity tester Self-powered bleeper or test light which indicates continuity.

Cp Candlepower. Bulb rating commonly found on US motorcycles.

Crossply tire Tire plies arranged in a criss-cross pattern. Usually four or six plies used, hence 4PR or 6PR in tire size codes.

Cush drive Rubber damper segments fitted between the rear wheel and final drive sprocket to absorb transmission shocks **(see illustration)**.

D

Degree disc Calibrated disc for measuring piston position. Expressed in degrees.

Dial gauge Clock-type gauge with adapters for measuring runout and piston position. Expressed in mm or inches.

Diaphragm The rubber membrane in a master cylinder or carburetor which seals the upper chamber.

Diaphragm spring A single sprung plate often used in clutches.

Direct current (dc) Current produced by a dc generator.

Decarbonization The process of removing carbon deposits - typically from the combustion chamber, valves and exhaust port/system.

Detonation Destructive and damaging explosion of fuel/air mixture in combustion chamber instead of controlled burning.

Diode An electrical valve which only allows current to flow in one direction. Commonly used in rectifiers and starter interlock systems.

Disc valve (or rotary valve) An induction system used on some two-stroke engines.

Double-overhead camshaft (DOHC) An engine that uses two overhead camshafts, one for the intake valves and one for the exhaust valves.

Drivebelt A toothed belt used to transmit drive to the rear wheel on some motorcycles. A drivebelt has also been used to drive the camshafts. Drivebelts are usually made of Kevlar.

Driveshaft Any shaft used to transmit motion. Commonly used when referring to the final driveshaft on shaft drive motorcycles.

E

ECU (Electronic Control Unit) A computer which controls (for instance) an ignition system, or an anti-lock braking system.

EGO Exhaust Gas Oxygen sensor. Sometimes called a Lambda sensor.

Electrolyte The fluid in a lead-acid battery.

EMS (Engine Management System) A computer controlled system which manages the fuel injection and the ignition systems in an integrated fashion.

Endfloat The amount of lengthways movement between two parts. As applied to a crankshaft, the distance that the crankshaft can move side-to-side in the crankcase.

Endless chain A chain having no joining link. Common use for cam chains and final drive chains.

EP (Extreme Pressure) Oil type used in locations where high loads are applied, such as between gear teeth.

Evaporative emission control system Describes a charcoal filled canister which stores fuel vapors from the tank rather than allowing them to vent to the atmosphere. Usually only fitted to California models and referred to as an EVAP system.

Expansion chamber Section of two-stroke engine exhaust system so designed to improve engine efficiency and boost power.

F

Feeler blade or gauge A thin strip or blade of hardened steel, ground to an exact thickness, used to check or measure clearances between parts.

Final drive Description of the drive from the transmission to the rear wheel. Usually by chain or shaft, but sometimes by belt.

Firing order The order in which the engine cylinders fire, or deliver their power strokes, beginning with the number one cylinder.

Flooding Term used to describe a high fuel level in the carburetor float chambers, leading to fuel overflow. Also refers to excess fuel in the combustion chamber due to incorrect starting technique.

Free length The no-load state of a component when measured. Clutch, valve and fork spring lengths are measured at rest, without any preload.

Freeplay The amount of travel before any action takes place. The looseness in a linkage, or an assembly of parts, between the initial application of force and actual movement. For example, the distance the rear brake pedal moves before the rear brake is actuated.

Fuel injection The fuel/air mixture is metered electronically and directed into the engine intake ports (indirect injection) or into the cylinders (direct injection). Sensors supply information on engine speed and conditions.

Fuel/air mixture The charge of fuel and air going into the engine. See Stoichiometric ratio.

Fuse An electrical device which protects a circuit against accidental overload. The typical fuse contains a soft piece of metal which is calibrated to melt at a predetermined current flow (expressed as amps) and break the circuit.

G

Gap The distance the spark must travel in jumping from the center electrode to the side electrode in a spark plug. Also refers to the distance between the ignition rotor and the pickup coil in an electronic ignition system.

Gasket Any thin, soft material - usually cork, cardboard, asbestos or soft metal - installed between two metal surfaces to ensure a good seal. For instance, the cylinder head gasket seals the joint between the block and the cylinder head.

Gauge An instrument panel display used to monitor engine conditions. A gauge with a movable pointer on a dial or a fixed scale is an analog gauge. A gauge with a numerical readout is called a digital gauge.

Gear ratios The drive ratio of a pair of gears in a gearbox, calculated on their number of teeth.

Glaze-busting see **Honing**

Grinding Process for renovating the valve face and valve seat contact area in the cylinder head.

Ground return The return path of an electrical circuit, utilizing the motorcycle's frame.

Gudgeon pin The shaft which connects the connecting rod small-end with the piston. Often called a piston pin or wrist pin.

H

Helical gears Gear teeth are slightly curved and produce less gear noise that straight-cut gears. Often used for primary drives.

Helicoil A thread insert repair system. Commonly used as a repair for stripped spark plug threads **(see illustration)**.

Installing a Helicoil thread insert in a cylinder head

Honing A process used to break down the glaze on a cylinder bore (also called glaze-busting). Can also be carried out to roughen a rebored cylinder to aid ring bedding-in.

HT (High Tension) Description of the electrical circuit from the secondary winding of the ignition coil to the spark plug.

Hydraulic A liquid filled system used to transmit pressure from one component to another. Common uses on motorcycles are brakes and clutches.

Hydrometer An instrument for measuring the specific gravity of a lead-acid battery.

Hygroscopic Water absorbing. In motorcycle applications, braking efficiency will be reduced if DOT 3 or 4 hydraulic fluid absorbs water from the air - care must be taken to keep new brake fluid in tightly sealed containers.

I

lbf ft Pounds-force feet. A unit of torque. Sometimes written as ft-lbs.

lbf in Pound-force inch. A unit of torque, applied to components where a very low torque is required. Sometimes written as inch-lbs.

IC Abbreviation for Integrated Circuit.

Ignition advance Means of increasing the timing of the spark at higher engine speeds. Done by mechanical means (ATU) on early engines or electronically by the ignition control unit on later engines.

Ignition timing The moment at which the spark plug fires, expressed in the number of crankshaft degrees before the piston reaches the top of its stroke, or in the number of millimeters before the piston reaches the top of its stroke.

Infinity (∞) Description of an open-circuit electrical state, where no continuity exists.

Inverted forks (upside down forks) The sliders or lower legs are held in the yokes and the fork tubes or stanchions are connected to the wheel axle (spindle). Less unsprung weight and stiffer construction than conventional forks.

J

JASO Japan Automobile Standards Organization JASO MA is a standard for motorcycle oil equivalent to API SJ, but designed to prevent problems with wet-type motorcycle clutches.

Joule The unit of electrical energy.

Journal The bearing surface of a shaft.

K

Kickstart Mechanical means of turning the engine over for starting purposes.

Only usually fitted to mopeds, small capacity motorcycles and off-road motorcycles.

Kill switch Handebar-mounted switch for emergency ignition cut-out. Cuts the ignition circuit on all models, and additionally prevent starter motor operation on others.

km Symbol for kilometer.

kmh Abbreviation for kilometers per hour.

L

Lambda sensor A sensor fitted in the exhaust system to measure the exhaust gas oxygen content (excess air factor). Also called oxygen sensor.

Lapping see **Grinding**.

LCD Abbreviation for Liquid Crystal Display.

LED Abbreviation for Light Emitting Diode.

Liner A steel cylinder liner inserted in an aluminum alloy cylinder block.

Locknut A nut used to lock an adjustment nut, or other threaded component, in place.

Lockstops The lugs on the lower triple clamp (yoke) which abut those on the frame, preventing handlebar-to-fuel tank contact.

Lockwasher A form of washer designed to prevent an attaching nut from working loose.

LT Low Tension Description of the electrical circuit from the power supply to the primary winding of the ignition coil.

M

Main bearings The bearings between the crankshaft and crankcase.

Maintenance-free (MF) battery A sealed battery which cannot be topped up.

Manometer Mercury-filled calibrated tubes used to measure intake tract vacuum. Used to synchronize carburetors on multi-cylinder engines.

Tappet shims are measured with a micrometer

Micrometer A precision measuring instrument that measures component outside diameters **(see illustration)**.

MON (Motor Octane Number) A measure of a fuel's resistance to knock.

Monograde oil An oil with a single viscosity, eg SAE80W.

Monoshock A single suspension unit linking the swingarm or suspension linkage to the frame.

mph Abbreviation for miles per hour.

Multigrade oil Having a wide viscosity range (eg 10W40). The W stands for Winter, thus the viscosity ranges from SAE10 when cold to SAE40 when hot.

Multimeter An electrical test instrument with the capability to measure voltage, current and resistance. Some meters also incorporate a continuity tester and buzzer.

N

Needle roller bearing Inner race of caged needle rollers and hardened outer race. Examples of uncaged needle rollers can be found on some engines. Commonly used in rear suspension applications and in two-stroke engines.

Nm Newton meters.

NOx Oxides of Nitrogen. A common toxic pollutant emitted by gasoline engines at higher temperatures.

O

Octane The measure of a fuel's resistance to knock.

OE (Original Equipment) Relates to components fitted to a motorcycle as standard or replacement parts supplied by the motorcycle manufacturer.

Ohm The unit of electrical resistance. Ohms = Volts ÷ Current.

Ohmmeter An instrument for measuring electrical resistance.

Oil cooler System for diverting engine oil outside of the engine to a radiator for cooling purposes.

Oil injection A system of two-stroke engine lubrication where oil is pump-fed to the engine in accordance with throttle position.

Open-circuit An electrical condition where there is a break in the flow of electricity - no continuity (high resistance).

O-ring A type of sealing ring made of a special rubber-like material; in use, the O-ring is compressed into a groove to provide the sealing action.

Oversize (OS) Term used for piston and ring size options fitted to a rebored cylinder.

Overhead cam (sohc) engine An engine with single camshaft located on top of the cylinder head.

Overhead valve (ohv) engine An engine with the valves located in the cylinder head, but with the camshaft located in the engine block or crankcase.

Oxygen sensor A device installed in the exhaust system which senses the oxygen content in the exhaust and converts this information into an electric current. Also called a Lambda sensor.

P

Plastigage A thin strip of plastic thread, available in different sizes, used for measuring clearances. For example, a strip of Plastigage is laid across a bearing journal. The parts are assembled and dismantled; the width of the crushed strip indicates the clearance between journal and bearing.

Polarity Either negative or positive ground, determined by which battery lead is connected to the frame (ground return). Modern motorcycles are usually negative ground.

Pre-ignition A situation where the fuel/air mixture ignites before the spark plug fires. Often due to a hot spot in the combustion chamber caused by carbon build-up. Engine has a tendency to 'run-on'.

Pre-load (suspension) The amount a spring is compressed when in the unloaded state. Preload can be applied by gas, spacer or mechanical adjuster.

Premix The method of engine lubrication on some gasoline two-stroke engines. Engine oil is mixed with the gasoline in the fuel tank in a specific ratio. The fuel/oil mix is sometimes referred to as "petrol".

Primary drive Description of the drive from the crankshaft to the clutch. Usually by gear or chain.

PS Pferdestärke - a German interpretation of BHP.

PSI Pounds-force per square inch. Imperial measurement of tire pressure and cylinder pressure measurement.

PTFE Polytetrafluroethylene. A low friction substance.

Pulse secondary air injection system A process of promoting the burning of excess fuel present in the exhaust gases by routing fresh air into the exhaust ports.

Q

Quartz halogen bulb Tungsten filament surrounded by a halogen gas. Typically used for the headlight **(see illustration)**.

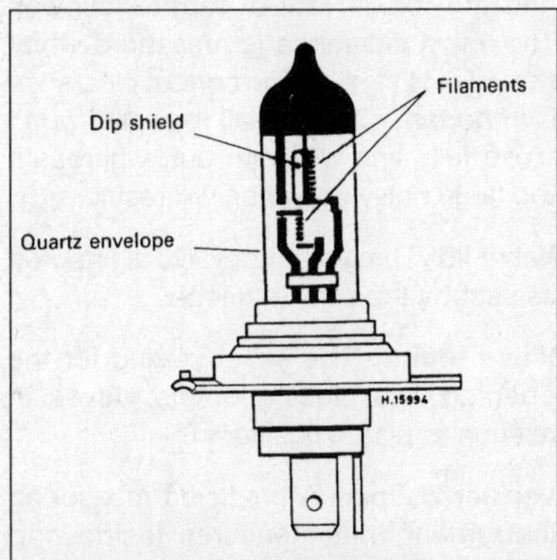

Quartz halogen headlight bulb construction

R

Rack-and-pinion A pinion gear on the end of a shaft that mates with a rack (think of a geared wheel opened up and laid flat). Sometimes used in clutch operating systems.

Radial play Up and down movement about a shaft.

Radial ply tires Tire plies run across the tire (from bead to bead) and around the circumference of the tire. Less resistant to tread distortion than other tire types.

Radiator A liquid-to-air heat transfer device designed to reduce the temperature of the coolant in a liquid cooled engine.

Rake A feature of steering geometry - the angle of the steering head in relation to the vertical **(see illustration)**.

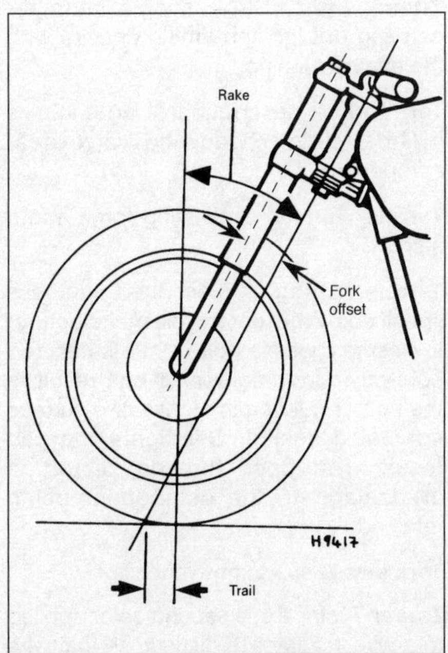

Steering geometry

Rebore Providing a new working surface to the cylinder bore by boring out the old surface. Necessitates the use of oversize piston and rings.

Rebound damping A means of controlling the oscillation of a suspension unit spring after it has been compressed. Resists the spring's natural tendency to bounce back after being compressed.

Rectifier Device for converting the ac output of an alternator into dc for battery charging.

Reed valve An induction system commonly used on two-stroke engines.

Regulator Device for maintaining the charging voltage from the generator or alternator within a specified range.

Relay A electrical device used to switch heavy current on and off by using a low current auxiliary circuit.

Resistance Measured in ohms. An electrical component's ability to pass electrical current.

RON (Research Octane Number) A measure of a fuel's resistance to knock.

rpm revolutions per minute.

Runout The amount of wobble (in-and-out movement) of a wheel or shaft as it's rotated. The amount a shaft rotates "out-of-true." The out-of-round condition of a rotating part.

SAE (Society of Automotive Engineers) A standard for the viscosity of a fluid.

Sealant A liquid or paste used to prevent leakage at a joint. Sometimes used in conjunction with a gasket.

Service limit Term for the point where a component is no longer useable and must be replaced.

Shaft drive A method of transmitting drive from the transmission to the rear wheel.

Shell bearings Plain bearings consisting of two shell halves. Most often used as big-end and main bearings in a four-stroke engine. Often called bearing inserts.

Shim Thin spacer, commonly used to adjust the clearance or relative positions between two parts. For example, shims inserted into or under tappets or followers to control valve clearances. Clearance is adjusted by changing the thickness of the shim.

Short-circuit An electrical condition where current shorts to ground bypassing the circuit components.

Skimming Process to correct warpage or repair a damaged surface, eg on brake discs or drums.

Slide-hammer A special puller that screws into or hooks onto a component such as a shaft or bearing; a heavy sliding handle on the shaft bottoms against the end of the shaft to knock the component free.

Small-end bearing The bearing in the upper end of the connecting rod at its joint with the gudgeon pin.

Snap-ring A ring-shaped clip used to prevent endwise movement of cylindrical parts and shafts. An internal snap-ring is installed in a groove in a housing; an external snap-ring fits into a groove on the outside of a cylindrical piece such as a shaft. Also known as a circlip.

Spalling Damage to camshaft lobes or bearing journals shown as pitting of the working surface.

Specific gravity (SG) The state of charge of the electrolyte in a lead-acid battery. A measure of the electrolyte's density compared with water.

Straight-cut gears Common type gear used on gearbox shafts and for oil pump and water pump drives.

Stanchion The inner sliding part of the front forks, held by the yokes. Often called a fork tube.

Stoichiometric ratio The optimum chemical air/fuel ratio for a gasoline engine, said to be 14.7 parts of air to 1 part of fuel.

Sulphuric acid The liquid (electrolyte) used in a lead-acid battery. Poisonous and extremely corrosive.

Surface grinding (lapping) Process to correct a warped gasket face, commonly used on cylinder heads.

T

Tapered-roller bearing Tapered inner race of caged needle rollers and separate tapered outer race. Examples of taper roller bearings can be found on steering heads.

Tappet A cylindrical component which transmits motion from the cam to the valve stem, either directly or via a pushrod and rocker arm. Also called a cam follower.

TCS Traction Control System. An electronically-controlled system which senses wheel spin and reduces engine speed accordingly.

TDC Top Dead Center denotes that the piston is at its highest point in the cylinder.

Thread-locking compound Solution applied to fastener threads to prevent loosening. Select type to suit application.

Thrust washer A washer positioned between two moving components on a shaft. For example, between gear pinions on gearshaft.

Timing chain See **Cam Chain**.

Timing light Stroboscopic lamp for carrying out ignition timing checks with the engine running.

Top-end A description of an engine's cylinder block, head and valve gear components.

Torque Turning or twisting force about a shaft.

Torque setting A prescribed tightness specified by the motorcycle manufacturer to ensure that the bolt or nut is secured correctly. Undertightening can result in the bolt or nut coming loose or a surface not being sealed. Overtightening can result in stripped threads, distortion or damage to the component being retained.

Torx key A six-point wrench.

Tracer A stripe of a second color applied to a wire insulator to distinguish that wire from another one with the same color insulator. For example, Br/W is often used to denote a brown insulator with a white tracer.

Trail A feature of steering geometry. Distance from the steering head axis to the tire's central contact point.

Triple clamps The cast components which extend from the steering head and support the fork stanchions or tubes. Often called fork yokes.

Turbocharger A centrifugal device, driven by exhaust gases, that pressurizes the intake air. Normally used to increase the power output from a given engine displacement.

TWI Abbreviation for Tire Wear Indicator. Indicates the location of the tread depth indicator bars on tires.

U

Universal joint or U-joint (UJ) A double-pivoted connection for transmitting power from a driving to a driven shaft through an angle. Typically found in shaft drive assemblies.

Unsprung weight Anything not supported by the bike's suspension (ie the wheel, tires, brakes, final drive and bottom (moving) part of the suspension).

V

Vacuum gauges Clock-type gauges for measuring intake tract vacuum. Used for carburetor synchronization on multi-cylinder engines.

Valve A device through which the flow of liquid, gas or vacuum may be stopped, started or regulated by a moveable part that opens, shuts or partially obstructs one or more ports or passageways. The intake and exhaust valves in the cylinder head are of the poppet type.

Valve clearance The clearance between the valve tip (the end of the valve stem) and the rocker arm or tappet/follower. The valve clearance is measured when the valve is closed. The correct clearance is important - if too small the valve won't close fully and will burn out, whereas if too large noisy operation will result.

Valve lift The amount a valve is lifted off its seat by the camshaft lobe.

Valve timing The exact setting for the opening and closing of the valves in relation to piston position.

Vernier caliper A precision measuring instrument that measures inside and outside dimensions. Not quite as accurate as a micrometer, but more convenient.

VIN Vehicle Identification Number. Term for the bike's engine and frame numbers.

Viscosity The thickness of a liquid or its resistance to flow.

Volt A unit for expressing electrical "pressure" in a circuit. Volts = current x ohms.

W

Water pump A mechanically-driven device for moving coolant around the engine.

Watt A unit for expressing electrical power. Watts = volts x current.

Wet liner arrangement

Wear limit see **Service limit**

Wet liner A liquid-cooled engine design where the pistons run in liners which are directly surrounded by coolant **(see illustration)**.

Wheelbase Distance from the center of the front wheel to the center of the rear wheel.

Wiring harness or loom Describes the electrical wires running the length of the motorcycle and enclosed in tape or plastic sheathing. Wiring coming off the main harness is usually referred to as a sub harness.

Woodruff key A key of semi-circular or square section used to locate a gear to a shaft. Often used to locate the alternator rotor on the crankshaft.

Wrist pin Another name for gudgeon or piston pin.

Notes

Note: *References throughout this index are in the form, "Chapter number"•"Page number"*